ORIENTING CANADA

ORIENTING CANADA
Race, Empire, and the Transpacific

JOHN PRICE

UBCPress · Vancouver · Toronto

20 19 18 17 16 15 14 13 12 11   5 4 3 2 1

Printed in Canada on FSC-certified ancient-forest-free paper (100% post-consumer recycled) that is processed chlorine- and acid-free.

Library and Archives Canada Cataloguing in Publication

Price, John
Orienting Canada : race, empire, and the Transpacific / John Price.

Includes bibliographical references and index.
Issued also in electronic format.
ISBN 978-0-7748-1983-1 (bound); ISBN 978-0-7748-1984-8 (pbk.)

1. Canada – Foreign relations – Pacific Area. 2. Pacific Area – Foreign relations – Canada. 3. Canada – Foreign relations – Asia. 4. Asia – Foreign relations – Canada. 5. Canada – Race relations – History – 20th century. 6. Asia – Race relations – History – 20th century. 7. Imperialism – History – 20th century. 8. Canada – History, Military – 20th century. I. Title.

FC244.P3P75 2011   327.710182'3   C2011-901704-0

e-book ISBNs: 978-0-7748-1985-5 (pdf); 978-0-7748-1986-2 (e-pub)

Canada

UBC Press gratefully acknowledges the financial support for our publishing program of the Government of Canada (through the Canada Book Fund), the Canada Council for the Arts, and the British Columbia Arts Council.

This book has been published with the help of a grant from the Canadian Federation for the Humanities and Social Sciences, through the Aid to Scholarly Publications Program, using funds provided by the Social Sciences and Humanities Research Council of Canada.

Parts of Chapter 6 appeared previously in John Price, "E.H. Norman, Canada and Japan's Postwar Constitution," *Pacific Affairs* 74, 3 (2001): 383-405.

UBC Press
The University of British Columbia
2029 West Mall
Vancouver, BC V6T 1Z2
www.ubcpress.ca

Contents

Part 2: Pax Americana – Race, Anti-Communism, and Asia

Illustrations

Acknowledgments

A book this long in the making incurs innumerable debts, and I would like to acknowledge the many people who helped me on what became a personal journey. In particular, I owe a huge debt of gratitude to Professor Suh Sung of Ritsumeikan University in Kyoto, Japan, whose research and activism have inspired me and whose assistance in doing fieldwork in Korea was invaluable. Similarly, Thekla Lit and Joseph Wong have made it possible for me to better understand the justice in the movement for redress for victims of war crimes in Asia as well as the complexities of the same. I also thank Tatsuo Kage for his assistance in Japanese translation and in educating me on the history of Japanese Canadians and the movement for redress.

Peter Baskerville, now retired from the University of Victoria's history department, helped me first craft the original research project that was supported by the Social Sciences and Humanities Research Council. Many other colleagues at UVIC, including Jo-Anne Lee, Zhongping Chen, Gregory Blue, John Lutz, and Patricia Roy, have provided invaluable assistance and support. Henry Yu at the University of British Columbia is a leading force in Asian-Canadian studies and it was a privilege to work with him, particularly around the conference on the hundredth anniversary of the 1907 race riots. Many thanks to those in the Asian-Canadian communities in Vancouver and Victoria with whom I have had the pleasure of working over the past decade: Judy Hanazawa, Grace Eiko Thomson, George Chow, Karin Lee, Hayne Wai, Harb Gill, Charan Gill, Rika Uto, Michiko "Midge" Ayukawa,

Stan and Masako Fukawa, and Gordie Mark. Many thanks to the Chinese Canadian Historical Society of BC, particularly Larry Wong, for helping to put me in touch with Dora Nipp of Toronto, who provided me with a number of pictures used in this book, including the cover picture of the 1930s demonstration in Victoria. Many in the Asian-Canadian literary and arts community, including Roy Miki, Joy Kogawa, Darcy Tamayose, Rita Wong, Chris Lee, and Alice Ming Wai Jim have made me appreciate the important role of art and literature in history. My thanks to them and also to Harley Wylie for educating me on First Nations issues.

Early on, John Hilliker and Greg Donaghy were especially helpful in enabling me to understand the history of Canada's Department of External Affairs. Denis Stairs was kind enough to share his knowledge of Canada-Korea relations. The late Arthur Menzies also gave valuable hours of his time to talk with me about his work in external affairs and about his old colleague, Herbert Norman. Kinuko Laskey kindly agreed to be interviewed not long before her death, as did her husband David, who now carries on the anti-nuclear work that Kinuko championed. Many thanks to Elsie Dean, Ken Woodsworth, Cyril and Marjorie Powles, George Fraser, and Stephen Endicott for agreeing to speak with me about their experiences during this period. Simon Nantais, Yuko Kimura, Venessa Stuppard, Kirsten Larmon, Sarah Romkey, and Meleisa Ono-George provided valuable research assistance over the years.

In Japan, I benefitted from the kind advice of Utsumi Aiko, Arai Shinichi, Nakano Toshiko, and Izumi Masami. Mr. Komatsu at the E.H. Norman Library in the Canadian Embassy was very helpful and allowed me access to the Ōkubo Genji collection. My heart-felt appreciation goes to the Naniwa family, who provided a home away from home on my many visits to Japan during the course of this project.

In Korea I am forever indebted to Kim Gwi-ok for rooting out the case of Shin Hyun-chan and for giving her valuable time to travel with me to Mr. Chan's place of residence and to interview him. I am also indebted to Chong Ae-Yu, who accompanied Kim Gwi-ok and acted as an interpreter for the Chan interview. Without their spirit of internationalism and sense of justice, the work on Korea would have been impossible. My appreciation also to Han Hong-Koo for taking the time to meet with me, along with Yoon Young-Mo, who provided many introductions to the new South Korea. Research assistant Alice Park undertook substantial book finding and translation, both of which were invaluable.

In China I am indebted to Niu Dayong, Yang Liwen, and Yang Kuisong of Beijing University, as well as to the Crook family, Isabel, Michael, and Carl, who have been unstinting in sharing their knowledge of their adopted country. David Hsieh helped in many ways, and my thanks to Hou Xiaojia for the important research assistance in the early stages of this project. Ningping Yu has provided remarkable insights and access to information and people in China. Many thanks to the anonymous reviewers of the manuscript. And a bow to Mark Selden and Noam Chomsky for giving me confidence in the manuscript in its early incarnation.

The staff at Library and Archives Canada have been extremely helpful over my many visits there. I would particularly like to thank Paulette Dozois, who was most generous with her time and who helped me solve problems as I went along. The Canadian Press kindly gave me extensive access to its files in Toronto. The assistance given me at Special Collections and the University of British Columbia Archives is greatly appreciated, as is the assistance received from Vancouver City Archives. In Tokyo, the staff at the National Diet Library and Foreign Ministry Archives were very helpful.

I want to thank the staff at UBC Press for making this book possible, particularly Randy Schmidt for supporting the manuscript through a difficult gestation; Holly Keller for bringing it into the print world; and Laraine Coates for helping to spread the word.

This book could not have been written without the understanding and support of my loving partner, Margaret McGregor, our children, Mae and Tom, my parents-in-law, as well as many close friends (the (un)usual suspects, they know who they are). Finally, my deep appreciation to Neil Burton, a friend and mentor who was unstinting in his assistance in editing an earlier version of the manuscript. Neil died before the manuscript went to print, and this book is dedicated to him.

Abbreviations

AEL	Asiatic Exclusion League
CCF	Co-operative Commonwealth Federation
CCP	Chinese Communist Party
CFM	Council of Foreign Ministers
CIA	Central Intelligence Agency
CLPD	Canadian League for Peace and Democracy
CPC	Combined Policy Committee
CPV	Chinese People's Volunteers
CYC	Canadian Youth Congress
DEA	Department of External Affairs
DRV	Democratic Republic of Vietnam
FEAC	Far Eastern Advisory Council
FEC	Far Eastern Commission
GMD	Guomindang (Nationalist Party)
GHQ	General Headquarters (of SCAP)
ICSC	International Commission for Supervision and Control in Vietnam
ICFTU	International Confederation of Free Trade Unions
ILO	International Labour Organization

IPR	Institute of Pacific Relations
IMTFE	International Military Tribunal for the Far East
NATO	North Atlantic Treaty Organization
NSC	National Security Council
PPS	Policy Planning Staff
PRC	People's Republic of China
PWC	Pacific War Council
ROK	Republic of Korea
SAC	Strategic Air Command (US)
SCAP	Supreme Command(er) of the Allied Powers
SFPT	San Francisco Peace Treaty
SWNCC	State-War-Navy Coordinating Committee
UNTCOK	United Nations Temporary Commission on Korea
VTLC	Vancouver Trades and Labour Council

A Note on Language

In general, I have conformed to East Asian usage in terms of people's names: family name first and given name second, except where the names are commonly used otherwise in the English language sources. Where necessary, I have provided the contemporary names of people and places as well as the terms used at the time.

ORIENTING CANADA

Map of East Asia

Introduction

This book examines how concepts of race and empire "oriented" Canada and the Transpacific in the first half of the twentieth century. The term "oriented" is used in both the conventional sense – providing a particular direction – and in a critical sense, turning Asia and its diverse peoples into a racialized "other," a notion initially developed by Edward Said in his now famous *Orientalism*.[1] I have purposefully chosen the term "transpacific." The welding together of "trans" and "Pacific" captures the geographic focus of the narrative as well as the notion of continuous movement and transformation. It best reflects the dynamic flow of ideas and peoples engaged in border-crossings on both sides of the Pacific. This particular study focuses on interactions among the peoples and governments of Canada, China, Japan, Korea, and Vietnam and, to a somewhat less extent, India.

How did concepts of race and empire come to occupy centre stage in *Orienting Canada*? An initial project examining Canada and the "Cold War" in East Asia ended in the uncomfortable realization that questions of race were essential to the telling of the story but that they were not easily written about or readily received by traditional diplomatic historians. Once broached, however, the concept of race demanded serious attention, and a close examination of its impact on Canadian foreign policies was imperative. This opened up very different horizons and fundamentally altered my views on Canadian and East-Asian history. It required a broader yet more focused inquiry that could capture enough of the past to actually map the contours of race and empires as they evolved.

The bookends for this volume are the 1907 race riots in Vancouver and the 1954-56 Geneva Accords for Indochina. *Orienting Canada* follows a seam that is clearly "Canadian," yet it also delves into substantive historical issues in East Asia that had an impact on transpacific experiences. The interconnections between the "Canadian" and the "East Asian" constitute this book's specific realm of inquiry. Thus, the voices of Korean comfort women and Canadian prime ministers, Chinese head tax payers and Japanese diplomats, Chinese forced labourers in Japan and Canadian feminists in China, Japanese "traitors" and Vietnamese communists, Japanese-Canadian soldiers and Hiroshima survivors are brought together in what might at first appear a dissonant chorus. In fact, they are what one scholar has recently called the "stories of an uncommon past," that is, the past "in the sense of rarely remembered, ignored, or erased, but also uncommon in terms of being unique, different, or not assimilated into a common narrative."[2] These unique stories offer a new frame, one that transcends commonly held views about Canada and Asia and that allows us to better perceive the often unspoken relationship between race and empire.

Looking back from the vantage point of another half century or more later, the shadows of this past remain perceptible – in the political landscape of East Asia, in continuing demands for redress and reconciliation in both Asia and Canada, and in ongoing battles connected with memory-making and foreign policy. As shifting economic dynamics turn the world's attention towards Asia once again, the present and the past come together to underscore a main theme of this book: the Transpacific has played a foundational role in Canadian and world politics in ways that are too often neglected and/or are poorly understood.

Anyone who teaches about Asia in North America is aware of the problem of Eurocentrism – how a persistent emphasis on European history or Canada's European links marginalizes Asia, not to mention Africa, Latin America, and the Carribean.[3] The research for this project not only underscores the pervasiveness of the problem but also goes to the heart of the matter – opening up the historical process that created the bias and that allows it to be continually reproduced. Indeed, much English-language scholarship often tends to refract the past and the world through a Eurocentric lens that eliminates, downplays, or denigrates the role of those excluded from the centres of power. As Erez Manela explains in his new study on the Versailles peace talks of 1919: "In the standard narrative of the peace conference, non-Western regions and peoples figure most often as inert masses of territory and humanity that the great powers carved up in an unprecedented expansion of imperialism."[4] This not only holds true for the prewar period but also continues to reproduce itself in histories of the wartime and postwar periods. Furthermore, it spans the political spectrum. A recent critique of the US role in the Second World War, for example, does an admirable job of demystifying the American role in Europe during the war but completely ignores its important contributions in the Pacific.[5]

Eurocentrism has relegated the story of the war in the Pacific to a minor spot behind the conflict in Europe, despite the fact the war there began in 1937 with the invasion of China, a full two years before the invasion of Poland. And if the Pacific War is given prominence of place, it is often contrived as a chronicle spanning Pearl Harbor and Hiroshima, highlighting the role of the United States, a protagonist determined in war, beneficent in victory. As a result, "Asian contributions to defeating the emperor's soldiers and sailors were displaced by an all-consuming focus on the American victory in the "Pacific War."[6] A similar problem affects the writing of the postwar Pacific, in which Asia is construed as a subject area of contention in a bipolar world dominated by the Soviet Union and the United States.[7] The wars in Vietnam and Korea are often portrayed as proxy wars, and, in many English-language accounts, this 1950s' Cold War perspective continues to shape both scholarly and popular perceptions of the past, denying those in Asia any substantial form of agency in world history.[8]

The Transpacific fares just as badly if not worse in Canadian history writing.[9] The crafting of this country's past has tended to be Atlantic-centred, focusing on European immigrant experience that displaces "First Nations peoples at the same time that it erases our Pacific past."[10] Social historians have made impressive strides in correcting this trend, particularly in regard to Aboriginal, class, and gender history, provoking Jack Granatstein, the *eminence gris* of traditional nationalist historians, to accuse them of "killing" Canadian history.[11] Yet, even among social historians, neglect of the Transpacific remains a problem.[12] And, although there have been changes recently, a Eurocentric narrative continues to grip Canadian diplomatic history, rendering Asia a "distraction" (at best) or, more often than not, relegating it to the oblivion of the omitted.[13]

Fortunately, streams of non-Eurocentric scholarship have also evolved, providing the basis for alternative perspectives on the past. For many years, Canadian scholars of Asia have authored important studies on Canada and the Transpacific, many of which I cite later in this book. From the 1970s on, scholars associated with the *Bulletin of Concerned Asian Scholars* (now *Critical Asian Studies*), including John Dower, Laura Hein, and Mark Selden, have published prodigious and widely acclaimed studies on US-Asia relations. The recent field of world history has also made its mark in overcoming past biases. Andre Gunder Frank's *ReOrient: Global Economy in the Asian Age*, among others, has made an important contribution to reassessing the world system from a five-hundred-year perspective.[14] As well, Asian-American studies and, more recently, Asian-Canadian studies have proven extremely fertile areas of innovative research.[15] Transnationalism has finally come of age and scholars in Asia, particularly in Japan, China, and Korea, are developing new and fascinating regional perspectives on the past.[16] The rise of postcolonialism, with its emphasis on the subaltern, has proven one of the most innovative fields of research, and a whole new generation of transpacific scholars is examining postwar history, including the Cold War in East Asia. I draw heavily on the insights offered in these critical perspectives, and they have helped frame the concepts of race and empire that I employ in *Orienting Canada*.

Concepts of Race and Empire

Redress for Japanese-Canadian internment, for the Chinese head tax, and for the abuse of Aboriginal children in residential schools has meant that, in Canada, few today would deny that injustices occurred in the country's past. Yet there remains a deep-seated reluctance, what might almost be termed an avoidance syndrome, to openly identify racism in Canada as a problem, past or present. One historian has termed this an "ideology of racelessness," part of a nationalist mythology that emphasizes Canada's difference from the United States.[17] Another problem is that, by the early 1900s, racism was being challenged internationally, and its advocates went to some lengths to code or mask their work. Once this is taken into account, however, it becomes apparent that questions of race permeated transpacific landscapes in ever-changing ways – from racist immigration laws in Canada to the collapse of Wilsonian ideals at Versailles; from the Chinese Exclusion Act to the opening of the Canadian Embassy in Tokyo; from the uprooting and destruction of the Japanese communities during the war to rampant bigotry during the Korean conflict. Observing and documenting race is one thing – understanding it as a process is another. How and why Asian Canadians finally won the franchise in the 1947-49 period, for example, turns out to be a question of immense complexity – the culmination of a historical process with local, transpacific, and global dimensions involving questions of race as well as other dynamics.

Recent theoretical developments in the scholarly understanding of race have proven useful in coming to grips with this issue, and I have adopted and integrated this concept based on the following premises.[18] There is little basis in reality for categorizing humans according to race. When used in *Orienting Canada,* the term "race" refers to social relations that have been defined by reference to it and that have thereby become social constructions reflecting power relations. In general, racism refers to an ideology that asserts a group's superiority or inferiority based on physical appearance, ethnicity, or culture. It usually involves the capacity to dominate. I employ the term "racialization" to refer to the process of constructing "race." Also of great importance is the term "white," which is often the invisible other of racialization. Also a social construct, it reflects the historical integration of groups of non-Anglo-Saxon European peoples as the dominant group in Canada's body politic. However, race also interacts with other factors, including class, gender, region, and religion, and is thus contingent and contextual, part of a complex matrix of power and privilege that is constant yet that changes with circumstances. For stylistic reasons, I generally avoid using quotation marks around terms such as "race," "racialization," "white," and so on. In any case, I believe the general anti-racist thrust of *Orienting Canada* outweighs the potential risks of misinterpretation.

The concepts of "empire" and "imperialism" are key to deconstructing the history of the Transpacific. As with questions related to race, few would deny the importance of British colonialism in Asia prior to, for example, the Second World War. However, until recently, there has been much less consensus regarding other types of empires. In the case of the United States, for example, that country's role in the Second World War, its anti-communism, its support of the Allies, its anti-colonial pronouncements, and its professed adherence to freedom and democracy made some scholars hesitate to talk of US imperialism. The war in Vietnam began to change this, but, for the most part, discussion of a US empire remained limited – if it was discussed, it was often done so through the use of terms such as "informal empire." However, the end of the Soviet Union left the United States in a position of global domination, without a clear adversary. Even before George Bush took office, Chalmers Johnson, a former conservative scholar and doyen of Asian studies in the United States, came to the conclusion that an ongoing global US military presence was "striking evidence, for those who care to look, of an imperial project that the Cold War obscured."[19] He suggested that this would inevitably result in some form of "blowback." In light of 9/11 and Iraq, his work was prophetic. Today, the discussion is not about the existence of an American Empire but, rather, about its nature. To some, such as Niall Ferguson of Harvard or Canada's Michael Ignatieff, the United States is a "liberal" imperial power, which they see as better than many alternatives.[20] To others, such as Hardt and Negri, globalization has meant a transition from imperialism to an empire that has "no territorial center of power and does not rely on fixed boundaries or barriers." Although the United States has a privileged position, the new empire lacks a nation-state at the centre of its imperial project.[21]

The debate on the nature of US power in the world reflects, among many things, the lack of any scholarly consensus regarding definitions of imperialism and empire. It may be that classical definitions have, as Mommsen suggests, run their course.[22] A plethora of models still remains – from the Leninist views of imperialism as the "highest" stage of capitalism to development theory, from world systems analysis to postcolonialism. In defining the term I draw on a number of insights. I agree with the thesis, cogently argued by Gallagher and Robinson over fifty years ago, that imperialism has both economic and strategic dimensions and, depending on specific circumstances, that it adopts formal (colonial) or informal (interventions short of colonization) means to achieve the desired aim of capitalist integration.[23] However, my focus is definitely not on economic aspects of imperialism; rather, I draw on a more recent dimension of scholarly inquiry, that is, the relationship between power and culture in imperial relations, particularly as articulated by Edward Said and then developed by various schools of "postcolonialism."[24] As an early proponent of postcolonialism suggests, imperialism has faced challenges before, including "nationalist rebellions against imperialist domination and Marxism's unrelenting critiques of capitalism and colonialism. But neither nationalism nor Marxism broke free from Eurocentric discourses."[25] Postcolonialism, he suggests, rejects the universalist discourse associated with Europe's historical experience. A "catachrestic combination of Marxism, poststructuralism, Gramsci and Foucault," postcolonialism seeks to undo the "appropriation of the other as History." The impact of these trends has now reached into diplomatic history, to the point at which many now accept the view that "racialized cultural hierarchies" were an integral part of imperial projects.[26] In this regard, Jane Jenson's study, *Race and Empire*, is of particular note for its attempt to provide an overview, based on Euro-American examples, of the historical links between imperialism and racism.[27] In *Orienting Canada,* I employ the term "imperialism" in its "modern" sense, that is, as a world system that produced and reproduces unequal relations between capitalist centres and peoples in the peripheries. Its existence is predicated on its projection and protection by state powers. Empire is the geographical and conceptual scope of specific instances of imperialism. Although the question of Soviet imperialism is addressed, it remains secondary, given the preponderance of Euro-American intervention in East Asia in the period under discussion. I also attempt to map Japanese imperialism into the trajectories of empires in Asia and to integrate questions of race as well as organized resistance to both racism and empire.[28]

Focusing on race and empires in a transnational study brings to light different questions about the past. How did concepts of race and empire change over time or, more concretely, why did Canada not have diplomatic relations with China until 1943? What are the implications of mapping Japanese expansionism onto the constellation of imperial powers that, in the postcolonial critique, are usually characterized as European, or "Western"? Did the struggle for Asian-Canadian equality reinforce the struggles for decolonization in Asia, as the struggle for Afro-American freedom reinforced the quest for African freedom?[29] Was there a "deep entanglement" between beliefs about race and modern imperialism and, if so, how did this affect Canadian relations with East Asia?[30]

Orienting Canada is the culmination of research undertaken over the past ten years.[31] It relies on archival materials from Library and Archives Canada, located in Ottawa, as well as on archival materials from London, Tokyo, and places in between. Field trips to Japan, Korea, and China provided an opportunity to interview both participants in and scholars of the events described. Where appropriate, I draw on newspaper accounts to illustrate popular perceptions related to specific issues. The book is organized into two sections, the first chronicles the wartime and immediate postwar period, and the second documents the period commonly referred to as the Cold War, but which I describe as the remilitarization of the Pacific. A prologue provides the historical background essential to understanding the wartime and postwar dynamics.

In focusing on these themes and areas, *Orienting Canada* spawns its own "others," those whose stories do not receive the attention they merit. Following a Canadian seam has meant concentrating on areas in which there was significant Canadian government intervention (i.e., China, Japan, Korea, Vietnam). This has meant that the roles of peoples in India, the Philippines, and other Southeast Asian states, as well as the Pacific Islanders, are not represented as they might be. Nor is there serious consideration either of the economic dimensions of imperialism or of its complex gender implications and intersections (i.e., the relationship between patriarchy and imperialism). In these and other ways, this book remains a very partial deconstruction of the politics of race and empire in the Transpacific.

PART 1

RACE, EMPIRE, AND WAR

1 Prologue to War: Migration, Race, and Empire

Prior to the Second World War, Canada's Department of External Affairs (DEA) was a small body, composed of staff officers made up almost exclusively of white men educated in elite universities in England or the United States.[1] Among this group was Lester Pearson, the son of a Methodist minister, a graduate of Oxford, a sporting enthusiast, and a man of good cheer. In 1935, Pearson was an up and comer in the DEA, responsible for British Empire affairs and the League of Nations before being sent to Great Britain as first secretary, where he attended the London Naval Conference of 1935, a follow-up to the 1930 meeting.[2] The 1935 conference ended with Japan's announcing its abandonment of the naval agreement after the United States and Great Britain refused to agree to the Japanese government's demand for complete parity in naval tonnage. Prior to the conference, Pearson, under the pseudonym "T," provided a detailed analysis of Canada's position regarding Japan and its expectations going into the 1935 Naval Conference. This analysis appeared in an important article in *Foreign Affairs*, the prestigious, mainstream journal published by the US Council for Foreign Affairs.[3] Entitling his essay "Canada and the Far East," Pearson argued that the Japanese government was angered because Japan "had played the game according to traditional rules, which some at least of her accusers have not yet themselves abandoned. She has wrapped herself in the mantle of injured pride, stirred up the militant patriotism of her people, and driven straight forward with her plans for hegemony in the Far East."[4] Japan was like

Germany at the end of the nineteenth century, Pearson argued. At the 1930 London Naval Conference, the United States had been given parity with the British Navy, and, "to Japanese eyes, Anglo-Saxon supremacy [had been] established in the Pacific." Now Japan demanded equality, which would be perceived by others as Japanese "supremacy in the Pacific."[5]

Pearson emphasized that the little Canadian interest in Asia that did exist was focused on matters of trade and immigration, particularly with regard to Japan. As had the United States, Canada restricted Japanese immigration, but, Pearson suggested, unlike the United States, it had done so without irritating the Japanese. The government, Pearson lamented, had no such qualms with regard to China. Pearson also pointed to Canadian prime minister Arthur Meighen's role in the 1921 Imperial Conference, at which Canada "imposed on a reluctant, even hostile, British Government, the abrogation of the Anglo-Japanese alliance."[6] He then argued that geography placed Canada between Japan and the United States in the north Pacific and that there was no question of a neutral Canada "to play the part and pay the penalty of 'gallant little Belgium.'"[7] That the Canadian government's loyalties lay with its southern neighbour was clear, but, at the same time, Pearson hoped to maintain some semblance of what was known at the time as the Washington treaty system: "Questions of fundamental import remain unsettled – Japan's need for markets, the recognition of Manchukuo, the Japanese 'Monroe Doctrine.' Agree on these questions, and a naval treaty becomes, if not easy, at least possible. Fail to agree on them, and the system built up at Washington and London will collapse." Pearson seemed inclined towards accepting Japan's control over Manchuria (northeast China), gained after it invaded in 1931, as the price of collective security: "The Anglo-Saxon states must realize Japan's special needs and interests in the Far East; Japan must realize that the collective system is in very truth 'the lifeline of civilization.'"[8] Canada, concluded Pearson, would back every exploration for an agreement based on "collective and internationalist ideals." However, if such an agreement were not achievable, everything would be done to ensure that "failure [would] not destroy or even weaken the close understanding and friendly cooperation between the Anglo-Saxon peoples."[9]

Pearson was very much a department man, and his views regarding the history of Canada and the Pacific are of considerable interest. In particular, his appreciation of the different treatment of Japanese and Chinese immigrants, Canada's role in ending the Anglo-Japanese alliance, the need to recognize Japan's "special needs and interests," and his emphasis on unity among the "Anglo-Saxon" states and peoples reflect a developed appreciation of the politics and values of that era. Anglo-Saxon unity as an ideal reflected not so much the ideas of Pearson as an individual as it did decades of racist exclusions and the edification of the Canadian state to the point that "whiteness," or Anglo-Saxonism, had become normative. In that sense, Pearson's views represented colonial knowledge, that is, they reflected the specific conditions that had evolved in Canada as a colonial settler state of the British Empire with close ties to the United States.

Race and Empire

In the past decade, Canadian historians have paid increasing attention to the history of colonial contact, that is, to the history of European-Aboriginal relations in the formative years of the Canadian state.[10] Such studies, and the struggles of Aboriginal peoples for justice, have changed the intellectual landscape and language of Canadian history. These developments have also created a new frame within which to view the history of Asian communities in Canada.

Over the past thirty years, important strides have been made in documenting the process of racializing peoples from Asia, the extensive discrimination that resulted, and the resilience displayed by such communities despite often perilous circumstances.[11] There have also been notable studies highlighting the local-global interconnections of such communities.[12] Recently, there have been important steps in the study of inter-raciality and in integrating questions of race with those of class and nation.[13] All too often, however, these histories have been siloed as ethnic histories or contained within the binary of European-Asian relations. To the extent that they have been integrated into a larger whole, it has been principally as part of "British Columbian" history. However, when taken with the growing body of newer contact literature, the history of Asian communities in Canada offers an opportunity to better appreciate the complex process of colonial state formation. This chapter offers a brief outline of that process, with a particular focus on the question of immigration and of racializing the "Oriental other," which, I suggest, was fundamental to state formation, to the creation of notions of "whiteness" in Canada, and to the construction of Anglo-Saxonism in international affairs as articulated by Canadian officials such as Lester Pearson.

Conventional notions about Asians in Canada centre on the idea that they were latecomers, that Canada had already been settled and that their arrival posed new questions in ethnic relations. To be sure, in Atlantic and eastern Canada, the early history of colonization and settlement is the story of early Aboriginal-European relations, dating from Cartier's early voyages of 1534-35, to the founding of Nouvelle France, to the British-French wars of the 1750s, and onwards. In terms of western Canada, however, settler colonization really only gains momentum after the 1840s. And from that perspective, Asians were present from the beginning. The first recorded arrival of Chinese is from the eighteenth century, when a group of Chinese carpenters was brought to Nootka in 1759. Mass migration begins in the 1850s. Colonization of the west coast opened up contact with the Pacific, and it was easier for Chinese to reach that area than it was for those coming from Europe. Thousands of Chinese migrants, almost exclusively males, arrived in Victoria in 1858, and, some years later, peoples from Japan and South Asia also began to arrive. From the outset, colonial officials on the Pacific coast faced new and complex questions.

As Bernard Cohn illustrates in his study of colonial India, the production of local knowledge through the interaction of imperial officials with local populations was integral to colonial rule.[14] This process involved creating racial classifications as well as other modes of knowledge. In a settler colony such as that of pre-Confederation Canada, officials and policy makers faced different conditions than did their counterparts in India. First and foremost was the foundational question of how to control the Aboriginal population. With the arrival of Chinese immigrants, however, new questions arose, and, as Renisa Mawani illustrates in her recent work, the colonial construction of their local identities was interwoven with that of Aboriginal peoples and others.[15] Often the local elite drew on previous colonial knowledges, initially from British and American sources. For example, the newspaper the *Victoria Gazette* declared that Californian and Australian experience had shown the Chinese were little more than slaves and were undesirable as permanent settlers.[16] This view was echoed by James Douglas, the colony's first governor, who perceived the Chinese as a class of people unsuited for settlement.[17] And the father of Confederation, John A. Macdonald, expressed similar sentiments at the founding of Confederation.

However, the racialization of Chinese took place against a backdrop of other factors, including class, gender, and religion. For example, to the consumers of Chinese labour – such as the Canadian Pacific Railway, the BC coal baron James Dunsmuir, or households who hired servants – Chinese labour was a valued commodity. James Douglas considered Chinese labour useful, but he distinguished between Chinese (who were not suitable for settlement) and African Americans (whom he welcomed as permanent settlers).[18] Race was unsettled terrain in these early years. In the mining fields, prospectors often reacted violently against the influx of Chinese miners. Within a few years, the preponderance of anti-Chinese sentiments outweighed the perceived benefits of their labour. A rising tide of racialization led to moves to limit the rights of Chinese, Indians, and others within the colonies. Shortly after Confederation, the BC legislature voted to disenfranchise Chinese and Indians, and, by 1875, they had been removed from the voters lists. By this time, anti-Chinese agitation was commonplace in the province.

The 1884-85 Royal Commission on Chinese Immigration was an important federal initiative whose purpose was to curtail Chinese immigration, and it followed on the heels of US legislation that completely barred people from China from entering the United States for a period of ten years. The commission held hearings in the United States as well as in British Columbia, and the testimony was varied and complex.[19] A number of people gave evidence regarding the contributions of Chinese migrants, yet others gave testimony that reinforced stereotypes about the Chinese as foreign, inassimilable, and inferior. In the end, the commission recommended a ten-dollar head tax to deter Chinese immigration, which the federal government arbitrarily increased to fifty dollars in legislation that summer. Not only did the local Chinese community protest, so did the Chinese government. Huang Sic Chen (Huang Cuxian), a consular representative, told the commission: "It is unjust in principle for Europeans to insist upon the right of unrestricted commercial relations with China, and at the same time to enforce unjust and unequal restrictions upon Chinese merchants and labourers."[20] Indeed, matters relating to immigration and trade had always been integrally connected in treaty negotiations between states. The evolution of the Chinese community, and the multifaceted identities associated with it, would reflect and affect these global interconnections, in particular, in the unfolding of the nationalist and anti-imperial movement in China.[21] At this time, however, China's international power was ebbing, and its capacity to stop the growing anti-Chinese movement in the United States and Canada was limited.

Racialization of the Chinese and the discriminatory measures associated with it were accompanied by new definitions of whiteness in Canada, in a way not dissimilar to the construction of whiteness in the United States.[22] In early colonial reports, for example, there were references to many "races," and the term was used as "ethnicity" is often used today. However, increasingly, a divide arose between people of colour (black, Aboriginal, Asians, mixed heritage, etc.) and the others – that is, whites. Settlement of the Prairies and British Columbia demanded large numbers of new settlers, and thus Canadian immigration policy changed its focus from exclusively emphasizing a dwindling supply of Anglo-Saxon immigrants to promoting the recruitment of non-Anglo Europeans.[23] For example, in the 1870s, 7,500 Russian Mennonites arrived in Manitoba, followed by Galicians (Western Ukrainians), and Doukhobors from Russia. The arrival of these European groups on the Prairies also provoked an ethnocentric response on the part of Anglo-Saxon settlers there. The newcomers were perceived as "second-class" and faced substantial discrimination. But their whiteness got them into the country and initially assured them of basic rights, including the right to vote and own land, at a time when migration from Asia was a distinct alternative but was rejected on the basis of racialized notions of the Chinese as inassimilable. Clifford Sifton, then in charge of Canadian immigration policy, defended these new white groups as appropriate farming settlers.[24] But Clifton had no such feeling towards peoples of Asian descent, and he, even more than Laurier, was prepared to bring in federal laws to increase the head tax on Chinese immigrants and, furthermore, supported a federal version of the Natal Act, a law that originated in Natal, South Africa, and that restricted immigration to those who could speak a European language.[25] Here we see a transition in concepts of race, from one that had been applied in some fashion to various ethnicities to one that created a rough institutional and legal divide between whites and non-whites. Within each of these broad categories were important distinctions and racial categories that reflected assessments regarding cultural hierarchy, labour, assimilability, and international power relations. Aboriginal peoples, already on the land, had to be contained and assimilated. Newcomers from southern and eastern Europe would face discrimination once in Canada but were generally welcomed as settlers. The Chinese, on the other hand, were classified as inassimilable and, thus, as a danger to the body politic.

Perils of the Colonial State

Despite the imposition of the head tax, disenfranchisement, and various other racist measures against the Chinese and Aboriginal populations, the Canadian state faced a crisis at the turn of the century that, in 1907, erupted in the form of race riots in Vancouver. The origins of this crisis can be found in important changes taking place both in terms of migration and international power relations. For one thing, the fifty-dollar head tax on Chinese in 1885 proved ineffective at limiting Chinese arrivals, and, within a few years, annual immigration was reaching two thousand per year.[26] Furthermore, migrants from Japan and India added new and complex dimensions to the question of race. The first recorded Japanese resident in British Columbia was Nagano Manzō, who arrived in New Westminster in 1877. Although Japanese communities would initially grow more slowly than Chinese communities, by the turn of the century, approximately fifteen thousand people from Japan (including Okinawa) had arrived in British Columbia. Most proceeded on to the United States, and, thus, the census figures record only 4,738 Japanese residents in Canada in 1901.[27] However, in the eyes of many in the white communities, the Japanese were, like the Chinese, part of a growing problem. Thus, the Japanese faced racialization and institutional discrimination on a scale similar to that faced by the Chinese, and, like the Chinese community, fought to overcome such challenges. For example, Homma Tomekichi, supported by the Japanese community, challenged the denial of voting rights and won in the BC Supreme Court only to see that decision overturned in 1902 by the British Privy Council.[28]

Pressure from the BC government obliged the federal government to convene another Royal Commission in 1901, this time focusing on both Chinese and Japanese immigration. The conclusions it reached were different for each. The commission deepened the critique of Chinese inassimilability and recommended a complete prohibition on Chinese labourers coming to Canada. This was to be done through "treaty supported by legislation," and, in the interim, the head tax was to be increased to $500. Regarding the Japanese, however, the commission reached different conclusions. On the one hand, it suggested that Japanese immigrants were in some ways more acceptable than Chinese immigrants; on the other, because they were keener competitors and had "more energy, push and independence, [they were] more dangerous in this regard than the Chinese."[29] However, the commissioners appended to their report extensive correspondence from Joseph Chamberlain, British minister of colonial affairs, indicating the British government's reservations regarding how to restrict Japanese immigration.[30] This correspondence revealed another dimension of the importance international relations had in such matters. The commissioners suggested relying on the Japanese government to restrict passports being issued for travel to Canada as a means of limiting immigration, but they also suggested that, should this not prove effective, legislative measures along the lines of the Natal Act should be adopted.[31]

The arrival of Japanese was accompanied by an influx of substantial numbers of immigrants from India.[32] Reports about Canada probably reached India after a number of Indian soldiers of the British Hong Kong regiment travelled through the country on their way back to Hong Kong after attending Queen Victoria's Diamond Jubilee in London in 1897.[33] Subsequently, approximately five thousand Indians – British subjects, almost exclusively male Sikhs from the Punjab – arrived in British Columbia at the turn of the century.[34] In the eyes of many, what had begun as a "Chinese" problem had now become an "Oriental" problem. The arrival of substantial numbers of Asians in British Columbia, particularly in 1906-7, and a surge in anti-Asian actions south of the border set the scene for hemispheric riots on the Pacific coast. Exacerbating the tensions were new developments in international power relations.

Joseph Chamberlain's concern not to offend the Japanese government, as expressed in the correspondence included in the 1902 report on Chinese and Japanese immigration, reflected the rise of Japan as an imperial power in East Asia and the resulting alliance with Great Britain. Adopting the slogan "fukoku kyōhei" (rich country, strong army), the Japanese government had forced marched Japan into industrialization and militarization. By 1895, the Meiji government succeeded in abolishing its semi-colonial status, overturning the unequal treaties first imposed by the United States in 1858 and defeating China in the 1894-95 Sino-Japanese War.[35] Its major deployment to quell the Boxer Rebellion in China in 1900 convinced the British government to strategically ally itself with Japan, and, in 1902, the two governments signed the Anglo-Japanese Alliance.[36] The alliance included a promise of military intervention if either party went to war and a third party intervened, exchanges of intelligence, and, potentially, British access to the ports and resources of Japan in times of war. From the perspective of Japanese policy makers, an alliance with Great Britain provided them with ample assurance that they could challenge Russia's appetite for territory in northeast China and Korea without fear of third party intervention.

Japan's victory in the 1904-5 Russo-Japanese War had a dual effect in the Euro-American world. On the one hand, British policy makers felt vindicated in their decision to sign the Anglo-Japanese Alliance of 1902. In the United States, Theodore Roosevelt expressed his admiration for the wonders of the Japanese war effort and Japan's continuing economic expansion. Yet, accompanying this praise was also trepidation for the future. Japan, Roosevelt mused, would one day become the arch competitor of European powers in Asia.[37] Even more significantly, Roosevelt and many others in both the United States and Canada worried about Japanese emigration. Japan's triumph in the war became a catalyst for renewed racialization, raising the spectre of a "yellow peril" in which Japanese immigrants would play the role of a fifth column for Japanese imperialism in North America. This was a new phase in the exclusion movement. Spearheaded by the *San Francisco Chronicle* in February and March 1905, while the Russo-Japanese War was still going on, it targeted what it perceived as the Japanese "menace."[38] A few weeks later, on 12 May 1905, exclusionists led by San Francisco trade unions gathered to form the Japanese and Korean Exclusion League. The fact that Chinese immigration had already been banned as of 1882 made their inclusion in the league's name appear to be unnecessary. A year later, on 18 April 1906, San Francisco was rocked by a major earthquake followed by fires. The catastrophe stoked racist passions, and in the aftermath Chinatown was threatened with elimination. In the meantime, the Exclusion League pressed home a campaign to force students of Japanese descent out of public schools, along with the Chinese who had already suffered the lash of school segregation. On 11 October 1906, the school board voted to segregate the Japanese students. This provoked an international crisis as the Japanese government vigorously protested such action to Theodore Roosevelt.[39] In the spring of 1907, Roosevelt brokered a deal in which the school board agreed to withdraw its segregation order for Japanese students and, in a quid pro quo, he passed an executive order prohibiting Japanese immigration into the United States via Hawaii, Canada, or Mexico.[40]

The surge of racism and Roosevelt's measures diverted many Japanese migrants heading for the United States to Vancouver, contributing to the perception of a Japanese "invasion" of that city.[41] The Asiatic Exclusion League (as the Japanese and Korean Exclusion League was renamed in 1907), reinforced by its success in the school board campaign, spread its influence and, by 1907, had made contact with labour organizations in Seattle and, subsequently, in Bellingham, Washington, as well as Vancouver, British Columbia.[42] The Vancouver Trades and Labour Council (VTLC) initiated the formation of a local Asiatic Exclusion League (AEL) in July, and, at a meeting on 12 August, the Vancouver AEL called for a parade to protest Asian immigration. In Bellingham, shortly after the 2 September Labor Day activities, a number of people began harassing South-Asian workers employed in that town's sawmills.[43] A few days later, the harassment escalated into wholesale attacks, and groups of workers raided sawmills and dormitories, beating up a number of people and forcing many South Asians to flee for their lives.[44] Exaggerated news reports immediately circulated (including in Vancouver), further fanning the already volatile situation preceding the 7 September parade.[45] The details of Vancouver's race riot have been recounted elsewhere and involved much of the city's populace in one way or another.[46] The Japanese and Chinese communities reacted by organizing vigorous defences, with a number of people taking up arms. A general protest strike was organized by the Chinese community. The race riots made headlines around the world, including in New York, London, Taiwan, Tokyo, and Beijing.[47] In Japan, all the major newspapers, including the *Asahi* and *Jiji shimpō,* reported critically on the riot.[48] However, both the Japanese government and the newspaper editors were mollified by a prompt apology on the part of the Canadian prime minister, Sir Wilfrid Laurier, and by his offer to create a commission to assess the damages to Japanese businesses with a view to providing compensation. This, and the Meiji leaders' belief in the strength of the Anglo-Japanese Alliance, helped to mitigate any immediate harm the riot might have had on Canada-Japan relations.

In other ways, however, the impact of the race riots were far reaching. Hitherto, the federal Liberal government under Laurier had tried to balance the demands for exclusion of Asians with the need to preserve and reinforce the Anglo-Japanese Alliance. Laurier had also hoped to increase trade with Japan.[49] After the race riots, however, the Laurier government shifted its policy, and control of Asian immigration became its main concern. The ramification of what otherwise might appear as a subtle shift in emphasis was dramatic. On the one hand, the government moved quickly to negotiate a formal agreement with Japan to limit immigration to Canada; on the other hand, it took decisive measures to prohibit South-Asian immigration to Canada. It also began to work much more closely with the US government to coordinate immigration policies and to promote closer Anglo-American relations. Gaining greater control over immigration demanded a higher diplomatic profile, better capacity to deal with the complex treaty issues involved, and greater autonomy within the British Empire. It is not surprising, then, that shortly after the Vancouver race riots the government moved to create the Department of External Affairs (DEA).[50]

Limiting emigration from Japan was not easily accomplished. Laurier had to dispatch his minister of labour, Rodolphe Lemieux, and secretary of state, Joseph Pope, across the Pacific to Japan in the hope of obtaining a commitment from the Japanese government to limit Japanese emigration.[51] The Japanese government tried to prevent the trip, but pressure from the British and Canadian governments obliged it to accept the delegation. Backed by the British government, Lemieux pressed Hayashi Tadasu, Japan's foreign minister, to adopt regulatory measures to limit Japanese emigration. The discussions concluded with a draft agreement to cap labour emigration at four hundred per year.[52] Lemieux was ready to sign the agreement on behalf of the government, but Laurier remained sceptical and ordered Lemieux and Pope home. The agreement was only ratified in January 1908 after Lemieux's return.

Closing Gates, Building Bridges

Laurier's fear that the Lemieux-Hayashi Agreement would be ineffective predisposed him to make common cause with the US government on immigration matters. Roosevelt had closely followed events in Vancouver, telling Henry Cabot Lodge that they would have two positive effects: (1) they would convince the British public that the dominions would take the same attitudes as the United States' west coast states, and (2) they would make Japan realize that "she [would] have to face the same feeling in the British Empire which she [did] in the American Republic."[53] Roosevelt criticized the illegality of the race riots but was very clear that "the attitude which [was] back of the movement [was] in each case sound." Roosevelt reached out to Mackenzie King, a deputy minister assigned to convene three commissions on the Vancouver riots, inviting him to Washington to discuss matters of mutual concern.[54] Shared interests in exclusion and hopes for a united front against Japan were the wellspring for this initiative.[55]

On 25 January 1908, Roosevelt met King in the White House. According to King's diary, during the course of the lunchtime conversation, Roosevelt suggested that if King were to visit England he might, on behalf of Roosevelt, ask for British assistance since Great Britain was allied with Japan. A word from an ally might go far as: "the Japanese must learn that they will have to keep their people in their own country."[56] Roosevelt believed that the Japanese government was refusing to limit immigration to the United States and he told King: "[The Japanese are] simply taking advantage of our politeness. I thought they had done this, and I decided to send the fleet into the Pacific, it may help them to understand that we want a definite arrangement."[57] The Great White Fleet was a battle fleet that made an around-the-world trip symbolizing the United States' arrival as a global naval power.[58] It was ironic that Roosevelt won the Nobel Peace Prize for brokering the peace settlement between Japan and Russia in 1905 and then proceeded to launch a major effort in gunboat diplomacy to intimidate the Japanese government and to prevent Japanese from coming to the United States.

Returning to Ottawa from his talks with Roosevelt, King reported to Laurier the president's suggestion that King act as a go-between with the British in the search for greater US-British collaboration. Laurier endorsed the idea and sent King back to Washington where he again met Roosevelt,

Mackenzie King's world tour in 1908-9 took him to Great Britain, India, China, and Japan, where immigration matters were his main concern. King (fourth from left) accompanied Sir John Jordan (sixth from left), British Minister to China, to Beijing to present Jordan's credentials to the Chinese Prince Regent on 27 March 1909. While in Beijing, King unsuccessfully tried to get the Chinese government to accept emigration quotas. | Library and Archives Canada, C-055525

along with Root and the British ambassador to Washington, on 31 January and 1 February 1908. Roosevelt informed Laurier in a personal letter written immediately afterwards that, in the course of the meetings, it was agreed that King would go to London to gain British support.[59] Roosevelt stressed the common interest not only of Canada, Great Britain, and the United States in regard to Asian immigration but also of Australia. As it turned out, Australian prime minister Alfred Deakin had invited the American battle fleet to visit Australia, an invitation to which Roosevelt had enthusiastically agreed because "such a visit would symbolize the unity of the English-speaking peoples of the Pacific."[60] Herein lies the wellspring for an alliance among the Anglo-Saxon states and an important impetus for what would later be called Atlanticism.

King did travel to England in the spring of 1908 and, furthermore, took a round-the-world trip to England, India, China, and Japan later that year to investigate and report on immigration issues.[61] A hemispheric agreement on exclusion proved elusive because British officials believed such an arrangement might be too transparent and offensive to its allies, particularly Japan. The elusiveness of a hemispheric agreement reflected the close but distinct relationship between race and empire. The British alliance with Japan in East Asia would remain an impediment to Anglo-American unity until the Canadian government finally took the initiative to subvert it in 1921.

King's voyages did have some immediate impact, however. He wrote an important report on South-Asian immigration, in which he articulates why Indians, nominally British subjects, are to be excluded. This is because: "a native of India is not a person suited to this country." Such people are used to a "tropical climate" and have manners and customs "so unlike those of our own people," along with an "inability to readily adapt." This results in "privation and suffering which render a discontinuance of such immigration most desirable in the interest of the Indians themselves."[62] King believed that policies adopted by the colonial government of India, pressure on the steamship companies, and the Canadian government's implementation of a continuous voyage stipulation would put an end to the problem.[63] Fortunately, concluded King, the restrictive measures contemplated meant that "enacting legislation either in India or in Canada which might appear to reflect on fellow British subjects in another part of the Empire ha[d] been wholly avoided."[64]

The Lemieux-Hayashi Agreement and the Continuous Journey Act were passed with the specific goal of adding Japanese and South Asians to the list of the excluded, thereby closing the gate to those deemed inassimilable and unsuitable to the emerging white body politic. This was soon followed by regulatory limits preventing African Americans from settling in Canada's west, completing the immigration colour bar that had begun with the head tax in 1885.[65] At the same time, however, resolving the crisis opened the door to a newly imagined role for Canadian diplomacy – as an honest broker between the "motherland" and its American cousins.

The Conservative Party, elected in 1911 and in power until 1921, embraced the racial politics of Laurier's Liberals. The Conservative prime ministers, Robert Borden and Arthur Meighen, stringently applied and reinforced the terms of exclusion while pursuing the role of honest broker in international relations. In regard to immigration, the *Komagata Maru* affair was the most notable event during Borden's first term.[66] The Conservative

The *Komagata Maru* departs Vancouver on 23 July 1914, pursued by the HMCS *Rainbow,* the first Canadian navy ship to be commissioned on the west coast. | Royal BC Museum / BC Archives, D-07570

government refused entry to Gurdit Singh and 375 other South-Asian passengers who arrived in Vancouver aboard a chartered Japanese vessel, the *Komagata Maru.* The ship anchored in Burrard Inlet, but, with the exception of twenty passengers who were returning residents, no one was allowed to land. For nearly two months, a running battle raged between the passengers and Canadian officials as the authorities tried to force the ship to leave. The Sikh community rallied behind their South-Asian brethren on the ship, providing food and legal support. On Sunday, 21 June 1914, the Khalsa Diwan Society and the United India League called a support meeting downtown – over four hundred South Asians jammed into the hall, along with 125 whites, mainly from the Socialist Party of Canada, for whom class interests theoretically trumped race interests.[67] On 21 July, in its first official commission, the fledgling Royal Canadian Navy sent the HMCS *Rainbow* to Burrard Inlet, where it trained its guns on the *Komagata Maru.* Two days later, the *Komagata Maru* departed. However, this was not the end of the affair. Upon the ship's arrival in India near the end of September, the British colonial police tried to force its passengers onto a train to the Punjab. A violent clash ensued, and twenty of the passengers were killed and many others wounded.

With the basic structures of exclusion in place, succeeding governments proceeded to tighten the restrictions. Loopholes in the Lemieux-Hayashi Agreement allowed a significant number of Japanese picture brides to arrive in Canada after 1908, but such was not the case for the Chinese and South-Asian communities.[68] Fears of miscegenation (specifically, of Asian men having sexual relations with white women) provoked an early debate regarding gender and family in which some advocated the loosening of the regulations to allow Asian women to enter the country.[69] However, the economic downturn after the First World War saw a resurgence of racist agitation, putting an end to any ideas of allowing Asian women into the country and increasing pressure for even stricter prohibitions against Asian immigration. In Halifax alone there were at least six violent incidents, including a riot involving hundreds of veterans and others that targeted Chinese restaurants.[70] Throughout the country, white supremacists began to agitate for more effective ways of excluding the Chinese. In 1920, the Vancouver Board of Trade and the Victoria Chamber of Commerce both called for exclusion as well as for school segregation. After the 1921 federal election that brought the Liberal government back to Ottawa, King moved to enact overt exclusion laws, using the excuse that the Chinese government could not control emigration.[71] This provoked further mobilization in Chinese communities across the country and led to the creation of the Chinese Association of Canada.[72] Over one thousand people attended a rally in Toronto, and a representative group travelled to Ottawa to lobby against exclusion (albeit to little avail). No one in Parliament opposed exclusion, and the Chinese Immigration Act, known in the Chinese community as the "43 harsh regulations," went into effect on 1 July 1923. The impact of this legislation was significant. With the exception of a few merchants and students, no Chinese immigrants were allowed into the country, and, in 1941, according to census data, the number of people of Chinese descent in British Columbia declined to 18,619, fewer than in 1911.[73] The community, however, proved to be much more resilient than anticipated, resorting to illegal means to circumvent the barriers and thus, according to the community newspaper *Dahan Gongbao* (*Chinese Times*), there were about thirty thousand people of Chinese descent in British Columbia.[74] Nevertheless, the new act was an additional impediment, and its effects were felt not only by those in Canada but also, and particularly, by women left behind in China.[75] In 1923, the re-elected Liberal government negotiated with the Japanese government to further limit the immigration quota for labourers from four hundred per year to 150, but no agreement could be reached on the inclusion of wives in this number.[76] In 1928, the King government moved to reduce the quota of Japanese immigrants from four hundred to 150 and closed the loopholes that had allowed many "picture brides" to come into Canada.[77] These changes capped twenty years of increasing regulation, under both Conservative and Liberal governments, the purpose of which was to cut off Asian immigration to Canada.

Race and Atlanticism

The aftermath of the First World War created a new era in international relations in which Atlanticism – the north Atlantic triangle of the United States, Canada, and Great Britain – came to the fore as an informal global network linking the American and British empires. Many scholars have identified this trend, but only recently have a few addressed the role of race in the edification of this international alliance.[78] What had begun as a Roosevelt initiative in the aftermath of the Vancouver race riots flourished after the First World War.

Canada, under Borden's Conservatives, embraced the goals of the British Empire and entered the "Great War" against Germany and Austria. The United States remained neutral until 1917, a source of tension with both the British and Canadian governments. The arrival of Japanese warships off the Pacific coast to protect Canada's western flank from German submarines, an action stemming from the Anglo-Japanese Alliance, resulted in some mitigation of anti-Japanese sentiments in British Columbia for the duration of the war.[79] However, in the secluded offices of imperial policy making, concerns were being expressed about Japanese attempts to expand influence in China.[80] These concerns were shared by the US government under Woodrow Wilson. With war raging in Europe, Japanese imperial forces were able to seize German colonial possessions in China (Shandong) and its island territories north of the equator. Shortly afterwards, the Japanese government tabled the infamous "Twenty-One Demands," which would have effectively reduced China to a Japanese protectorate. Both the American and Chinese governments became part of the Allied forces in 1917. Unknown to them at the time, the British government had signed a secret memorandum with the Japanese regarding postwar treaty talks. In it Great Britain agreed to support Japan's claim to the German territories in Shandong and the Pacific Islands in exchange for Japan's recognition of

British control of the south Pacific Islands.[81] These issues would be thrashed out in Versailles in 1919.

Canada's prime minister Robert Borden led its delegation to Versailles. Besides reinforcing Canada's autonomy in international relations, Borden continued to pursue the idea of Canada's acting as an honest broker in harmonizing US-British relations while seeing to it that its own racist legislation was not threatened by new international regulations.[82] In preparation for the Versailles peace conference, Borden wrote to British prime minister Lloyd George, extolling the merits of Atlanticism:

> You know my own conviction that there is at least possible a League of the two great English speaking commonwealths who share common ancestry, language and literature, who are inspired by like democratic ideals, who enjoy similar political institutions and whose united force is sufficient to ensure the peace of the world. It is with a view to the consummation of so great a purpose that I should be content, and indeed desire, to invite and even urge the American Republic to undertake worldwide responsibilities in respect of undeveloped territories and backward races similar to, if not commensurate with, those which have been assumed by or imposed upon our own Empire.[83]

Versailles represented a step in this direction. Conventional accounts of Versailles, including the well known *Paris 1919* by Margaret MacMillan, have largely focused on the European implications of the peace treaty.[84] Omitted or downplayed have been the enormous implications of Versailles for the forces of decolonization in Asia and the rest of the world.[85] These played out at Versailles in the marginalization of Afro-Asian liberation movements, the rejection of a racial equality clause, the ceding of Chinese and Pacific Islander territories to the Japanese and British empires over the objections of Chinese representatives, and the gutting of equality clauses in the charter for the International Labour Organization (ILO).

Concerning the racial equality clause, the governments of Great Britain and the United States refused to endorse a Japanese proposal despite vigorous and prolonged lobbying by the Japanese delegation.[86] When the delegation then proposed a watered-down clause, brokered by Robert Borden, it passed by a majority (eleven out of seventeen votes) in the League of Nations Commission. Wilson, with British support, used his position as chair of the session to veto the resolution. The defeat of the racial equality clause was not the end of discussions related to race at Versailles. The issue resurfaced as part of discussions related to the labour-related proceedings.[87] According to the labour commission's original draft of a charter for the ILO, an institution that continues to this day, clause 8 included the statement: "In all matters concerning their status as workers and social insurance, foreign workmen lawfully admitted to any country and their families should be ensured the same treatment as the nationals of that country."[88] Borden, Hughes, and others in the British Empire delegation decried this suggestion because it would give Asian workers the same rights as white workers. Borden wrote to Lloyd George on 27 March 1919 complaining that Canadian conditions were not being fairly considered: "For example, in British Columbia there is Provincial legislation which reserves certain industries for white labour. Apparently the eighth article of the proposed report would call upon us to override this legislation. Any such proposal would arouse the fiercest resentment and might lead to the most serious consequences."[89] In one of the darker moments of Canadian diplomacy, Borden secretly substituted his own draft charter for the ILO, which effectively nixed equal treatment for workers regardless of race.[90]

The final item at Versailles that had profound consequences was the resolution of the Japanese demand to retain the former German colonial holdings on the Shandong peninsula in China and the Pacific Islands north of the equator. The Japanese delegation already had the support of the British, and Wilson, fearful the Japanese would reject the creation of the League of Nations if they were defeated on both racial equality and Shandong, decided to allow the concessions despite strong opposition from the Chinese representatives as well as from his own advisers. In the process, Wilson, having effectively scuttled the racial equality clause, had the temerity to lecture Wellington Koo, the Chinese representative, on matters of race: "A long time ago, the Kaiser set himself up as the enemy of your race, and we all remember his famous speech on the Yellow Peril. He would not have tried to govern France and England; it would have been enough to vanquish them to seize all that pleased him afterwards. One of the results of this war was to save the Far East in particular."[91] Lloyd George was not far behind Wilson in rationalizing the beneficence of the West. In discussions with Wilson and Makino, the Japanese representative at Versailles, Lloyd George declared: "China's stagnation justifies a great part of what foreigners have done there. The Chinese are like the Arabs, a very talented race, but at a stage that doesn't allow them to progress further. China would have been destroyed by the Taiping Rebellion if Gordon hadn't been there to organize her army."[92]

In the end, the US Senate failed to ratify the peace treaty and the United States remained outside the League of Nations. Many scholars and commentators have perceived this failure to ratify the Versailles Treaty and the subsequent decision not to join the League of Nations as the onset of American "isolationism." As Asian specialist John King Fairbank points out in his memoirs, such a view of American foreign policy distorts reality: "We actually had three policies at once: east toward Europe, no entangling alliances, 'we keep out'; south toward Latin America, the Monroe Doctrine, 'you keep out'; and west across the Pacific, the Open Door, 'we all go in.'"[93] Across the Pacific, however, was also Japan.

Japan's representatives at Versailles had won their demand for further concessions in China, but this, and the Japanese military's prolonged occupation of Siberia as part of the Allied intervention against the Soviet Union, raised warning flags among its imperial rivals. As Antony Best shows in his study of British military intelligence between the wars, racism remained strong within the British defence and foreign policy communities. Distrust of the Japanese prompted the Committee of Imperial Defence to recommend the building of a major base at Singapore, noting "the most likely war for some time to come would be one between the white and yellow races whose interests lay in the Pacific."[94]

Canadian prime minister Arthur Meighen, who had replaced Borden as head of the Conservative Party, played a key role in putting the final nail in the coffin of the Anglo-Japanese Alliance during the 1921 Imperial Conference in London.[95] As early as February that year, Meighen had written Lloyd George suggesting abrogation of the treaty and the convening of a "Conference of Pacific Powers."[96] Otherwise, Meighen cautioned, renewal of the treaty risked being seen by the US government as an "unfriendly exclusion and as a barrier to an English speaking accord." Meighen's motivations for actively advocating abrogation are not difficult to ascertain. Earlier in the month, Newton Rowell, a prominent lawyer and founder of the League of Nations Society in Canada, had met with advisors to president-elect Warren Harding and communicated to Meighen Washington's antipathy towards the Anglo-Japanese Alliance.[97] In Washington, leading opposition to the renewal of the alliance came from Henry Cabot Lodge and William Howard Gardiner. In 1912, Lodge had spearheaded a racist anti-Japanese corollary to the Monroe Doctrine, and he had led the opposition to US ratification of the League of Nations. For his part, Gardiner was a former president of the English-Speaking Union.[98]

Arthur Meighen was assisted in the preparations for the conference by Loring Christie, the legal advisor to the DEA. According to one scholar, Christie was the "principal architect of the Canadian assault on the Anglo-Japanese Alliance."[99] Immigration, trade, and ending the Anglo-Japanese Alliance constituted the focus of Canadian officials.[100] Meighen's intervention at the meeting effectively prevented the Imperial Conference from extending the Anglo-Japanese Alliance, and, furthermore, it prompted the colonial secretary, a young Winston Churchill, to declare against renewal of the treaty.[101] In the United States, President Warren Harding unofficially announced on 10 July 1921 that his government would welcome an international forum on Pacific problems to be held in Washington the following year. The Washington Conference opened on 12 November 1921 and lasted almost three months. In Japan, both hostility and fatalism greeted the events.[102] The conference ended with the signing of numerous accords, including the Four Power Treaty among the United States, Great Britain, Japan, and France, replacing the Anglo-Japanese Alliance; the Five-Power Naval Limitation Treaty, aimed at curbing the naval arms race then taking place among Great Britain, Japan, and the United States; and the Nine-Power Treaty regarding China.[103] Most commentators on these treaties either herald them as an impressive achievement in a new internationalist, multilateral order or as acts of folly that left the major powers unprepared for Japanese aggression. However, another perspective is possible.

The end of the Anglo-Japanese Alliance was met with mixed feelings on the part of Japanese officials. From the perspective of people such as Shidehara Kijūrō, there was little to be done: "We would only embarrass the British government if we insisted on the alliance being continued."[104] Charles Elliot, British ambassador in Tokyo, reported that the Washington Conference was seen there as "a secret coalition between Great Britain and the US at the expense of Japan."[105] The limits imposed on the Japanese navy created fertile fields of resentment within its ranks. The following year, in fact, a revised national defence policy suggested that the "Asiatic" policy of the United States was based on an "economic invasion" of China and racial prejudice against Japanese and that "sooner or later a clash with our Empire [would] become inevitable."[106] Fifteen years after the Vancouver race riots, the efforts to build an Anglo-Saxon accord regarding East Asia culminated in the Washington agreements, rendering Japan a subordinate imperial power while keeping China open for imperial business.

Even the establishment of the Canadian legation in Tokyo a few years later reflected the intensified racism of the era. Writing in his diary in

October 1927, King rationalized the opening of a Canadian legation: "It seems to me that our only effective way to deal with the Japanese question is to have our own Minister in Japan to vise passports. This will be the way to meet the Tory policy of 'exclusion' which we can never consent."[107] Respect for Japan's imperial status and hopes for trade were also significant in King's decision to open a legation, but his desire to enforce exclusion through passport and visa controls in Tokyo came first, and this reflects the institutionalization of state racism during this era.

Diaspora, Nationalism, and Decolonization

The origins of the Second World War in Asia are often traced to Japanese militarism and expansionism in East Asia and rightly so. But too often conventional English-language histories portray the Washington treaties through the lens of Japan-US relations, that is, as an era of multilateral internationalism in the joint exploitation of China, a process interrupted in 1931 by the Japanese invasion of northeast China. But just as Eurocentric views of Versailles displace its fundamental relationship with decolonization (or, to be more precise, its lack thereof), so, too, the liberal interpretation of the Washington treaties displaces a fundamental character of the period – the rise and, indeed, triumph of anti-colonialism in China. The movements that shaped this emerging force had a major impact not only on Chinese politics but also on imperial policies and Canadian attitudes.

In 1925, thousands of people in the Chinese communities in Toronto, Vancouver, and Victoria gathered together to protest the killing of Chinese anti-imperial demonstrators in Shanghai in what is known as the May 30th Incident. The incident, which saw British forces in Shanghai fire on unarmed protestors, reflected a burgeoning nationalist movement in China that challenged imperial control. In the meetings in Canada, the Chinese raised thousands of dollars to support the new Guomindang (GMD), or Nationalist, government that was taking shape. They also demanded that any settlement with the imperial powers in China include a deal to repeal Canada's Chinese Exclusion Act, 1923.[108] For many, the transnational linkage between imperialism abroad and racism at home was transparent at this time. Understanding these connections is as important for understanding the origins of the war in the Pacific, where Canadian troops first saw action in the Second World War, as it is for understanding the evolution of racialized communities in Canada.

In the wake of Versailles and the May 4th protests in China that were its result, GMD and communist forces united to create the first united front and a northern expedition to vanquish warlordism and to unite China. This movement was pushed forward by popular actions such as the Hong Kong Seaman's strike of 1922, an action in which race was key in so far as the strikers demanded wage parity with white sailors. On 15 May 1925, a demonstration against the firing of two Chinese workers at a Japanese-owned cotton mill in Shanghai led to the murder of Ku Cheng-hung.[109] This provoked mass protests, and on 30 May Shanghai military police under British direction fired on Chinese demonstrators, killing eleven and wounding scores of others. The confrontation escalated after a confrontation in Shanghai's international settlement, and the Shameen (Shamian) massacre of 23 June saw fifty-two Chinese protesters killed by British-led forces near Guangzhou. A general strike in Hong Kong-Guangzhou, mass protests, and a boycott movement swept the country, with British imperialism the main target. This was soon to change, however. As Chinese military forces approached northern China, Japanese imperialism came under increasing attack, particularly after three military interventions by Japanese troops in the Shandong region in 1927-28. The tensions that arose led some in Japan's elite to question the maintenance of its "formal" empire (i.e., colonial control over Korea, Taiwan, and northeast China). For others, however, the way out of the crisis was increased military intervention. The global economic depression of the early 1930s further exacerbated these contradictions, and, in 1931, military officers stationed in northeast China took matters into their own hands.[110]

Northeast China: The Invasion of Manchuria

Japan's invasion of Manchuria, or China's northeast provinces as they are referred to in Chinese, began on 18 September 1931 with an explosion near the Japanese-controlled rail line outside of Shenyang (Mukden).[111] Japanese authorities blamed "Chinese bandits" for this act of terror, but, in fact, it was Japanese military officers who were responsible. The fighting spread to Shanghai in early 1932, with the Chinese army waging a valiant effort against Japanese imperial forces – an effort that inspired many Chinese both at home and abroad. In the end, however, the GMD decided not to carry on the war, and soon Japanese forces controlled most of the region, establishing the puppet kingdom of Manchukuo and enthroning the last Chinese emperor, Pu Yi. The invasion provoked much resentment among Chinese abroad. In Canada, Chinese communities across the country organized support leagues and raised thousands of dollars to support the resistance in China.[112]

The Canadian government did little to support China at this time, refusing to establish diplomatic relations with China until 1942. Consular services were under the jurisdiction of Canada's legation in Japan. Canada's first ambassador to Japan, Herbert Marler, a former Cabinet minister in the Mackenzie King government in the early 1920s, was an unabashed anglophile and pro-Japan.[113] The British war and foreign offices agreed that the main problem regarding Japan's invasion was that pro-League of Nations opinion might damage relations with Japan and that League sanctions against Japan would have a disastrous effect on "our interests in the Far East."[114] That Japan should expand in northeast China did not overly concern the British foreign ministry, given that British interests were mainly concentrated in the Yangtze Valley. In fact, there was a distinct advantage: Japanese expansion created a larger force as a buffer against the Soviet Union, which the British government, as well as the Japanese, perceived as trying to undermine its interests in China and elsewhere.

In 1932, delegates gathered at the League of Nations in Geneva to debate the conclusions of the Lytton report, the League-commissioned study of the situation in Manchuria. C.H. Cahan, secretary of state in the Conservative Bennett Cabinet, addressed the assembly and largely supported Japan's position, declaring its actions as being similar to those of Great Britain in China in 1927, questioning China's right to a seat at the League, and supporting Japan's denials of any attempts to split Manchuria from China.[115] Cahan had been influenced to some degree by the British foreign minister, and the Canadian government was so unhappy with this transparent appeasement that it disavowed his position, lobbying instead to bring together the British and American positions.[116] Canadian officials were convinced that all they could do was duck and run. In Tokyo, Hugh Keenleyside remarked on the continual pull towards the British: "The minister spent Saturday afternoon playing golf with the British Ambassador and is consequently back again in his anti-Chinese, anti-League, pro-Japanese attitude from which he varied only after a lot of hard work on the part of Kirkwood and myself and some indirect comments from Dr. Skelton." The racism that underscored Marler's views did not go unnoticed: "The minister is still talking about the 'oriental mind' and the fact that we must not judge the orient by the occidental standards – especially with relation to such things as the Kellogg Pact, the Covenant of the League, etc., etc. This I cannot swallow. The inscrutability of the Orient and the 'oriental mentality' are largely a fiction of lazy minds."[117] The dissension over Manchuria rendered the Institute of Pacific Relations (IPR), a transpacific think tank in which Canadians actively participated, less effective than it might otherwise have been.[118] In the end, the Japanese Empire extended its grip in northeast China, consolidating the state of Manchukuo and extending its military control to just outside of Beijing.

Lester Pearson thus arrived in London in late 1935 to observe the Japanese delegation withdraw from the Naval Conference after the Euro-American powers rejected its demand for naval parity. Pearson's predictions regarding "the close understanding and friendly cooperation" of the Anglo-Saxon peoples had indeed proved prescient. The Chinese people, at home or in the diaspora, remained the excluded "other" and were left to their own devices to face the armed Japanese Empire.

2 China and the Clash of Empires

The sprawl that is today's Beijing has reached far into what was until quite recently rural countryside, even to the famous Lugouqiao, known in English as the Marco Polo Bridge, where Japanese troops clashed with Chinese on 7 July 1937, leading to an all-out invasion. Earlier Japanese aggression in Shandong and in northeast China had ignited a sense of indignation among many Chinese, and, unlike the 1931 invasion of Manchuria, the Chinese army dared to fight back against Japanese imperial forces.[1] For their part, both Japan's general staff and the Cabinet of then prime minister Konoe Fumimaro were prepared to expand the war, agreeing to dispatch three divisions if there was not a quick settlement. Local Chinese authorities in Hebei and Qahar provinces agreed to Japanese conditions for settling the incident, but Chiang Kai-shek hesitated and on 17 July called on the Chinese people to be prepared to fight against the latest aggression. On 26 July, the Japanese government dispatched the three promised divisions and heavy fighting broke out shortly thereafter. The 29th Corps fought back but was soon forced out of Beijing to the southwest city of Baoding. In Shanghai, using the pretext of a fight between a local Chinese security officer and a Japanese sailor, the Japanese imperial forces went on the offensive. Sporadic fighting in Shanghai lasted for three months until the Japanese landed a major force at Hangzhou Bay, south of Shanghai, forcing a pull-back of Chinese units to the then capital Nanjing. As the evening edition of Sunday's *Yomiuri shimbun* for 8 November 1937 stated at the time, a million Japanese troops had landed in

Hangzhou Bay just south of Shanghai, and, in a brilliant propaganda ploy, the army had sent a large air balloon over Shanghai announcing the landing of the troops accompanied by one hundred warships and calling for cooperation in bringing about "order."[2] With the arrival of reinforcements the Japanese military waged a fierce campaign to take Shanghai and then moved up the Yangtze River (Chang Jiang) towards Nanjing. Faced with overwhelming odds, the Chinese government decided to abandon the city and followed the Yangtze inland to escape the enemy forces. A token number of Chinese soldiers had been left behind in Nanjing as a rear guard, and, as the Japanese troops approached, many discarded their uniforms and attempted to meld into the civilian population. On the evening of 12 December 1937, the Japanese troops breached the walls surrounding Nanjing and entered the city. The cataclysm that ensued is recounted by a survivor.

Li Xiuying was seventeen years old when Japanese troops breached the walls of Nanjing. Li, seven months pregnant at the time, fled from the city centre to Wutai Mountain, where she found refuge with many other women at an American-run schoolhouse. The women, about a hundred in all, crammed into a cellar, hoping to avoid discovery by Japanese soldiers. On 19 December 1937, however, armed soldiers entered the schoolhouse, and, while conducting a thorough search, came across the cellar. The soldiers forced the women to leave the cellar, and while some stood guard, others proceeded to rape and humiliate them. Li was determined to resist. When a soldier tried to assault her, she rammed her own head against a wall and fell unconscious. The soldiers kicked her but she survived. Taken back inside, Li rested and attempted to come to terms with her situation. Before long, however, another group of soldiers arrived, and Li, rather than wait to be assaulted, grabbed for a soldier's sheathed bayonet and attempted to stab him. Others grabbed her, however, and in an orgy of reprisal, with their bayonets the soldiers proceeded to systematically slash Li over her entire body. She mercifully lost consciousness but awoke to find that she had miscarried.

Li's story was documented at the time by John Rabe, a German national and member of the Nazi Party, who helped organize an International Safety Zone in the city. On 24 December 1937, Rabe recorded in his diary his visit to Kulou Hospital, where Dr. Robert Wilson, another member of the International Safety Committee, was ministering to the injured: "Dr. Wilson used the opportunity to show me a few of his patients. The woman who was admitted because of a miscarriage and had the bayonet cuts all over her face is doing fairly well."[3] Many years later, Li's story remained consistent: "Now, after fifty-eight years, the wrinkles have covered the scars," Li recounted, "but when I was young, the scars on my face were obvious and terrible."[4] Even Japanese courts have been obliged to recognize the outrage perpetrated against Li.[5] Tens of thousands of civilians and soldiers lost their lives in Nanjing, with women suffering the added cruelty of wide-scale rape. The story of the massacre, and the organization of a safety zone, eventually filtered through the fog of propaganda, but it was soon only one of many in the chaos of protracted war.

During the siege of Nanjing, Japanese planes bombed and strafed American and British gunboats, the *Panay* and *Ladybird*, respectively, stationed in the Yangtze to enforce foreign treaty rights. The Japanese government soon apologized, but there was no respite in the attacks on GMD forces. Continuing Chinese resistance led the Japanese government to announce on 16 January 1938 that it would no longer have direct contact with the GMD government. In the spring, the Japanese forces continued their offensive, pursuing retreating Chinese forces along the Yangtze. The campaign to capture Xuzhou (Hsuchow) lasted nearly five months, focusing initially on the battle at Taierzhuang in March and April that year. Through tremendous effort and with strong popular support, the Chinese forces were able to inflict severe setbacks to the Japanese army. The scale of these battles was immense. In the first Chinese victory over Japanese forces, 100,000 Chinese troops inflicted approximately 20,000 casualties. The Japanese Imperial Army responded by dispatching reinforcements, eventually totalling about 300,000 troops. Moving to take Xuzhou itself, they met fierce resistance as the town's people united with the GMD armies to become "a city of courage under fire."[6] Besieged from six directions, the Chinese forces retreated and Xuzhou fell on 19 May 1938. The people of the region suffered enormously in the aftermath of this battle. Missionary reports from the battle zone indicate that Japanese troops engaged in an extensive massacre of civilians. In one case alone, Japanese troops rounded up 670 men in Yanwo, both locals and refugees, herded them into the courtyard of a large house, then burned it to the ground, shooting all who tried to escape the flames. Only five of the 670 survived. Dozens of similar massacres were also recorded, often by missionaries who, because their home countries had appeased Japan, were given immunity by the Japanese military in China. Then, in early June, peoples of the region faced a new disaster. Hoping to slow the Japanese forces, Chiang Kai-shek ordered his forces to blow up the Yellow River dykes, inundating 3,000 square kilometres in Henan, Anhui, and Jiangsu provinces and causing hundreds of thousands of people to drown. In the fall of 1938, Chinese troops continued to resist, facing a determined attempt by the Japanese

Imperial Army to pursue and destroy the GMD government. In October 1938, major confrontations took place around Hankou, the temporary capital of Chiang's forces. Again, the Nationalists retreated after inflicting significant losses on the enemy forces.

Accounts of Chinese resistance against the Japanese invasion, and the costs of that resistance, have not received the attention they deserve outside of China. In Japan, however, a number of scholars and journalists did endeavour to document the tragedy. In 1972, the publication of Honda Katsuichi's revelations about Nanjing in an *Asahi* newspaper series, "Chugoku no Tabi" (Journey to China), allowed many Japanese to hear for the first time the nature of the Imperial Army's aggression. On the other hand, English-language works on the Second World War in the Pacific have been preoccupied with the American role after Pearl Harbor. This, and military history's focus on the island-hopping battles of Midway, Leyte, Okinawa, and so forth, have tended to displace accounts of Chinese resistance. To the extent the larger questions of the war in China are discussed, they are often perceived through the prism of GMD-communist rivalry, with more than a few acerbic accounts of GMD corruption.[7] First-hand accounts of communist resistance, based in Yan'an, gained some currency at the time and received renewed attention in the 1960s and 1970s, during the war in Vietnam, only to recede into the shadows after the Sino-Vietnam border war in 1979.[8] The 1997 publication of Iris Chang's *The Rape of Nanking: The Forgotten Massacre* began to lift the shroud of English-language silence regarding what happened in China in the 1930s and 1940s. Many subsequent accounts have dealt with the atrocities committed by the Japanese imperial forces in China and the tragic plight of civilians.[9] Takashi Yoshida, in a recent study of Nanjing, suggested that the brutalities that took place there came to symbolize the cruelty and barbarism not just of the Japanese military but also of the Japanese people as a whole. The varied images of Japanese military atrocities involving the use of swords and bayonets were fuel for the "anti-Japanese imagination." Yoshida concludes: "The Japanese atrocities in Nanjing contributed to the image of inherent Japanese cruelty, as the stories about Nanjing were coupled with information about other atrocities." A monolithic perception of the Japanese among Americans led to 10 to 13 percent of polled respondents calling for the extermination of the Japanese. In other words, the reporting at the time seemed to contribute to intensified racialization. Yet, Yoshida's generalizations are questionable: an examination of reactions in Canada to this early period of the war reveals a complex landscape in which issues of race and empire became interwoven with local racisms, resistance, and the interactions of daily life.

Canada and the War

The clash outside Beijing quickly caught the attention of Canada's newspapers. The *Vancouver Sun* deployed an essentialist and gendered view in which Japan possessed a national temperament that, for historical reasons, was "quarrelsome": "Japan was pitchforked into the modern world as mediaeval child and grew up too fast. Today she is like a child suddenly elevated without preparation to one of the high offices of adulthood. She mistakes arrogance for dignity, vanity for pride, violence for energy." Against this, the *Sun* editorialist posited the superiority of the other imperial powers: "She is demonstrating a nasty genius for outlawry, for conquest, for oppression and for all those feudal abuses that white nations abandoned, at least in theory, many years ago."[10] As Japanese troops overran coastal cities and approached victory in Shanghai, the editorial tune changed to one of resignation: "She has taken Shanghai by force of arms, a process as legal as the purchase of a house. And just as the new landlord of a rented house may expel the tenants, if he so chooses, so, in our view, may Japan force the evacuation of those Occidental nationals who have been the tenants of China in Shanghai." Again, the *Sun* editorialist invoked racialized hierarchies with the British Empire, on the one hand, and India and China, on the other: "If a few brigades of well-armed and single-purposed Englishmen can hold all India, a comparatively small number of well-armed and single-purposed Japanese can hold the ill equipped hordes of China, who may be a race, but who have never been a unified nation."[11]

Editorials in the *Toronto Daily Star* reflected a slightly varied spectrum of opinion among the Anglo elite. On the one hand, an editorial in mid-July trumpeted the paper's support for Chiang, who, the paper suggested, "ha[d] gained an extraordinary hold upon the Chinese people."[12] Chiang, the editorial stated, was now a devout Christian and it quoted him as follows: "I have been a constant reader of the Bible. Never before has this sacred book been so interesting to me as during my two weeks' captivity in Sian ... I have dedicated my soul and body to the state." The paper concluded: "The national affairs of China are in good hands." Yet, just over a week later, another editorial proclaimed: "Japan's expansion, as this man sees it, is as irresistible a force as that which carried our own ancestors from the Atlantic seaboard to the prairies and beyond; but we found nothing in the way, except Indians and buffaloes, whereas China is nearly as overpopulated as Japan itself. They don't want to try to govern what this man calls 400,000,000 rugged individualists. 'But' ... it is this plethora of 'buts' that is bringing sleepless nights to many more besides the premier of Japan."[13] The French-language daily *La Presse* pointed to Soviet concern and suggested that, because the United States and the United Kingdom had interests in China, the situation would become similar to that of the Spanish Civil War: "Les repercussions ne tardent pas a se faire sentir a l'exterieur. Et alors viennent les interventions que les diplomates ont toutes les peines du monde, comme on le voit dans les affaires d'Espagne, a empecher de degenerer en guerre entre plusieurs nations."[14]

As the war continued, stories of atrocities reached Canada and the United States, but the attention devoted to them was as short-lived as the focus was diluted. In the month of December, there were approximately 150 items related to the events in China published in ten newspapers across Canada. These included news articles, editorials, cartoons, and letters to the editor. Of the approximately 150 items, only about 10 percent (or fifteen items) were related to casualties, military and/or civilian, in Nanjing. There was no mention of the raping of women in any of the articles.

For example, the *Vancouver Sun* ran two articles related to Nanjing, on 16 and 18 December 1937, respectively. The first, written by Paramount newsreel photographer Arthur Menken and entitled "Nanking Strewn with Corpses When It Fell," recounted how the capital was strewn with soldier and civilian corpses but noted that the "Japanese refrained from shelling and bombing the safety zone which was set aside for foreigners." It also noted that "more than 100,000 Chinese sought refuge in the zone."[15] Menken highlighted the heroic role of a Chinese private who, after telling Menken to get off the road, died in a hail of bullets from a Japanese tank that had just arrived. This article was buried on page 27. Two days later, the paper ran a second wire story by C. Yates McDaniel, an Associated Press correspondent, based on extracts from his diary for 8-16 December, revealing incidents of atrocities: "Some Japanese's sense of humor: Decapitated head balanced on a barricade with a biscuit in the mouth; another with a long Chinese pipe." On 13 December, McDaniel urged Chinese soldiers to shed their uniforms and to enter the safety zone to avoid being shot. Two days later, he recorded: "Saw some of the soldiers I helped disarm dragged from houses, shot and kicked into ditches. Tonight saw group of the civilians and disarmed soldiers, hands tied, marched from safety zone by Japanese carrying Chinese 'big swords.' None returned." On leaving the city, McDaniel wrote:

"My last remembrances of Nanking: 'Dead Chinese, dead Chinese, dead Chinese.'"[16] But even more shocking, in a certain sense, is his last entry on 17 December: "Arrived in Shanghai on the Japanese destroyer *Tsuga*."

The *Vancouver Daily Province* published an editorial entitled "Sack of Nanking."[17] Citing *London Times* reports from Nanjing, the editorial chastised Japan and its soldiers for conducting an undeclared and unprovoked war on China, and for breaking their original League of Nations commitments not to resort to war. It then provided a definition of "sack" and a historical reference inferring that sacks occurred only in a previous age. The only reference found relating to civilians was a 4 December 1937 page 1 article with a banner headline: "Attempt to Rescue Nine Canadian Nuns Foiled as British Ship Shelled." This was an Associated Press wire story that told how a Québécois missionary, Reverend Adrien Sansoucy, and a British consular official had attempted to "rescue" nine "French-Canadian Nuns," using the ship *Siushan,* which was turned back by machine gun fire, resulting in the death of the Chinese chief officer and the wounding of a number of passengers.[18]

On 18 December 1937, the *Calgary Herald* ran a front-page story from the Southam correspondent A.C. Cuming under the heading "Orgy of Looting, Murder Marked Nanking's Capture," with the subheading "Americans Subjected to Humiliation by Japs." The article described looting by Chinese soldiers, the collapse of the resistance, and how the Japanese "began wholesale executions of all those they suspected of being soldiers even though most real soldiers had already discarded and burned their uniforms. Japanese military police arrested and shot out of hand refugees and soldiers who came forward to them offering to surrender. No mercy was shown."[19] According to the article, this was followed by a reign of terror.

The *Globe and Mail* emphasized empire in a different way, portraying the danger to foreigners in Nanjing: "Fear Felt for Whites in Nanking" ran its first-page headline on 15 December 1937.[20] The fear arose not only out of an absence of information but also from "unverified accounts of tremendous casualties among Chinese civilians and troops since the attack on the capital proper was launched December 10th." In *La Presse* there were no specific stories on the seizure of Nanjing. To the extent there were any stories related to civilian casualties, these had to do with the fate of missionaries.

La Presse, like many other papers, dwelled on the bombing of the American and British warships the *Panay* and the *Ladybird*, respectively. It was this issue, more than any other, that got the attention of newspapers in Canada. The bombing of the *Panay* and the *Ladybird* gave rise to great consternation. The *Victoria Daily Times*, like *La Presse*, had no articles on what happened specifically in Nanjing, choosing instead to emphasize the attacks on the *Panay* and *Ladybird*. It suggested that talks between Great Britain and the United States were an indication that "just as soon as circumstances [were] considered bad enough to justify the substitution of the sword for the pen, that change [would] take place with full co-operation on the part of Westminster and Washington."[21] Less than a week later, an editorial hit harder, stating that the "time for mealy-mouthed platitudes had passed" and that unless measures were taken Japanese forces would "continue week by week to add to the territory dominated by the Rising Sun."[22] *La Presse*, in a 15 December editorial entitled "Un empire s'organise," suggested that Europe and the United States should start to worry as, in China, Japan was gaining a large empire with huge new lands and a population triple that of Japan itself.[23] Initially, newspaper commentaries in the Canadian mainstream press paid little attention to the atrocities in Nanjing, choosing, instead, to indicate the threat that an expansionist Japan posed to Euro-American imperial interests.

Reactions in Chinese and Japanese Communities

In Japanese and Chinese communities in Canada, the 1937 war provoked a variety of responses. These communities had evolved: resilience in the face of adversity had brought greater respect and growing ties with whites in many localities; furthermore, second and third generations had begun to organize and to challenge both white supremacy and the simplistic nationalist rhetoric of earlier generations.[24] The war both exacerbated and attenuated these differences.

As early as 1931, at the time of the invasion of northeast China (the Manchurian Incident), the Chinese community began to organize patriotic projects. In Victoria, for example, community leaders initiated the Resist Japan and Save the Nation Association.[25] This movement was not huge at the time, but it did lay the groundwork for future organizing. After the July 1937 invasion, across the country, in large communities and small, people of Chinese descent contributed substantial sums to agencies in China through cash donations and the purchase of war bonds to help fund the resistance to Japanese imperialism. This amounted to about $5 million over the course of the war, from 1937 to 1945.[26] However, during the Pacific phase of the war (1942-45), the same communities purchased over Cdn$10 million in Victory Bonds, which were issued by the Canadian government.[27] The attack on

China prompted a tide of sympathy with what many considered their motherland, especially as reports of war damage, famine, and deaths began to circulate. For some young people, this created a strong desire to join in the defence of China, and a number, like the "Oriental Wingbird" Charles Wong of Winnipeg, trained to join China's air force.[28] The Vancouver Chinese Benevolent Association and the Resistance Association initiated a call to boycott commercial dealings both with Japan and Japanese Canadians. Political divisions in the community faded into the background as people united to assist China in the war. Representatives from the GMD arrived in cities across the country to help with organizing. Even today, family reminiscences of the past often focus on the effects of the war and the movement to support the resistance.[29]Although the Canadian government did little to support China at the beginning of the Sino-Japanese War, others in the white community did speak out and worked with the Chinese community. As the editorials on the war show, there was a massive shift in the portrayal of China, which went from being the "sick man of Asia" to being the noble victim. In the process, figures such as Wong Foon Sien (Wong Mun-po) in Vancouver and E.C. Mark in Toronto gained some prominence (and elicited some resentment) as their English-language skills gained them admiration among many in the white community.

The war's impact in the Japanese-Canadian community was somewhat different. In recent times, the necessity of refuting deeply embedded racialized notions of members of the community as spies and potential saboteurs has given rise to what might fairly be described as the counter-portrait of Japanese Canadians as loyal Canadians.[30] Examining community newspaper coverage of the Sino-Japanese War provides important insights into the diversity within the community at the time and provides us with a broader view of Canadian reactions to the war, in particular, to the events in Nanjing. There were three Japanese-language community newspapers at the time of the war: the *Tairiku nippō* [Continental Times], founded in 1907; the *Kanada shimbun* [Canadian Daily News], founded in 1923; and the *Nikkan minshū* [Daily People], founded in 1924.[31] Of these three, the *Tairiku nippō* had the largest circulation at about four thousand households, the *Kanada shimbun* had twenty-five hundred households, and the *Nikkan minshū* had fifteen hundred. In 1938, the *nisei* (second-generation Japanese Canadians) started an English-language paper called the *New Canadian*.

Prior to the onset of the Sino-Japanese War in 1937, much of the international news carried in *Tairiku nippō* focused on conflicts along the

Manchukuo-Soviet border. The outbreak of war in 1937 resulted in an increase in international coverage from approximately one page per eight pages to four or five pages per eight, with the focus on the progress of the Japanese imperial forces in China. Much of the war coverage originated in Tokyo, with the *Dōmei tsūshinsha* [Domei News], the main wire service. The pro-imperial perspective was clear in the stories about the war. At the outset, the Chinese army was blamed for the initial skirmishes on 7 July 1937, and subsequent escalations were characterized as actions of self-defence on the part of the Japanese military. Local coverage highlighted examples of patriotic support. For example, the paper documented the story of Uta Zenkichi, a Vancouver businessman, who had donated one thousand yen (Cnd$292.50) to the Japanese Imperial Army.[32] A few days later, the paper also reported how Hinatani Yoshinori, a thirteen-year-old Templeton High School student, had saved up money from berry picking and given ten dollars to the imperial forces after hearing from his father about their sacrifices in China. The article also listed donations of one hundred yen from a Buddhist women's organization and a fifty-yen donation from a Mr. Kobayashi.

Regarding Nanjing, on 18 December 1937 the *Tairiku nippō* quoted reports originating from the Shanghai Expeditionary Force that there were eighty to ninety thousand corpses in the capital and that about one thousand prisoners of war had been captured.[33] On 27 December these figures were revised: eighty-four thousand Chinese troops were reported killed, and 10,050 were taken as prisoners of war.[34] But the Japanese community in Canada in 1937 was not the same community of earlier years. Labour organizing had begun in the 1920s, with the formation of the Japanese Labour Union (later the Camp and Mill Workers' Union). A key player at this time, Suzuki Etsu, also took the initiative to form the *Daily People* (*Nikkan minshū*).[35] Even this paper was swept up to some degree in the surge of nationalist pride in Japan's victories, but voices of opposition to the war, such as that of Umezuki Takaichi, could also be heard. Umezuki put his hopes in the next generation, or *nisei,* whom he believed would be less influenced by Japanese propaganda. His hopes were not misplaced. As early as 1936, *nisei* had begun to organize, and, on 22 May of that year, a delegation appeared before a House of Commons committee to argue its case for the franchise.[36] Out of this movement emerged the new English-language voice representing the second generation of Japanese immigrants – the *New Canadian,* founded in November 1938.

The *New Canadian* was dedicated to demonstrating that *nisei* deserved Canadian citizenship, and it went out of its way to display Canadian patriotism. For example, the paper prominently displayed a photo of a Japanese-Canadian float, constructed in the form of a huge crown and covered in flags, in honour of King George VI's 1939 visit to Vancouver. Evolving into a very professional weekly journal, the paper carried regular coverage of community events but little of the propaganda that was so prominent in the *Tairiku nippō*. This is not to say that it did not have any international coverage. In April, the *New Canadian* announced that its chief editor, Shinobu Higashi, was sailing for Japan en route to Dairen, where he was to take up a new editorial position with the *Manchurian Daily News,* an English-language paper.[37] Higashi, a graduate of the University of British Columbia's English honours program, had attended the Co-operative Commonwealth Federation (CCF, the precursor to the New Democratic Party) summer school in May 1938 as a delegate for the Japanese Canadian Citizens Association. The paper also reprinted a critical review of Japanese militarism written by Pearl S. Buck.[38]

When tensions between Great Britain and Japanese forces mounted as a result of a clash in Tianjin, the *London Daily Express* asked for the views of Vancouver's Dr. Edward C. Banno. In a front-page article reprinting the exchange, the *New Canadian* quoted Banno: "As Canadians of Japanese descent it grieves us profoundly that Great Britain and Japan should engage in serious discord in the Orient or elsewhere."[39] In its next issue, the paper reported on an interview with Japanese parliamentarians visiting Vancouver. Funada Naka, the paper reported, was firm in his belief that there would not be war between Japan and Great Britain. In response to a question regarding *nisei* loyalties, Funada told the paper that "the Nisei would best qualify as responsible citizens of Canada, and would be in a position to make their greatest contribution by studying Japanese culture and retaining the characteristics of the Japanese race, which made possible the rise of modern Japan."[40]

The *New Canadian* spared no effort to take on racism directed at their community. It took square aim at the *Vancouver Sun* for its assertion that Japanese Canadians were "not assimilable and [did] not properly belong in this country." It suggested that the *Vancouver Sun* should change the slogan on its masthead to: "A newspaper devoted to reaction and intolerance, hypocrisy and the persecution of racial minorities." It criticized and rebutted Ontario Conservative Party leader George Drew's suggestion that, if the

Japanese forces in Tientsin (Tianjin) did not accommodate the British authorities, "then we shall be obliged to order all of the Japanese in Canada to leave our country."[41] As these quotes indicate, the war had provided new possibilities for those dedicated to the eradication of the Japanese community. Accusations that "Japanese" or "Orientals" were not assimilable, that Japanese interests were buying up resources for Japan's war effort, or that Japanese people were acting as spies regularly made the rounds.[42] British Columbia's premier, T.D. Patullo, told a royal commission that all "Orientals" had to be excluded and those already in the province "repatriated."[43]

Despite the resurgence of racialization at this time, the Canada of the 1930s was not the same as the Canada of 1907. Asian communities' resilience in the face of adversity began to shine through the prejudice. The Asahi baseball team and a Chinese soccer team stood out for their skills and fair play, garnering favourable press coverage. The founding of unions among workers of Chinese, Japanese, and South Asian descent, and changing attitudes among some left-wing unions, led to increasing cross-community actions. A few Liberals and many CCF politicians condemned the rising attacks on Japanese Canadians, accusing those doing the attacking of acting like Hitler. The *BC Lumber Worker* warned against making Japanese Canadians scapegoats for the aggression of the Japanese Imperial Army. And the CCF candidate in a provincial by-election defeated Halford Wilson, a rabid anti-Asian alderman from Vancouver, accusing him of planning a "pogrom against the Japanese."[44]

The Movement for Sanctions

Japanese aggression in China had stoked the anti-Japanese imagination among many white Canadians, and the rise of such agitation created complex dynamics within social movements of the time, including the movements to impose an embargo on Canadian exports to Japan and to boycott Japanese goods coming into Canada. The movement for sanctions against Japan was spearheaded by the League for Peace and Democracy. This was the second incarnation of the League against War and Fascism, which was formed in 1934 by communists but had broad-based support that included intellectuals at the University of Toronto, groups from a number of churches, and well known groups such as the Fellowship of Reconciliation and the Women's International League for Peace and Freedom.[45] CCF members of Parliament Tommy Douglas and William Irvine sat on the national executive for a period. In 1937, the League against War and Fascism changed its name to the League for Peace and Democracy. The Canadian Youth Congress

(CYC) also formed in this period, with a cross-section of support, including the YMCA, the YWCA, and the Student Christian Movement. Its first pan-Canadian meeting took place in May 1936 with 455 delegates. The CYC participated in the first World Youth Congress in Geneva, and among the delegates were William Kashtan, secretary of the Young Communist League; T.C. Douglas of the CCF; and Paul Martin (senior), a future minister of foreign affairs.[46] Ken Woodsworth, a nephew of the founder of the CCF, J.S. Woodsworth, was the chair of the CYC.

One hundred and sixty delegates attended the Congress for Peace and Democracy in Toronto, which began on 19 November 1937 in Toronto's Victoria Theatre. Dr. Heng Shih Tao, dean of the University of Nanjing, brought greetings from China. The Chinese had the same belief as did Canadians, he stated, in a "government of, for and by the people."[47] He knew, he told the attentive audience, that Canada was exporting minerals to Japan and that the "people of Canada [did] not agree with this." He concluded his address with a historical reference: "Napoleon said: 'Let the sleeping giant lie': But I tell you the giant of the east has awakened. Your fight is our fight and your success our success."

This marked the beginning of an intense campaign to force the Canadian government to halt its shipments of strategic goods to Japan. On 7 December 1937, the *Toronto Daily Star* published a letter from H.A. Potter, secretary of the Canadian League for Peace and Democracy (CLPD), calling the Japanese invasion of China and the bombing of "helpless women and children" a crime against civilization. He called for an embargo on exports of war materials and a boycott of goods produced in Japan.[48] The *Winnipeg Free Press* highlighted the boycott issues in front-page stories about a major meeting on Wednesday night, 15 December 1937, sponsored by the "joint committee" cooperating with the Chinese Patriotic League. Calling it "one of the most representative in the city's history with men and women from religious, political, labor, youth and peace organizations," the meeting passed resolutions calling on the Canadian government to ban exports of war materials to Japan and on Canadians to boycott the purchase of goods "imported from Japan."[49] The paper also noted that the CCF had introduced a motion in the Manitoba legislature that sparked lively debate before being tabled by the Conservative government.[50]

The CLPD reported in the January 1938 edition of its newsletter, the *Amplifier*, that the embargo campaign had distributed seventy-five thousand cards demanding that the government halt shipments of war materiel to Japan and that another seventy-five thousand were being distributed, with a goal of sending fully 500,000 such cards to the government.[51] The campaign also mobilized supplies to aid the resistance. From Vancouver, for example, the CLPD's BC branch managed to ship thirty thousand surgical dressings and clothing for six hundred people.[52] Madame Chiang Kai-shek (Soong Meiling) wrote to A.A. McLeod, the national chairman of the CLPD, in the spring of 1938 acknowledging the work of the CLPD with "appreciation and our warmest gratitude." Mme. Chiang stressed that the world had never before seen "the barbarities which the Japanese ha[d] committed and [were] still committing in China," and she insisted that the support of peoples around the world encouraged the Chinese people in their resistance, even though foreign "governments ma[d]e no practical move to show that they condemn[ed] and [would] expose the inhumanities and ruthlessness of the Japanese." She pointed out that the Chinese resistance had prevented Japan from securing a quick victory and had been able to "destroy the myth of their invincibility."

Within Canada, the Chinese communities had been extremely active in raising support for China's war of resistance against Japan. In a number of cities they were instrumental in promoting the embargo and boycott campaign and were enforcing sanctions on a local level. Jean Lumb recalls from her childhood years: "My best friend was still Japanese, although my parents would say, 'You can't go into their store to buy candy anymore.' We didn't have much money to buy candy anyway."[53] The boycott created consternation among many in the Japanese-Canadian community who believed Chinese merchants were taking advantage of the situation. In its 1 February 1939 edition, the *New Canadian* reported on the boycott of rhubarb produced on farms owned by people of Japanese descent, citing Y. Ebata of the Farmers Products Distributing Company: "A Chinese green grocer was in to see us this morning and he expressed the desire to handle our rhubarb. But it seems that they are intimidated by hired thugs and ruffians, and if they are caught they are fined heavily for dealing with the Japanese."[54] Ebata said he regretted that the "Chinese should discriminate against the Japanese because of hostilities in the Orient." But the *New Canadian* wavered in opposing the boycott openly. On 15 March 1939, the editors reprinted an article from the *Financial News* on the Embargo Council, an organization that was promoting a boycott of exports to Japan. They were reprinting the article, they stated, because many *nisei* organizations were being asked to participate in its activities and were having a hard time coming to any decision.[55] The article, entitled "Take It or Leave It," advised: "The Embargo Council in British Columbia, with which some respectable citizens have ill-advisedly

Chinese-Canadian women prepare for a tag day to collect funds for war relief during the China War. The Canadian government declined to establish diplomatic relations with China, refused to send war relief or aid, and refused to take actions to sanction the Japanese government for its invasion of China. | Dora Nipp collection, Multicultural History Society of Ontario

become associated is just such a [Communist] movement." It was sponsored, stated the *Financial News,* by the League for Peace and Democracy, a communist offspring originally known as the League Against War and Fascism. On the other hand, some *nisei* retained ties with the left, as illustrated by the photograph of Tom Shoyama and Kunio Shimizu, Japanese Canadian Citizens Association president and vice-president, respectively, with Bill McConnel, Maurice Rush, Young Communist League secretary, and Val Bjarnason, Vancouver Youth Council executive secretary, upon their return from the fourth annual Canadian Youth Congress, displayed prominently on the front page of the 15 July 1939 edition of the paper. Herein lies the complexity of the situation: the CYC continued to promote the demand for an Asian-Canadian franchise but it also supported the embargo and boycott.

Support for some form of economic sanctions against Japan, an embargo on materials to be used in war, or even a boycott of incoming Japanese products spanned the political spectrum and the movement gained momentum in 1938-39.[56] As in the United States, women often took a leading role in demanding some sort of action to oppose the war.[57] To be sure, some racists saw sanctions as a vindication of their views, but many of those involved were actively fighting discrimination against Asian Canadians and perceived sanctions as an act opposing imperialism and war. The sanctions movement achieved limited success, however, in the 1937-39 period.

The Canadian government under Mackenzie King pushed back hard against the intensive lobbying for Canada to take a more active stance against Japanese aggression. Earlier conceptions (i.e., that Japanese aggression was simply a means of whipping an unstable China into shape) once again made their appearance in comments by R. Randolph Bruce, the Canadian minister in Japan, in an interview with the *Toronto Star*.[58] As in the past, King and his key foreign affairs officials, O.D. Skelton and Loring Christie, remained reluctant to take any action and looked to their Anglo cousins, Great Britain and the United States, for direction. Much was at stake, including Canadian commercial interests, trade, and the possibility of war. But one element that is seldom emphasized is how the question of race fitted in. In his diary, King describes a dream in which he interprets the unfolding of the war in Asia as a pig in a poke, in which armed intervention by the British Empire would be inappropriate: "The animal instincts are asserting themselves, & are best left to work themselves out, & others to abstain therefrom. It is an appaling [sic] world situation – but not worth the lives of white men for 'Business Interests.'"[59] King's candid revelation in his diary reflects how accommodation of Japanese aggression in China was also a function of racialization, of his assumption that Asians were supposedly reverting to their animal instincts and that "white men" should simply let them fight it out. While this particular piece of evidence is confined to King, we should not presume that he was alone in harbouring such assumptions. Indeed, the thrust of Canadian foreign policy since the Vancouver race riots of 1907 had been to solidify an Anglo-Saxon alliance between the American and British empires.

A September 1937 report suggested that few Canadian interests in China were threatened and that, therefore, it was not necessary to consider sanctions or an embargo, a demand the Chinese government introduced at the League of Nations on 13 September of that year. All this slowed down the rush to accommodation that the King government had signalled with the decision to allow R. Randolph Bruce to return to Tokyo as ambassador after having ordered him to delay doing so.[60] In October, the government supported a weak League of Nations' resolution criticizing Japan and calling for a meeting of the Washington Treaty signatories at Brussels. Despite the strong pressure at home for some type of sanction against Japanese expansionism, the government refused to budge. And since the British and

American governments refused to challenge what had hitherto been their junior partner in the Pacific, despite great dissatisfaction with the war on China, the Brussels conference ended with an empty declaration criticizing Japan.[61] The King government resisted calls for Canada to withdraw from the Anglo-Japanese Treaty of Commerce and Navigation and, in fact, encouraged the continuation of trade. In May 1939, Hideo Iwasaki wrote on Canada-Japan trade in the *New Canadian,* noting: "instead of a radical decline expected in the export of Canadian goods to Japan, there has actually been a comparative increase."[62] This would continue, Iwasaki suggested, because of the demand for "actual reconstruction in China and also for delayed normal building activities throughout Japan." Such trade would continue to "flourish and expand, provided that undesirable and artificial obstacles such as tariffs, embargo and boycott movements, and trade wars [were] not deliberately provoked." He concluded that "Canadians, on [their] part, should endorse the sane attitude of the Dept. of Trade and Commerce," which had, in an advertising program, reinforced the need for expanded trade. Not only was it business as usual, but the Sino-Japanese War was also a business opportunity. The billowing clouds of moral condemnation were inversely related to government action. In fact, overall trade as well as metal exports to Japan peaked in 1939.[63]

In March that year, King reflected on Canada's historical role in the imperial politics of East Asia:

> There is no doubt the [Anglo-Japanese] alliance would not have been ended but for Meighen's insistence at the Conference of 1919 or 1920. Had it not been ended, Japan and Britain would have continued to be friends, probably China and the US ditto, with the result that England and the States could have held the Orient in a stable condition, and avoided the war that is taking place there. With conditions steady in the Orient, England could have handled the European situation. We would not have had Germany, Italy and Japan allied against the democracies. It shows how one mistaken step, even in a country as remote from the scene as Canada, may affect the whole world situation.[64]

King's reflection on Canada's role is of some interest in that it embraces a number of important concepts and poses challenges to conventional views about King's foreign policies. King suggests that ending the Anglo-Japanese Alliance in 1921 and replacing it with the Washington treaties had been a mistake. However, we know from King's earlier activities that he himself had worked avidly for an Atlantic alliance based on shared Anglo-Saxonism. This raises the question of how King viewed the role of the powers in East Asia. King hoped the British and American governments could have exercised paternal authority over Japan and China. This reflected a racial hierarchy and it also negated any independent role for the Japanese government or for the Chinese movement for independence. Given that King had travelled in China and Japan and had been impressed by the force of Japanese imperialism, his retrospective view about Meighen and Canada's role in ending the alliance seems to have more to do with his penchant for chastising the actions of his former nemesis than anything else. King believed that he had proven his capacities as a conciliator and knew when intervention was called for.

The reaction of the other imperial powers to China's plight was pragmatic: as long as the Japanese forces were prepared to tolerate Euro-American interests in China, there would be little or no assistance to the Chinese government. Instead, the Japanese would not only be appeased but also actively assisted. Roosevelt made his now-famous "Quarantine speech," calling for an end to lawlessness but then vetoed a proposal at a Brussels conference calling for economic sanctions. Trade continued unabated, fuelling Japan's aggression. The only country that came to the assistance of Chiang Kai-shek's GMD government was the Soviet Union. Its fitful relations with Japan after 1931 had seen it sell to the Japanese the Chinese Eastern Railway, on the one hand, and engage in brutal fighting against Japan at Nomonhan, on the border with Inner Mongolia, on the other. After 1937, it signed a treaty of non-aggression with Chiang, affording the GMD government – not the communists – credits of $250 million and providing it with hundreds of airplanes and aviators as well. Germany, which had hitherto tried to work with Chiang's government, withdrew from China and, on 20 February 1938, in his infamous Reichstag speech, Hitler praised Japan for fighting communism.

In late 1938, the Konoe government supplemented its military strategy with a new propaganda initiative, calling for the creation of a "new order in East Asia" based on cooperation among China, Manchukuo, and Japan to "carry out a common defence against communism, create a new culture, and bring about an economic combination in East Asia." This was a political appeal for a united front against white imperialism and communism, and it reflected a belief among Konoe's advisors that it was necessary to win Chinese political support and that a military solution alone was impossible. It did have some effect, as a number of Chinese leaders, including Wang Jingwei, went over to the Japanese side, providing the Japanese imperial cause with a veneer of legitimacy. Chiang, however, rebutted Konoe's proposals, declaring that the "so-called new order would be based on the intimate relations that would tie enslaved China to the Japanese-created Manchukuo and Japan herself."[65] The only impediment to Japanese control of China was continued determination on the part of the GMD and communist forces to resist.

Transnational Support to China

Among the less well known aspects of resistance in China is the defection to the Chinese side of large numbers of Japanese soldiers who had been captured as prisoners of war. The story of these "turncoats" has been told by Japanese historians.[66] Over twelve hundred former soldiers or support workers worked actively with the Yan'an communists and the so-called "red" armies to defeat their own compatriots. Maeda Mitsukei was employed as a railway supervisor and, in the spring of 1938, was dispatched to China to oversee railways in the occupied areas. Told one day by villagers that the 8th Route Army was nearby, he didn't know what to make of it: "I had never heard of the 8th Route Army; this was the first I knew of it. I went back to the barracks and in the middle of the night the village headsman woke me to say that the 8th Route Army was close and an attack on the railway was imminent."[67] Maeda reported this to the railway police and offered to help them but was told to stay out of it. Returning to the railway offices, he went to bed only to be roused to find the barrel of a pistol in his mouth. The 8th Route Army took him prisoner. Maeda was reported dead by Japanese officials, and his parents erected a gravestone for him. According to Maeda, the Japanese prisoners of war (POWs) who went over to the Chinese usually took a year or two to decide to do so. But after being talked to by another POW, and having been shown what the Japanese army did after a battle, he began to change his views. Because of his Buddhist background, and because as a civilian he had not received the indoctrination so common in the army, Maeda began to have second thoughts. Within six months of being captured, he came to the conclusion that Japan's invasion was wrong. And so for the rest of the war, he worked against Japan's imperial forces, writing leaflets in Japanese to the Japanese soldiers. These men were engaged in what their own state considered treasonous acts; however, for the most part, they were men of conscience who had rejected the rationale of an imperial war.

Canada, Great Britain, and the United States had rejected taking an active stand against Japan's invasion of China, but among the Chinese and

Dr. Norman Bethune (right) with Dr. Richard Brown and soldiers of the Eighth Route Army, Northern China, 1938 | Library and Archives Canada, PA-116874

Japanese there were a number of people who decided to join the resistance. Among the most prominent Canadians to work in solidarity with the Chinese in their struggle against the invasion was Norman Bethune.[68] A Montreal physician, Bethune became radicalized in the 1930s and was among the contingent of Canadians (the MacKenzie-Papineau Battalion) that went to support Republican Spain in the fight against Franco. There he developed a technique for delivering and administering blood transfusions at the front. By the time he returned to Canada, he had become a left-wing folk hero. On 18 June 1937, over eight thousand attended a Montreal rally to hear Bethune report on his experiences in Spain. In Vancouver, Bethune spoke to a packed house at the Orpheum Theatre on 1 August, a few weeks after Japan's invasion of China. Bethune would soon leave for China to bring supplies and to apply his skills as part of an international medical mission. Bethune was not alone.

Jean Ewen found herself being recruited by the LPD to return to China and work alongside Bethune. Ewen, the daughter of Tom MacEwen, a prominent leader in the Communist Party, was resentful of her father's neglect of the family. After completing her nursing training, she went to China as a medical missionary and learned to speak fluent Chinese. After a number of years working in rural areas, she returned to Canada only to be recruited once again after the Japanese invasion. She did not suffer fools gladly, particularly those of the male persuasion. She recalled joining Bethune on the *Empress of Japan* in Vancouver, piped up the gangplank "by a fellow Scotsman, Jimmy Mitchell, in full Highland dress. As [she] came aboard [she] noticed Dr. Bethune and Dr. Parsons leaning on the rail. [She] shook hands with them and Dr. Bethune asked, 'Who the hell is the oatmeal savage piping, anyway?' 'Me, of course,' [she] answered. He gave a contemptuous sneer saying, 'I don't believe it! Tom's daughter a Scottish Nationalist.'"[69] Ewen recalled that she "assured him [she] didn't care what he believed." On 8 January 1938, they departed for China, where their relationship would remain a stormy one. Volunteering to help the 8th Route Army, a communist-led force, Bethune and Ewen were in the thick of the action: "The Japanese airmen were out early every day, dropping bombs on any small village that might have a soldier quartered. We watched them from a distance, flying very low. Each time a bomb dropped, a wall of earth rose skyward with a thud, and houses and trees were no more. Their favourite game was strafing anything that moved, be it a dog, a child, or a soldier."[70] They travelled to Yan'an, where they delivered urgent medical care. Eventually, the stress of war and working with a male hero-martyr such as Bethune took its toll, and later the same year Ewen returned to Canada. Bethune, a Communist, and Ewen, an early feminist, were but two of a growing number of people in Canada who joined the worldwide outcry against the invasion of China. Norman Bethune died in November 1939, after he contracted blood poisoning while operating on a patient in a remote area of Shanxi Province. The following tribute, written by Mao Zedong after he learned of Bethune's death, made the Canadian doctor a household name in China.

> Comrade Norman Bethune, a member of the Communist Party of Canada, was around fifty when he was sent by the Communist Parties of Canada and the United States to China; he made light of traveling thousands of miles to help us in our War of Resistance Against Japan. He arrived in Yan'an in the spring of last year, went to work in the Wutai Mountains, and to our great sorrow died a martyr at his post. What kind of spirit is this that makes a foreigner selflessly adopt the cause of the Chinese people's liberation as his own? It is the spirit of internationalism, the spirit of communism, from which every Chinese Communist must learn.[71]

What is often forgotten is that there were also a large number of Chinese Canadians who, after the 1937 invasion, wanted to fight as part of the Chinese resistance. But the refusal of the Canadian and British governments to come to the assistance of Chiang, not to mention racist barriers to enlistment, made it extremely difficult. Missionaries such as Robert McClure and James Endicott also assisted the resistance in their own ways.[72] And they were not alone.

Favourable reports of communist actions, both in fighting the Japanese and in their treatment of peasants, attracted the attention of many non-Chinese supporters of China's struggle for independence. One of the more memorable characters involved was Rewi Alley, a New Zealander who had landed in Shanghai in 1927.[73] In 1938, Alley began the "Gung Ho" (Gong He) movement of industrial cooperatives as a means of maintaining production in areas of resistance. However, even support from members of the Soong family, Chiang Kai-shek's own in-laws, did not always protect the movement from anti-communist zealots in the GMD regime. Alley recalled an attack by GMD forces on the Gung Ho office in Maolin on 4 January 1941: "They came to the front of our office and opened up with their machine-guns and wounded our accountant, who was busy inside. Fortunately, some of the staff had not arrived at the office that morning. They went to the hills and marched off with the remainder of the New Fourth Army across the [Yangtze] river."[74]

Regional Wars in Europe and Asia, 1939-41

In a dramatic reversal, the Soviet Union ended its policy calling for a united front against fascism and signed a non-aggression pact with Germany's Nazi government on 23 August 1939. The Soviet Union and Germany together occupied Poland, triggering an end to the British policy of appeasement. Within a few days, Great Britain declared war on Germany, followed by other British Commonwealth countries, including Canada. However, none of the British-allied countries at war with Germany and Italy declared war on Japan at this time. What took place in the years between 1939 and 1941 were separate regional wars, one in Asia and the other in Europe.

The Canadian government began mobilizing people and resources to support the British Empire and other European allies in the fight against Germany and Italy. That King and the Canadian government should support the British Empire in 1939, even though it did not support the Chinese against Japan in 1937, seems almost common sense, but it was also a reflection of the long process of the "whitening" of Canada, that is, the exclusion of Asians and other peoples of colour and the encouragement of European settlers, including those who, in the past, had been considered second-class whites – the Ukrainians, Doukhobors, and Italians. Canada's gaze towards Europe was not "natural"; rather, it was a feature of the conscious exclusion of those whose gaze might have been westward, to the Transpacific.

The decision to declare war on Germany immediately posed the question of recruitment of large numbers of soldiers, particularly if conscription, the bugbear of Mackenzie King, was to be avoided. Numerous Japanese and Chinese Canadians, as well as those of South-Asian descent, had either volunteered for the armed forces or were called up after modified conscription began in mid-1940. The South-Asian community was lobbying hard at this time for the franchise and, in the face of prevarication by military authorities regarding its recruitment, stopped enlistment as part of a "no vote-no war" campaign.[75] The government later responded by issuing indefinite deferment for those of South-Asian descent. Regarding recruitment from the Japanese- and Chinese-Canadian communities, the Cabinet War Committee appointed a "Special Committee on Orientals in British Columbia" on 1 October 1940 to examine issues related to national security and military recruitment. The creation of the committee was in response to intense pressure from exclusionist politicians such as British Columbia's premier Dufferin Patullo, Ian McKenzie, Halford Wilson, and others. After holding hearings for two months, the committee, which included representatives from the Department of National Defence and the RCMP, as well as Hugh Keenleyside from the DEA and Sir George Samson, a British historian of Japan, reported to the government. The investigation targeted both Japanese and Chinese Canadians, but, in practice, it focused on the Japanese-Canadian community. On the one hand, the report stated clearly that charges of disloyalty were unsupportable and were based on "unsubstantiated rumour and hearsay."[76] The report reflected the communities' efforts to survive and to display their loyalty to Canada as well as the important degree of solidarity with Asian Canadians that had developed in the 1930s. On the other hand, it also recommended that neither people of Chinese nor people of Japanese origin be allowed to serve in the military, that all Japanese Canadians be registered, that measures be taken to diminish anti-Japanese propaganda, and that a standing committee on "Orientals" be established to continue the working of the special committee.[77] Recommendations to end Oriental immigration at an appropriate time, and to intern "suspicious" Japanese in the event of war with Japan, were not included in the report but were, in fact, under active consideration.[78] King met the Japanese minister in early January to provide him with details of the proposal to register all Japanese Canadians. Tomii told King that he thought that those who wanted to enlist in the Canadian military should be allowed to do so. King responded that this was just a temporary measure.[79] He reminded Tomii that "Japan and China were at war and [that] we might be encouraging a little civil war if we supplied both Chinese and Japanese with rifles, etc. in BC at this time." Tomii, reported King, "laughed very heartily at that." King worried that the minister might be offended that only the Japanese were being registered.

Much manoeuvring took place as the imperial and fascist powers tried to decide how to best approach the specific conflicts in the two theatres. Within this complex mix, the question of what to do about the Soviet Union was key, particularly for Japan but also for Germany. The Soviet Union continued to aid Chiang Kai-shek's GMD government, now based in Chongqing (Chungking), and serious clashes between Soviet and Japanese troops took place along the frontier separating China and Mongolia from the Soviet Union. As the spectre of war rose in Europe, the Japanese military used the opportunity to challenge British power in Asia, blockading the British concession in Tianjin in June 1939 and forcing the British ambassador to recognize Japan's special rights during the war with China. On a number of occasions, the British government took concrete measures to appease the Japanese government. Meanwhile, the Japanese government entered into talks with Germany about a mutual assistance treaty in 1939, but it was hesitant to move ahead with a pact that might embroil it in a war with European powers while it still faced serious Chinese resistance as well as Soviet power in northeast Asia.

As the fighting continued, Japan's imperial headquarters dispatched reserves, and, by early 1940, nearly a million troops were in China. That so many troops were required is testimony to Chinese resistance to the occupiers. This resistance took many forms and often led to terrible retribution being visited on the civilian populations. One such case occurred on Chongming Island in the Chang Jiang (Yangtze) River delta, not far from Shanghai. There, in the spring of 1940, a guerrilla unit planted mines on the highway and succeeded in blowing up a troop carrier, killing twenty-six Japanese soldiers.[80] The Japanese garrison commander called in the Japanese navy to seal off the island and obliged the local collaborators to call together the citizenry at a local temple. Of the two hundred or so civilians that assembled, the majority were stabbed or shot after being unable or unwilling to say where the guerrillas were located. The bodies were then burned and left to rot in the temple. This was only one of hundreds of massacres that Japan's imperial forces perpetrated during the war.

The war had divided China into three distinct areas. The Japanese were in full occupation of northeast China and major parts of China's eastern coast down to Hainan Island; the GMD government, based in Chongqing, was in control of parts of west-central and southern China; and the communists, based in Yan'an, dominated the Shaanxi-Gansu-Ningxia border region in northwest China. The communist-led armies included the 8th Route Army, the New Fourth Army, and what was known as the South China Guerrilla Detachment. According to Chinese sources, these latter three armies were responsible for inflicting approximately 175,000 casualties among Japanese troops in 1939-40.[81] While the South China Guerrilla Detachment was ostensibly a part of the GMD army, the Chinese Communist Party (CCP) directed its operations. By July 1940, there were reportedly 500,000 troops in these contingents, CCP membership had reached 800,000, and the population in the liberated areas totalled about 100 million.

The spring of 1940 was a turning point in the European war, as German troops rapidly took over Belgium, the Netherlands, and France. The establishment of the Vichy regime in France, under German direction, had a direct bearing on the war in China. The Japanese imperial government was never willing to recognize that its inability to conquer China was a result of strong Chinese nationalism, a nationalism that, whatever else might characterize it, was infused with a determination to end colonial control of China. Instead, the Japanese government believed that foreign assistance was all that was sustaining the Chinese regime centred in Chongqing. Hence, it manoeuvred to take advantage of the war in Europe to consolidate its position in Asia. In May, it approached the government of the Dutch East Indies with demands for a guarantee of oil supplies to supplant US fuel oil, which was increasingly difficult to obtain. Japan's forces then moved to cut off the two supply routes into Chongqing and the areas still controlled by it. That summer, the French submitted to pressure by agreeing to block supplies moving through Indochina and to allow the stationing of Japanese troops to monitor the situation, while the British agreed to close the Burma Road.

These moves prompted new responses from the United States, which had earlier made some token gestures of support for China, providing a $25 million loan, announcing the abrogation of its treaty of commerce and navigation with Japan, and allowing Claire Chennault to work with the Chinese air force. However, for the most part, it had refused to make any substantial moves to support the Chinese resistance or to apply sanctions against the Japanese Empire. American aviation fuel continued to power Japanese planes engaged in the indiscriminate bombing of Chinese cities. However, in 1940, Roosevelt responded to Churchill's appeal for Anglo-American unity and began creating the framework for substantial economic and military support of Great Britain. There were spin-off effects in the Asian theatre as the US government began to provide more aid to Chiang Kai-shek's GMD regime. In Canada as well, demands for sanctions against Japan increased, and eventually the government began to take measures.[82] The signing of the Tripartite Alliance among Germany, Japan, and Italy on 27 September 1940 marked a further polarizing of world alignments.

The German attack on the Soviet Union in June 1941 created confusion in Japan, where the government had only months earlier signed a neutrality pact with the Soviet Union, hoping to stave off northern threats to its continental expansion. However, the German attack did create the basis for a strengthened anti-fascist coalition. A first step in that direction was Churchill and Roosevelt's August 1941 signing of the so-called Atlantic Charter during a summit held on naval craft off the coast of Newfoundland. This charter was the basis for the ensuing collaboration among the liberal imperial powers:

> First, their countries seek no aggrandizement, territorial or other;
>
> Second, they desire to see no territorial changes that do not accord with the freely expressed wishes of the peoples concerned;
>
> Third, they respect the right of all peoples to choose the form of government under which they will live; and they wish to see sovereign rights and self government restored to those who have been forcibly deprived of them;
>
> Fourth, they will endeavor, with due respect for their existing obligations, to further the enjoyment by all States, great or small, victor or vanquished, of access, on equal terms, to the trade and to the raw materials of the world which are needed for their economic prosperity.[83]

These are key ideals and are reminiscent of the Wilsonian moment of 1919. They reflect a step towards universalizing Roosevelt's and the US's idea of the "open door," a keystone of US economic expansion, and self-determination, a point that thrilled many in the developing world.[84] The only question, as Filipino general Carlos Romulo put it at the time, was: "Is the Atlantic Charter also for the Pacific?"[85] This question was not rhetorical, and Churchill in particular was unabashed in his views. As British historian Christopher Thorne describes him: "Forthrightly racist in private, he assumed that not only Britain's empire but also those of other European powers in Asia must and would be restored at the end of the war." Furthermore, Churchill "made it clear to Roosevelt that he did not regard the Atlantic Charter as applying to Africa and Asia."[86] The implications of Churchill's views were enormous and would play out over time, but the Axis agreement (i.e., the Tripartite Alliance) did allow Roosevelt to move forward with his preparations to bring the United States into the war against Germany. The United States also moved to impose economic sanctions on Japan.

In Canada, King met with the new Japanese minister, Yoshizawa, on 26 July 1941 to explain to him the reason for the freezing of Japanese assets in Canada.[87] He also informed him that the government was giving the twelve months notice required to end Canadian adherence to the British Empire treaty of trade and commerce with Japan. A month before the attack on Pearl Harbor, King was disheartened by the approach of war with Japan: "China has made it quite clear that without further assistance, she cannot hope to effectively resist and that her resistance will end unless such assistance is speedily given. If China's resistance fails and breaks, Japan will have a free field, no enemy at her rear in Asia, and will be able to go after both the British and Russians but what is worse is that a break in Chinese resistance will probably mean a break in Russian resistance. If that comes, Hitler would along with Japan and Italy have all his own way in breaking up the British empire. The U.S. would become more tenacious than ever of her own security in the face of that danger."[88] Despite King's fears, Chinese resistance did not end, although attempts on the part of Japanese forces to appeal to Chiang's anti-communism did have some impact as the united front between the GMD and the CCP began to fray.[89]

3 December 1941 and World War

Don MacPherson was a Canadian farm boy, only nineteen years old when he decided to enlist. After being recruited by a smooth-talking army agent, MacPherson became a Winnipeg Grenadier. He was sent to Jamaica in May 1940 for garrison duty guarding German and political prisoners, returning to Canada in the fall of 1941. After some leave in Vancouver he shipped out on the *Awatea* for Hong Kong, arriving there on 16 November. Don recalled that, after debarking, his unit marched to the Sham Shu Po camp in Kowloon, but not without help: "It must have looked pretty foolish to see two regiments of soldiers marching and all these Chinese carrying their gear."[1] Not all was work and often the soldiers would go to a bowling alley where "there would be at least a dozen beautiful Chinese prostitutes outside." According to Don, "They would come up to us and say 'Good time one dollar?' and some of the younger ones would say 'First time five dollars?' And to think we still went bowling!" There were other distractions. One day he found himself looking on as "about six Canadian soldiers" took over one of the main streets: "They were having a race down the street. The funny thing about it was that they were pulling rickshaws and the coolies were sitting in the rickshaws scared out of their minds!" White soldiers were generally given free rein in British colonies such as Hong Kong, but cavorting such as this would soon come to an abrupt and deadly end.

Carl Vincent and others have documented the senseless deployment of Canadian troops to Hong Kong.[2] The decision came as a result of an "old boys" network within the Commonwealth military. Canadian-born major general A.E. Grasett was appointed the commanding officer of British forces in China in November 1938. He became fixated on defending Hong Kong, even though the British chiefs of staff and Winston Churchill had clearly decided that Hong Kong was indefensible and that additional troops were not to be sent to bolster Hong Kong defences. Grasett, however, like many others in the British government and military, had an extremely low opinion of the qualities of Japanese soldiers – a reflection of the endemic racialization described in the previous chapter. His racist views convinced him that a few more reinforcements added to the Hong Kong garrison would allow the British to hold the colony. After his command of Hong Kong ended in July 1941, Grasett travelled to Canada where he met with the Canadian chief of staff, Major H.D.G. Crerar, with whom he had attended Royal Military College in Kingston, Ontario. Grasett apparently convinced Crerar of the advisability of reinforcing Hong Kong. Upon his return to England, Grasett then lobbied the British authorities to reverse their view on the defensibility of Hong Kong and suggested that Canada might be willing to supply the troops. The idea that Canadians might bolster the Commonwealth forces in the Asia Pacific caught on with the British leaders, and they subsequently requested that the Canadian government send two battalions to Hong Kong, a suggestion that the Mackenzie King government, on the advice of Crerar, took up with fateful results.

On 8 December 1941 (Hong Kong time), three weeks after Canadian troops had arrived, the bombs began dropping and the city soon faced a full-scale assault by Japanese imperial forces. MacPherson and his thirty mates in the Winnipeg Grenadiers platoon engaged the Japanese army in constant skirmishes, with heavy casualties. On Christmas morning at five o'clock the Japanese army attacked their position frontally: "We were able to hold them with small arms fire and a lot of grenades." Later in the morning, a two-inch mortar landed between MacPherson and his brother-in-law, Wilf Barrett, sending shrapnel into Barrett's head and killing him instantly. After intense fighting, the allied defence forces surrendered on Christmas day 1941. The defence of Hong Kong, as seen through the experience of a Canadian soldier stationed there, captures some of the complexities of war that continued into its next phase. For the hundreds of Canadians captured at Hong Kong, however, life would never be the same. Their experiences in the POW camps were horrific and many perished from disease, neglect, and, in some cases, direct abuse at the hands of their captors.[3]

The Japanese attacks on Pearl Harbor, Manila, Hong Kong, and Malaya, as well as the Pacific Islands of Guam, Midway, and Wake, on 7 December 1941 marked the beginning of an entirely new phase of the war, for now Japan was at war not only with China but also with the Euro-American powers and independence movements in Southeast Asia.[4] The Hong Kong experience illustrates how the multiple layers of colonialism, racism, and anti-fascism blended into a single objective – defeating the enemy. Yet these layers did not disappear, and once Japanese imperialism was defeated they reappeared, affected, to be sure, by the forces of decolonization and anti-racism, but persistent nonetheless. Immediately after the attacks on Pearl Harbor, not only the Americans but also the British and other Allies declared war on Japan. In other words, regional conflict in Asia now became fused with the regional conflict in Europe and North Africa, resulting in a worldwide war. On the one side were the Axis powers of Japan, Germany, and Italy and their associated allies and collaborators, and, on the other side, were the liberal imperial powers, including Great Britain and the United States. The Soviet Union was also part of this coalition, although it continued to adhere to the terms of its treaty of neutrality with Japan until near the end of the war. Among the peoples of Asia, the war produced both collaboration and opposition to Japanese imperialism. The respected Indian nationalist leader Subhas Chandra Bose perceived the war as an opportunity to end British colonialism, and he actively collaborated with the Japanese Empire, establishing the Indian National Army to fight alongside Japanese troops. Others, particularly left-wing nationalists such as Ho Chi Minh, organized armed resistance in opposition to Japanese expansion.[5] Among the non-imperial members of the coalition was China. This was the first time that what is now referred to as a "developing" country became a significant player at the diplomatic table of the Big Powers. China achieved this status, and became known as one of the Big Four, mainly because of its resistance to Japanese aggression since 1937.

Both the Canadian and the Chinese governments signed the Declaration by United Nations of 1 January 1942. Based on the Atlantic Charter, it allowed any country to become part of the anti-fascist coalition in so far as they abided by the following terms:

> (1) Each Government pledges itself to employ its full resources, military or economic, against those members of the Tripartite Pact and its adherents with which such government is at war.

> (2) Each Government pledges itself to cooperate with the Governments signatory hereto and not to make a separate armistice or peace with the enemies.[6]

The idea that there could be no separate deals with the Axis powers would have major implications for the postwar peace treaty with Japan. The charter also reflected and was instrumental in establishing the terms "Allies" and "United Nations" as part of the wartime and postwar lexicon.

The United States' entry into the war brought to the Allied cause the power of concentrated mass production and unprecedented technological innovation. Despite the losses in Pearl Harbor, the US military soon rebounded, and war production went into high gear. The battles of Guadalcanal and Midway, in the spring of 1942, only weeks after Pearl Harbor, put an end to the Japanese offensive in Southeast Asia and the Pacific and signalled the start of a dogged campaign by US forces to displace the Japanese. From the south, Douglas MacArthur began his island-hopping campaign. In the central Pacific, the navy and marines moved to capture strategic islands. Tens of thousands of American lives were lost, and many more Americans were wounded in the course of a series of ferocious battles. The justification put forward for this sacrifice was twofold: first, the war was readily sold as an exercise in retribution for the "infamy" of Pearl Harbor; second, it was touted as assisting the countries of Asia, especially China, to liberate themselves from Japanese occupation. The American war effort was an important contribution to the defeat of the Axis powers. Unfortunately, the reasons and motivations behind US participation were more complex than these official justifications might lead us to believe.

As leaders of an imperial power, US policy makers also articulated another aspect of their war agenda: to extend US influence in the Pacific, ostensibly to maintain "peace and stability." This was the role of the "imperial guardian." Washington also desired, as had preceding administrations, to assure access to the economies of China, Japan, and other Asian countries. From one perspective, such a vision was almost common sense. However, in the context of the previous one hundred years of extra-territoriality and the contemporary struggles for decolonization, these goals were arbitrary and self-serving. Another difficult dimension to the war was the racism that exploded with the attack on Pearl Harbor. As *Time* magazine put it in the immediate aftermath of the attack: "Over the US and its history there was a great unanswered question: What would the people, the 132,000,000, say in the face of the mightiest event of their time? What they said – tens of thousands of them – was: 'Why, the yellow bastards!'"[7] This was but the tip of what would became a systematic campaign to demonize all Japanese. It is not surprising that passions were aroused by war, particularly by reports of the Japanese treatment of US POWs. However, the racialization of this era was not some externally imposed imperative but, rather, a welling up of racism that had been embedded in American culture from earlier times and that the war then exacerbated. The picture becomes even more complex, however, because the vulgar racism exhibited towards the Japanese (and Japanese Americans) was accompanied by a transformation in public attitudes towards Asian allies, including the Chinese. These people were recast less as part of the "yellow hordes" and more as victims who required benevolent rescuing by the United States. This was merely a different type of racialization, a paternalistic form that reworked the relationship from one of innocent person versus antagonistic alien into one of parent and child, with the more mature and knowledgable "West" leading the childlike Asian along the road to modernity. This was a manifestation of the "bad-Asian, good-Asian" syndrome, and there were important transfer mechanisms that allowed it to occur. One of these was religion. The great attraction of Chiang Kai-shek's regime was the fact that both Chaing and his wife were ostensibly Christian, a metaphor, many believed, for the necessary transition from a pagan to a modern state.[8]

Canada at War in the Pacific

In the aftermath of the attack on Hong Kong and Pearl Harbor, Canada quickly declared war on Japan, even before the United States and Great Britain. King signed the order-in-council at 9:15 PM, 7 December 1941, on the basis of an earlier declaration that, when Canadian troops went to Hong Kong, they were "part of the defence of Canada and of freedom [against] any attack which might be made by the Japanese against British Territory or Forces in the Orient."[9] In other words, King and the government declared war on Japan as part of its defence of the British Empire.

The mainstream press responded to Japan's offensive on 7 December with righteous indignation and fear at the massive nature of the assault. The possibility of attacks on the west coast of North America appeared real. Soon the question of what to do with people of Japanese ancestry in British Columbia became a burning issue. The path that led to the uprooting, dislocation, dispossession, and attempted deportation of those of Japanese ancestry in British Columbia is well documented.[10] However, understanding the relationship between the war and racism and subsequent Japanese-Canadian internment continues to pose important challenges. In short, more than a few people cling to the view that the "war made them do it," that the uprooting and dispossession was regrettable but inevitable given the circumstances, and that reconciliation requires putting the past to rest. Such views, however, do violence to the historical process and impose today's agenda on a past that is still misunderstood in many ways.

As described in the previous chapter, the Canadian government, through its special committee, had already identified racism in the white community as a major problem but had then put in place measures, including registration of all peoples of Japanese race while denying them (and peoples of Chinese descent) the opportunity to serve in the armed forces. For a short period, these measures silenced some of the more vociferous voices of racism, but they also projected the view that the Japanese were a race apart, despite substantial attempts by *nisei* organizations (in particular) to assert their loyalty. The outbreak of war created new circumstances, and the government immediately ordered thirty-eight Japanese nationals to be detained on suspicion of disloyalty, twelve hundred fishing boats owned by Japanese Canadians to be rounded up and brought to Ladner, Japanese-language schools to be closed, and Japanese-language presses to be shut down.[11] Many people in local communities in British Columbia were fearful of what the war might mean, and these fears were quite understandable. But, as discussed earlier, not all people identified the Japanese population in the province as a problem: the years of bridge building during the 1930s had led to important changes in attitudes. This was reflected in the heated debate that took place in Ottawa on 8-9 January 1942. Assembled for the meeting were members of the Standing Committee on Orientals in British Columbia, BC provincial politicians, DEA representatives, and officials of the armed forces and the RCMP. According to accounts of that meeting, the RCMP, army, navy, and the DEA considered the situation to be under control and believed that further restrictions on persons of Japanese ancestry were unnecessary. Provincial politicians, on the other hand, were outraged with what they viewed as complacency towards the Japanese threat. Their attitudes prompted Escott Reid, who represented the DEA at the meeting, to later state: "I felt in the committee room the physical presence of evil."[12] In the aftermath of the meeting, Ian Mackenzie and provincial politicians were able to lobby the prime minister and to obtain some satisfaction: on 14 January, the government announced the evacuation from the coast of all male Japanese nationals between the ages of eighteen and forty-five. On 16 January, PC 365 allowed the government to designate certain regions as protected areas, and, shortly afterwards, the area from the coast to one hundred miles inland was so designated.

The major factor behind the move towards uprooting all Japanese Canadians was the active campaign waged by men like Ian Mackenzie, A.W. Neill, Thomas Reid, Howard Green, and others as well as the mainstream press, which, by this time, was actively promoting uprooting. Brigadier Sutherland Brown of the Victoria Conservative Association captured the tenor of the times in declaring: "every little slant-eyed Jap will wave the flag of the Rising Sun if his countrymen invade this coast."[13] Working with them were institutions such as the Pacific Coast Security League, the Citizen's Defence Committee, numerous municipalities, and many legion branches that became active champions of expelling the Japanese on the coast. For many, that was only the first step to getting rid of them altogether.

Contributing to the furor were the constant reports of Japanese advances in the Pacific and the fact that the US administration was also contemplating uprooting the Japanese on the coast, a decision that Roosevelt finalized with executive order 9066 on 19 February 1942. A few days later, the Canadian government followed suit, passing PC 1486, which extended the evacuation order against Japanese nationals to all peoples of Japanese ancestry, regardless of birth or citizenship. Announced publicly on 26 February, this was followed by the decision on 28 February to impose a curfew on Japanese Canadians. The die was cast, and it was not long before hundreds of Canadians were being rounded up and herded into the former livestock building at the Pacific National Exhibition grounds on Hastings Street. The first evacuees arrived on 16 March, and, as the numbers increased, other buildings were also taken over. Over eight thousand passed through these holding tanks before being dispersed into the interior – men, women, and children alike. In one manner or another, over twenty thousand of the total 23,149 people of Japanese descent were uprooted and sent into exile from the coast by the end of October 1942.[14]

If the war fanned the flames of anti-Japanese racism it also made it more difficult to protest the treatment of Japanese Canadians. A very few, including Howard Norman and W.R. McWilliams, spoke out, but, for the most part, those who had actively campaigned in support of the community fell silent regarding its uprooting, including the CCF. Within the community there were diverse reactions. Many Japanese Canadians saw no alternative, and the voice of the *nisei*, the *New Canadian*, counselled obedience. A few protested vigorously and were quickly rounded up and shipped off to the

A classroom in the internment camp in Slocan, BC, in 1943. Japanese Canadians organized an autonomous school system in the camps throughout British Columbia. | National Film Board of Canada / Library and Archives Canada, C-024454

POW camp in Angler, Ontario.[15] There was deep dissatisfaction with the original evacuation plan because it called for males to be shipped out to work at road camps, separating them from their families. Protests about the evacuation eventually led to the Security Commission's revising the regulations and allowing men to join their families. Camps housing nearly ten thousand of the evacuees were established in the Slocan Valley, including Bay Farm, Popoff, Lemon Creek, Tashme, New Denver, Roseberry, Greenwood, Kaslo, and Sandon. The conditions were harsh and the winters long, and some died without ever seeing their homes again. Even when the war ended, exile would continue for another four long years and, for some, forever. Defending the British Empire and uprooting the Japanese communities were the primary goals of the Canadian government in the Pacific theatre at this time.

Pressure to recruit a large number of military personnel for overseas duty eventually put into question the armed forces' colour bar, a fact it later recognized: "Unfortunately, racism was systemic in the armed forces. The Royal Canadian Navy and the Royal Canadian Air Force refused to enlist Asians until political direction given midway through the war forced them to change their practices."[16] The army held similar policies, although a few Asian Canadians were able to enlist in provinces outside British Columbia and Saskatchewan. Even after conscription began, people of Asian descent were not to be conscripted for fear this would strengthen their case for winning the franchise afterwards. However, the war in the Pacific and the demands for replacements in the European theatre finally resulted in the piecemeal disintegration of the colour bar. The story of Kam Len Douglas Sam illustrates both the challenges and the triumphs.[17] Born in Victoria in 1918, Sam was one of nine children and, when growing up, he had always wanted to be a pilot. In fact, his high school yearbook bore the inscription: "Doug has aspirations to become the Chinese Lindbergh." In 1938, with war ravaging China, Sam applied to the British air force but was refused because of the colour bar. The same happened in 1941, when he applied to the RCAF. However, after Pearl Harbor, the situation changed, and, on 21 October 1942, Sam enlisted. Although he was qualified for officer training, the air force continued to discriminate against people of colour and did not employ them in such high-end roles. As a result, Sam received training as an air gunner and was eventually promoted to sergeant. He went to England as part of 426 Squadron and flew Lancaster bombers over Europe. After twenty-eight successful missions, Sam's luck ran out, and, on 28 June 1944, he was shot down over Reims, France, and was reported as presumed dead.

Upon hearing the news, Sam's grandmother went to the Chinese temple in Victoria and prayed for her grandson, lighting incense sticks on his behalf. Her prayers were rewarded; as it turned out, Sam had parachuted to safety, landing near a German air base in France. Rescued by the resistance, Sam was instructed to stay in France and began what can only be called a heroic mission, posing as an Indochinese student stranded in France by the war. He became a key liaison person among the resistance groups, helping to distribute arms and equipment dropped by Allied aircraft and organizing escape routes for Allied service members. As the war in Europe entered its final stage, guerrilla actions began against German convoys. So it was with some surprise that an American commander jumped from his lone tank in front of the Café-Bar de l'Univers in Reims to be greeted by a Chinese-Canadian partisan fighter. The French government honoured Sam's contribution with a Croix de Guerre. Sam returned to Canada, where he volunteered for Tiger Force, a combined air operation being readied for the final assault on Japan. Over six hundred Chinese Canadians eventually joined the armed forces. Private Edna Silaine Lowe, Corporal Lila Wong, Private Marion Laura Mah, Private Mary Ko Bong, and Private Helen Hoe joined the Women's Army Corps, while Jean Suey Zee Lee joined the RCAF as Aircraft Woman 1. Yet, it is only recently that their contribution and the discrimination they faced have really been discussed. The Canadian treatment of those of Chinese descent was institutionalized to a degree that far exceeded the situation in the United States.

Regarding the recruitment of Japanese Canadians, King and his Cabinet repeatedly delayed making a decision due to their biases and fear of a backlash. Finally, after pressure from "Intrepid" – William Stephenson, the head of British wartime intelligence in the United States – the Cabinet capitulated, and, on 17 January 1945, allowed the formation of a special segregated unit of Japanese Canadians in the Canadian army.[18] There were many Japanese Canadians, even after having been effectively dispossessed from their homes and interned, who still wanted to enlist and join in the battle against Japanese imperialism.

Harold Hirose was one of the first to join up.[19] Born in Cumberland, British Columbia, where his father worked in the coal mine, Harold was one of seven children. Harold went to public school but also attended Japanese-language school in the evening. He eventually moved to Vancouver, working as a servant for his board and room while attending Lord Byng Secondary School. After graduating he attended a commercial school and then found a job as an accountant in an insurance firm. In 1934, the Hirose family moved to Surrey, where Harold became the secretary-treasurer of the Surrey Berry Growers Cooperative Association. After Pearl Harbor, however, Harold was rounded up with others and sent to Manitoba, where he and the rest of the family worked on a beet farm. They later moved to Winnipeg, where they faced what seemed like insurmountable barriers to finding a place to live. Eventually, they did find a place, and Harold got work as a dishwasher in a Jewish seniors home that had previously employed Japanese. Later, he found a job as an accountant. In April 1945, Hirose signed up, despite protests from friends that, given how Japanese Canadians had been treated, he had no obligation to do so. After completing training and receiving his army uniform, Hirose and three others went for dinner at a Chinese restaurant. They were refused service but kicked up such a fuss that eventually they were given their meal. The divisions among communities remained deeply engrained. From Toronto, Harold was sent to Bombay to join in the British-led invasion force. He waded ashore onto the beaches of Port Dickson, thirty kilometres north of Singapore, to help take the Japanese surrender. Moving inland to Kuala Lumpur, Hirose worked as an interpreter and communications officer. When criticized for errors in his *kanji* [Chinese characters] he "merely snapped back, 'What do you think I am, a Jap?'" By the end of the war, approximately 150 *nisei* had enlisted in the Canadian army.

The China Factor

Prior to the Japanese attacks of 7 December 1941, the Canadian government did little to help the Chinese resistance and, instead, continued to accommodate Japan. A decision by King to try and improve relations with the Japanese government by sending a minister back to Japan in the summer of 1941 prompted Escott Reid, then a second secretary in the DEA, to point out that perhaps it was time to consider establishing a legation in Chongqing.[20] King brought the proposal to Cabinet, which, on 31 July 1941, approved of the posting of a minister. The idea of opening such a legation had been raised years earlier, but nothing had been done, even though this would have provided a clear signal of Canadian government support for China in its war with Japan. In this light, the conventional discourse regarding the debate over sanctions against Japan, and Canada's not being able to take the lead in light of British and American reluctance to impose them after 1931 or 1937, obscures the fact that reticence over sanctions was not just a matter of paucity of multilateral will; rather, it reflected a deep ambivalence towards China, an ambivalence that cannot be separated from the racialization of Chinese people that, for nearly a century, had been prevalent in Canada. Respect for Japan, on the other hand, so present in the actions of King, who continued to meet and have cordial relations with Japan's minister to Canada right up to Pearl Harbor, reflected not only King's affinity for the rituals of protocol but also his identification with empire and power. That was about to change, and with it would come major upheavals, including what Asian-American scholar Ronald Takaki and others have termed the "double victory" coming out of the war.[21]

The opening of diplomatic relations with China was an important step. King invited the previous Chinese consul general, Shih Chao-Ying, who was being replaced by a new minister appointed by the GMD, to tea on the eve of his return to China. King recalled that Shih had been in Ottawa for two and half years: "I felt humiliated that I had never had him and his wife to dinner during all this time."[22] China would remain steadfast in its resistance to the Japanese, King believed, and was exuberant in his meeting with Shih: "I expressed the great admiration I had for them, for their long resistance of aggression." Shih, on the other hand, told him he hoped there would be an end to the Chinese Exclusion Act and that the people of China would be allowed a quota for immigration purposes. King told the parting consul general that he agreed. Here, King was not being duplicitous – he had in the past indeed lobbied for exclusion based on strict quotas and in 1923 only voted for outright exclusion on the basis of expediency. Now the tide was beginning to turn. Before Shih left, King told him that, if the Chinese government "wanted wheat from Canada, not to hesitate to let us know."

In February 1942, the arrival of the first Chinese minister to Canada, Dr. Liu Shih Shun, brought King to the train station to greet him. "Quite a pretty sight to see the station filled with Chinese in their best clothers [sic], carrying Chinese flags, all present to greet their new Minister," recalled King.[23] In a way, Liu was indeed "their" new minister since those of Chinese ancestry had little standing in the Canadian polity. For King the Chinese remained at this point a race apart. Two weeks later, however, King spent a whole day meeting with T.V. Soong and Laughlin Currie, Roosevelt's special assistant on China. Soong, the former minister to Washington, was to represent China in discussions with the Canadian government regarding munitions-related contracts. The Canadian-born Currie had just returned from a fact-finding mission to China, where he had met with Chiang and with Zhou Enlai. According to King, Currie revealed how their smugness and sense of superiority had led the British to refuse "the Chinese offer of troops to help them in Malaya and Singapore, feeling so sure they could do things themselves and not wanting it to appear that they needed the aid of the Chinese."[24] The British sense of superiority, based on stereotypes of the Japanese, was brought up a number of times recounted King, and Currie "endorsed what Lady Brook Popham said about the way daily routine of life was going on, the British unwilling to use some of the Chinese troops on the score that the Japanese could not get through a narrow path in the woods."[25] Soong reiterated similar anecdotes and told King that the British needed to grant self-government to India if they wanted the support of the Indian people. According to King's diary, Soong confided in him that the Chinese had intercepted Japanese aircraft communications that pointed to possible attacks on the *Repulse* and the *Prince of Wales* due to their lack of air support. Although they had communicated this to British contacts, no action had been taken.[26] Soong told him not to trust "any of the Japanese no matter how honourable they might appear to be, or how long they may have been away from Japan, naturalized, or even those who were born in the country. Every one of them, he thought, were saboteurs and would help Japan when the moment came."[27] King noted: "I agreed with him." Having just decided to uproot and intern all Japanese Canadians, King no doubt felt vindicated by Soong's remarks. At dinner that evening, hosted by C.D. Howe at the Ottawa country club, King recalled that he spoke of the Chinese and their "heroic part in the war – ten years of fighting, with loss of live [sic], between soldiers and civilians, equal to that of the total population of Canada." He concluded: "It is a terrific story when it is told."

Exactly at this time, the British government was attempting to secure a reaffirmation of extraterritoriality in China. In response, the undersecretary for external affairs, Norman Robertson, in consultation with others in the DEA, noted that such a measure was not appropriate, particularly given the fact the Canadian government had just established its mission in Chongqing.[28] That fall T.A. Crerar, the minister of mines, wrote to King suggesting that Canada try to improve its standing in China by sending an RCAF squadron there and by eliminating the Chinese Immigration Act.[29] Crerar hoped to put Canada in at "least as good a position as the United States" to participate in postwar trade. King replied that he was wholly sympathetic to repealing the Chinese Exclusion Act and reiterated his hope for a negotiated agreement with the Chinese government regarding limited immigration. An RCAF squadron was another matter – personally, he was sympathetic, he said in reply, but felt other allies would not be so receptive.[30]

Despite King's newly gained appreciation for the role of the Chinese resistance, the government dragged its heels in appointing a Canadian minister to Chongqing, a point not lost on the Chinese minister in Ottawa, who formally urged the speedy appointment of the Canadian representative. The issue was also raised by the Chinese ambassador to Great Britain.[31] Finally, King appointed General Victor Odlum, a veteran of the Boer War and the First World War as well as the former high commissioner to Australia.[32] In the first months of 1942, George Patterson (the director of the YMCA) and Ralph Collins, both of them "mish" kids (i.e., children of missionaries in Asia), were also appointed to assist in setting up the embassy. Chester Ronning would later join the embassy as first secretary in the summer of 1945.[33] In the interim, King and Robertson had informed the Chinese minister in Ottawa that they hoped to sign a treaty abolishing extraterritoriality for Canadians, as the United States had done and as Great Britain, after further reflection, decided was also in its best interests. DEA officials had also reviewed the immigration file in the hope of finding a solution that would "in fact retain the ban on permanent Chinese immigration in to Canada but would do so in such a manner as to spare Chinese sensibilities."[34] To that end, they dusted off an old plan developed by Hugh Keenleyside that called for "reciprocity," an idea that had already been tried in discussions with the Japanese government and discredited. Indeed, King himself had tried the same tactic in his negotiations in China in 1909. Despite changing circumstances, the government was loathe to abandon its exclusion policies, and this was made clear to Odlum as he made his way to China. Arriving in Chongqing at the end of April 1943, Odlum carried instructions that included four points outlining the Canadian government's "wishes," namely:

(a) to establish and maintain in China an attitude of friendship and respect for Canada;
(b) to assist China, as opportunity offers, in the prosecution of the war and in the adoption of enlightened policies at home and abroad;
(c) when the time comes, to strengthen the economic relationships between the two countries to their mutual advantage; and
(d) to do whatever may be politically feasible and socially wise to meet Chinese views in regard to immigration and other subjects in the field of racial relations.[35]

As matters turned out, extraterritoriality was ended quite rapidly, but the questions of immigration and race would prove to be more difficult.[36]

On 1 April 1942, pressure from smaller states obliged Great Britain to accept the formation of a Pacific War Council (PWC) to be based in Washington. Although Canada was nominally a member, it was not present at the first meeting. Other PWC members included the United States, Great Britain, China, Australia, New Zealand, and the Netherlands, reflecting the predominantly colonial nature of the alliance. Later, India and the Philippines were given representation. King, however, attended the second meeting while in Washington on 15 April 1942. In private discussions with Roosevelt, he learned that the president felt that Great Britain no longer had much of a role to play in Asia and that matters would have to be handled by China and the United States. King recorded that Roosevelt felt that the United States had "been very fair in its dealing with China" and that it was prepared to give self-government to the Philippines.[37] According to King, Roosevelt believed that there were "no possessions in the East to which self-government could not be given immediately except North Guinea and possibly Borneo for a hundred years."

King's interaction with Chinese government representatives as well as with Churchill and Roosevelt reveal an important tension in the Allies' relationship. A visit by T.V. Soong to Ottawa on 22 April provided another occasion for King to reflect on Canada's relationship with China and also reveals his changing perspective on Churchill. Soong, reported King: "[believes] the Chinese today sense a very different type of human attitude on the part of the white man through the kind of speeches Roosevelt and myself have made as contrasted with what they have been used to in the past. In this connection, he does not feel that Churchill has yet caught the same spirit."[38] At the PWC meeting in May in Washington, King saw first-hand the struggle being waged between Soong and a recalcitrant Churchill when Soong accused the British troops of "not attacking the enemy as had been agreed upon at the Casablanca conference."[39] Churchill denied any such agreement existed, despite Soong's claim that the agreement had been signed by Sir John Dill. What was important, King recalled, was that Soong "took direct issue" with Churchill, stating he "could not understand how Churchill had no knowledge of it." Roosevelt helped to calm things down, but King felt that Soong had made a very fine presentation: "He was in an extremely embarrassing position but spoke most patriotically. Churchill was too positive the other way and really must have been in error in part." The debate continued afterwards during a private conversation among King, Churchill, and Roosevelt. In response to Roosevelt's claim that, after all, the Chinese had basic principles and sound ideas, Churchill, according to King, "looked over at me and said: as between Jesus Christ and Confucius, I think there was more of the mystical and of life and action in Christ than there was in the reflective moods in Confucius, and that what He expressed meant more to mankind than the reflection and contemplation of Confucius."[40] King did not respond directly but later talked about the ten commandments and the Nazi's rejection of them. Churchill, King recorded, stated: "Hitler is anti-Christ. The whole fight is against Anti-Christ." King weighed in, observing: "today it was a conflict of the same forces that had met around the Cross at the time of the crucifixion." With Soong absent from the discussion, the emphasis seemed to shift to ideology and religion, which were fused as the basis for opposition to Hitler. However, the tensions would become transparent again when Churchill and Roosevelt came to Quebec City in late summer for the Quebec Conference.

In anticipation of a visit to Ottawa planned for June 1943, King met with Madame Chiang Kai-shek (Soong Meiling) in Washington before returning home. The two exchanged pleasantries, and Chiang's social skills left a lasting impression: "I confess I do not recall ever having had an interview in which I instantly felt so much at home and which revealed so much of careful briefing beforehand on the part of the one giving the audience."[41] Two weeks later, King received Soong at Laurier House. After giving her a guided tour, during which she had remarked, upon seeing a portrait of King's mother, how much he resembled her, King and Chiang sat down to discuss the war situation. In response to King's query about how Canada might be of assistance in China's relationship with Great Britain or the United States, Chiang stated that some people in China believed Great Britain might resume its friendship with Japan after the war. She did not think that but told King that "those in authority in England must realize that the China of today is very different from the China of former years."[42] The younger generation had a different outlook than did their ancestors: "They are much more modern." The following day, 16 June 1943, Madame Chiang Kai-shek addressed a joint session of Parliament. In introducing her, King extolled both the woman and the "heroic people of China, the first great power to resist axis aggression."[43] He asked that she convey to the men and women of China: "how unbounded is our admiration of their unswerving fortitude. Their uncomplaining courage has not been surpassed in the annals of human resistance."[44] In her address, Chiang wowed the audience by her command of English and her clear knowledge of the history of parliamentary democracy. Regarding the war, she discussed why China was important to Japan and how the Occupation had meant the appropriation of 100 million tons of raw materials, not including food. She stated: "for six years [China] has hung like a millstone around the neck of the Japanese military, and has succeeded in preventing Japan from utilizing several millions of her armed forces and workers in other parts of the world."[45] A warm response from all parties as well as the media greeted her speech.

The Quebec Conference took place from 17-27 August 1943. Hosted by King, it brought Churchill, Roosevelt, and their staffs together to clarify global military strategy. Canadian representatives had minor roles, but King's interactions with Churchill and Roosevelt provide further insights into the dynamics and tensions regarding the war in the Pacific. King recalled a private exchange between Roosevelt and Churchill in which the US president recalled how his grandfather had been to China and, when trying to arrange a contract to export tea, had offended a Chinese official. His grandfather had apologized in a humble manner and the contract was won. According to King, "Churchill's reaction to the story was, that his grandfather was wrong to offer an apology & should have been offended because it was asked. He should have shown them the power & might of the US & demanded that it be carried out."[46] King noted that there was much that he could not recall of the dinner conversation but that this anecdote had stuck. The next day, King introduced the two heads of state for a noon press briefing at the conclusion of the conference. Churchill had made quite a speech, King recalled: "He had spoken of Britain, the US and Russia, but had made no mention of China. I whispered to him to say a word on China. This he did in a very satisfactory way. He had missed that reference, as the omission of any mention of China in his address before Congress had raised a great deal of comment when he was last in the US."[47] In a private conversation with King in Ottawa after the conference, Roosevelt suggested that it was important to keep China in the picture and that it might act as a "buffer State" between Russia and the United States: "He regrets that Winston looks at the Chinese as so many pigtails. [Churchill] Does not realize how different the new generation are from the old."[48] A few months later, after listening to a Churchill speech on the radio, King lamented that the British leader failed to recognize Canada's contribution during the war: "I confess that the closing portion of his speech filled me with indignation and made me sick at heart."[49] Nor had Churchill made any reference to China, King noted, recalling having had to remind him to do so at Quebec City a few months earlier: "It is the John Bull and his island attitude of self-sufficiency and unconscious superiority of certain of the British stock."

King's observations regarding Churchill's recalcitrance towards China confirms the observations of other historians, who indicate that Churchill "unashamedly and partly on the basis of racist convictions, remained until the end of the war profoundly opposed to any change in the white-dominated order of things."[50] Churchill was not alone in his beliefs, and these, along with other factors, would shape the British attitude towards decolonization in the latter stages of the war. As for King, his newly found empathy for China and its resistance was partially related to his own feelings about Churchill and the British tendency to take Canada and its war contribution for granted. In other words, there was some small grain of anti-colonialism within King's psyche that allowed him to side with Chiang and Roosevelt against Churchill. This did not mean, however, that King saw immigration issues any differently than he had before: the "Chinese" were best appreciated from afar or in diplomatic parlours where the rituals of protocol dominated.

The Imagined and Unimagined

The intensification of the war, stimulated by the Japanese attack on the United States and Great Britain, brought substantial aid to Chiang's government but little relief to the people trapped in occupied China. For their part, the Japanese avoided mounting any major offensive against Chiang's redoubt in Chongqing and transferred some of their units to theatres in Southeast Asia. At the same time, they resorted to brutal measures to maintain their control in China. The use of chemical and biological weapons was envisaged as a possibility by both sides in the war. Indeed, at a Cabinet war committee on 8 July 1942, King and his colleagues discussed the matter: "There was further discussion on chemical warfare. Ilsley, St. Laurent and myself all strongly insisted on not permitting gas to be used by Canadians offensively until it was quite clear it had been used in that way by an enemy who might be attacking us. In other words, if the Japanese use it against China or the British, we would be free to use it in protecting ourselves and using it offensively should they attack Canada."[51]

In China, the Japanese imperial forces were already engaging in extensive use of both chemical and biological weapons to consolidate control over occupied China. The story of the development and deployment of biological weapons in China during the war only became public knowledge through the dedicated efforts of a small group of researchers and activists in China, Japan, the United States, and Great Britain.[52] When one takes into account that, according to both governments' sources, between 700,000 and 2 million canisters of chemical and biological weapons remain buried in the Chinese countryside, the scale of the special weapons program becomes evident. But only survivors can relate the real meaning of the use of such weapons. Xu Jiaxie, a resident of Zhangtan on the Zu River in Zhejiang Province, was fourteen years old in 1942.[53] In June and July that year, Japanese soldiers had arrived and were pillaging the village. Xu and his family escaped to an islet in the river but were eventually discovered and Xu was detained on two occasions. He personally witnessed the rape of four eleven- or twelve-year-old girls. Finally, the troops left the region that August and soon after the whole family became ill: "Grandfather, who had stayed behind at home, and my mother suffered from festering boils, their whole bodies were swollen up. My three-year-old baby sister had two egg-sized festering holes on both sides of her forehead. I was suffering from malaria, scabies, and festering legs." Not long after, Xu's grandfather died, as did his baby sister. Xu's leg also broke out into festering sores: "A small red patch gradually developed into a blister. When the blister broke open, it turned into a rotting hole. The rotting flesh oozed out smelly liquid and was attracting flies; even chickens came to peck at it when I sat down." Xu was able to gain some temporary relief by stealing some medicinal herbs from the traditional medicine store he worked for, but the disease never disappeared. Indeed, in the area in which Xu lives, there is a village that is known as the "rotten legs" village. American physician Martin Furmanski later visited the village and concluded that the agent used at the time was glanders. Only today are we finding out about the scale of death and destruction due to the use of biological weapons during the Second World War.

As the Pacific stage of the war intensified, the Japanese government stepped up its recruitment among its colonial subjects, including the recruitment and conscription of soldiers and civilians from Japan's colonies, particularly Taiwan and Korea. According to Japanese government statistics, the military directly employed over 240,000 Koreans as soldiers or support personnel.[54] Mass recruitment began in 1938. According to Japanese propaganda at the time, "The China incident was the storm that breathed new life into the Korea that had broken out of its old shell. This storm stirred awake the Japanese consciousness that had been sleeping deep within the hearts of our Korean brethren."[55] Promises of good wages and honour lured many volunteers into this system, but, as Japanese losses mounted, conscription began on 1 March 1943. Many Koreans were employed as guards in POW camps, and a number abused the POWs under their watch. For native Taiwanese, the story was somewhat different, but it had many parallels with the Korean experience.[56]

Colonized women also became the target of recruiters, to be used in what became known as the "comfort women" system, in which women were either lured or forced into becoming sexual slaves for the soldiers of the Imperial Army.[57] Young women throughout the Pacific were at risk of being dragooned into service. For Ahn Jeomsun, the war would soon become a nightmare, one with which she has continued to live for sixty years.[58] In the fall of 1942, Ahn was a thirteen-year-old living in Seoul with her family. One day Ahn accompanied her mother to a gathering called by the local neighbourhood organization. When she arrived, a dozen other girls were already there, along with neighbourhood people and Japanese soldiers: "Those girls

One of the survivors of the system of sexual slavery, Ahn Jeomsun, became active in the movement for redress in the 1990s. She is pictured here in 2008 during a human rights training session on Jeju Island, Korea. | Photo courtesy of Ahn Jeomsun

were all being weighed on the rice scale one by one. Tall girls and healthy ones were being put in a truck. Japanese soldiers were putting the girls in the truck, lifting them up. My turn came. I went up on the scale and I weighed in around fifty-five or sixty kilograms. From when I was very young I had a heavy frame, so even now I'm a little over sixty-two kilograms, and so then, at the age of fourteen, I was sixty kilograms. So those damned soldiers put me in the truck." Ahn didn't know what it was all about, but she did know she wasn't about to leave her family and her home: "No matter how much I struggled, I wasn't able to resist the strength of the soldiers. As my mother cried and screamed 'Why are you taking my daughter; where are you taking her?' she clung to the truck along with other mothers, fighting with the fury of demons. But it was no use. With our mothers crying and crying without end behind the truck, in this way I was forcibly carried away from Boksagol Street."

Taken by train and truck to the west of Beijing, young Ahn couldn't believe where she ended up: "My god, I'd never seen such a place in my life. There were no mountains, no trees, no water, just covered with yellow sand like a complete desert." Ahn's life changed irrevocably at that moment: "From the very first day, they wouldn't leave me alone. As soon as I got there, they threw around all kinds of curses and were doing that horrible, unspeakable thing. That ... you know. How was I supposed to know anything? All those bastards who were there then are probably dead by now." Ahn continued to resist, running away and hiding, but eventually other women already at the "comfort station" persuaded her that there was little choice: "As soon as the Japanese soldiers finished their breakfast, they would begin to descend upon us. There was no night and day for us. Saturday and Sunday were resting days, so the weekends were especially bad. I think I had to deal with about ten soldiers per day on the weekdays but more than that on the weekends." Not all went along with the regime: "There were some good Japanese soldiers, too, though. I can't remember their names now, but there was one Japanese soldier who would always hold my hand, telling me how sorry he was for me. In Japanese, it was "kawaiiso, kawaiiso" ("You poor thing, you poor thing"). He didn't try to sleep with me but would just sit." But that was the rare exception. Unless Ahn went along with her rapists, she would be beaten.

The medical effects of this torture were damaging both psychologically and physically. Ahn recalled: "Below, I was torn, turned inside out, bleeding ... Oh, just thinking about it." There was little medical attention: "I never even saw a 'satku' (condom). Also, where's the time to use it? When I think about it, that was why I couldn't help but be infected with so many diseases." Within six months she was infected with venereal disease. Ahn would survive but many did not. The comfort women system, initiated in the 1930s, would consume tens of thousands of young women from across Asia before the war came to an end.

An Ally of a New Type

Discussions between Canadian officials in Chongqing and the Chinese government proved fruitful, at least on a symbolic level. On 14 April 1944, King signed the first treaty between Canada and China that ended extraterritoriality, a gesture, in the prime minister's mind, of "friendship and goodwill." Having just received a telegram from Madame Chiang, King recalled that he had it in hand at the signing ceremony: "It was interesting also to see one's name added to the agreement in Chinese characters."[59] King made a last-minute decision to attend a celebratory dinner at the Chinese Embassy that evening. Key officials, including Escott Reid, Hugh Keenleyside, Norman Robertson, and Arthur Menzies, attended, as did their spouses. In response to Dr. Liu's toast to Canada and King's health, King made an impromptu speech in which he recalled that it was exactly thirty-five years ago that he "was in China negotiating an agreement between the two governments to remove discrimination so far as Canada was concerned."[60] In his mind, King believed that removing the head tax, a measure that targeted the Chinese alone, would end discrimination, even though the Chinese Immigration Act, which replaced it in 1923, was even more draconian. King consistently disassociated diplomatic questions (the form of discrimination) from the question of immigration policy, which remained, as always, based on a white Canada. The capacity to disassociate was not unique to King, but it could only exist because many others shared his values. Many layers of justification – that labour would not put up with Asian immigration, that the races could not get along, that children of mixed race would suffer, and so forth – added a benevolent sheen to the ideology. One of the ultimate arguments was that exclusion was necessary in order to avoid riots that might lead to attacks against the community. The legacy of the 1907 race riots cast a long and enduring shadow, which extended from the west coast to Parliament Hill.

Nowhere was this more evident than in the discussions on immigration that continued between the Chinese and Canadian governments. As described earlier, there was a will to change the superficial aspects of exclusion by amending the Chinese Immigration Act. Furthermore, complaints about the flagrant discrimination that Chinese who tried to enter Canada faced were increasing. The Chinese ambassador to the United States, Hu Shih, even spoke out against holding meetings of the Institute of Pacific Relations in Canada because of the harassment faced by Chinese delegates. Matters were further complicated by the fact that the US government had repealed the Chinese Exclusion Act, provided an annual quota for 105 Chinese immigrants, and recognized their right to naturalization.[61] Messages from Odlum, who was in Chongqing, called for reducing impediments to merchants and students. These were sent after he had learned that "Chinese [thought] they ha[d] to suffer more indignities, and be more crudely treated, when going to Canada than when entering the United States."[62] When Odlum's status was elevated to ambassador and the legation became an embassy, an upgrade in diplomatic ranking, the government presented the Chinese government with its new draft immigration law. It got no further than had King thirty-five years earlier. On the morning of 2 June 1944, the Chinese ambassador Liu Shih Shun met with Norman Robertson and informed him that his government could not accept the proposed treaty because, although in form it suggested reciprocity, "in fact [it was] discriminatory because it would establish a distinction in Canadian policy between the admission of Chinese and of other foreigners to Canada."[63] Robertson told Liu that it was impossible to afford equality to Chinese immigrants. He then informed King that at least they had tried and that the Chinese, on second thought, might accept it rather than face "an indefinite continuance of the present situation." Robertson was wrong, and immigration restrictions continued despite protests from Odlum immediately after the war ended. The conflict over immigration might have led to serious problems in Canada-China relations had it not been for the aid being provided by Canada to China.[64] Newspaper editorials expressing support for the Chinese resistance on the seventh anniversary of the war, 7 July 1944, were widespread.[65] At an anniversary meeting at the Oriental Theatre, organized by the Chinese Benevolent Association and the Chinese National Salvation League, Vancouver's mayor, J.W. Cornett, praised the Chinese war effort, adding: "We know the Chinese well in Vancouver. We have more of them resident here than any other Canadian city. We get along well with them. We like them and as our allies in this fight for word [sic] liberty, we admire them."[66] Compared to his earlier views favouring the segregation of Vancouver's Chinese population, Cornett seems to have changed; however, his newfound admiration for "the Chinese" remained contingent and reflected a turn towards paternal benevolence, an increasingly common form of racialization after the war.

By the end of the war, both Roosevelt and King had become less enthusiastic in their support of Chiang and the Guomindang because of the perceived weak military role the latter had come to play. Nevertheless, King and his Cabinet resolved in September 1944 to participate in the anticipated invasion of Japan. They were reacting to a report from the chiefs of staff recommending participation as a way of "avenging Hong Kong, saving face in the East and restoring Canadian military prestige."[67] King stipulated, however, that he did not want Canadian forces being used to recapture British colonies, a reflection of how his views had changed since declaring war on Japan in 1941. A Canadian army division and twenty-five fighter squadrons were preparing to join in the invasion of Japan after Germany's surrender in May 1945.

The war in the Pacific had finally obliged the Canadian government to establish diplomatic relations with China, and some in the government came to realize that continuing the Chinese Immigration Act would not be possible. But change would come neither quickly nor easily. The war had focused the hatred of the "other" on the Japanese-Canadian community, but challenges to the racialized order, based in cross-community solidarity that had emerged in the 1930s, would challenge the government's policies after the war.

Defeating Japan, Dividing the World

The world war that commenced in December 1941 fused uneasy coalitions between colonizers and colonized, on both the Axis and Allied sides. But there were important differences among the industrialized powers as well. As the war progressed, leaders of Great Britain, the United States, the Soviet Union, and even China, a junior partner to be sure, became linchpins of the Allied coalition. With the tides of war running in their favour, they organized a series of summit meetings to work out agreements on the conduct and aims of the war. These conferences were held in Cairo and Teheran in 1943, in Yalta in early 1945, and at Potsdam just outside Berlin in July-August 1945, in the wake of victory in the European theatre.

An account of a dinner meeting between Roosevelt and Chiang Kai-shek on 23 November 1943 provides amazing insights into the evolving US-China relationship. According to the minutes of the Cairo meeting, Roosevelt invited China to become a member of the "Big Four" (the United States, Great Britain, the Soviet Union, and China), which would, in effect, become the steering committee for the Allies. Chiang agreed. In response to Roosevelt's query regarding the fate of the Japanese emperor, Chiang advised that the Japanese people themselves should decide that question, otherwise there might be problems later. Roosevelt also proposed that "China should play the leading role in the post-war military occupation of Japan." Chiang responded that China "was not equipped to shoulder this considerable responsibility, that the task should be carried out under the leadership of the United States" and that China would play a supporting role if necessary.[68] At this same dinner meeting, Chiang stressed the importance of granting independence to Korea after the war, and helping Indochina as well as Thailand achieve independence. Roosevelt agreed, but the conference communiqué released on 1 December 1943 put Korea's fate this way: "Japan will also be expelled from all other territories which she has taken by violence and greed. The aforesaid three great powers, mindful of the enslavement of the people of Korea, are determined that in due course Korea shall become free and independent."

The handling of Korea represents an interesting example of the nuances of words and diplomacy and – with the benefit of hindsight – demonstrates the potentially explosive impact when a few people gather in a room to determine the fate of a country whose people are not represented. The first draft of the communiqué called for Korean independence at the "earliest possible moment," which was then changed to "the proper time," and finally to "in due course." This reflected the influence of Churchill, Roosevelt, and their advisors, who, although knowing next to nothing about Korea, including the fact that it had been independent for hundreds of years, believed that it would require tutoring before it could become independent. The repercussions of these decisions would be felt long into the future.

Discussions among Roosevelt, Churchill, and Stalin took place at Yalta in February 1945. Stalin came to an agreement with Roosevelt and Churchill that the Soviet Union would enter the war in the Pacific within three months of the end of the war in Europe. Its aims, like those of the United States, were twofold: to assist in the combined effort to defeat the last of the Axis powers and to increase its influence and standing in the region. This latter goal, as expressed in the Yalta Agreements, included keeping Outer Mongolia within the Soviet sphere; acquiring southern Sakhalin and adjacent islands; "internationalizing" Dairen (Dalian), with Soviet "preeminent interests" safeguarded; leasing Port Arthur (Lushunkou) as a Soviet naval port; establishing a joint Sino-Soviet enterprise to run the Chinese Eastern and Southern Manchurian railways; and acquiring the Kuril islands.[69] These imperial aims reclaimed territories or concessions formerly held by the Russian tsar. This was well understood by both Roosevelt and Churchill when they agreed to them. Chinese representatives, however, were not directly involved in these talks, even though many of the Soviet demands directly affected Chinese sovereignty. The Soviet state would be required to negotiate the terms that affected China with the GMD, but it would have the support of the United States and Great Britain in these negotiations.

Roosevelt's death on 12 April 1945 and Truman's ascent to power further complicated matters as policy elites grappled with how to conclude a war that was clearly going to end in Japan's defeat. With Germany's surrender on 8 May, decision makers in the respective countries began to assess how best to take advantage of Japan's imminent defeat. Key considerations in Washington at this time included defining what unconditional surrender actually meant, deploying atomic weapons, and reimagining postwar relations with the Soviet Union. It was at this moment that the potential of atomic weapons made itself felt. The bomb was not yet ready, even for testing purposes. To maximize US advantage, Truman decided to delay engaging the Japanese in a surrender process, and he postponed the Allied meeting planned for Potsdam that June. Meanwhile, in Moscow, Stalin avoided any engagement with Japanese surrender initiatives in order to intensify preparations to enter the war. The destruction of Japanese forces in Okinawa, accompanied by huge and unnecessary civilian casualties, ratcheted the vise of defeat up another notch.[70] The die-hards in the Supreme War Council prepared for the final battle to resist a land invasion. However, as the situation became increasingly desperate, the decision was made to approach the Soviet Union with a clear request to mediate. When this initiative failed to bear fruit, Hirohito and Kido again intervened, this time by arranging to have the Supreme War Council accept that the Emperor would dispatch a personal envoy to Moscow. This decision was taken on 7 July, and, five days later, Hirohito received Konoe Fumimaro at the imperial palace, appointing him special envoy. But by this time it was too late. Truman had already boarded the presidential yacht en route to Potsdam, where he would meet with Churchill and Stalin beginning on 17 July. On 16 July, the first atomic bomb exploded in the desert of Alamogordo in New Mexico. At the beginning of the summit, Stalin announced that Soviet forces would join in the war by mid-August. The Soviet leader had no interest in engaging in a surrender process prior to the launch of a Soviet attack in northeast Asia. For this Truman was thankful: if an invasion were necessary, Soviet participation in the war would, he hoped, reduce American casualties. However, upon receiving details on 21 July of the successful atomic test, Truman saw less need for Soviet assistance. Both sides were rushing towards final assaults against Japanese forces, and neither had any interest in promoting a surrender process. On 26 July, the British and US governments released the Potsdam Declaration demanding unconditional surrender. No mention was made of possible continuation of the monarchy, despite pressure from the Joint Chiefs of Staff and Secretary of War Stimson to include something besides the demand for unconditional surrender. The Potsdam Declaration was a warning prior to the dropping of the bomb: it was not an offer to engage in a process leading to surrender. Stalin, however, was not invited to sign the declaration, a decision that infuriated him in so far as he had hoped to use the declaration as a rationale for abrogating his treaty of neutrality with Japan and declaring war. Stalin's absent signature, and the ambiguity regarding the future of the imperial household in the Potsdam Declaration, convinced Hirohito and the Supreme War Council to ignore the declaration and continue instead with requests that Moscow intervene on their behalf. This delay would have tragic consequences.

4 Hiroshima and War's End

Kinuko Doi was born in Hiroshima in 1929. Her parents ran a bookstore in the city to support the sizable family: Kinuko had three brothers and two sisters. Her father loved the written word, and students in the city appreciated his passion for books, dropping by to read and chat. That he didn't mind if they went home without buying anything was no doubt an added incentive for them to visit the store. Kinuko's father dreamed of going to California one day, but Kinuko's imagination did not stray to lands so far. As a child, she was captivated by the disciplined, uniform-clad soldiers marching by her house: "Every time I saw the soldiers walking down the street, I used to march along with them and get lost, and so they had to bring me home. But, I was crazy about soldiers, I liked the look and everything, and I was kind of ... you know ... strong-minded – I guess ... stubborn."[1] Kinuko's memory of such episodes highlights the fact that Japan in the 1930s was becoming a militarized society. The quest for empire was rationalized on the basis that Japan was simply doing what other imperial powers had already done in India, in China, in the Philippines. The fact that the United States, Canada, and other settler states passed racist exclusion laws against Japanese and Chinese immigration provided an additional rationale for making Asia into Japan's backyard. The problem was that numerous Koreans, Chinese, and others resisted Japan's imperial appetite, just as many Filipinos, Indians, and others had resisted Euro-American colonialism.

As Japan's "advance" into the Asian mainland progressed, the difficulties of sustaining the military effort grew, and everyone was gradually dragged in. After the global war began, young students were mobilized as support personnel. Kinuko and her classmates were periodically sent out to help work in munitions factories. Kinuko used to cry when faced with the war work, which she hated. And so she applied to become a nurse as she wanted to tend the sick and wounded, not help to kill people. Her sister, Tomoko, was outspoken, and, as the war continued, she told her father in unequivocal terms that Japan had lost and should surrender. Kinuko laughingly recalls how her father used to chase Tomoko around their house, terrified by her brashness. Indeed, her demand for surrender was treasonous and could have imperilled the family had it become known. The family had seen other young students arrested and marched off in handcuffs by the *Kempeitai* (secret police). The repression was real, and its effects disastrous. The stifling of dissent was a key ingredient in allowing militarism to gain a lock on the Japanese people.

Asia was already a holocaust by the end of the war. Japanese imperial troops had laid waste to large parts of China, and the United States had systematically fire-bombed key Japanese cities. Hiroshima and Nagasaki had been spared such fire-bombing – only to face a worse fate. In the early morning of 6 August 1945, Kinuko walked to work. Her father had told her he might meet her for lunch. As she walked, the air-raid sirens sounded, and, high up in the sky, she spotted a silver plane, too high to be launching bombs, she thought. She had reached her post at the civilian hospital where she worked when the world's first operational A-bomb detonated. Looking out a window, she was blinded by the sudden flash but did not lose consciousness:

> No. It's not that easy [laughing]; as soon as I looked up and then ... okay ... and then a few seconds maybe ... a few seconds ... just my eyes going like that, and then ... flash ... and so I feel my eyes cut open because the light ... cut my eyes ... and, I always thought I gonna hide underneath the counter because that counter was built onto the wall, and you can't move [it], and it's safe. So, if anything happened I just gonna go down here ... you know. So I thought that's what I did. I covered the head ... you know ... hold the head and get down ... but that air blast came and took me out into the hallway. But I didn't know that, so I thought I'm down there ... and I'm bouncing my head to the under the table and going like this ... like a ball. Then I came to

> a little bit ... motion stopped so I was sitting up and what was happening ... and I was looking, and the countertop is not there and I can't feel anything, and then the bigger window glass broke ... and then you hear the crashing and it came down on me, so that time I got pincushioned with window glass. Then all the window broke, so all the smoke started going out the window, then I could start seeing everything. And I was sitting in the hallway, and I wasn't in the room at all where I was, I was in the hallway. And then I could see the smoke going out and dust going out and then when the doctor was ... eye doctor ... he was running down the hallway, trying not to step on dead body or whoever ... and almost like ... you know ... he shouting ... go out the front ... you know ... "Get out, get out!" So, I wanted to get out, so I got up and started going towards the front ... and back way to go front. Then I saw my friend worked in that same room ... I saw her ... I could see her cheek is down ... hanging down here and you could see her teeth. And I said to her, "Oh you're injured and I can see your teeth," and then I lifted her cheek up for her and ... "We better get bandage" ... and she said ... "Oh you, you look awful too, you know." And I said, "Oh my goodness" ... and then the washroom was right there so we both went to washroom, but I couldn't see ... she just run out right away ... she saw what happened. And I can't see because blood coming down ... so I wipe it off and I saw that myself ... two pigtails stand up like a horn, and all gray and dusty and coated with blood and everything and so I wanted to go back and get the bandage, but I couldn't find anything. So her ... and she ... I hang myself on the curtains and pull them down and tear in pieces and tied each others face and we went out in the front.

Kinuko lost consciousness a number of times:

> After the black rain I don't know how long the next time I wake up ... is cleaning that ... start cleaning ... all the doctors and nurses ... you know ... whoever help ... soldiers, some soldiers came and helped the hospital too. Cleaning everything and disinfected everything, and dead bodies had to be cremated, because we don't want to have a sickness to come over. They start doing that, taking our rings and our watches and little piece of clothes and the name and write down where they found them and put in the hole to cremate every night. And so I was waiting in that hole when I wake up. I could see the blue sky, but it was kind of deep in there ... and the dead body all over ... so I crawl over the dead body and crawl up to the street. And I

Six years after barely surviving the atomic bomb, Kinuko Doi met her Canadian husband-to-be, David Laskey, in Hiroshima. | Photo courtesy of David Laskey

> looked where am I and I saw the hospital still standing there, but I don't see anybody ... no people and around there the communication hospital in between there is cleaning ... so I started crawling.

Ottawa

As Kinuko Doi crawled out of the mass grave in the living hell of Hiroshima, Canada's prime minister was contemplating the arrival of the atomic age. Even though the Cabinet had not discussed the dropping of the bomb on Japan, Mackenzie King knew about the imminent attack. On Saturday evening, 4 August 1945, he wrote in his diary: "I have been thinking a great deal of the moment for the dropping of the atomic bomb. Believe it will come immediately after the return of the President and Stimson. It makes one very sad at heart to think of the loss of life that it will occasion among innocent people as well as those that are guilty. It can only be justified through the knowledge that for one life destroyed, it may save hundreds of thousands and bring this terrible war quickly to a close."[2]

As the prime minister rehearsed a speech on Sunday afternoon and evening, the atomic bomb flattened Hiroshima. The next morning, King and other officials gathered in an Ottawa hotel for a federal-provincial conference. They were still unaware of the terror that had arrived in Hiroshima. At 11:30 AM, Malcolm MacDonald, British high commissioner in Ottawa, sent a handwritten note to Minister of Munitions and Supply C.D. Howe: "The thing has gone off and the President's statement has gone out. Stimson's will be issued in about 3/4-of-an-hour, and yours should go out about half-an-hour after that." MacDonald asked Howe to come out of the conference to discuss "two or three points" because, stated the British official, there were "one or two ways in which we should like to help you."[3] Howe left the conference and, after talking with MacDonald, met reporters and released his statement regarding the dropping of the bomb. Howe first acknowledged Truman's statement, released a few hours earlier, announcing that US forces had dropped "the first atomic bomb on Japan and ha[d] at a single stroke destroyed a large part of the great Japanese army base of Hiroshima."[4] Howe said it was his particular pleasure to "announce that Canadian scientists and Canadian institutions ha[d] played an intimate part and ha[d] been associated in an effective way with this great scientific development." While the Canadian effort could not be compared with the American, Howe stated, "nevertheless Canadian scientists and engineers in co-operation with distinguished workers from Britain and America have played a part that guarantees us a front line position in the scientific advance that lies ahead." Howe cited a staff complement at the ministry's Montreal facility of over 340, over half of whom were Canadian. He also pointed to Canada's Chalk River facility as a pioneer in developing "one of the methods of making material which is required for the atomic bomb."[5] Howe explained that the Canadian government had taken over the Eldorado Mining and Refining Company to guarantee a government supply of uranium. When it became evident that a functioning bomb was indeed feasible, the three partner governments – the United States, Great Britain, and Canada – "regarding closest cooperation to be in the interests of the Allied Powers, agreed that all work should be more intimately integrated, and a Combined Policy Committee was set up under the chairmanship of Secretary of War Stimson to exercise general supervision of the joint effort of the countries concerned."[6] The three countries, Howe explained, also created a joint technical committee to supervise the Canadian Chalk River project. Everyone could take pride, Howe insisted, in the sizeable Canadian contribution to the atomic project.

Having skilfully scooped the prime minister, Howe proceeded to finally inform Mackenzie King, who was still in the federal-provincial conference, of the momentous developments. King recorded in his diary:

> Now for the two great events of the day. Just about noon, as I was presiding at the morning's proceedings at the Conference, I received a note from Howe saying a bomb had been dropped and that he was giving a report to the press. I had only, just immediately before, placed Drew's letter on record and received from Mackenzie a note saying "good work." When I read the reference to the bomb dropping I thought at first it had reference to my having shown up Drew by his own letter. Then I suddenly realized it was the atomic bomb in Japan. I felt that all present would be interested in the news but being fearful that the report might be premature, I sent word to Howe to say that I had thought of making a statement to the conference and asking what he would suggest. He then sent me down a copy of his own statement which he had prepared.[7]

The prime minister recalled:

> At about 12:30 I saw him getting cuttings from the ticker which he handed to Mackenzie to look at. I asked Mackenzie to let me have them. Saw that they were an account of Truman's statement, so waited until it came to 1 o'c. and then adjourned the proceedings. I told those present that I had a world shaking announcement to make. I then mentioned in a word the dropping

> of the atomic bomb. Read Howe's statement and later the paragraph from the ticker. I mentioned that as there were no afternoon papers today, it being Civic Holiday, I felt all present would be especially interested in this news. The statement was listened to in dead silence. I mentioned having Mr. Churchill's statement in my possession and arranged to read it when the proceedings opened at three. The statement is a little long but I feel it was all of historic significance. Felt it was proper to read all the statements in full. Naturally this word created mixed feelings in my mind and heart. We were now within sight of the end of the war with Japan. In this connection I should note that yesterday in revising the speech from the conference I struck out the word, in reference to the ending of the Japanese war, substituted the word "hope" for "believe" before "swiftly." I had it in my mind that there was no doubt that this would come very soon and that the atomic bomb would be used this week. Strangely enough it must have been about ten-thirty when I read this to the conference. The word of the use of the bomb came at 12. While I was speaking it had already descended. The whole business was referred to as the greatest achievement in science. In this it was an equally great achievement in secrecy – a tremendous secret to have kept over four years. It shows what control by a government of publicity can effect.

Mackenzie King continued:

> It is quite remarkable that it should have been given to me to be the first in Canada to inform my own colleagues and the premiers of the several provinces and their ministers of this most amazing of all scientific discoveries and of what certainly presages the early close of the Japanese war. We now see what might have come to the British race had German scientists won the race. It is fortunate that the use of the bomb should have been upon the Japanese rather than upon the white races of Europe.[8]

King's musings may have offered him some comfort, but on the other side of the world there was little relief from the ensuing carnage.

Hiroshima and Nagasaki

Tsuda Eichi, Fukuoka Hajime, and Ueda Masayuki were thirteen, fourteen, and twelve years old, respectively. They, along with most of the other 350 students of their junior high school, had been organized to clean up the debris from a demolished building on 6 August 1945.[9] They and most of their classmates died instantaneously when the bomb was dropped. Of Hiroshima's 350,000 or so residents at the time, no more than forty thousand were soldiers. The victims of Hiroshima, like those of Nanjing a few years earlier, were mainly civilians, despite claims by C.D. Howe and others that Hiroshima was "a great Japanese army base." The US Strategic Bombing Survey team estimated that the atom bomb killed only 3,243 troops out of the seventy thousand persons who, the team said, died instantly. [10] The total casualty figures for Hiroshima included an additional sixty thousand who died by November and another seventy thousand by 1950. This is not to deny that there were legitimate military targets within Hiroshima, but those who planned and made the decision to drop the bomb were well aware that its tremendous power would create huge losses among civilians. Indeed, the bomb was set to explode at an altitude of just under six hundred metres specifically to maximize its explosive impact for evaluation purposes. Three days later, another atomic bomb, this one made from plutonium, was dropped on Nagasaki. The impact was devastatingly similar to that experienced in Hiroshima, except that the city's hills disrupted the firestorm's path. Still, an estimated seventy thousand residents died in Nagasaki, with similar levels of casualties afterwards. What has often been neglected in the telling of the bombings' horrors, however, has been their effects on the thousands of Koreans who lived in the two cities at the time of the bombing. Of an estimated fifty thousand Koreans living in Hiroshima at the time of the bombing, thirty thousand are believed to have died.[11] In Nagasaki, an estimated twenty thousand Korean residents were casualties, including ten thousand deaths.

The Bombs and Racism

The news of the dropping of the atomic bombs was widely covered in Canadian newspapers at the time, prompting an outburst of editorial comment and letters to the editor. The day after Hiroshima, the *Vancouver Sun* editorialized that the atom bomb heralded "the age-old dream of superpower come true, for evil or for good." It would be used for constructive purposes, the editorial suggested, because if "this ... war [wasn't] the last the next one probably [would] be – ... the triumph of western civilization [would] be complete in one way if not another."[12] One reader was aghast at Truman's announcement concerning Hiroshima and the subsequent British threat: "We will withhold use of the atomic bomb for 48 hours in which time you can surrender. Otherwise you face the prospect of the entire obliteration of the Japanese nation." In response to this news, Gerald Bonwick pleaded: "In the name of humanity, I protest with every fibre of my being against any ultimate aim in war as is now indicated. We have execrated the German Nazi Party for their deliberate extermination of five million Jews. How can we possibly contemplate the massacre of over seventy million Japanese?" The Toronto man also enquired whether Koreans, a people "enslaved" by the Japanese, were to be part of the "general massacre that is promised."[13]

In response, Fred Gregg wrote:

> Have the Japanese, in any way, or at any time, practiced humane methods of warfare against us? The whole record of the Japanese war bristles daily with horrible reports of their fiendish treatment of the white races, even their allies the Germans ... [T]o be wiped out by atomic bombs is certainly a swift and merciful way of clearing a heap of filth from the path of human progress. Let's hear no more of this maudlin talk. Are the white races, as an alternative, to pour out the flower of their manhood for years, to teach this nation of inhuman rascals that honest purposes and plain dealing are what get nations places even as they get individuals where they have the right to be.

Gregg was joined in his views by George Watkin Evans: "For my part I would like to see a master atomic bomb so large and so effective that it would blow every military minded Jap straight into Hades so that there would be no language in Hell for the next thousand years, other than Japanese." W. Hopkins agreed: "[The bombs would] shorten the war and save the lives of hundreds of our boys – yours and mine ... The fact is also that Japan has never accomplished any deed, or created any culture except that which the people have copied off others, to warrant their continuing as a nation. If we destroy them we only destroy the most evil thing that has ever existed." Cherrebeth Gordon suggested that the solution to the atomic dilemma was to elect "representatives who daily practice the principles of the Sermon on the Mount from the international level of perception, as well as from the individual level of perception.[14]

The racism embedded in these letters, and King's suggestion that it was better to bomb the Japanese rather than the white races of Europe, suggests that race was indeed a significant factor in peoples' attitudes towards the use of the bomb. US author Ronald Takaki has made the case in his study, and the evidence above reinforces it.[15] Despite the complexity of understanding how race affects particular individuals, a problem Takaki acknowledges in his study of Truman's views, racism directed against perceived enemies such as the Japanese intensified during the war, with the Japanese constantly being portrayed as inhuman. Of course, Japanese war crimes provided much grist for that mill, but this only added fuel to older racist fires already raging in the United States (and Canada) at this time. The tenor of the war created a biased and dehumanizing climate that facilitated the decision to use atomic weapons against the Japanese people. It was not the only factor, nor was it as all-pervasive as some might believe. The Depression and ongoing anti-racist struggles in the years before the war had made important inroads among some people, and this came out, in both the United States and Canada, in the debate on using the bomb.

Indeed, Eva Sanderson of Toronto retorted that the use of the atomic bomb was a "fiendish act." She continued: "[Hiroshima is] made up of women and children, old people and men who have absolutely no power over their Government or their cruel militarists and are in no way responsible for the war. Mr. Gregg and Mr. George Evans are much more responsible for the Japanese war than these people. What protest did they make to our Government when the Japanese went into Manchuria?"[16] A similarly intense debate was also taking place in Great Britain and the United States. The Toronto *Globe and Mail* published news of protests emanating from Christian groups, the London Women's Parliament, and the Bombing Restriction Committee.[17] Winston Churchill finally weighed in on the debate, declaring: "The atomic bomb saved 1,000,000 American and 250,000 British lives by making an invasion of Japan unnecessary."[18] Regarding the legality of the war, editors at the *Vancouver Sun* suggested that they agreed with the Inter-American Judicial Commission's view that the German missiles directed against London were "terror weapons pure and simple," whereas the atomic bomb could be controlled and that the targets selected were strictly military in nature. The fact that its power also killed civilians and destroyed non-military targets was unfortunate: "[but] it is just as true to say that no means of war can be so controlled as entirely to spare civilians. This was as true in the days of Caesar and Napoleon as it is today."[19] Civil deaths and damage, it would seem, were embedded in an immutable logic of war. Indeed, the concept of "collateral damage" originates in this logic. However, this justification fails to stand up to historic scrutiny.

Fifty years after the dropping of the atom bomb, J. Samuel Walker, chief historian of the US Nuclear Regulatory Commission, concluded: "The consensus among scholars is that the bomb was not needed to avoid an invasion of Japan and to end the war within a relatively short time. It is clear that alternatives to the bomb existed and that Truman and his advisers knew it."[20]

This does not mean that scholarly debate has ended but, rather, that the preponderant view among scholars is critical of the use of the bomb.[21] The historical consensus regarding the first use of atomic weapons obliges us to pose some serious questions: What were the alternatives to using the bomb or invading Japan at a great cost to Allied lives? And why, if such alternatives existed, were they not chosen? In regard to the first question, alternatives to an invasion or using the bombs on Hiroshima and Nagasaki were numerous. First, it was quite conceivable, and, in fact, was suggested at the time, that the Allies simply continue the more conventional bombing campaign and their strict naval blockade of Japan. Second, it was quite possible to encourage Soviet intervention and to await its effects. As it turned out, the Soviet attack on Manchuria, beginning on 8 August 1945, was, according to Tsuyoshi Hasegawa's recent study, the decisive factor that precipitated Japan's surrender.[22] Indeed, the surrender might well have occurred quickly even without the atomic bombs. Third, it was proposed at the time that defining the terms of "unconditional" surrender, for instance by pointing out that it did not necessarily mean the immediate toppling of the Showa Emperor (as in fact was agreed at the time of surrender), would have induced a quick capitulation. This approach, promoted by Joseph Grew, the former US ambassador to Japan, and others was rejected by the new US secretary of state, James Byrnes. Fourth, the Allies could have pursued Japan's own peace moves at the time, in particular the official proposal to send the former prime minister of Japan, Konoe Fumimaro, to Moscow for discussions to end the war. Finally, it was well within the realm of possibility to demonstrate the power of the bomb not by obliterating Hiroshima but by dropping it in, say, Tokyo Bay or close to a naval base, as was suggested by a number of scientists at the time. Given that there were a number of reasonable if not foolproof alternatives, why were they all rejected in favour of immediate use of the bomb?

Scholarly research, particularly that conducted by Gar Alperovitz in the United States, has shown that one of the reasons for using the bomb was to intimidate the Soviet Union.[23] This factor is now generally recognized by most scholars, although there remains much debate regarding its relative importance. Another important factor was the disregard for civilian lives, which had become an entrenched part of the psychological landscape of the Allied leaders. It wasn't that they didn't know there would be civilian casualties; rather, it was that, in the heat of the moment, they didn't give it that much thought. The problem of civilian casualties was simply not an issue; or, if it was, it was secondary to other concerns. The fact is that the Allied governments had already adopted a policy of what effectively amounted to terror bombing in order to induce an early surrender. Killing civilians was not just an unfortunate by-product of war: it was a deliberate policy whose purpose was to terrorize the population and to bring about surrender. One spokesman for the air force stated at the time: "There are no civilians in Japan."[24] The planned use of indiscriminate bombing is illustrated both in Germany (Dresden and Hamburg) and in the fire bombings of Japanese cities. This willingness to use total war, to obliterate cities and civilian populations, was shared by many, but not all, in positions of power.[25] It was exactly this point that drew the editors of the *Vancouver Sun* to comment: "Two atomic bombs have dropped upon Japan, and in Allied countries, but particularly Britain, the United States and Canada, many people who were utterly unmoved, or hardly moved at all, by the 1000-plan RAF and AAF raids on Germany or, indeed, by raids of nearly similar size on Japan, are beginning to have qualms."[26] The editors did not themselves have qualms, arguing that, in terms of civilian casualties, the atomic bomb differed from conventional bombs in "degree only," that the atomic bomb risked fewer Allied soldiers, that the enemy would have used the weapon against "us" first, and that it would actually save Japanese lives by shortening the war.

Under pressure to maximize the damage inflicted on Japan, some believed that the bombing of cities was justifiable, rationalizing this view by suggesting that, in cases of total war and total mobilization, there were no longer distinctions between civilians and soldiers. To the public, however, the issue was often masked by the use of misleading language, as when C.D. Howe referred to the "great army base of Hiroshima." Kinuko Doi's story illustrates the fallacy of that view. The pressures of war, technological imperatives, and disregard for civilians all contributed to the decision makers not really caring about civilians. Racialized notions of the Japanese as beasts and demonic savages, discussed earlier, further exacerbated the disregard for civilian lives in Japan. Truman carried these notions with him, as did James Byrnes, his secretary of state. So, too, did Canada's prime minister, Mackenzie King, and many others.

Hiroshima in Memory

Popular views on the bomb remain bound to place, person, and time. In the United States, for example, nearly 85 percent of Americans supported the use of the atomic bombs against Japan at the time, and the proportion did not change significantly until the 1960s.[27] By the 1990s, however, approval of use of the bomb had fallen to 59 percent, based mainly on an increasingly critical assessment by African Americans and women in the United States. Men and seniors substantially supported the use of the bomb even fifty years later. These deep divisions are reflected in ongoing controversies over the atomic bomb, including the 1995 debate over the *Enola Gay* exhibition at the Smithsonian's National Air and Space Museum.[28] In Japan there exists a consensus, both scholarly and popular, that the atomic bombings were a war crime. Indeed, in the 1950s, residents of Hiroshima and Nagasaki launched a lawsuit against the Japanese government for damages suffered from the atomic bombings. They claimed that they were illegal and that the Japanese government, having waived any claims against the United States when it signed the 1951 peace treaty, was itself responsible for damages. In 1963, the Tokyo District Court (Judge Toshimasa Koseki presiding) ruled that the bombings of Nagasaki and Hiroshima, as undefended cities, were illegal acts.[29] It denied the survivors damages, however, ruling that claims by Japanese nationals had been waived both internationally and domestically. Thirty-three years later, the International Court of Justice in The Hague ruled (in an 8-7 decision) that the threat or use of nuclear weapons would generally be contrary to the rules of international law.[30]

In Canada, however, discussion about the bombs and Canada's role in their development and deployment has been muted if not extinguished from public memory. Traditionalist Canadian historians have ignored or downplayed this seamier side of Canadian participation in the war. Instead, they deal with the atomic bomb with taciturn observations like: "Those bombs killed tens of thousands of Japanese, but spared tens of thousands of Allied soldiers' lives, including those of the many Canadians who would have been killed in the final battle for Japan."[31] Even a history of atomic energy in Canada gives short shrift indeed to the impact of the nuclear bomb: "The Japanese war ended in August when the Americans dropped atomic bombs on Hiroshima and Nagasaki."[32] Simply repeating what Winston Churchill and Mackenzie King said decades earlier, without reconstructing the context within which those statements were made, is hardly the mark of critical scholarship. A preoccupation with Canadian participation in the European theatre – the "good" war – and aspirations towards "peacekeeping" have tended to bury Canada's role in Hiroshima. Thankfully, a few Canadian diplomats hinted that something might be amiss. For example, John Holmes, a key figure in the DEA until he was purged in 1960 for being gay, suggested that the question of the morality of the bomb and Canadian involvement might require further reflection: "The record then does not provide solid grounds for arguing Canadian innocence of 'complicity.' Nor is there a good case for arguing that Canada could have done anything to prevent Hiroshima or Nagasaki. This was an instance in which Canada, on functionalist grounds, might have claimed a voice but preferred silence."[33] Hugh Keenleyside, who had been instrumental in opening Canada's first embassy in Tokyo in 1929, was much more critical of the decision to use atomic weapons: "It then became clear that the holocaust at Hiroshima and innumerable other deaths that it had averted might equally have been avoided by warning the Japanese that this weapon existed and even disclosing its power by some demonstration other than the massacre of the innocent victims who died in its first use."[34] Since these memoirs were written, it has been left to the marginalized to remind us of a past that should not be forgotten.

Canada's Hiroshima

Cindy Kenny-Gilday is an Aboriginal activist of the Deline Dene Band. Sah Tu, or Great Bear Lake, as it is known in English, is the ancestral home of this First Nation. In 1998, Kenny-Gilday was the chair of the Dene of Deline First Nation Uranium Committee, which had been formed to advocate on behalf of its people for the damaging affects of radiation: "Our sad story of how the uranium mining has brought death and fear to our people is finally being told to the world after all these years."[35] Today, their territories and, indeed, the huge lake itself are contaminated with uranium for this is the place where, in the early 1930s, radium and uranium were first discovered in Canada. One conventional story cites Gilbert Labine as having discovered the first deposits in March 1930, while another gives the credit to Boris Pregel, a Russian-born French metals speculator.[36] However, according to indigenous accounts, it was a Dene man, Beyonnie, who first discovered the radioactive pitchblende ("money-rock," as it was known among Aboriginal peoples) and showed it to a white trapper.[37] A year later "the trapper came back with more white people who gave Beyonnie flour, baking powder, and lard for the money rocks."

A flurry of further exploration led Gilbert Labine to establish a mine at Somba K'e (Port Radium) on Great Bear Lake (Northwest Territories) and a refinery at Port Hope in Ontario, run by Eldorado Gold Mines. During the 1930s, the radium and uranium from the mine and refinery were mainly used in radiography (X-rays) and the ceramics industry. In 1940, with markets in decline, the mine closed, only to be reopened by government order in 1941. The race to produce the bomb had begun, and, in January 1944, the Canadian government effectively nationalized the mines and other facilities, renaming the company Eldorado Mining and Refining Limited. Even before Kinuko Doi found herself writhing in pain in Hiroshima that 6 August 1945 morning, atomic radiation was already doing its destructive work on the bodies of the people of the Sahtugot'ine First Nation, who, for thousands of years, had inhabited the shores of Great Bear Lake just south of the Arctic Circle. It was to their village, Deline (de-la-nay), or Fort Franklin as it was known then, that Eldorado turned to recruit people as ore carriers for the mine at Port Radium.[38] The ore, packed in forty-five kilogram bags, was transported down the Great Bear River, with the First Nations transporters playing a crucial role in loading and unloading the heavy sacks. George Blondin, whose family lived on fish caught near the mine, recalled: "I thought it was gold, they were going to make rings or something."[39] Since then, Blondin has lost three of his brothers, his wife, and four of seven children to cancer. Today, many of the men of that group of Dene are dead, their bodies ravaged by cancer from their exposure to uranium, a danger of which the Canadian government was aware but which it neglected to pass on to the Dene ore carriers.[40] Given Canada's history of expropriation and racialization it is, in one sense, not surprising that Canada's own atomic victims would be indigenous peoples. What is surprising, however, is how few Canadians are aware of this history.

How much Canadian uranium went into the first three atomic bombs – the Trinity test bomb and those used on Hiroshima and Nagasaki – is not clear. According to one press report, "a shipload of Congo ore sitting in New York harbor eventually made up the bulk of the supplies because Eldorado had trouble filling both American and British orders for the war effort. But the Manhattan Project mixed ores from Great Bear and Africa and all the uranium was refined at Port Hope."[41] The Canadian involvement in the atomic bomb development project (code-named the Manhattan Project, or Tube Alloy) was not limited to simply providing uranium. Heavy water ("water" consisting of molecules with an extra hydrogen atom), a medium to moderate the speed of the neutrons that induce nuclear fission, was also a key ingredient in early atomic experiments. It was first produced in 1943 at the Cominco plant in Trail, British Columbia, and from there it was shipped to the US facilities, contributing to the production of enriched uranium and plutonium.

Canadian participation in atomic development also included a significant scientific component, as C.D. Howe was proud to point out in announcing the dropping of the bomb. Between March 1940 and July 1941, key research in atomic bomb development took place mainly in Great Britain, not in the United States. Emblematic of this was the creation of the top secret British MAUD committee, which examined whether the development of an atomic weapon, the releasing of the enormous amounts of energy projected by theoretical physics, was practical or not. Its report, issued in July 1941, spurred the US government to undertake a major initiative in atomic bomb development. In the meantime, the visit of a British scientific mission headed by Sir Henry Tizard to North America in the summer of 1940 also encouraged British, American, and Canadian scientific collaboration, and this later became institutionalized.[42] Otto Maass, head of McGill University's chemistry department and later the head of Canada's chemical and biological warfare program, met Tizard when he arrived in Montreal on 15 August 1940.[43] The concrete expression of this nascent collaboration was the decision to move much of the British experimental project to Canada. Thus, at the end of 1942, Canada's National Research Council established a Montreal laboratory for nuclear experimentation as a joint project of both Canada and Great Britain.[44] With a staff of over 340, the government claimed it was "by far the largest organization ever created in this country to carry out a single research project."

Tri-country collaboration in actual nuclear weapons development was institutionalized after Churchill and Roosevelt met during a summit in Quebec City that led to the signing of the Quebec Agreement on 19 August 1943. The agreement included the decision to create the Combined Policy Committee (CPC), and, as Churchill stated in a letter to Mackenzie King: "the President has accepted the suggestion that Mr. Howe [minister of munitions and supply] should be invited to become a member of the Combined Policy Committee as a representative of Canada."[45] Although not present at formal meetings of the CPC in its earlier months, C.D. Howe was in communication with its members and fought to gain better access to the formal sessions.[46] On 17 February 1945, the CPC created a subcommittee to make recommendations regarding a joint development of a heavy water "pile." C.J. Mackenzie participated in the subcommittee proceedings, and, on 13 April, this group recommended to the CPC that there be no increase in the facilities producing heavy water, that the Chicago and Montreal research into heavy water piles continue, and that a joint US-British-Canadian heavy water pilot pile be established in Canada.[47] At its meeting on 21 April 1944, Canada's Cabinet War Committee approved expenditures of $4 million for capital costs and $750,000 for operations, and thus began the Chalk River

British prime minister Clement Attlee, US president Harry Truman, and Canadian prime minister W.L. Mackenzie King met at war's end to discuss atomic matters. The wartime atomic partnership later dissolved as the US government pursued nuclear weapons supremacy. | Harris and Ewing, photographers / Library and Archives Canada, C-023271

mega-project, harbinger of a nuclear Canada. The CPC also spawned specific subgroups to work on special projects. For example, in June 1944, the Canadian government appointed George C. Bateman, already a deputy member of the Combined Production and Resources Board and associate metals controller, as Canadian representative on the Combined Development Trust, an offshoot of the CPC designed to gain control over world uranium sources.[48] C.D. Howe, in appointing Bateman, pointed out that "Canada ha[d] an interest through being an important source of supply of the material."

The CPC was the transnational forum in which the United States submitted its proposal to drop the bomb on Japan. At 9:30 AM on 4 July 1945, the four members of the CPC – US secretary of war Henry Stimson, British field marshal Sir Henry Maitland-Wilson, Canada's C.D. Howe, and US scientist Vannevar Bush – gathered at the Pentagon to discuss the use of the atomic bomb, which had been successfully developed and was about to be operationally tested for the first time in Alamogordo, New Mexico. According to the minutes of that meeting, Maitland-Wilson told the committee that the "British Government concurred in the use of the T.A. weapon against Japan."[49] The minutes are silent regarding Howe's views, and there is no record of a Canadian Cabinet discussion on the topic. However, Howe was ready to intervene during the meeting when it came to the planned public release of information once the bomb was dropped, suggesting that Canada's scientific representative, Dean MacKenzie, "should also be brought into consultation" prior to the release of any information on the technical aspects of the bomb. There seems little alternative but to conclude that Howe supported the CPC's decision to drop the bomb.

Clearly, Canada's role in the development of the atomic bomb was considerable. So, too, was that of Great Britain. In this sense, the development of atomic weapons, and the decision to use them, was neither an exclusive American enterprise nor an exercise in unilateralism. Great Britain and Canada were intent on being part of the atomic action and, in many ways, participated in the making of, and in the decision to drop, the bombs. This point has both theoretical and practical significance. On the practical side, it helps illustrate that the atomic era was not simply an American creation but, rather, that of a transnational "coalition of the willing," in effect, an exercise in multilateralism. This was, to be sure, a US-led coalition, but the values expressed in it – that is, the willingness to use total war to obliterate cities and civilian populations – was shared by many in positions of power.[50] Limiting discussion on the first use of the bomb to the American government alone ends up reinforcing US exceptionalism, on the one hand, and creating conditions conducive to the demonization of the United States, on the other.

In the end, it was the Soviet attack on 8 August 1945 that shocked the Japanese elite into immediate surrender: "the two atomic bombs on Hiroshima and Nagasaki alone were not decisive in inducing Japan to surrender. Despite their destructive power, the atomic bombs were not sufficient to change the direction of Japanese diplomacy. The Soviet invasion was."[51] The reason the Soviet Union's declaration of war played such a key role has to do with the Japanese elite's fear that the Soviet Union would occupy part of Japan, that the Communist Party in Japan would re-emerge, and that their ultimate nightmare – the abolition of the *kokutai* and the imperial system – would come to pass. To those raised on the idea that the awesome power of the atomic bomb was the "clincher" in what was clearly a no-win situation for Japan, this claim may seem incredible. From the other side of the retrospective prism, however, the assertion makes sense. US officials had become increasingly ambivalent about invoking the Soviet Union's commitment to get involved in the Asian theatre mainly because they feared an increase in Soviet influence at the expense of American influence. This concern prevented them from emphasizing the threat of imminent Soviet involvement (e.g., by having Stalin sign the Potsdam Declaration), which might have brought about an earlier surrender on the part of the Japanese. Instead, the Americans decided to try and conclude the war independently through the use of the atomic bombs. This had the effect of accelerating the Soviet timetable for launching its offensive against Japanese troops in northeast China and Korea. The race for regional influence and the reluctance of the Japanese elite to face defeat prolonged the agony of soldiers and civilians alike. Finally, at noon on 15 August 1945, the Emperor's voice, hitherto unheard by the people of Japan, emanated from thousands of radios, announcing surrender. At 5:00 PM in Washington, US officials learned from Swiss officials that the Japanese government had formally accepted the Allied terms. And at 7:00 PM Washington time, Truman announced that the war was over.

5 Shades of Liberation

Shock, jubilation, and tribulation heralded the end of the war in Asia. Those areas most affected by the Second World War, including China, Korea, Vietnam, the Philippines, and Indonesia, were left devastated by years of warfare that only intensified towards war's end. Not only Hiroshima and Nagasaki but most of Japan's cities were in ruins after months of fire-bombing. From the wreckage, survivors groped to stand and move forward, to find lost family members, and to find the means to sustain themselves. Few were expecting such a rapid end to the war, and quickly the politics of race and empire reasserted themselves. Policy makers in the victorious countries – the United States, the Soviet Union, and Europe (including Great Britain) – rushed to find ways to assert their own countries' agendas in the region. On the other hand, forces determined to achieve independence in countries such as Vietnam and Korea also moved to consolidate their presence. In China, one of the victorious allies, Chiang Kai-shek and the Guomindang tried to gain control over the whole of the country but quickly ran into opposition from Mao Zedong and the Chinese Communist Party, a force that had grown substantially through the war. Change was afoot, but none felt the effects of victory more profoundly than those who survived the worst effects of Japanese militarism.

Survivors

One who survived the war in Asia was the Canadian Don MacPherson. Interned as a POW in Hong Kong and then taken to Japan in 1943, MacPherson recalled: "[the camp commander called for a] parade and said that the war was over and now we were all friends again. He then had a large pig delivered to the gate and let it go into the compound. I don't think that pig had time to squeal before it was in the pot."[1] Three American fighters "flew in low over the camp and dropped packages of canned coffee, cream and sugar wrapped in women's underwear!" Later, B-17s dropped one hundred ninety-litre drums of food: "I ate 32 of those large Hershey bars and 11 large cans of peaches in two days! I just ate and threw up and ate and threw up." Interned in Hong Kong for nearly two years, his weight had dropped from seventy-seven kilograms to forty seven. In August 1943, MacPherson had been transported to Oyama, Japan, where he had been obliged to work in a coal mine and, later, in an open-pit nickel mine. The conditions were extreme. "Hunger dominated our lives," stated MacPherson: "The Japs had a whole warehouse of our Red Cross parcels but refused to let us have them." The POWs received only three and a half parcels each during the four years they were interned.[2] "We never had any solid food other than rice," and many of the POWs suffered from beri-beri, pellagra, dysentery, and diarrhoea. MacPherson himself began to lose his eyesight. Little wonder that his body was unable to process chocolate bars! Not all POWs suffered to this degree, but all were thankful to be free and to be quickly repatriated when Occupation forces arrived in Japan at the end of August.

Surrender meant something different for people of Asian descent who had been brought to Japan as forced labourers during the war. Of the innumerable cases that might be cited, perhaps none is more moving or enlightening than that of Liu Lianren.[3] Born in Zhucheng County on China's Shandong peninsula in 1913, Liu grew up in the region. He was twenty-four at the time of the Japanese invasion of China in 1937 and continued to farm in Shandong during the early years of Japan's occupation. His wife was pregnant when, in September 1944, Chinese conscripts working for the Japanese army arrived at his farm. They arrested Liu, thirty-one at the time, and sent him to Japan, where he was deployed as a forced labourer at the Showa Mining branch of the Meiji Mining Corporation. Conditions in the mine were appalling: the Chinese labourers were forced to work twelve hours a day without adequate food or shelter. Safety conditions in the mines had deteriorated, making the work extremely dangerous, and mine bosses frequently resorted to beating the workers to keep them in line. In July 1945,

Canadian POWS, veterans of the battle at Hong Kong in December 1941, suffered severely during internment in Japan. In September 1945, a few weeks after being liberated, they received new clothing in Yokohama. | Canada. Department of National Defence / Library and Archives Canada, PA-114876

the terrible conditions and death threats uttered by the conscript labourers' overseers prompted Liu and four others to flee for their lives. Escaping into the mountainous terrain of Hokkaido, they lived from hand to mouth off the land – in the case of Liu, for years – oblivious to the fact that the war had ended. Liu became separated from his three comrades in 1946 but continued his life in hiding, using a cave as his home. Finally, a hunter from the region discovered Liu and brought him down from the mountains. As incredible as it may seem, this was in January 1958: thirteen years had passed since he had fled the mines.[4]

Liu's story is unique, but there were thousands of forced labourers from China and Korea who suffered extreme deprivation. At Mitsui's Miike coal mine, the largest in Japan with twenty-four thousand employees, miners left the seams en masse after the war because of the deplorable conditions. Of these, six thousand were Chinese and Korean forced labourers or Allied POWs. According to the company's own records, the white POWs were immediately repatriated, but many Chinese and Korean forced labourers were obliged to continue to mine coal for the Occupation![5] Over thirty thousand Chinese forced labourers were still in Japan after the war. The Japanese government reported to the Supreme Commander of the Allied Powers (SCAP) that "their agitations since the termination of the war ha[d] become so violent as to constitute a great menace to peace and order."[6] The Chinese labourers had the temerity, reported Japanese officials, to "disregard the terms of contract which they accepted as reasonable and satisfactory but also demand 'special' treatment as nationals of a victorious Power." The Chinese labourers were even rioting to back their "excessive" demands, stated the report. Eventually, most of the forced labourers were repatriated but the injustices they suffered were neither addressed nor forgotten.

For the "comfort women," war's end meant death for many at the hands of their overseers. Even those who survived faced great perils. At war's end, Ahn Jeomsun recalled:

> It was when I was seventeen that the war ended but at first we didn't even realize it.[7] We could never meet people like civilians; Japanese soldiers made up our entire world. However, I did see Chinese people attacking and killing Japanese soldiers with their fists and knives. We were almost killed by the Chinese, too, but thankfully they realized that we weren't Japanese women but Chosun [Korean] women who had been forcefully taken to those camps to serve as comfort women. Because of that, the Chinese people actually helped us instead of attacking us. For that reason, several other women and I were able to walk out of there with the help of the Chinese.

Having left the comfort station, Ahn had to find her own way home to Korea: "On the way, I would sleep in empty houses and eat the food that I could get from others. In that way I walked for a little over one week and finally came to Beijing. It was there that I met a man in the Independence

Army, a Mr. Yoon from Chuncheong Province. Upon hearing about my situation, Mr. Yoon and his wife said how pitiable it was and said that from then on I should travel with them."

Ahn collapsed upon arriving home and stayed in bed for three months:

> They said it was malaria: one day my whole body would feel as if it was on fire; another day I wouldn't hurt at all and would be fine. At that time, my whole family thought that I was going to die. Since there was no special kind of medicine back then, I barely recovered after eating all different kinds of medicinal herbs that my mother got for me. Also, from then on I began to work hard in order to eat and live again. I helped out at other people's stores, worked as a maid in wealthy people's homes, and lived in that way.

Ahn was only seventeen years old and soon found herself being pressured to marry: "A woman in my neighborhood kept nagging me so once I finally went out to meet the son of the family that ran our neighborhood Western-style clothing store; I guess he fell for me because he would wait in front of my house every day. But I really hated seeing him. If you just said the word 'man,' I would shudder."

These survivors, all of whom were victims of crimes against humanity, would live with their experiences for the rest of their lives. And they were but the tip of an iceberg. As we shall see, redress for them and hundreds of thousands of others like them was not taken seriously, either through the war crimes tribunal process or in the final negotiations that led to a peace treaty with Japan a few years later. Survivors in Asia faced not only their own memories but also the devastation wrought by war in their homelands. Moreover, instead of peace, Asian survivors often confronted civil war or a colonial war in which Euro-American powers attempted to reimpose their control.

Canada at War's End

People in Great Britain and its dominions, as well as in the United States, swept into the streets with the formal announcement of surrender. Apprised of the imminent announcement, Mackenzie King in Ottawa prepared a radio address, which was then inadvertently released, to King's great embarrassment, on Sunday night, 12 August 1945. On Wednesday, 15 August, King convened his Cabinet and then declared the day a national holiday. For both the government and for the armed forces surrender was a relief, guaranteeing the immediate release of Canadian POWs and also avoiding the dispatch of troops returning from the European theatre to the Pacific for the invasion of Japan.

The *Vancouver Sun* editorialists declared the surrender marked the end of "six years of the most frightful conflict the world ha[d] ever endured."[8] In other words, the war had begun in 1939 with the declaration of war against Germany. On 7 December 1941, Japan had, according to the same editorial, put themselves "beyond the pale when, in cynical disregard of law, they treacherously attacked a nation with which they were at peace." This account did not reflect the experience of the people of China, for whom the war had begun much earlier, nor that of the Chinese-Canadian community, which had been actively engaged in the defence of China since 1937 or even earlier. The "Canadian" narrative of the war was being constructed in the reflection of the Eurocentric gaze.

None was more exuberant in celebrating Japan's defeat than Chinese Canadians. Having mobilized the community for eight long years, and having overcome the impediments to enlisting, community leaders began to turn their minds to reaping the rewards of their efforts and the new climate in Canada. On 16 February 1945, even before the war ended, the Chinese Canadian Association submitted a memorandum and petition to John Hart, the premier of British Columbia, requesting the franchise for "all Canadian citizens of Chinese descent" in the province.[9] The group declared: "In the present war, the Chinese community has over-subscribed its quota in each of the Victory Loan Drives, and the Vancouver Chinese achieved the distinction of contributing more per capita than any other single group in Canada!"[10] The provincial government awarded the franchise to war veterans of Asian descent but to no others. It would take another two years of lobbying by the community and its allies before the franchise was finally won.

Nor did war's end bring relief to the Japanese Canadians uprooted, interned, or dispersed across Canada. They were not allowed to return to their homes. In the United States, however, Mitsuye Endo had challenged internment, and the US Supreme Court ruled that it was unlawful to detain a law-abiding US citizen and ordered Endo released. The War Department announced that the evacuation orders would be rescinded effective 2 January 1945.[11] Why did the Canadian government continue to pursue racialized policies after the war despite the developments south of the border? As Ann Sunahara documents in her book *The Politics of Racism*, the BC chapter of the Canadian Legion and Vancouver mayor J.W. Cornett demanded that the "Japanese and their children be shipped to Japan after the war and never be allowed to return here."[12]

In the Soldiers' Vote Bill of 1944, which enabled overseas soldiers to vote in the general election, the Liberals had included a clause that disenfranchised any person "whose racial origin [was] that of a country at war with Canada."[13] The furious debate that ensued concluded with amendments to allow those of German and Italian descent to vote but continued to deny the vote to Japanese Canadians. According to Mackenzie King, this avoided "racial favouritism" towards Japanese Canadians. The persistence of discrimination even after the war prompted activist and writer Muriel Kitagawa to take pen to paper shortly after Japan's surrender:

Freedom

MacArthur stands,
a colossus astride the cursed men
who used the "sacred" name of "heaven descended"
to gild the scourge that drove a muzzled people.
MacArthur orders: Freedom!
Where freedom never lived before,
where freedom died in prisons.

And here?
where Freedom is the motto
inscribed upon the cornerstone of democracy?
The edifice is built so grand,
the busy men-in-office on the topmost floors
sometimes forget their very elevation
rests upon that cornerstone.

The inscription still remains
for brooding fingers to trace again
the imprint of the blood, the sweat, the tears
carved deeply there ...
each letter carved as deeply on our waiting hearts.[14]

Kitagawa's verse captures not only the ironies of an occupying force implementing democracy by fiat but also rings with the anguish of a people still waiting for an end to an era that continued to scar a whole community – and a country.

Recasting the Empire

As the Allies competed for strategic advantage, the US agencies in charge of planning for the occupation of Japan deliberated on the mechanisms of control. Various contingencies were envisaged, but central to all of the various plans was what might be termed a foundation belief, that is: "The major share of the effort in the war against Japan has been, and will continue to be made by the United States."[15] As discussions progressed, this belief evolved into one of the strategic platforms of US policy in East Asia, namely: "The United States had primary interest in and responsibility for security in the Pacific and Far East. In order to protect that interest and discharge that responsibility, the control of Japan should be exercised throughout the entire period of occupation by a Supreme Commander designated by the United States."[16] This view of the war in Asia, and its implication that peoples in Asia themselves were incapable of safeguarding their own security, was more than a little self-serving. However, complicating the scene was the fact that the Chinese government had declined to play a predominant role in the occupation of Japan. Invited to do so by Roosevelt, Chiang Kai-shek had asked that the United States take on that role. The United States had gained much good will because of its role in the Pacific war, and this reinforced its imperial inclinations under the guise of benevolence.

Yet, for a decade the Chinese people had been left to fend for themselves against Japanese aggression. Until 1941, their resistance, whether armed or passive, was the single most important factor in determining the nature and indeed the outcome of the war. After Pearl Harbor – that is, from 1942 on – US involvement was substantial, and its contribution to the defeat of the Axis, including Japan, deserves full recognition. However, in 1931 or 1937, when China first faced aggression, and even after the European regional war broke out in 1939, the major powers, including the United States, remained in an uneasy partnership with Japan, protecting their own imperial interests in Asia. And, as is well known, the US government also remained largely on the sidelines with respect to the European theatre, despite repeated requests for assistance. The formulation quoted above, that the United States made the major effort in the war and that, as a corollary, it had primary interest in the region is a reflection of how the US government appropriated to itself a victory that belonged to many.

Thus, at war's end, Japan came under the control of the US government through General Douglas MacArthur, appointed by Truman as Supreme Commander for the Allied Powers.[17] This was a legal occupation, its authority being derived from the Potsdam Declaration, the terms of surrender negotiated between the Truman administration and Japanese authorities between 10 and 14 August, and subsequent agreements reached at the Council of Foreign Ministers meetings in London and Moscow in September and December 1945, respectively. Stalin had acquiesced to a US-led occupation, although he had hoped for a zone of occupation, as in Germany, but this was rejected by the Truman administration. MacArthur arrived in Japan on 30 August, and on 2 September 1945, the formal surrender of Japanese forces took place on the USS *Missouri* anchored in Tokyo Bay. Unlike in Germany, where the US government had abolished the existing German governing structures, in Japan the US government decided to leave the existing government intact and to exert control via the General Headquarters (GHQ) of SCAP. MacArthur was all-powerful and could order the Japanese government to do anything he determined was necessary. That fall, the general moved to protect the Emperor from war crimes prosecution and worked to have him reinvented as a constitutional monarch. But MacArthur was also constrained – by Washington, by the other Allied powers (including Canada), but, most important, by developments in Japan itself.

In Japan the shock of defeat and surrender was accompanied by another shock – the arrival of American and Allied soldiers.[18] Astonishingly, there was little resistance to the Occupation. Some people resented their arrival, others welcomed them; but most people felt powerless and were too busy trying to keep body and soul together to worry about their new overseers. The spectre of starvation was real. For its part, the Japanese government was worried about arriving GIs molesting Japanese women, and so organized a semi-official system of "comfort stations" for US soldiers under the "Recreation and Amusement Association." Initially sanctioned by MacArthur, the Association was later disbanded because of high rates of venereal disease, among other reasons, and the sex trade moved into the streets and bars of Occupied Japan.[19] Meanwhile, popular movements involving tenant associations, labour unions, women's groups, and left-wing political parties re-emerged to demand changes. In some cases, demands were radical and tactics more so: employers were challenged for their wartime conduct and for hoarding. For the most part, the Occupation tolerated and even encouraged these developments, but the situation would soon change.

Herbert Norman and the Early Occupation of Japan

Canadian participation in the Occupation was based on its relatively minor military contribution in the Pacific theatre. Although limited, this military role included the sending of troops for the defence of Hong Kong; the participation of Canadian soldiers – including Japanese Canadians and Chinese Canadians – in the Pacific, usually under the direction of the British Southeast Asia Command; and the participation of the naval vessel *Uganda* in the final stages of naval operations against Japan. Unlike Great Britain and Australia, Canada did not send troops to participate in the Occupation. Its role was mainly political.

A number of Canadians represented the Canadian government during the Occupation, including E. Herbert Norman, J.J. McCardle, Ralph Collins, and A.R. Menzies, as well as military officers posted to the Canadian mission in Tokyo during the Korean War. There has not been any definitive study of Canada's role in the Occupation, but there are a few published essays on the topic, and related diplomatic documents have been published in the series *Documents on Canadian External Relations*.[20] For the most part, these studies tie Canadian policy during the Occupation to the work of E. Herbert Norman.[21]

Norman, a scholar of Japanese history, worked as a language officer in the Canadian Embassy until Pearl Harbor. He was repatriated in 1942, and for the duration of the war worked as the head of Canada's small wartime intelligence agency (the Examination Unit). After Japan's defeat, he travelled to Manila and from there to Japan, where he was seconded to MacArthur's intelligence staff from September 1945 to January 1946. During the spring of 1946, he acted as Canada's delegate to the Far Eastern Commission, based in Washington, before returning to Japan in August 1946 as head of the Canadian mission to Occupied Japan. In October 1950, he was recalled from Tokyo after accusations that he was a communist and suspected spy surfaced in the United States. Cleared of the charges, he continued to play an important role in Canada's Department of External Affairs until 1952, when further accusations made his position increasingly untenable. In 1953, he became Canada's high commissioner to New Zealand, and in 1956 he became Canada's ambassador to Egypt. Old accusations followed him in his new post, and he committed suicide in Cairo in April 1957. While the major works on Norman in English do not provide a thorough account of his role in the Occupation, they do provide invaluable insights. Recently, Katō Shūichi and Nakano Toshiko made a significant contribution to research on Norman by publishing, in Japanese, a compendium of Norman's dispatches from Tokyo for the period from 1946 to 1948.[22] Norman's actions in the first year of the Occupation were primarily concerned with the assessment of war responsibility and revision of Japan's Constitution.[23]

Norman had been assigned to work on MacArthur's staff while still in Canada, and he arrived in Yokohama in early September. Working as an intelligence officer, Norman provided detailed reports on the involvement of the Japanese elite in the war. His findings would have a major impact as he used his knowledge of Japan's history to trace the trajectory of Japanese expansion. Norman's appreciation of the stages of the war and those responsible for it differed significantly from the views of MacArthur and most of his advisors. He saw the earlier phase of the war – that is, the Japanese aggression against China – as being just as important as the post-1941 stage (i.e., after Pearl Harbor). Furthermore, he felt that responsibility for this war of colonial aggression should be assigned to Japan's oligarchy, in which he included the monarchy, the financial conglomerates (*zaibatsu*), the government bureaucracy, and the military. Although Norman used the terms "military" and "military clique" as a form of shorthand, he was quite clear that civilians such as Konoe Fumimaro (the former prime minister, who was considered part of a "peace" faction at the end of the war) had to be held accountable for the war.[24]

Norman's submission to George Atcheson regarding the war responsibility of Konoe and others was critical in forcing SCAP to distance itself from Konoe, who was subsequently listed as a suspected war criminal.[25] The former prime minister committed suicide on 16 December 1945. In their accounts of this incident, both Nakano and Bowen make reference to what they consider Norman's personal attacks against Konoe in his report.[26] Their point is well taken, but it should not obscure the more significant issue. Norman pursued Konoe not out of personal pique but, rather, from a profound difference with MacArthur over the nature of, and responsibility for, the war. And while Norman, like MacArthur, did not call for putting the Emperor on trial, he did call for a full investigation into the monarchy and the Emperor, a move that MacArthur blocked. Calling the monarchy a form of "Japanese Caesarism," Norman argued that it may have played the same role as had Fuhrerism in Nazi Germany with regard to transfer of responsibility for war crimes:

> Thus, no matter how abominable the act, all sense of guilt is shifted to the Fuhrer. Similarly, Japanese atrocities can perhaps be explained in part by the same psychological trick: to kill captured enemies in cold blood, does not strike them as inhuman since it is done in the name of the Emperor. Perhaps this would not make the Emperor a war criminal, but it is difficult to see how such a dehumanizing and barbarizing institution could ever be

> converted by some act of political legerdemain into an instrument making for peace and humanistic enlightenment.[27]

Norman suggests that more information would be required to decide on whether Hirohito should be tried as a war criminal. There were hints that the Emperor may not have been 100 percent behind the decision to go to war with the United States and Great Britain, but Norman suggested that he took an active interest in military affairs, particularly in the war in China, and that it would be hard to believe that he was not informed of Japanese acts of terror in that country: "Thus, although some Westerners may be willing to give the Imperial House a clean sheet as regards war guilt in planning Pearl Harbor, the Chinese might well be less disposed towards charity in the experiences of Japanese Imperial benevolence." In light of the ongoing controversy regarding Japan's war responsibility, Norman's views can only be deemed prophetic. At the time, however, he also warned that the Allies should not themselves depose the Emperor, nor should they endorse the institution or absolve the Emperor of war guilt: it was up to the Japanese people to work out their political problems. In a related point, Norman warned that to support the monarchy would encourage the wartime leaders "to take the full blame upon themselves, not for the wanton slaughter and destruction they ha[d] wrought but for the defeat and humiliation which they [would] have brought on Japan, and for the evil counsel they ha[d] given the Emperor."[28] There was indeed something distinct in Norman's views, derived perhaps in part from the social gospel of his missionary family but also from his socialist beliefs, which he developed in the 1930s. These critical views would initially have some impact; however, as tensions between the Soviet Union and the United States developed, the Canadian government and Norman would learn to temper their views in regard to US policies not only in Japan but also in China, Vietnam, and Korea.

Race and Recolonization: Vietnam

The US government initially deferred to the British in policy making for South and Southeast Asia after the war. At the Potsdam Conference in July 1945, Truman and Churchill had approved a military plan that allowed British forces to take the surrender of Japanese forces in Vietnam south of the 16th parallel and Chinese forces to take the surrender north of that parallel.[29] This reflected a major shift in US policy regarding French colonialism, which hitherto had been quite critical because of Roosevelt's perception that the French had been poor colonial administrators. The British government fully supported a return of French colonial control in Indochina since it wanted to do the same in Malaya, Burma, Hong Kong, and other areas. From the perspective of French officials, US opposition was based not on a concern for the well-being of the Vietnamese people but on other interests: "It is possible that the American government favours independence in certain colonial territories only in order to gain possession of bases."[30] By the time of his death in April 1945, Roosevelt himself had shifted substantially, allowing for French recolonization but on the condition that France carry out the "obligations of a trustee" and commit to independence as the ultimate goal.[31]

However, the imperial consensus favouring recolonization did not take into account the rising strength of independence forces led by Ho Chi Minh. After hearing news of Japan's offer to surrender, on 12 August 1945, the Viet Minh called for a national insurrection and capture of the Japanese troops.[32] At the same time, pro-Japanese forces that had collaborated with the Japanese occupation pushed to create the Committee for National Salvation to support Bao Dai, the former Vietnamese emperor to whom the Japanese had turned for support after their March coup against the Vichy-backed French colonial regime. In Hanoi, Viet Minh forces arrived in the city and engaged in an ongoing battle for the allegiance of the town's people, about half of whom apparently supported the Viet Minh. On 19 August, the Viet Minh mobilized thousands of peasants from surrounding areas to come to Hanoi, and, in a ceremony in front of the municipal theatre just before noon, the Vietnamese liberation flag was hoisted.[33] By the end of the day, the Viet Minh had won control of Hanoi in a bloodless coup. The remaining Japanese troops agreed not to interfere and the Committee for National Salvation dissolved soon after.

In the south, the Viet Minh were somewhat weaker, but the success in Hanoi and the decision by Emperor Bao Dai to endorse the Viet Minh government in Hanoi inspired non-communist nationalists in Saigon to dissolve a "national united front" and to replace it with a new liberation organization led by Viet Minh leader Tran Van Giau. On 25 August, a general insurrection on the Hanoi pattern occurred, the streets filling with both the townspeople and peasants from the surrounding districts. Shouting the slogans "Down with imperialists, down with French colonialists" (*da da de quoc, da dao thuch dan phap*), people of all political stripes and religious persuasions celebrated liberation from both the Japanese and the French. Marring the triumph were a number of cases in which crowds took revenge against French expatriates, with a number beaten and a few even lynched.

Such acts of revenge, also common in Europe after the war, should not mask the fact that the August Revolution saw the Vietnamese people take control of their own country. As Canadian foreign affairs officials put it in their own handbook of Vietnam's history, the widest coalition after the war was "the League of Annamese Revolutionary Parties, the strongest component of which was the Viet Minh, itself a combination of smaller groups including the Communist party."[34]

At war's end, an American official, Archimedes Patti, who arrived in Hanoi on 22 August 1945, became an official conduit between the Viet Minh and the Truman administration. He provided Ho Chi Minh with a translated version of the US Declaration of Independence and, indeed, on 2 September, when Ho stood before a mass meeting to declare Vietnam independent, the first words of the declaration were: "We hold truths that all men are created equal, that they are endowed by their Creator with certain unalienable rights, among these are Life, Liberty and the pursuit of happiness."[35] The declaration went on to decry the French colonial legacy, concluding: "Vietnam has the right to be free and independent and, in fact, has become free and independent." Indeed, the former emperor, Bao Dai, abdicated at this time, calling on all his former subjects to cooperate with the nationalist revolution. He set an example by accepting the position of "supreme counsellor" to a broadly based revolutionary government in Hanoi in which both Viet Minh and non-Viet Minh participated. The broad-based support for the Viet Minh reflected the respect of a people who had suffered terribly under the Japanese and Vichy French joint wartime occupation. Occupation policy of seizing rice harvests for use as fuel or as food shipments to Japan led to a massive famine that killed as many as 2 million Vietnamese in the north.[36]

While a number of US representatives in Vietnam at the time expressed great admiration for the Vietnamese efforts to gain independence, reports sent to the State Department tended to be much more critical. Patti, for example, wrote quite positively in his memoirs about the Viet Minh, but his reports to the US administration differed. An encounter between Vo Nguyen Giap and Jean Sainteny, the senior French official in Hanoi, is described in Patti's memoirs in the words "Saiteny [sic] had been outplayed and was visibly annoyed," but his report to the administration described the same encounter differently, suggesting that "the French had the upper hand and that during course of negotiations Annamites lost considerable ground mainly due to inferiority complex when confronted by a European."[37] In fact, many US reports from the field display a remarkable core of ingrained racism towards the Vietnamese, describing them as having "no sense of solidarity," being politically "immature," lacking executive ability, and not being ready for independence. Of course, being politically immature, they had succumbed to communism and were therefore "pure imports from Moscow."[38] Here we see an important juncture between racism and anti-communism. Unwilling or unable to imagine that Asians might be communists because they equated Euro-Americans with imperialism, people such as Patti instead racialized the Vietnamese as immature and susceptible to foreign manipulation. Such allegations persisted despite the fact that there was no Soviet help for the Viet Minh at this time, just as there was no American help.

British officials led by General Gracey, accompanied by Indian troops under British command, arrived in Saigon at the end of August 1945. The British quickly helped reorganize the French troops who had been imprisoned. On 22 September, French legionnaires led a large group of French civilians to retake control of Saigon. Running gun battles took place, but the combined imperial forces obliged the Viet Minh to retreat to the countryside. In the north, Chinese Nationalist troops who had entered the country to take the surrender of the Japanese, displaced the Viet Minh as well. Ho Chi Minh and the Viet Minh were being seriously squeezed. Faced with the return of French colonial power, Ho proposed compromise, even travelling to France for negotiations for an autonomous if not independent Vietnam. Part of the deal was to restore French control in order to remove Chinese Nationalist troops. This retreat was bitterly criticized by many in the Viet Minh, but Ho retorted: "You are forgetting your past history. Whenever the Chinese came, they stayed a thousand years. The French, on the other hand, can stay for only a short time."[39] To a French historian he put it somewhat more bluntly: "It is better to sniff French shit for a while than to eat China's for the rest of our lives." In February 1946, the French displaced the Chinese troops in the north, but the truce with the Viet Minh could not hold. In a dispute over collection of customs duties in Haiphong, fighting broke out between Viet Minh and French colonial soldiers. The French forces decided to provide a lesson in force. On 23 November 1946 they bombed and razed the town of Haiphong, killing six thousand people, mainly civilians. A few weeks later, Viet Minh resistance fighters struck back, destroying Haiphong's electrical plant and assassinating French officials. The war against French colonialism had begun. General Etienne Valluy declared: "[if] those gooks want a fight they'll get it."[40] For the next eight years, Vietnam would be ravaged by French colonialism, the restoration assisted by the British and supported by the United States. As the "liberal" Dean Acheson in the US State

Department described it, the US had "no thought of opposing the re-establishment of French control in Indochina and no official statement by US Government ha[d] questioned even by implication French sovereignty over Indochina."[41]

The politics of race and empire converged in Vietnam to support the reimposition of colonial control. The Allies had raised the banner of self-determination in the Atlantic Charter as part of the effort to defeat the Axis forces, but, in practice, the opposite was occurring, and not only in Vietnam. Many of the policy makers and power brokers in London, Paris, and Washington shared a deep belief in the superiority of Anglo-European civilization, and this went a long way towards mitigating whatever differences might have existed regarding the pace of decolonization.

Dividing a Nation: The Korean Peninsula

In the last days of the war, hasty decisions were made regarding who was to oversee the Japanese surrender.[42] The decision to divide Korea at the 38th parallel was a unilateral American decision recommended by Dean Rusk and Charles Bonesteel, two young military officers. This recommendation was then integrated into the surrender order announced by Douglas MacArthur on 15 August 1945. The Soviet government was not consulted, nor were any Koreans. The Soviet Union accepted the division in order to strengthen its hand in other regions, and Soviet forces thus dutifully halted at the 38th parallel as they moved down the Korean peninsula. US forces, not having anticipated the early surrender or the necessity of occupying Korea, had to scramble to get to Korea, a force of twenty-one ships arriving in Inch'on Harbour near Seoul only on 8 September. Under the command of General John Reed Hodge, US troops disembarked and arrived in Seoul the next day: a formal surrender ceremony took place that noon.

In the interim, a revolution was taking place throughout Korea, in both the north and south. People organized marches on the colonial jails to force the release of political dissidents. Within a few days after Japan's defeat, hundreds of "People's Committees" had been created, and on 6 September 1945, the Korean People's Republic was proclaimed in the south. This popular movement never gained the support of US occupation forces but, instead, became a target of conservatives and US authorities. Hodge and his staff arrived determined to take control. Fearful that the popular movement was controlled by communists, the US military quickly came to rely on the conservative Korean Democratic Party for its information while demanding from Washington more "staff who [were] experienced in governmental affairs and who [knew] orientals."[43] Hodge was known for his view that Japanese and Koreans were the "same breed of cat."[44] By the end of September, Hodge's political advisor informed Washington that Korea was divided into two camps, communists and the "democratic or conservative group."[45] This group, centred on the Korean Democratic Party and Syngman Rhee, soon gained substantive influence over the colonial bureaucracy, including the police, with the support of US forces. Popular resistance continued, however, and Rhee increasingly turned to repression to cope with widening discontent, even within the conservative camp.

There were approximately 250,000 Japanese in occupied Korea at the end of the war, over 200,000 of whom were civilians. They became refugees, fleeing towards the ports to try and find some way back to Japan. The Soviet forces interned many of the soldiers, and, in a number of cases, they were sent to the Soviet Union rather than being repatriated to Japan, as were many in northeast China. There was also some looting and numerous acts of rape, particularly of "enemy" women, that is, Japanese women in northern Korea.[46] On the whole, the Soviet army did not use its control to extract from Korea its economic capital. An American investigative team that visited northern Korea in 1946 concluded that the region's industrial equipment was left intact and was indeed functioning.[47] If anything, it was the fleeing Japanese troops who engaged in acts of sabotage, at times to forestall the Soviet offensive and at times simply to take vengeance for their defeat.

Soviet forces in Pyongyang, like their US counterparts in the south, did exercise significant influence over the emerging administration of northern Korea. But Stalin did not advocate radical changes, instead favouring those that would be friendly to the Soviet Union, with the goal of reinforcing Soviet security. Unlike the US military, the Soviet administrators allowed the indigenous People's Committees (although they often went under different names) that began to spring up across Korea to continue, while trying to influence them. It was in this context that Kim Il Sung emerged from the hills of northeast China to take on a key role.[48] The Soviet authorities established the Soviet Civil Administration, which acted as a parallel administrative body until February 1946, after which indigenous structures took over. Soviet advisors were appointed to the provincial and central People's Committees.

In Pyongyang itself, the People's Committee was led initially by Cho Mansik. Cho, a Presbyterian elder who had promoted the indigenous Korean production movement in the 1920s, was a conservative nationalist with support within the business and Christian communities. He formed the conservative-leaning Korean Democratic Party in November 1945. However, after the December 1945 Moscow conference of foreign ministers rejected immediate independence for Korea, Cho became increasingly outspoken against the Soviet-dominated trusteeship and was placed under house arrest in January 1946.

The patterns of interactions between the occupying powers and the indigenous political movements in north and south Korea shared a basic similarity: both the Soviet Union and the United States displayed a bias towards those elites who most shared their worldview. However, the dynamics and outcomes differed. In the case of the south, the US government imposed a US military government and refused to recognize or accord any legitimacy to the People's Committees, which, in both the north and the south, were an expression of indigenous popular control. In the north, the Soviet Union reduced its military presence relatively early and worked with the People's Committees. What resulted was a populist, communist-dominated indigenous regime whose reforms were on the whole welcomed by most Koreans in the north. In the south, the US military administration's refusal to accord any legitimacy to the popular movement, and to use coercive measures to suppress the left, isolated it from the majority of the Korean people. It ended up favouring the conservative elite and was obliged to rely on the old Japanese colonial institutions in order to effect control. Thus, reforms that occurred in the north did not occur in the south, and an increasing amount of repression was required in order to maintain control.

From Surrender to Civil War: China

In China, surrender brought Japanese occupation of large sections of the continent to an end. Immediately, however, new problems arose. Soviet troops in northeast China took the surrender of Japanese troops, but the Chinese Communist Party also attempted to consolidate its own power base by disarming its former enemies. The US government directed its military forces to land in major Chinese ports and strategic centres to assist Chiang's forces in consolidating control over the whole country.[49] The Soviet Union, however, had agreed at Yalta to negotiate a friendship treaty with the GMD, and, on 14 August 1945, the two sides initialled the agreement. This treaty gave the Soviet Union territorial concessions it had demanded at Yalta, but it also obliged Stalin to recognize Chiang's government as the sole authority within China, thus constraining any assistance the Soviet government might want to give to its CCP ally.[50] For his part, Harry Truman was appalled by the Yalta Agreements once he read them after taking office. While obliged to support them formally, he and his ambassador, Patrick Hurley, forcefully intervened both diplomatically and militarily to support Chiang. They also advised him, however, that it was absolutely essential to negotiate with the CCP to bring them into a coalition government. This proved difficult, and when Ambassador Patrick Hurley resigned, Truman appointed General George Marshall as his envoy to China. Former secretary of war Henry Stimson warned Marshall that his mission would be difficult: "Very few white men have ever understood the Chinese political mind."[51] The new ambassador worked assiduously to bring about a coalition government in China; however, this was to little avail as Chiang decided to push home the apparent advantage of US support by asserting military control over the whole of China. At first hard pressed, the CCP forces later regrouped and achieved a number of important victories that eventually provided them with the base necessary to go on an offensive against Chiang's forces.

The Canadians in China, including the ambassador Victor Odlum, were attentive observers of this period. Odlum had plunged into things Chinese and was reporting in more than a little detail on the efforts to form a coalition government between the two major political forces in the country: Chiang Kai-shek's Nationalist government and the CCP. In long and carefully worded dispatches, he informed the Department of External Affairs that the tentative agreement that had been reached had broad support: "The Communists assure me that they are delighted with the settlement. Fighting they say has stopped and will not recommence."[52] Odlum reported that GMD officials had told him: "The agreement is real and will be vigorously put into effect. They believe the Communists will give sincere cooperation, certainly for the present. The crisis will come when their army has to be effectively merged with the National Army." Odlum concluded: "I am satisfied that the agreement marks another definite step towards the inevitable ultimate adoption of the Western democracy towards which Chiang Kai-shek is consciously leading China. *Fear of the North and appreciation of dollars are relentlessly driving China forward.*"[53] At the same time, Odlum was gently pressing MacKenzie King to relieve him, noting: "in one month I will have been away from home for 6 years!" But, although Odlum advised that a new ambassador be sent immediately, he was to continue in the post until the embassy was moved from Chongqing to Nanjing following Japan's defeat.[54] Odlum was never to waver in his loyalty towards Chiang and his wife as individuals, but this did not mean that he became an apologist for the Nationalists. From time to time he would cast a pox on both houses: "Both parties are authoritarian and not truly liberal and democratic. I am a liberal democrat through and through, and my great regret is there is no real liberal party in China."[55] The rejection of anything but liberal solutions would become a hallmark of white superiority.

The end of the Second World War made transparent the multiple agendas at work in East Asia. On the ground, survival, reunification, and repatriation were the overwhelming concerns for many. For European powers, including Great Britain, the end of the war brought to the fore their plans for the recolonization of their former territories. The US government went along with these plans for the most part and, in a number of cases, directly intervened to assist recolonization efforts. In Japan and in South Korea, not to mention the Philippines, the United States was the principal power involved, and, as such, it articulated a rationale for its continuing presence that was classically imperial.

The perception that the world was dividing into two hostile camps rendered the developing world into oblivion. Here the ideologies of race and anti-communism converged. Decolonization was no longer a product of indigenous desire for independence but, rather, a communist-led insurgency under the direction of the Soviet Union. Racialization assisted in the construction of this paradigm in its caricaturization of leaders such as Ho or Kim as, at best, misguided by communism or, more frequently, as puppets for their Soviet masters. The utility of such ideas was not lost on men such as Winston Churchill. When he took the stage on 5 March 1946 at Westminster College in Fulton, Missouri, in the company of Harry Truman, it was to deliver a clarion call for a new global agenda. The speech, entitled "The Sinews of Peace," has often been quoted for its fundamental assertion: "From Stettin in the Baltic to Trieste in the Adriatic, an iron curtain has descended across the Continent."[56] Less quoted, but more prescient in the context of Asian history, is the fact that he "felt bound to portray the shadow which, alike in the west and in the east, falls upon the world." He did not dwell on the dangers in Asia because, he stated, Americans were "so well-informed about the Far East, and such devoted friends of China, that [he did] not need to expatiate on the situation there." To combat the "iron curtain" in east and west, Churchill proposed:

> Now, while still pursuing the method of realizing our overall strategic concept, I come to the crux of what I have traveled here to say. Neither the sure prevention of war, nor the continuous rise of world organization will be

> gained without what I have called the fraternal association of the English-speaking peoples. This means a special relationship between the British Commonwealth and Empire and the United States ... If the population of the English-speaking Commonwealth be added to that of the United States, with all that such co-operation implies in the air, on the sea, all over the globe, and in science and industry, and in moral force, there will be no quivering, precarious balance of power to offer its temptation to ambition or adventure. On the contrary there will be an overwhelming assurance of security.

As Thomas Borstelmann has suggested, this was a renewed call for "racial and cultural unity."[57] The world, however, was not the same place as it had been in 1907 when Mackenzie King had made a similar appeal. In both the United States and Canada, struggles against racism were ascendant, and decolonization was under way in a number of countries. In this context, the racial character of the emerging imperial coalition had to be rendered opaque. This coalition took on the mantle of liberalism, of freedom and democracy, in the name of combating totalitarian communism. Yet, the makeup of this renewed coalition was at its core essentially what King and Borden had called for in the past. Harkening back to wartime solidarity, Churchill's appeal found a strong resonance in Anglo-European countries, but it was a much harder sell in what we know today as the global South.

Many people in Korea and Vietnam rebelled at the continuing paternalistic denial of their right to self-determination. Meanwhile, Allied representatives such as Norman articulated alternatives to US policies. But differences among the Allies would be subordinated to the perceived imperative of reinforcing US power in the Pacific. This coalition consensus was built on the basis of shared goals as well as expediency. Even though there were those – including the Chinese GMD government – that advocated policies based on the notion of self-determination rather than imperial overlordism, the die had been cast, breathing life into the belief that the United States had won the war and should be given controlling influence over much of the Pacific. Faced with insurrections in Korea and Vietnam, the US administration increasingly adopted Churchill's program of anti-communism as justification for its continuing military presence in the region.

6 Boundaries of Race and Democracy

US ascendancy as a global power had its roots in the Pacific. The Japanese navy had provoked the powerful country at Pearl Harbor, and it was in the battle for East Asia and the Pacific Islands that American military might had been deployed on a massive scale. It was there that atomic weapons were used for the first time. The US policy makers, corporations, and military conceived of China and Japan as part of their new sphere of influence, paid for with American blood. The competition, in some US eyes, was the Soviet Union. US power derived not only from its large military presence and its economic prowess but also from the support it gained from its wartime allies, particularly from what Winston Churchill called the "English-speaking peoples." In both formal and informal ways, the United States and its Anglo allies did form the nucleus of a new world order in which the Canadian government would play a small but significant role. Canada's transpacific policies, particularly during the occupation of Japan, became closely aligned with those of the Truman administration. Yet, at home, the King government pursued the biopolitics of eliminating Japanese Canadians as a community. Challenged by a new postwar coalition of social groups, the King government was forced to relent; however, by then the communities had been dispersed, forced to leave Canada for Japan, or to migrate east of the Rockies.

The Diplomat, the General, and Imperial Democracy

Some scholars have suggested that, in the early period of the Occupation, Herbert Norman was largely in agreement with and a fan of Douglas MacArthur, that he wielded substantial influence over Occupation policy in this initial phase, and that his later fall from grace occurred because, after 1948, he became more critical of the Occupation.[1] However, the evidence suggests that Norman clashed with MacArthur on numerous occasions during the early Occupation. In the end, however, the Canadian government and Norman lined up to support the renovated US Empire.

Norman had spent the first half year after Japan's surrender working for MacArthur's headquarters in Tokyo before being recalled by the Canadian government in February 1946 to become its main representative on the Far Eastern Commission (FEC) based in Washington.[2] The FEC would include eleven countries (later thirteen), including Canada, while the United States, Soviet Union, China, and Great Britain would carry a veto.[3] The United States was authorized to issue interim orders in the case of non-consensus. While the FEC would later become powerless in the face of US intransigence, when its formation was first announced in December 1945, it appeared that it would have some powers, particularly in constitutional matters. Though its makeup reflected the colonial heritage, the presence of China and the Soviet Union, and the later addition of India and Pakistan, provided for some diversity in its makeup.

MacArthur had initially invited the FEC to work on the question of a new constitution for Japan.[4] However, within a few days, MacArthur reversed himself and directed his US staff to begin drafting a model constitution for Japan. On 5 February 1946, SCAP's Government Section chief, General Courtenay Whitney, convened select staff to inform them that they would sit as something of a "constitutional convention" to draft Japan's postwar Constitution. While MacArthur's determination to quickly assert control over the process seems to have been primarily aimed at thwarting the FEC, it may also have been a ploy to protect the Emperor.[5] In any case, MacArthur's reversal on the constitutional issue was to create havoc.

Lester Pearson, as Canadian ambassador to the United States, was the formal Canadian representative to the FEC, but he relinquished much of the responsibility to Norman, his alternate. From March until June 1946, Norman would serve as Canada's main spokesman on the FEC in Washington. Besides standing in for Pearson on the steering committee, Norman sat on FEC committee no. 3 – the Constitutional and Legal Affairs Committee – charged with the responsibility of assuring democratic constitutional change. However, before the committee could even meet, MacArthur's staff finished drafting its own constitution for Japan. Within two weeks MacArthur's staff had fleshed out a full draft constitution that was then translated and handed to Japanese government representatives for Diet "consideration." Needless to say, FEC representatives, including Norman, were not happy with the news that MacArthur had embarked on his own constitutional gambit after having told FEC representatives that they would be in charge. On 20 March they adopted a policy statement in which they argued that any constitutional proposal would have to be approved by the FEC before being adopted by the Diet, that the Diet should consider other constitutional proposals, and that MacArthur's public support of the proposed constitution did not reflect FEC approval. Upon receiving the gist of FEC policy, MacArthur delivered a tirade to Major General Frank McCoy, the chair of the FEC, accusing the international body of "reversing American policy" by insisting on its right to approve the final draft constitution. Challenged by the FEC, MacArthur was a firm believer that the best defence was a good offence. In a most remarkable declaration of American imperial interests, MacArthur concluded his message to McCoy by stating that the FEC was putting in jeopardy not only the Occupation but also the safety of the United States:

> What is at stake in this matter? It is not merely the unimportant question of a division of authority between various agencies but is the retention of American influence and American control which has been established in Japan by the American government in a skillful combination of checks and balances designed to preserve American interests here. There is a planned and concerted attack to break this down. It exists in the Far Eastern Commission in a most definite and decisive form under the veneer of diplomacy and comradeship therein. There is an implacable determination to break down the control of the United States which that country exercises through SCAP. I beg of you to protect in every possible way, including the veto power, the position and policy of the United States Government. Appeasements, small as they may seem, rapidly become accumulative to the point of danger. If we lose control of this sphere of influence under this policy of aggressive action, we will not only jeopardize the occupation but hazard the future safety of the United States.[6]

MacArthur's statement might be dismissed as simply a bellicose response to a perceived threat to his authority. But it contains within it important concepts that underpinned US policy. The first is that the Occupation was not an Allied undertaking but a US one; that its purpose was not simply to democratize and demilitarize but also to assert American interests; that Japan was within the American "sphere of influence"; and that such control was necessary for the "safety of the United States." Here we can perceive how US military power, achieved during the war, translated into effective, unilateral control over another nation in "American interests." The classic imperial concept of "spheres of influence" was a useful linguistic device that persisted even after the war.

Norman continued to challenge MacArthur as the FEC deliberated on constitutional issues in April and May 1946, putting forward proposals for a constitutional process that would allow substantial input from Japan's people. Informed that MacArthur had cast the Emperor as head of state, the FEC subcommittee recommended: "The Japanese should be encouraged to abolish the Emperor Institution or to reform it along more democratic lines."[7] In May, Norman and the FEC were in the hot seat as the constitutional issue came to a head. In a remarkable series of memoranda, Lester Pearson outlined the dynamics shaping the debate in the FEC. The major dispute centred on principles that the FEC would adopt to guide it in its deliberations on the Constitution. Referring to Article 2 of the draft, which would deal with the legitimacy of the new Constitution, the Constitutional Committee (supported by Canada but with the United States and Great Britain reserving judgment) stated that it would not be appropriate "if the new Constitution is either considered or adopted solely by the present Diet":

> The present Diet should be, however, encouraged to initiate popular and governmental discussion and study of a new Constitution. Since, however, the Japanese people did not elect the present Diet to serve as a Constituent Assembly it will be necessary for them in due time to elect either a Constituent Assembly or a new Diet charged primarily with the task of formulating a Constitution. Following the formulation of a Constitution by a new Diet or by a Constituent Assembly, the Japanese people should have an opportunity to express their will on that Constitution through a referendum.[8]

The committee further recommended that the existing Diet be empowered to amend the Meiji Constitution as necessary. After heated exchanges in the

FEC, Pearson remarked: "The view of the majority of the members of Committee No. 3 had been that if such a draft Constitution (to all intents and purposes prepared at SCAP headquarters) were adopted by the present Diet, which was not elected as in any sense a constituent assembly, it could hardly be 'the free expression of the will of the Japanese people.'"[9] Such a challenge could not go unanswered

The issue would come to a head after Norman left Washington for Ottawa on 7 June to prepare to take up his new position as head of Canada's liaison mission to Occupied Japan. Canada's Washington Embassy requested direction from the DEA regarding the final vote. After intense discussions in the department, J.R. Maybee wrote to Hume Wrong, the associate undersecretary of state for external affairs at the time.[10] Maybee was very clear on the nature of the dispute. After outlining the respective positions of the US and Soviet governments and the terms of reference, he advised: "On the basis of the controlling documents neither the United States nor the USSR appears to have a clear-cut case. While it is in our interest to maintain the authority and prestige of international bodies such as the Far Eastern Commission, it would probably not be desirable to oppose the United States in this constitutional issue since their interest in internal Japanese affairs is far greater than ours." On 18 July, Maybee cabled Pearson in Washington and made the point even more clearly: "It is realized and regretted that under the United States interpretation of the basic documents on this point the scope of the Commission's authority will be somewhat reduced and the United States will continue to be in a position to block effective Commission action on constitutional matters. It is felt, however, that it would not be in Canada's interests to oppose the United States on this issue."[11] The decision to not oppose the United States on the issue of constitutional process, when the Canadian position was both distinct and principled and dealt with another nation's Constitution, was an important example of how the Canadian government was willing to sacrifice the interests of democratic process and multilateralism to the imperial aspirations of the United States. Few Canadians, however, knew that these developments were even taking place. Events in Japan seemed far away and irrelevant to many – except when it came to dealing with Canadians of Japanese descent.

Biopolitics and Japanese Canadians

Departing from Vancouver Harbour on 12 August 1946, a former troop carrier, the *General M.C. Meigs,* pushed its way past Stanley Park and through the narrow straits separating Burrard Inlet from English Bay and the Gulf of

Exiled to Japan, Japanese Canadians on board the SS *General M.C. Meigs* at CPR Pier A, Vancouver, 16 June 1946. Watching are Corporal R.A. Davidson of the RCMP, C.W. Fisher, and T.B. Pickersgill. Two months later, E.H. Norman would depart on the same ship for Japan. | Library and Archives Canada, PA-119024

Georgia. Destined for Japan, the ship carried a roster of over thirteen hundred passengers. As it steamed out of Vancouver under the Lions Gate Bridge, many had gathered on the ship's deck, craning their necks upwards to gaze at the steel girders that seemed suspended directly above them. On board that warm summer day in August was Herbert Norman. Relieved of his responsibilities in the Far Eastern Commission, he was bound for Tokyo to set up and assume charge of what was formally known as the Canadian Liaison Mission to Occupied Japan. Also on board the *General Meigs* that day was Irene Kato, a twenty-year-old Canadian woman. Hers was a different mission than Norman's: she was looking for a place to call home. In very different ways, the politics of race and empire had brought both Norman and Kato on board the *General Meigs.* Indeed, their destinies intertwined, bound by time, history, and circumstances not of their own making.

Who was Irene Kato?[12] Born in 1925 in the Powell Street area that was the centre of the Japanese community in Vancouver at the time, and where her parents ran a shoe store, Irene, an only child, attended Strathcona School as well as the Alexander Street Japanese-Language School. Interned with her parents at the Tashme camp in 1942, Irene had been able to complete Grade 11. By 1944, the tides of war were clearly running in favour of the Allies. Like other Japanese Canadians interned at the time, the Katos were given the "choice" of either moving east or "returning" to Japan. Returning to Vancouver or the BC coast was still prohibited. For Irene's parents, neither of whom was physically well, the idea of moving and starting over in eastern Canada was too much. Given no other choice by the Canadian government, they decided to leave for Japan, where at least they had family in the countryside and thought they could survive. Irene, who had been to Japan with her parents when she was six, didn't want to leave Canada. For both Irene and her parents, the idea of separating was unacceptable, but Irene insisted that her parents agree that they, or at least she, return to Canada at the earliest opportunity.

The decision that the Kato family made, and that resulted in their being aboard the *General Meigs* on 2 August 1946, was thus not really a choice but, rather, an act of desperation forced on them as part of a series of racist actions against Japanese Canadians prior to, during, and even after the Second World War. The story of Irene and her family is only one of many; however, like the others, it challenges the often-heard claim that the discrimination faced by Canadians of Japanese descent during this time period was caused by the war. The distortion in this claim is all the more transparent when we consider that Japanese Americans were allowed to return to their homes in January 1945 and, furthermore, that, because of the citizenship protections afforded by the US Constitution, they were on the whole not forced into the large-scale exile experienced by Japanese Canadians.

As described in the previous chapter, the government had forced all Japanese Canadians to fill out a "repatriation" survey, even though most of them were Canadian citizens. Labour Minister Humphrey Mitchell used the results of the survey to demand new powers under the War Measures Act, namely, to make the repatriation results binding; to strip those to be repatriated of their citizenship; and to set up a loyalty commission to further screen "Japanese aliens." On 17 December 1945, the government introduced three orders-in-council: PC 7356, stripping those going to Japan of their citizenship; PC 7357, creating a loyalty commission to investigate other suspicious cases; and PC 7355, authorizing, based on survey results, deportation of

Japanese nationals and naturalized citizens who had not revoked their survey request by 1 September 1945 and Canadian-born who had not revoked their request prior to receiving the deportation order.[13] Cloaking its actions in the garb of "repatriation," the government used its earlier survey to coerce Japanese Canadians into leaving the country.

Resistance against what was in effect deportation mounted both within the community and among white allies. Muriel Kitagawa, an activist who wrote often in the Japanese-Canadian journal the *New Canadian*, responded angrily to the actions of the Canadian government: "Though we have not, at any time, made any application for removal to Japan now or after the war, nevertheless, we received, through the mails, a letter from you accompanied by a notice from the Department of Labour concerning voluntary 'repatriation to Japan' ... Every effort and devious method tried to persuade us that Canada is no place for us, that we would be better off in Japan."[14] The newly formed Japanese Canadian Committee for Democracy and a broader coalition, the Cooperative Committee on Japanese Canadians, began a public campaign against deportation. Acting on behalf of the committees, Andrew Brewin challenged the legality of the deportation orders in the Supreme Court. However, after taking evidence on 24-25 January 1946, the Supreme Court ruled in favour of the government legislation, although minority opinions questioned the legality of deporting Canadian-born wives and children. In 1946 Muriel Kitagawa penned a poetic response to the decision, a response that echoed the anguish of others who had fallen before, victims of ethnic cleansing or genocide:

Weep Canadians!

(Headline in *Toronto Star*, Feb. 20: RULE SOME JAPS DEPORTABLE)

The Cabinet stands white-washed.
The judgement reads in banner headlines:
"Japs Deportable!"

Weep Acadians!
The bitter tears of 1755
You shed in vain
Evangeline will mourn again for Gabriel
Gabriel will die again, calling,
"Evangeline!"[15]
Weep, ye murdered Jews!

Ye homeless of this earth!
The total of your suffering is not enough
To pay the price of liberation!

Weep, Canadians
For now it seems you need the blood
Of one billion coloured men
To bring Christ back to earth again![16]

Kitagawa's ability to grasp and represent in her poetry the historical and global politics of race is perhaps unique in Canada's literary landscape of the era.

Like Muriel Kitagawa and Irene Kato and her family, thousands of others experienced these trying times. Though tears were seldom shed, at least not openly, the wounds ran deep. Imprisoned in the Angler concentration camp for resisting internment, Robert Okazaki recorded the dilemma his father felt in the New Denver camp: "There are rumours that all internees will be deported to Japan. If you both go, I feel I should remain in Canada until you are settled ... Each day my friends leave, either voluntarily or coerced, to areas east of the Rockies. I feel sad and lonely as I see them off. Still, I cannot make up my mind. These are very unsettled days."[17] In response, Okazaki wrote: "We have no homes to return to, and no country to call home."

Despite the swelling protest, the ships of exile sailed out of Vancouver one after the other in the spring and summer of 1946. On 31 May 1946, the *Marine Angel* slipped under the Lions Gate Bridge with 668 exiles; on 16 June, the *General Meigs,* with 1,106, to return and then leave again on 12 August with 1,377. On 2 September, the *Marine Falcon* departed with 523, then made another voyage on 24 December with 240. Sixty-six percent of the 3,964 deportees were citizens of Canada.[18] This episode of liberal ethnic cleansing is not well known, yet it is the clearest evidence that the injustices perpetrated against Japanese Canadians were not an issue of fear instigated by the war in the Pacific; rather, they were a reflection of the racism that persisted in Canada in the 1940s and 1950s, a racism that made a mockery of democracy by physically expelling those whom a white elite considered undesirables. While the deportations would be halted in 1947, it would be years before those expelled were able to come home.

For those stranded in Japan, life was difficult. Although Irene Kato was able to get by, she felt like a stranger in that country. She worked in order to support her parents, first in Odawara and later in Yokohama, all the while yearning to return to Canada. Nor was she alone. By 1947 there were thousands of Japanese Canadians in Japan, the majority of whom were Canadian citizens, and many of whom were knocking on the doors of the Canadian Liaison Mission. Unlike Irene, who had found a relatively good job as a translator and receptionist at an American military facility in Yokohama, many of the Japanese Canadians were literally starving to death in a country that they had never known. Initially, their appeals, through the Canadian Liaison Mission, and through letters to friends and family back in Canada, fell on deaf ears in Ottawa. And once the regulations were lifted, Japanese Canadians stranded in Japan subsequently encountered continued racist immigration regulations constructed to keep Asians out of Canada. Even though she was a Canadian citizen born in Canada, Irene Kato had to find a sponsor in order to qualify to return. Furthermore, to purchase passage to Canada required dollars (yen was not accepted), and since possession of foreign currency was strictly regulated in Japan, Irene's family had to turn to friends in Canada to put up the fare. The Tsuyuki family, friends of Irene's father, offered accommodation for Irene, and, with this, her parents agreed to her returning to Canada alone. By the end of 1949, only 174 Japanese Canadians had been able to make their return, Irene among them. She returned to live in Lillooet with the Tsuyuki family and, in 1950, married Norman Tsuyuki. The following year they moved to Vancouver in the Lower Mainland.

Irene struggled long and hard to help her parents return to Canada. Although naturalized Canadians, her mother and father had been stripped of their citizenship when they "volunteered" to return to Japan. And because emigration from Japan remained prohibited, the only way her parents could come back to join Irene in Canada was through special permission granted on "compassionate" grounds. Irene applied for such permission but was refused. She then applied to have her mother come on a visitor's visa, and this was arranged. But just as Irene was preparing to leave for Japan to accompany her on the return trans-Pacific crossing, her mother fell ill and died without ever again setting eyes on Canada. Irene then applied to the Canadian government to allow her father, now widowed and alone in Japan, to return to Canada on compassionate grounds. That request was finally granted. Before the permit arrived in Japan, Irene's father, too, had died. Not all of the exiles shared the same fate, but many faced desperate circumstances, and more than a few found their way to the Canadian Liaison Mission to demand repatriation.[19]

As a diplomat, Herbert Norman's experience in Japan differed radically from that of Irene Kato. But he soon had to come to grips with the humanitarian crisis that grew in tandem with the arrival of Japanese Canadians on the doorstep of the liaison mission in Aoyama, Tokyo. Norman had received instructions upon arriving that he was not to "(a) help persons of Japanese race to obtain exit permits or buy passage, (b) issue visas to Japanese aliens even if they have technically retained Canadian domiciles and (c) issue or renew passports to Canadian citizens of Japanese origin, except in special circumstances."[20] However, Norman took up the issue, reporting to the DEA that he considered there to be five to six thousand Japanese Canadians in Japan who could be considered Canadian citizens. He urged that this issue be addressed squarely, and his recommendation was taken to the Cabinet Committee dealing with the issue.[21] Unfortunately, no major changes ensued until 1947. How Norman reconciled his own personal views on this issue with the limits imposed by the Canadian government is not recorded.

Having undermined the power of the FEC, and having no presence on the Allied Council, the Tokyo-based FEC representative body, Canada's liaison mission basically became responsible for three tasks not dissimilar to those it undertook in its prewar role: trade, immigration, and intelligence. Of these, the first two were limited because both trade and immigration were, for the most part, prohibited at this time. The two major tasks were thus dealing with exiled Japanese Canadians who wanted to return to Canada and intelligence related to the Occupation. Norman excelled in the latter role, and his insightful reports provide a fascinating window into Occupation politics. But Norman also began to spend more time studying and writing about Japanese history and, in the process, built friendships with many people in Japan – one of the reasons why, even today, Norman is held in much esteem by so many. His major effort at this time, aided by his erstwhile assistant Ōkubo Genji, was to research and write about the Tokugawa antifeudal figure Andō Shōeki, hoping to counter the view among "Westerners, especially those lightly tinctured with a knowledge of Japanese culture and history, that Japan never produced an original thinker."[22] It had become apparent to Norman that, despite the best intentions of reformers during the Occupation, many held deeply ingrained stereotypes about Japan, its history, and its peoples. The idea that Japan could only imitate the "West" was one of those deeply rooted assumptions, but there were many others. Norman continued to fulfill his role as diplomat, cultivating his relationship with MacArthur and, at the same time, providing extensive reports on the shifting landscape in Japan. These reports, along with later historical

Canadian diplomat Herbert Norman chats with General Douglas MacArthur during a Dominion Day reception at the Canadian Embassy, 1 July 1947. | External Affairs (Canada) / Library and Archives Canada, PA-187690

accounts of the Occupation, provide new insights into the dynamics of the Occupation.

Talking to the Occupation

Although Norman had been away from Japan for only about six months, much else had changed by the time he returned to it in late summer 1946.

Elections in April had seen the return of conservative parties to power. Women, having won the franchise for the first time, turned out in substantial numbers to cast their ballots (14 million of an eligible 21 million), and 39 out of 79 female candidates were elected.[23] Shortly afterward, the Liberal Party formed a coalition with the Progressive Party, and Yoshida Shigeru became prime minister.[24] In May, the International Military Tribunal for the Far East (IMTFE) began proceedings against twenty-eight alleged war criminals, including the wartime prime minister Tōjō Hideki. Among the eleven judges was a Canadian, E. Stuart McDougall.

On the surface, the Occupation seemed to be proceeding without major problems. To be sure, the food shortages were severe, and many were in a state of *kyodatsu*, or "exhaustion and despair," as John Dower translates it in his book *Embracing Defeat*.[25] This partly explains the surprisingly weak resistance to the Occupation and the willingness of many in Japan to work with the Allied forces despite having been in a life-and-death struggle with them only a few months earlier. Recent historical enquiry, however, provides a different lens for looking at the Occupation and reveals new dimensions to the complex politics of this period. Yukiko Koshiro's important study, *Trans-Pacific Racisms and the US Occupation of Japan*, suggests that there was a concerted effort on the part of the Occupation to reinforce what she calls Japan's "double vision," that is, the tendency for some Japanese to view themselves as "superior to other Asians and coloured races but inferior to the white race."[26] Such a generalization can be overdrawn, but it does have some explanatory power. Certain US authorities thought along these lines, and they instructed officials to use what they believed to be "jealousy or envy" towards "Westerners" to motivate further emulation, in this case, to obey the directives of the Occupation.[27] On the other hand, US officials were so worried about race issues that they imposed blanket censorship on any discussion in the media of race issues along with other issues, including the atomic bombings.

The renovated racial hierarchy meant that blatant acts of racist hostility towards the Japanese were detrimental to the image of the beneficent victor willing to act as tutor to the vanquished. On the other hand, the legacy of a century of racism meant that race could not so easily be cast aside: it reproduced itself, in both old and new forms, naturalized through the metaphors of gender (Japan as geisha) and immaturity (Japan as child) as brilliantly elucidated by Naoko Shibusawa.[28] The US-led forces had their own forms of double vision, which, at times, meshed with those of the Japanese. The most obvious manifestation of this was the continued segregation of Allied forces in Japan. Even after Truman, in 1948, ordered that the armed forces be desegregated, MacArthur refused to comply. Thus, from the beginning of the Occupation, black troops in Japan operated as segregated units and were barred from many facilities designated for whites only. So too were *nisei*, second-generation Japanese Americans who were often employed in translation services. Back in the United States, moves were afoot to end the total ban of Asian immigration that had been in effect from before the war. It was concluded that outright discriminatory treatment did not reflect well on the United States and might be used to advantage in Soviet propaganda. Thus, in 1947, Walter Judd, a Minnesota congressman, introduced a bill to allow one hundred emigrants per year from each country in Asia. This was a change indeed, yet it was also a new form of discrimination, given that emigrants from Europe were being allowed into the United States in substantial numbers. More than a token but less than a substantive change, the immigration regulations were a unilateral move by the US government (since the Japanese government was no longer in a position to negotiate). The continuing hierarchy of race was contingent on the existence of other under-groups. For the Americans it was the Japanese; for the Japanese it was the Okinawans, Ainu, and Asians, particularly Koreans.

The occupation of Japan introduced numerous reforms, many of which were supported by large numbers of people. But often, race meant that the same reforms had different impacts on minorities than on others. Take, for example, the land reform law, which resulted in many impoverished tenant farmers being able to purchase and farm their own land. However, in Hokkaido, where the minority Ainu people had been squeezed in successive waves of northern colonization, the Ainu were forced to give up 34 percent of their remaining lands.[29] As the Occupation evolved, MacArthur moved to halt "fraternization" between Allied troops and the Japanese. Prompted by concern about extensive sexual liaisons between Japanese women of "immoral character" and US troops, the anti-fraternization order expanded to cover many aspects of soldier-civilian relations.[30] Japanese were banned from US-run mess halls, and segregated railway cars or separate compartments were set up as part of the rail system. Separate entrances existed for Allied personnel and Japanese at the war crimes tribunal. Although there were many reasons for these regulations, what resulted were clear lines of racial demarcation between the victors and the vanquished. MacArthur himself went out of his way to avoid contact with the Japanese, yet he believed that his unique understanding of "Oriental" psychology would allow him to lead the people in a spiritual revolution.[31]

Non-fraternization, however, could not prevent GIs from finding sexual partners, and this gave rise to new issues, including what to do with the thousands of "mixed-race" babies that were born as a result.[32] Colonel Crawford Sams, head of the Public Health and Welfare Section of SCAP, put a stop to a proposed survey of the issue. American fathers of these children were allowed to eschew all responsibility, and mothers had no recourse. Sams ordered that the babies be brought up as Japanese, and many ended up in orphanages. Both Americans and Japanese viewed such babies as a problem, a reflection of a mutual dislike for miscegenation.

During the Occupation, race had a severe impact on minorities such as the Ainu (see above) as well as on the Okinawans, whose lands were being confiscated by US military forces. These peoples were treated as expendable by many on Japan's mainland. And the Koreans in Japan found themselves in tragic circumstances.[33] Faced with the denial of their voting rights, imposition of a war tax, and other issues, Korean residents in Japan demonstrated in front of the Imperial Palace on 20 December 1946. After a scuffle with police, ten leaders where arrested, tried, convicted of acts prejudicial to the Occupation, and deported to southern Korea.[34] Nor did Occupation forces do anything when the media allowed vitriolic press reports against Koreans to be aired. Koreans in Japan established autonomous schools so that their children could receive an education in Korean and not be subjected to textbooks that denigrated them or whitewashed Japanese colonialism. SCAP encouraged the Japanese education ministry to clamp down on these schools, a move that provoked protests and skirmishes with police. On 28 April 1948, Koreans organized another protest to protect their schools in Osaka. Little did they know that SCAP had authorized Japanese police to use lethal force. Two Koreans, a sixteen-year-old boy and a fourteen-year-old girl, died in the confrontation, and ten others were severely wounded.[35] Chang Du-sik, a Korean resident in Japan for most of his life, wrote in a magazine: "Why are we Koreans not allowed to educate our children in our own language? Why could the self-righteous action by the Japanese authorities determine our future unilaterally? Someday, we shall wipe away this Japanese sense of superiority."[36] The US censor's knife assured his anguished cry for justice never saw the light of day.

Part of the problem, Norman mused, was the omnipotent presence of MacArthur: "While SCAP is scrupulously careful to refrain from exploiting this position, any Japanese leader today must feel as if some Olympian figure were constantly looking over his shoulder, whose very proximity diminishes his stature in the popular view and disturbs his own self-respect."[37]

This report was given wide circulation in the government and in Canada's diplomatic posts abroad. It prompted Lester Pearson to write a personal note to Norman, complimenting him on his report and suggesting that, while many in the government might not pay attention to Japan because it was under the control of allies, "whether or not Japan learns the lessons intended from her defeat will have an important bearing on future peace in the North Pacific area and consequently on our own country."[38]

The next day, 1 February 1947, Norman reported that Yoshida's attempt to form a coalition with the Japan Socialist Party had failed. He also pointed out that MacArthur had issued a statement banning the proposed general strike: "No mention of threat to occupation was in statement but that strike would have caused unnecessary suffering to Japanese."[39] Although not spelled out in his brief memo, Norman's point was that MacArthur had no authority to ban a general strike unless it was a threat to the Occupation itself.[40] In the midst of the fray at the time, Norman did not realize that the prohibition of the general strike represented a turning point in the Occupation. SCAP's labour division began a campaign to undermine left-wing unions and, at the same time, began to support the re-establishment of employers associations. Employers and conservative policy makers began to lobby much more aggressively for changes in SCAP policies. In this sense, class conflict in Japan was an important factor that led the US government to change Occupation policy, a view that was transmitted to Washington by what became known as the "Japan lobby," a group of conservative businessmen, lawyers, and media types in the United States.[41] On 7 February 1947, MacArthur, after nominal discussion with the Allied Council, released a letter he had sent to Yoshida suggesting the time was ripe for new elections.[42]

At the end of December 1947, Norman forwarded a copy of notes from discussions with Patrick Shaw, head of the Australian mission in Japan, along with his own comments on Japan's evolving democracy. Based on discussions with Suzuki Yasuzō, a member of the Committee for the Popularization of the Constitution and the editor of *Chuō Kōron*, Norman stressed that, despite the Japan Socialist Party's victory (a plurality) in April, conservative forces remained active in the Imperial Household, the Upper House, and in other institutions.[43] Norman stated that Suzuki worried about a nationalist resurgence after the withdrawal of the Occupation forces. Suzuki, Norman reported, hoped for a more interventionist SCAP, and he had challenged him on this: "Mr. Suzuki admitted that it was undemocratic to *order* people to carry out reforms, but he maintained it was utopian to expect the Japanese in their present state of political development to initiate themselves the necessary reforms."[44] As Norman's report reveals, both resistance to and dependence on the Occupation were important components in what had become an extremely complicated political landscape. It would become even more complicated as US officials and corporations decided that reforms in Japan had gone too far and began planning to reincorporate Japan as an armed and resuscitated ally in the Pacific.

Canada: *Plus ça change?*

Japanese Canadians faced extremely tough circumstances in both Japan and Canada during this period. In the first year after Norman returned to Japan, significant changes took place in the Canadian political landscape. The foundations of the white walls of exclusion that had been reinforced with the 1907 race riots finally began to crumble. As early as 1943, when King went through his metamorphosis over China, he had declared the 1923 Chinese Immigration Act "a mistake."[45] King's admission reflected not only his own changing views but also the changing image of the Chinese in Canada. As described previously, the 1930s had seen important bonds of solidarity grow as many progressive whites worked with Asian-Canadian communities on both economic issues and the struggle for the franchise. The war in China in 1937 and the resistance on the part of many Chinese altered the internationally generated images of China. The double patriotism on the part of the Chinese in Canada, supporting Chinese resistance as well as the Canadian war effort in Europe, further enhanced the reputation of the community. At war's end, the Japanese-Canadian community remained an excluded other, but the Chinese and South-Asian communities were able to capitalize on the changing images and successfully pressed for changes in Canada's laws.[46]

Perhaps no one better personified the altered mood in white Canada than Victor Odlum, the former ambassador to China. In 1921, he had run on a "White Canada Forever" ticket in the federal elections, unsuccessfully, as it turned out. Yet, in early 1947, he spoke at a reception in the Chinese community for T.C. Davis, the newly assigned ambassador, where he railed against the Exclusion Act and called for intensified efforts to change it.[47] No organization better reflected the growing support for the Chinese community than the Toronto-based Committee for the Repeal of the Chinese Immigration Act. Its letterhead listed seventy-one names of supporters, the large majority of whom were non-Chinese.[48] This group, along with many others from across the country, lobbied hard for repeal of the federal act. At the same time, provincial-level organizing was taking place. In British Columbia, in November 1946, a joint delegation from the Chinese and South-Asian communities presented before a legislative committee its case for the right to vote. As Patricia Roy documents in *The Triumph of Citizenship*, these domestic efforts were supplemented by continued efforts on the part of the Chinese government for a new immigration agreement with Canada as well as by the impact of UN standards, which induced fear in the government that it would be taken to task internationally for its racist policies. The lobby efforts in these changed circumstances led to significant breakthroughs that began to alter the fabric of Canadian life.[49]

In December 1946, the King Cabinet discussed the Chinese Immigration Act, and, by then, it had become clear that its defence was not an option. King met the Chinese ambassador to Canada in January the following year and informed him that the exclusionary act would be repealed.[50] And so it was in May 1947. In the interim, the government passed the Citizenship Act, which gave citizenship to all naturalized citizens regardless of race. The BC legislature amended its election act that spring, and people of Chinese and South-Asian descent finally won the right to vote. This measure also meant an end to multiple prohibitions in employment that had been contingent on having voting rights. For those affected, these legal changes ushered in a new era of at least nominal equality. Success on these fronts also encouraged those demanding an end to the harsh and discriminatory treatment of Japanese Canadians. For example, the Co-operative Committee on Japanese Canadians, initially formed by women in June 1943, focused its early efforts on helping those uprooted to resettle in the Toronto area.[51] However, the group grew quickly and consulted closely with Japanese Canadians, and it soon became embroiled in the fight against "repatriation." Faced with mounting criticism of its policies, the federal government, in January 1947, finally rescinded the trio of laws, enacted in December 1945, that had been upheld by the Supreme Court. The minister of justice and soon-to-be prime minister, Louis St. Laurent, railed against the retreat at a Cabinet meeting on 22 June 1947, insisting that, unless the Japanese were deported, they would create trouble.[52] The government still did not rescind its regulations barring Japanese Canadians from returning to British Columbia. A review of the restrictions in early 1948 left intact the ban against residence in British Columbia and on the holding of fishing licences.[53] On 1 April 1949, the restrictions against Japanese Canadians finally expired. By that time, much of the community had been effectively dispersed, many living in the Prairies and eastern Canada and the rest, like Irene Kato, living in Japan.

Terminating a number of overtly racist laws and regulations marked a turning of the tide against white supremacy, but it was only the start of a process of changing normative standards. Indigenous peoples bore the brunt of the legacy of colonial expropriation, but all peoples of colour, including Asian Canadians, continued to face barriers related to race. In announcing the repeal of the Chinese Immigration Act, for example, King reiterated his commitment to keeping Canada white. The people of Canada, he stated, do not wish "as a result of mass immigration, to make a fundamental alteration in the character of [their] population. Large-scale immigration from the Orient would change the fundamental composition of the Canadian population."[54] Not only did people of colour need to fight to bring even close relatives into Canada, they also had to deal with systemic incidents of discrimination. Racism remained an everyday occurrence in postwar Canada. Nevertheless, the fight again racism and colonialism had made an impact, even in the backrooms of the DEA, where concern was mounting about how the Soviet Union might use the issue:

> The Soviet Union is today posing as the principal defender of the rights of coloured and colonial peoples. It is also posing as the principal defender of the sovereignty of small powers. It would seem probable that, if the Western powers are unable to remove racial discriminations rapidly and to satisfy the demands of colonial peoples for self-government, the Western powers may have the great majority of the colonial and coloured peoples hostile or unfriendly to them in the event of war with the Soviet Union or at least doing their best to fish in troubled waters.[55]

Similar signs were evident on the left. On the one hand, the Canadian Congress of Labour embraced a postwar Atlanticist vision, emphasizing "Canada's historic role as a keystone in the arch of Anglo-American understanding, and the necessity of Canada's continuing to act in that capacity for many years to come."[56] On the other hand, David Lewis, a labour lawyer and national secretary of the CCF, recalled confronting the British Labour Party during a first Commonwealth labour party conference in 1944, insisting "that India and other colonies had to be given their freedom once the war was won."[57] At a follow-up conference in Canada in 1947, the CCF "felt strongly that the conference should include Asians and Africans and not be a purely white gathering." The CCF's pleas for "even a token presence to signify that the Commonwealth was not a white man's club even in 1947" fell on deaf ears. Decolonization clearly was on the global agenda, but it continued to face formidable resistance.

7 Elusive Justice
Canada and the Tokyo Tribunal

Three years after escaping from the Showa Mining Corporation in Hokkaido in 1945, Liu Lianren continued to eke out a precarious existence in the hills of Hokkaido, unaware that the war that had snatched him from his native Shandong Province had come to a cataclysmic end.[1] Struggling to stay alive, and cut off from all communication, Liu was unaware that hundreds of kilometres away, in far-off Tokyo, Tōjō Hideki and six other Japanese wartime leaders had breathed their last, having been hanged on 23 December 1948 in Sugamo Prison by Occupation authorities after having been convicted by the Tokyo Tribunal (formally, the International Military Tribunal for the Far East [IMTFE]) of personal responsibility for war crimes. Nor was Liu aware that the next morning, the man who had designed and implemented the policies of forced labour, Kishi Nobusuke, dressed in the uniform of a private in the Japanese army, had climbed into an army jeep to be driven by a GI to the gates of the very same prison. After showing authorization papers, he walked out through the barbed-wire gates a free man. After holding Kishi for thirty-nine months on suspicion of having committed major war crimes, the Allied forces declared there would be no further prosecutions for such crimes.[2] While Liu shivered in the Hokkaido woods, Kishi quickly re-established himself on the Tokyo political scene, and, in 1957, he became the leader of the Liberal Democratic Party and Japan's prime minister. Shortly afterwards, Liu was found in the Hokkaido forests, thirteen years after his escape from the mining corporation. He was sent back to China with little fanfare. Kishi continued as Japan's prime minister for the next three years. He even travelled to the United States and Canada in 1960. "Stag Dinner for Jap Premier" was how the *Ottawa Journal* described the glittering Rideau Hall banquet given by Governor General Georges Vanier for Kishi on 21 January 1960.[3] Kishi's visit to Canada, the first ever by a Japanese prime minister, lasted only twenty-five hours, but Kishi and Canadian prime minister John Diefenbaker got along well according to press reports at the time.[4]

The contrasting fates of Liu Lianren and Kishi Nobusuke highlight the failure of the judicial process that took place in Japan after the Second World War, including trials for "minor" war crimes and the major trial known as the Tokyo Tribunal.[5] Few Canadians are even aware that the Canadian government was one of the sponsors of the major tribunal or that a Canadian judge, E.S. McDougall, sat on the bench.[6] As the trial evolved, issues of race and empire played out in a complex dance that saw the bench divided, with a group of four justices from the Anglo-American states playing a decisive role. In the end, there were serious miscarriages of justice, Asian victims of Japanese war crimes were sidelined, and many suspected war criminals (such as Kishi Nobusuke) were exonerated and went on to play important political roles in postwar Japan.

In Japan, critics of the Tokyo Tribunal abound, but there is a chasm separating their views. Most scholars and commentators agree that the trials suffered from serious flaws and were an example of "victor's justice." But conservatives in Japan use the flawed process to bolster their contention that Japan's war was a "defensive" war and that there was little to distinguish the actions of their country from those of the Allies. Media star Kobayashi Yoshinori put it this way: "Throughout the world, it is recognized that the Tokyo Tribunal was, in the light of conventional international law, nothing but theatre – the theatre of barbaric revenge and of political melodrama. In Japan, however, if you repudiate the Tokyo trials, you are still called a 'reactionary' or accused of harbouring 'dangerous thoughts denying the war.'"[7] Kobayashi, a part of Japan's new generation, works with an older generation of historians, such as Tanaka Masaaki and Hayashi Fusao, who have long termed Japan's Occupation as nothing more than "victor's revenge."[8] On the other hand, progressive scholars in Japan are critical of the trials but from a radically different perspective.[9] They agree that many aspects of the trials were biased, but their main concern is what they failed to do: "Besides the non-indictment of the Emperor, there were a lot of issues that the [Tokyo] tribunal did not deal with including biological warfare conducted by the Kanto Army's Water Purification Unit (Unit 731), the use of poisonous gases [chemical warfare], and responsibility for US atomic bombing, an issue introduced by the defense. Furthermore, issues related to Japan's colonial control of Korea and Taiwan were not even discussed. In this Tribunal, controlled by the Allies, above all the Americans, Asian countries that directly experienced the Japanese invasion were not present. The Republic of China and the Philippines may have participated in the trial but it cannot be said that Japanese military atrocities in Asia were adequately dealt with."[10] As suggested by Japan scholar Utsumi Aiko, many people who were victimized in Asian countries during the war tend to share this view. On the other hand, scholars in the United States and Canada tend to focus more on the flaws of the trial, emphasizing that it was an exercise in victor's justice.[11] While not denying the extensive atrocities that took place, they emphasize that those punished were not given a fair trial, thus throwing into doubt the sentences of those convicted. No easy reconciliation of these views is possible.

The Tokyo Tribunal: An Overview

Representatives of Allied countries met in London in January 1942, at which time they defined punishment of war crimes as one of their wartime objectives. Later that same year, Roosevelt and Britain's Lord Chancellor agreed on the creation of the United Nations War Crimes Commission, which began meeting the following year. And, after Germany had surrendered, Truman and Churchill reiterated in Article 10 of the Potsdam Declaration their determination to prosecute Japanese war criminals. Shortly afterward, representatives of the United States, the Soviet Union, France, and Great Britain met in London and, on 8 August, agreed to convene an international military tribunal and issued the charter for such a tribunal. This was the origin of the Nuremberg Trials as well as the Tokyo Tribunal.[12]

On 19 January 1946, SCAP issued a special proclamation establishing the International Military Tribunal for the Far East and, the same day, issued a charter governing its conduct.[13] The charter was amended in April after the Far Eastern Commission, sitting in Washington, adopted its own policy on war crimes in Asia. The amended charter called for eleven justices from those countries represented on the FEC to sit as judges. The countries included Australia (Sir William Webb), Canada (E. Stuart McDougall), China (Mei Juao), France (H. Bernard), India (R.B. Pal), the United Kingdom (Lord Patrick), the Netherlands (B.V.A. Roling), New Zealand (E.H. Northcroft), the Philippines (D. Jaranilla), the USSR (I.M. Zaryanov), and the United States (Higgins, replaced by Myron Cramer). According to the amended charter, trials in Asia would sit in judgment not only on major war criminals – those charged with waging aggressive war – but also on "minor" war criminals: those charged with violations of the laws of war.[14]

The eleven nations also appointed prosecutors, with the United States appointing Joseph B. Keenan as the chief prosecutor and Canada appointing H.G. Nolan as an associate prosecutor. On 29 April 1946, twenty-eight Japanese leaders, including Tōjō Hideki, were indicted on fifty-five specific charges. The accused were arraigned on 3 May 1946, at which time they all entered "not guilty" pleas. The trial proceedings lasted from 4 June 1946 to 16 April 1948, after which the judgment was written. The court reconvened on 4 November 1948, at which time the judgment was read, and individual verdicts and sentences were handed down on the closing day, 12 November. On 22 November, General MacArthur summoned the representatives of the FEC powers to consult on the sentences as he had been empowered to reduce them (but not increase them) as he saw fit. Two days later, on 24 November, he confirmed the sentences, but two of those sentenced to death, Doihara and Hirota Kōki, appealed to the US Supreme Court, which agreed to hear the case on 16 December. After hearing the appeal, the court decided in a 6 to 1 decision that it had no jurisdiction over the Tokyo Tribunal and dismissed the appeal. The sentences were carried out on 23 December 1948. The judgment and sentences were determined by majority decision of the eleven judges.

In his assessment of the trial at the time, Herbert Norman did not try to obscure the fact that there were dissenting opinions, including partial dissents by the judges from the Netherlands and France, and a completely dissenting opinion by the Indian judge, in which he exonerated all the accused and opined that the Tribunal was not properly constituted to try them. The Tribunal president, William Webb, while concurring with the majority opinion, offered his personal views of the death penalty (he was opposed) and of the impropriety of not having indicted Emperor Hirohito, whom he considered the ringleader in conspiracy to wage aggressive war.[15] In comparing the Tokyo Tribunal to the Nuremberg Trials, Herbert Norman pointed out that there were eleven judges in Tokyo compared to four in Germany; that the Tokyo Tribunal took two and a half years to complete while the Nuremberg Trials took less than a year; that the linguistic problems were greater in Tokyo than they were in Germany and that the volume of evidence was also much greater. The basic difference between the two trials, Norman asserted, was that the state structure in Germany was relatively simple, "from the Fuerher [sic] at the top down through descending chains of command to the lower organizations of state and party, whereas no such simple state structure existed in Japan."[16] Rather than trying to delve into the complex legal problems associated with the trial, Norman stressed its contribution to understanding Japan's history. The proceedings provided material that consisted "chiefly of hitherto secret documents which might otherwise never have seen the light of day, together with the testimony of witnesses." Among the important documents from the trial were records of imperial and liaison conferences; memoranda and secret notes on Japanese policy towards China from 1932 to 1939; plans for total warfare and economic regimentation in East Asia; and proof of widespread narcotics trafficking. These, thought Norman, along with transcripts of communications between Japanese ambassador to Washington Nomura and his government, peace feelers towards China, Tōjō's resignation, and the unsuccessful attempt to send Konoe Fumimaro to Moscow in 1945 would all provide important grist for the historian's mill. Norman emphasized that two diaries, the Saionji-Harada memoirs and the diary of Kido Kōichi, were of particular significance for their insights into the inner politics of the ruling groups in wartime Japan.

Tokyo Tribunal records reveal how difficult it was to find a centre of gravity within the Japanese state. Constant interaction between different factions of the military, government branches, and ultra-nationalists resulted, by 1941, in the government's accepting the full program of the extremists. This occurred within the existing constitutional framework, and thus it was difficult to pinpoint when Japan became a "fascist or aggressive state" or when the decision to go to war with the Western powers was finalized. Norman suggested that perhaps the die had been cast in September 1940, when Japan, with a full understanding of the ramifications, joined the Axis powers.[17] Norman seems to go to some lengths to note the Emperor's role. For example, in reference to the decision-making process regarding aggression in China or joining the Axis, Norman noted that such decisions were initiated by junior officials and then ratified by a conference of senior officials, "perhaps in the form of an Imperial conference, that is to say in the presence of the Emperor." Norman cautioned, however, that the "mantle of the historian is not cut to fit the judge" and that, because of this, much "evidence" that might be taken into account by historians was not examined by the court. In almost a postcolonial moment, Norman remarked: "To put it another way, Japan was not only acting upon others but in some fashion was being acted upon and this highly complex inter-relationship could not adequately be explored. Thus perhaps the least satisfactory aspect of the judgement for the historian's purpose is the section which deals with Sino-Japanese relations." Norman's summary introduces some of the historical issues addressed during the trial, but he purposefully omitted dealing with the internal dynamics of the trial process or with the complex legal issues. Today, much more information is available regarding both of these issues, including the role that Canadians played during the trials.

Canada and the Tokyo Tribunal

The Canadian government had not been eager to participate in war crimes prosecutions. This stemmed from fear that publication of the intent to conduct war crimes trials would act as a disincentive for the Axis to end the war. Further, there was a belief that there was no legal basis for the creation of an international war crimes tribunal. Thus, the Canadian War Crimes Advisory Committee, created in November 1943, maintained a low profile and limited its inquiries to crimes committed against Canadian nationals. And only with reluctance did the Canadian government participate in the London-based United Nations Commission for the Investigation of War Crimes created in 1943. However, towards the end of the war, evidence of wide-scale atrocities began to make news, and demands for the punishment of those who had committed them were becoming insistent. Nevertheless, the Canadian representative to the United Nations War Crimes Commission abstained when the question of whether crimes against peace and crimes against humanity were actually war crimes was put to the vote.[18] Nevertheless, when the Tokyo Tribunal began deliberations in May 1946, with twenty-five alleged war criminals in the dock, sitting on the bench representing Canada was E. Stuart McDougall, a superior court judge from Montreal. Acting as associate prosecutor was Harold Nolan, who had arrived in Tokyo in February 1946, a few weeks before McDougall. Nolan was housed in the Canadian Embassy, a structure that remained intact despite the surrounding destruction, while McDougall lived in the Imperial Hotel, just across from the Imperial Palace. McDougall wrote to the Department of External Affairs in April, just before the trial began, informing the government that he expected the indictment to be submitted soon. "I might add," he wrote, "that the relations of the judges is excellent every one showing the best spirit of cooperation. There is every indication that even if the indictment is presented next week we cannot expect to have a judgement ready before the autumn if then." Even this cautious view of how long the trial might last proved to be wildly off the mark.[19]

Despite McDougall's upbeat assessment of his colleagues, less than a year later a crisis erupted on the bench. Early in the trial, the defence had filed two motions, the first challenging the legality of the Tribunal itself and the second questioning whether aggressive war was actually illegal under existing international law. The judges debated these issues but were unable to come to a clear agreement. However, the majority were prepared to reject the defence arguments, although their reasons differed. In the event, Justice Webb informed the trial participants that the motions had been rejected but that the legal reasoning would be provided later. The trial thus proceeded with the prosecution, presenting its case from 4 June 1946 until 24 January 1947. During this period, the judges attempted to work out the details of their earlier rulings on the motions regarding the legality of the Tribunal and whether aggressive war was indeed a crime. These issues split the bench, and by March the divisions had deepened to the point of rupture. The problems prompted the Canadian justice, McDougall, to write an extraordinary letter to External Affairs Minister Louis St. Laurent on 19 March 1947. According to McDougall, given what had happened over the past year, as well as for other reasons "which [he] prefer[red] not to commit to writing, [he was] convinced that the accused ha[d] not had and [could not] have [had] a fair trial."[20] McDougall stated that it would be best if he were to resign as then Canada would "avoid in the future the opprobrium of having her representative participate in a judgment that [would] do credit to no nation and in future cases, should they arise, [would] be used to justify the vengeance of a successful belligerent."[21] He justified laying his views at the feet of St. Laurent, stating: "a situation has been gradually developing which may require action on my part either alone or with two of my colleagues." The problem, according to McDougall, was that the trial had been unduly prolonged because of inefficiency and a lack of leadership on the part of the prosecution and defence. The responsibility for this lay with the US government, which, for lack of seriousness or for repercussions from Nuremberg, "did not see fit to send qualified men to take charge of the preparation and handling of the case."[22] Although told by Keenan when he arrived that the trial would be over by summer 1946, McDougall mused that, unless there was a repeat of the 1923 earthquake, which would "swallow Sugamo Prison in which twenty-five of the surviving accused are confined," the trial would drag on for many more months.

Not only was the trial futile, stated McDougall, but the final judgment would "have the effect of detracting from rather than adding to useful jurisprudence in International Law."[23] As an example, the Canadian justice cited the infighting that had occurred over the challenge to the court's jurisdiction, specifically in regard to whether or not aggressive war was a crime. Two of the other justices, McDougall railed, held the "extraordinary view" that aggressive war was not a crime, despite its elucidation as such in the IMTFE charter upon which they had been appointed. McDougall then chastised the Australian president of the bench, William Webb, stating that he had failed to defend the charter based upon international precedents. When it was clear no agreement could be reached, the bench had issued an interim denial of the defence motion, opting to defer its reasoning for the final decision. As a result, McDougall concluded: "it is impossible to hope that the final judgement with an indictment of fifty-five counts and twenty-six accused can be anything but a complete failure even from a political point of view."[24] To make matters worse, said McDougall, "we have a President in whom no one has any trust or confidence; his lack of experience and ability, we know; and his sincerity, we suspect; a man who insists that he will prepare the final judgment without help or advice; if necessary standing alone; in fact, by preference."[25] Webb has so antagonized the other justices, McDougall observed, that "two of the most able and experienced [were] prevented from working with him at all."[26] McDougall feared that the final judgment would be made up of a number of separate opinions or judgments that would, in the end, undermine not only the Tokyo but also the Nuremberg judgment. The Tokyo Tribunal was a "tragedy in the making," and even at that point, McDougall suggested "that the experiment [was] a failure."[27] After Webb had suggested that he alone would write the final judgment, McDougall told St. Laurent: "a number of us tried on several occasions to organize a group which would work out a majority judgment independently of the President but found even that impossible." McDougall stated that his colleagues from New Zealand and the United Kingdom shared his views and would also be communicating with their respective governments.

A factor further complicating the situation was his own health, McDougall said, and he was going to propose that the Tribunal adjourn from 15 May to 15 September of that year (1947). He did not believe the proposal would be accepted, but, if it was, he would return to Canada for rest and for further discussions with the government. Three courses of action were open: to resign now with the approval of the Canadian government; to return to Canada if a three-month recess were to be allowed, with a final decision on resignation to be made after consultation; or to resign immediately for reasons of health. He would never have accepted the assignment had he known the trial would last longer than six months, McDougall stated, and, having already served for a year, he wondered whether he had not done his duty and should now be entitled to be relieved from what, in his words: "I am convinced will be an international tragedy."

St. Laurent forwarded McDougall's letter to his deputy, Lester Pearson, commenting that it "seemed to reveal a pretty serious situation."[28] Who was the tribunal president, he queried, suggesting that further inquiries be made in writing to "our man" in Japan and to the High Commissioner in London. Lester Pearson consequently wrote to the Canadian ambassador in Washington, Hume Wrong; to Herbert Norman in Tokyo; and to Norman Robertson in London to solicit their views and to establish whether British and American authorities had heard similar complaints regarding Webb and the Tribunal from their respective justices in Tokyo. Pearson heard back first from Herbert Norman, who emphasized the difficulties Webb encountered, including having to attempt to bring about consensus among a panel of judges who often had "sharp differences of opinion" and came from different legal traditions.[29] Some of the defence counsels were also "deliberately using tactics of delay" in the hope that this might benefit their clients. The trial itself was extremely complex, covering "not only events leading up to Pearl Harbor, but in Manchuria, China and other parts of Asia."[30] Acknowledging criticisms of Webb's manner in court, Norman emphasized the magnitude of Webb's task. Regarding possible withdrawal of Canadian representation from the bench, Norman cited criticism of the previous withdrawal of US justice Higgins, even though he had been quickly replaced, and suggested that, given the late date, it would be impossible to replace McDougall: "That would leave the Tribunal without Canadian representation, would certainly tend to impair the prestige of the court, and in view of the fact that it is in its closing phases, even though it may still last for some time, would make such a unilateral withdrawal on Canada's part exceedingly difficult to justify." Norman concluded: "I sincerely hope that it will not be necessary to follow such a course." Wrong reported from Washington that he had been unable to garner much information, and this indicated that there was "no widespread concern on the matter here, but this may well be due to ignorance of the facts."[31] The only definite information he had obtained, wrote Wrong, was regarding the chief prosecutor, Joseph Keenan, and that was "that by reason of his intemperance, if not for other causes as well, he [was] a definite menace to the success of the trials."

On 8 May 1947, Norman Robertson wrote from London that the British government had finally heard from Lord Patrick, his reply confirming "in all respects the misgivings which Judge McDougall reported to you."[32] Indeed,

Lord Patrick's six-page letter to Britain's Lord Chancellor, now available in the British archives, provides further detail to McDougall's accusations. He states that he had read the trial's charter before arriving and had agreed with its essence – that the "planning or waging of a war of aggression is a crime and (second) its declaration that there shall be individual responsibility for what used to be considered acts of state, for which there was no individual responsibility."[33] However, when the defence had moved that the indictment be dismissed because it had no basis in law, it became apparent, stated Lord Patrick, that a number of the judges tended to agree with the defence motion. Nevertheless, in the end the judges decided unanimously that they did exercise lawful jurisdiction over the case, and it was agreed to dismiss the motion with reasons to be given later. "Our reasons for this judgement should have been promptly delivered," stated Lord Patrick, and the wavering judges could, at that point, with proper leadership, have been "induced to sign a single judgement." The problem, he suggested, was that "the President could not be got to prepare such a judgement." Webb's own views were far from clear, and he was waiting at the time to see what Nuremberg would say: "Meanwhile he antagonized every member of his Tribunal. I have told you what a quick-tempered turbulent bully he is, how resentful of the expression of any view differing from his own."[34] As a result, stated Patrick, the judges were divided and reduced to writing their own opinions. "The result is that we shall have a little core which will be on the same lines as Nurnberg," and the others would go their own way: "Far from adding weight to the Nurnberg judgement as a precedent in International Law, the judgement will cast doubts on its soundness. It is a deplorable situation."[35]

To the Lord Chancellor's idea of possible recall, Patrick took the same view as Norman, stating: "I don't see how that can be done. It is certain that my recall would be followed by a request by at least two other judges for their recall. The trial would be quite discredited." In his note from London to the DEA, Norman Robertson indicated that the New Zealand judge had also written to the chief justice of New Zealand. Robertson relayed a British request that no action be taken without further consultation and that British officials had asked the British judge, Lord Patrick, to consult confidentially with the US judge, Myron Cramer, "who does not appear to be so defeated by the situation as United Kingdom, Canadian and New Zealand judge[s]." On 20 May 1947, McDougall again wrote St. Laurent, informing him that Lord Patrick had apprised him of the communications that had been taking place among the governments. He concluded: "Unless I am forced by reasons of health to resign, I propose to carry on and to the utmost of my ability to reconcile differences of opinion which may arise from time to time. My first letter to you was prompted by a sense of duty to the Canadian government and having fulfilled that duty I can now consider the matter closed."[36] This correspondence, when read with reports of the New Zealand judge, today provides us with a clearer picture of the internal dynamics on the bench.[37]

Even at the time, defence counsel was aware of the divided bench. In their appeal of the verdict, they stated: "The verdict is not that of the tribunal, but of a clique of it," a seven-member majority that had excluded four judges, including Pal, Bernard, Roling, and Webb, from deliberations regarding the final judgment.[38] They were only partially correct. We now know that the drafting was done principally by an inner core, including Patrick, Northcroft, and McDougall, along with the US judge Cramer but excluding the president of the tribunal, Webb, whom they had come to dislike so intensely. This inner core reflected the intimacy that could arise among men who shared the same language and cultural traditions, although this cannot be assumed, as the exclusion of Webb from the inner circle illustrates.

After having recessed to consider the evidence and write their judgment, the justices reconvened the court on 4 November 1947 for the reading aloud of their 1,218-page document. This took over a week. In the end, eight of the eleven judges concurred fully with the majority view, two of them (Webb and Jaranilla) writing supplementary, concurring opinions – Webb arguing that the Emperor should have been tried and Jaranilla arguing for stiffer sentences. Roling of the Netherlands filed a dissenting opinion regarding the reasoning for finding aggressive war a crime and for assigning civilian responsibility for acts of state. Bernard of France filed notice of dissent in reaction to the release of the judgment not as a majority opinion but, rather, in the name of the Tribunal as a whole. He also argued for trying the Emperor and objected to certain procedural matters. Finally, Justice Pal submitted a 250-page separate opinion rejecting the very legal basis for the trial and finding all those indicted not guilty. His trenchant criticism of the hypocrisy of imperial politics won him few friends on the bench, although he was later venerated by Japanese conservatives.

Thinking about Justice

Among the older generation of Japanese historians who wrote about the trials is Ienaga Saburō, a historian of note who confronted the government over its handling of war history in Japanese textbooks. Regarding the Tokyo

Tribunal, Ienaga considers that the dissenting opinions of the Tribunal contained some sound arguments but that Pal's "justification of Japan's aggression against China reeks of the prejudices of his vehement anti-Communist ideology."[39] Stating that, in Japan, people failed and continued to fail to deal with war criminals, Ienaga argues: "we must view with great doubt any wholesale repudiation of the Tokyo trial as 'victor's justice.'" Ienaga agrees with defence attorney Takayanagi Kenzō that the trial was based on retroactive law, but he does not agree that therefore the acts scrutinized should have been exempt from punishment. At the time, Herbert Norman opined that other alleged war criminals still being held at Sugamo Prison should be tried. He informed the DEA that, although "they are not as well-known as the major suspects being tried presently and whose judgement will soon be announced, this second group is in its own way as representative a selection of prominent Japanese war-time leaders in the field of military, bureaucratic, propagandist and ultra-nationalist activities as could be made."[40] Iwamura Michiyo and Kishi Nobusuke were "included primarily because they were members of Tōjō's Cabinet," Norman informed his superiors. And although it was a "grave reflection on the administration of the war crimes trials in Japan that this second group had to wait trial for so long," Norman cautioned that the "unfortunate handling of their case ... should not blind one to the fact that this group includes some of the most fanatical and unsavoury leaders of aggressive Japanese imperialism."[41] However, within a month, the US government made the decision that there were to be no further trials. The rules of procedure of the Tribunal assigned the chief prosecutor, US attorney Joseph Keenan, the final decision regarding whether or not to prosecute. With MacArthur's approval, he recommended that those still being held in Sugamo Prison as suspected war criminals be released. Subsequently, the FEC endorsed this decision and resolved that there would be no further trials of those charged with crimes against peace and that any further trials for conventional war crimes or crimes against humanity should be completed by 30 September 1949.[42] This contrasts with how things were handled in Germany.

The Scales of Justice

On 24 December 1948, Kishi Nobusuke walked out of Sugamo Prison a free man. Yet, half a world away, the former German minister Albert Speer remained behind bars, having been found guilty of war crimes by the court at the Nuremberg proceedings for, among other things, having developed economic plans that he knew would require the use of forced labour. That Speer, who had held a position not dissimilar from that of Kishi, remained imprisoned while Kishi walked free is but one example of how the treatment of war crimes committed by the two former Axis states differed. Yet, the prosecution of war crimes in both countries originated from common perceptions that emerged among the Allied powers regarding the treatment of former enemies. These perceptions, today known as the Nuremberg process, differed in significant ways in their respective application in Germany and Japan.

In the case of Germany, twenty-two German war criminals were tried by the Nuremberg International Military Tribunal, with nineteen of them ultimately being found guilty. Twelve were sentenced to death, seven were given prison sentences, and three were acquitted. Moreover, in both Germany and Japan (and the former occupied territories), Allied military commands convened military tribunals for crimes committed against their soldiers. There the parallel ends, however. In Germany, the Allied Control Council passed Control Council Law No. 10, which authorized the convening of further tribunals to try alleged war criminals. These military tribunals subsequently tried 177 alleged war criminals in thirteen separate trials. These lesser trials included the so-called "Doctor's Trial," the prosecution of medical staff (including the infamous Joseph Mengele), who engaged in pseudoscientific experiments on prisoners leading to death and severe injuries. Of the 177 alleged war criminals charged in these lesser Nuremberg proceedings, 142 were convicted, with twenty-four receiving sentences of death. Furthermore, between the end of the war in 1945 and 1988, prosecutions by both East Germany and West Germany resulted in ninety-one thousand individuals being charged for war crimes.[43] In terms of compensation for victims of war crimes, the German government institutionalized a process by which victims of Nazi crimes were able to present claims without having to resort to the courts. While this process has not always been easy, and there remain significant problems, it has at least given victims a voice and a means by which to present their case. Indeed, redress for Nazi victims continues to this day and includes such examples as the "Hardship Fund," a special fund created for previously uncompensated victims in the Soviet bloc; the 1981 Koeln Fund for previously uncompensated, non-Jewish victims; and the 1995 Princz Agreement for US victims of Nazi persecution. Although not fully satisfactory, these agreements were achieved because of pressure from victims' organizations, although certain groups, such as the Romani ("Gypsies"), continue to face discrimination in terms of redress.[44] Most recently, the foundation representing the German government and German companies that employed forced labour allocated over US$6 billion to compensate 1.5 million victims of forced labour.

In Japan's case, the situation, both in terms of prosecutions of war crimes and compensation for victims of war crimes, was dramatically different. Aside from the Tokyo Tribunal itself, there have never been any subsequent trials of suspected war criminals. And, for the most part, the Japanese government has steadfastly refused to compensate victims who came forward after Japan became independent in 1952. This has led to ongoing resentment on the part of those who suffered from Japanese war crimes. Because there has been no channel for redress, victims have been forced into costly and timely court cases. And the absence of prosecutions of war criminals has meant that victims and their advocates have had to resort to alternative means to air their cases against suspected perpetrators. Part of the reason for the difference in treatment and outcomes is related to the fact that Nuremberg proceeded relatively quickly, facilitating the institutionalization of the redress and reconciliation process. And, as has been pointed out by numerous commentators, the chain of command and culpability was relatively clear in the case of the Nazis. Furthermore, the scale of the atrocities in Europe was perceived as being on a magnitude that demanded redress. In the case of Japan, the challenges in terms of establishing war responsibility and understanding the magnitude of war crimes were much greater. And, unlike in post-surrender Germany, in Occupied Japan, the United States was preponderant. Furthermore, the Tokyo Tribunal continued into the period when the Cold War was rapidly intensifying and thus the politics of anti-communism came to dominate. The impact was to marginalize the Asian victims of Japanese war crimes and, as the movement swung towards Japan's rehabilitation into the Western bloc, to sweep certain crimes under the carpet.

The Trials That Never Happened

According to the official transcript of the Tokyo Tribunal, on Thursday, 29 August 1946, David N. Sutton, an assistant to the Chinese associate prosecutor, introduced evidence related to Japanese wartime experiments on human subjects as follows:

The President: Mr. Sutton:

Mr Sutton: (Reading)
"The enemy's TAMA Detachment carried off their civilian captives to the medical laboratory, where the reactions to poisonous serums were tested. This detachment was one of the most secret organizations. The number of persons slaughtered by this detachment cannot be ascertained."
...
The President: Are you going to give us any further evidence of these alleged laboratory tests for reactions to poisonous serums? That is something entirely new, we haven't heard before. Are you going to leave it at that?

Mr Sutton: We do not at this time anticipate introducing additional evidence on that subject.[45]

That the Japanese Imperial Army had engaged in biological warfare, hinted at in the excerpt above, was finally confirmed fifty years later when 180 victims filed suit against the Japanese government in Tokyo District Court (Cases 16684 and 27579 Compensation Claims). Another five years later, on 27 August 2002, a panel of Japanese judges (Koji Iwata presiding) delivered its ruling regarding the survivors' claim that, between 1940 and 1942, Unit 731 and other units of the Japanese Imperial Army(s) had attacked Chinese villages with biological weapons leading to thousands of deaths and untold suffering.[46] As to its interpretation of the evidence, the judgment noted that the Japanese government did not even try to challenge the evidence submitted by the Chinese victims. The judges concluded that the court had sufficient evidence to establish the following facts:

- The Epidemic Prevention Department of the Kwantung Army, established in 1936, was reorganized as the Epidemic Prevention and Water Purification Department of the Kwantung Army in 1940, when it became known as Unit 731;
- The unit established its major facility in the City of Pingfan, on the outskirts of Harbin in northeast China, and had branches in other parts of China, Unit Ei-1644 and Unit 1644 in Nanjing being the major ones;
- The principal task of this unit was the development and manufacture of biological weapons;
- Anti-Japanese resistance fighters were sent to Unit 731, where they were subjected to experimentation;

- Unit 731 "conducted war using biological weapons (biological warfare) in various regions of China," including Quzhou, Meiwu, Dongyang, Chongshan, Taxiazhou, Ningbo, Changde, and Jiangshan;
- "The use of such biological weapons as a means to wage war was part of the overall war as prosecuted by the Japanese military and was thus in accordance with orders from central army command."

The court concluded that victims' suffering "was truly immense and the former Japanese military's wartime actions were clearly inhumane."

The story of Unit 731 and the cover-up that ensued during the Occupation has been told elsewhere.[47] What remains to be documented, however, is the extent to which there was coalition collaboration in the cover-up. Until there is full disclosure of the relevant documents by the respective governments, it is difficult to state categorically that coalition partners such as Canada were fully involved. Enough evidence from the Tokyo Tribunal and the FEC exists, however, to point to such a conclusion. According to Soviet reports, documents related to the Nanjing "Tama" detachment were handed to the IMTFE in Tokyo and suggest that a Tribunal representative had asked the "American Prosecution to supply additional proof."[48] In the transcript quoted from above, Sutton may have been referring to the Soviet evidence, but we know that Chinese officials had also collected related evidence in China. How or whether this evidence was kept from the Tribunal remains unclear, but we do know that US officials at the highest levels worked to prevent the perpetrators from being prosecuted. Interrogations of suspects took place as early as 1946 in Tokyo and continued into 1947. On 2 June 1947, Major General Alden Waitt, who worked closely with Otto Maass, a Canadian scientist deeply involved in biological warfare testing in Canada, phoned the head of US intelligence in Tokyo, Charles Willoughby, to emphasize the importance of the information being obtained from Ishii Shirō and others. Three weeks later, Waitt and representatives from the departments of war, state, and justice met in Washington, where they accepted Waitt and MacArthur's recommendation of immunity for suspected perpetrators of biological warfare – this despite the fact that the International Prosecution Section of the Tokyo Tribunal had confirmed that a "Japanese BW group, headed by Ishii, did violate the rules of land warfare."[49]

So, were the Canadian prosecutor and judge part of the conspiracy to suppress the evidence against Unit 731? In 1980, one judge, V.A. Roling of the Netherlands, reflected upon learning of the conspiracy of silence: "The first information about these Japanese atrocities became known through the trial at Khabarovsk, December 25 to 30, 1949. I remember hearing about it, and not believing its contents. I could not imagine that these things had happened, without the Court in Tokyo being informed."[50] Thus, if Roling did not know about the use of biological weapons at the time of the trials, it is quite conceivable that McDougall did not know either.[51] The evidence poses further questions. As already explained, McDougall was part of an inner circle of judges at the Tribunal. Furthermore, in July 1946, the US Joint Chiefs of Staff had formulated a policy restricting access to information: "Under present circumstances, intelligence relating to research and development in the field of science and war material should not be disclosed to nations other than the British Commonwealth (omitting Eire) without specific authorization of the Joint Chiefs of Staff."[52] Thus, Roling and others could have been excluded from the information loop while the inner group of anglophones were privy to it. The same may be true of the Canadian prosecutor, Henry Nolan. We know, for example, that the associate prosecutor for China and his assistant, David Sutton, had access to information related to biological warfare and that the head of the prosecution decided not to prosecute. Indeed, Joseph Keenan, the head prosecutor and man whom Roling blames for the cover-up, later attested that Nolan had been "the outstanding Associate Prosecutor in many ways" and was also "a painstaking and conscientious contributor in the matter of adjustment of these different points of view, and wise and valuable in giving counsel."[53] Furthermore, Nolan was "a member of the Executive Committee that formulated the policies of the prosecution."[54] Further research, focusing on the Executive Committee as well as on the justices, will eventually reveal the details of this sordid affair at the level of the Tokyo Tribunal.

Further suggestion of a Canadian cover-up comes from a related war crimes trial that is seldom discussed in Canada. As the rivalry between the Soviet Union and the United States intensified, the former decided to take matters regarding suspected Japanese war criminals into its own hands. As the Netherlands judge attested, in 1949 the Soviet government decided to proceed with charges against members of Unit 731 for having conducted biological warfare against the Chinese. Soviet troops first discovered the charred remains of the Japanese factories of death in Manchuria when they began their offensive on 8 August 1945. They brought their evidence forward in a trial that took place from 25 to 30 December 1949 in Khabarovsk.[55]

In early January 1950, an official at Canada's Moscow Embassy informed the DEA about the Khabarovsk trial and included with his report extensive translations of Moscow press accounts of the trial and its judgment. On 1 February 1950, A. Panyushkin, the USSR representative on the FEC, passed to Hume Wrong, Canada's ambassador in Washington, a full copy of a Soviet note submitted to Dean Acheson recounting the Soviet findings from the Khabarovsk trial. This fourteen-page report outlined in detail the operations of Unit 731 and was forwarded from Washington to the DEA.[56] It identifies the "Water Supply and Prophylactic Department for the Units of the Kwantung Army" as the early sponsor of the program and cites "Unit 731" and "Unit 100" as later incarnations. It also correctly indicates that Unit 100 was concerned with warfare against plants and animals. It identifies Pingfan as the main site for the program and correctly estimates the number of personnel at about three thousand. It also suggests that about three thousand people were killed in experiments but that biological weapons were also used in actual warfare, including the 1940-42 campaign in China. It describes in detail the role of Ishii Shirō, the godfather of Japan's biological warfare program; Kasahara Yukio, chief of staff of the Kwantung Army; Kitano Masazō, head of Unit 731 for a couple of years; and Wakamatsu Yujiro, head of Unit 100. In retrospect, this document, and indeed much of the information regarding Japanese use of biological warfare that was placed in evidence at the Khabarovsk trial, has since been verified. And this evidence was in the hands of Canadian officials almost immediately after the trial.

In May 1950, Canadian officials in Moscow sent further reports to the DEA, which included press reports related to the Khabarovsk trial and Japanese biological warfare.[57] The press reports at the time included, however, Soviet accusations that "tests of means of bacteriological warfare were being carried out by the Americans on Canadian territories with the knowledge of the Canadian government and that an unprecedented plague epidemic among the Eskimos was the direct consequence of these experiments."[58] These reports were supplemented with reports supplied to the Canadian and other representatives in the FEC. After the Khabarovsk trial, the Soviet Union presented governments represented on the FEC with a detailed note regarding the use of biological warfare and suggesting that the FEC convene further trials. This note and a second one, delivered to the US State Department on 31 May, prompted a flurry of correspondence between Washington, Ottawa, and Tokyo. On 1 June, a Canadian representative in Washington asked the DEA for advice regarding how to respond to US representations on the subject. He had informally obtained a confidential document entitled "Notes for Conversations with other FEC Delegations

Regarding the Soviet Proposal to try the Japanese Emperor and Four Generals for War Crimes."[59] This fascinating document indicates that the US State Department suggested that to try the Emperor, as the Soviets were suggesting, would "turn the Japanese against the Occupation." It continues: "To attack the Emperor as proposed would be to throw away one of our strongest supports in Japan and to inflict upon ourselves a great and needless injury." It further recommended that it was too late to try the four generals. What is most remarkable in this document, however, is what is missing. Nowhere is there any attempt to even suggest that the charges against the Emperor and the four generals were unfounded.

From Tokyo, Canadian diplomat Herbert Norman, himself secretly under investigation by this time as a possible spy, responded to DEA queries regarding the Soviet information on biological warfare by stating that the government view that Soviet proposals were "primarily a propaganda move possibly to embarrass the United States before other Asiatic nations, [was] absolutely sound."[60] The DEA also requested an opinion from its legal division on 9 June, and two weeks later the legal advisor responded with his view that it was quite possible for the FEC to issue a special directive that would make it possible to try Hirohito and others for war crimes even at this late date. As for the FEC policy decision of 31 March 1949 calling for the conclusion of war crime trials by 30 September 1949, the DEA legal advisor perceived this as non-binding because of its wording. He further pointed out that the Australian government was already in breach of the policy since it was continuing trials of lesser war criminals that summer, nearly a year after the recommended conclusion of trials.[61] In other words, the Canadian government could have recommended that the FEC indict the perpetrators of biological warfare but it chose not to do so. Canada, in close cooperation with the United States government, had shut the door on justice for the Chinese victims of biological warfare. This door would remain closed for fifty years.

PART 2

PAX AMERICANA
Race, Anti-Communism, and Asia

8

Mr. Kennan Comes to Ottawa

As the Tokyo Tribunal proceeded, General Douglas MacArthur dined with foreign press correspondents at the Press Club in Tokyo on 17 March 1947. It was an unusual move for this imperial consul, who was renowned for sticking close to home and headquarters. Although he had indicated that he was not there to answer questions, he magnanimously agreed to be interviewed. In fact, the general wanted to get out a message: "The time is now approaching when we must talk peace with Japan. Our Occupation job here can be defined as falling roughly into three phases – military, political and economic."[1] Citing the demobilization of Japan's troops, demilitarization of the country, and the tearing down of military installations, MacArthur concluded: "[the] military purpose, which was to ensure Japan will follow the ways of peace, and never again be a menace, has been, I think, accomplished." MacArthur told the assembled reporters: "[the] political phase is approaching such completion as is possible under the Occupation." Regarding the economic aspect of the Occupation, MacArthur stated that the economy could not be revived as long as Japan's trade was restricted: "We do not allow Japan to trade. She must be allowed to trade with the world. Japan is only permitted the barter system through the bottleneck of SCAP." Thus, suggested the general: "It would be advisable for the world to initiate at this time peace talks with Japan." Asked when the peace treaty should be concluded, MacArthur replied, "I will say as soon as possible."

MacArthur's public advocacy of the need to begin negotiations for a peace treaty created shock waves in world capitals. It was exactly what he had hoped for. His political adviser, George Atcheson, Jr., had informed him in February that a draft treaty was being prepared by the US State Department and that discussions about a treaty might soon take place at an upcoming meeting of the Council of Foreign Ministers. Furthermore, President Truman had just been on radio, outlining what was to become known as the Truman Doctrine. The president told the world that there were only two choices – to follow the path of freedom or to follow the path of totalitarianism – and that the US government would take on the role of world police officer to ensure that freedom triumphed. Worried by Truman's declaration that even Asia was not immune to Soviet influence, and angered by accusations that Occupation economic policies were at best ineffective and at worst undermining the managerial elite and providing sustenance to communism, MacArthur struck out on his own, a tactic that he had employed on numerous previous occasions. As a result of MacArthur's announcement, other governments began to make inquiries with the State Department regarding the substance of its draft treaty and the process that was being envisaged for adopting it. This accelerated the treaty-drafting discussions in Washington, where there was strong agreement with MacArthur's view that it was time to conclude a peace treaty with Japan.[2] In June, US secretary of state George Marshall informed MacArthur that the State Department was ready to initiate discussions for the conclusion of a peace treaty. Marshall envisaged the treaty's being hammered out in an eleven-power conference made up of representatives of the countries that formed the Far Eastern Commission. He stated: "although Dept prefers a voting procedure requiring only two-thirds majority of the 11 powers, it would be prepared to consider provision for unanimity among interested powers if the suggestion came from a substantial number of the powers consulted and if the provision for unanimity could be limited to four powers – the US, USSR, China and UK or Australia."[3]

On 1 July 1947, State Department representatives met with representatives of the FEC countries in Washington to invite them to attend a peace conference on 19 August. That date was chosen out of a "desire for a treaty for Japan as soon as possible."[4] Ralph Collins represented Canada at that meeting, and, although the Soviet representative was unable to attend, the invitation had been sent to the Soviet Embassy. After consultations with the respective governments, most countries with the exception of the Soviet Union and China agreed to an eleven-power conference, with decision making by a simple two-thirds majority. However, the Australian government, intent on gaining a larger say in the peace treaty discussions, had already invited Commonwealth countries to attend a preliminary conference in Canberra beginning in late August. In light of this, the British government informed the US State Department that the proposed 12 August date for the peace conference was not realistic. As a result, the State Department considered rescheduling its proposed meeting to 8 September 1947. As we shall see, its plans ran into heavy turbulence.

The Canberra Conference

MacArthur's 19 March 1947 press conference had put negotiations for a peace treaty into high gear, and, on 26 August 1947, representatives of Commonwealth countries, including Great Britain, Australia, India, New Zealand, Pakistan, and Canada, convened in Canberra in peace treaty consultations.[5] The Canadian delegation was led by Brooke Claxton, the minister of defence, and included Herbert Norman. The Canadian external affairs department provided extensive documentation for the delegation. Included in these briefing materials were extensive reference documents prepared by Norman in Tokyo.[6] Solicited by the Department of External Affairs, Norman's recommendations are to some extent unique in that they were not diplomatic observations but, rather, informed opinions about Japan's future based on his understanding of Japan's history and his sense of the durability of reforms to that point.

Norman envisaged a post-treaty supervisory mechanism in the form of a control council that would be based in Tokyo and would report to the United Nations.[7] Its membership would be composed of signatories to the treaty and would operate by majority vote. It would have powers to observe and inspect post-Occupation Japan, but only the United Nations would be able to enforce any corrective sanctions thought necessary. Regarding Japan's reintegration into the world community, Norman suggested that Japan would be able to resume diplomatic relations with all countries once the peace treaty was ratified. Norman also provided detailed recommendations regarding the settlement of territorial questions, first citing the Cairo Declaration and the agreement that Japan would relinquish sovereignty over Formosa and Manchuria, returning them both to China, and that Korea would become independent.[8] As for Occupation reforms, Norman mused on possible challenges likely to be faced by either conservative or socialist governments if they were presented with a treaty that specifically demanded the retention of SCAP directives. Norman suggested that such a demand "would be to fit a straight jacket upon the body politic of the Japanese nation, which should be encouraged to grow as much as possible through its own efforts and political leadership, provided the direction of its growth is peaceful and fundamentally democratic."[9] In lieu of such a demand, he posited that a general clause be inserted calling on Japan to promote democratic and human rights.[10] On trade issues, Norman felt that there would have to be increased production for export and access to world markets but that "some form of control over Japan's exports and imports should be maintained for some years."[11]

Norman's briefing papers significantly influenced the Canadian position that Claxton brought to the table at Canberra, and Norman was himself invited to address ministers and officials attending the conference. In his address to the conference on the afternoon of 27 August, Norman reviewed the factors facilitating and inhibiting democratic growth in Japan.[12] He told the Commonwealth ministers that "the balance [was] in favour of democratic growth provided there [was] reasonable economic stability and guidance [was] available from the victor side."[13] As he had in the past, Norman pointed to the fact that women, intellectuals, and trade unions would have an ongoing interest in seeing the reforms sustained, but, he cautioned his audience: "a generation or so is required before these reforms can take firm root."[14] In his report to the Canadian government, Claxton stated that Norman's presentation was "thoughtful and penetrating" and "indeed generally recognized as one of the most useful of the conference."[15] Claxton's report stressed that the conference was very amiable and that Australia no longer advocated a hard peace.[16] According to Claxton, the conference envisaged a meeting of the FEC, plus Pakistan and perhaps Burma, to be held in October at the latest; voting would be by a two-thirds majority and the treaty should be completed by 1948.[17] Claxton's report reflected the general view in Canberra that a "peace conference should be called without delay."[18] The end of 1948 came and went without the completion of a treaty. Indeed, it had fallen completely off the international diplomatic agenda.[19] What happened?

Most English-language historical accounts point to Soviet objections to the July 1947 US proposal as the major stumbling block to an early peace. While it is quite true that the Soviet Union objected to the US proposal, so too did the Chinese government. As it turns out, their objections had considerable merit and solutions could have been found, but the fact was that the US administration no longer wanted a peace treaty, despite the earlier international consensus that Japan had fulfilled the Potsdam conditions. This poses serious questions regarding the legality of the Occupation after 1948.

The Soviet Union's objection to the US proposal that the treaty be drawn up by FEC members, with a two-thirds majority necessary to resolve disputes, was not so unilateral as it was later made out to be. In response to this proposal, the Soviet memorandum stated that it should "be provisionally examined by [the] Council of Foreign Ministers" and that the council should meet in Washington as early as possible. Soviet representatives put this position forward because the US formula denied the USSR and the other powers (China, Great Britain, and the United States) a veto. While the merits of vetoes for large powers was and remains an issue to this day, at the time, providing the powers a veto was standard operating procedure both in the UN Security Council and within the FEC. In that sense, the US proposal that the treaty be negotiated by the FEC powers but outside of the FEC (because, within the FEC, the veto operated) was justifiably viewed by Soviet representatives as a suspect innovation. Far from trying to block the negotiation of a treaty, however, the Soviet representatives counter-proposed that the Council of Foreign Ministers (CFM) handle the treaty, at least in the initial stages. That the Soviet representatives suggested this was quite understandable in light of the fact that even the US working group on the peace treaty envisaged the CFM as a possible venue for drawing up the document.[20] Moreover, in correspondence with the Soviet Union, the United States recognized that "the CFM was constituted on a basis which would have permitted its use for the preparation of a Treaty of Peace with Japan, provided the members of the Council subsequently agreed." But the United States itself did not agree, suggesting that the FEC was the most appropriate body.[21] This was another repudiation of wartime agreements. Citing the minutes from the Potsdam meeting, the State Department's legal advisor informed the department that it was then US secretary of state James Brynes who had suggested in 1945 that China become part of the CFM but that its participation be "limited to problems concerning the Far East or problems of world-wide significance." If the war with Japan ended soon, the Potsdam conferees "would in this manner have established the organization to deal with the problem of peace in the Far East."[22] The legal adviser suggested that the agreement reached was, however, a "political understanding" and not an international agreement. He advised the State Department that, if circumstances had changed, it was not bound by this political agreement.

That the United States was now moving the goalposts becomes even clearer when the 1947 position of China's Guomindang leadership is taken into account. On 17 November 1947, the Chinese government endorsed the US proposal that a special session of the FEC be convened on a date to be decided by the four Big Powers and, furthermore, that those same powers be accorded a veto in the deliberations. In other words, the Chinese government had come part way in meeting the concerns of the Soviet Union that it retain a veto and that the Big Powers retain some role in the process.[23] This attempt at compromise reflected the fact that China had signed a friendship treaty with the Soviet Union (14 August 1945) that expressly prohibited the signing of a peace treaty with Japan that excluded either of the signatories.[24] The Soviet Union, unwisely as it turns out, rejected this proposal, but so too did the United States and, more particularly, the Commonwealth countries (New Zealand, Australia, and Canada), which took umbrage at their relegation to middle power status without a veto. The Chinese government, on the other hand, was clearly perturbed by developments in Canberra: "Even though British Commonwealth denied existence of bloc, result was same as they could be expected to vote alike. Chinese public opinion, [the Chinese vice foreign minister] said, would never consent to relinquishment of right of veto under these circumstances."[25] And even within the State Department, as late as May 1947, the Office of Far Eastern Affairs recommended that the United States accept a formula that allowed for a veto.[26] What scuttled the peace treaty was not Soviet obstinacy regarding the veto, a right that the Chinese government was also demanding, but, rather, a remarkable shift in US foreign policy towards imperial anti-communism that had been building throughout 1946 and 1947. Thus, while Commonwealth representatives prepared for and met in Canberra to discuss the treaty with Japan in the summer of 1947, conservative US forces, with George Kennan as the sword bearer, began a major offensive within the US administration to implement the policies of imperial anti-communism in Asia just as decolonization was gaining momentum.[27]

George Kennan: Imagining a Cold War

Rivalry between the Soviet Union and the United States had, as described in earlier chapters, existed even during the wartime alliance. Yet, there was a strong desire in what might be described as the centre-left of the political spectrum to maintain a cooperative relationship with the Soviet Union to preserve peace in the world. Those on the centre-right, however, cast the

Soviet Union as the new enemy of freedom, a caricature invoked by Churchill in his Fulton speech in March 1946. George Kennan's brief role as a leading ideologue began around the same time. A career foreign service officer since 1926, Kennan was posted to Moscow from 1944 to 1946. In February of that year, while still in Moscow, Kennan wrote what later became known as the "long" telegram in which he articulated the necessity of quarantining the Soviet Union, spurning the policy of co-existence that had mainly characterized the wartime and immediate postwar relationship. As part of his proposed grand strategy, Kennan called for the strengthening of both Germany and Japan as regional centres of capitalist development. In July 1947, Kennan's views were published under the pseudonym "X" in the journal *Foreign Affairs* in an article that is now generally accepted by historians as one of the founding documents of the Cold War.[28] Many have commented on the seminal nature of these documents, but recently the impact of race and gender on Kennan's views has come under scrutiny.[29] In his long telegram, for example, he attributes the Soviet Union's despotic tendencies to its "attitude of Oriental secretiveness and conspiracy."[30] Also in his *Foreign Affairs* article, Kennan suggested that the Soviets' problems stemmed from a fanaticism derived from the "Russian-Asiatic world" that was unmoderated by "Anglo-Saxon traditions of compromise."[31] Some might dismiss such points as secondary to the article's main concern (which they were) and see them as a legacy of the racist past. In fact, however, Kennan's views reflected the continuing inability of many in imperial centres to understand resistance to racialization and empire, and it displays a rather desperate search to find rationales that would justify an ongoing global role for the United States. Although under attack mostly from peoples of colour, both at home and abroad, racism still had some purchasing power within the cohort of elite white men who dominated diplomacy and government. Increasingly important at this time, however, was the discursive power of anti-communism, particularly in colonial settler states. The proximity of the Soviet Union to Europe and, indeed, the presence of Soviet forces in Germany, Poland, and Austria had brought communism into close contact with what most white diplomats considered the old country, the hearth of "civilization" – Europe. Thus Churchill's speech in Fulton focused on the dangers of potential Soviet influence and called on Anglo-Saxon peoples to form a united front. By 1947, the Truman administration responded vigorously. The president made his famous 12 March speech outlining new US commitments in Greece and Turkey, and the administration then announced a massive stimulus package for Europe (the Marshall Plan) on 5 June. The introduction of the National Security Act that July consolidated the mechanics of foreign policy and defence administration.

In the process, George Kennan's views gained increased currency with the White House and he took charge of the Policy Planning Staff (PPS), a high-powered think tank within the State Department, in May 1947. Under Kennan's supervision, the PPS began a review of US policy in Japan, and in mid-August Kennan and the PPS staff had reviewed the draft treaty. Informing Undersecretary of State Robert Lovett that it "causes us some concern," Kennan recommended that the State Department "should try to delay the opening of these discussions until this matter [could] be systematically thrashed out, United States objectives agreed upon at a high level, and our peace treaty draft related strictly to those objectives."[32] Lovett immediately responded, telling Kennan: "[I have] sent the 'treaty' back as being wholly inadequate in present form. Your views are being passed along."[33] In other words, by the time the Commonwealth countries came together in Canberra, Kennan had already succeeded in putting peace treaty initiatives on hold within the United States. Kennan clearly had the ear of the administration, and he used this to advantage.

After securing a freeze on the peace initiative, Kennan followed up with a detailed report recommending that the US administration prolong the Occupation.[34] The main conclusion of the eight-week PPS study was as follows: "[The PPS] sees great risks in an early relinquishment of Allied control over Japan. It has no satisfactory evidence that Japanese society would be politically or economically stable if turned loose and left to its own devices at this stage. If Japan is not politically and economically stable when the peace treaty is signed, it will be difficult to prevent communist penetration."[35] Kennan's lack of confidence in the Japanese people, which at least partially derives from his racialized views of them, transforms them into the perfect victim for the imagined communist conspirators. Here we see the subtle intersection between race and anti-communism.

Kennan warned, however, that these were interim views that required verification through a fact-finding visit to Japan. In the meantime, any talks related to a peace treaty, if held at all, should be exploratory and non-binding. While supposedly an interim report, the PPS memorandum had immediate effects. Discussion of a peace treaty came to a standstill, and, as early as January 1948, the United States announced within the Far Eastern Commission that its main priority was the development of a "self-supporting

DIVISION OF CENTRAL SERVICES TELEGRAPH SECTION

DEPARTMENT OF STATE

INCOMING TELEGRAM

INFORMATION COPY
ACTION MUST BE ENDORSED ON ACTION COPY

PEM-K-M
No paraphrase necessary.

8963

Moscow via War

ACTION:EUR
INFO:
S
U
C
A-B
A-C
A-D
SA
SPA
UNO
EUR/X
DC/R

~~SECRET~~

Dated February 22, 1946

Rec'd 3:52 p.m.

Secretary of State,

Washington.

511, February 22, 9 p.m.

Answer to Dept's 284, Feb 3 involves questions so intricate, so delicate, so strange to our form of thought, and so important to analysis of our international environment that I cannot compress answers into single brief message without yielding to what I feel would be dangerous degree of over-simplification. I hope, therefore, Dept will bear with me if I submit in answer to this question five parts, subjects of which will be roughly as follows:

(One) Basic features of post-war Soviet outlook.

(Two) Background of this outlook.

(Three) Its projection in practical policy on official level.

(Four) Its projection on unofficial level.

(Five) Practical deductions from standpoint of US policy.

I apologize in advance for this burdening of telegraphic channel; but questions involved are of such urgent importance, particularly in view of recent events, that our answers to them, if they deserve attention at all, seem to me to deserve it at once. THERE FOLLOWS PART ONE: BASIC FEATURES OF POST WAR SOVIET OUTLOOK, AS PUT FORWARD BY OFFICIAL PROPAGANDA MACHINE, ARE AS FOLLOWS:

(A) USSR still lives in antagonistic "capitalist encirclement" with which in the long run there can be no permanent peaceful coexistence. As stated by Stalin in 1927 to a delegation of American workers:

"In course

~~SECRET~~

DECLASSIFIED
E.O. 11652, Sec. 3(E) and 5(D) or (E)
Dept. of State letter, Aug. 10, 1972

George Kennan, the author of the now famous "long telegram" (pictured here), secretly visited Ottawa at the end of May 1948 to assure Canadian support for delaying the peace treaty with Japan. | George Kennan to George Marshall ["Long Telegram"], 22 February 1946, Harry S. Truman Administration File, Elsey Papers. Courtesy of Truman Library and Museum.

economy in Japan."[36] In the spring, Kennan himself travelled to Japan to determine whether the PPS interim conclusions were correct. During his stay in Tokyo, he told MacArthur that he should feel neither bound by the Potsdam Declaration nor constrained by the FEC: "However, the terms of the Potsdam Declaration were substantially carried out at the present time, and what remained to be done could be done in a very short time. This meant that in actuality the policy-making functions of the FEC were substantially completed." At the time, Kennan summarized the agreement he reached with MacArthur in these words: "The terms of the surrender have been executed; therefore the policy-making functions of FEC are exhausted. We cannot, however, abolish the regime of control, in so far as it relates to the occupation of Japan, until we have a treaty of peace. In other words, the occupation is continued, not for the enforcement of the execution of the terms of surrender, but to bridge the hiatus in the status of Japan caused by the failure of the Allies to agree on a treaty of peace."[37] In his 1967 memoir, Kennan reiterated this view, that is, that the Occupation had reached a hiatus and that "the United States government and [MacArthur] as its commander in Japan had to exercise an independent judgment." He continued: "I saw no need for him, in these circumstances, to consult the Far Eastern Commission or to feel himself bound by views it had expressed at earlier dates with a view to implementing the terms of surrender."[38] Kennan recalled that this idea "appeared to please the general mightily; he even slapped his thigh in approval; and we parted with a common feeling, I believe, of having reached a general meeting of the minds." If international supervision of the Occupation through the FEC had been ephemeral in the past, from this point on it became almost completely irrelevant. Kennan and MacArthur had, without consultation, relegated not only the FEC but also the entire legal basis of the Occupation – the Potsdam Declaration and implementation of the terms of surrender – to the scrapheap.

Kennan also wrote in his memoir that he saw the Occupation as "parasitical" – as a burden on the Japanese people, with Occupation costs "absorbing approximately one-third of the Japanese budget" – even claiming that exactions upon the Japanese for "the personal enrichment of members of the occupation [were] not always absent." Interestingly, in visiting centres outside Tokyo, Kennan and his fellow investigators "were kindly given the use of a private railway car, and every effort was made, so far as [Kennan] could see, to provide [them] with whatever information [they] wanted."[39]

Whether Kennan felt any qualms about this personal addition to the burden on the Japanese people is open to question.

Kennan, in a manner somewhat different from MacArthur, reiterated his Eurocentric and racist view of the people he was so intent upon saving from communism. The cold warrior comments upon his trip: "[It was] instructive rather than gratifying to get a glimpse of this vast oriental world, so far from any hope of adjustment to the requirements of an orderly and humane civilization, and to note the peculiarly cynical and grasping side of its own nature which Western civilization seems to present to these billions of oriental eyes, so curious, so observant, and so pathetically expectant."[40] This biased perspective was reiterated on numerous occasions.[41] Upon his return to Washington, Kennan submitted his report, PPS 28, concluding: "This Government should not press for a treaty of peace at this time."[42] Kennan's belief in a bipolar world in which the Soviet Union had to be contained in order for Western civilization to survive, and his racialized view of Asia and Asians, was the basis upon which he built his contention that, although the aims of demilitarization and democratization had basically been met, the Occupation could be extended even without legal grounds. By allowing the Soviets to be made the scapegoat for the failure of initial treaty talks, he would kill two birds with one stone: he would reinforce anti-communism and construct a rationale for extending the Occupation.

The Cold War and the United Nations

The ideological frame that Kennan was constructing was not dependent solely on his ideas or on the State Department. US policy makers at numerous levels were grappling with a host of problems that had arisen in the aftermath of the war. Although the idea that the Soviet Union was the source of US problems was seductive, it did not necessarily result in smooth policy making. One of the most important examples of this dilemma was the situation in Korea, which, at the time, remained divided along the 38th parallel. How the United Nations and Canada became involved in Korea in 1947-48 offers a fascinating window on US policy making as well as on how the Canadian government came to adopt the priorities and policies of US containment.[43]

As described earlier, Korea had been divided into two zones, with Soviet troops taking the surrender north of the 38th parallel and US troops moving into the south somewhat later. Unable to come to agreement on how to unify the country, US strategists decided to use the United Nations to create a separate, pro-US regime in the south of Korea. While conventional commentators view the United States' use of the United Nations as an example of multilateralism, the decision to turn to that institution arose because US intervention in the south of Korea was a fiasco, prompting a search for an alternative strategy.

Regardless of how the North Korean regime is viewed today, there is considerable evidence that the regime that arose there had considerable popular support – certainly much more than did the US-dominated south. For example, Canadian diplomats Ralph Collins and Herbert Norman wrote from Washington in July 1946 that US officials reported: "[there is] no evidence of the three Russian-trained Korean divisions which have been reported on various occasions ... there seemed to be a fair amount of popular support for the Russian authorities in northern Korea, and the Russian accusations against the conservative character of the United States occupation in civilian Korea had a certain amount of justification, although the situation was improving somewhat. There had been a fair amount of repression by the Military Government of left wing groups, and liberal social legislation had been definitely resisted."[44] This situation was also recounted in what was known as the State-War-Navy Coordinating Committee (SWNCC), the predecessor to the US National Security Council. There, Secretary of War Robert Patterson reported: "General Hodge was in a mess and his reports were becoming more and more strident. He [Patterson] doubted the efficacy of fiscal relief. Korea represents the most urgent of any of our occupation problems by far. Until recently, we have had the support of the Rightist elements in Korea but now we have even lost that."[45] The discussion then moved to an examination of alternatives, and Patterson indicated that the army was working on the problem but that officials who had been in Korea were suggesting that it might be better to pull out than to let the situation blow up: "If we adhere to the Moscow Agreement, he [Patterson] sees no hope of any solution. An alternative is to set up a South Korean Republic. General Eisenhower said he was inclined to favour a separate republic."[46] Herein lies the origins of a separate entity in the south of Korea.

For its part, the army was looking for an exit strategy since it did not perceive Korea as strategically important, that is, as necessary to its military posture in Asia. But others in the government, including then secretary of state George Marshall, felt that "US prestige in the Far East would greatly suffer if we should withdraw."[47] In the spring, the State Department announced a three-year $500 million aid plan for Korea that would be submitted to Congress. In July, the department's John Allison sketched out a plan

to push the Korean issue into the United Nations.[48] And, on 17 September 1947, the US government announced that it intended to bring the issue of Korea before the United Nations – a violation of the Yalta Accords regarding Korea.[49] On 17 October 1947, the United States submitted a detailed proposal to the United Nations calling for elections to be held in each zone no later than 31 March 1948, with a view to forming a national assembly and government of Korea to which power could be handed over.[50] To implement the proposal, the United States proposed the formation of a commission to observe elections in each zone and to consult with the new government.

The Soviet Union, on the other hand, proposed that all foreign troops leave Korea and that further negotiations over unification be left to the Korean people. The Soviets argued that, if the United Nations was to deliberate on the matter, it should hear from Korean representatives from both the northern and southern zones. Indeed, in cases involving conflict, the UN Charter prescribed hearing from both sides to a dispute. The United Nations voted to adopt the amended proposal to include "elected representatives of the Korean people" in resolving the issue of Korean independence and to create the United Nations Temporary Commission on Korea (UNTCOK) to facilitate participation and to assure that the representatives in the debate were duly elected.[51] UNTCOK would travel, observe, and consult throughout Korea. The second part of the resolution designated Australia, Canada, China, El Salvador, France, India, the Philippines, Syria, and the Ukraine Soviet Socialist Republic as UNTCOK members. This second part also recommended "that the elections be held not later than 31 March 1948 on the basis of adult suffrage and by secret ballot to choose representatives with whom the Commission may consult regarding the prompt attainment of the freedom and independence of the Korean people and which representatives, constituting a National Assembly, may establish a National government of Korea." The elections were to be "under the observation of the Commission," and, "as soon as possible after the elections," the National Assembly should convene, form a national government, and notify UNTCOK of its formation.

The proposal for Canada to participate in UNTCOK caught the DEA off guard, and officials hurriedly put together a position paper regarding Korea and the United Nations, dated 24 October 1947.[52] The document, approved by Pearson and St. Laurent, was replete with anti-communist caricatures of the left in the north and south and paternalistically called for "moderate Korean leaders imbued with a spirit of genuine Korean nationalism."[53] Most important, it aligned Canadian and American foreign policy: "There is a close similarity between and interdependence of Canadian and United States security interests in the North Pacific. Canadian interests would not be served, therefore, by any settlement of the Korean question that would impair the United States strategic position in the Northwest Pacific."[54] The Canadian delegation to the United Nations was ambivalent about participation in the proposed commission. According to DEA documents: "Before nomination of Canada to the Korean temporary commission, the delegation sought to have Canada excluded. However, the United States urged us not to withdraw on the grounds that it would upset the geographical balance of representation and would seriously weaken the Commission."[55] With this the Canadian delegation accepted the nomination. Clearly, pressure from the United States was a key factor that swayed the Canadian delegation in its decision to accept nomination to UNTCOK. Lester Pearson subsequently nominated George Patterson, in China at the time, to serve as the Canadian representative. However, before Patterson could take up his post, Mackenzie King got wind of the proposal and aggressively intervened to prevent Canadian participation, sparking one of the most serious cabinet crises in Canadian history. Pearson and St. Laurent worked assiduously to change King's mind, and finally an agreement was reached in which King acceded to Patterson's participation on the condition that the Soviets gave the commission permission to enter the north. King wrote to Truman on 8 January 1948, stating: "Commission should operate in North Korea as well as South Korea and will require the co-operation of the USSR authorities in the northern zone; and that the Commission will at once get into touch with the Soviet authorities with a view to securing, if possible, such co-operation. *Should such co-operation not be forthcoming, and the Commission not return its mandate to the United Nations in view of the impossibility of carrying out that mandate in the whole of Korea, our representative will be told to withdraw from the Commission.*"[56] As it turned out, such cooperation was not forthcoming, and Patterson subsequently withdrew from commission proceedings. However, the US press got wind of this development, and this resulted in a campaign of vilification against Patterson. Pearson and St. Laurent went into damage control, and, engaging in anti-communist tactics and bureaucratic manipulations, they convinced King and the Cabinet to reverse the earlier position and Patterson stayed on UNTCOK.

The Cabinet decision to reverse the Canadian position regarding Korea was motivated primarily by a desire to please its US ally and was based on the premise that anything the United States might decide would be advantageous in the context of a global showdown with the Soviet Union. This was imperial politics of the highest order, predicated on the assumption that what was best for the West must be good enough for the Korean people. In one sense, the strategy worked. UNTCOK, with Patterson participating, gave its stamp of approval to the May 1948 elections that brought Syngman Rhee to power. The significance of UNTCOK's role in this matter has often been overlooked or misconstrued by prominent Canadian historians.[57] The legitimacy UNTCOK afforded these elections was the basis upon which the Rhee regime declared itself the national government of Korea in August 1948, a move that the United States government quickly endorsed. It then went even further, recognizing the Rhee regime as the only legitimate government on the peninsula. Furthermore, the United Nations (with Canadian agreement) supported the Rhee regime's application for membership in the world body, and, although the Soviet Union vetoed the admission of the South at that time, the Canadian government subsequently officially recognized the Rhee government on the basis of its supportive vote in the United Nations. The scene was set for Canadian and UN condemnation of North Korea as an international aggressor when its troops crossed the 38th parallel in its quest to unify Korea. However, we now know that the elections themselves were wrought with problems, and, in a more immediate sense, they provoked an uprising on the island of Cheju, off Korea's southern coast, which was brutally repressed. [58] Over seventeen thousand people died in a bloody crackdown engineered by Rhee and backed by the United States.

Mr. Kennan comes to Ottawa

Although the Canadian government had reversed its previous policy regarding elections in Korea, thereby aligning itself with US containment plans, not everyone was convinced that Canada was fully on board. Indeed, while in Japan in March 1948, George Kennan had met with Herbert Norman, who duly communicated Kennan's policy intent to Ottawa.[59] Of particular interest, however, is the fact that Kennan came away from his meeting with Norman convinced that the Canadian government might not be on the same page regarding his proposal to prolong the Occupation. Writing in May 1948 to US secretary of state George Marshall, Kennan and Walton Butterworth jointly advised taking "the first opportunity to impress on the Canadians the necessity for a new approach to the questions of occupational policy in Japan and the peace treaty." They continued: "We believe that there is at present a serious divergence of view between the Canadians and ourselves on the subject, which should be corrected as soon as possible."[60] Marshall and Lovett approved Kennan's proposal that he visit

Ottawa for discussions with Canadian officials, and they also approved his suggestion that, should the opportunity arise, he take Canadian officials and even Cabinet-level politicians into his confidence so that they would "feel that we were taking them in to our confidence generally." Canadian ambassador Hume Wrong met Kennan in Washington ten days before his Ottawa visit and confirmed Norman's earlier reports about Kennan's views: "The main problem now was to prevent Japan becoming an easy prey of the Soviet government. ([Kennan] had no doubt that from the Russian point of view Japan would be a far more valuable prize than the whole of China inasmuch as Japanese industry and skills would go some of the way to fill Russian deficiencies.)"[61] Kennan, said Wrong, did not believe this necessarily meant "the indefinite maintenance of an Army of Occupation in Japan, because from the military point of view forces stationed at Okinawa and other Far Eastern points were a sufficient safeguard." More important, from Kennan's point of view, was economic reform. And, with regard to the Peace Conference, Kennan "said the pressure for an early Conference had disappeared. He did refer once or twice to indefinite continuation of some sort of occupation regime, but he also said that peace might be concluded within two or three years."[62]

Before Kennan arrived in Ottawa, M.E. Dening, British Foreign Office undersecretary for the Far East, visited the DEA on his way to Washington. Dening told Arthur Menzies that Great Britain fully sympathized with the anti-communist strategy of the United States: "[He] could not understand, however, why the Americans now appeared to be contemplating continuing their occupation for a two to three year period and were unwilling to insist upon the convening of a Japanese peace conference in the near future."[63] The Japanese, Dening told Menzies, had complied with the terms of surrender, and "he wondered what moral right the United States thought it had to unilaterally continue the Occupation of Japan."[64]

In preparation for Kennan's arrival in Ottawa, Menzies put together a short memorandum for Lester Pearson outlining the stakes in the discussion. The US objectives, he wrote Pearson, "now appear to be: (a) to deny the country's industrial potential and trained manpower to the Soviet Union, and (b) see an end to the expenditure of $400 million annually for relief."[65] The US strategy, Menzies suggested, was to postpone the peace conference, "to be able to continue to station troops in Japan," to reduce reparations that Japan must pay, to promote industrial reconstruction, and to reduce interference with the Japanese government. By contrast, Canadian objectives, Menzies stated, were to ensure Canadian participation in a broad-based settlement; continuation of democratic, anti-militaristic reforms; sensible demilitarization measures, including prohibition of war-supporting industries; and an open-door commercial policy. Great Britain, Menzies told Pearson, agreed with the US objectives but felt a peace conference would be the best venue for achieving them.

On 1 June 1948, Kennan, accompanied by US ambassador Ray Atherton, joined Canadian officials for in-depth discussions of the peace treaty. Kennan told these officials that the United States was consulting particularly with the United Kingdom and Canada in regard to a revised strategy for the Occupation: "The United States was apprehensive lest Japan, turned free by a peace treaty, should lack the economic and military resources to resist Soviet interference. The Unites States was now thinking in terms of prolonging the pre-treaty occupation period."[66] Kennan had much to say that Menzies, an inveterate recorder of detail, summarized: "While in Tokyo Mr. Kennan had had an opportunity to speak to a number of the heads of Allied missions there to get their views on developments. He found that the various Allied observers that he talked to sized up the situation in Japan much the same as he did." On his return to Washington, Mr. Kennan had gone ahead with his planning for Japan: "Their studies were now sufficiently advanced that they wished to have preliminary exchanges of views with the United Kingdom and ourselves."[67] Regarding the treaty negotiation process, Kennan suggested that, although "they had considered the problem[,] they had not been able to find any means of breaking the deadlock at this time." Menzies himself raised China's desire for a veto and "wonder[ed] what Soviet minimum demands were, perhaps measures could be taken to assure them 2/3 majority would not be abused."[68] Kennan, however, responded with a stereotype: "The Chinese had made a tremendous fuss over the concessions in Manchuria which President Roosevelt had offered Premier Stalin to come into the war against Japan. Once they got hold of a handle of that kind the Chinese would never stop working it."[69] Ralph Collins then asked whether any of the other countries had given any informal indication that they would be prepared to move in the direction of meeting the Chinese suggestion that the conference should follow the FEC voting procedure. As regards the Soviet Union's views, "he pointed out that the suggestion had been made that the language of the Soviet notes might be interpreted as leaving the way open to a compromise through a meeting of the Council of Foreign Ministers to discuss procedural problems only, and that if the Russians really were willing to go ahead with a peace settlement at all they might be willing to agree at such a meeting to a procedure for the Conference itself which would be acceptable to the other FEC countries." Kennan responded that he thought there would be "some difficulty in confining discussions in the Council of Foreign Ministers to procedural matters. Mr. Menzies said that he was pretty suspicious of this approach to the subject and thought that Australia and some of the others would be even more suspicious of such an approach."[70]

However, Menzies recorded: "Mr. Kennan said that they had given very careful consideration to the question of going ahead with a Peace Conference without Russia if the Russians were unprepared to accept our procedural terms. They had concluded that it would be inadvisable to do so." Kennan also said that, "as a result of their studies[,] they were swinging round to the view that it would probably be unwise to try to get agreement on a peace treaty now."[71] Menzies added to the record that "it was apparent throughout the trend of the conversation that Mr. Kennan wished to convince us of the undesirability of trying to conclude a peace treaty with Japan in the near future." The minutes concluded: "Mr. Collins asked whether it was really necessary to delay the peace settlement with Japan in order for the United States to continue to furnish financial assistance for the economic rehabilitation of the country. He wondered whether the United States could not furnish the same economic assistance and views after a peace treaty through arrangements similar to those arrived at with the European countries in connection with the Marshall Plan. Mr. Kennan had no very satisfactory rationalization to offer." Kennan emphasized: "The United States would not stand for irresponsible meddling in Japanese industrial recovery through some 'frivolous' reparations programme while she was paying out $500,000,000 a year to get Japan on her feet again."[72]

According to Menzies' record, Kennan believed that "a good number of the internal reform measures in Japan had gone much too far," and he suggested it was wrong to try to make the Japanese over "like ourselves ... All we were doing was tearing apart the closely woven fabric of Japanese society. Some of the young officers in GHQ/SCAP were out-doing the Russians in their enthusiasm for uprooting traditional structures."[73] Kennan asserted that the reforms meant that it was possible "for Communists to infiltrate local elected governments and local police forces and for the central government in Tokyo to know nothing about it."[74] The purge came "under an especially heavy attack from Mr. Kennan," who suggested that the dissatisfied elite might be used by communists. Challenged by Ralph Collins, however, Kennan backtracked, clarifying that "conservatives" would be the source of instability, which the communists could use to their advantage. After Kennan suggested that the business de-concentration program should be watered down, Menzies intervened, stating that he thought it was wrong to abandon the reform program. In reply, Kennan stated: "while we were worrying about Japanese reforms, we were giving the Russians an opportunity to extend their influence in Japan."[75] Kennan concluded by saying: "as we could not really count on very extensive reforms in the outlook of the Japanese, it would be necessary to maintain certain minimum security controls for quite a time."[76] There was no Canadian comment on Kennan's assertion about the unchanging nature of the Japanese mind.

Canadian officials in the DEA clearly had doubts about this new US approach. Kennan's defence of the US administration's radical change in Occupation policy reveals that there was no desire on the part of the United States to reach a compromise on the peace treaty, either with Canada or with anyone else. This becomes particularly clear if British objections and the Canadian government's reaction to those are also factored in. On 21 July 1948, Clement Attlee wrote a top secret and personal note to Mackenzie King, emphasizing that the British view was that the US administration appeared to "be dominated by what they believe to be the aim of the Soviet Union, viz. to obtain control of Japan as being the only Far Eastern country at present with any real industrial potential."[77] The Truman administration, Attlee suggested, was intent on an "indefinite prolongation of United States occupation which [would] enable them to retain the United States strategic position in Japan." Attlee supported this analysis of Soviet intentions but suggested that the idea of fully restoring Japan's economy was open to "grave objection." The British PM proposed that an early peace treaty was still the best solution and that the United States could ensure its position in Japan "by the conclusion simultaneously with Peace Treaty of defence pact [sic] between United States and Japan to which other friendly Powers might perhaps accede." Attlee warned: "Indefinite occupation by the United States without a treaty would on the contrary be difficult to defend except on grounds of pure expediency."[78] Pearson drafted a reply for Mackenzie King that, although not sent, became the basis of the Canadian position.[79] The government concluded: "The present United States policy of denying Japan's industrial potential to the Soviet Union is of great importance and should be supported. While we had hoped that it might have been possible to convene a Japanese Peace Conference at an early date we do not think we would be justified in pressing the United States Government unduly to push forward with a conference at this time if they do not think this wise."[80] And that was that. Pearson and the Canadian government effectively rejected the

British appeal for a continued, cooperative lobby to pressure the United States to conclude a peace treaty.

Today, the position that Pearson articulated might seem reasonable: Canadians had an independent view but weren't going to battle the United States on this. Indeed, many scholars continue to justify this as a reasonable Pearsonian approach to internationalism. In fact, however, there were serious problems with this position. As is now known, the Soviet threat was exaggerated. Even at the time, many opposed the way containment theorists were characterizing Soviet actions. MacArthur stated unequivocally that the Soviets had no designs on Japan, nor was domestic communism in Japan a significant threat. Furthermore, extending the Occupation as advocated by US officials was in all likelihood illegal because the authority of the Occupation was based on the Potsdam Declaration, an international covenant, as well as official US policy as expressed in the US "Initial Post-Surrender Policy for Japan."[81] Indeed, according to Article 12 of the Potsdam Declaration: " The occupying forces of the Allies shall be withdrawn from Japan as soon as these objectives have been accomplished and there has been established in accordance with the freely expressed will of the Japanese people a peacefully inclined and responsible government."[82] In other words, the people of Japan could have regained their sovereignty in 1948, but because of the Cold War, the Occupation would drag on for nearly another four years. Despite having a position of privileged access to US policy makers such as Kennan, and having the option of working with the British government to offset some aspects of the new US approach, Pearson chose not to. In rejecting Attlee's appeal, Pearson confirmed what was to become the cornerstone of Canadian foreign policy: that, in so far as Japan was concerned, the Canadian government perceived that country to be mainly the responsibility of the United States, even after the Occupation reforms had been largely achieved. The persistent emphasis on this point reflected a continuing adherence to old imperial notions of spheres of influence in which the views and values of the people concerned, in this case the Japanese, mattered little. It was Big Power politics, and Pearson knew which side he was on, even if the British offered an alternative course of action.

Secure in the knowledge that the Canadians would not support a separate British or Commonwealth position, Kennan and the State Department effectively killed peace treaty discussions, extended the occupation of Japan, and began a program to roll back a number of the reforms that had already been or were now in the process of being implemented. As Kennan recounted in his memoirs: "In the refusal of the Russians and Chinese to go along [with the peace treaty], we had been luckier than we deserved."[83] The Japanese government and people do not figure prominently in Kennan's views: Japan was manifestly a prize to be won by the main contenders in the Cold War. As long as capitalism revived, and Japan became allied with the United States, little else mattered. However, in Japan it did matter – a great deal. The business and conservative elite, once assured by people such as George Kennan, William Draper, and others that change to a more conservative course was imminent, were more than happy to work under a continuing Occupation that would promote their interests by ending the reparations and *zaibatsu* deconcentration program, weakening organized labour, and ending the purge and war crimes trials then taking place. What is often left out of this discussion is the fact that the reverse course was implemented as a replacement for a peace treaty.

Resistance and Change

The ascent of imperial anti-communism within the US policy-making elite coincided with the rise of vigorous social movements in Japan in 1945-47 and continuing challenges to US control in southern Korea. In Japan, the new emphasis on economic reconstruction allowed the business community there to regroup and to launch an offensive against a labour movement that at the time represented a phenomenal 50 percent of all workers in Japan.[84] The origins of the campaign can be traced to a shift in Occupation policy that occurred after labour leaders refused to cancel a proposed general strike on 1 February 1947, despite numerous appeals from US officials. MacArthur was forced to ban the strike himself, and, from that point on, the Occupation worked to help re-establish business organizations and to assist them in a concerted effort to weaken the labour movement. US conservatives in what was known as the Japan lobby assured political support for this new agenda.[85]

Anti-communism was a key component in this campaign. Communists were active in many unions, but the offensive aimed at reinforcing managerial rights and weakening trade unions regardless of political orientation. The campaign began with a concerted effort to break a strike at the Tōhō movie studios in the summer of 1948. MacArthur supported the effort by sending in Occupation troops against the strikers. The previous month MacArthur had ordered an end to government employees' rights to bargain and strike. In 1949, employers worked with the Yoshida government, which had come to power after January elections, to mount a full-scale campaign that included revising labour laws, breaking unions, and laying off hundreds of thousands of workers. Parallel to this process, the Occupation also began to roll back its political program, putting a halt to the dissolution of wartime conglomerates, ending reparations to countries victimized by Japanese imperial conquests, prohibiting further attempts to punish war criminals, and relaxing controls over those "purged" because of war responsibility. In 1949, economic retrenchment received a boost from MacArthur and the US administration through the establishment of the so-called "Dodge Plan" for financial reform, named after the American banker Joseph Dodge, who was sent to implement a more conservative agenda.

Many people in Japan were affected by these changes, and they did not simply roll over and accept them. There was a huge outcry against MacArthur's July 1948 order to deny public-sector workers the right to strike, a right introduced in the original labour reform of 1945. Workers went on strike, organized protests, and constantly confronted employers and the government. In many ways, the labour movement lost the battles of this period. Indeed, union membership had declined from 6.7 million in 1949 to 5.7 million in 1951, and the number of unions that actually had contracts with their employers also declined by nearly half. The paradox, however, was that radical unions in particular were weakened, but then a backlash occurred that inspired a major political realignment within the left. A renewed and militant labour federation, Sōhyō, emerged in 1950, and the left-wing faction in the Socialist Party gained control of the party's leadership. These were harbingers of new challenges to conservatives in Japan as well as to US attempts to align Japan with the policies of imperial anti-communism. The Occupation would continue, but as it did, critics became more vociferous in their opposition.

In southern Korea, however, the crackdown in Cheju heralded the onset of authoritarian regimes and a repression of the left that would continue for decades. Even Lester Pearson recognized this state of affairs, stating in his biography: "Rhee's government was just as dictatorial as the one in the North, just as totalitarian. Indeed, it was more so in some ways, based as it was on Rhee's strong personal appeal as leader in exile for many years."[86] Even at the time, Pearson was aware from field reports that there were enormous problems. Canadian policy in East Asia, however, was predicated not on the needs of people in the region but, rather, on the belief that Canadian interests required reinforcing US power in the Pacific.

Canada, Asia, and "Pax Americana"

There was both continuity and change in how the Canadian foreign policy community imagined "Asia" after 1947. On the one hand, Asian immigration continued to be viewed as a threat to the "fundamental composition of the Canadian population," as the Canadian prime minister put it in his statement on immigration of 1 May 1947. This was a euphemistic way of expressing the desire to maintain a "white" Canada. On the other hand, the repeal of the Chinese Exclusion Act meant the government now allowed for a small number of wives and children of Chinese-Canadian citizens to apply to come to Canada, but it was unwilling to allow even a small quota of non-relative immigrants from China, something the United States had done in 1943.[1] Japanese under the Occupation were prohibited from emigrating, which took care of that issue, and those from South Asia remained excluded from the quota system completely until 1952.[2] Many people in the affected communities protested against an institutionalized bias that was glaring in light of the expedited passage being organized and financed for European refugees after the war.[3] An end to the racist quota system would not come until the 1960s.[4]

As the experiences in the Far Eastern Commission, in the United Nations Temporary Commission on Korea, and in the peace treaty consultations with George Kennan, reveal, the Canadian government displayed a strong inclination to support the US agenda in the Pacific regardless of the implications for the peoples there, for democracy, or for multilateral institutions.

The rationale for this conduct was that Japan and Asia were within the US sphere of influence, an imperial concept that still held sway. Underpinning this view was the fact that Canada had only limited interests or resources in Asia and regarded its continental ties with the United States – economic, military, and political – as strategic. This became increasingly clear as the Department of External Affairs conducted an internal discussion regarding future strategy based on a working paper, "The United States and the Soviet Union: A Study of the Possibility of War and Some of the Implications for Canadian Policy," drafted by Escott Reid.[5] Lester Pearson circulated this paper to ranking staff in Ottawa as well as to missions abroad.[6] Even at this time, Pearson and Reid were acquainted with George Kennan's article in *Foreign Affairs,* and they had a growing appreciation of the thinking behind US foreign policy. Casting the Soviet Union as a police state and the United States and its allies as democracies, Reid contended that both the Soviet Union and the United States were engaged in an endless extension of their defence boundaries and that this was the basis for the rivalry and the possibility of war. The solution was for the US-led coalition to gain a preponderance of power and to force the Soviet Union to retreat. Reid proposed that the coalition needed to end racial discrimination at home and to offer independence to colonized peoples, even though there were dangers in giving colonial people self-government "before they were ready for it."[7] The threat of Soviet control of independence movements increased the longer self-determination was delayed, stated Reid. Although conflict between the two powers stretched from "Korea to Finland," it was Europe that would be decisive. Herein lay the foundation for a renewed Canadian commitment to Atlanticism. Incorporating suggestions from L.D. Wilgress, Reid concluded: "Canada is being brought into still greater dependence upon the United States. The 'Atlantic Community' advocated by Mr. Walter Lippmann in his book on 'United States War Aims' is coming into existence. That Atlantic Community was one dominated by the United States but in the same benevolent fashion as Great Britain in the nineteenth century dominated a world which was susceptible to sea power. The Pax Britannica of the nineteenth is to be replaced in the later twentieth century by a Pax Americana."[8] Reid suggested that if war were to occur, Canada would have no freedom of action in any matter the United States considered essential, but otherwise it might exercise considerable influence in Washington. Canada's integration into the US-led coalition was not so much a coercive process as one in which there was substantial Canadian consent: "We were all Atlantic men," was the way the Canadian diplomat Charles Ritchie put it.[9] The

Anglo-Saxon unity that King and Roosevelt had imagined in 1908 was being reinvented.

The long-time prime minister MacKenzie King relinquished power in the fall of 1948, and Lester Pearson became the minister for external affairs under King's successor, Louis St. Laurent. Both Pearson and St. Laurent ushered in the shift in Canadian foreign policy in which increasing attention was given to reinforcing strategic ties with the United States, while still targeting Europe as the most important region outside the continent. The creation of the North Atlantic Treaty Organization (NATO) in 1949, in which Canadian officials played a key role, was both the instrument and symbol of the continuing European focus of the "Atlantic men."

The implications of the Cold War and its Eurocentric thrust had an important impact on how other areas of the world were perceived. Asia remained a secondary region of concern but was of increasing importance. The impact of anti-racism struggles and decolonization meant that the overt policies of racism and colonialism were in decline. However, it was not the ideals of self-determination, popular sovereignty, or the equality of nations that triumphed but, rather, an informal empire in the form of a benevolent "Pax Americana." In this light, Asia once again became a pawn, albeit a valuable one, in a game of world one-upmanship. What really gave shape to the reimagining of Asia was its potential as a threat to the new empire. In countries such as China, Vietnam, Korea, and elsewhere, anti-imperialism, nationalism, and communism were on the march. Many there did not share the perception of a benevolent Pax Americana, and the movement for decolonization was picking up steam. Hopes for American assistance were also being dashed as the white, male world of the Atlanticists tried to squeeze this movement into the confines of their Cold War paradigm. The powerful term "the East" was taking on new meaning as the tattered portrait of "the yellow peril" was overlaid with a new stain – this time with a reddish hue. Anti-communism increasingly became the main weapon in an imperial arsenal.

The fact that the Canadian government dealt with Asian affairs through its "American and Far Eastern" division, established in the first major reorganization of the DEA in 1941, meant that American concerns about developments in Asia were constantly tracked.[10] Pearson in particular hoped that post-independent India, a member of the renovated British Commonwealth, would act as a hedge against communism in Asia, and this translated into a long-term commitment through the Colombo Plan. Canada's historical ties to France would also have some bearing on Canadian policy, particularly in regard to Vietnam. Pearson focused his own efforts on developing Commonwealth relations, particularly with India, and, for a short period, it appeared that Canadian diplomacy might still track that of Great Britain and that the US policy of imperial anti-communism would itself be contained. This created ongoing tensions in the making of Canadian policy as it seemed that peaceful co-existence between the socialist and capitalist worlds was still considered an option.

Intervening in China

The story of US intervention in China during that country's civil war has been told many times.[11] Efforts to broker a coalition government seemed to be making progress, but the resistance within the conservative faction of the dominant Guomindang, along with the Chinese Communist Party's reluctance to lay down its arms, made civil war all but inevitable. In retrospect, the CCP-led victory in the civil war reflected the credibility it had gained in the struggle against Japanese imperialism as well as the support gained among the peasantry because of the communists' dedication to land reform. However, for both the Canadian and American governments, the spectre of communists gaining power in China was anathema, and they actively intervened to support Chiang and the GMD. US support for the GMD angered Mao and other CCP leaders, and by the time the CCP emerged victorious in 1949, thoughts of tempering the envisaged alliance with the Soviet Union by developing ties with the United States had vanished. The estrangement hardened when the United States continued to work closely with Chiang after his retreat to Taiwan. Ideology played its part in the estrangement, of course, but there was ideology on all sides, not only on the communist side. This becomes evident in the Canadian reports from that era, discussed below. The rise of communist China created new global dynamics, and for a period it seemed that Canada and Great Britain, in the hope of creating some stability in the world, were willing to afford recognition to the new republic.

Canada's first ambassador to China, Victor Odlum, returned home to Vancouver in October 1946, and the government appointed Ontario justice T.C. Davis to replace him. Following his arrival in China in the spring of 1947, Davis reported that the GMD foreign minister, Wang Shih-chieh (Wang Shijie), had told him in an initial interview that Great Britain and the United States were great powers and that "these two nations in their relationship to China might have some ulterior motive, or might try to wield an influence upon China's policy due to their power and size. In other words, [Davis thought Wang] had in mind what is commonly termed the application of 'imperialism.'"[12] Canada, on the other hand, was not a great power, and this made for easier relations. Shortly after arriving in Nanjing, reclaimed by the GMD as China's postwar capital, Davis received a report about purported communist atrocities from the reverend G.K. King, secretary of the Canadian Church Mission, who was based in Kaifeng, Honan Province. Davis passed the report on, notifying Ottawa that he found it authentic, based on "the fact that the writer thereof [was] a Canadian, a member of a Canadian Christian Church, and consequently that it could be taken for granted that he [was] thoroughly reliable and responsible." King's information, the ambassador said, was based on "first-hand knowledge gathered from eye witnesses and other reliable witnesses," and he, Davis, therefore concluded: "we can take the statements to be completely true."[13] However, the new ambassador was persuaded by arguments from experienced aides George Patterson and Chester Ronning that both the GMD and the CCP were guilty of cruelty and brutal practices, and so that fact alone could not be the criterion for policy decisions. Davis went on to reflect on other factors and came to the conclusion that he would personally support the GMD government because he thought that "seeds of democracy" existed there. However, his main argument was that he was philosophically opposed to state control (as exercised by communist regimes) and the suppression of opposition. He feared that if the communists gained control of China, they would dominate "the whole of the South Seas" and perhaps even India. And as he saw matters, "If Communism controlled this part of the world, then the outlook for our Western way of life would be bleak indeed."[14]

As Davis continued his journey into things Chinese, he came to believe that the GMD was trying to cast the civil war as a proxy war between "Russian communism on the one hand and American capitalism on the other" and that having cast it in such a light it was now impossible for them to compromise in a coalition with the communists because to do so would undermine their argument that the conflict was international. Davis opined that the real agenda was one in which: "the reactionary elements in the government, within and without, [desire] to exclude Western influences and have China continue to exist under the feudal system which prevails, as against the Liberal elements who want to let the light of the West in and fit our Western civilization into the Chinese way of life."[15] He concluded change would be slow: "Nothing will ever happen here in a hurry." Events would soon prove just how wrong Davis's stereotypical views were.

Davis spent his first summer in Nanjing setting affairs of the new embassy in order and then travelled to Shanghai to do the diplomatic rounds, arriving there on 10 October 1947. His report of his activities there is fascinating, not least for its observations regarding a large reception for Canadians he hosted at the landmark Cathay Hotel. To his amazement, Davis later reported, as many as 150 to two hundred Canadians showed up. But his real astonishment was in reaction to the significant presence of Chinese Canadians:

> You would swear in talking to one of them that you were speaking to a Canadian of Anglo Saxon extraction. One chap, an Engineer, was out installing refrigeration plants, another was a Medical Doctor, a third was a College Professor, and so on down the line. To see them in their native land beside their Chinese counterparts, makes one realize that our educational system can turn out real Canadians regardless of race. All these men are helping China and mighty proud of their Canadian citizenship. Educate these Chinese in Canada and they will make good citizens.[16]

As the civil war continued with the GMD beginning to lose control in the northeast (Manchuria), Davis began to waver in his support for Chiang. He had believed that US aid to the GMD had to be without strings, but, as the situation deteriorated, he thought conditions needed to be attached to any aid to up the ante and force liberalization of the regime.[17] He pinned his hopes on former leaders of the Democratic League: "A liberalized government might be able to defeat Communism in China, by political means. No one can by military means." The final outcome, Davis stated, "lies within the control of the Congress of the United States of America."

Canadian shipments of arms to China became an issue in Canada, first arising in November 1946 after Odlum had left China and Davis had not yet arrived. Ronning reported that stories in the press out of the civil war zone in northern China had quoted the GMD general Fu Zuoyi (Fu Tso-yi) as saying: "Many friends have suspected that we get arms from the United States. As a responsible officer of the Government I can say that we did not get one single gun from the Americans. All we had besides our own stuff were a few Canadian light machine guns, a few small arms from Soviet Russia, and a few arms made in Germany 30 years ago."[18] Since the end of the Second World War in Asia, permits for arms exports had been approved "for export to the United Kingdom and China where provision had been made under

Mutual Aid."[19] A financial agreement signed 7 February 1946 had allocated CDN$25 million for "completion of orders for military and other supplies placed originally under the Mutual Aid programme."[20] But the Cabinet Committee on External Trade had decided in March the following year to allow the Canadian monies to be used to finance new requests for arms sold as surplus by the War Assets Corporation.

George Patterson, then the Canadian chargé d'affaires in Nanjing, reported earlier in the year that there had been critical press comment about recent arrivals of US military aid. He went on to say: "[it was also] known that a shipment had been received from Canada, but no press comment was, fortunately I believe, forthcoming."[21] Meanwhile, the Canadian military attaché suggested that ammunition, or the lack thereof, would become critical over the next period. The Nationalist government subsequently placed an order for fifty Bofors machine guns and for construction of an ammunition plant, using Canadian machinery, to be financed under the Canadian line of credit. The armaments plant project actually proceeded to the point where the Chinese government had sent six to eight technical personnel to "participate in the engineering and development of the plant" to be constructed in Canada and shipped to China. It also provided $200,000 to the Canadian Commercial Corporation to cover initial costs.[22] However, the transaction ran into opposition from Robert Bryce in the Department of Finance, eliciting an angry response from C.D. Howe, who complained bitterly about the lack of coordination among departments. When the arms export issue came before the Cabinet Committee on External Trade, it recommended that all shipments of arms to China be halted but that a permit be issued for China to purchase "single-purpose machines" for the ammunition plant. Approval by Cabinet came on 16 April.[23] This decision was rationalized by the speculation that "it would probably take the Chinese many years to complete the arsenal for the production of ammunition." A month later, the government extended the terms of its credit line to the Nationalist government to allow orders to be placed until 31 December 1948. As the civil war progressed and the GMD suffered major losses, the United States lifted its embargo on supplying arms to the Nationalists. C.D. Howe wrote to St. Laurent, Canada's secretary of state for external affairs at the time, suggesting that the "War Assets Corporation be instructed that the door is open to sale of guns and ammunition, fighter planes, armed frigates and other items ... in which the Chinese have indicated an interest."[24] This suggestion did not gain the support of either Pearson or St. Laurent, but Cabinet overruled their objections and authorized the sale of 174 military aircraft and thirty-five air frames, ostensibly because this would bring US$6 million to Canada.[25]

The following year, the defeat of GMD units in Shenyang (Mukden) allowed communist-led forces to quickly gain control of northeast China. Escott Reid reported to Lester Pearson, the acting and soon-to-be-permanent secretary of state for external affairs, that the situation was disheartening but that the approximately 850 Canadians in China had been advised of possible dangers and had received recommendations to leave China. Reid warned: "Communist control is being rapidly extended over a great area of Northeast Asia. This development will have grave implications for the world."[26] Cabinet subsequently authorized the use of an RCAF transport plane based in Tokyo for the evacuation of Canadians, although a charter plane was later found to fulfill evacuation requirements. In December the government decided to withhold further draws against the line of credit that had been established.

The communist-led forces crossed the Yangtze River in the third week of April 1949 and quickly occupied Nanjing. Chester Ronning described the event in his memoirs:

> After months of certainty that the Nationalists would eventually topple, Nanking was liberated on April 23. Following a thunderous night of cannonading, I finally dropped off to sleep only to be suddenly awakened by Top, who burst into my room. Off we went in his jeep to stand inside the North West Gate to see the first thousands of PLA troops walk, at ease, into the city carrying their war equipment and *pei-wo*, sleeping bags, to take possession of the capital of China with no fanfare or triumphant pomposity.[27]

A few days later, Ronning and a fellow embassy officer, J.R. Maybee, had their first contact with the city's new masters, after which Maybee wrote a memo to the ambassador:

> At 12.50 on April 27 the gateman came to the office to inform us that some Communist soldiers were at the gates and wished to pass through the compound ... We asked the [communist] corporal to state his business. He said that he and his squad wished to go to the top of the hill at the rear of our compound to examine the surrounding area of the city. We asked him if they wished, either on that day or on any other occasion, to construct any defences on our hill, but he assured us that they had no such plan. We further asked him whether he knew that this was the Canadian Embassy. This

took a bit of explaining, as the corporal evidently had never heard of Canada, though he did have a rough idea of what an embassy was.[28]

Ambassador Davis departed China that July, leaving the Nanjing Embassy under the stewardship of Chester Ronning. As the communists continued to extend their authority over the whole of China, and especially after their proclamation of the People's Republic of China (PRC) on 1 October 1949, Ronning pressed Lester Pearson to have the Canadian government recognize the new reality. His prodding of the DEA and Pearson was finally rewarded. Memoranda from the American and Far East division in June and November 1949 all recommended recognition.[29] And in November, Cabinet decided in principle to recognize the new regime. Shortly afterwards, Pearson departed Ottawa on his first trip to Asia.

The Colombo Conference

Representatives of governments of the Commonwealth countries met at the Colombo Conference on Foreign Affairs from 9 to 14 January 1950. India, Pakistan, and Ceylon, by then having won independence from Britain, now counted as full members. Escott Reid's detailed report on the first day's proceedings reflected a new colour consciousness: "Of the twenty-two people who were seated at the conference table, ten were coloured and the coloured members on the whole were much more good-looking than the non-coloured members. There were various shades of colour among the coloured members, even within delegations. Most of the Ceylonese are dark chocolate with pitch-black hair and usually very fine-featured. The Indians vary from Mr. Nehru's pale gray to Mr. Menon's dark black."[30] The five-day conference was replete with the usual formalities at such events, but behind the scenes there were some frank and illuminating discussions about international relations in general as well as issues related to Asia. Among the key problems in Asia that the conference addressed were how to deal with the Soviet Union and communism, whether or not to recognize the PRC, and the situation in Indochina (including Vietnam). In a prelude to the conference, India had officially extended recognition to the PRC on 30 December 1949 and the British government did so on January 6, 1950, only a few days before the start of the conference.

Canada was represented in Colombo by a sizable delegation led by its foreign minister, Lester Pearson. One of the main reasons given for Canada's participation was that "Canada had a general interest as a world power, and a special interest as a Pacific power[,] in discussing the difficult current problems in Asia and in ascertaining the views of the Asian Commonwealth Governments on these problems."[31] In an interview for CBC radio at the time, Pearson emphasized: "[It is] natural for us to devote the greater part of our time to the problems of Asia and particularly Southeast Asia ... In effect the centre of gravity of the world is shifting to Asia. Here you have countries with immense populations such as India, Pakistan, Ceylon and Indonesia, which has recently won independence, and China, which has just become a communist state."[32] He told Canadians that Canada could not isolate itself from world events and that Canadian foreign policy "was based on the consciousness of two dangers – first, the aggressive imperialism of the Soviet government and secondly, and less immediately, the fear that Communism would increase through the inability of countries to deal with their own economic and social problems." Pearson stressed that, in relation to the current problems in the world, Canada was in a "middle position."[33]

In an exchange on international affairs, British foreign secretary Ernest Bevin told the gathered foreign ministers that if it was possible for a social-democratic country like Great Britain to cooperate with the free enterprise government of the United States, it should also be possible in the future to cooperate with the Russians on the same "let-live" terms.[34] India's prime minister, Pandit Nehru, followed Bevin and agreed with his projection that co-existence without interference in the internal affairs of a country was a realistic goal. However, he also told the conference that, with regard to Russia, many countries "were too obsessed with their fears."

Pearson wrote to his undersecretary that he himself "was greatly impressed by the arguments put forward by both the United Kingdom and India for recognition of the Communist government of China."[35] Regarding Indochina, Bevin had apparently informed the French government that Great Britain was prepared to recognize the French-controlled government of Bao Dai, but his position "did not seem to make any converts among the Asian states."[36] Nehru had told the conference that he was "firmly opposed to any kind of recognition of the Bao Dai regime in the Asian states." Pearson speculated that Nehru was irritated with the French government because of its clinging to its colonial outposts and because he did not believe the French would give Bao Dai any real independence of action.

In a more detailed report to Prime Minister Louis St. Laurent, Pearson elaborated on recognition of China. He told St. Laurent that Great Britain, as well as India, Pakistan, and Ceylon, had extended recognition prior to the conference and that this had brought a lashing from the Australian and New Zealand representatives who claimed non-consultation and expressed the

India's prime minister, Jawaharlal Nehru, with Mackenzie King during Nehru's state visit to Canada in October 1949. Although Lester Pearson perceived India as an important non-communist ally in the postwar period, in fact, Canadian and Indian foreign policies diverged after 1950. | National Film Board of Canada, Phototheque / Library and Archives Canada, PA-122477

desire for a shared Commonwealth position. These arguments were refuted, said Pearson, with Bevin suggesting that the "failure of United States policies in China made it difficult for them to take any leadership at this time, [their recognition] ... would make it easier for the United States government to follow along in due course as they must inevitably do."[37] Bevin also claimed, said Pearson, that recognition would reduce the possibility that "local Chinese" in other parts of Asia would ally themselves with China and, furthermore, that "if Mao wanted to pursue a policy independent of the Soviet Union his bargaining power in his Moscow discussions would be increased if his government was recognized rather than being held at bay by

Herbert Norman greets Lester Pearson on his arrival in Tokyo in January 1950. Pearson and Norman would meet with General MacArthur and other Occupation officials during his stopover after the Commonwealth Conference in Colombo. | Rare Books and Special Collections, Department of the Library, University of British Columbia

the West." Pearson also reported to St. Laurent that Nehru believed the Chinese communists promised to do something about peoples' grievances and had delivered on those promises: "United States financial and military assistance to the Nationalists had failed because the Nationalists were unwilling to give the people the reforms they wanted. He warned against the repetition of this policy elsewhere in Asia." Pearson concluded by telling St. Laurent that all the other Commonwealth governments agreed to recognition, therefore: "If we are to get any advantage out of recognition I think we should avoid being the last to do so." Clearly, Pearson and the government were predisposed to go forward with recognition, reassured in the knowledge that not only India but also Great Britain had already done so.

China was not the only subject of discussion at the Colombo Conference. The Canadian delegation also participated in side sessions on economic issues out of which developed the Colombo plan for assistance in technical training and provision of capital goods. This assistance plan was aimed at forestalling communist inroads in developing countries.[38] As articulated by the Canadian administrator of the plan shortly afterwards: "We cannot hope to raise the standards of living of these peoples except by using the methods by which we ourselves have become wealthy, we must aid the man by the machine."[39]

Upon his return to Ottawa, Pearson held a press conference at which he expressed the fear that "Soviet imperialism might overrun the whole of the Far East" and that the establishment of the PRC was "a dramatic indication of this growing strength."[40] Pearson went so far as to suggest that "there was no doubt that the top leaders in China had been trained in Moscow and that their policy was to tie the Chinese government closely to Moscow." Pearson appeared to be publicly reinforcing his anti-communist credentials while preparing to bring to Cabinet concrete plans for Canada's recognition of the PRC.

Despite strong DEA recommendations for recognition, Cabinet refused to act. Opposition came from Finance Minister D.C. Abbott, who was fearful of financial losses on pre-existing loans and investments in China and, more important, from the prime minister, Louis St. Laurent, who did not want to break with the "West," a "rather flaccid cover for his fear of annoying the Americans," as one Canadian scholar has put it.[41] Indeed, Hume Wrong, Canada's ambassador in Washington, wrote of the mounting anti-communist winds in America and counselled delay in recognition.[42] Pearson, Ronning, and Escott Reid worked assiduously to try and overcome Cabinet hesitations, but the continual delays added up to another act of deference to US concerns. This action, however, must be attributed to Cabinet and not to Pearson who, at this time, was very much influenced by what he perceived as an opportunity for peaceful co-existence. Pearson's experience in Colombo also had an impact on other issues, particularly on the question of support for the French in Vietnam.

Vietnam

The French government continued to reassert its former colonial prerogatives in Vietnam immediately after the war, with the blessing and support of the British government, which attempted to do the same in its former colonies. This had forced Ho Chi Minh to abandon Hanoi and Vietnam's provincial capitals.[43] Yet, from bases in the rural areas the Viet Minh forces waged guerrilla warfare in 1947-48, continuing the struggle for Vietnamese independence. During this period they were largely on their own, the Soviet Union being preoccupied with Europe, and the communists in China fully engaged in their own civil war. With little support from these potential allies, and cut off from urban supply lines, the Viet Minh reached out to Asian neighbours and even to the United States for support. As early as 1946, Nehru had been in direct contact with Ho Chi Minh, expressing a desire for close ties between Vietnam and India.[44] In April 1947, Gandhi stated that he was in full sympathy with Vietnam in its quest for independence. For a period, governments in Indonesia, Burma, and even Thailand offered at least moral support for the Viet Minh government. Democratic Republic of Vietnam (DRV) representatives participated actively in the anti-colonial 1947 Asian Relations Conference in New Delhi as well as in the Southeast Asia League organized in Bangkok the same year. Herein we find the postwar origins of the incipient Non-Aligned Movement that would come to play an important international role. The immediate upshot of these deliberations, however, was that an official DRV mission was established in Bangkok, where the Vietnam News Service produced weekly reports on the situation in Vietnam. Later, a mission in Rangoon, Burma, became the main liaison centre for the DRV. The Viet Minh government also tried to develop ties with the Chinese Nationalist government in Nanjing with little success.

One of the most significant aims of this DRV outreach was to obtain arms with which to fight the French forces in Vietnam. The DRV sent Pham Ngo Thach to Bangkok to meet with US representatives, and it offered major concessions to US businesses in return for US recognition. From Washington, Secretary of State Marshall attempted to learn more about Ho and the Viet Minh, requesting reports from US missions abroad. According to the American consul in Saigon, the Vietnamese people were not ready for self-government: they were not "particularly industrious," nor were they known for their "honesty, loyalty or veracity."[45] They were thus susceptible to domination by a Ho-led government and by Soviet leaders whose manipulation appeared to be by "remote control rather than one of open support." Reports came not only from the region but also from the US ambassador in France, who was categorical in his assessment that the Vietnamese people lacked democratic traditions and were therefore susceptible to manipulation.

The US government, while remaining critical of French colonial administration, made its fateful choice in September 1948. After reviewing its policy options, the State Department concluded: "We have not urged the French to negotiate directly with Ho Chi Minh, even though he probably is now supported by a considerable majority of the Vietnamese people, because of his record as a communist and the communist background of many of the influential figures in and about his government."[46] In other words, regardless of what the Vietnamese people thought, the US government knew what was in their best interests. Colonized peoples could exercise a right to self-determination only in so far as they repudiated any affinity with the Soviet Union. On the one hand, this reflected the geo-strategic orientation of the US government; on the other hand, it also reflected the persistence of a racialized view of Asian peoples as being incapable of deciding what was in their own best interests. According to George Kennan, those who had turned to socialism were "racially and socially embittered against the West."[47]

In the face of the US refusal to afford any support, Ho Chi Minh had turned increasingly to the Chinese communists for assistance, particularly after their victory in the Chinese civil war in 1949. In December 1949, Mao had left Beijing for Moscow for talks with Stalin. On 14 January 1950, the Viet Minh declared themselves the sole government of Vietnam, and, four days later, the government of the newly founded PRC offered them recognition.[48] A few days later, after walking for seventeen days to reach China, Ho arrived in Beijing for talks with Liu Shaoqi and military staff. He then received Stalin's agreement that he travel to Moscow for talks: on 3 February, Ho left for Moscow with Zhou Enlai.

Ho's experience in Moscow reveals that American officials were not alone in their racialized views. While attending the signing ceremonies for the Sino-Soviet friendship treaty, Ho suggested to Stalin that he consider signing a similar treaty with Vietnam. When Stalin demurred, citing the informal nature of Ho's visit, Ho suggested that he take a helicopter ride and return on a formal visit. At which point, Stalin barked: "Oh, you Orientals. You have such rich imaginations."[49] Nevertheless, Ho did manage to obtain Soviet recognition of the Viet Minh government and promises of assistance. Stalin told Ho, however, that China would be its main benefactor.[50] As in the case of Korea, Stalin hoped to put China on the spot so that the Soviet Union could focus on Eastern Europe. In this preoccupation with Europe, Soviet and Euro-American foreign policies converged. Faced with a growing insurgency, the French government, for its part, finally decided to go through the motions of according some autonomy to Vietnam. In March 1949, the Elysee Agreement gave Vietnam the status of an "associated state" within the French union. Bao Dai, the former emperor, was appointed head of state.

The escalation of violence in Vietnam in the late 1940s finally caught the attention of the international community, including the Canadian government. Within the DEA, Arthur Menzies attempted to argue that the French might have been making the same mistake as the Dutch in Indonesia when they refused to negotiate with Sukarno.[51] However, with no personnel on the ground in Southeast Asia, the Canadian government turned to its ambassador to France, Georges Vanier, for information regarding Vietnam. Vanier disagreed with Menzies, arguing in January 1949 that the former Emperor Bao Dai was the "only political figure with whom the French could negotiate."[52] Such negotiations would not be easy "since one of the negotiating parties was Oriental" and could not lose face. Nor, stated Vanier, could the French afford to "lower their prestige." At the end of August, the French government informed its Canadian counterpart that it had formally established direct relations with Bao Dai and hoped for Canadian support. The government shuffled off a non-reply, reflecting the ongoing struggle within Canadian officialdom. In the meantime, the French continued to press for Canadian recognition of Bao Dai, as did Georges Vanier, who advised that granting recognition would encourage France to grant further concessions but, more important, it would help the French government in its quest for funds from "a US military aid bill." In other words, recognition would help the French obtain more arms and weapons to kill Vietnamese nationalists. The debate continued within the DEA after the PRC and the Soviet Union recognized the Viet Minh government in January 1950. At the time, argued Charles Ritchie, there was little legal basis for bestowing recognition on Bao Dai. Vietnam was still not an independent state, and Bao Dai did not have effective control. However, more important were the political considerations. Lester Pearson had learned at the Colombo Commonwealth leaders' conference in January that India's prime minister, Jawaharlal Nehru, refused to recognize Bao Dai and had been scathing in his indictment of the French government for its recolonization attempt. Given that the French government was refusing to relinquish control of its colonial outpost Pondicherry in India, Nehru's attitude was hardly surprising. Pearson at this point was unwilling to split with India on this question.

The French government formally requested that the Canadian government recognize its newly formed "Associated States" on 3 February 1950. In a memorandum to Cabinet on the matter of recognition, the DEA pointed out that the main reason for supporting recognition was *political,* that is, it was the need to support the French government against communist threats both within France and in Southeast Asia.[53] Against recognition was the fact that Vietnam did not fulfill the legal requirements for recognition of a state. France retained a large measure of control over "foreign affairs, defence and finance" and, moreover, Bao Dai had only limited control over small parts of Vietnam, while "Ho Chi Minh, on the other hand, control[led] a large area and for the present appear[ed] to have the acquiescence of a considerable portion of the inhabitants of th[at] area." Furthermore, given opposition to the Bao Dai government on the part of Asian countries such as India, Canadian recognition would "result in an undesirable 'white versus Asiatic' alignment within the Commonwealth" on this issue. Given little Canadian direct interests in Indochina, there was not the "political necessity" to focus on recognition and, furthermore, withholding recognition might pressure the French government into transferring effective power to Bao Dai. In order to preempt any negative effects on the anti-communist united front, however, the memorandum further recommended that, in the House of Commons, Pearson make a "brief and sympathetic reference" to the Associated States as part of the French Union.[54] He did so on 22 February 1950.[55] The next day, Cabinet rejected extending recognition to the Associated States.[56] Was the government misleading Parliament in saying one thing and doing (or in this case, not doing) another?

At this point, Pearson's inclination was to follow the lead of the Asian states in the Commonwealth on this question, but for political reasons he felt it necessary to reinforce the government's anti-communist credentials to appease both the Conservatives and their allies to the south. Thus the parliamentary double-speak. However, Pearson was not able to develop a coherent rationale for peaceful co-existence upon which to articulate an alternative to a simplistic and bellicose anti-communism. This was, in large part, because of his own tendency to embrace anti-communism whenever it seemed to serve his interests. His fear of a possible "white versus Asiatic" alignment in the Commonwealth deserves close scrutiny. It suggests that Pearson was aware not only of the upsurge in pan-Asian solidarity against colonialism but also of the fact that, in Canada, overt, state-sponsored discrimination against peoples of Asian descent was no longer politically viable. Consequently, officials perceived a danger that developing nations would associate racism with imperialism and that this would eliminate "Western" influence with the emerging Non-Aligned Movement. This new appreciation added an additional veneer of equality to diplomatic machinations, but the earlier layers of racism had not been directly repudiated and would resurface in new forms at important moments. The race card was only one element in what was essentially a contested view of the future.

Pearson and many in the Euro-American coalition believed in a modernist approach to development, in which capitalism and electoralism were the linchpins of democracy. From the perspective of many in Asia, however, other aspects of modernity – empires and racism – were just as real and, at that particular historical moment, socialism and communism appeared to offer a possible alternative. Pearson was not unaware of these dynamics, but he was also acutely aware of expectations in other quarters. Thus, on the one hand, the Canadian government withheld support from Bao Dai, while, on the other, it provided armaments to the French government – armaments that were being funnelled to French forces in Vietnam, where the fighting was becoming intense and brutal. As one Vietnamese soldier recalled when describing his first encounter with napalm: "An intense flame which seems to spread for hundreds of meters, sows terror in the ranks of the fighters. It is napalm, the fire which falls from the sky."[57] The fire from the sky was falling not only in Vietnam but also in Korea, the first testing ground for this weapon of terror.

10 America's Prestige, Korea's War

On 25 June 1950, North Korean forces crossed the border in a military offensive to take Seoul. The Truman administration responded quickly and aggressively, sending in air and naval support and, shortly afterwards, ground forces to resist the attack from the north. It also called on the United Nations to intervene. At the time, many believed in the existence of a Soviet conspiracy to take over the world. The banner headlines in the *Globe and Mail*, "UN Declare Reds Guilty, WAR IN KOREA" appealed to an imagined "war against communism." The news article informed readers that the US Department of Defense was scanning secret reports for "any indications that the Russian Army or Air Force might choose this time to come into the open."[1] The following day, Anthony Leviero of the *New York Times* reported in the *Globe and Mail:* "President Truman warned Russia and her satellites today that the United States took a very serious view of the act of aggression in Korea." Although not named in the statement, "officials made it clear they [held] the Soviet Union responsible as the motivating power behind the North Korea government."[2]

The UN Security Council, acting on a request from the US administration, met at 2:00 PM on 25 June and concluded, without hearing from any Korean representatives, that the attack was an act of North Korean aggression and a clear breach of the peace.[3] The Soviet Union, boycotting the Security Council because of UN refusal to allow Chinese representatives a seat in the United Nations, was absent, and Yugoslavia abstained. Two days after the outbreak of hostilities, the *Globe and Mail* published an editorial on the conflict: "Clearly it is Soviet Communist imperialism that is waging war on the Republic of Korea and, according to late messages, waging it with marked success. It is just as clear that this aggressive action is a challenge and a test for the West. For historians writing a dozen years hence it may be plain that the real beginning of the Third World War was this attack, just as Mussolini's unchecked invasion of Abyssinia in 1935 was the real beginning of the second."[4] The *Vancouver Sun* provided its own backgrounder: "Russia is supporting Northern Korea, a Communist puppet state which attacked American-supported Southern Korea before dawn Sunday in an attempt to win control of the whole country ... Under American sponsorship, the (South) Korean Republic was proclaimed August 15, 1948, with Syngman Rhee as president. The United States turned over the reins of government to the new republic."

On the fiftieth anniversary of the war, Canada's *Maclean's* magazine projected its assessment of that conflict: "The Korean conflict was largely a product of Cold War tensions. It began when the Communist North invaded the newly democratic South in late June, 1950. That violated the UN sanctioned division of the Korean peninsula at the 38th parallel where Soviet and US forces had met in August, 1945, after defeating the Japanese forces."[5] In a more subtle but similar vein, one Canadian historian concluded that "Korea constituted the first effort by a Communist state to take control of a non-Communist neighbour, against the will of its people, by force of arms. The UN stopped that effort cold and held the line. Korea never became the Munich of the Cold War. In a very real sense, the first real victory of the West in the Cold War was won in the bloody hills of central Korea, and 516 Canadians paid the ultimate price for that victory."[6] These recent views and those of fifty years ago are hauntingly similar. It would seem that all was clear then and all is clear now. No ambiguity and not much new to be learned, according to some scholars and media outlets. Such an approach reflects the power of conventional memory-making and the fact that, far from being over, the Cold War lingers on, bolstered by the self-righteousness of nationalist historiography. Recent scholarship on the war, including recent critical perspectives on US foreign policy, post-Soviet analyses from the former communist bloc and China, as well as emerging critical perspectives from democratized South Korea, reveals a different past and helps explain why Korea, of all places, became the killing field that changed the world.

The Origins of War: Korea

Today, we are much better placed to understand the origins of the war. It is not a simple story – in fact, its complexity is daunting. It requires an understanding not only of the domestic circumstances within Korea but also of Chinese, Soviet, and American foreign policy. Luckily, much more evidence has been gathered from Soviet and Chinese sources, and this has shed substantial, if not definitive, light on the origins of the war.[7] Although the interpretations of these materials differ, there seems to be an agreement on certain facts regarding the decisions for war taken by both sides.

The first salient point is that Kim Il Sung, a fervent nationalist and communist, was as determined as was Syngman Rhee to unify the Korean peninsula. However, it was Kim and the Korean Workers Party who conceived of and carried out the attack across the 38th parallel. He was no puppet, however, and the regime that arose in the north of Korea after 1945 had a strong base of popular support. Hints of this were even found in Canadian reports of the time. Writing in *Maclean's*, Blair Fraser suggested that, while both north and south had committed atrocities, in terms of popular support, the "Communist Government of North Korea actually seem[ed] to have done a better job than the so-called democracy in the south."[8] It had brought in land reform, whereas in South Korea "land reform was consistently sabotaged by the Syngman Rhee government right up to the outbreak of the war." However, Kim was not acting alone when he decided to attack the south. Indeed, he had overt support from the Soviet Union, the original occupying power in the north, as well as tacit support from the new Chinese republic. That there were bonds of solidarity between the CCP and the Korean Workers Party is not surprising, given that many Korean resistance fighters had found refuge in China during the long struggle against Japanese colonialism. There had also been, however, very serious internal battles and defeats at the hand of the Japanese forces – so serious that Kim and a number of other partisans in 1941 shifted their base of operations to the Soviet Union, which, as a neutral state in the war with Japan, offered greater protection from Japanese attacks.[9]

Kim persistently requested Stalin's support to reunify the peninsula by force, including during a visit to Moscow in March 1949. Stalin initially refused to support Kim's plan. In the meantime, the Korean Workers Party developed ties with the CCP, and, in January 1949, after a meeting between the two parties in Harbin, twenty-eight thousand troops of Korean descent repatriated to North Korea.[10] In May, Kim Il Sung met with Mao Zedong in

Beijing, at which time Mao agreed that further troops of Korean ethnicity could repatriate to North Korea, and this was repeated in January 1950; this time Mao approved the sending of arms with the troops.[11] These exchanges reflected historical ties between Korean and Chinese independence fighters, but they did not indicate any specific plan for an attempt at forced reunification. However, globally significant developments, including the ascent to power of the CCP in 1949 and the Soviet testing of an atomic bomb, signalled a shift in the balance of forces, particularly on the Eurasian continent. Three critical Sino-Soviet summit meetings occurred between November 1949 and 17 February 1950, at which time the two countries concluded an alliance, the Soviet Union returning concessions it had been granted at Yalta and also providing economic credits for Chinese development.[12] These negotiations had been difficult, and, in the midst of the talks, Kim Il Sung again wired Stalin, requesting permission to see him to discuss a northern offensive to reunite the peninsula. Stalin mentioned this to Mao, who, according to Shi Zhe, his interpreter, indicated that both the Soviet Union and China should help Kim but that the situation was complicated.[13] Mao left the Soviet Union on 17 February, three days after the announcement of the Sino-Soviet alliance. Kim Il Sung travelled to Moscow and met with Stalin, probably in late February, at which time Stalin appeared to give the green light to a northern offensive but cautioned Kim that Soviet troops would not become involved in any fighting. He also told Kim that he had to obtain the support of China before precipitating any action. Kim travelled to Beijing in May 1950, at which time he met with Mao. Startled by Kim's news that Stalin had agreed to the plan, Mao declined to take Kim's news at face value and wired Stalin for confirmation. Stalin informed Mao that he had agreed, but only on condition that the CCP also agree. What emerged from the Mao-Kim talks was an agreement in principle for the attack to proceed, but Mao wanted a friendship treaty with North Korea first. Details of the planned attack were not discussed nor does it appear that there was any agreement regarding specific aid that China might provide. In June, the CCP cancelled the planned demobilization of 1 million Chinese troops. However, no concrete measures were taken militarily until after Kim initiated hostilities on 25 June. These events have led Chen Jian to conclude that the "Korean War was in the first place the North Korean Communist leader Kim Il Sung's war. The war's peninsula origin [was] as important as its international origin."[14] Kim Il-sung and the north initiated the armed offensive, crossing the 38th parallel to try and unify the peninsula. Yet, this was not the action of a puppet government acting under the instruction of some

Soviet directive but, rather, one by a determined and popular Korean regime that was able to convince Stalin and the Soviet leadership of the viability of such a plan. Changed world circumstances suggested to Stalin that there was little risk in agreeing to the plan, but he also limited Soviet exposure by making it clear that, if the plan failed, the Soviet Union would not intervene on behalf of Kim. Stalin further limited Soviet responsibility by insisting that Kim obtain the support of the new Chinese government. This interpretation is further bolstered by Korean historians, who perceive the conflict mainly as an extension of a civil conflict that had begun after liberation and entered an armed phase in 1948, with the Cheju and Yeosu rebellions of that year.[15] Hoping to regain control over Taiwan, the Chinese communists perceived Kim's gambit as a vehicle for weakening US influence on the Asian continent, thus paving the way for a military offensive against the remnants of Chiang's army. The desire and the decision to go to war was, in the final analysis, Kim's. Neither he nor Singman Rhee recognized the legitimacy of the division of Korea. The fact the United States, with the support of Canada and other allies, manipulated the United Nations to create a separate state in the south of Korea was not seen as a legitimate exercise of international authority. The decision on the part of the Chinese and Soviet leadership to provide support for Kim's plans was also related to developments in the United States, in particular to an intense debate taking place in the highest echelons of government policy making. This debate, only partially open, ended up sending mixed signals about US intentions – signals that were misinterpreted by Lester Pearson as well as by Kim Il Sung, Stalin, and Mao.

The Origins of War: US

By 1949 decolonization movements in East Asia, often under the leadership of communists, were posing new challenges for the US government's policy of "containment" as articulated by George Kennan and elaborated in a host of anti-Soviet policies. Many of these policies stemmed from strategic economic and political considerations related to expanding global capitalism under US leadership. Often they found their ideological roots in the classical anti-communism that evolved in antipathy to the Russian Revolution in 1917. This had been pushed to the background by the wartime alliance with the Soviet Union but quickly re-emerged as the postwar clash to define spheres of influence gained momentum. Europe was seen as the strategic nexus, and the US government had agreed to intervene there through the Marshall Plan and by joining in the creation of NATO. Canadian and US military plans based their operational preparations on the view that the

Soviet Union was seriously considering invading Europe, although such a scenario was not perceived as imminent. In 1949, however, serious disagreements arose within US policy-making circles regarding how best to confront the Soviet Union, how to deal with emerging movements for decolonization, and how to characterize the relationship between nationalism and communism. This debate had many dimensions, but its focus was on the "loss" of China, that is, the defeat of the US- and Canadian-backed forces of Chiang at the hands of the communist-led forces of Mao in 1949. The outcome of the debate was a major policy development centred in the brokering of what became known as National Security Council Paper No. 68 (NSC-68). The adoption of this policy represented the ascent of aggressive US military expansion and was the culmination of complex policy debates among various bureaucratic factions in the US government, including the State Department, the Department of Defense, the Joint Chiefs of Staff, up to the president himself. At issue were the respective roles of conventional and nuclear weapons, Asian nationalism, China and Taiwan, and military aid for Korea. The process was heavily influenced by the public debates regarding the "loss of China," pressure from the pro-Taiwan lobby in the United States, and by the rise of McCarthyism and anti-communist hysteria, which came to affect so many, including those in Chinese communities.[16]

Initially, Dean Acheson and the State Department triumphed in the debate, and it appeared the United States would refuse to back Chiang on Taiwan. To reinforce this position, Acheson scheduled a presidential press conference for 5 January 1950. Truman backed Acheson to the hilt at the press conference, but this only precipitated further backlash. William F. Knowland initiated a five-hour debate in the Senate in which he stole a march on Senator Joseph McCarthy by accusing a small group of men in the Far Eastern Division of the State Department of being responsible for the China "disaster."[17] That same day, Acheson made a major speech at the National Press Club on US foreign policy in Asia. He analyzed in some detail the emerging Asian landscape and suggested that nationalism was on the rise across the area and that, if people failed to understand what happened in China, it was because of their "failure to understand this basic revolutionary force which is loose in Asia."[18] Acheson went on to assert that, although the "military menace" was not immediate, the United States did have a military policy and that it ascribed a US "defensive perimeter" descending from the Aleutians, to Japan, through the Ryukyu Islands (Okinawa), to the Philippines. Acheson was faithfully reflecting the US military's strategic view. Interestingly, after he finished his speech, he was specifically asked by reporters about the defence of Korea, a question which he declined to answer, suggesting that it should be redirected to the Department of Defense.[19] In response to a question on Taiwan, Acheson reiterated his view that he wanted the Chinese people to see what the Russians were doing in China and not to deflect their attention "to some silly adventure which some people in [that] country [were] urging."[20] Press reports were generally favourable towards Acheson's speech, but this only fanned the flames, and, on 19 January, the House of Representatives defeated a $60 million aid package for Korea. It was out of the frying pan into the fire. Shortly afterwards, on 31 January, Truman ordered a review of national security policy under the aegis of both departments – defence and state – hoping that the joint project would help reconcile the warring factions.

Directed by Paul Nitze, the new chief of the Policy Planning Staff and advocate of expanding conventional military forces, the policy study that would become NSC-68, the basis for imperial over-reach and for what many US scholars have referred to as the "national security state,"[21] got under way. However, key to the adoption of the new policy was winning over Acheson and others who were reluctant to promote military options over diplomacy. At this critical juncture, other actors also appeared on stage. On 9 February 1950, Senator McCarthy picked up where Knowland had left off in his speech in the Senate. Addressing a Lincoln Day dinner of the Ohio County Women's Republican Club in Wheeling, West Virginia, McCarthy told the audience that he held in his hand a list of 205 communists in the State Department.[22] Among those publicly vilified by McCarthy were Owen Lattimore, Philip Jessup, and John Carter Vincent, all, in one sense or another, China experts who had worked with the State Department. Meanwhile, Alger Hiss, accused and tried on charges of disloyalty and spying for the Soviet Union, was convicted on a lesser count of perjury. In this same intense period, the Chinese government's campaign against US policy intensified in retaliation for US lack of recognition of the new regime. These events, and especially the continuous attacks against the State Department, put Acheson on the defensive. As Nitze worked on what would become NSC-68, Acheson moved to rebuild his bridges with conservatives.[23] He replaced a number of his key officials, and, in early April, Acheson recommended to Truman that John Foster Dulles, a Republican lawyer, be appointed as a consultant to the State Department to handle peace treaty talks with Japan.

On 14 April, Truman submitted NSC-68 to the National Security Council for approval and subsequently gave it the go ahead in May.[24] In it, Nitze imagined a world situation in which the Soviet Union, "unlike previous aspirants to hegemony, [was] animated by a new fanatic faith, antithetical to our own, and [sought] to impose its absolute authority over the rest of the world."[25] NSC-68 suggested that "any substantial further extension of the area under the domination of the Kremlin" would render allied resistance inadequate and that the United States now stood in its "deepest peril." The fate of not only the United States but of "civilization itself" was at stake. The solution was to rapidly increase the strength of the "free world" and to adopt a policy to "check and roll back the Kremlin's drive for world domination." The "comprehensive and decisive program" it envisaged was expected to involve:

> (1) The development of an adequate political and economic framework for the achievement of our long-range objectives.
> (2) A substantial increase in expenditures for military purposes ...
> (3) A substantial increase in military assistance programs ...
> (4) Some increase in economic assistance programs and recognition of the need to continue these programs until their purposes have been accomplished.
> (5) A concerted attack on the problem of the United States balance of payments ...
> (6) Development of programs designed to build and maintain confidence among other peoples in our strength and resolution, and to wage overt psychological warfare designed to encourage mass defections from Soviet allegiance and to frustrate the Kremlin design in other ways.
> (7) Intensification of affirmative and timely measures and operations by covert means in the fields of economic warfare and political and psychological warfare with a view to fomenting and supporting unrest and revolt in selected strategic satellite countries.
> (8) Development of internal security and civilian defense programs.
> (9) Improvement and intensification of intelligence activities.
> (10) Reduction of Federal expenditures for purposes other than defense and foreign assistance, if necessary by the deferment of certain desirable programs.
> (11) Increased taxes.[26]

In some ways, as Melvyn Leffler has argued, NSC-68 was not a radical departure from previous positions. What was different was its ideological tone, the preponderance given to military means, and its advocacy of major budget increases. These were more than nuances, they represented Nitze's belief that the United States needed to be much more aggressive in expanding its influence and his willingness to defy the administration's existing budgetary priorities in order to provide resources to the military. At the time, few would take issue with NSC-68 – certainly not Acheson, who was now aggressively seeking Republican support and displaying a renewed willingness to adapt to the changed circumstances. Still, few were willing to go to bat for its financial implementation.[27] NSC-68 was, as American historian Walter LaFeber put it, a policy in search of an opportunity. And that opportunity was not long in coming. Acheson and his aides later stated: "Korea came along and saved us."[28]

Pearson, Canada, and the Korean War

Lester Pearson recounted in his memoirs: "[At] almost the exact time on 26 June when President Truman was deciding that the United States would be giving air and sea support to the South Koreans, I was talking to some press people in Ottawa and telling them, off the record, that I did not expect a US military response to the invasion."[29] Pearson did not expect a response because neither he nor DEA officials were privy to NSC-68 and were relying on earlier analyses regarding US policy. In that regard, the Canadian ambassador to Washington reported fully on Acheson's National Press Club speech, noting that it emphasized the dynamics of Asian nationalism and that US policy, particularly in South Asia and Southeast Asia, would be one of "friendly and helpful non-intervention."[30] The report emphasized how Acheson had cast communism "against the revolutionary nationalism of the area as the new imperialism" and that it "would be folly, through ill-conceived adventures (in Formosa) to obscure the reality of this fact."[31] With regard to the defensive perimeter, the Canadian ambassador noted only that it was the first time the US government had suggested it might put Okinawa under a UN trusteeship. The Canadian report interpreted Acheson's message as one that emphasized non-intervention in China and Southeast Asia while defining a clear military perimeter. Such a policy would turn the forces of nationalism against Soviet imperialism and not jeopardize US influence by unwarranted intervention. The Canadian ambassador suggested that

Privates A.F. Proulx and J.M. Aubin of the Royal 22e Regiment (anglicized as the Van Doos) on patrol in Korea, December 1952. | Marwick, photographer, Canada, Department of National Defence / Library and Archives Canada, PA-166881

Acheson's speech and the press coverage that followed might help pave the way to recognition of the new Chinese regime.[32] Thus, in June, Pearson and the DEA officials continued to believe that Korea was not included within the US "defense perimeter."

Thus, it was not surprising that Pearson was also unhappy about Truman's 27 June statement committing air and sea forces in Korea and directing the US 7th Fleet to intervene in the Taiwan straits.[33] Pearson was not "so much concerned about the wisdom or unwisdom of such intervention as about the way in which it might be brought about."[34] As described earlier, Pearson had long conceded to the US administration leadership in Asian affairs, and thus he was willing to follow Truman's lead regarding military intervention in Korea.[35] His concern about the way in which armed intervention might take place related to the fact that Truman had committed his forces without first consulting with other Cold War allies or bringing the issue to the United

Fishermen captured by the HMCS *Nootka* off the west coast of Korea, 13 May 1951 | Canada, Department of National Defence / Library and Archives Canada, PA-151996

Nations. It was maintaining the imperial coalition, and providing a legal justification for intervention, not the nature of the war that concerned Pearson. In other words, he saw the specific conflict in Korea as subordinate to maintaining an alliance against perceived Soviet aggression. The immediate repercussion of this attitude, however, was that Pearson also rendered Korea invisible except as a battlefield in the Cold War, and, ironically, he also limited his own ability to understand what was happening in the United States. Further complicating the picture was the reluctance of Canada's prime minister to lend military support for the venture.[36]

Under Pearson's leadership, however, the Canadian Cabinet came on side despite initial reservations, particularly about sending ground troops. Canadian military participation in the war began in July with the assignment of three Canadian destroyers, HMCS *Cayuga,* HMCS *Athabaskan,* and HMCS *Sioux* to naval operations off the coast of Korea. Shortly afterwards, the government ordered the Air Force's 426 "Thunderbird" transport squadron to participate in air lift operations out of McChord Air Force base in the United States. After considerable hesitation, the government finally created the 25th Infantry Brigade as a special unit to serve in Korea. According to government statistics, 26,791 troops (the third largest contingent) served under UN Command, suffering 516 fatalities.[37] The Canadian government's actions found broad support within Canadian society, including not only the media but also the Chinese community, the social-democratic CCF, and the labour movement. In Chinese communities, where many organizations were led by pro-Guomindang representatives, there was strong antagonism towards the new Chinese regime.[38] Support for Taiwan predisposed many in the communities to uphold Canadian participation in the war.

Canada's two national labour federations issued a joint statement on 10 August 1950, calling for "full support" for the UN Security Council in its attempt to counter the attack from North Korea and to "re-establish peace and democratic government in Korea."[39] The statement called on the affiliates of the federations to provide unqualified support for the war effort: "As is now well known, the armies of Stalin's puppet government of North Korea invaded South Korea on June 25th, after having resisted all efforts of the United Nations to re-unite Korea under stable democratic government." Shortly afterwards, delegates to one of the labour federations, the Trades and Labour Congress, gathered at the Mount Royal Hotel in Montreal from 11 to 16 September 1950 for the union's sixty-fifth convention. Invited to address the convention, the Liberal minister of labour, Milton Gregg, stated: "Korea is a cross-roads in human affairs. Korea today; Indo-China or Malaya or Iraq, or Europe tomorrow – anywhere they can get a foothold, with satellite armies preferred, until they consider the timing opportune to commit their own forces in a more ambitious timetable."[40] Percy Bengough, president of the Trades and Labour Council, did not mince words in his opening address: "We are fighting Stalin's Russian Soviet dictatorship in South Korea. We must fight its willing dupes right here at home, and most particularly, it is our job to expose them and destroy their influence inside our own trade unions."[41] The Cold War international labour federation, to which Canadian unions were affiliated, the International Confederation of Free Trade Unions (ICFTU), reacted swiftly to the war in Korea, characterizing it as a "flagrant and unprovoked armed attack launched by Communist forces on Southern Korea ... This is clearly the latest move in a systematic plan for enlarging – by armed force, if necessary – the totalitarian sphere of influence."[42] In September, the ICFTU circulated millions of copies of an open letter to unionists throughout the world, stating: "The last war was started by Hitler, and the present Communist aggression in Korea was unleashed on the direct instructions of Moscow. Hundreds of Russian tanks were waiting in North Korea, together with over 100,000 fully equipped and well-trained troops, ready for the invasion of the south, which was unprepared even to defend itself, let alone attack."[43]

There was dissent. Within Parliament, a number of Québécois representatives, including Jean-Francois Pouliot, Raoul Poulin, and Paul Gagnon, delivered a subtle and perceptive critique that, as we shall see, turned out to be on the mark.[44] Pierre Elliott Trudeau, then working in the Privy Council Office and later to succeed Lester Pearson as Canadian prime minister, argued against participation in the war. In hearing Pearson announce Canadian participation in the war, Trudeau wrote: "I've just heard Pearson's speech on Korea in the House. Not a single original thought."[45] The Canadian Peace Congress, led by the resolute and provocative James Endicott, suggested that it was South Korea that started the war. Although not everyone believed this, there remained a relatively active current of antipathy to the war within organizations such as the Women's International League for Peace and Freedom and local peace groups working to bring about a ceasefire.[46]

Border Crossings

The Korean War went through a number of phases in the first seven months: the initial North Korean offensive driving US/Republic of Korea (ROK) forces down to the Pusan region; the US/UN counter-offensive, including the landing at Inchon on 15 September 1950; the crossing of the 38th parallel in early October and the march north to the Yalu; the three Chinese offensives of 25 October, 25 November, and 31 December that brought the Chinese/North Korean forces to the 38th parallel and then across to capture Seoul on 4 January 1951; and the US/UN counter-offensive in late January, which basically brought the conflict to a stalemate around the 38th parallel, an imaginary line conceived originally as a divider for different armies accepting the Japanese surrender. Northern Korean forces had initially been very successful in pushing through to Seoul, and there is some evidence to suggest that they hoped at that point to negotiate, using their battlefield gains as a bargaining chip for a deal to reunite the country. In any case, the decision on the part of the United States to intervene with reinforcements meant the battle was joined. Still, by August the US/UN forces had been pushed down the peninsula to a small perimeter around Pusan. The limited support offered by the Soviet Union meant that US forces dominated the seas and air and, with supply lines stretched, the northern Korean forces were unable to press home their offensive. In the meantime, MacArthur planned a comeback.

MacArthur launched his military counter-offensive with a naval landing at Inchon behind North Korean lines, successfully dividing North Korean forces and allowing the US/UN forces to sweep back up the peninsula and capture Seoul. But the offensive did not end there. Instead, MacArthur, with Truman's blessing, made the decision to cross the 38th parallel and to destroy the DPRK, a measure that was endorsed by the UN General Assembly despite opposition from countries such as India.[47] Even before this, South Korean troops crossed the 38th parallel on 30 September, followed by UN troops on 7 October. In the heat of a bitter conflict, the decision to move north reflected a determination to try, through the use of force, to resolve the Korean division once and for all. This was exactly the rationale of the North Korean regime three months earlier. The difference was that the Koreans had acted mainly on their own, while the counter-offensive to destroy the DPRK was undertaken by a UN force led by the most powerful state on earth, the United States. The US military presence 8,000 kilometres from home, and its intervention in support of Chiang Kai-shek during and after the Chinese civil war, prompted the newly established Chinese government in Beijing to issue repeated warnings that China would intervene if US troops crossed into North Korea. Although not consulted about battle plans by Kim's forces before the invasion, the CCP monitored the situation carefully and, in August, had bolstered its forces in the China-Korea border area. On 17 September, two days after the Inchon landing, China sent five representatives into Korea for first-hand observations.[48] After ROK troops crossed the 38th parallel, Mao issued provisional orders that the Chinese "volunteer" force be prepared to cross the Yalu River into Korea by 15 October. On 8 October, after US troops crossed the demarcation line, Chinese troops were given orders to cross into Korea. The Chinese troops first encountered South Korean troops in late October, but after an initial clash they retreated, hoping to entice the enemy into their embrace. When MacArthur launched his final offensive on 24 November, the Chinese/northern forces struck back en masse, forcing the US/UN forces into an all-out retreat. MacArthur's promise to Truman that his troops would be home by Christmas now appeared a pipe dream. Canadian troops – troops that MacArthur had first thought would not be necessary – were now rushed into combat. As the Chinese/northern forces headed south, the Korean War had become not only a military but also a political crisis.

US coalition partners, including Canada, were extremely worried about the escalation of the war because, as US/UN forces lost ground, aggressive counter-measures, including the bombing of China and the possible use of the atomic bomb, were being contemplated. Such possibilities raised the issue of the reliability of commanders in the field and how much autonomy they had – or might assume – in making decisions that could widen the war. The question of autonomy of field command and overflights into China had come up earlier in the fall when the Chinese government accused the US forces of invading its air space. Writing from Nanjing in September 1950, Chester Ronning informed Ottawa of these charges and chastised the US administration for refusing to issue UN credentials for representatives of "one fifth of the world's population living in China," saying that this was "rapidly making friends for the USSR."[49] The issue of breaching Chinese air space arose again in a more dramatic manner when Truman, during a press conference on 30 November, responded that the use of nuclear weapons had always been under "active consideration" and that commanders in the field had "charge of the use of weapons," a statement that appeared to contradict the statutory regulation that only the US president himself could order the use of nuclear weapons. The spectre of another atomic holocaust was such that British prime minister Attlee travelled to Washington on 4 December 1950 for consultations with Truman over the use of the bomb and regarding conventional attacks against Chinese territory. Although Truman offered Attlee an oral promise of prior consultation before using the bomb, this was not part of the summit statement. Visiting Ottawa on his way home to London, Attlee assured the Canadian Cabinet that, while there were differences with the Truman administration over China's involvement in the Korean War, the "underlying unity [between the United States and Great Britain] was so great and so fully recognized" that they were able to act jointly.[50] Canadian officials were not so complacent about the risks. The DEA had called for a military appraisal related to possible attacks on China, and the reply was not reassuring. The Joint Planning Committee recommended to the Canadian Chiefs of Staff that UN forces "undertake unlimited tactical air operations without regard for the Manchurian border" but added that strategic bombing would not be necessary so long as the struggle was not prolonged.[51] The Chiefs of Staff advised the DEA that they concurred with the Joint Planning Committee's recommendation, but they also stated unequivocally that a field commander, if in a battle for survival, "must be allowed to use all weapons at his disposal whenever and wherever he sees fit in order to provide the necessary security for the survival of his force."[52] An exasperated Escott Reid wrote on the document: "even if this means precipitating the outbreak of the third world war at a time when there is a good chance of our being beaten!" He suggested that the Chiefs of Staff reread Clausewitz so that they might understand that war is an instrument of policy. What Attlee and the Canadians may or may not have known was that the Central Intelligence Agency (CIA) had already organized clandestine attacks on Chinese territory. Jay Lovestone, a former leader of the American Communist Party who had recanted and become an official of the American Federation of Labor as well as a CIA agent, was running a spy operation on the Chinese mainland in 1950 that, among other things, blew up a Shanghai dock on 8 November 1950.[53] The edge of the abyss was closer than anyone knew.

Imagining a Global Nuclear War

In the early morning of 11 November 1950, a US B-50 bomber ran into engine trouble as it flew from Goose Bay, Labrador, to Tucson, Arizona. Having lost one engine, and with a second starting to backfire, the pilot made the fateful decision that it was necessary to dump its payload in order to successfully land. As the plane dropped earthward, it crossed over the St. Lawrence River not far from Riviérè du Loup in Quebec. Its bombardier set a fuse to its payload and jettisoned it into the St. Lawrence. The bomb contained just under 2,300 kilograms of high explosives that detonated as it hit the river, sending shock waves through the surrounding area.[54] There were political shock waves as well: the jettisoned bomb had been a Mark IV atomic weapon, minus its atomic core.[55] Defence liaison officers in the DEA, in the dark regarding atomic deployment, suggested to their superior that the American ambassador be called onto the carpet and questioned by what authority the US aircraft was carrying "live bombs" over Canadian territory, a practice allowed only with the express permission of Canadian authorities. The aggressive tone soon quieted, however, when it was discovered that, unknown to even the Cabinet, St. Laurent had agreed that atomic weapons be stationed at Goose Bay, Labrador, at the emergency request of the United States Strategic Air Command (SAC) in response to developments in Korea. The request had been made not through diplomatic but through military channels (through Canadian air marshal Curtis) after Truman had requested the transfer of the nuclear bombs, minus their cores, from the US Atomic

Energy Commission.[56] Atomic bombs had earlier been sent to Guam for possible use in Korea, but deployment to both Canada and Great Britain also went ahead, based on the assumption that the Korean War might be the first shot in what would become a general war in which Europe would be the central theatre. Atomic bombs were considered part of the strategic response in the case of war in Europe.

The nuclear accident that occurred over the St. Lawrence River is an example of how tenuous civilian control of military matters can become, particularly in emergencies. Furthermore, there remain unanswered questions. The agreement to station SAC bombers at Goose Bay, armed with nuclear components, was authorized in mid-August when the US/UN forces were being pushed down the Korean peninsula and defeat seemed imminent. But this authorization was only good for six weeks, and inclement weather and lack of facilities meant the nuclear weapons were to be transferred back to the United States in October. How was it that nuclear-equipped bombers were still flying over Canada on 11 November 1950?

The deployment and threat to use nuclear weapons reflected the intersection of strategic responses to perceived Soviet threats and to actual conditions on the ground in Korea. Truman's utterances on 30 November let the cat out of the bag and reflected not only the reality of the nuclear option but also the increasing stress created by the successful Chinese offensive. And as the offensive continued throughout December, tensions continued to mount, provoking a crisis of unprecedented proportions and a deepening pessimism on the part of those involved. The December despondency was captured in a report by Arthur Menzies, who had replaced Herbert Norman as the head of the Canadian mission in Tokyo. Menzies presented his credentials to MacArthur on 14 December, and, after intoning a few lines of introduction, he worried that MacArthur "seemed not to be listening." He went on:

> [This] gave me a sinking feeling, wondering if I should repeat my lines or try to rise to higher peaks of eulogy, but then he stopped reading and, seizing me by the arm, said in a husky voice, 'Now, that is very kind of you to say those things. Sit down, sit down.' And, with that, he slumped into a brown leather-upholstered chair with the sigh of a tired man. He raised a thin long-fingered hand, through whose parchment-coloured skin veins and bones stood out, and ran it over the top of his head, in such a way as not to disarrange the covering hairs. He looked up with a smile and said, 'You know, it's not easy to be a defeated general.'"[57]

MacArthur was "brusque in his dismissal of the South Koreans as useful fighting units," continued Menzies' report, and he had to assign to them American military advisers who would "butter them up" and tell them they were better than they really were. The problem was that these advisors began to feed HQ the same view, but MacArthur believed that "South Koreans could not be relied on."[58] MacArthur also complained that he was not permitted to use the air force to bomb northeast China. He also spoke with feeling about the "devastation in Korea which was now being fought through for the third time. Each side, as it gained the upper hand, was liquidating its enemies and potential enemies."[59] Remarkably, MacArthur was blunt about the importance of Korea. It was, he told Menzies, important as an emblem in order to uphold the morale of the allies, "but in case of general war Korea should be abandoned with problem to be solved by victor in the general war."

As the Chinese and North Korean forces continued towards Seoul in December, the US administration sent a circular document to its embassies in allied countries in which it declared its determination to have the United Nations declare China an aggressor if its troops should cross the 38th parallel. Pearson, informed of this possibility while in Ottawa, began a furious round of discussions at the United Nations to try and avoid such a development. They were unsuccessful. A discouraged Pearson wrote to St. Laurent, confessing that he was coming closer to the tragic conclusion that a "general war is closer than it has been at any time since 1945, and that it [would] now be a miracle if it [could] be averted."[60] The Americans, declared Pearson, were moving towards total preparation for and widespread acceptance of war, while the Chinese were determined to defend their revolution just as the Russians had in 1918-19. Pearson believed that the United States had now committed itself to becoming far stronger than it had ever been in peacetime, but he thought there was still a very good chance that, if "accompanied by wise and unprovocative diplomacy, it [might] prove to be an effective deterrent against war."[61] Enmeshed in negotiations, Pearson noted he was not in much of a Christmas mood and that the situation was "depressing, almost frightening."

There is no question that, early on, Lester Pearson was playing a role of mediator and peacemaker within the United Nations. But a careful examination of the rationale for Pearson's actions, and Escott Reid's for that matter, helps illuminate the understandable but ultimately erroneous assumptions that underpinned them. In response to the crossing of the 38th parallel, the

Chinese army intervened and the successful Chinese/northern counter-offensive precipitated a December crisis in the US/UN countries. This obliged Pearson and Canada's defence minister, Brooke Claxton, to bring the issue before Cabinet, which they did in a joint submission on 28 December 1950.[62] Their top secret memorandum suggested that the danger of general war, previously estimated to arrive in late 1953 or 1954, had already arrived and that "peace [was] now in jeopardy." The two men spelled out the reasons for their strong views and the necessity of avoiding becoming embroiled in a war with Communist China: "In such a war a decision would be almost impossible to secure. Even the atomic bomb would probably not be decisive since suitable targets are few, life is cheap and manpower virtually inexhaustible." Becoming bogged down in such a war, draining resources, would prevent the strategic bolstering of Western Europe, where the "initial Soviet attack would probably be made in the event of a general war."[63] Instructions to the Canadian mission in Tokyo reproduced the strategic outlook that Korean decisions had to reflect "global strategy" and the "present balance of armed forces between Soviet world and democratic world."[64] The relative weakness of the West's armed forces dictated the need to "play for time," to avoid needless confrontation over Korea, and to make strategic decisions based mainly on what was happening in Europe.[65] Even if a general war could be avoided, the ministers informed their Cabinet colleagues, "[the] defeat which the United Nations have suffered in Korea makes more likely Communist attacks on other parts of Asia, the Middle East and Eastern Europe." A full-scale attack on Indochina was an early possibility, and "if Indo-China is lost, the whole of South-East Asia, including Burma, Malaya and Indonesia with their important natural resources, might well fall under Communist control."[66] In this context, proposed the two men, it was essential that non-communist countries be provided with external financial assistance for economic development.

Not only was this analysis an early and clearly articulated version of the "domino theory" that became the justification for US intervention in Vietnam but it was also riddled with stereotypes about Asia and about communism. Caution in going to war in China was based not on the fact that it might be unwarranted but, rather, on the fact that it was a losing proposition: how could one defeat the hordes whose lives meant so little? The priority had to be Europe. These views highlight how stereotypes and Eurocentrism persisted even after the Second World War. Applied to southeast Asia, they rendered Indochina and other Asian countries prey to external aggression, hapless "victims" of an external "other" – Soviet imperialism. These caricatures were related to those that, for similar reasons, were invoked by a number of US officials.[67] Providing imagined justification for Canadian policies, such rationalizations played the additional role of diverting attention from the reality that Canada's ally, France, was waging a bloody war against the Vietnamese independence movement at the very moment that Pearson and Claxton were elaborating on the supposed Soviet threat to Indochina. Pearson's mediation efforts were not simply a question of building bridges: they also reflected a lack of confidence in the US administration's capacity to maintain a strategic perspective in the heat of war. Europe, feared the Canadians, would be sacrificed by expanding the war in Asia to the point that the allies would be unable to mount a successful defence of Europe through NATO. Was this not another phase in the historical role of Canada's acting as a bridge for trans-Atlantic unity?

At the same time, Pearson felt caught between the developing world and its US ally. Pearson was not happy. He lashed out in frustration in late February, asking Hume Wrong to communicate to Dean Rusk that "US Government representatives and officials should stop talking about the armed conflict in the Far East as one against communism." He continued: "It is, of course, not that at all, but armed resistance to aggression." Although Pearson suggested that this was one of the most disturbing features of US policy, he failed to recognize that the ideological approach he espoused on numerous occasions reinforced the US belief that it was waging a just war, regardless of the legal niceties. The inherent contradictions between the imagined and the real meant that consistency was often a rare commodity.

Pearson was not acting alone, nor was he solely responsible for the policies adopted by the Canadian government. Three months after the start of the Korean War, Canada's prime minister, Louis St. Laurent, speaking to the graduating class at the University of Toronto, emphasized the importance of "preserving civilization." At the dawn of the twentieth century, mused St. Laurent, civilization was "advancing steadily over the face of the globe" and only "ignorance and barbarism" stood as obstacles in that path.[68] That "Fascism, Nazism and Communism" arose in the very heart of the civilized world came as a great surprise, he told his young audience, and now the Soviet Union, with its population and resources, was a "menace to civilization." Its theoretical promise of increased material welfare and its propaganda in favour of racial equality constituted a great ideological danger. Armed strength was a necessary deterrent to potential Soviet aggression, St. Laurent claimed, as was aid to the untold millions of the less fortunate, particularly in Asia.[69] "We in the Western world have adopted the conception of good and evil from the Hebrew and Greek civilizations. This concept has been transformed and transmitted to us through our Christian traditions," St. Laurent said. The role of universities was to educate people in that "liberal and humane tradition which is the glory of our Christian civilization."[70] By casting the Christian "West" as the sword bearer of civilization, and communism as a totalitarian and imperialist threat, St. Laurent was creating an essential "them-and-us" scenario in which the US-led coalition represented the forces of light and the communists the forces of darkness. Hence, the masses of Asia required benevolent assistance even if it killed them. In his equating of imperialism with civilization, St. Laurent showed that he was at times blind to the fact that those schooled in the art of anti-imperial resistance – in China, Korea, India, and Indochina as well as many other colonies – had quite a different view of "civilization." For many in Asia "Western civilization" had symbolized an imperial modernity that implied dispossession, poverty, imprisonment, and death.

Faced with the vagaries of US policy, Pearson did criticize his southern ally, but while so doing he continually worked to reinforce Canada's alliance with its imperial partner. In a famous speech to the Canadian Club in April 1951, Pearson suggested that the world was "in arms, and in conflict."[71] There were two sides, "freedom vs. slavery," with the US leading the former and the USSR the latter. In that confrontation, both arms and diplomacy were necessary. "War without warfare" might continue for years: "We are faced now with a situation similar in some respects to that which confronted our fore-fathers in early colonial days when they ploughed the land with a rifle slung on the shoulder. If they stuck to the plough and left the rifle at home, they would have been easy victims for any savages lurking in the woods."[72] That Pearson would make such a public analogy with Canada's indigenous peoples is indicative of the persistence of racism in the 1950s. His sentiments were part of the bond he shared with US officials who often perceived the war in Korea, and later wars in Vietnam, as an extension of the frontier wars to conquer the American West.

Pearson contended that, on strategic issues, Canada must respect US "leadership ... in the conflict against Communist imperialism" and that there would "be times when [Canada] should abandon [its] position if it is more important to maintain unity in the face of the common foe." Speaking to the Sudbury Chamber of Commerce and Kiwanis Club a few days later, Pearson lashed out at the peace movement, targeting in particular the Canadian Peace Congress, which, Pearson told the local blue-chip audience, had become the agent of a "foreign aggressive imperialism."[73] The Peace Congress had been leading a campaign for signatures to the Stockholm Appeal, which called for the total banning of the atomic weapon; establishment of strict international control to ensure the implementation of the ban; and determination that any government that first used the atomic weapon against any country whatsoever would be committing a crime against humanity and should be dealt with as a war criminal. Calling the appeal a "misleading and dishonest" document, Pearson stated that armed aggression alone was a war crime: "A victim is just as dead whether he is killed by a bayonet or an atom bomb. War – aggressive war – is the supreme crime – not the use of any particular weapon."[74] The peace movement's demand for withdrawal of all foreign troops from Korea elicited a sharp retort from Pearson, who, having been involved in the attempts to arrange a ceasefire in the United Nations, concluded that "responsibility for failure rests on the shoulders of those countries who plotted and engineered the aggression in Korea."[75] Pearson concluded that Canada would have to re-arm and that Canadians would have to pay higher taxes, work harder, and forgo some of the luxuries that they had looked forward to. He commended fifty applied science students who attempted to take over a University of Toronto chapter of the Canadian Peace Congress.[76] Pearson's foes in his battle with the peace movement were people such as I.G. Perkins of Donlands United Church in Toronto and the well-known Canadian missionary to China Dr. James Endicott, who was also a former advisor to Chiang Kai-shek (Jiang Jieshi) and sometime agent for the Office of Strategic Services.[77] Endicott, as president of the Peace Congress, actively campaigned for an end to the war and promoted the Stockholm Appeal. Not only Pearson but also the Liberal and Conservative parties of the day denounced the petition, accusing Endicott of being a dupe for the Soviet Union. Even the CCF national council advised its members to avoid becoming involved in the peace movement. Still, thousands refused to be intimidated, including the premier of Saskatchewan, Tommy Douglas.[78] In the face of a decision by the Truman administration to dispatch National Guard units to Japan because of fears of a Soviet invasion, Herbert Norman rebutted the suggestion that the Soviet Union would try to covertly land in Hokkaido, given other "weaker links in our defensive chain than Japan."[79]

The Elusive Armistice

The first attempt at mediation of the Korean conflict failed, and the Chinese and North Korean forces crossed the 38th parallel on 31 December 1950 in what the Chinese military histories refer to as the "third offensive." On 4 January 1951, Seoul once again changed hands. As part of a UN special three-person committee, Pearson helped articulate five principles for a ceasefire. The Chinese government rejected this – a mistake on the part of the communist leadership according to Chinese historian Chen Jian.[80] The US and Canadian administrations were not the only ones making serious mistakes. Mao and the CCP leadership believed that the Chinese/northern forces, with their superior numbers, could push the US/UN troops off the peninsula despite warnings from Peng Dehuai that it was becoming increasingly difficult to maintain any offensive.[81] But Kim Il Sung and other Korean officials insisted on pushing on. Within a week after Zhou Enlai formally rejected the peace initiative, on 17 January the Chinese/northern forces faced a US/UN counter-attack that drove them out of Seoul yet again that April.

At this time, Escott Reid emphasized in a communication with Pearson that the idea of autonomy of command was dangerous not only in general but also in particular. And here he had in mind none other than Douglas MacArthur – "Douglas MacArthur who has proved himself insolent and insubordinate to his own government and to the United Nations and whom we strongly suspect of desiring to transform the present United Nations operations in Korea into a war led by the United States against communism in China."[82] In fact, even more was at stake than Reid imagined. Having reached an agreement with the Senate to send US troops to Europe, thus reinforcing the US commitment to military deployment and defence of Europe, the Joint Chiefs of Staff immediately demanded that MacArthur be authorized to attack air bases in northeast China in the case of a major attack on UN forces.[83] A few days later, Truman approved this proposal and, in addition, authorized the dispatch of nuclear weapons to Okinawa. It was in this context – preparing for a major onslaught against the north – that Truman made the decision to fire MacArthur in April 1951 and to replace him with General Matthew Ridgeway. It was impossible to engage in controlled escalation of the war while MacArthur was publicly calling for attacks on China. After the firing of MacArthur, Dean Acheson stated clearly that the British should not interpret this act as conceding to the British point of view but, rather, as placing Great Britain in the "position to support or at least acquiesce in certain US Far Eastern policies which thus far [the] British have adamantly opposed."[84]

The failure of the Chinese/northern forces' fourth and fifth campaigns in late April 1950 prompted the Chinese and northern forces to review their strategy in May. In June, Kim Il Sung visited Beijing. There he reluctantly went along with the Chinese insistence that reunification of the peninsula was now impossible and the time for negotiations had arrived. Kim and China's Gao Gang next travelled to Moscow, where, on 13 June, they consulted with Stalin, all three parties agreeing that negotiations were necessary. On 23 June 1950, Soviet ambassador to the UN Jacob Malik called for an immediate ceasefire and an armistice. Achieving this, however, was not so easy.

On the US side, military opposition to a ceasefire was strong. Ridgeway recommended against one, citing "communist duplicity and faithlessness." Later in the summer he accused communists of being "treacherous savages," guilty of "murderous conspiracy," and insisted that, "as representatives of an enlightened and civilized people," negotiation with them was "to deride one's own dignity."[85] Shortly after replacing MacArthur as commander of UN forces, he wrote the rector of his church, who read his letter to the congregation of St. Bartholomew's Protestant Episcopal Church. This letter was picked up in the press. America, claimed Ridgeway, "seems not to know" about the reality of the Korean War, in which hundreds of thousands of poor Koreans were fleeing, "driven to all this by one seemingly overpowering fear, the fear of government by communists."[86] He concluded by asking: "[Is the issue not] truly whether some day our women, our babies, our sick and our aged are to be driven forth by Asiatic masters, or now while yet there's time, this America and our Allies may extinguish all petty issues and unite with all they have to destroy the greatest peril we have ever known." From Ottawa, Herbert Norman enquired of Arthur Menzies whether it might not be possible to determine whether Ridgeway's remarks represented a form of "yellow peril" argument or whether he was referring to the Russians as "Asiatics." Menzies consulted with others, who described Ridgeway's views as a "gaff," and it was left at that.

Despite such ideological impediments, a ceasefire was eventually achieved and armistice talks began on 10 July 1951 in the town of Kaesong near the 38th parallel. Ridgeway nominated Vice-Admiral Charles Turner Joy to represent the US/UN forces, while generals Xie Fang and Nam Il represented the Chinese and North Korean sides, respectively. The adversaries agreed on a five-point plan for discussions: (1) approving an agenda for the talks, (2) establishing an armistice line and demilitarized zone, (3) making ceasefire arrangements and inspections, (4) dealing with prisoners of war, and (5) making recommendations to their respective governments.

The talks stalled over differences in placement of the armistice line and then ruptured completely in late August when US/UN forces, in a covert operation, bombed the neutralized territory around Kaesong.[87] In earlier incidents, armed Chinese troops had also breached the perimeter of the same zone. Talks finally resumed on 25 October and, in the ensuing months, agreement was reached on a demarcation line along the existing battlefront and on holding a political conference for resolving outstanding issues within ninety days of an armistice. However, the talks bogged down over the question of the repatriation of POWs. According to the Geneva Convention of 1949, all POWs were to be repatriated to their country of origin. However, under pressure from army hardliners, the US negotiators decided to repudiate the Geneva stipulations and argue for select repatriation based on the personal choice of the individual prisoners. At first, the US/UN negotiators suggested that 116,000 of the 132,000 POWs would be returned, but later that number was reduced to seventy thousand. According to their surveys, many Korean and Chinese POWs did not want to return to North Korea or to China. There were in fact many POWs who did not want to be repatriated for a number of reasons. However, the numbers were flawed and were based on figures obtained under duress in the POW camps, where chaos reigned. The rebellion that took place on Koje Island, just east of Pusan, and the ensuing diplomatic crisis involving Canada symbolized the situation in the camps.[88]

At the same time as the POW issue erupted, Chinese and North Korean officials charged the US/UN forces with the use of biological weapons. The details of this episode and recent revelations regarding biological warfare are discussed in Chapter 12. The truth regarding the use of such weapons of mass destruction remains elusive. However, a historian of Chinese foreign policy who reviewed the documentation in Chinese archives argues that he "found enough evidence to show that in early 1952 both CPV commanders and Beijing's leaders truly believed that the Americans had used biological weapons against the Chinese and North Koreans."[89] This belief, and the extensive propaganda campaign developed around it, added another insoluble issue to the already complex armistice talks. In the meantime, the war dragged on and, although there was little change in the battlefront on the ground, the air war intensified.

On 5 December 1952, Canadian fighter pilot Andrew (Andy) Mackenzie was flying an F-86 Sabre jet at 13,000 metres near the Yalu River.[90] On exchange to the US forces, Mackenzie was flying with the 139th Squadron,

51st Wing of the 5th Air Force, when he was shot down by an attacking MiG squadron. Bailing out at high speed, Mackenzie was stripped naked; descending by parachute, he reportedly took over half an hour to reach the ground. Captured, Mackenzie spent two years in a POW camp in Shenyang (Mukden), where he endured difficult conditions, although he stated upon his release that he had not been subjected to torture.[91] According to Mackenzie, his Chinese captors accused him of flying into Chinese air space, although he denied this. Based on press reports at the time, Mackenzie was forced to sign a confession stating that he "had been shot down while invading Chinese air space, but had landed in North Korea. In fact, he was not briefed to fly over China and did not knowingly do so."[92]

Recently discovered documentation indicates, however, that there may have indeed been a policy of breaching Chinese air space. Certainly, the Chinese command believed that to be the case, and scholars who edited their memoirs confirm that US/UN forces sent air reconnaissance missions into China as early as August 1950.[93] Documents from the Canadian archives also suggest that US overflights into China became more common as the war progressed. This issue had been the subject of intense debate in April 1951, at which time the US State Department told the Canadian government that it would consult before conducting such operations except in the case where the US/UN command was at stake. On 22 May 1952, the Canadian mission to Japan sent two reports on overflights that led Pearson to believe that there were "good grounds for suspecting that at some level there has been a decision to ignore the restrictions which have been placed on air operations in Korea."[94] The reports indicated that fighter aircraft had been dispatched on organized flights "across the Yalu, possibly as far as Mukden [Shenyang]." Pearson found the reports "another disturbing development" in Korea, and, although he believed that such flights were the result of "excessive zeal" on the part of local commanders, he felt they were still dangerous and asked Canada's ambassador in Washington to raise the issue with the State Department. However, he warned Wrong not to reveal the sources of the reports, one of which was a drunk fighter pilot on leave in Japan. The second source, however, was much more convincing, as Wrong put it, involving the "questioning by Group Captain McNair of Flying Officer Nixon of the RCAF."[95] In other words, Canadian pilots on exchange with the American air force appear to have verified a policy of breaching the border with China. The Canadian officials felt that to reveal this source would compromise the pilot exchange program with the United States and otherwise jeopardize defence relations. The unwillingness of the

Canadian government to reveal its sources meant that both the US and British authorities declined to pursue the matter. However, the matter would arise again at the 1954 Geneva Conference, by which time it was apparent that there had indeed been numerous violations of Chinese air space.[96]

One of the important casualties of the US administration's rollback policy was Norman himself. NSC-68 highlighted the importance of intelligence, and, subsequently, the US "national security" establishment intensified surveillance and internal security reviews. In April, the FBI reopened Norman's file after his name arose in US Senate hearings on subversion, with the RCMP cooperating with the FBI and the DEA in undertaking its own investigation.[97] On 14 October 1950, Arnold Heeney, the undersecretary of state for the DEA, issued an urgent recall of Norman after authorizing the dispatch of a faulty RCMP report on him to the FBI and without even giving Norman the chance to respond to the allegations of impropriety. Although Norman was cleared of any wrongdoing, the allegations made in the RCMP report would resurface on a number of subsequent occasions – with devastating results.

Ending the War

Finally, on 27 July 1953, all sides signed the armistice document, bringing the three-year war to a conclusion. Over 3 million had died in what can only be called a conflagration of the greatest magnitude, while the country remained divided. For the most part, Canadian historians have examined Korea either as a military exercise or as a venue for Canadian diplomacy. In particular, they have been interested in the role of Lester Pearson at the United Nations, where he first intervened in October 1950 when a decision was being taken regarding US/UN forces crossing the 38th parallel into North Korea and attempting to forcibly unite the peninsula, a move that ran into Indian opposition. Pearson intervened a second time in December, when the joint Chinese/North Korean offensive reached the 38th parallel and Asian/Arab nations proposed a ceasefire, and a third and final time in February, when the United States wanted to brand China as an "aggressor" after its forces crossed the 38th parallel. Pearson and the Canadian government, as a member of the Commonwealth and as a country only recently emerging from under the imperial blanket of Great Britain, had some sensitivity to the concerns of non-communist decolonized countries, particularly India. Pearson thus attempted to mediate between what was essentially the emerging Non-Aligned Movement and the Western powers. However, in every case, Pearson and the Canadian delegation ultimately voted with the

United States and the other imperial powers against their own best instincts. For example, in the debate regarding the resolution that would have authorized US/UN forces to cross the Yalu River, Pearson voted with the Americans, despite being bombarded by telegrams from Escott Reid and even a personal telephone call from Norman Robertson (then clear of the Privy Council), to whom Pearson replied: "Norman, you have no idea of what the pressure is like here. I can't possibly oppose the resolution."[98] As Reid later found out, many in the US State Department and the CIA were also advising against going into North Korea. If only someone had leaked these documents, Reid concluded, "the disastrous error of the crossing of the 38th parallel might have been avoided."[99]

Pearson was intent not so much on building bridges as on bringing representatives of countries such as India on-side. In this there was a strong paternalistic aspect to Pearson's initiatives, and to the Indians this became transparent in the UN debate over possible ceasefire proposals. Pearson outlined the rationale for Canada's position in a statement prepared for the debate on the resolution in which he concluded that the Asia/Arab resolution failed to "embody the conception of an orderly sequence of events."[100] The US resolution, on the other hand, stated a vital truth: "The armed forces of the People's Government of China continue their invasion of Korea."[101] The resolution, branding China as an international aggressor state, opened the door to escalation and represented a clear positioning of the Canadian government in opposition to what was to become the Non-Aligned Movement. As Pearson himself later recounted: "[The Canadian delegation was] faced with great American pressure to support their resolution of condemnation. We succumbed to that pressure."[102] These decisions went against the advice of his top advisors, and the passing of this UN resolution further increased the dangers of the war's expanding, since the branding of China as an aggressor provided a legal fiction for attacks on China itself. And it was precisely such attacks that MacArthur had contemplated. The Chinese government accused Canada of succumbing to US pressure and trying to "trap" the Chinese. Although Pearson did try to reach out to the adversaries, his own inclination and his government's policies were to support the US administration at every crucial moment, bound by a deep belief in the righteousness of the Western cause. But the experience to that point also created fear that the US administration would involve the United Nations in a war with China and, possibly, with the Soviet Union. Such a war would be, in Pearson's view, just but (because of perceived military weakness) untimely.

Paradoxically, in his insistent advocacy for moderation even in defiance of US pressure, Escott Reid began to articulate the need for a more independent foreign policy for Canada. Reid was acting undersecretary from September 1948 until March 1949, but Pearson bypassed him as his own replacement in the position of undersecretary when he, Pearson, decided to enter politics as the new minister for external affairs. Arnold Heeney, the former clerk of the Privy Council, took on the position of what today is called deputy minister.[103] Reid did not agree with Heeney's appointment and had hoped Hume Wrong would get the posting. In the event, Reid had become deputy undersecretary, a position in which he came to play the key policy role during the Korean War.[104] When MacArthur threatened to expand the war, Reid, as deputy undersecretary, pushed Pearson to articulate publicly their reservations regarding US failure to adequately consult its coalition partners. On 31 March 1951, Pearson obliquely chastised MacArthur and, during his 10 April address at the Canadian Club in Toronto, he stated that the days of "relatively easy and automatic political relations with our neighbour" were over and that the preoccupation was "no longer whether the United States [would] discharge her international responsibilities but how she [would] do it and how the rest of us [would] be involved."[105] These statements caught the attention of the press because they appeared the day after Truman fired MacArthur. In this same period, Pearson also heeded Reid's call for an internal review of Canadian foreign policy. The review, labelled "A Re-Examination of Canadian Foreign Policy," was centred on a series of policy papers focusing on key fields that presented challenges for Canadian policy makers.[106] Pearson, in endorsing the initiative, hoped that the studies would be "short, not too academic; guides for the future based on analyses of past experience."[107] This exercise was an oblique attempt to come to grips with the United States as an imperial power. The study would later be shelved, but Pearson's misgivings regarding US foreign policy remained and would resurface later with unintended but significant consequences for Canadian foreign policy.

11

The San Francisco Peace Treaty and Re-Militarization of the Transpacific

The adoption of NSC-68, and the Korean War that gave it life, also resuscitated the moribund peace treaty process with Japan. The conservative forces that had come to the fore through the "reverse course" reflected the re-establishment of corporate alliances between Tokyo and Washington.[1] Their interests dovetailed well with the anti-communist policies of Kennan, who, as one of his first acts, had intervened to stop the negotiation of a peace treaty in 1947, even though the wartime powers had agreed that the conditions for ending the Occupation had been fulfilled. The politics of the "reverse course" were, however, a double-edged sword. On the one hand, the idealistic radicalism of the early postwar period receded; on the other hand, as the impact of the economic reforms took hold, there was intense, popular resistance that had important political repercussions and was reflected in growing dissatisfaction with the Occupation. Miyazawa Kiichi, a future prime minister of Japan, revealed how disenchantment with the prolonged Occupation precipitated a renewed interest on the part of the Japanese government in obtaining a peace treaty: "The economic recession was perceived as having been engineered by a heartless foreigner called Dodge in the name of the Occupation; thus the sense of oppression felt by ordinary folks transferred into growing dissatisfaction towards the Occupation."[2] This same dissatisfaction also marked a shift in progressive politics in Japan as many people began to realize that anti-communism disarmed not only communists but also socialists of all stripes. Within the Japan Socialist Party, the changing circumstances led its left wing to articulate its vision for post-Occupation Japan based on: (1) the signing of a "comprehensive peace treaty," that is, one that was acceptable to the Soviet Union, China, and Asian countries as well as the United States and its Cold War allies; (2) permanent neutrality for Japan in global politics; and (3) opposition to foreign military bases in Japan after independence.[3] A fourth component, rejection of rearmament, was added the following year. Thus, growing disenchantment with the Occupation coalesced with a growing unease over the notion that Japan might be drawn into the Cold War, a feeling that, as Japan's pre-eminent historian of the Occupation points out, was growing among "intellectuals, students, citizens groups, religious groups and so forth."[4] Among these groups, women's groups were especially active. Hiratsuka Raichō, who in 1911 had helped found the "Bluestockings," one of Japan's earliest women's groups, co-authored an appeal for a disarmed, neutral Japan based on a comprehensive peace treaty.[5] This appeal also made a special request for ongoing friendship with China – for "historical, geographic, economic and other reasons." She and her comrades declared: "We will not cooperate in any country's war, we refuse to send our husbands and sons to the killing fields." To US officials in Japan, however, the upsurge in demands for a comprehensive peace settlement was dismissed simply as a response to a "persistent and fairly effective communist party line in Japan opposing a 'separate' peace and the granting of bases to the United States."[6] It was against this backdrop that conservative prime minister Yoshida Shigeru sent a special mission to Washington, led by the up-and-coming and newly minted finance minister Ikeda Hayato, ostensibly to discuss economic matters but in fact to transmit an extremely important message: the Yoshida government was prepared to allow US military bases in Japan even after a peace treaty was signed. Under pressure to restart treaty negotiations, Truman had appointed John Foster Dulles, a Republican with bi-partisan connections, to break the impasse within US government branches and to broker a treaty that would be acceptable to both Democrats and Republicans.

The Commonwealth foreign ministers had earlier discussed the peace treaty issue at their January 1950 conference in Colombo, Ceylon, and decided to convene a Commonwealth working party on the treaty.[7] Consultations began in London on 1 May 1950. Canada's high commissioner in Britain, L.D. Wilgress, was in charge of a Canadian delegation that included S.F. Rae and Ralph Collins, Canada's representative on the Far Eastern Commission. The Department of External Affairs issued instructions to the delegation a week before the meeting, stressing that the government "must take into account the view of the United States Government."[8] Nor did the government want the working party to create the impression that the Commonwealth was developing a common position that, within the FEC, would effectively give it a veto over a treaty. This would "prejudice their relations with the US" and would be "most undesirable."[9]

The Korean War created new dynamics in the peace treaty process. Given Japan's central role as a US forward base in Korean operations, the State Department gave up its opposition to continued military occupation of Japan and aligned itself with the Department of Defense in its quest for maximum access and flexibility for military operations in post-treaty Japan. While the Korean War diverted energies away from the peace treaty in the short term, in September 1950 the US began intensive consultations with its allies regarding a treaty. The war in the Korean peninsula had rekindled US interest in a peace treaty with Japan, but the effects of the war had a different impact on Canada's DEA. In a remarkable memorandum penned on 13 October, nearly four months after the start of the Korean War, the DEA cabled a memorandum to Pearson, who was at the United Nations in New York in anticipation of a meeting with Dulles regarding the peace treaty. In it, the DEA recommended a policy that still reflected the ideal of peaceful co-existence that Pearson had experienced at the Colombo Conference. It suggested that a peace treaty "whose provisions because of their reasonableness and soundness should be acceptable to all interested parties" would have obvious advantages compared to a treaty acceptable only to US allies. Furthermore, the memorandum suggested that the peace treaty was an Asian issue, that the People's Republic of China fulfilled the conditions for de jure recognition and that its exclusion from the treaty would create difficulties with other Asian countries and for the treaty's long-term prospects; and, furthermore, that the treaty itself could not contain anything about US-Japan security arrangements, although this would not preclude post-treaty negotiations.[10] This document articulates an approach to the peace treaty that was in many ways similar to what opposition parties in Japan were advocating – a comprehensive treaty that included the Soviet Union and China, with any military arrangements to be negotiated separately from the peace treaty. Unfortunately, there is no record of Pearson actually discussing this proposal with Dulles or with anyone else at the time, but it does reflect the ongoing tension within the DEA regarding Asia policy. After China entered the Korean War, however, such a proposal became a dead letter.

Over the course of treaty discussions in 1950-51, Dulles travelled to Japan four times. In early 1951, Dulles began a major tour in his quest for a treaty, beginning with Japan in late January and continuing with stops in the Philippines, Australia, and New Zealand, and then visits to London and France. With the exception of the Philippines, those countries most victimized by Japan's imperial conquests remained peripheral to the consultation process. In Japan, Dulles met with MacArthur, with Prime Minister Yoshida Shigeru, and with officials of the foreign affairs ministry. The topics ranged far and wide and touched on territorial issues, including Okinawa (which the United States had taken over completely), reparations, trade, the stationing of US troops in Japan, and Japanese rearmament.[11] One key issue that arose in the discussions was Japan's relations with Korea, including the rights of the Korean minority in Japan. Meeting on 23 April 1951, Dulles told Yoshida that he had heard that the Japanese government objected to Korea's being a signatory to the treaty. Yoshida replied that "the Government would like to send almost all Koreans in Japan 'to their homes' because it had long been concerned by their illegal activities."[12] Dulles stated that he could see the wisdom of deciding that "Korean nationals in Japan, mostly Communists, should not obtain the property benefits of the treaty." As a result of these discussions, hundreds of thousands of Koreans in Japan were excluded from the treaty benefits that other Allied civilians received under the San Francisco Peace Treaty (SFPT).

While in Japan, Dulles also met Sir Alvery Gascoigne, the British political representative in Occupied Japan, at which time the two held a revealing discussion regarding the creation of an "elite Anglo-Saxon club." Gascoigne suggested that he had seen the term in one of the peace-related dispatches, to which Dulles replied, "that phrase is I think quite possibly one that I used."[13] Dulles went on to explain: "The Japanese have felt a certain superiority as against the Asiatic mainland masses ... [and] that the Western civilization represented by Britain, more latterly the United States, is perhaps sharing in that, represents a certain triumph of mind over mass which gives us a social standing in the world better than what is being achieved in terms of the mainland human masses of Asia, and that they think they have also achieved somewhat the similar superiority of mind over mass and would like to feel that they belong to, or are accepted by, the Western nations." Dulles stated that it was important to "encourage that feeling" in order to offset the economic attraction of developing bonds with the mainland (i.e., China). That Dulles should propose to encourage Japanese ethnocentrism after what Japan's imperial forces had wrought in China and other Asian countries reflects how disingenuous he could be and how, once again, racism on the part of Allied representatives encouraged the same on the part of many Japanese officials.

Dulles next went to the Philippines, where he met then president Quirino, who indicated an interest in some form of Pacific military pact but who mainly emphasized the Filipino demand for compensation for the estimated $8 billion in damage inflicted by Japanese imperial forces.[14] Quirino argued that Japan's rehabilitation had progressed much more rapidly than had that of the Philippines and that Japan should contribute to the rebuilding of the Philippine economy. If this were not possible immediately, then perhaps payments might be spread over a number of years. Dulles had the temerity to argue with the Philippine representatives that there appeared no effective way reparations could be paid, even though he had already argued on behalf of Allied property claims in Japan despite MacArthur's admonitions that such claims would make it "look as though the United States and England were feathering their own nests at the expense of these other countries."[15] In a personal letter to MacArthur summing up his trip and written shortly after he arrived home, Dulles underscored how the Philippine people were preoccupied with the issue of reparations and that, while the leaders he met seemed to understand the complexities of reparations, there remained "the problem of overcoming the emotional prejudices of the people and explaining to them why the relief to which they have looked forward for so long cannot be had."[16]

Norman and the 1951 Consultations

On 23 March 1951, the United States finally issued a second draft treaty.[17] It was at this point that Herbert Norman once again became involved in treaty discussions. After being exonerated of accusations of disloyalty in the winter of 1950, Norman took charge of preparing the Canadian position in the upcoming talks. Pearson had appointed Norman the head of the American and Far East Division in December, and he took up his duties after receiving top security clearance on 23 January 1951. Norman's division discussed the American draft on 6 April.[18] There seemed to be consensus that the draft treaty "foreshadowed a very generous peace settlement for Japan," which would make it difficult to offer Germany lesser terms in a future peace treaty.[19] At this time, Norman pushed for a war guilt clause in the treaty, a suggestion that the division had taken up on grounds that the absence of such a clause would add to cynicism on the part of other countries. Not only would others look askance at the lengths to which the United States was willing to go to "gain the cooperation of an ex-enemy," but China and the Soviet Union would be able to use the omission in their propaganda.[20] Regarding territorial issues, the department recommended that Japan renounce its claim to former territories but that the treaty not specify to whom they were ceded (the Formosa issue), and it accepted US control of Okinawa. The US draft contained no limitation on Japan's rearmament, an omission that concerned the department and that might have set a precedent for Germany as well. Also suggested was a draft human rights clause. Other provisions discussed included most favoured nation treatment (to which the department agreed if certain reservations were permitted), shipping, and aviation. The department recommended that a fisheries clause (to control the north Pacific fishery) be inserted in the treaty.

On 18 May, Norman sent a copy of the Canadian government's formal reply to the US draft treaty to the Canadian Embassy in Washington.[21] He noted that Hume Wrong, Canada's ambassador to the United States, was in Ottawa at the time and would personally take several copies of the fourteen-page memorandum with him back to Washington so that it would be in Dulles's hands before he left for London for talks with the British. The memorandum expanded on certain points that had been made in earlier exchanges with the State Department. In terms of process, it called for a special meeting of working parties of experts for fisheries and war claims. Regarding the substance of the US draft, the Canadian memorandum referred repeatedly to the treaty of peace with Italy as a benchmark. For example, it continued to stress Norman's suggestion concerning war responsibility, but, in light of adamant US opposition, it chose a watered-down form. It suggested that a phrase similar to one used in the Potsdam Declaration be included: "Japan bears its share of responsibility for precipitating a war of aggression into which her people were deceived and misled by irresponsible and self-willed militarists."[22] On territorial issues, the note recommended that all territories acquired through conquest be relinquished without distinction but that they not be specifically assigned to other countries. Regarding the Nansei Islands (including Okinawa), the government was prepared to have Japan renounce sovereignty over the islands and to reassign control to the United States, with the possibility of a future UN mandate. It suggested that Japan recognize Korean sovereignty, including sovereignty over Quelpart (Jeju, Saishuto in Japanese) Island. Regarding security, it welcomed a bilateral US-Japan military pact that limited Japan's offensive potential, but it questioned the wisdom of specifying Japan's right to such potential in the treaty.

The government objected to discussion of Japan's accession to the General Agreement on Tariffs and Trade until terms of accession were defined. It suggested that Japan should spell out its renunciation of special rights and privileges in China, with a separate provision renouncing any such rights in Manchuria. The Japanese government, it suggested, should be bound to accept the decisions of the Tokyo Tribunal and there should be no provision for pardon of convicted war criminals. It reserved Canada's right to take protectionist measures if necessary. Regarding reparations, the government called for a special working party to examine and reinforce these clauses (Canada wanted access to the "Gold pot" for those countries with claims to reparations). Furthermore, it wanted to reduce the types of seized properties that it might have to return to Japan. The government considered Article 15 (return of Allied property in Japan) "most unsatisfactory," proposing instead Article 78 of the Italian treaty as an alternative.

Regarding disputes over reparations claims, the Canadian government suggested that special conciliation commissions or tribunals be created to deal with disputes: these would be appointed by the president of the International Court. Finally, the Canadian brief suggested that there be no mention of the FEC as part of the ratification process and that there be special provision for Korean participation. Japan should take responsibility for maintaining Allied war graves. Of particular concern to Canadian authorities was the fisheries issue, but when Minister of Fisheries R.W. Mayhew met with Dulles in May, Dulles reiterated his opposition to a fisheries convention as part of the treaty. A compromise was reached whereby the Japanese government agreed that no fishing would take place in Pacific waters until a new fisheries convention had been signed.[23]

On 23 May 1951, Norman prepared for Pearson a reply to a British query regarding the final stages in the treaty-making process. Norman suggested that there seemed little alternative to continued negotiations via normal diplomatic channels since the United States "would not be likely to show any greater concern for the views of other governments at a conference than is the case under the present method of procedure."[24] However, he suggested that they request a definition of the principal parties that were to draw up the treaty, in the erroneous belief that there was still a possibility of an enlarged meeting of the moribund FEC to work out final details. Pearson approved Norman's note to the British High Commissioner's Office in Ottawa, and shortly afterwards Norman left Ottawa for London, where he attended Commonwealth consultations with the British government as the British negotiated with John Foster Dulles on the final treaty proposal. The object of these discussions was to try to reach consensus between Britain and the United States regarding the draft peace treaty. DEA officials sent reports on a regular basis back to Ottawa. Dulles and the British foreign office reached agreement on a draft treaty on 14 June. As part of the agreement, it was decided that Britain would abandon its demand for Chinese participation in exchange for the United States' doing the same regarding Formosa.[25] This caught the attention of Chester Ronning, who had returned to Ottawa from Nanjing in the spring of 1951. He fired off a memo to Pearson, in which he foresaw the outcome of the new British-US entente. He suggested that the British view that Japan would be free after the signing of the treaty to work out agreements with both Guomindang and communist governments was extremely unrealistic because: (1) the United States would pressure the Japanese government to sign an agreement with Chiang Kai-shek, and (2) the communist regime would not deal with a regime that tried to have relations with both the mainland and Taiwan.[26] The United States was getting what it wanted "with little compromise involved." Ronning warned that a treaty that did not include the Soviet Union and China could not "provide for stable relations in the area." The treaty terms would make it more difficult to settle the Korean War, and therefore it was wrong to rush the treaty even though it was long overdue. The deputy undersecretary, Escott Reid, took this point up with Pearson, who agreed that Hume Wrong might raise the points informally with the State Department.[27] Hume Wrong in fact met Dean Rusk to inform him of Canadian concerns, but Rusk rejected these, telling Wrong that Great Britain did not share Canadian worries.[28]

Unknown to the Canadians, the US administration was then in the process of making a U-turn regarding the Rhee regime in South Korea. On 9 July 1951, Dulles met with the South Korean ambassador to the United States, Yang Yu Chan, to inform him that the South Korean government would not be permitted to be a signatory to the peace treaty since "only those nations in a state of war with Japan and which were signatories of the United Nations Declaration of 1942 would sign the treaty."[29] Yang was astounded by this news and protested that a division of Korean troops had fought against Japan from China and that the Korean Provisional Government had issued a declaration of war. To this, Robert Fearey of the State Department's Far Eastern Division replied that the US government had never recognized the Korean Provisional Government. Why had the United States reversed its position?

According to one view, the United States changed its view on South Korean participation because the British government had convinced the State Department that its participation would provide a pretext for the Soviet Union to object to the treaty.[30] This analysis is only partially convincing. The idea that only signatories to the 1942 UN Declaration would sign the treaty was transparently false. This became vividly clear when the US government decided to permit the newly created French neocolonial regimes – the Associated States of Vietnam, Laos, and Cambodia – to participate in the conference, despite the fact that they were never signatories to the Allied Declaration of 1942 and that many countries had refused to recognize them.[31] In light of the trouble to which the United States went to include these adjutants of French colonialism, to which the Soviet Union could equally object, why, we might ask, was the United States unwilling to go to bat for the South Korean regime? Two other factors must be considered. First, Dulles mistrusted Korean nationalism and worried that South Korean delegates might upset his carefully crafted conference by attacking Japanese imperialism. Furthermore, Dulles was also determined to exclude Korean nationals in Japan from having Allied national status, an issue that the Yoshida government had insisted on and to which Dulles had already agreed.

The ROK did not take the US decision lying down, and, on 18 July 1951, Yang issued a press statement warning that the Japanese government could not be trusted. In a follow-up meeting with Yang on 19 July, Dulles chastised him for his statements to the press. Yang's outburst was a reflection of the deep antipathy that many Koreans held towards Japanese imperialism, an antipathy that Rhee might well play to during a peace conference. Such an eventuality could not be countenanced. But there was a related reason for Dulles's reversal. In replying to Dulles during the meeting on 19 July, Yang defended the ROK's right to attend the peace conference by explaining that the Japanese government, still smarting over its loss of Korea, was discriminating against the 800,000 Koreans who were still residing in Japan.[32] To this Dulles replied that "many of these Koreans were undesirables, being in many cases from North Korea and constituting a center for Communist agitation in Japan. He believed, therefore, that probably a legitimate Japanese fear of certain of these Koreans was involved in any action taken against them by the Japanese authorities."[33] That Dulles would take such a position against the Korean minorities in Japan is not surprising given his previous discussions with Yoshida on this issue.

By early summer 1951, echoes of growing resistance to the treaty began to reach Ottawa. On 27 July, Heeney informed the Cabinet that the DEA had "doubts about the timing of the treaty" because of the difficulties it might create for a settlement in Korea.[34] But another factor also gave the DEA pause. As expressed in Heeney's memorandum, "The Asian states appeared to be divided in their attitude towards the treaty." The memorandum also notes that Burma was refusing to sign and that the Philippines was also unhappy with the "lack of provision for substantial reparations." On the other hand, it reassured Cabinet that India, Pakistan, and Indonesia appeared to be on side. Despite the drawbacks to the treaty, the memorandum recommended that Canada sign because the treaty was "part of the United States' arrangements for the defence of the Pacific, and the responsibility for appearing to threaten those arrangements by refusing to sign would be very grave."[35]

In early August, Heeney reported to Pearson on new, "important" developments since the 27 July memorandum. The US State Department was finally making "a belated attempt at fulfilling at least the proprieties of consultation." The views of the Asian states were now clearer, Heeney informed Pearson, and India had made it plain that it would not sign a treaty "which would in effect make Japan a United States bastion against China."[36] Heeney assured Pearson that the DEA had informed Washington of its concerns about the timing of the treaty as well as about its doubts about the security clauses. These clauses, Heeney stated, "[are not] legally necessary and are the ones to which China and the USSR could not reasonably be expected to agree."[37] Heeney also explained that there was opposition to the treaty from other countries, such as the Netherlands, but, more important, he told Pearson: "Legal Division is of the opinion that renunciation by Japan of her rights and titles in Formosa, the Pescadores, Sakhalin and the Kuriles provides China and the USSR respectively with legal title to the territories."[38] This view, one with which the British foreign office also agreed, had not been shared with the State Department, Heeney reported. Given the problems with the treaty, any statement in support of it should be moderate, he advised Pearson. He concluded by asking Pearson whether the DEA should "support India's stand in respect to the security clauses or whether [it] should leave it to the Indian government to argue this point alone with the United States government."

With Pearson mulling over this question, on 16 August, the PRC published a statement by Zhou Enlai, then minister of foreign affairs as well as prime minister, regarding the proposed treaty and conference. The treaty, he stated, violated the United Nations Declaration of 1 January 1942, the Cairo Declaration, the Yalta Agreements, the Potsdam Declaration and Agreement, and the Basic Post-Surrender Policy of the Far Eastern Commission. According to Zhou: "The United Nations Declaration provides that no separate Peace should be made. The Potsdam Agreement states that the 'preparatory work of the Peace Settlements' should be undertaken by those States which were signatories to the terms of surrender imposed upon the Enemy State concerned."[39] The PRC, he said, supported the Soviet proposal that all states whose armed forces had participated in the war effort against Japan should prepare the treaty. Instead, the United States had monopolized the task of preparing the treaty and was now proposing to exclude China even though, in "the war of resisting and defeating Japanese imperialism, the Chinese people, after a bitter struggle of the longest duration, sustained the heaviest losses and made the greatest contribution."[40] On the specifics of the proposed treaty, the PRC: (1) took particular exception to the clause on reparations for Allied property because it rendered Japan liable for damages only after 7 December 1941, ignoring the fact that China was at war with Japan much earlier; (2) refuted the territorial clauses that gave the United States control over Pacific Islands and neglected to assign sovereignty for Taiwan and the Pescadores as well as the Kuriles to China and the Soviet Union, respectively; (3) underscored the absence of safeguards to limit Japan's armed forces, to prevent the resurgence of militaristic organizations, and to ensure democratic rights; and (4) rejected US predominance over Japan's economy and the exclusion of normal trade relations with the PRC.[41] China, Zhou declared, reserved its right to demand reparations from Japan and would refuse to recognize the treaty.

The DEA received the note the following day, and Pearson cited it and the Soviet Union's decision to participate in the San Francisco conference in a memorandum to his Cabinet colleagues on 21 August 1951.[42] Cabinet approved the treaty the following day. In his note to Cabinet, however, Pearson did not raise any of the substantive objections of either the Soviet Union or the PRC in their opposition to the treaty. Nor does he even mention the reservations expressed by India, Burma, and the Netherlands that Heeney had emphasized in his note to Pearson on 8 August. One is left with the distinct impression that Pearson consciously avoided bringing the Cabinet into the debate over the treaty and instead relied on anti-communism (if the Soviets and PRC oppose the treaty it must be good) to gain Cabinet approval.

The day after Cabinet assented to the treaty, on 23 August 1951, the Indian government formally informed Dulles that it would refuse to accede to the peace treaty. The telegram was very explicit regarding the reasons for its rejection of the treaty. It considered: (1) that the provision giving the United States control of Okinawa and the Bonin Islands was not justifiable; (2) that the military provisions of the treaty (and the security treaty to be signed with it, should only be concluded after Japan became fully independent; (3) that Formosa (Taiwan) should be returned to China directly; and (4) that the deliberations to be held in San Francisco would not allow for negotiation of the treaty. Dulles, Acheson, and Truman were stunned by the news as they had anticipated Indian participation. The Indian reply provoked Truman to scribble in the margins of the Indian note: "Evidently the 'Govt' of India has consulted Uncle Joe and Mousie Dung of China!"[43]

Singing at the Opera

Pearson was not happy as he, fisheries minister Mayhew, and Herbert Norman made their way to San Francisco in early September. Word of India's objections to the treaty had leaked to the press. Furthermore, it was precisely at this time that Norman came under fire, for the second time, from McCarthyism in the United States. Testifying before the Senate Internal Security Subcommittee on 7 August 1951, Professor Karl Wittfogel publicly named Herbert Norman as a communist, and Robert Morris, legal counsel for the subcommittee, used this opening to launch a scurrilous attack against the Institute of Pacific Relations. Pearson, to his credit, defended Norman, issuing a press statement and complaining to the State Department. Upon his arrival in San Francisco, a US reporter asked Pearson whether he thought the Senate "sub-committee should invite Norman to testify," to which Pearson replied, "We have already indicated to the proper United States' authorities what we think of Dr. Wittfogel's statement and no further action seems to be required."[44]

As the 4 September opening of the conference approached, the work of Dulles and the State Department bore fruit in rapid succession. On Thursday, 30 August, with Philippine president Quirino and US president Truman in attendance, representatives of the US and Philippine governments signed the Mutual Defence Treaty, the price of Philippine adherence to the peace treaty.[45] On Saturday, 1 September, officials from the United States, Australia, and New Zealand gathered at the Presidio overlooking San Francisco Bay to sign the ANZUS pact. These military treaties represented an important step in what historian Akira Iriye has referred to as the militarization of

President Truman addressing the opening of the San Francisco Peace Conference, September 1951. | Courtesy of Truman Library and Museum

the Pacific, or the San Francisco system.[46] The next evening, four hundred conference delegates and eight hundred media crowded into the main hall of the Opera House to hear Truman make his opening address. The previous day, he had set the tone in a major speech to launch the sale of new defence bonds. "Communists may try to resume the offensive in Korea at any time," he warned. "Red rulers" he said, "are capable of launching new attacks in Europe, the Middle East, or elsewhere in Asia, whenever it suits them." That evening, however, Truman took a more statesman-like tone, befitting the opening of an international conference that was to be carried live on television from coast to coast in the United States, the first such broadcast in history. He told the assembled delegates that the conference would show who wanted peace and who wanted war. Japan, he said, would take up full responsibilities in the United Nations in the future.

Commenting on Truman's speech at the conference, a *Vancouver Sun* editorial writer suggested that the president's contention that Japan would take up a full role in the United Nations "implie[d] a Japanese force in Korea at some date."[47] The editorial concluded: "It seems wasteful and uneconomical that a holding war should be fought with troops brought from across the Pacific and even across two oceans and a continent. The Japanese, once they are full members of the UN, are the natural guardians of UN integrity in the Far East." Not everyone was so willing to embrace Japan. The transpacific disconnect was highlighted when Truman's South Korean ally and cold warrior par excellence, Syngman Rhee, stated, upon hearing that the United States was intent on rearming Japan and hoped to send Japanese troops to fight in Korea: "On this occasion I declare to the world that we will fight the Japanese before we expel the Chinese."[48]

With the major victims of Japanese aggression absent from the conference and those who did attend acting in concert with Dean Acheson and John Foster Dulles, there was little hope of making any substantive changes in the draft treaty. In the end it was signed by forty-eight countries, with the Soviet Union, Czechoslovakia, and Poland refusing to sign. Even so, a number of non-communist representatives were obliged to raise important items of disagreement with the treaty. For example, Carlos Romulo, secretary of foreign affairs of the Philippines and its head of delegation at San Francisco, demolished the US argument that Japan, for economic reasons, lacked the ability to pay reparations. He noted that Japan's economy had recuperated to the point that industrial activity was 32 percent above prewar levels, that its fiscal position showed a surplus, and that its balance of trade had moved into the black.[49] That the Japanese government had much more economic leeway than either Tokyo or US representatives were willing to admit, and even more than Romulo thought, is confirmed in discussions that took place between Finance Minister Ikeda Hayato and Joseph Dodge just prior to the peace conference. In their discussion, Ikeda admitted a budget surplus of over 100 billion yen, 40 billion yen of which he hoped to return to Japanese taxpayers in a rebate.[50] He was also at this time considering "compensation to Japanese nationals for loss of overseas assets and veterans' allowances." The governor of the Bank of Japan, in another meeting with Dodge, had also to try to convince him to accept Japanese gold holdings (with an estimated worth of over 200 million yen) because he feared "that the Filipinos might try to attach the gold as reparations."[51] The Japanese representatives confided with American representatives in such ways, knowing full well that US officials were seeking to minimize any reparations payments by Japan, insisting that its costs during the Occupation (the exclusive nature of which was at Washington's own insistence), estimated at US$2 billion, were to come before any other claims.

With respect to compensation claims, a last-minute exchange during the San Francisco conference between the US, Japanese, and Netherlands delegations reveals that the SFPT did not preclude the payment of private claims. Under pressure from citizens who felt they were victims of war crimes when incarcerated by the Japanese in the Dutch East Indies during the war, the Dutch representatives explained to Dulles that they were under instructions from their government not to sign the peace treaty unless a means was found whereby private citizens could file claims for alleged atrocities committed against them.[52] After a series of meetings, the Japanese delegation apparently agreed that, while Japan would not accept private claims through the machinery of the SFPT, "there [were] certain types of private claims by Allied nationals which the Japanese Government might wish voluntarily to deal with."[53] It was based on this agreement that the Netherlands representative claimed in his presentation: "[Article 14(b)] does not involve the expropriation by each Allied Government of the private claims of its nationals so that after the treaty comes into force these claims will be nonexistent."[54] In the end, intense pressure from the United States to the contrary, the Philippine government made a formal reservation to its support of the treaty, declaring it would negotiate a reparations agreement "any provision of the present treaty to the contrary notwithstanding."[55] Indonesia, at this period still with relatively strong ties to the US government, also advanced an alternative proposal regarding reparations and ultimately rejected the SFPT, concluding a separate peace treaty with Japan in 1958. Burma simply refused to attend the conference in protest against the lack of reparations.

Canada, however, fell in behind the United States – totally. In disregard of his subordinates' recommendation of only moderate support for the treaty, Pearson instead went all out, launching a vigorous defence of the treaty, including substantial praise for Douglas MacArthur and John Foster Dulles, and even going so far as to refute India's arguments regarding the SFPT.[56] His support for the US government was undiluted: "It [the treaty] reflects also the wisdom and basic democracy of the United States government and people in refusing to embark on the imperialistic course of making Japan a mere appendage to the United States; or more subtly perhaps, of attempting to refashion Japan in the image of America."[57] That China was not at the conference, he suggested, was China's own fault because it had committed its forces in Korea: "The Peiping government must realize that it cannot shoot its way into the United Nations," he stated, echoing the very words of the US State Department.[58] The *Vancouver Sun* opined: "The treaty will have no value at all for the people who are on our side in the struggle to maintain peace in the Pacific Ocean unless it is made the forerunner of a general Pacific Defense Pact similar to the North Atlantic Pact ... The Philippine proposal for a full-blown Pacific Pact to match the Atlantic Pact is now due."[59] The recently signed defence pacts "merely highlight the need for a larger pact into which at least Indonesia, Siam, Indo-China and possibly Japan – as well as Canada and Britain, might also be drawn."

On Saturday, 8 September, Lester Pearson and R.W. Mayhew stepped up to the podium to sign the treaty, along with representatives from forty-seven other states. Pearson then handed the gold pen, specially manufactured for the signing ceremony, to Herbert Norman as a gesture of his respect for Norman's work. A few hours later, US and Japanese representatives met to sign an alliance, the US-Japan Security Treaty, completing a military alliance network in the Pacific.

The next day Lester Pearson and other members of the Canadian delegation boarded an RCAF transport plane that took them to Vancouver. Within a few hours, Pearson and Mayhew were gazing out over a capacity crowd that had filled Vancouver's venerable Orpheum Theatre on Granville Street.[60] Apprised by the *Vancouver Sun* of Pearson's visit, nearly three thousand people had come out to hear his report on the peace treaty. While they patiently waited to gain entrance, members of the BC Peace Council handed out a leaflet with the headline "An Open Letter to Hon. Lester B. Pearson," in which they suggested that the peace treaty was really a step backward.

Pearson began his speech at the Orpheum by recognizing the special interest shown in the treaty by people in British Columbia: "I suppose this is a part of Canada which is most interested in Pacific problems," Pearson said, "but there should be no part of Canada that should not be interested in the Pacific. We are becoming more conscious in the East that Canada is a Pacific power." He told the audience that the treaty aimed at bringing peace and stability to Asia and that this would ensure the same for the rest of the world. However, Russia, Poland, and Czechoslovakia had gone to San Francisco specifically to obstruct and delay the treaty, he opined. Hearing this, hecklers immediately opened up to challenge Pearson: "Where was China?" "Why didn't the Soviet Union sign?" For the most part he ignored the taunts, but at one point he suggested that, unlike his own reception in Vancouver, delegates from the Soviet Union had been given the courtesy of an uninterrupted hearing in San Francisco. In light of the press reports and records of the San Francisco proceedings, this seems to be more fancy than fact. Undaunted, Pearson related how the United States had just completed mutual assistance treaties with the Philippines, Japan, Australia, and New Zealand, and he added: "one agreement covering them all may be drafted." "I am sure that Canada will take a part as we have already done in the North Atlantic Treaty," he told the crowd. Canada had taken "a very active" part in drafting the treaty. Pearson brushed aside the fact that India and Burma had not attended the meeting, stating that their reasons for not attending were contradictory. Burma thought the terms were too lenient, India, that they were too harsh. Pearson said he was troubled by the Russian threat that the responsibility for whatever the Reds might do in Asia now rested on the shoulders of the rest of the world.

The Yoshida Letter

Pearson's fierce defence of the treaty was not reflected in E.H. Norman's report on the conference at the Heads of Division Meeting upon his return to Ottawa. The treaty had been signed by forty-eight countries, he reported, but the meeting "was not in any sense a real conference"; rather, it was a meeting at which representatives expressed their views regarding an already-agreed-upon draft treaty. Communist opposition was half-hearted, he stated, and the communists had not taken full advantage that the discussion on rules of procedure might have afforded them. He concluded: "The greatest interest was displayed in the statements of the Asian Delegates at the Conference. The delegates from Indonesia and the Philippines indicated their dissatisfaction with the reparations clauses of the Treaty and reserved the position of their Governments with respect to implementation of these clauses. It was apparent from the speeches of most of the Asian delegates that those countries, which must live in proximity to Japan, were not completely convinced that the 'peace of reconciliation' with Japan would be entirely successful. Each of them offered cause why it would be difficult for their countries to forget Japanese wartime aggression."[61] In an unpublished article, "Japan since Surrender," Norman reiterated his view that the San Francisco peace conference was little more than a signing ceremony.[62] Treaty affairs did not end with the 8 September 1951 signing. For Norman, however, the situation became more difficult personally as attacks against him mounted. He was ostensibly reassigned while retaining his nominal title of head of the American and Far East Division, but he faced further internal interrogations in January 1952. He nevertheless continued to participate in DEA affairs and was intimately involved in fashioning the Canadian response to what became known as "the Yoshida letter."

This letter, signed on 24 December 1951 by Yoshida Shigeru and addressed to Dulles, was made public on 15 January 1952 and immediately created an uproar because it suggested that Japan would recognize Taiwan despite a gentlemen's agreement with Great Britain that Japan would be free to determine its relations between the two Chinese regimes. We now know, of course, that Dulles forced Yoshida to sign a letter drafted by Dulles himself guaranteeing that Japan would recognize the Taiwanese regime and isolate the PRC.[63] This, Dulles told Yoshida, was necessary in order to get Republican senators to ratify the peace treaty. When the British government vigorously protested against Dulles's actions in Tokyo, Dulles lied to the US Secretary of State, suggesting that Yoshida himself had proffered the ideas and that Dulles had only encouraged him to put his ideas on paper.[64] The bill for Republican support for the peace treaty had come due, and Dulles was determined to have it paid in full. Norman, in response to Great Britain's protests against what was perceived as undue US pressure on Yoshida, informed Pearson regarding the developments.[65] Pearson was also exercised by the US power play, and, in response to Norman's memo, wrote: "This is very stupid policy on the part of the USA and will not work out as they plan. The Japs will see to that. It is surprising that Dulles can be so naive! I think we should tell Wrong what we think about it in case he has a chance to discuss the matter in Washington."[66] Norman prepared a message to that effect, quoting, on the advice of Escott Reid, the minister's comments in full (the racist term "Japs" was changed to "Japanese"). In his memorandum on the subject, Norman noted that arbitrary measures similar to the Yoshida letter had "marked the latter years of the occupation." Hume Wrong objected to the idea of raising the idea with the State Department, pleading that it was too late and would do little good.[67] He suggested Pearson might express the policy disagreement in a press conference, but, according to Pearson, this had not been possible. Regarding the US argument that Japanese support for Chiang Kai-shek was necessary in order to obtain ratification of the peace treaty, Pearson responded that he found it hard to believe that over one-third of the US Senate would "vote against the ratification of a treaty which was in effect drafted by the United States and which was supported by so many countries merely out of deference to the United States, especially in view of the frequency with which this treaty ha[d] been produced as proof of the willingness of the United States to make peace as against the Soviet determination to be obstructive."[68] Wrong eventually complied with the instructions, meeting with State Department representatives on 14 February. Wrong reported that Allison "rose to the bait," defending the Yoshida letter and stating that the Yoshida government had informed them in June 1951 that it intended to recognize the Chiang regime.[69] A month later, Pearson reported: "[Dulles] denied emphatically that this intervention violated any agreement previously reached with British Foreign Secretary Herbert Morrison, and he claimed that Eden accepted this. I doubt, however, whether the London version of this episode would be the same as that given to me by Dulles."[70]

The peace treaty and military agreements signed in 1951 had important repercussions. After much jockeying, enough of the respective legislatures ratified the treaties to bring them into force. Japan formally became independent on 28 April 1952. However, most Asian countries either did not sign the treaty or refused to ratify it, and for many years relations between the Japanese and other Asian governments were strained. There were no diplomatic relations between Japan and the Soviet Union for a number of years; the same with South Korea and China. Important territorial issues, including the fate of the Kurile Islands under Soviet control, were left unresolved.[71] Furthermore, many people in Japan objected to the terms of the treaty, particularly the continued presence of US bases and the seizure of Okinawa by the US government. The Korean minority in Japan protested what was in effect the denial of citizenship. In the end, NSC-68, the Korean War, and the military pacts signed in 1951 contributed to transforming what in Europe had been a Cold War confrontation into hot wars and the militarization of Asia. For Yoshida Shigeru, however, it was a chance for redemption, not with China or the other Asian countries that had suffered so much at the hands of Japan's imperial forces, but with the Anglo-Saxon powers: "As I have stated, and history confirms, ever since the opening of Japan's doors to the Western world more than a century ago, the basic principle of Japanese policy has been the maintenance of close and cordial political and economic ties with Great Britain and the United States. That Japan departed from this basic principle, and became allied with Germany and Italy, was the prime cause for my country being pushed headlong into a reckless war."[72] Yoshida may well have thought the treaty represented a vindication of his life, and, in a way, it did. Just as Yoshida discounted the history of Japanese aggression in China and Asia, so the peace treaty excluded the peoples of those countries from redress or reconciliation. Yoshida had embraced not only defeat but also the US-led imperial alliance that was waging war only a few hundred kilometers from Tokyo – with devastating results.

12 Racism, War Crimes, and the Korean War

Uijongbu is a suburb in the north of metropolitan Seoul. In the ancient past, it was a centre of officialdom in the Korean kingdoms. Today it is the site of a large army base, a reminder that, despite the democratization of South Korea in the late 1980s, the country remains highly militarized. Continuing further into the countryside, the military presence becomes even more pronounced. Along the winding Imjin River, not far from the border dividing South Korea from North Korea, young soldiers stand at attention in sentry posts erected every thousand metres or so. Between each of the elevated, wooden lookouts is a large chain fence topped with razor wire. The shadows of war are not far from the small village Hwang Bang-li, Yangjun County, in northern Kyongi Province. Here, at the top of a hill overgrown with grass, is a small earthen mound. Shin Hyun-chan, a retired farmer, tells the story of how his father came to be buried in this unmarked grave.[1]

Shin displays a petition that he submitted to the Ministry of Defence. It is signed and dated, with the names, dates of birth, and seals of eleven others from the village verifying his story. Shin recounted the moment that changed his life and that of his family forever. It was September 1951. Armistice talks between the warring antagonists had begun, but fighting continued. A UN engineer unit was stationed only two or three hundred metres from Shin's old house, constructing roads and support facilities for the war effort. Shin's family farmed, growing rice and beans on their land until the war came. The

UN troops were living in tents in an adjacent field, and some Korean soldiers were staying in a house nearby. He recalled: "It was the middle of the night; I remember because there was a full moon, and it must have been the eighth month [according to the lunar calendar] and he came into our house and told us to come out. The soldier first asked my father something, but he had no idea what he was talking about because he couldn't speak the language, so my father called me to help with communication, and that's when the shooting started ... the soldier had this machine gun in his hands, and there must have been about thirty bullets in it ... and so we went out, and then he starts shooting." The soldier was standing in the middle of the courtyard, a common feature of Korean houses of the era. Shin's younger siblings and mother were in their respective rooms at the time. Shin doesn't remember much after being shot but he did recall the weapon that was used: "You could see the bullets," he said, "about thirty bullets that go into the cartridge and you feed it from the bottom." His only other recollection was that other soldiers came into the courtyard and that he was transported somewhere with his father, Shin Yong-Dok. He was sure the shooter was a Canadian: "The way he was dressed, the uniform and all, was Canadian."

Shin's mother, Park Chong-Soon, now eighty-eight and crippled by age and a life of hardship, recalled: "The soldier shot towards the room so that the bullet skinned my ten-year old daughter in the neck. I ran out of the room and looked to see my husband lying down covered with blood on his stomach area. I tried to cover his stomach but others came and said it wasn't going to do any good. My son was also bleeding ... Soldiers came in after my husband and my son got shot, and they took them to the hospital. The next day soldiers came and took me to where my husband was, but by the time I got there he had already died. I then looked for my son but he was transferred to another hospital. So my situation ... of course it was horrible." Park said that she had no photograph to remind her of her husband, that she was left with nothing: "When I came home [from the hospital] they brought my husband's body back. He was totally stripped, he had nothing on, and he was just wrapped in a blanket. The next day I went to look for my son again, and so the villagers and friends came in and just took him and buried him."

The younger Shin was hospitalized for twenty-five or twenty-six days, twenty days in a Norwegian field unit at Tuk Kye-Ri and then another five days in a Red Cross hospital in Seoul. Shin found out later that a soldier accused of the crimes was to be court-martialled. He and his sister attended the trial. A translator told him afterwards that the perpetrator had been sentenced to ten years and sent back to Canada: "But we didn't really know

Shin Hyun-Chan stands beside his father's grave in Hwang Bang-li, Kyongi, South Korea, in April 2004. He was wounded and his father was killed by a wayward Canadian soldier in 1951. Dozens of soldiers faced court-martials for similar war crimes but were then released upon return to Canada. | With permission, photograph by author

and there was no way to verify it." Life was not easy for the Shin/Park family after losing their father. They tried to eke out a living from farming but eventually had to sell the farm. In 1956, Shin served an obligatory three years in the military, but his disabilities from the shooting were such that he ended

Shin Yong-Dok's widow, Park Chong-Soon, has not forgotten the fateful events that left her husband dead and her son seriously wounded. | With permission, photograph by author

up incapacitated much of the time. After recounting his ordeal, Shin displayed the scars from his wounds, an entry scar on his abdomen and the exit wound on his back, as well as another scar near his elbow.

Shin might have taken his tragic story to his grave had it not been for the fact that a political revolution in 1987-88 finally toppled the corrupt and repressive juntas that had ruled South Korea from 1948 until the end of the 1980s. The flowering of democracy released spirits that had long been repressed. Kim Dong-choon, associate professor of history at Songkonghue

University in Seoul, is one of the founding members of the Truth Commission on Civilian Massacres during the Korean War.[2] According to Kim, hundreds of victims of atrocities committed during the war have come forth to tell stories not unlike those of Shin, and in every part of the country, regional advocacy groups for the victims have been established with the assistance of local NGOs. Atrocities were committed by all sides during the war, but after forty years of only hearing allegations of North Korean atrocities during the authoritarian period, the new stories were dramatically changing the portraits of the past in South Korea. Indeed, what prompted Shin to finally go public with his own story, and to file a claim for redress, were the 1998 revelations of a massacre that had taken place at No Gun Ri.

The Massacre at No Gun Ri

A month after northern forces began their attack, they overran Seoul, the southern capital, and pushed as far south as Yongdon, a village half-way between Seoul and the southern tip of the Korean peninsula.[3] US ground forces that had been rushed to the battlefront were forced to turn back and head south in the face of the North Korean assault. Covering the retreat of US forces was the 2nd Battalion of the 7th Cavalry Regiment. Accompanying the retreating US and southern troops were thousands of refugees fleeing the war zone. On 26 July 1950, some six hundred of these refugees, most of them women, children, and elderly people from small villages that had been caught in earlier crossfire, approached a train trestle near the small village of No Gun Ri. It was around noon on a hot, muggy, but clear day when they reached the trestle at No Gun Ri, a few kilometres from their own villages. There they paused to try to collect their wits and to make something to eat after the kilometres of trekking. Thoughts of food or home quickly vanished when jets howled in towards them and an explosion suddenly tore into the group, sending mud and body parts flying into the air. Machine gun fire from troops in the hills spattered around them. Yang Hae-sook, a thirteen-year-old girl, survived the first blast, hidden under the skirts of her mother, who had dragged her under an acacia tree. Her uncle was not so lucky. Hae-sook recalled: "He was flipping over in pain. I saw the intestines coming out of his belly. They were blue. He screamed three times and then he was silent."[4] A shell exploded near the acacia tree where Hae-sook hid, shrapnel blasting her in the face. When she gained consciousness, she found her eye dangling before her. Screaming, she begged those around her to tear it off. Stunned, none responded, so Hae-sook grabbed her eye, pulling it to sever the last ties to her face, and proceeded to throw it away. She and the other villagers plunged into a culvert near the trestle, but it offered little protection as troops aimed machine gun fire and mortars directly at the refugees. During lulls in the fire, many escaped from the culvert to gather in the two tunnels under the rail tracks only to be attacked again. The carnage continued intermittently for over a day. By the end, hundreds had been killed or maimed.

Confronted by Associated Press revelations about No Gun Ri, the US Department of Defense initially denied any wrongdoing. But with mounting evidence of atrocities, including confessions by American soldiers who were present at No Gun Ri, the department eventually opened its own investigation and, in January 2001, published its findings.[5] The investigators concluded that they could not "exclude the possibility that US or allied aircraft might have hit civilian refugees in the vicinity of No Gun Ri during an air strike/strafing on July 26, 1950" but that the attacks were not deliberate. It further concluded that some US soldiers of the 1st Cavalry Division may have fired out of fear but that there had been no order to kill civilians.[6] "What befell civilians in the vicinity of No Gun Ri in late July 1950," the summary concludes, "was a tragic and deeply regrettable accompaniment to a war forced upon unprepared US and ROK forces." Since the publication of this report, however, further evidence has come to light that casts doubt on the army's account. This includes a previously unknown memorandum written by the American ambassador to South Korea, John J. Muccio, stating: "If refugees do appear from north of US lines they will receive warning shots, and if they then persist in advancing they will be shot."[7]

That the US Army and Air Force to some extent adopted policies that either targeted refugees or allowed them to become targets gains further credence as an increasing number of claims of atrocities come forth within Korea. Yet, very few Canadians or Americans have ever heard the story of No Gun Ri, despite the fact that the authors of *The Bridge at No Gun Ri* won the Pulitzer Prize for investigative journalism for their work in breaking the story. Stories, no matter how truthful, have difficulty becoming ingrained in public memory if they go against dominant interpretations of wars. At best they are integrated into conventional narratives as tragic but isolated incidents, perpetrated by soldiers who are considered bad apples. Life goes on. War itself is inhumane, or so the story goes. In South Korea, however, that response does not suffice. The incidents are so numerous and widespread that, as the tragedy of the war is finally brought to light, we find that No Gun Ri and the murder of an innocent civilian north of Seoul are only the tip of a large, blood-stained iceberg. The ongoing democratic revolution is melting that iceberg, and, as it disappears, the bloody past is re-emerging and telling a new generation in South Korea different stories, reinforcing a sense of nationhood long denied. It is a past that leads from Korea to Washington and to other capitals, including Ottawa.

War Crimes and Impunity

It took a team of dedicated reporters with a supportive editor to track down and verify the events at No Gun Ri. As it turns out, it was possible to verify Shin's story much more easily through Canadian sources. On 6 December 1951, Canadian army headquarters in Ottawa announced that John Murray Steeves, a sapper with the 57th Independent Field Squadron of the Royal Canadian Engineers, would be tried for the murder of Shin's father.[8] Army headquarters had appointed Brigadier A.B. Connelly, commander of the Canadian military mission in Tokyo, as court president, and he arrived in Seoul on 13 December. The court martial began the following day. According to press reports, those who had found Steeves testified that he had appeared incoherent and complained that "a Korean had stolen his watch."[9] The watch had been recovered, but the two soldiers who produced it and the investigating warrant officer were both undergoing psychiatric treatment in Japan. Another witness testified that Steeves had left his bed muttering, "Unless I get my wife back tonight somebody's going to die." Steeves had been drunk going to work on 16 September and was even more drunk upon arriving back from work around 4:00 PM, when he was put to bed. He had been assigned guard duty beginning at 3:00 AM the next morning. Two other sappers testified that they had accompanied Steeves into the village where they had taken over an unoccupied house so they could have a party where they "couldn't bother anybody."[10] According to Shin's testimony at the time, three soldiers had visited their home seeking "women and liquor."[11] According to a medical officer, a third victim was a sapper of the Republic of Korea's 1st Division. On 16 December, a Canadian army psychiatrist testified that Steeves had a mild form of "repressed hostility" that might cause him to "explode" if intoxicated. Steeves himself testified on 17 December, during his court martial in Seoul, that he could not remember anything about the incident. The following day, the court convicted Steeves of manslaughter and sentenced him to fifteen years in prison. It appeared that the rule of law, a liberal touchstone, was functioning even during a war fifty years ago. Subsequent events, however, fail to sustain that premise.

On 13 June 1952, Canadian Press reported that a Canadian "found guilty of manslaughter in the death of a Korean civilian and sentenced to 15 years in prison ha[d] been freed by the Defence Department."[12] John Steeves was freed "some time ago," after Judge Advocate General Brigadier W.A. Lawson ruled that he had been wrongfully convicted at the December court martial, basing his ruling on the law involving "circumstantial evidence." In other words, Steeves didn't serve even six months of his fifteen-year sentence. News of this development never reached the Shin family. Was the court martial really that flawed? Was Steeves really innocent? We may never know the answers to those questions. As it turns out, what happened to Shin and his family, and the impunity that the perpetrator received, was not an isolated incident. Six months prior to the Shin murder, Glen Blank, Alan Davis, and Donald Gibson of the Princess Patricia Regiment left their camp near the village of Chung Woon Myon.[13] They had just come back from the front for a two-week rest period and had been partying. They came across a farmhouse and decided that this was their stop. Inside they found a farmer, several South Korean soldiers, and two women, one of whom was the sister of one of the soldiers. The Canadian soldiers demanded that the women have sex with them. The women were beaten when they refused, then they were dragged off and raped. The South Korean soldiers tried to intervene but were beaten senseless at gunpoint. On their departure, Glen Blank tossed a grenade into the farmhouse, and, for good measure, the Canadian troops fired their weapons into the building as they left the scene. Local authorities complained and rumours started, attracting the attention of Bill Boss, a Canadian Press correspondent. Ten days after the crimes, Boss had finally pieced the story together and had sent it to his head office. It never arrived. A few months later, *MacLean's* revealed what had happened to Boss's story, written nearly half a year earlier. It had been censored by officials in Tokyo, who forwarded it to Canadian army headquarters, where it languished. To add insult to injury, Boss himself "was subjected to a campaign of vilification from United Nations public relations officers. He was called 'subversive' and an abortive attempt was made to oust him from the Korean theatre."[14] Finally, on 1 August 1951, defence headquarters announced that Blank, Gibson, and Davis would be court-martialled that fall. After a week of trials, military judges found Blank guilty of manslaughter, and Gibson and Davis, of attempted rape. Blank received a sentence of life imprisonment, while Gibson and Davis received two years less a day and eighteen-month terms, respectively. They were shipped home to Canada to serve their sentences. Yet, on 8 July 1952, Blank was released, and Gibson and Davis saw their sentences set aside.[15] There were hundreds and perhaps thousands of such violent crimes committed by UN forces. Of the sixty or so Canadian cases that actually came to trial and resulted in convictions, most of those convicted, like Steeves and Blank, were released upon their return to Canada.[16] In another example, two soldiers, Vincent Francis Carlisle and Donald James Ferrier, were convicted of raping a Korean woman and sentenced to ten and fifteen years, respectively, in 1951. The court-martial appeal board ordered a new trial for these men on 4 September 1952.[17] The pattern of conviction in Korea and exoneration in Canada casts doubt on the integrity of the military justice system. Indeed, a Canadian military historian recently concluded that the record of remission and release was a travesty of justice and "another example of the institutional racism that seems to have permeated the upper echelons of the Department of National Defence."[18] It is an assertion that, if anything, understates the problem.

Racism, War, and Crimes against Humanity

Many Canadian soldiers conducted themselves with discipline and integrity while in Korea, and the Korean Veterans Association had to overcome serious impediments to have their sacrifices remembered.[19] Indeed, some of the Canadian soldiers displayed a strong sense of humanity towards the Korean people. For example, Sergeant-Major Maurice Juteau of the Royal 22nd Regiment was distraught at the pitiable conditions he found in a Korean hospital and decided to take matters into his own hands. He organized what became known as the "khaki charities." Juteau asked his comrades to donate clothes and food that had come from Canada. Not only did soldiers respond, they also began to donate part of their rations and were able to provide thousands of supplementary meals for Koreans. Donations were being picked up twice a day in the wake of the overwhelming response.[20] Such acts of benevolence need to be acknowledged. But they should not be counter-posed to acts of criminal behaviour, as if one offsets the other. The question the historian must answer is why a substantial number of soldiers committed crimes against civilians, and why these acts went unpunished. Today, thanks to the efforts of critical scholarship, we now know that the commission of atrocities is often just an extreme reflection of a broader social problem. A new generation of military historians is today acknowledging the problem of racism, but there remains much to be done to understand how racism interacts with other variables to produce some of the most horrific crimes. The release and exoneration of Canadian soldiers who committed war crimes in Korea did reflect a structural problem of racism in the upper echelons of the National Defence establishment. But it was hardly confined to that group. In fact, even a cursory examination of reports by journalists during the Korean War suggests that racism was rampant and that the crimes against humanity may well have been reflections of what we now refer to as a toxic environment, made even deadlier by war.

On 21 August 1951, the day before the first Canadian court martial began in Seoul, George Barrett sent a dispatch to the *New York Times,* outlining the crimes and concluding: "Details of the crime of which the Canadians are accused are particularly shocking. The greatest ill effect from this crime is its seizure by the Koreans as a symbol of the widespread contempt held by many United Nations soldiers for the people of this country, a contempt emphasized every day in the way the Koreans are pushed around."[21] Bill Boss and Barrett were not the only journalists who pointed to the problem. Pierre Berton, a fledgling correspondent who later became one of Canada's major literary figures, was sent to Korea in the spring of 1951 to report for *Maclean's* magazine. At that time, the US-led forces were pushing once again northward, "moving back up the peninsula through villages roasted by our napalm and cities crumbled by our shells."[22] Berton later recalled:

> I have some vivid memories of Korea and many of them I wish I could forget. There is the memory of the old Korean who stumbled unloading a crate from a C-54 in Pusan, and the little pipsqueak of a GI private who seized him by the faded coat lapels and shouted in his face: "You sonofabitch if you do that again I'll punch you in the nose!" There is the memory of the wretched young man with his feet half eaten away, dying of gangrene and refused medical assistance by a succession of MOs because he was a Korean and didn't count. There is the memory of the Canadian private who emptied his Bren gun into a Korean grave and the memory of the GI in the bus at Pusan who shouted loudly at a comrade about how much he hated the gooks and the look on the face of the Korean bus driver who overheard him.[23]

Berton continued: "There is above all the memory of the serious young Korean university graduate gazing solemnly and sadly at me across the remnants of a chow mein dinner that had cost the equivalent of two months' wages in Korea, and saying: 'You Americans are so stupid. You have made prostitutes of our women and beggars of our children. Surely you are not going to make the mistake of thinking the Koreans love you?'"[24] Berton had tried to take this Korean colleague, with two others, to an American mess hall, but they ended up "eating in a native restaurant because this young man could not eat with [him] in the officers' mess where all the other war correspondents [ate]. Yet he was an accredited war correspondent, too, who wore the United Nations patch and uniform. But he was a Korean. Sorry."

Bill Boss, on leave from his reporting duties from Korea, told Ottawa's Canadian Club: "Canadian soldiers have shared in a general Western contempt for the Korean people that stems from a superiority complex."[25] Syndicated columnist Elmore Philpott also took up the criticism: "The terrible truth is that in the battle for men's minds and souls, the Western leadership is losing out everywhere in Asia and Africa mainly because it, so far, has nothing solid and well reasoned to offer anybody but the white man."[26]

Prodded by these and other newspaper reports at the time, the government responded by ordering an internal inquiry and by sending a delegation of church leaders to Korea. On 15 October 1951, Defence Minister Brooke Claxton announced that Maurice Roy, archbishop of Quebec; W.F. Barfoot, primate of the Church of England and Canada; C.M. Nicholson, moderator of the United Church; and N.D. Kennedy, moderator of the Presbyterian Church, would be going to Korea at the minister's invitation.[27] Upon landing back in Montreal, Roy was quoted as being convinced "that reports of Canadian troops 'mistreating and looking down on Koreans' [were] incorrect."[28] Roy acknowledged that Korea was ravaged almost beyond description by the war but that the Koreans were a proud people and versatile, whose houses, although made of mud and straw, had heating in the floor. According to the religious leaders, reporters such as George Barrett, Bill Boss, and Pierre Berton were exaggerating isolated incidents. Shortly afterwards, acting chief of the General Staff, Major General H.A. Sparling, reported that the internal inquiry showed that Canadian soldiers were friendly towards Koreans and gave them food, clothing, and medical attention.[29] The combination of military denial backed up by clerical testimony was enough to bury the problem of crimes perpetrated by Allied soldiers despite the fact that Canadian reporters had pointed not only to specific incidents but also to the problems of systemic racism that existed among the Canadian troops.[30] This point was addressed neither by the military nor by the religious leaders. Indeed, the Canadian Army's official history of its participation in the war, published in 1966, reflected the persistence of racism in its account of the capture of a number of Chinese troops: "Three days later the platoon captured three more Chinese and in the words of the platoon commander 'it was rumoured at the time ... that the poor fellows had heard that there was a laundry in the vicinity and had merely come in looking for a job.'"[31] Here we see how the history of racism in Canada, expressed through the stereotype of Chinese as "laundry workers," became translocalized across the Pacific, with tragic consequences for Koreans and Chinese. Not only were individual acts of inhumanity encouraged through direct orders to bomb and strafe civilians, they were also encouraged by the atmosphere of contempt that stemmed from the ongoing legacy of white supremacy in Canada. The inhumanity, however, was not confined to individual acts.

Total War and Indiscriminate Bombing

The abuse of Koreans and individual war crimes committed by UN forces were systemic and reflected, among other things, a racist bias against Koreans that in a war theatre, where fear and death were everywhere, contributed to the many crimes that have been noted. These individual actions, however, were reproduced on a much more massive scale through the actions of the UN air forces. The bombing and strafing of civilians at No Gun Ri described earlier was but one example of how air power was used to tactically support troops on the ground.

The Associated Press revelations regarding No Gun Ri suggest that this was not simply a "friendly fire" accident or a case of a few soldiers having run amok, although that too occurred. In the case of No Gun Ri, the atrocities committed appear to be linked to US policy towards refugees. On 24 July 1950, 1st Cavalry orders instructed: "No refugees to cross the front line. Fire everyone trying cross lines. Use discretion in case of women and children."[32] This policy was predicated on the belief that any civilian left in a war zone that was supposed to have been cleared was to be considered an enemy and action taken accordingly. Furthermore, the army had requested that the air force "strafe all civilian refugee parties that [were] noted approaching [their] positions," and the air force had, as of 25 July, complied with the army request.[33] Colonel Turner C. Rogers, reviewing this policy, noted: "[such operations] involving the strafing of civilians are sure to receive wide publicity and may cause embarrassment to the US Air Force and to the US government in its relations with the United Nations."[34] According to an official army source, on 3 August 1950, on orders of Major General Hobart R. Gay, the US Army bombed the Naktong River Bridge at Waegwan while it was crowded with refugees, killing hundreds.[35] Nor did it end there. On 9 January 1951, an Associated Press report out of Tokyo reported: "United Nations airmen today were ordered to kill any one moving behind

Communist lines in Korea – in or out of uniform – except women and children."[36]

Further research on the topic of military directives related to civilians in Korea is necessary. However, evidence from Canadian sources also backs up the revelations related to No Gun Ri and points to problems in the treatment of refugees fleeing the war. For example, on 24 April 1951, Canadian private Wayne Mitchell gazed into the valley near Kapyong and saw "hundreds of thousands of people, mostly refugees" streaming towards his position: "Orders were to stop them, because the enemy was in there among them. I felt horrible, but I set up ... and fired low."[37] Mitchell was soon relieved of his gruesome task when "three American fighter aircraft swooped down over his position and began strafing and bombing the people in the valley." Mitchell's account has serious implications because it suggests that American jets continued to strafe and bomb civilians even a year after No Gun Ri and that infantry units were also being ordered to fire on refugees. If so, then many Korean civilians injured or killed during the conflict were not some sort of "regrettable accompaniment" to war (i.e., "collateral damage") but, rather, the victims of a policy of deliberately targeting refugees.

The use of air power in support of close ground operations and the deliberate targeting of refugees was but one example of a breach of conventional warfare committed by UN forces. But the air forces were engaged in more than just "tactical" operations. They also engaged in "strategic" bombing, that is, in the targeting of strategic sites that, although not in an immediate theatre where fighting on the ground was taking place, were considered key military targets. The Joint Chiefs of Staff decided to dispatch units of the Strategic Air Command against targets in North Korea. Emmett O'Donnell and Curtis E. LeMay immediately proposed to MacArthur that SAC bombers be allowed to conduct fire-bombing of large urban areas as they had in Japan at the end of the war. MacArthur had been instructed to avoid fire-bombing, however, and he declined O'Donnell's request. Nevertheless, he did agree to the bombing of urban military targets and stated that, if SAC bombers missed their targets "and kill[ed] people or destroy[ed] other parts of the city, [he] accept[ed] that as part of war."[38] In other words, although MacArthur did not authorize fire-bombing as a general strategy, he did allow for the bombing of cities and villages. Thus began the first wave of strategic bombings of North Korean targets. B-29s dropped thirty thousand tons of bombs in just over three months in the early stage of the war. By October 1950, UN forces had regained the offensive and were moving into North Korea. Strategic bombing targets had become so scarce that one bomber, finding no justifiable target, chased a motorcycle rider on a road, dropping bombs until one finally vaporized the "target."[39] The lack of targets prompted officials to authorize the return of two bomber groups to the United States.

MacArthur had to reverse himself quickly when Chinese troops with their North Korean counterparts began their counter-offensive in response to the invasion of the north. This prompted MacArthur and Stratemeyer to reassess the situation, and they authorized the use of fire-bombing. The first attack occurred on 5 November 1950 when two dozen bombers fire-bombed the city of Kanggye, destroying 65 percent of it. Stratemeyer rationalized the attack this way: "Kanggye was virtual arsenal and tremendously important communications centre, hence decision to employ incendiaries for first time in Korea."[40] The destruction of Kanggye through fire-bombing was but the start of what can only be described as the most systematic and deliberate campaign of terror bombing in world history. [41] Although MacArthur and his air command would continue to state publicly that they were bombing only military targets, the truth was that MacArthur had instructed his fliers "to destroy every means of communication and every installation, factory, city and village" in North Korea, except for hydroelectric plants and the City of Rashin (sites that had been put off limits because they bordered on China and the Soviet Union, respectively).[42] When the JCS tried to cancel the planned fire-bombing of Sinuiju near the Chinese border, MacArthur railed against the chiefs and finally got his way: seventy bombers burned down 60 percent of the city. Eight more towns followed, including Hoeryong, which was burned to the ground. MacArthur was determined, he told the US ambassador to south Korea, to turn the territory between the UN front and the border into a "desert," barren of anything that might support the other side. Chafing at the restrictions that prevented his air forces from crossing the Yalu River into China proper, MacArthur announced that, to counter this advantage to the enemy: "command, communication and supply centers of North Korea will be obliterated."

The carnage that ensued was immense. In early 1951, George Barrett, the *New York Times* journalist, described in graphic detail the grim reality that he encountered at one Korean village in the aftermath of a US-led bombing raid: "A napalm raid hit the village [north of Anyang] three or four days ago when the Chinese were holding up the advance, and nowhere in the village have they buried the dead because there is nobody left to do it. This correspondent came across an old woman, the only one who seemed to be left alive, dazedly hanging up some clothes in a blackened courtyard filled with the bodies of four members of her family." Barrett continued: "The inhabitants throughout the village and in the fields were caught and killed and kept the exact posture they had held when the napalm struck – a man about to get on his bicycle, 50 boys and girls playing in an orphanage, a housewife strangely unmarked, holding in her hand a page torn from a Sears-Roebuck catalog with markings at a $2.98 'bewitching bed jacket.' There must be almost 200 dead in the tiny hamlet."[43]

The civilians that perished were the victims of napalm. Invented during the Second World War, napalm was a combustible gel formed by adding napthenate and palmitate to gasoline (the name is derived from the "na" of napthenate and the "palm" of palmitate). The horrible effects of the napalm attacks that Barrett's article describe did not go unnoticed. Indeed, his article caught the attention of Lester Pearson, who wrote a personal note to Hume Wrong in Washington, noting that the Anyang description would "have nothing but unhappy repercussions in Asia."[44] Pearson wrote that he knew of nothing that could indicate more clearly "the dangerous possibilities of United States and United Nations action in Korea on Asian opinion than a military episode of this kind, and the way it was reported. Such military action was possibly 'inevitable' but surely we do not have to give publicity to such things all over the world. Wouldn't you think the censorship which is now in force could stop this kind of reporting?" Pearson also complained about language and terms such as "Operation Killer" and "putting the Chinese through the meat chopper." In reply, Wrong agreed with Pearson about the need for better censorship and suggested that an approach might be made in Tokyo. But, he noted, the term "Operation Killer" was not a problem of defective censorship: it was the name assigned by military command. He concluded, "Nearly all Koreans, both North and South, must now rue the day on which they became the victims of collective security."[45] Pearson and Wrong were not alone in their concerns. Brooke Claxton, the minister of defence, also made clear that he worried about the use of bombers and artillery to destroy defenceless villages.[46] But none pursued the matter, and the blood of innocent civilians continued to flow. If anything, the prohibitions on flights across the Yalu River intensified the indiscriminate bombing, and, by the time the armistice talks began in July 1951, Curtis LeMay would recall: "We burned down just about every city in North and South Korea both – we killed off over a million civilian Koreans and drove several million more from their homes."[47]

When the armistice talks became deadlocked over the issue of repatriation of POWs, rather than pursue diplomatic means to resolve the deadlocked discussions, the US military seized on the opportunity to promote a new wave of bombing. In May 1952, US commander Mark Clark promoted "air pressure," that is, the use of massive air strikes as a means to bludgeon the North Koreans and Chinese into agreeing to US terms in the armistice talks then deadlocked in Panmunjom.[48] In June 1952, massive air raids largely destroyed the hydroelectric system in North Korea, beginning with the Suiho facilities, Aoji and Hoeryong on the Soviet border, and the monzanite mines that, like the Canadian uranium mines in Eldorado, supplied their country with uranium ores. And, on 11 July and 27 August, the US Air Force launched massive raids on the northern capital, Pyongyang. The August raid was the largest single raid of the whole Korean War. Indeed, the destruction was so extensive that, once again, further bombing was considered inadvisable because all potential targets had been destroyed. Having exhausted their strategy of destruction from the air without winning concessions, the UN/US representatives abandoned the Panmunjom talks. Yet, even after all that destruction, the thirst for victory remained impossible to quench. In May 1953, with the armistice talks still deadlocked, the allies decided on a more devious tactic, bombing the dams that provided water for field irrigation. Air force analysts had discovered that rice was a key source of food for people in the north, and, with this in mind, they proposed bombing the dams that were the centrepieces of the irrigation system for crops in Pyongan and Hwanghae provinces. But Far East Air Force commander Otto P. Weyland and Mark Clark hesitated, knowing that the Nazis' destruction of dikes in the Netherlands during the Second World War had been declared a war crime by the Nuremberg Tribunal. In order to obscure the nature of the attacks, they decided only to blast irrigation dams that were in the vicinity of "military targets," and, on 13 May 1953, US bombers attacked the Toksan Dam, north of Pyongyang. A few hours later the dam collapsed, releasing a torrent of water that destroyed rice fields as well as some rail lines and bridges.[49] Two days later, the bombers attacked the Chasan Dam, just north of Pyongyang, leading to massive flooding not only of the rice fields but also of Pyongyang itself.

Biological Warfare

On 24 February 1952, Chinese premier Zhou Enlai publicly charged the US government with using biological weapons in the Korean War, a charge that elicited a hot denial by US secretary of state Dean Acheson a little more than a month later. Canadians were soon drawn into the debate, as the Reverend James Endicott, visiting China at the time, cabled Lester Pearson, informing him that his personal investigations in northeast China revealed that there indeed was "continuing germ warfare on Chinese mainland."[50] What ensued was a major propaganda battle by the two sides in the Cold War, a battle in which truth became a casualty. Years later, the debate continues. Some scholars, using recent but partial records from the Russian Presidential Archive, suggest that the allegations of germ warfare in Korea were completely fabricated.[51] Canadian scholars Stephen Endicott and Edward Hagerman have contested this conclusion and recently published an in-depth study of US involvement in biological warfare preparations.[52] While final resolution of the matter will only come with the opening of all countries' related archives, a reprise of the events and reactions of that period is instructive because, although key documents remain classified, related materials are becoming increasingly available. What is clear today is that, in response to the allegations of biological warfare, the coalition governments engaged in a carefully orchestrated and massive propaganda campaign.[53] In the process, the Canadian government misled Parliament, encouraged censorship of the press, and intimidated the peace movement.

Speaking in the House of Commons on 12 May 1952, Lester Pearson told Parliament that the charge that UN forces in Korea had engaged in germ warfare was "so false and so fantastic that it would normally be unwise to dignify it by official denials." However, because it had become an issue, Pearson addressed the matter: "So far as our own position is concerned, it is, of course, a slanderous falsehood to say that Canada has participated in any way in any form of germ warfare. It is equally false and equally slanderous, but more cowardly and despicable, to imply without stating it in so many words that Canada is making any preparations in this field except for defence against such warfare."[54] Pearson assured Parliament that some of Canada's "best qualified scientists" had already examined the so-called evidence and had "pronounced it, in an oral report to [him], to be a transparent and clumsy hoax." The following month the minister of justice introduced three letters from C.E. Atwood, A.W. Baker, and W.H. Britain, respectively, testifying that the evidence of biological warfare was implausible. Their views and the painting of James Endicott as an anti-Christ reflected the fact, as one scholarly source puts it, that the media had "willingly joined in a McCarthyite campaign that was sanctioned by the highest authorities in the land."[55]

At the same time, Justice E. Stuart McDougall, who had represented Canada on the Tokyo Tribunal and had returned to Montreal to become a judge in the Court of King's Bench, wrote to Lester Pearson after the biological warfare storm broke. He had, McDougall wrote Pearson, received a Beijing news report that contained a letter written by Mei Juao, his Chinese counterpart on the Tokyo Tribunal.[56] In the letter, Justice Mei had expressed his opinion on "Germ Warfare," and McDougall told Pearson that it amounted to "quite a bit of Communist propaganda": "Having spent nearly three years with Judge Mei in Tokyo, we became quite friendly. I may add that his present attitude comes as a complete surprise, for during our Tokyo experience there was no stronger supporter of the so-called Nationalist Government of Chiang Kai Shek. However, in truly oriental fashion I assume he has come to the conclusion that 'one must live' and the easiest living in China these days is obtained by supporting the Communist Regime."

What was not revealed at the time was that the DEA, prompted by the US State Department, had solicited scientific opinions to back the government's case while at the same time concealing more reliable and informed views regarding biological weapons. This is clear from a memorandum prepared by Dr. Guilford B. Reed of the Defence Research Board in conjunction with the DEA.[57] Reed was the key Canadian scientist involved in biological warfare research at this time and worked with the DEA to assess the plausibility of the evidence offered by Chinese and North Korean forces. In the memorandum, Reed suggested that there were a number of anomalies in the evidence he had reviewed, mainly with regard to the fact that the insects claimed to be used as carriers were reportedly active in temperatures of -20 degrees Celsius – far below the temperature at which such insects were normally active. The idea that these insects had been cold-conditioned was, however, "biologically conceivable," though it would require considerable time and study to develop such a modification. The charges of germ warfare and accompanying propaganda, stated the memorandum, had been "carefully prepared and there [were] no obvious impossibilities with regard to the diseased and the carriers with which they [were] supposed to be associated." The delivery of biological warfare agents by artillery would present insurmountable difficulties, but, the memorandum continued: "[The] dropping of insects from the air is entirely feasible. Such objects as rotten fish and bags of pork are rather unorthodox B.W. weapons but again they are not entirely impossible. The use of feathers has been experimented with in Canada, although anthrax, which the Communists link with them, was not used in our experiments."

Despite having received and read Reed's memorandum, Pearson persisted in promoting the views of Atwood and the other Canadian scientists, even introducing their letters in Parliament and releasing them to the press in June, while Reed's views were kept under lock and key. That Pearson did not release or share Reed's findings is not surprising since they indicated the allegations had some foundation. Moreover, Reed's memorandum indirectly suggests that the Canadian government was indeed involved in biological warfare research – research that has since been revealed to have been conducted in concert with Great Britain and the United States and that included the development of offensive biological weapons. This aspect of Atlanticism was one that Pearson had specifically denied in his speech to Parliament, even though, as we shall see, he was fully informed of the development of biological weapons.

Not only were the allied governments actively recruiting scientists to provide plausible denials, Canadian politicians and officials were also working to manipulate the press and even to censor it. In reaction to a 2 May *Ottawa Citizen* article revealing that tri-national meetings of military scientists to discuss biological warfare were being held in Ottawa and other Canadian cities, Escott Reid noted that Pearson felt that such articles played into the hands of communist propagandists and that he now felt he had to write to Mr. Southam (owner of the *Citizen*) to complain.[58] Omar Solandt, head of the Defence Research Board, reported Reid, had told Pearson at a meeting to discuss the fallout from the accusation, that "as soon as he heard of the story he had taken measures to see that it was not carried further and had it killed in the *Ottawa Journal* and over the CP wires." On the grounds of national security, the truth about Canadian involvement in biological warfare preparations remained hidden. Canada had, after all, signed and ratified the 1928 protocols prohibiting the use of chemical or biological weapons. Today, we now know part of the story.

Canada and Biological Warfare

The Canadian Peace Congress launched a campaign against biological warfare that was part of a coordinated effort of the World Peace Council, the leading anti-war organization of the time, which included in its executive such figures as Pablo Picasso, Jean-Paul Sartre, Salvadore Allende, Pablo Neruda, Jorge Amado, Bertolt Brecht, and Linus Pauling.[59] It put the Canadian and American governments on the defensive because it raised not only the question of biological warfare but also the larger issue of the morality of the war in Korea. For its part, the Soviet Union capitalized on the peace effort within the United Nations, and the attendant biological warfare issue became a worldwide one that the Canadian government could not avoid. But neither could it reveal the truth because, unknown to most people then – and even today – was the fact that Canada was deeply involved in a tri-country program developing weapons of mass destruction. The story of how this collaboration began during the Second World War has been told already.[60] What has not been revealed is the depth of Canada's involvement and the fact that it not only continued but accelerated into the 1950s.

At the heart of Canadian collaboration were two eminent scientists, G.B. Reed and Otto Maass of McGill University. Canada's highest military body, the Chiefs of Staff Committee, confirmed that Otto Maass, director of Chemical Warfare and Smoke and a top scientist, was acting as the main liaison with US officials on matters pertaining to biological warfare.[61] As a consequence, George W. Merck, chair of the US Biological Warfare Committee, informed Harvey Bundy, assistant to the secretary of war, that the committee met on 22 November 1944, and he "expressed its wish to have a Canadian representative attend the next meeting and all subsequent meetings of the Committee." He continued: "The suggestion is offered that Dr. Otto Maas (sic), Director of Chemical Warfare and Smoke, be invited as the Canadian representative because of his knowledge and position."[62] R.M. Macdonnell, a Canadian member of the Permanent Joint Board of Defence, consulted with C.J. Mackenzie, president of the National Research Council, who thought Maass's participation in the US committee would be an excellent thing: "Dr. Maass has directed work of the most important nature in the field of biological warfare, and the work done in Canada is considered to be outstanding."[63] On 2 January 1945, Macdonnell informed his US counterpart on the Permanent Joint Board on Defence that Canadian authorities "heartily approve[d]" of Maass's representing Canada on the US biological warfare committee.[64] In other words, a Canadian scientist, appointed by the Canadian government, became an integral member of the US team. Similar exchanges took place with the British program as well. In his capacity as a member of the US program, Maass was in a critical position, with access to key officials and top secret US documents. For example, Maass worked closely with Major General Alden Waitt, chief of the chemical corps at Fort Detrick, the home base of US biological weapons testing, and a key figure in negotiating immunity for Ishii Shirō and other Japanese perpetrators of biological warfare in China.

The biological warfare program did not end with the Second World War. Under Maass's direction, Suffield Experimental Station in Alberta became the centre for testing – testing in which both Maass and Reed personally participated. Liaison with the US program was an integral part of the process, and, on numerous occasions, Canadian, American, and British scientists gathered at Suffield and other locations to discuss the results of their top-secret work. Maass remained a key figure in liaison with US biological warfare officers. In late January 1949, he wrote to Major J.C. Bond in Montreal regarding an apparently serious security breach: "Leaving the American aspect which DMI [Director of Military Intelligence] tries to promote out of account, as I believe you do, we are left with a very serious situation, that is, there is somebody in or out of our organization who was acting for Russia."[65] The events relating to the unexplained security problem had prompted the cancellation of Alden Waitt's planned visit to Ottawa. Maass appended a transcript of his discussion with Waitt by phone a few days earlier. The transcript reveals that Maass was "terribly worried about it." As Maass put it: "I am not worried about your officer, what I am worried about is that apparently there is some activity, some second-hand play ... on the part of somebody who is sniffing around and I can't get to first base with our Intelligence Officers in the Army."[66] The files relating to this security breach have not been released, but the incident may well be connected with revelations that came out of Moscow in May 1950. According to this report, newspapers in Canada had reported in the summer of 1949 that "tests of means of bacteriological warfare were being carried out by the Americans on Canadian territories with the knowledge of the Canadian government and that an unprecedented plague epidemic among the Eskimos was the direct consequence of these experiments."[67] This report was news to the Canadian officer in Moscow but was dismissed as nothing of "great importance" and, in fact, as an example of the type of propaganda emanating from Moscow.[68]

The tri-country program in biological warfare accelerated in the early 1950s.[69] Fewer than ten days after the Korean War began, the JCS, in a special meeting on 3 July 1950 in Ottawa, heard a report from the British vice-chief of air staff, Air Chief Marshal Sir Ralph Cochrane of the Royal Air Force, in which he emphasized that "UK Chiefs of Staff were agreed on the importance of biological warfare and were anxious to continue offensive as well as defensive research in this field."[70] To this end, they had decided to construct a new plant at Porton for "bulk production of agents," but, before proceeding, Cochrane told those assembled, the UK chiefs of staff wanted to have the views of the US and Canadian chiefs of staff on the "operational value of this form of warfare and the degree of priority that it should be given." Attending this meeting were not only the joint chiefs but also A.D.P.

Heeney, undersecretary of state for the DEA; Norman Robertson, secretary to the Cabinet; and Guilford Reed himself. Reed had prepared for the meeting a summary of Canada's work in the development of "Special Weapons." The report, which had been sent to Arnold Heeney and the others, revealed that field tests had been conducted using five agents – anthrax, brucella, tularemia, pestis, and botulinum – and that these trials had yielded "reasonably accurate estimates of their effectiveness."[71] Mass production of these agents in Canada had been restricted to "anthrax spores and botulinum toxin." The tri-country collaboration was far enough advanced "to justify the opinion that large scale operations [were] altogether feasible."[72] Although no completely satisfactory method of dispersal had been devised, there had been substantial field trials using bombs and insects, and the "infecting of killing dose for animals [had been] determined." Representatives in the field of special weapons, Reed reported, would be meeting in Canada in October 1950 to review the work to date and to plan the research programs for the following year. After discussion, the committee agreed to support the Porton project on the understanding that Canadian participation would be reviewed again in October. The scope of cooperation in fact expanded over the next year.

In the wake of the failed armistice talks in the fall of 1951, the US administration stepped up its operational preparations for the use of biological weapons and, on 21 December 1951, Secretary of Defence Robert Lovett directed the JCS to achieve readiness for biological warfare. Prior to this, in October, the air force representative on the Canadian Joint Staff wrote the chief of air staff in Ottawa, informing him that, because the United States was pursuing "a more vigorous policy on BW/CW," tests and trials had to be planned ahead and that the US agencies wanted to examine the suitability of both Cold Lake and Suffield as test sites.[73] In what was an "out of channel" request, the United States asked for detailed information on both Cold Lake and Suffield. In December, A.L. Wright, the Canadian Defence Research member of the Canadian Joint Staff, informed the Defence Research Board that the "USAF [was] giving serious consideration to the probable use of special weapons," acknowledged that detailed survey information regarding Cold Lake had been forwarded, and reiterated the request for detailed information on Suffield.[74] This was provided.

Even without full documentation, it is clear that the Canadian government was deeply involved in developing offensive weapons of mass destruction, including biological warfare, and that Parliament was misled by Lester Pearson at the time the accusations of biological warfare in Korea were first raised. We know also that the US military was stepping up preparations for deployment and use of biological weapons in late 1951 and that Canadian officials were well aware of this and actively supported it. To avoid revealing the nature of the biological warfare program and Canadian collaboration, which would have lent credence to the charges levelled by the Chinese and Korean governments, the Canadian government attempted to discredit the peace movement.

13 Vietnam
Departures in Canadian Foreign Policy

By the end of the Korean War, the Canadian government's international strategy had come to rest squarely on two pillars – a close alliance with the United States and assisting NATO in Europe. However, that was far from the end of the story. Its historical ties to Great Britain, its Commonwealth connections, and its determination to restrict Asian immigration continued to influence foreign policy. Furthermore, ongoing decolonization in Asia, with the attendant US attention to that area, meant that the region retained some importance in Canadian foreign policy. The hope invested in India as a non-communist example of decolonization began to turn to bitterness, however, as India under Nehru engaged in a policy of non-alignment and Asian-African solidarity. While still sensitive to the India factor, Canadian foreign policy in Asia under St. Laurent and Pearson had largely converged with that of the US government. Despite reservations, the Canadian government supported the reverse course in the occupation of Japan; it had joined the war in Korea under pressure from the United States; despite British recognition of China, the Canadian government had resolutely supported the US boycott of the People's Republic of China; and Pearson had personally gone out on a limb to support the United States during the San Francisco peace treaty proceedings, despite admonitions from his officials against active support of the flawed treaty. The energies, commitments, and entanglements that had ensued from these policy decisions were enough to convince Pearson that it was time to impose limits on Canadian engagement in the region, and by 1953 he began to distance the government from suggestions that Canada should take part in a NATO-like treaty in the Pacific. With the Korean War winding down, the occupation of Japan over, and recognition of China put off, Asian affairs might have been relegated to a minor position. Internally as well, the Department of External Affairs began to see a consolidation of conservatism within its own ranks. The appointment of Arnold Heeney over Escott Reid for the position of under-secretary, the attacks against Herbert Norman leading to his effective exile to New Zealand in 1953, the death of George Patterson in Boston in 1953, the departure of Escott Reid as high commissioner to India in 1952, and the appointment of Chester Ronning as ambassador to Norway meant that the "mish kid" experiences of Asia as well as the social-democratic trend within the DEA began to dissipate. All the more surprising then, that, in 1954, the Canadian government should decide to take on a new role in Asia: of international peacekeeping in Indochina.

The Challenge of Decolonization

Despite substantial and growing economic and military support from the United States, France suffered setbacks in its colonial war with the nationalist movement in Vietnam. The French government intensified its lobbying of NATO allies for further military and diplomatic support. By the fall of 1952, the DEA had decided that recognition of the Bao Dai regime was overdue. In a 1 November memorandum, Brook Claxton, minister of defence and acting foreign minister (Pearson was UN president at the time), presented the case for and against recognition:[1] "Indochina continues to be one of the most critical soft spots in Asia which the Communists are probing. The struggle being waged by the French and Indochinese to hold them in check is relentless and costly. In the context of the cold war, particularly of its intensification in Asia, there is now some political urgency for Canada to reconsider its stand on Indochina."[2] Vietnam, stated Claxton, "[is] largely under the control of the Vietminh which has the support of a strong anti-colonial nationalist movement. Many of the moderate nationalists are still adopting a 'wait and see' attitude toward the struggle for control of the country. There is no apparent alternative to the Bao Dai regime at the present time except that of Communist Ho Chi Minh. Moreover, although the French have not given Bao Dai enough power to satisfy the nationalist aspirations of even some of his supporters, they have given him as much as, or perhaps more than, his weak administration can manage." France, stated Claxton, was facing grave "difficulties in supporting major military efforts in both Europe and Indochina and in maintaining its position in North Africa ... Accordingly, any encouragement which [could] be given to the Franco Vietnamese forces to hold on would be desirable."[3] In France, a feeling existed that it "alone must bear the responsibility of safeguarding western strategic interests in Indochina," while it must also promote NATO and European unity. Recognizing the Bao Dai government would "contribute towards a manifestation of the political solidarity of the democracies on cold war problems in Asia." However, Claxton also cited the arguments against recognition: "Vietnam, Laos and Cambodia do not fulfil the customary legal requirements for the recognition of states. Nor do their governments fulfil the customary legal requirements for the recognition of governments." French control continued, and "the three states [could not] be considered as independent." Further exacerbating the situation was the fact that even non-communist states of Asia and the Middle East opposed recognition because, according to Claxton, there seemed to be some "distrust of French intentions." Canadian recognition, he suggested, might be criticized and "might weaken [Canada's] advantageous position as a 'neutral' on colonial questions. The undesirable 'white versus Asian' alignment, already too prevalent in the Commonwealth, might recur on this issue."

Cabinet was made painfully aware of the dilemma it faced: "In essence the question of recognizing the states of Vietnam, Laos and Cambodia and their governments is one in which our reluctance to recognize governments, which do not fulfil the customary legal requirements and which are frowned upon by most of the neighbouring countries in Asia, must be weighed against our desire to assist a NATO colleague, sorely tried by foreign and domestic problems, and to bolster such limited independence as the governments themselves now possess. My opinion is that the political factors, in particular the NATO considerations, override the legal and other objections."[4] Cabinet accepted Claxton's recommendation, reversing the earlier neutralist position, but delayed implementation for fear of the "undesirable effects of such recognition on friendly Asian countries."[5] Cabinet decided to offer recognition on 30 December 1952: "The Assembly is now in recess, and the period from that date until it again convenes will afford an opportunity for any unfavourable reaction in these countries to subside." Recognition of Bao Dai also made South Vietnam eligible for Canadian foreign aid as part of the Colombo Plan. Pressure from the French government and other NATO allies successfully reversed the previous wait-and-see attitude that had reflected Pearson's recognition of the Indian government's critique of French colonialism.

What is of note in the rationales expressed in this policy decision is not only the fact that the Canadian government was knowingly disregarding its own guidelines regarding recognition but also the fact that the Canadian government hoped to occupy a space of "neutrality" regarding decolonization, and how little this actually meant when faced with serious pressure from a European NATO ally. It is within this context that the role of anti-communism can be best understood: that is, as a means to completely reframe a situation so that what had been an important and legitimate regional anti-colonial movement was now part of a universalized communist conspiracy, thereby providing a rationale for continued imperial intervention in the postwar era. At the same time, the government policy paper reflected its desire to stake out some type of middle ground in the developing struggle between the north and the south. Herein lies the origins of the Canadian quest to distinguish itself as a distinct if loyal ally of the United States. This was articulated as an attempt to maintain some semblance of a "middle power"; however, as we shall see, in practice Canada rejected that role whenever it conflicted with its strategic alliance with the United States.

Despite support from its NATO allies, including Canada, the French government was unable to defeat the Viet Minh on the battlefield. Throughout the period from 1952 to 1954, the Viet Minh became increasingly effective in their military operations. This was partially due to Chinese military support, but it would be a mistake to interpret this as evidence of a communist conspiracy emanating from Moscow or from Beijing.[6] To be sure, Ho Chi Minh, who spoke Chinese and had long been associated with Chinese revolutionaries, had requested and received substantial Chinese aid. But as almost every source recognizes today, and as the Canadian government recognized at the time, the Viet Minh was an indigenous movement (with substantial popular support) confronting a colonial regime. Faced with this armed resistance, the French government attempted to put in place a façade of Vietnamese control through its establishment of the Associated States in Indochina. Bao Dai, the former emperor and newly appointed head of the associated state in Vietnam, was utterly dependent on France's colonial apparatus, including its army.[7]

As the Viet Minh gained the upper hand, major fissures began to appear in the postwar imperial coalition. The British and French governments hoped to find some sort of negotiated settlement to the war for independence in Vietnam, thereby minimizing its impact. The US government, on the other hand, hoped to retrieve the situation and instead attempted to convince its coalition allies to create the conditions for armed intervention in support of the French forces while forcing the latter to grant at least nominal independence to Vietnam. The US military explored the possibility of immediate intervention (Operation Vulture) while Dulles projected a new coalition entente under the slogan "United Action."[8] The centrepiece of Dulles's plan was the creation of a coalition of the United States, Great Britain, France, Australia, New Zealand, the Associated States, the Philippines, and Thailand. This was the formula for the liberal empire in which formal if nominal independence would be granted to Vietnam, local and regional forces would do the ground fighting, and the US-led coalition would provide resources as well as air and naval support.[9] This formula would eventually come to fruition, but for the time being it was a non-starter. The French government refused to accept "United Action" because of its implied end to France's influence in Indochina. And because the French government was also being asked to accept the revival of an armed Germany through the formation of the European Defence Community, it retained considerable leverage over the situation. French rejection of "United Action" and British government refusal to intervene militarily meant Dulles was unable to persuade Congressional leaders of the necessity of armed intervention. Here, the lessons and sacrifices of the Korean War had a direct bearing. Meeting with Dulles on 3 April 1954, US congressmen emphasized that there would be "no more Koreas, with the United States furnishing 90 percent of the manpower."[10] Defeats on the battlefield intensified contradictions among the imperial powers, and, as prospects for a military victory disappeared, the necessity of a negotiated settlement became all important. On 7 May 1954, the French forces surrendered at Dien Bien Phu, by which time negotiations were already under way in Geneva.

Geneva 1954

Further complicating the situation for the Euro-American powers was the fact that, after Stalin's death, the Soviet government began to promote peaceful co-existence much more aggressively. This was apparent in its agreement to a Korean armistice and also in its willingness to promote a peaceful resolution of the conflict in Indochina. On 18 February 1954, representatives of the United States, Great Britain, France, and the Soviet Union met in Berlin and agreed to hold talks on Korean reunification, as had been stipulated in the armistice agreement, as well as on Indochina, at a conference to be convened in Geneva on 26 April. France and Great Britain had pushed for inclusion of Indochina on the agenda and for participation by the Chinese government in the conference, despite objections by the United States. The European powers hoped for a compromise on Indochina that would leave the French with some influence and also lead to some regional stability, a key goal for the British government in its quest to retain its colonial interests in Malaya and Hong Kong.

Lester Pearson, John Holmes, and Chester Ronning all participated in the Geneva Conference that took place from 26 April to 21 July 1954.[11] The conference was co-chaired by Anthony Eden, foreign minister of Great Britain, and Vyacheslav Molotov for the Soviet Union.[12] The Canadians had official representation only in the Korean portion of the conference because of Canada's participation in the war in Korea. This first part of the conference lasted from 27 April until 15 June, with the talks ending without progress in terms of reunification of the Korean peninsula. Beginning on 8 May, parallel discussions began on Indochina. These talks continued after the talks on Korea broke off, and they ended on 21 July 1954 with the declaration of the Geneva Accords. These accords included a proposal that Canada participate on a commission to supervise their implementation, which I contend, was the first major exercise in Canadian peacekeeping.

The reasons behind Canadian involvement in a peacekeeping capacity in Indochina are complex, related both to the Korean experience and to developments leading up to the conference. In early 1954, Canada's prime minister Louis St. Laurent travelled to India for discussions with Nehru. In a press conference on 24 February, St. Laurent endorsed Nehru's appeal for peace in Vietnam "without any reservation or hesitation whatsoever."[13] In response to a reporter's query whether NATO obligations included support for a NATO member if its colonies were attacked, St. Laurent replied with a categorical "No." The unnamed Indian reporter clarified his concern: "I have in mind the Portuguese settlements in India," to which St. Laurent said: "No. No, it certainly does not include the Portuguese colonies in India." This public renunciation of NATO support for European colonialism impressed the Indian government, despite the fact that Canadian recognition and support for the Bao Dai regime contradicted St. Laurent's contention. Nehru and Krishna Menon, chair of India's UN delegation, would later promote Canadian participation in the International Commission for Supervision and Control in Vietnam (ICSC), tasked with supervising implementation of the Geneva Accords. However, the affinity between Canadian and Indian foreign policy should not be overdrawn. Anglo-Saxon solidarity at the expense of Asian countries continued, and in the lead-up to the Geneva Conference, British foreign minister Anthony Eden hosted a lunch in Paris for Canadian, British, and Australian representatives to discuss procedural problems expected to be posed by the conference. No announcement regarding procedures and participating countries would be made "lest an opportunity be given to Nehru to point to the exclusion from these discussions of the countries represented in Colombo."[14] The Colombo powers, meeting at this time, included Burma, Ceylon, India, Indonesia, and Pakistan, and they constituted one of the emerging groups that would help found the Non-Aligned Movement. Eden took great pains to keep the Asian countries out of any official role in the Geneva talks while courting their support.[15]

From Geneva, Pearson reported to St. Laurent on 6 May during the first phase of the conference focusing on Korea.[16] Pearson first made contact with Zhou Enlai at this time, reporting that Zhou had wanted to meet him: "so I had myself introduced to him one afternoon at the buffet. He was friendly enough, but I have made no move to follow this up."[17] John Foster Dulles, Pearson told the prime minister, "had come and went without having even nodded to Chou [Zhou] En-lai." Chinese sources provide further detail.[18] Ronning, who spoke Chinese well, had been chatting with Chinese delegation members Wang Bingnan, Qiao Guanhua, Gong Peng, and Huang Hua, as well as drinking coffee with Zhou during a conference break. As "the only Western delegate capable of communicating in Chinese with the Chinese delegates," Ronning was told by Zhou that he (Zhou) "would be interested in getting to know Pearson, so Ronning went over to Pearson and passed on the message. Pearson followed Ronning back over to Zhou, the two shook hands, drank coffee together, and chatted. As they got up to return to the conference hall, Dulles walked towards Pearson thinking to accompany him, at which time Zhou stretched out his hand to Dulles. But Dulles didn't respond and turned away, while presenting an unhappy face to Pearson."[19]

In his report to St. Laurent, Pearson went on to discuss Korean affairs, telling the prime minister that the communist positions were impossible to accept and that their attitude was "hard and unyielding." However, the real stumbling block was "the reluctance of the South Korean Government to accept free elections for all Korea" and, furthermore, the US unwillingness to push the Rhee regime on this issue.[20] Given the circumstances, Pearson mused, the only solution might be to criticize the communist positions and not put any counter-proposals forward. That was not very satisfactory but "better than to have open disagreement in our own ranks."[21] Indeed, that was what happened. The implications of the Canadian and US positions require some reflection. The Canadian and US governments were willing to subordinate liberal goals (i.e., the establishment of an electoral system in South Korea) in order to maintain the authoritarian Rhee regime. Was there anything that justified their actions other than imperial interests under the guise of anti-communism? As we shall see, a similar question must be posed regarding Vietnam.

The Indochina section of the conference began in May while the Korea section was still under way and just when the French were on their way to defeat at Dien Bien Phu. Pearson went to some lengths to explain to St. Laurent that he was not lobbying to be included in the Indochina section of the conference but, rather, was working to avoid giving the impression of "indifference," on the one hand, and of "commitment," on the other. However, the Canadian delegation was "completely informed" about what was going on and had even participated in "a good many of the preliminary and formal discussions."[22] Indeed, a week after Pearson wrote to St. Laurent, Eden invited the Canadian and Australian representatives to an urgent meeting at which he informed them that he had just seen General Walter Bedell Smith, the American representative in charge at Geneva after Dulles left. Bedell Smith confirmed newspaper reports that the US government had "formally approached French with a proposal that they would be prepared to intervene in Indo China with ground forces."[23] The conditions for intervention would be that: no agreement be reached in Geneva or that the French ask for assistance; the French agree to give full independence to the Associated States (including the right to secede); a collective defence organization, to include Thailand, Philippines, Australia, New Zealand, "and if possible, the United Kingdom" be established; and the French agree not to reduce their forces.[24] Eden, stated the report, was very upset and worried that they were repeating the crisis of three weeks earlier, when the United States had proposed joint military action to relieve the siege of Dien Bien Phu. Pearson himself met with Bedell Smith on 20 May, advising him that the United States should reconsider its suggestion for a southeast Asia treaty organization to provide a security guarantee "to states like Laos and Cambodia, or even Vietnam – if it didn't go completely Communist – when such states were weak and divided and whose people didn't, possibly, want such a guarantee."[25] He also told the general: "We, for one, could not associate ourselves with the earlier South Korean proposals and therefore felt the time was coming when we would have to put forward our own views."[26] However, this never happened, and both Pearson's and Ronning's presentations at the conference were more obstructionist than anything else.[27] The Korean section of the conference ended with no agreement. Pearson and Ronning both then departed Geneva, as did John Holmes shortly thereafter. The focus of the conference then shifted to Indochina.

Pearson's search for a way out of the dilemma found a unique outlet as negotiations in Geneva came to a conclusion in July. These negotiations became more frantic as a French-imposed deadline of 20 July approached. The final agreement regarding Vietnam established the 17th parallel as a provisional military demarcation line; established "two regrouping zones" south and north for the respective forces, zones in which political and administrative measures would be established pending general elections to reunify the country; prohibited the introduction of "fresh troops, military personnel, arms and munitions"; and called for general elections to be held in July 1956 based on consultation between the respective administrations, to begin in July 1955.[28] The agreements and the elections would be supervised by an international commission made up of Poland, India, and Canada. This news came as a surprise to the Canadian government. Indeed John Holmes, in charge of the delegation after the departure of Pearson and Ronning, had already left Geneva, and the talks were being monitored only by the Canadian representative to the United Nations in Geneva.

The key to the resolution of the Geneva negotiations was a trip taken by Zhou Enlai to India, Burma, and then home to China in late June and early July, while the conference was in recess. Zhou met with Ho Chi Minh in Liuzhou from 3-5 July. While the accounts of Zhou's meetings with Ho and other Vietnamese leaders differ, the outcome was definitely a softening in the communist position and acceptance of a temporary division of Vietnam.[29] While in India, Zhou met with Nehru. Afterwards Krishna Menon, who was at the United Nations in New York, lunched with the Canadian representative. He reported that Zhou and Nehru's talks had been successful and that Zhou had seen that "India and Burma, Asian countries, had their own distinctive way of life, neither Communist nor American."[30] The report also noted that "Zhou Enlai had told Menon that though he knew on what side Canada stood he nevertheless appreciated [its] independent attitude." This perception of Canada's having a somewhat independent view on international affairs was related in part to the presence of long-time China hand Chester Ronning at the Geneva Conference. As mentioned earlier, Ronning had introduced Pearson to Zhou Enlai early in the conference. Moreover, on the strength of the close rapport he had built with Chinese communist representatives during his earlier stints in Chongqing and Nanjing, he had helped facilitate the return of Canadian soldiers in the Korean War who had been detained in China as POWs. Indeed, after the Korea portion of the Geneva Conference ended on 15 June, and before returning to Oslo to resume his duties as ambassador to Norway, Ronning visited the Chinese delegation's residence. This 19 June visit was intended to allow Ronning to say goodbye to Zhou, but, according to Chinese accounts, it also had another motive. Ronning had been entrusted by the Canadian government to use his China connections and go through the "back door" to help gain the release of Andy Mackenzie, a Canadian pilot who had been captured after his fighter had been shot down near the Yalu River and who remained interned in China (see Chapter 12).[31] After pleasantries, Ronning raised the Mackenzie question with Zhou, who told him that the case could be resolved through special measures but that, because Mackenzie was a prisoner of war, it involved going through certain legal procedures. He agreed to look into the matter after returning to China so as to better understand the circumstances. Ronning later wrote to Zhou from Norway and, in mid-December, Mackenzie was back in Montreal. Ronning's visit to the Chinese residence ended with Zhou mistakenly sending Ronning back to the Canadian Embassy in his own car because Ronning's driver hadn't entered the Chinese compound but had waited outside the gate.

In a sense, the nomination of Canada to the supervisory commissions reflected the efforts of Ronning's work with the Chinese and Pearson's attempts to articulate, behind the scenes, an independent view of the world, one in which co-existence of differing social systems was possible. Of course this view was rife with contradictions and limitations because of Canada's participation in NATO and its commitment to its alliance with the United States. But because Great Britain and the United States differed regarding the use of military force in Indochina at this particular time, a space had been created in which Canadian views could be expressed. Thus it became known that the Canadian government had eschewed the Dulles-led attempts to construct a coalition of the willing to intervene militarily in Indochina and that Lester Pearson was sceptical about the creation of a collective security pact in Southeast Asia. This point is reinforced by archival accounts of Pearson's views after returning from Geneva. Speaking at a private gathering at the Canadian Embassy in Washington, Pearson suggested: "[If] an Asian security pact could muster the adherence from Asia of only the Philippines and Thailand, it would be better to have no such pact ... Outright communist aggression in Asia did not seem likely in the immediate future."[32]

In assessing Dulles, Pearson "suggested that Mr. Dulles regarded Communism as something not to be tolerated; that he could not face the idea of co-existence; and that it was his policy to bring about the overthrow of the Peking regime."[33] Yet, in a conversation with Krishna Menon the next month, Pearson recorded that he had "explained that Canadian commitments, particularly in NATO, would likely prevent [Canada's] active participation in the proposed pact. Nevertheless, [Canada] favoured a treaty organization for the area, in which both Western and Asian countries would be represented."[34] Pearson reported that Krishna Menon "stated flatly that his country would join no Southeast Asian pact to which only one side of the Cold War adhered." Was Pearson simply playing devil's advocate in the informal atmosphere of a dinner party? Or was there more to it than meets the eye? My view is that Pearson was a consummate diplomat, quick to perceive potential problems and cognizant of the tension between a renewed trans-Atlantic coalition, on the one hand, and the growing power of developing countries, on the other. He regularly spoke to these tensions, but, when it came down to brass tacks, Pearson and Canadian policy sided with the imperial coalition.[35] This was partly due to Pearson's own identity, to his belief in the need for a strong coalition, and to the constraints of intense anti-communism that existed in this era, both within the US government and within Canada itself. This anti-communism, which Pearson himself had made use of on numerous occasions, came back to haunt him when he came under attack from conservatives, both in the press and in the House of Commons, when he suggested that the Canadian government did not, because of its NATO commitments, intend to join a security pact for Southeast Asia, although the government supported the formation of such a pact.

The news of Canada's nomination to the supervisory commissions came as a shock to Pearson and the DEA. After having already expressed disinterest in joining a collective security pact for the region, and having reinforced Canada's commitment to working through the United Nations, the proposal that Canada participate in a supervisory commission outside the framework of the United Nations created both challenges and opportunities for the government. Pearson carefully consulted the governments of the United States, Great Britain, and India before recommending that Canada accept the nomination to the supervisory commission. The Canadian Cabinet approved the decision on 28 July 1954, with the understanding that the three countries would "later be asked to assume responsibility for supervising the elections."[36] In the discussion, Cabinet was informed that both France and the United States were anxious that Canada participate; that "no other

International Commission's truce team in Indochina on inspection of an ammunition ship, 1955. *Left to right:* Captain Allen (Canada), Major Hanspal, Lieutenant-Colonels Panum and Wysocki, Mr. Swierkocki, and Captain Lamarre (Canada). | Canada, Department of National Defence / Library and Archives Canada, PA-146523

Western country" could work as well with India; that the mission might lead, unlike in the Korean situation, to a permanent settlement because "the Chinese had now demonstrated that they could defeat the white man" and didn't want to resume fighting in Indochina. The Chinese position was flexible because it was possible "that completely free elections would produce Communist regimes in Indo-China." The Cabinet also heard the suggestion that the only "hope of salvation for Asia was the election of truly national governments" and that free elections should be held "even though such elections might result in the establishment of Communist regimes."

The decision to take on this peacekeeping role requires careful scrutiny because, on the surface, it appeared to be quite inconsistent with previously stated policy: the assignment was not related to the United Nations, it required a substantial commitment of both diplomatic and military personnel, and it entailed commitments to a region in which Canada did not have substantial interests and about which it had limited knowledge. It also came at the same time as the government was eschewing any military role in the region through the proposed collective security agreement known as the Southeast Asia Treaty Organization. Even Pearson commented, "This is really something new for Canada."[37] Indeed it was. Contradictions between the British and American governments, between colonialism on the decline and a rising liberal empire, created a space into which Pearson, in his enthusiasm for an autonomous Canadian role, rushed. Because of Pearson's quiet but distinct criticism of US policy on Korea, the US representatives in Geneva had not been advocating for Canada.[38] In fact, Dulles actually opposed the creation of a supervisory commission, just as he opposed the Geneva Accords, but apparently he felt that if there had to be one at least Canada would be able to exercise a veto in its deliberations. He would not be disappointed.

Religion, Propaganda, and Covert Actions

Implementation of the 1954 Geneva Accords proved to be extremely difficult, and they eventually foundered. However, the initial challenge of disengagement of the combatants proceeded relatively smoothly, and the Viet Minh quickly consolidated their control of the north. The French forces regrouped in the south but then had to contend with the rising star of Ngo Diem, backed by the US government. In the ensuing months, two key issues emerged. The first was the question of freedom of movement of the civilian population, which, under the terms of the Geneva Accords, was to be facilitated in the first three hundred days following their ratification. The second major challenge was the holding of national elections in 1956, preparations for which were to begin in July 1955.

As for the movement of civilians, the operative clause had been inserted to allow civilians in both the northern and southern parts of Vietnam to migrate into the opposite zones according to choice. There were indeed many in the north of Vietnam, mostly Roman Catholics, who did not want to stay there. However, according to early US reports: "The clergy have been advising their flocks against evacuation and so far relatively few have left. According to reports from the US Embassy in Hanoi, the Communists are behaving very correctly towards the Roman Catholic population."[39] However, within a few months this picture would change dramatically, and, eventually, nearly a million people would abandon the north for the south. Furthermore, the Democratic Republic of Vietnam would be systematically assailed for supposedly violating the Geneva Accords by trying to obstruct the migration. Recent studies indicate that there was indeed sectarianism and discrimination developing among the Viet Minh cadres in the north towards the Catholic population.[40] Other revelations reinforce earlier questions regarding exactly how "free" this movement actually was and to what degree it was manipulated.[41]

On 1 September 1954, the Roman Catholic Delegatio Apostolica, the Roman Catholic Church's representative in Ottawa, presented Lester Pearson with a note stating that people in Vietnam were ignorant of Article 14 of the Geneva Accords allowing for the transfer of populations and that this brought "great harm to the Christian population, particularly to the Catholics who wish[ed] to be transferred."[42] He suggested that the Holy See would be very grateful if the Canadian representative on the ICSC would promote fulfilment of the clause. Pearson responded that the commission was insisting that the signatories to the agreement promote the rights accorded to the population by "radio, press, and handbills."[43] The Vatican was not the only institution determined to see its adherents moved south. It was clear from what happened in Geneva that peaceful co-existence was not on the Eisenhower government's agenda, and it had no intention of abiding by the Geneva Accords, even though the Viet Minh had made major concessions to arrive at them. Early in 1954, Dulles had told Edward Lansdale, a high-level CIA operative whose last assignment had been to put down the armed resistance movement in the Philippines, that he would be going to Vietnam.[44] After a stop in the Philippines, Lansdale proceeded to Vietnam in late May. A month after the conclusion of the Geneva Accords, the US National Security Council met and approved new initiatives to "protect its position and restore its prestige in the Far East" and to prevent further losses to communism.[45] The measures to be taken included "covert operations on a large and effective scale" and the creation of the Southeast Asia Treaty Organization, which included the United States, Great Britain, France, Australia, New Zealand, and three Asian countries (Thailand, the Philippines, and Pakistan).

Lansdale, already on the ground and working with Vietnamese psych-ops (psychological operations) teams formed under the French, became intimately involved in organizing covert operations to persuade northerners to move south. He and his cohorts helped edit and distribute flyers – by the thousands – entitled "Christ Has Gone South" and "The Virgin Mary has Departed from the North." A central evacuation committee circulated the following leaflet: "Dear Catholic brothers and sisters, hundreds of gigantic airplanes are waiting to transport you gratis to Saigon. In the South the cost of living is three times less, you will receive twelve piastres a day and in addition you will be given fertile rice fields and other means of livelihood. By remaining in the North you will experience famine and will *damn your souls*."[46] This type of propaganda proliferated in what a US historian recently called "one of the most audacious propaganda campaigns in the history of covert action."[47] In a mission dubbed by the US Navy "Passage to Freedom," hundreds of navy ships were rushed into Haiphong, the port adjacent to Hanoi, to transport the refugees to the south. To what extent this migration reflected indigenous factors and to what extent it was a manufactured crisis remains open to question. Regardless, the crisis presents an interesting intersection between the questions of race and broader geo-strategic concerns.

Dr. Tom Dooley, a US Navy doctor who assisted in "Passage to Freedom" from September 1954 through May 1955, recorded many of his experiences in letters to his mother and went on to write a book entitled *Deliver Us from Evil*.[48] The book sold millions of copies, was translated into a score of languages, and was serialized in *Reader's Digest*. What is remarkable is the resonance that his stories elicited by invoking paternalistic images of the downtrodden and oppressed Vietnamese people; presenting caricatures of the horrible, torturing communists; and, most significantly, mythologizing the life-saving role of the good-hearted doctor from America. This postwar portrait of the imagined Vietnamese differs from earlier Orientalist caricatures and reflected a significant change in the imperial gaze.[49] Whereas American diplomats had previously described the Vietnamese as lazy, childlike, and susceptible to communist manipulation, in their new incarnation the Vietnamese were cast as victims with agency, that is, they were hardworking and dreamed of "freedom." In other words, they were just like Americans. This type of Orientalist imagery projected US interests as representing the interests of all humanity and, as a universalist project, tended to restrain overt forms of racialization, substituting in their stead a paternalism that mimicked the gendered relations within the patriarchal family. The effects of this Cold War "Orientalism" were to create and to sustain a pervasive paternalism towards developing countries and peoples in Asia and a rabid anti-communism that, I would suggest, became the prism through which many people in Canada and the United States came to view Vietnam and, indeed, the world. The contingent term "the East" was now invoked as a euphemism for communism as well as for the non-Western world.

Pearson, as indicated earlier, had been subjected to religious lobbying to provide greater promotion of migration out of North Vietnam. Under the influence of the church and covert operations organized by the CIA, the trickle of refugees became a flood, seemingly validating the accusations that Christians were suffering under the harsh whip of communist repression. Given the propaganda being aimed at them, it would hardly be surprising if Ho Chi Minh and the Viet Minh were offended and tried to stem the tide. However, the DRV decided that it had little choice but to allow the migration. Yet, there were many instances in which northern officials, local and otherwise, took it upon themselves to try to impede those fleeing. It was precisely those cases that the Canadian representatives in the ICSC seized on. In fact, in the commission's third report of April 1955, the Canadian delegation inserted a separate note underscoring its dissatisfaction with the progress related to freedom of movement and suggesting that Article 14 (d) of the Geneva Accords would not necessarily be fulfilled within the prescribed time constraints.[50] Indeed, this single issue pushed many Canadian officials "into a lasting posture of determined anti-communism."[51] No better reflection of this consolidation can be presented than that given by Escott Reid. High commissioner to India at the time, Reid returned to Ottawa in the summer of 1955. While there he presented his views on Canada-India relations to senior DEA officials. Regarding Indochina, Reid reported on what he considered to be the Indian government's perspective, that is, that both Great Britain and France had, in signing the Geneva Accords, come to accept that Vietnam might well come under the leadership of Ho Chi Minh and the Viet Minh, that while it might be possible to prevent Laos and Cambodia from becoming communist states, Ho would likely win the elections in Vietnam. That was the Indian view of these matters, and he agreed with it. Reid later recounted: "The roof fell in on me. Officer after officer at the meeting attacked me for my callous, immoral proposal which would betray millions of anti-communist people in South Vietnam into the clutches of the communists of North Vietnam. (Twenty years and millions of deaths later not only they but also the Laotians and Cambodians would be 'betrayed' into the hands of the communists.)"[52] Reid might have added that the view he had expressed at the time had, only a few months earlier, also been the position of the DEA and, indeed, the Canadian Cabinet.

The Election That Never Happened

The second major issue that scuttled the Geneva Accords was that of the general elections scheduled for 1956 in both the north and south of Vietnam.

Again, the US government, having refused to sign the Accords, was instrumental in preventing the elections from proceeding and instead worked towards the creation of a separate state in the south, as it had done in Korea previously. Central to the US strategy was finding a leader for the south and providing the military assistance to bolster a separate southern regime. To that end, the US government chose to back Ngo Dinh Diem, a Roman Catholic nationalist who had become an official in the French administrative apparatus in Vietnam during the 1930s.[53] As a district chief and a Catholic, Diem was dismayed by his first contact with communists, who were organizing peasants to challenge French colonial control, and he helped the French suppress the budding insurgency. But after the French rejected his suggestions for administrative reforms, he abandoned the colonial regime and looked for ways of promoting Vietnamese independence. However, he spurned an approach by Ho Chi Minh, who invited him into his coalition government, and chose instead to lie low until the end of the war. Afterwards, at the urging of the US government, the French-backed president of Vietnam, Bao Dai, appointed Diem prime minister of South Vietnam. The choice of Diem was grounded in US perceptions that, as a Christian, he was eminently suited to become the leader of a "free" Vietnam. Dulles and Eisenhower, it seems, were convinced that a leader of Buddhist faith would be unreliable since Buddhism, in their perception, was too passive for the job at hand.

Some people in South Vietnam were prepared to at least give Diem a chance. Truong Nhu Tang, a nationalist living in Saigon at the time, explained that it was hard to take the measure of Diem: "Foreign attempts to manipulate Vietnam were hardly a novelty, but manipulation was always a two-way street. The classic example of this was Ho Chi Minh himself, who had used Chinese and Soviet support in pursuit of his own goals, but had done this without relinquishing his stature as a nationalist."[54] Before long, however, Tang and many others came to the conclusion that Diem was more of an autocrat than a nationalist. In April 1954, Diem, with American backing, launched a military offensive against the Binh Xuyen, a powerful clandestine network based in the Cholon area on the outskirts of Saigon. This was the opening shot in Diem's confrontation with non-Catholics in South Vietnam, including groups such as the Cao Dai and the Hoa Hao as well as Buddhists. Backed by the CIA's covert operations, Diem's military offensive ravaged Saigon, but Diem emerged victorious. This military victory was crucial because a US presidential envoy, General J. Lawton Collins, had soured on Diem, and the US administration was on the verge of withdrawing its support for his regime.[55] Hailed by US newspapers and magazines, including *Time* and *Life,* Diem's military victory breathed new life into the regime. An editorial by *Life* publisher Henry Luce claimed that Diem deserved the support of every "son, daughter, and even distant admirer of the American Revolution." Luce continued: "[Diem] has not one enemy but several: the communists, the French, the Binh Xuyen gangsters, the sects, and probably others lurking in the rice fields, to say nothing of the backwardness of his own people."[56] Diem "brooked no opposition and expected total obedience, nothing more, nothing less."[57] After his April 1954 victory, Diem went on to consolidate control, although the measures taken spawned new and growing opposition within South Vietnam.

Outside of Vietnam there were critics as well. French premier Edgar Faure considered Diem a complete liability despite his military victory. With France nominally still in control of the south, Faure met John Foster Dulles in Paris in July 1955 during NATO consultations. The French leader suggested that his government was willing to completely withdraw from Vietnam, but he warned Dulles that, under Diem, the south had no future. Dulles, like others in the US administration, was pleased to dissociate the US liberal empire from the taint of French colonialism and, thus, happy to hear that the French would leave. Although no formal announcement was made at the time, by the end of 1955, nearly all French forces would be gone. But Dulles defended Diem to the hilt, both to Faure and to the National Security Council, with whom he met immediately upon returning to Washington: "In the Orient it was necessary to work through a single head of government rather than through a coalition in which various personal interests had to be submerged in a common loyalty."[58] One-man governments were the rule, he stated, pointing to Syngman Rhee in Korea and Ho Chi Minh in North Vietnam. In the event, and with US backing, Diem soon called for the abdication of head of state Bao Dai and the creation of a republic with himself as president. Diem articulated his own agenda for change in the national referendum campaign, but he also received some additional help.[59] Diem received 605,000 votes among Saigon's 405,000 registered voters, and 99 percent of the vote across the south as a whole. On the basis of what many historians now consider a rigged election, Diem declared the founding of the Republic of South Vietnam on 23 October 1955, creating yet another divided country. While his military control depended heavily on the US-financed and trained army in Vietnam, Diem's social base at this time included the minority Roman Catholic population, whose numbers had swelled because of the flow of migrants from North Vietnam. A large portion of US aid went to the refugees, northern Catholics were given privileged positions in the army and the government, and the Roman Catholic Church enjoyed special rights to acquire and to own property.[60] On 16 July 1955, Diem declared in a radio broadcast that his government was in no way bound by the Geneva Accords.

Canada and the ICSC

The Canadian government sanctioned and participated in the undermining of the Geneva Accords in two ways. As we have seen, it portrayed the DRV as being completely uncooperative in the implementation of Article 14 (d) governing the freedom of movement, and it refused to take any responsibility for assuring that the elections prescribed in the final declaration were actually held. There were complicated legal arguments related to the latter issue, which have been discussed elsewhere.[61] But the documentary record regarding these events suggests that it was not legal but, rather, political considerations that were preeminent in the actions of the Canadian representatives. The bias regarding the Canadian pressure exerted on the freedom of movement issue has already been touched upon above. The flip side of the coin was Canadian unwillingness to confront the authoritarianism of the Diem regime.

Pearson's choice as Canada's first commissioner to the ICSC was Sherwood Lett, a lawyer and former military officer from Vancouver.[62] Pearson's initial instructions to him indicated that the government perceived the Geneva Accords as a means by which to stop communism in Asia. However, the decision to participate in the ICSC was said to be prompted by the desire to contribute "to the establishment of peace and security in Southeast Asia."[63] On the one hand, Pearson emphasized that a "NATO pattern pact might not befit the facts of Southeast Asia," but, on the other hand, he told Lett that it was Canadian policy to encourage a Southeast Asia defence organization.[64] Poland, Canada's counterpart on the ICSC, "ha[d] no independent foreign policy" and could be expected to put on a "devious performance" combining a "show of cooperativeness with varying degrees of obstruction, deceit and bad faith" – at least according to Pearson, who, in official policy documents, continued to project the official anti-communist line. Ironically, Canada's interim commissioner, R.M. Macdonnell, who stood in for Lett until his arrival in Hanoi, reported that, contrary to Pearson's expectations, the Polish representative had been "cooperative, friendly and easy in his manner ... and ha[d] shown the same impartiality as his Indian and Canadian colleagues."[65] Although Pearson thought this was a charade, in fact, over the life of the ICSC, the Polish representatives appeared no more biased than the Canadian representatives.[66]

Lett quickly took up his duties in the fall of 1954, setting up his headquarters in Hanoi, where he would spend most of the next year.[67] As for the freedom of movement issue, Sherwood Lett wrote on 7 July 1955 that any charge against the Viet Minh for impeding freedom of movement could "readily be matched by reciprocal action by Polish commissioner (with which the Indians might well be in agreement) to charge the other party with failure to carry out provisions of Article 14 (c)."[68] Lett clarified: "The investigations which have been conducted by mobile teams in South (including reports now being received) provide an ugly picture of beatings, tortures and murders of former members of the resistance which took place last fall ... security of our teams cannot be guaranteed. A fair picture, therefore, of the operations of Geneva agreement would reflect what can only be described as a shocking state of law and order in many areas of Vietnam."[69] Nothing better illustrated Lett's point than the anti-ICSC riots that occurred in Saigon two weeks after Lett wrote the above memorandum. An urgent telegram arrived at the DEA at 7:00 AM 20 July 1955: "Organized mob demonstration occurred this morning Saigon with mob violence directed upon Hotel Majestic and commission personnel. All Canadians are safe and well for the present."[70] Apparently, several hundred young men armed with knives, sticks, and hammers had gathered outside the Hotel Majestic and then entered it, destroying furnishings and then looting the rooms over a period of one and a half hours. Almost all personal belongings of the forty-four ICSC personnel staying at the hotel were stolen. ISCS cars parked outside the hotel were torched, and one Indian staff member was attacked and injured.[71] According to US sources on the spot in Saigon, the Indian and Canadian members of the ICSC blamed the Diem government because it had fomented anti-ICSC feeling through a long press campaign, had failed to provide security outside the hotel despite numerous requests, and had failed to respond to urgent requests for protection on the day of the riot. Furthermore, the police who were at the hotel had failed to intervene.[72] The reaction of the Canadian government to this signal event was simply to counsel "patience," despite the fact that the riot reflected Diem's antagonism to the ICSC and to the Geneva Accords generally, an antagonism that was shared by the US government. As early as February 1955, Dulles expressly told Pearson that "the difficulties in the way of holding elections in two parts of a country which were so hostile to each other would likely prove insuperable."[73]

The Canadian government never seriously challenged the Diem government over the Saigon attacks or over its rejection of the necessity for political preparations for national elections. To the contrary, the Canadian government recognized the Diem regime and continued to articulate its concerns about the Geneva Accords at a meeting of representatives of Great Britain, India, and Canada during a Commonwealth leaders meeting: "Mr. St. Laurent and Mr. Pearson raised certain questions regarding the work of the Vietnam armistice commission, indicating Canadian concern over the obstacles in the way of the free movement from the North to the South and over the responsibilities of the Commission powers in respect of the forthcoming elections. The Canadian Ministers tried to make it clear that we did not wish the commissions to be used as a cloak for elections which were not completely free."[74] Given the government's ability to turn a blind eye to electoral fraud then going on within South Vietnam, the issue, it would seem, was not concern for the integrity of liberal electoralism but, rather, who might benefit from such elections. In the end, the government again had departed from its supposed affinity with India's neutral foreign policy. Pearson was no doubt able to rationalize this not only on the basis of maintaining the West's strategic interests but also on the basis of his view of those with whom he disagreed: "Nehru was quite bitter about American policy, and resented, as an Asian, their bullying and threatening tactics. He obviously doesn't feel the same resentment when Chou bullies and blusters, because Chou is not so much a Communist as an Asian."[75]

Andrew Preston has pointed out that there is a small but hotly contested literature on the role of the Canadian government in Vietnam.[76] On one side of the debate are those who argue that the government was complicit in abetting American aggression in Vietnam.[77] On the other side are those who suggest that Canadian actions were quite appropriate. Key among the latter's work is the 1984 study by Douglas Ross, who summarized the Canadian government's stance as

> informed by a rational conception of the country's interests: minimization of the risk of escalation of the conflict to tactical nuclear warfare, given Canadian, British, and Indian fears that this would precipitate a third world war; termination of the Franco-Vietminh war at the earliest possible date by negotiated concessions to the communist side if necessary, so as to end the depletion of French military strength that was preventing an effective

> French contribution in NATO; encouragement of further international tension reduction, now that Korea was stabilized and now that Moscow and Beijing seemed inclined towards detente; and last, the prevention of direct Canadian military involvement in the conflict should the Geneva talks fail, but in such a way that Canada's NATO allies would not be offended.[78]

Ross went on to assail other researchers who took a more critical view of the Canadian role in Vietnam, stating: "[those] who would search only for the roots of Canadian 'complicity' in America's later intervention err by applying a standard of evaluation that is both reductive and unhelpful." The evidence brought together in this chapter suggests that what was anomalous in Canadian actions was the very fact that Canada took on this commitment when all the evidence pointed to Pearson's desire to reduce Canadian government exposure in Southeast Asia. The reason Canada acceded to the request for Canadian participation was because it struck a minor chord, that is, the aspiration for some semblance of a foreign policy role that was distinctively Canadian. The peacekeeping niche afforded by participation in the Indochina commissions was tailor-made to give the appearance of a middle force in international diplomacy. The long-term effect of this decision was extremely important in Canada and is discussed further in the conclusion. In the short term, however, Pearson's preoccupation with appearing on-side with the Americans, and his anti-communist affinities, contrived to ensure that Canadian commissioners on the ICSC would, regardless of their individual observations and perceptions, align Canadian positions with the agenda of the American Empire in the south of Vietnam. This early collaboration could only reinforce the US administration's belief in the righteousness of its actions. Few at the time could have imagined that this righteousness would lead the United States to deploy 500,000 troops to Vietnam and engage in indiscriminate bombing on a scale unknown in human history. No doubt Pearson and others felt that their positions were dictated by the need to maintain Western solidarity.[79] Yet, it was precisely this imagined Western solidarity against a Soviet conspiracy that led to the continuing subordination of the Vietnamese peoples' quest for self-determination. Later, maintaining US prestige as the core of Western solidarity became the rationale for escalation of the war, with its deadly and tragic results.

Conclusion

The episodes and stories described in this book confirm Jane Samson's suggestion of a "deep entanglement" between race and empire. Discerning the contours of this entanglement, however, is not so simple. Canada's past is enmeshed in a complex web of socio-economic intersections shrouded by an established nationalist discourse of progress from colony to nation and, in terms of foreign policy, from isolationism to internationalism. *Orienting Canada* approaches the past from the margins, and its findings suggest that such an approach offers different and valuable ways of reframing Canadian history.

Given the direction of postwar Canadian foreign policy, it is not surprising that a traditionalist interpretation might conclude: "In a homogenizing decade, there was no basic difference among Canada's major political factions on the Cold War, or NATO, or the confrontations with Soviet Russia. Nor was there any serious disagreement that Europe and of course the United States were the proper focus of Canadian attention. Canadians were in overall agreement as to what constituted 'their' world. Asia was a source of mystery and danger but in the 1950s concerns on that continent counted only as a distraction."[1] In one sense, such a characterization seems to make sense of Canadian foreign policy. As history, however, it fails to go beyond the obvious to probe or problematize the underlying processes that led to the results described. Furthermore, by wielding the term "Canadian" in such an unqualified manner, this approach to history again marginalizes Canadian "others," those for whom events in Asia were of great importance – people such as Irene Kato, who was stranded in Japan by a government intent on expelling people of Japanese heritage from the west coast; or Wong Foon Sien, who continued to journey to Ottawa to lobby for immigration from China. Such people find themselves excluded from traditional Canadian narratives, forgotten entirely or relegated to "minority" status and therefore irrelevant given the majority view. In this and other ways, conventional narratives refract reality so that it is "whiteness that is centered and assumed. Difference is understood in relation to it."[2] What is at times forgotten is that in reproducing "whiteness," traditional histories racialize not only peoples of colour but also peoples of European descent, if in a somewhat different fashion. So Chester Ronning, of Norwegian descent, may be counted as one of the "Canadians" described above, but in so doing, his life-long concern for China is denied; so too, Herbert Norman, whose affinity for Japan and its peoples is legend in that country, is also denied a place in the dominant narrative in which "Canadians" were unconcerned about Asia. Such biases do not help in crafting history. It is time for different stories to emerge, to decentre our history and to relocate its margins.

The episodes and stories compiled for this book do not constitute an alternate history of Canada-East Asian relations, but they do suggest that Asia was an important focus for Canadian foreign policy, and, furthermore, they challenge the entrenched narrative regarding Canada's being "isolationist," only to emerge after the Second World War as a "middle power," associated with "Pearsonian internationalism," multilateralism, and a collaborative world order.[3] By way of conclusion, I examine these issues in the context of continentalism and Atlanticism in Canadian foreign policy and then explore the implications of mapping Japan and Asian-Canadian history onto the past. I hope this will precipitate renewed discussion about our collective memories and facilitate innovative research in Canadian, transpacific, and world history.

Continentalism and the Transpacific

In many critical decision-making situations in which the Canadian government had an independent position regarding developments in postwar East Asia, it withdrew or reversed its position even when it had support from others, including, at times, Great Britain. This was true in the Far Eastern Commission debate on Japan's Constitution, when the government abandoned its proposals for a participatory democratic process for the Japanese people in the face of US intransigence; in the UN Temporary Commission on Korea, when it reversed its commitment to holding elections for the whole of Korea and not just in the south; in its decision to support George Kennan and the regressive "reverse course" in Japan despite its own and British misgivings; in the decision to go to war in Korea despite Pearson's initial view that Korea was not strategic; in its refusal to extend recognition to China or to establish diplomatic relations despite British efforts in that direction; in its support for the US position during the drafting of the San Francisco peace treaty in 1951 despite British misgivings and objections from many countries in Asia, including India; in the decision to support the Bao Dai regime in Vietnam despite opposition from Nehru. In almost all of these cases there was the possibility of support for alternative Canadian positions, and, indeed, on numerous occasions DEA staff articulated alternatives or warned against courses of actions under consideration. Yet in each instance the Canadian government withdrew or subsumed its views in favour of support for US government positions. For some, the explanation for such actions lies in the realm of common sense: Canadian interests in its bilateral relationship with the United States far outweighed its interests in Asia. To accept this view, however, jeopardizes the cherished view of Canada as internationalist and multilateral. For, in the instances cited above, the Canadian government supported actions that were contrary to its own policies and, as even the government acknowledged at the time, might undermine multilateral institutions. Can one argue that sacrificing the interests of democratic constitutional processes for the people of Japan, defeated and occupied at the time, was "internationalism" in action? What I am proposing is not just that the Canadian government played a supporting role in the emerging global order in which US power would predominate, a position that others have argued before, but, rather, that it actively encouraged the United States to take on this role, and that it did so due to the values shared by the men in the foreign policy establishment of both countries – values that reflected ideas about race and empire, reinforcing their belief that the Euro-American powers had to play a significant role in Asia as well as elsewhere. In an era of decolonization, the Canadian government aligned the country with American imperialism.

For Pearson and others, the instability of the 1930s, the war with Germany (beginning in 1939), and the desperate search for American support prior to Pearl Harbor were important factors that shaped their views. For them, the attack on Pearl Harbor and the American declaration of war against the Axis was a huge relief in that it brought US resources and commitment to the war effort. They tragically believed, as did a US president sixty years later, that the attack on Pearl Harbor was the start of a long and terrible war for America: "Yet out of that surprise attack grew a steadfast resolve that made America freedom's defender."[4] Indeed, the resources, commitment, and sacrifices of the American war effort contributed greatly to defeating Japanese imperialism. However, if taken in isolation – that is, if it is removed from its spatial and temporal context – this truth obscures much more than it reveals. It masks the fact that, historically, the US government had abetted the rise of Japanese imperialism, particularly in facilitating its annexation of Korea and later in collaborating in the joint exploitation of China. A unilateral emphasis on Pearl Harbor and the US response can conceal the fact that the essence of the conflict in the Pacific was essentially a struggle of the Korean, Chinese, and Asian peoples for independence from both Japanese and Euro-American imperialism, as illustrated by vociferous demands across Asia for decolonization and the termination of unequal treaties. It was a war that depended on the resistance of the Chinese people to Japanese aggression – resistance that extracted a terrible toll, first on the Chinese peoples and later on the many others in Asia who suffered under Japanese colonialism after 1941. Yet, from the vantage point of Ottawa or Washington, too often the war appeared to be America's war, and the victory America's victory. The cataclysms of Hiroshima and Nagasaki left no doubt of that in the minds of many, all but erasing the decisive role that Soviet entry into the war had on Japan's defeat.

Buttressing the Canadian government's views was the belief, articulated regularly in policy documents, that the postwar Pacific was an American sphere of influence. Indeed, for the Atlantic men who dominated in the DEA, the postwar era was seen as a shift to a global Pax Americana. These were classic imperialist concepts, rooted in a view of the world in which the Big Powers could, and indeed would, determine the future of peoples in Asia or elsewhere. This was not perceived as imperialism per se since, at the time, "imperialism" was mainly equated with colonialism (i.e., the direct political control of a country or region by a metropole). Pearson often went to great lengths to deny any imperial role on the part of the United States and even went so far as to present Canada-US relations as evidence of the non-imperial nature of US intervention. To separate oneself from colonialism in this way, while endorsing US power abroad, reflected not only the growing force of decolonization but also an abiding belief that peoples in the developing world were incapable of navigating their own way. A guide was necessary, and the trans-Atlantic powers, with the United States in the lead, were ready to serve. The spectre of increasing communist influence provided an additional rationale for maintaining spheres of influence and even for justifying what was to become US military colonization of Okinawa and many Pacific islands. China had forced imperial powers to put an end to the unequal treaties, and, in their place, was born the postwar era of "collective security," in which new military alliances and status of forces agreements replaced yet, in some ways, replicated the unequal relations of the imperial past.

Race remained a potent force in this postwar world. To be sure, anti-racism and anti-colonialism, not to mention the fear of communism, forced some blatant forms of racism, such as the vicious wartime propaganda against Japan, into the shadows. And there were victories, including the achievement of the franchise for many Asian Canadians and the overturning of the Chinese Exclusion Act. Fear of trouble for Canada arising in the United Nations in response to racist policies towards Japanese Canadians also inspired the government to take a more judicious stance on some issues. This was not a recognition of Canada's racist past: it was its sanitization. As Sophie Bessis suggests, "the collective consciousness was more convinced then ever, after victory over the Beast, that it was the repository of humanist universality, while at the same time retaining its certainty of superiority."[5] This was not the end of white supremacy but, rather, its recasting in different moulds.[6]

Thus racism continued to shape Canadian and American policies in the postwar, both at home and in East Asia. The war in Korea revealed the continuing norms of vulgar racialization among many soldiers, American and Canadian alike, contributing to the wanton disregard for Korean civilians on the part of American and Canadian officials. And, despite the participation of Indonesia and the Philippines, the 1951 San Francisco Peace Treaty was a reflection of a more subtle but deeply racialized view of the world in which the United States and its allies appropriated the victory in the Pacific War to themselves and excluded from the peace process the Asian peoples who had fallen victim to Japanese aggression. In so doing, they played on the deeply held view among Japanese leaders such as Yoshida Shigeru that Japan's great error in the war was not its imperial expansion in Asia but, rather, its misguided attack on its imperial allies, the United States and Great Britain. Using a combination of blandishments and coercion, Dulles played on Yoshida's belief that the Japanese differed from other peoples of Asia. Indeed, the reintegration of Japan into the American-led treaty system post-1952 signalled another *datsu a ron*, a leaving of Asia not dissimilar to that of the 1880s, when the Meiji government articulated its belief that Japan had to break with its neighbours to join the "civilized" West. The problems associated with the peace treaty endure to this day in territorial disputes and in the continuing demands for redress and reconciliation on the part of victims of Japanese war crimes during the Pacific War.

Yet, there were also important divergences between the Canadian and American governments on racial issues.[7] With regard to the treatment of Japanese Canadians, the Canadian government had embarked on a postwar program of what amounted to the deportation of Japanese Canadians and persistent attempts to bar them from the west coast. Yet, in many cases, in the spring of 1945, Japanese Americans had been able to return to the west coast and reclaim their possessions and property. In the Endo decision, the US Supreme Court ruled on 19 December 1944 that incarceration in the camps without trial was illegal, and, shortly afterwards, the incarceration order was rescinded.[8] The persecution of Japanese Canadians, on the other hand, persisted and in some ways intensified even after the war had ended. This difference highlights the relative lack of any effective institutional curbs on state power in Canada compared to what existed in the United States. The treatment of Japanese Canadians from 1945 to 1949, which effectively completed the destruction of many communities in British Columbia that began during the war, is a distinct and shameful chapter in Canadian history. It highlights the intensity and grip of racism over both federal and provincial institutions in this era, including the Supreme Court, and it suggests that ethnic cleansing can also take place in liberal regimes, where state coercion short of physical extermination can achieve similar ends. That Japanese-Canadian communities later reformed in different ways does not obviate this fact; rather, it is testimony to the resilience of imagined communities and the power of redress.[9]

Difference with the United States also arose in regard to immigration. Whereas the US Congress began to take minimal measures to implement a quota system for immigration from Asia, the Canadian government refused at this time to even consider quotas for new emigrants from Asian countries. Immigration was restricted to relatives only, narrowly defined.[10] In the United Nations, the Canadian government was reticent to endorse the Universal Declaration of Human Rights despite strong endorsement by the US government and despite the involvement of the Canadian lawyer John Humphries in the writing of the declaration.[11] Race continued to cast a long shadow in policy deliberations into the 1950s, as underlined by Escott Reid's recollection: "[I was] particularly depressed in New York by what I learned about the line which Canadian delegations to the Assembly had been taking in the last years of the Liberal regime on racialism, colonialism and trusteeship question."[12] Research on the question of race and postwar Canadian foreign policy is embryonic to say the least, and much more systematic inquiry is essential to gain a better understanding of this intersection.

Of particular historical concern is the complex question of the role of anti-communism and postwar foreign policy, both in its strategic dimension as well as in its relationship to questions of race. Whitaker and Marcuse argue persuasively that anti-communism resonated in the postwar period because of historical antecedents as well as the legacy of a "them-and-us" mentality that emerged during the course of the war.[13] There were legitimate grounds for criticism of communism, both internationally and in Canada. As historians have shown, the Soviet Union had its own imperial aspirations in East Asia, as reflected in the Yalta Agreements. But Soviet willingness to allow US forces to control South Korea and to exercise predominant control in the occupation of Japan reflected its adherence to wartime agreements dividing the world into spheres of influence. What upset that balance was not principally Soviet actions but, rather, I would argue, European attempts to restore colonial regimes in Southeast Asia; acute civil wars in which the United States intervened (on behalf of Chiang in China and Rhee in South Korea); and Anglo-American intransigence in their relations with the Soviets in postwar Germany.[14] We need to look beyond obvious Soviet-American hostility and locate the postwar both spatially and temporally as an era when peoples in liberal regimes such Canada and the United States wanted peace and stability after years of war, as a time when capitalism was unstable, decolonization was intensifying, and communism had gained prestige and legitimacy. In this context, people such as Acheson and Truman believed they had to scare the hell out of people to produce the support necessary to finance an emerging global Pax Americana.

International anti-communism had many prewar antecedents, but in the postwar world it necessarily evolved in stages after extensive wartime collaboration. The first phase, beginning in May 1945, was one of escalating rivalry related to occupation policies, the use and control of atomic weapons, and jockeying for position in the clashes between the forces of recolonization and decolonization. Hopes for an era of peaceful co-existence remained strong, but criticism of Soviet actions served both as a means to mobilize a diverse array of people and a way to deflect criticism of the gross injustices being perpetrated by Euro-American empires in their attempts to regain control, by direct or indirect methods, of much of the globe. By the spring of 1947, what were real tensions were being used to remanufacture a world scenario in which there were supposedly only two camps: communism and democracy. This was initially an ideological campaign that, in the context of the 1949 Chinese revolution and the Soviet Union's successful testing of an atomic weapon, soon evolved into a fierce campaign to demonize communism at home and abroad. The Korean War and NSC-68 were both symbols and instruments of the extremism of anti-communism in this third phase, in which the dangers of appeasement became a caricature of the lessons of the earlier war.

These phases were reflected in the Canadian experience. The delay in the release of information during the Gouzenko affair of 1945 and the sensationalism that later surrounded the whole issue reflected the instability of the postwar situation. By 1947, Canadian officials were fully embracing the concept of a bipolar world with Europe at its centre while continuing to debate the respective roles of the Soviet and American powers. The December 1947 Cabinet crisis regarding the United Nations Temporary Commission on Korea was resolved the following spring, when the Canadian government reversed its position on elections in South Korea alone. Lester Pearson had one of his first tastes of the effectiveness of anti-communism in the process, and, despite misgivings, he became an effective cold warrior. It was not hard for George Kennan, therefore, to persuade the Canadian government to alter its views regarding occupation policies for Japan. Pearson was a key figure as both under-secretary of state for external affairs and, later, as the minister for external affairs. Under his and St. Laurent's guidance, the Canadian government actively pursued the creation of NATO, while continuing to recognize the importance and complexities of Asia. US government concern for the region, and a renovated Commonwealth that now included India, Pakistan, and Sri Lanka, underscored its importance. Pearson also understood Japan's strategic role within a north Pacific that included the Soviet Union. Anti-communism predisposed Pearson to view India in particular as a positive alternative to communism, leading to Canadian support for the Colombo Plan. But Nehru and the Indian government's refusal to accept the concept of a bipolar world created constant tension in India-Canadian relations. Nevertheless, the Canadian government continued to pursue certain elements of peaceful co-existence and tried to distance itself from the taint of colonial projects.

The Korean War, however, fundamentally altered the world as well as the Canadian scene. Anti-communism took on a life of its own, fed by the blood shed by soldiers and civilians alike during three years of protracted war. Eurocentrism in Canada may have later rendered the conflagration into

Canada's "forgotten war," but it was a definitive moment in world history, marking the consolidation of American leadership of a resurgent coalition and the ascendency of a new form of liberal militarism – the national security state.

Pearson and the Liberal government embraced anti-communism partially out of expediency but also because it provided a new indispensable enemy against which to project liberal values. It was an effective means to discredit political adversaries and to achieve political objectives that might otherwise not have been possible. Ironically, Pearson himself, not to mention Herbert Norman, Chester Ronning, and George Patterson, came under fire from McCarthyism in the United States. The extremes of anti-communism, and of American imperial over-reach, encouraged Pearson and others to think again about reinforcing autonomy in Canadian foreign policy. But there was little space for this in the 1950-54 period. Only after the British and French governments reached out to the Soviet Union in the 1954 Berlin meetings would space again emerge for initiatives that were not determined by US policies and anti-communism.

The relationship between anti-communism and racism is daunting in its complexity. On the one hand, postwar anti-communism targeting the Soviet Union was partially inspired by the notion of the Soviet Union as a "semi-Asiatic" race. Its Eurocentric thrust reflected the premium attached to Europe and a concomitant downgrading of the importance of anti-imperial struggles that, for the majority of the world's peoples, were the main instrument for gaining freedom. White statesmen such as Acheson or Pearson treated their counterparts in the global South, communist and non-communist alike, with a paternalism that reflected the continuing influence of white superiority. On the other hand, the US rise to globalism in a decolonizing world demanded the construction of a multi-racial, international coalition. This, and the persistent assertions of the superior freedoms of liberal regimes, left the latter vulnerable to criticisms of racism. These factors facilitated progressive change, and, thus, the relationship was one of constant tension and negotiation, shaped not only by international requirements but also by local and regional dynamics. However, within the ensuing international coalitions, old hierarchies tended to reproduce themselves.

Race, Altanticism, and the Transpacific

Suggesting that postwar Canadian foreign policy in the Transpacific was driven by continentalism is not to deny the ongoing importance of Europe, and particularly Great Britain, in postwar Canadian foreign policy. A 1945

Canadian Congress of Labour memorandum to the government on foreign policy articulated what many believed was a foundation of Canadian policy: that Canada must function "as a keystone in the arch of Anglo-American understanding," and, further, that it must continue to do so "for many years to come."[15] It was precisely at this time that the Canadian scholar J.B. Brebner, a historian at Columbia University, articulated the notion of "Atlanticism" in his landmark study *North Atlantic Triangle: The Interplay of Canada, the United States, and Great Britain*.[16] The significance of Brebner's work was not so much an original analysis as it was his ability to put in academic terms what had indeed become conventional wisdom for many in Canada. Brebner's thesis was that Canada and the United States were "Siamese Twins," that the two countries' relationship could not, however, be explained in "merely North American terms" and that, essentially, it was part of a triangle that included Great Britain.[17] Geography, demographics (Canadians and Americans were "of the same human stock except for their proportions of French and Negro elements") and different historical trajectories meant that the relationship could not be taken for granted. Canadians, suggested Brebner, often sought to differentiate themselves from Americans by seeking refuge in Catholicism or a "real or imagined Britoness."[18] By the 1940s, however, relations had matured, founded, according to Brebner, on a bedrock of closer economic integration. At the time, the noted scholar James T. Shotwell heralded Brebner's study as a landmark work that dealt with "the three great branches of the English-speaking peoples, Great Britain, Canada and the United States," and that illuminated the "greatest single chapter in the history of international intercourse anywhere in the world."[19] Brebner's concept of a triangular Atlanticism has endured. Michael Fry, the noted Canadian scholar of Canada-Japan relations took up Brebner's notions in his examination of the 1921-22 Washington Conference.[20] In it he hinted at the racialized basis for the drive to end the Anglo-Japanese alliance that was presented at that conference. In a co-authored study entitled *The North Pacific Triangle*,[21] Fry went on to adapt Brebner's concept to Canada-Asia relations. Recent studies of Canada's relations with the United States and Great Britain also acknowledge both Brebner and the concept of Atlanticism.[22] *Orienting Canada* goes further in explicitly identifying and exploring race as a fundamental factor in shaping this north Atlantic triangle and, in so doing, both confirms and modifies the notion of Atlanticism.

Theodore Roosevelt's reaction to the 1907 race riots (described in the prologue), his proposal to send King to London as a go-between with the express objective of developing closer Anglo-American cooperation in the Pacific, and his determination to confront the Japanese government are important instances of Atlanticism in the making. As the Asian-American historian Erika Lee suggests, the 1907 race riots, and indeed anti-Asian racism in general, were not limited to specific cities or states but, in fact, constituted what she calls "hemisperhic Orientalism."[23] And recently, Lake and Reynolds have extended the boundaries even further in their study of the global colour line.[24] The fact that there was also competition between British and American imperial centres, with the Canadian government often caught in the middle, may obscure but does not contradict the common anti-Asian bias in those two countries. In that sense, *Orienting Canada* takes issue with Kohn's study, in which he argues that Anglo-Saxonism was extremely important in creating continental affinities but that it went into decline in the post-1903 period and, furthermore, that postwar Anglo-American policy rhetoric was not "racially based."[25] It may well be that Anglo-Saxonism was less present as a popular phenomenon, but it hardly disappeared. What came to overlay, but not entirely to replace, Anglo-Saxonism was the notion of "whiteness," the idea that Canada was to become a "white man's country." This notion fired the popular imagination as well as government policy. White superiority became a social norm. Rooted originally in conflict between Europeans and Aboriginal peoples, it rose to preponderance in the twentieth century as a social construct created mainly out of persistent ideological and juridical efforts to racialize "Orientals." Contested and challenged, particularly during the 1930s, the presumption of white superiority nevertheless continued to dominate socially and politically into the Second World War. Even after the war, Anglo-Saxonism continued as an informal but resilient strand within the cultural lattice of whiteness, binding networks of power and influence inside and outside of government.

Atlanticism, with its racializing bias and Eurocentric orientation, persisted into the postwar period. This can be most readily perceived in immigration policy. In the immediate aftermath of war, the Canadian embrace of large numbers of refugees and displaced peoples from Europe is often noted as a significant humanitarian gesture. However, there was an even greater number of refugees or displaced peoples in Asian countries, from Indonesia to the Philippines and China, yet they remained purposefully excluded. Canadian humanitarianism remained colour coded. Close to 2 million people came to Canada from Europe in the fifteen years after the war, of whom British immigrants continued to represent the largest single group. The predominance of European immigration, combined with the baby boom in

Canada, meant that between 1941 and 1961, the number of Canadians of European (including British) origins increased from 11.2 million in 1941 to 17.7 million in 1961 – an increase of 6.5 million people of European heritage in this twenty-year period.[26] This policy buttressed Canada's whiteness at the same time as it reinforced trans-Atlantic links to Europe.

It comes as no surprise then that strong echoes of prewar Atlanticism could be seen at work in postwar international relations. Churchill, in his Cold War speech in Fulton in 1946, appealed for the unity of "English-speaking peoples" and a global military alliance between the Commonwealth and the United States. This did indeed become an informal but effective core of the broader coalition constructed to oppose the perceived threat of the Soviet Union and communism. Anglo-Saxonism had been purposefully dropped from Cold War vocabulary to be replaced by what was to become the international language of "whiteness." In this sense, Atlanticism came to represent the constantly shifting and negotiated spaces between the British and American empires. The Canadian government perceived its own role as a mediator and guide for the British and Americans and, at other times, for the newly independent India and the United States.

Canadian involvement in policy making in the Pacific offers a window into the functioning of Atlanticism in this region. Was it coincidence that the four men empowered to write the final judgment of the Tokyo Tribunal were judges from Canada, New Zealand, Great Britain, and the United States? Was it coincidence that George Kennan felt it important to consult mainly with Great Britain and Canada with regard to his proposal to re-invent Japan and to reverse engines with regard to Occupation reforms? Was it coincidence that Great Britain and the United States governments were the sponsors of the San Francisco Peace Conference in 1951 and that the Chinese governments were excluded? Atlanticism facilitated the co-ordination of imperial interests in East Asia, and, when this coordination broke down, as it did over Vietnam in 1954, different outcomes occurred.

Many in Canada's foreign policy establishment perceived that their role was to work with US diplomats to assure a global role not only for America but also for the trans-Atlantic alliance. For Canadian diplomats, the priority within this global agenda was Europe, and this was reflected in the drive to create NATO, a military alliance that began in Europe but that grew to include the United States and Canada. At the time, its geographic scope was limited specifically to Europe and North America. However, Atlanticism in its postwar, global guise can be perceived more broadly as a layered network in which Great Britain and the colonial settler states (including the United States) played a key role, in concert with European and other allies, including non-Europeans from the global South.

In the postwar period, Atlanticism had to contend with the rapid onset of decolonization, and this changed to some extent the complexion of alliances in the Transpacific. They began to include at least nominally independent countries such as the Philippines or Thailand, and these allied states in the periphery could, depending on the circumstances, play an important and at times decisive role in imperial politics. The participation of Indonesia and the Philippines in the 1951 San Francisco Peace Treaty provided an essential veneer of Asian participation in a process that was otherwise deeply flawed. In this we find striking evidence of how anti-communism and race intersected in ways that, in traditional analyses, have often been obscured. Focusing on communism allowed the creation of cross-racial alliances while leaving intact Atlanticist priorities. In Asia, however, the legacy of anti-colonial struggles meant that many leaders, including Nehru, were not convinced of the altruism of anti-communism, and his pan-Asianism was a bitter pill for Pearson to swallow.

In painting radical anti-colonial movements as being under communist or Soviet influence, the resurgent Euro-American coalition attempted to discredit the ongoing struggle for decolonization or to subordinate it to other goals. That this battle was not expressly cast in racial terms renders it more complex but does not alter its production of a racialized global hierarchy in which "Anglo-Americans were still on top, followed by the various European peoples. Then came the 'Third World.'"[27]

Understanding the persistent yet changing forms of Atlanticism in the Pacific helps to deconstruct the discourse of multilateralism and, at the same time, to highlight what amounts to shameful anti-Americanism in which the United States alone is held responsible for global hegemony. To be sure, the unilateralist impulse on the part of the American Empire was real, and transparently so in the handling of the Korean War, with Truman decided on military action even before consulting his allies or the United Nations. But for the most part, such examples are exceptions to the rule of multilateral consultation and collaboration. Whether it be the dropping of atomic bombs or the establishment of the San Francisco system of military alliances, the United States worked in concert with its allies. In other words, it is erroneous to suggest that successive US administrations were acting unilaterally in projecting a powerful presence across the Pacific. Atlanticism plus – that is, the historical Anglo-American alliance plus the new postwar allies – worked collectively towards maintaining a powerful US presence in East Asia.[28] On the other hand, there were many people in the United States who opposed the trajectory their country was taking, a fact anti-Americanism overlooks.

Mapping Japan onto Postcolonialism

In suggesting that it was necessary to map Japanese imperialism onto the postcolonial map, Choi emphasizes what he perceives as a Eurocentric tinge among postcolonial scholars who tend to focus almost uniquely on European imperialism to the exclusion of Japanese imperialism. This is ironic given that the postcolonial critique seeks, as one of its leading proponents argues, to "undo the Eurocentrism produced by the institution of the West's trajectory, its appropriation of the other as History," and accuses "colonialist, nationalist, and Marxist interpretations of robbing the common people" of their agency.[29] In fact, Choi's critique raises a number of issues that require unpacking and discrete inquiry. Some scholars have begun the process of subjecting Asian nationalisms to postcolonial analysis. Feminist scholars examining the postwar trajectory of the "comfort women" as well as more general studies of gender and nationalism have now been published in English, yet they offer important new insights into Japanese-East Asian relations.[30] Much is to be learned from this expanding repertoire of postcolonial critiques of nationalisms and Japanese imperialism. The focus here, however, is on race and empire, particularly in relation to the Transpacific. This, and the fact that I mainly address issues that arise in English-language scholarship, are important limiting factors in this study. But, as Choi points out, Japan's postwar image has largely been mediated by US accounts, and this holds true in Canada as well, where such accounts have also had a large impact on teaching about Japan. Despite efforts by critical US and Canadian scholars, much of the content of school and even university curricula remains conventional, rationalizing without fully probing the transformation of Japan's image from one of implacable enemy to erstwhile ally (and the reverse in the case of China).

As Alexis Dudden points out, Japanese imperialism's roots can be traced back to earlier decades, when states such as the United States and Great Britain had often "approved and, in many cases, instructed" Japan's colonial aspirations, particularly in its annexation of Korea.[31] Mapping the rise of Japanese imperialism means setting aside the prism of the Second World War and retrospective history and re-establishing the context of the prewar era. In Japan, in particular, the aggregate impact of continuous racism in North America and its subordination in imperial alliances (e.g., the

Washington treaties) reinforced nationalist and ethnocentric notions among officials, policy makers, and the popular press. This includes the concept that Japan's "surplus population" needed an outlet on the Asian mainland. Many believed that Japan had a civilizing mission there not unlike Euro-American imperialism's mission in India or the Philippines. That vision had ancient origins but was reinforced as part of Meiji-era notions of "modernity."[32] Other imperial powers validated the vision through their support for Japanese colonialism after the victory over Russia in 1905. From the perspective of Japanese leaders, subsequent British and American protests against Japanese expansion, beginning in the First World War, were perceived as self-serving and hypocritical. In this, Japanese imperialists were quite right. Nationalistic military officers and civilian groups used such fault lines for their own ends and went on to become the cutting edge of a reinvented imperial destiny that further exacerbated tensions.

Tracing Japan's imperial trajectory also demands an understanding of the resistance that it provoked. That resistance first took shape in Korea but was bitterly repressed. In China, however, it was more difficult to crush the movements for independence. The 1920s was a tumultuous period, in which great anti-imperial movements, including the Hong Kong seaman's strike, the anti-British boycott, and the May 30th movement challenged the power of colonialism. Imperial powers tried to play on the differences between the political factions, and anti-communism was a powerful inducement to force non-communist nationalists to compromise and cooperate. To be sure, collaboration did arise, yet a general compromise proved elusive because popular anti-imperialism remained strong – to defy it was to deny the emerging "imagined community" of an independent China. In the end, British and Japanese imperial responses to the anti-imperialist movements diverged – the former choosing to compromise and retreat when necessary and the latter choosing confrontation and violence. After 1928, Japanese imperialism became the main target of the anti-colonial movement in China. This narrowed focus created the basis for the second united front in 1936, the force of which led Japanese officials to believe that they had no choice but to put down the resistance once and for all – precipitating the 1937 invasion of China. The cumulative effect of decades of racializing the Chinese, in conjunction with militarism and patriarchy, precipitated systemic abuses – war crimes against soldiers, civilians, and, in particular, women, became endemic.

Among the Euro-American powers there was an ongoing debate about the attractions of Japanese control (eradication of communism, law and order, etc.) versus the problems. And thus, for over four years, resistance against Japanese aggression was based almost entirely on the efforts of the Chinese peoples aided by the diaspora and a transnational assortment of others. The impact in the long term would be far-reaching, but US intervention after Pearl Harbor came to dominate later accounts of the war. However, buried in the archives is important evidence of a different type. For example, Mackenzie King's diaries are an extremely important source as they highlight the transformative influences of Chinese resistance. Although King's appreciation of that resistance really only began after December 1941 when the Japanese attacked the British Empire, his contact with Soong Meiling, Wellington Koo, and T.V. Soong, as well as with Chinese government representatives in Canada, altered to some extent his attitude towards China, towards people of Chinese descent, and towards British colonialism. This, in turn, contributed to the establishment of diplomatic relations with China, the abolition of extra-territoriality, and the view that Canadian forces, if dispatched to the Pacific, should not be used to reimpose colonialism. Later, King would waver on many of these issues, but that change occurred at all can be attributed to the power of decolonization. In unexpected ways, mapping Japanese imperialism and its resistance offers rich rewards in understanding Canada as well as East Asia.

Asian Canadian History and Canada's Foundations

The construction of "race" within Canada was a protracted process that affected peoples of colour and also shaped, in very fundamental ways, Canada as a whole, including its foreign policies. In that sense, there exists a foundational character to race in Canadian history. Aboriginal peoples know this, and many others in Canada are beginning to acknowledge it with regard to First Nations. I suggest that an understanding of race in Canada cannot be achieved without adequately integrating the histories of Asian Canadians. This is because it was principally with them as protagonist that race was constructed and the Canadian demography emerged. By going to what some would consider the "margins," by discerning the trajectory of Asian-Canadian and transpacific history and their intersections, we can newly engage conventional as well as social histories, some of which have failed to adequately position themselves, thereby inadvertently reinforcing Eurocentric or nationalist tropes.

A significant finding that arises from *Orienting Canada* is the resilience of race. The Second World War may have been a pivotal moment to the extent that it marked a shifting of tides against racism. But what was surprising was how Canada, on the whole, did not change in any substantive sense – if anything, in some important ways, it became even more of a "white man's country." This, in turn, provoked ongoing contestation into the 1950s and beyond.[33] To be sure, some of the modes of racialization changed, but this was no linear process in which racism simply began to be beaten out of Canadian society. Race, it would seem, is remarkably malleable and resilient and is bound up with core concepts about Canada as a country. Understanding and explaining the nature of this resilience is itself an important challenge for scholars.

Largely unknown to most Canadians, the 1907 Vancouver race riots were a defining moment in Canadian history. Not only did they bring into sharp relief the polarization between the many who believed in a white Canada and the demonized "Oriental other," the aftermath saw renewed and decisive state intervention with regard to immigration. If the 1885 and 1902 royal commissions represented the institutional foundations of racialization and discrimination, the aftermath of the 1907 riots saw the consolidation of the notion of "Orientals," which included not only the Chinese but also the Japanese and South Asians. Furthermore, immigration matters came to trump trade and even strategic considerations, and the federal government put in place comprehensive yet distinct policies and regulations to achieve its aims. The varied treatments (negotiated quotas, regulatory exclusion, statutory bans, and so forth) reflected, inter alia, the different positions the home countries represented within the racialized constellation of nation-states as well as the varied tropes invoked in racializing Asian peoples. It cannot be over-emphasized that these were negotiated processes involving other state actors and that immigration has never been solely a question of domestic politics. It is impossible, in other words, to understand Canadian state policies without understanding the interstate relationships that were at play. This is why the federal government, not provincial politicians, became the main agent in defining a white Canada. It is time to put to rest the oft-repeated caricature that racism was strong in British Columbia and that the role of the federal government was to exert a moderating influence. Lemieux, Pope, King, Laurier, Sifton, Borden – these men of impeccable "Eastern" origins were the ones who, after 1907, defined the reasons for Oriental exclusion. They, together with provincial politicians, became architects in the institutionalization of a white Canada. The determination of the federal government to both define and to regulate this complex racialized hierarchy reinforces the point that the powers of racialization only achieve "full structural and systemic power when they are legally defined and enforced by state power."[34] In Canada, that required substantive federal government intervention.

In edifying the ideological foundations of the construction of race at this time, it becomes clear that the government perceived the issues as not simply or primarily economic, but rather as fundamental for white people wherever they lived. The Oriental was being excluded, and the notion of a bloc of people of lighter complexion was supplanting earlier notions that associated race with ethnicity. Contrary to what multicultural mythology would suggest today, this was not simply the elaboration of a hierarchy of competing ethnicities – race in the sense of colour mattered. The movement to prevent settlement of African Americans in the Prairies just after the 1907 race riots suggests that, despite the fluidity of the colour line, by the time of the First World War, Canada had embraced many of the features of a white supremacist state.[35] For specific reasons, whiteness was defined in particular relation to the "Oriental other" at this specific conjuncture, and it is for this reason that Asian-Canadian history deserves much more attention than it has received to date. However, state policies and racial taxonomies were also informed by perceived interactions of Orientals with Aboriginal peoples.[36] Further research into the intersections of racialization and the resistance of peoples of colour, including Aboriginal peoples and peoples of African descent, is required to better understand the stages and transitions of racialization in Canada.[37] Establishing how such intersections relate to Quebec history is also a major challenge for the future.

Family, community, and support from those in the old countries imparted the resilience that allowed racialized immigrant communities to endure and, indeed, to grow despite the difficult challenges of living in a hostile atmosphere. Everyday lives involved much more than how they reacted, or not, to discrimination. But resistance was part of many stories. It and many other aspects of the communities' histories deserve much greater recognition and exploration. In the context of this study, the struggle against discrimination took many forms, through direct means such as petitions and other methods of government lobbying, through building community connections, and through extralegal means, including undocumented or falsely documented immigration. Such perseverance in the face of state power prompted the King government to completely prohibit Chinese immigration in 1923. The gendered dimensions of these interactions, particularly regarding the inclusion or exclusion of Asian females to Canada (fears of permanent settlement versus fears of miscegenation) further complicate the scenario.[38] In the case of the Japanese community, the arrival of substantial numbers of picture brides after 1907 and the growth of Japanese-Canadian communities prompted further restrictions limiting Japanese immigration in 1928. Despite a growing number of whites who challenged anti-Asian policies, exclusionist policies intensified, putting the communities' very survival at risk. On the other hand, opposition to racialization was also increasing among a growing number of whites, and, by the 1930s, momentum was building to change Canada's racist laws. However, as the threat of war grew in the 1930s, new problems arose.

Historians such as Thomas Borstelmann in the United States have suggested that the African and African-American freedom movements "moved on parallel tracks."[39] This dynamic also arose within Canada. However, Asia was not Africa and Canada was not the United States. The differential treatment of the communities reflected not only local circumstances but also the impact of the transnational. In the case of the Chinese, the movements for China's independence and justice for Chinese Canadians was closely linked and mutually reinforcing. Similarly, the South-Asian community closely identified with anti-imperialism in India. For the Japanese community, however, the matter involved different dynamics. Rather than mutual movements reinforcing justice, Japan's imperial status meant that the diaspora had slightly more leverage with the Canadian government, on the one hand, but, on the other, the community also faced increasing discrimination as the status of the homeland transformed from imperial ally into enemy.

Japan's invasion of northeast China in 1931 and then its full-scale invasion of 1937 mobilized many in the Chinese community to lend solidarity to those in their homeland, and the same may be said for the Japanese community, if to a lesser extent. The war in China drew a sharp line between the Japanese and Chinese communities in Canada. Although some in the Japanese community were uncomfortable with what was happening on the continent, there were others who supported the efforts of the Japanese imperial forces, a fact that has been at times neglected in historical accounts because of the necessity to refute charges of disloyalty as part of the campaign for redress.[40] It is indeed important to draw a line between disloyalty, of which there were no proven instances, and actions in support of Japanese imperial forces in China. In that regard, Japanese-Canadians who supported Japan's war of aggression were no more "disloyal" than were the nickel producers or the government that fuelled Japan's imperial war machine. However, for many in the Chinese communities, Japanese-Canadian actions in support of the invasion of China were a slap in the face, and they acted angrily, and at times inappropriately, labelling all Japanese spies and supporting their uprooting and dislocation.

Attempts by Asian Canadians to enlist in the Canadian military were, for the most part, rebuffed until the latter stages of the war. Nevertheless, hundreds did finally enter either the Canadian or British forces, and many served with distinction. Actions to gain the franchise and to end the Chinese Exclusion Act began even during the war and were rewarded in 1947. However much the "double victory" of the Second World War represented new opportunities for peoples of Asian descent in the postwar period, there was no repudiation of Canada's racist past. Instead race was driven underground, obfuscated, giving rise to the notion of a raceless Canada. Yet racializing norms remained strong. The postwar treatment of Japanese Canadians, their exile and the refusal of the government to allow them to return to Canada was but one example. Race continued to shape immigration policy, and the dramatic demographic effects of this are captured in census data. While the populations of European descent increased by 6.5 million to 1961, the total number of peoples of "Asiatic" descent in Canada increased by a total of forty-eight thousand, less than three-quarters of 1 percent of the increase in those of European descent.[41] In other words, the government's policies continued to reinforce the overwhelming domination of those of European descent, despite the changes coming out of the war. This resilience of race in the face of challenge is the legacy of whiteness, a power able to reproduce itself through what scholars in the recently evolving field of white studies define as "*exnomination*, that is the power not to be named; *naturalization*, through which whiteness establishes itself as the norm; and *universalization*, where whiteness alone can make sense of a problem and its understanding becomes *the* understanding."[42] Creating new spaces and new conversations, in which the oft-ignored voices of the past can mingle with those of the present, will provide the crucible from which all may achieve their rightful place.

Chronology

1871	Chinese and First Nations denied rights to vote in British Columbia.
1885	Royal Commission on Chinese Immigration (head tax begins).
1894-95	Japan defeats Chinese land and sea forces in Korea, Manchuria, and Yellow Sea, ending Chinese influence over Korea; Japan takes China's Liaodong Peninsula and Taiwan as war prizes (Liaodong later relinquished due to German/Russian/French pressure).
1898	United States takes Philippines from Spain in course of Spanish-American War, crushes Filipino independence movement.
1900	8-power multilateral "relief expedition" suppresses "Boxer Rebellion" for targeting foreigners, imposes harsh penalties on China's ruling Qing Dynasty.
1902	Establishment of Anglo-Japanese Alliance (renewed until abrogated in 1922).
1903	Chinese head tax increased to $500 per person entering Canada.
1905	Japan defeats Russia's land and sea forces in East Asia (Manchuria, Korea); United States provides venue for peace negotiations: Portsmouth, NH.
	US recognizes Japan's "special interests" in Korea (Taft-Katsura Agreement); Korea becomes Japanese "protectorate."

1906 Laurier government accedes to Anglo-Japanese Treaty of Commerce and Navigation.

San Francisco School Board moves to segregate Japanese schools.

1907 [September] Race riots in Vancouver, Bellingham; King hearings on damages and causes continue into 1908.

[November-December] Rodolphe Lemieux and Joseph Pope cross Pacific to negotiate with Hayashi Tadasu, Japan's foreign minister, to limit Japanese emigration.

1908 [January] Parliament passes Hayashi-Lemieux Agreement; similar agreement signed between Japanese and US governments.

Government adopts "Continuous Journey" regulations prohibiting South Asians from immigrating to Canada.

King meets with Theodore Roosevelt in Washington, discusses hemispheric approach to restricting emigration from Asia.

[April] King departs for London at request of Roosevelt for closer British-American ties.

[December] King departs for Great Britain, India, China, and Japan.

1909 [March] King negotiates with Qing representatives for quotas on emigration.

1910 Japan annexes Korea, which remains a part of Japanese Empire until Japan defeated in 1945.

1911 China's Qing Dynasty collapses; newly established republic soon dissolves into regional warlord enclaves.

1914 Outbreak of First World War; Japanese imperial forces capture and retain German possessions in Shandong (Qingdao) and Pacific Islands north of the equator.

1915 Japan makes "21 Demands" on government of Chinese president Yuan Shikai in attempt to secure special position in China while European Powers are embroiled in First World War.

1917 [March] Chinese government declares war on Germany; 100,000 Chinese labourers sent secretly across Canada by train on way to front.

[November] US secretly recognizes Japan's "special interests" in China.

1918 International forces (including American, Japanese, and Canadian troops) intervene in Siberia on side of "Whites" against "Reds" in Russian Revolution (Japanese troops remain until 1923).

1919 [March] Korean patriots declare independence from Japanese rule; Japan brutally suppresses the Korean movement for independence.

[Spring] Paris Peace Conference ignores Korean, Vietnamese, and other calls for independence; Wilson accedes to Japanese demand to take over German concessions in Shandong Province; British and US governments conspire to defeat Japanese call for racial equality; Canadian PM Borden works to ensure Canadian discriminatory immigration and labour policies are upheld during peace talks.

[May] Chinese nationalists react to Treaty of Versailles by staging street demonstrations and anti-Japanese boycotts in Beijing and other major cities (later known as "May Fourth Movement").

1921 [May]Formation of Chinese Communist Party (Shanghai).

[July] Canadian prime minister Arthur Meighen leads criticism of Anglo-Japanese Alliance at Imperial Conference in London.

1921-22 Washington Conference brings end to Anglo-Japanese Alliance and concludes with new treaties, including limits to Japanese naval power; confirmation of Japan's WW I acquisitions; China's interests largely ignored.

1923 Canada bans all Chinese immigration, ending head tax.

1923-25 Sun Yat-sen's Nationalist (Guomindang) Party establishes secure foothold in Guangdong Province after several attempts.

1924 United States legislates anti-Japanese Immigration Act.

1926-27 Nationalist-led armies – including significant communist contingents – stage "Northern March," wresting much of south and central China from warlord control.

1927 Canada establishes first legation abroad: Washington, DC; Minister: Vincent Massey.

[April] Nationalist army leader Chiang Kai-shek engineers bloody coup against communist allies, particularly in Shanghai.

1928 Japanese troops engineer assassination of Manchurian warlord Zhang Zuolin, who appears ready to "cut a deal" with Chiang Kai-shek.

Canadian government further reduces quota of Japanese immigrants to 150 despite protests by Japanese government.

1929 Canada establishes its third overseas legation in Tokyo; first minister is Herbert Marler.

1930 London Naval Conference makes adjustments to allowable fleet ratios of major naval powers, criticized by military in Japan.

1931 Japanese troops in Manchuria stage provocation, invade and occupy much of northeast China (Manchuria).

Japanese forces attack Shanghai, ostensibly in retaliation for anti-Japanese actions there.

1933 Japanese client state of Manchukuo established; last emperor of China installed as puppet emperor.

1937 [July] Japan launches full-scale advance through north and coastal east China (Operation Ichigo), following "Marco Polo Bridge" (Lugouqiao) incident southwest of Beijing.

[December] Chiang Kai-shek's Nationalist capital Nanjing occupied by Japanese troops following government's withdrawal; "Rape of Nanking"/Nanjing Massacre ensues.

1938 [January] Canadians, including Norman Bethune and Jean Ewen, depart Vancouver to aid anti-Japanese forces in China.

1941 [October] Japan's civilian Konoe Cabinet resigns; Tōjō Hideki, Chief of General Staff, becomes premier concurrently.

[7 December] Japanese bombing of Pearl Harbor brings United States into Second World War.

[10 December] Japanese bombers sink key British battleship and cruiser, breaking back of British Far East Fleet, after Britain declares war on Japan.

[25 December] Japanese forces defeat British-led forces in Hong Kong, Canadian Hong Kong contingent suffers heavy casualties, interned as POWs.

1942 [2 January] Japanese expeditionary force occupies Manila.

[January-March] Japanese Canadians suffer restrictions on movements and eventual uprooting, dispossession, and internment.

[15 February] Singapore surrenders to Japanese forces.

[5 March] Batavia (Jakarta) occupied by Japanese force (Netherlands has also declared war on Japan).

[8 March] Rangoon falls to Japanese forces.

[5 June] US carrier squadron surprises, sinks four Japanese carriers off Midway.

[7 August] US forces land on Guadalcanal.

1943 Quebec Conference; agreement between Churchill, Roosevelt provides for British, American, Canadian cooperation on nuclear experimentation, among other things.

US and Britain relinquish extraterritorial privileges in China, now a wartime ally; Canada follows suit a year later.

[Spring] Canada establishes Legation in Chongqing; 1st Minister/Ambassador, Maj. Gen. Victor Odlum, arrives in fall.

[June] Madame Chiang Kai-shek addresses joint session of Parliament.

[27 November] Cairo Conference of major Second World War allies (Great Britain, US, China) discusses postwar territorial and other arrangements.

[November] Teheran Conference; Stalin agrees USSR will enter war against Japan when conditions permit.

1944 [June] Battle of the Philippine Sea seriously cripples Japanese naval capacities.

[June] Japanese forces repelled in attack on India; British forces follow up with push into Burma.

[July] Tōjō Cabinet forced to resign; Koiso Kuniaki becomes premier.

[October] US forces land on Leyte.

[November] US air raids on Tokyo commence.

1945 [January] US forces land on Luzon.

[February] Yalta Conference in Crimea of major Second World War allies (Great Britain, US, USSR) outlines disposition of European and Japanese-held territories.

[Spring] Canadian government undertakes "repatriation" survey among Japanese Canadians, a disguised attempt to permanently ban their communities in BC.

[April] US forces land on Okinawa; huge civilian casualties over next two months.

[April] Suzuki Kantarō Cabinet formed.

[8 May] Germany's surrender ("VE Day").

[June] United Nations Charter signed in San Francisco.

[July] Potsdam Conference specifies surrender terms for Japan.

[6 and 9 August] Atomic bombings of Hiroshima and Nagasaki.

[8 August] USSR enters war against Japan, pushes into Manchuria, Sakhalin, northern Korea.

[15 August] Japan's surrender ("VJ Day"), followed by occupation until 1952 under Supreme Commander of the Allied Powers (SCAP) General Douglas MacArthur.

[10-15 August] US proposes temporary division of Korea along 38th parallel, with Soviet and US troops accepting surrender of Japanese forces in respective zones; USSR accepts decision, waits for US troops.

[August] Herbert Norman flies to Manila, proceeds in early September to Japan.

[September] Vietnamese declare independence, British-French intervene.

1945-50 Soviet-allied North Korea and US-allied South Korea contend for control of entire Korean peninsula.

1946 [May] Tokyo Tribunal begins hearings, E. Stuart McDougall of Canada sits as one of eleven justices.

1947 Chinese Exclusion Act repealed, some relatives allowed.

Chinese and South Asians in Canada gain right to vote.

[August-September] Commonwealth Conference in Canberra, Australia, on peace treaty with Japan; Claxton and Norman address conference for Canada.

[14 November] US-sponsored UN resolution calls for UN-supervised elections throughout Korea; George Patterson represents Canada on UN commission.

[December-January 1948] Canadian Cabinet crisis regarding Korea.

1948 [3 April] "Cheju-do 4.3 Massacre" in South Korea.

	[May] Elections in South Korea for National Assembly legitimize Syngman Rhee's rule.
	George Kennan visits Ottawa to gain Canadian support for "reverse course" in Japan.
	[15 August] Republic of Korea (ROK) proclaimed; Syngman Rhee 1st president (South Korea).
	[September] Democratic People's Republic of Korea (DPRK) proclaimed (North Korea).
1948-49	Restrictions on Japanese Canadians rescinded, gain right to vote.
1949	[1 October] Proclamation of founding of People's Republic of China (PRC).
1950	[25 June] Outbreak of Korean War with all-out invasion from north.
	[October] Herbert Norman recalled from Tokyo after charges of communist leanings and suspected disloyalty are aired in US Senate.
1950	[October-December] Chinese troops, designated as "volunteers," enter Korean War as US forces cross 38th parallel, approach China's Yalu River boundary.
	Canadian Cabinet sees spectre of world war.
1950	US recognizes government of Bao Dai in Vietnam, begins aid to French forces.
1951	[Spring] Canadian troops see action in Korea.
	[September] Reports of Canadian soldiers' war crimes surface in newspaper reports; Shin Yong-dok murdered, Shin Hyun-Chan wounded.
	[September] San Francisco Peace Treaty ending state of war between Japan and Allied powers; signed in conjunction with US-Japan agreements on maintenance of US bases and forces in Japan.
1952	[April] Japan regains its independence.
1953	[July] Korean Armistice signed in Panmunjom.
1954	[May-July] Geneva Conference convened to deal with Korean and "Indochina" conflicts.

[May] French forces defeated by communist-led Viet Minh forces at Dienbienphu in northern Vietnam.

[July] Agreement reached in Geneva on temporary "military" division of Vietnam until country-wide elections held; nine countries sign, US and Bao Dai government refuse, tighten grip on south.

Canada assumes first major peacekeeping mission as one of three members of International Supervisory Commission and Control for Indo-China.

[September] US sponsors formation of Southeast Asia Treaty Organization (SEATO) inaugurated in Manila.

1956 Failure to hold elections in Vietnam signals breakdown of Geneva Accords and escalating US involvement in South Vietnam.

Suez Crisis.

Notes

Intoduction

1 Edward Said, *Orientalism* (London: Routledge, 1978).

2 Henry Yu, "Introduction: Refracting Pacific Canada – Seeing Our Uncommon Past," *BC Studies* 156/57 (2007/08): 6.

3 The study of Europe is not in itself Eurocentric. It is when such studies fail to qualify their geographical limitations, project an unwarranted universalism, or marginalize or underestimate contrary experiences that studies related to Europe become Eurocentric.

4 Erez Manela, *The Wilsonian Moment: Self-Determination and the International Origins of Anti-Colonial Nationalism* (New York: Oxford University Press, 2007), x.

5 For example, despite its title and otherwise critical insights, Jacques Pauwels' *The Myth of the Good War: America in the Second World War* (Toronto: James Lorimer, 2002) is almost completely focused on Europe, ignoring the American deployment in Asia from 1942 to 1945.

6 John Dower, *Embracing Defeat: Japan in the Wake of World War II* (New York: W.W. Norton, 1999), 27.

7 Michael Yahuda, *The International Politics of the Asia-Pacific, 1945-1995* (London: Routledge, 1996), 26.

8 Ki-baik Lew, Carter J. Eckert, Young Ick Lew, Michael Robinson, and Edward W. Wagner, *Korea Old and New: A History* (Seoul: Ilchokak Publishers for the Korea Institute, Harvard University Press, 1990), 335.

9 For example, in Desmond Morton's *A Short History of Canada,* 5th ed. (Toronto: McClelland and Stewart, 2001), Asian Canadians are hardly mentioned, and, when they are, Morton minimizes the discrimination they faced: "British Columbians clamoured against Oriental immigration, but so long as Sir James Dunsmuir, the

province's chief mine owner, wanted cheap labour for his coal mines, the Chinese suffered no more than a head tax and a ban on bringing their wives" (60).

10 Yu, "Introduction," 6.

11 Jack Granatstein authored a traditional nationalist broadside against social history in *Who Killed Canadian History?* (Toronto: HarperCollins, 1998).

12 For example, Franca Iacovetta's *Gatekeepers: Reshaping Immigrant Lives in Cold War Canada* (Toronto: Between the Lines, 2006) does not address the racist laws creating the European bias in immigration – laws that her book otherwise analyzes so creatively.

13 Robert Bothwell's treatment of this subject is a good example of the evolution of traditionalist diplomatic historians. Robert Bothwell, Ian Drummond, and John English's *Canada, 1900-1945* (Toronto: University of Toronto Press, 1987) has little on the Transpacific. In 1998, Bothwell begins in a confused fashion to examine the Transpacific in "Eyes West: Canada and the Cold War in Asia," in *Canada and the Early Cold War 1943-1957*, ed. Greg Donaghy, 59-70 (Ottawa: Department of Foreign Affairs and International Trade, 1998). He addresses Asia in a more systematic way in his recent *Alliance and Illusion: Canada and the World, 1945-1984* (Vancouver: UBC Press, 2007). Much of the impetus for change can be attributed to Greg Donaghy and Patricia Roy, who have worked to bring Asia into the Canadian picture.

14 Andre Gunder Frank, *ReOrient: Global Economy in the Asian Age* (Berkeley: University of California Press, 1998).

15 Asian-American studies has long been associated with the *Amerasia Journal*. For recent developments in Asian-Canadian studies, see two volumes edited by Henry Yu, "Pacific Canada: Beyond the 49th Parallel," *Amerasia Journal* 33, 2 (2007); and "Refracting Pacific Canada," *BC Studies* (double issue) 156/57 (2008).

16 Of particular note is Hamashita Takeshi's work on maritime networks and the tributary system in East Asia. Two contemporary regional initiatives include the International Symposium on Human Rights in East Asia, led by Suh Sung of Ritsumeikan University, and a novel approach to textbook writing that brought together scholars and social activists from China, Korea, and Japan, who met over the course of two years – a process that culminated in the simultaneous publication in three languages (Korean, Chinese, and Japanese) of a common account of East Asia's past: Nihon, Chūgoku, Kankoku kyōdō henshū, Nitchūkan 3-goku Kyōtsū Rekishi Kyōzai Iinkai, *Mirai o hiraku rekishi: Higashi Ajia 3-goku no kin-gendaishi* [A History of the Future: A Modern and Contemporary History of Three Countries in East Asia] (Tokyo: Kōbunken, 2005).

17 Constance Backhouse, *Colour-Coded: A Legal History of Racism in Canada, 1900-1950* (Toronto: Osgoode Society for Canadian Legal History/University of Toronto Press, 2001), 14.

18 Augie Fleras and Jean Leonard Elliot, *Unequal Relations: An Introduction to Race and Ethnic Dynamics in Canada*, 4th ed. (Toronto: Prentice Hall, 2003); Sean P. Hier and B. Singh Bolaria, eds., *Race and Racism in 21st Century Canada* (Peterborough, ON: Broadview Press, 2007); Himani Bannerji, ed., *Returning the Gaze: Essays on Racism, Feminism, and Politics* (Toronto: Sister Vision Press, 1993), and *The Dark*

Side of the Nation: Essays on Muticulturalism, Nationalism and Gender (Toronto: Canadian Scholars' Press, 2000); Enakshi Dua and Angela Robertson, eds., *Scratching the Surface: Canadian Anti-Racist Feminist Thought* (Toronto: Women's Press, 1999); Tineke Hellwig and Sunera Thobani, eds., *Asian Women: Interconnections* (Toronto: Women's Press, 2006). On race and the Pacific War, see John Dower, *War without Mercy: Race and Power in the Pacific War* (New York: Pantheon, 1986); Ronald Takaki, *Hiroshima* (Boston: Little, Brown and Co., 1995); Christopher Thorne, *Racial Aspects of the Far Eastern War of 1941-1945* (London: Oxford University Press, 1982); Gerald Horne, *Race War: White Supremacy and the Japanese Attack on the British Empire* (New York: New York University Press, 2004). On postcolonial perspectives, see Anne McClintock, *Imperial Leather: Race, Gender and Sexuality in the Colonial Contest* (New York: Routledge, 1995); Ann Laura Stoler, *Carnal Knowledge and Imperial Power: Race and the Intimate in Colonial Rule* (Berkeley: University of California Press, 2002); Mary Louise Pratt, *Imperial Eyes: Travel Writing and Transculturation* (London: Routledge, 1992).

19 Chalmers Johnson, *Blowback: The Costs and Consequences of American Empire* (New York: Henry Holt, 2000), 5.

20 Niall Ferguson, *Colossus: The Rise and Fall of the American Empire* (New York: Penguin Books, 2004); and Michael Ignatieff, *Empire Lite: Nation-Building in Bosnia, Kosovo and Afghanistan* (London: Penguin, 2003).

21 Michael Hardt and Antonio Negri, *Empire* (Cambridge: Harvard University Press, 2000), xxii-xxiv.

22 Wolfgang J. Mommsen, *Theories of Imperialism* (Chicago: University of Chicago Press, 1980), 143.

23 John Gallagher and Ronald Robinson, "The Imperialism of Free Trade," *Economic History Review* (second series) 6, 1 (1953): 1-15.

24 On postcolonialism, see Said, *Orientalism;* and Edward Said, *Culture and Imperialism* (New York: Vintage, 1994). See also Benedict Anderson, *Imagined Communities: Reflections on the Origin and Spread of Nationalism* (London: Verso, 1983); H.K. Bhabha, *Nation and Narration* (London: Routledge, 1990); Arif Dirlik, *The Postcolonial Aura: Third World Criticism in the Age of Global Capitalism* (Boulder: Westview Press, 1997); Ania Loomba, *Colonialism/Postcolonialism* (London: Routledge, 1998); G.C. Spivak, *A Critique of Postcolonial Reason: Toward a History of the Vanishing Present* (Cambridge, MA: Harvard University Press, 1999); Robert J.C. Young, *Postcolonialism: An Historical Introduction* (Oxford: Blackwell, 2001).

25 Gyan Prakash, "Subaltern Studies as Postcolonial Criticism," *American Historical Review* 99, 5 (1994): 1475.

26 This is central to Said's work but has also been integrated into diplomatic history, for example, in Mark Bradley, *Imagining Vietnam and America: The Making of Postcolonial Vietnam, 1919-1950* (Chapel Hill: University of North Carolina Press, 2000).

27 Jane Samson, *Race and Empire* (Harlow, UK: Pearson Longman, 2005).

28 This challenge was issued by Jung-Bong Choi in "Mapping Japanese Imperialism onto Postcolonial Critique," *Social Identities* 9, 3 (2003): 325-39.

29 Thomas Borstelmann, *The Cold War and the Color Line: American Race Relations in the Global Arena* (Cambridge: Harvard University Press, 2001).

30 This term is invoked by Samson in her *Race and Empire*, xiii.

31 Earlier versions of some aspects of the research results have been published in scholarly journals, including *Pacific Affairs, Canadian Historical Review*, and *BC Studies*.

CHAPTER 1: PROLOGUE TO WAR

1 A second group in the Department of External Affairs was the support staff – white, female secretaries who, in that era, were essential to the recording and transmission of diplomatic information.

2 Details of postings are from John Hilliker, *Canada's Department of External Affairs*, vol. 1, *The Early Years, 1909-1946* (Montreal and Kingston: McGill-Queen's University Press, 1990).

3 Lester B. Pearson ("T"), "Canada and the Far East," *Foreign Affairs* 13, 3 (1935): 388-97. My appreciation to John Meehan for finding this document.

4 Pearson, "Canada and the Far East," 388.

5 Ibid., 390.

6 Ibid., 394.

7 Ibid., 396.

8 Ibid., 397.

9 Ibid.

10 Among the many studies in this field, see Adele Perry, *On the Edge of Empire: Gender, Race, and the Making of British Columbia, 1849-1871* (Toronto: University of Toronto Press, 2001); and, more recently, John Sutton Lutz, *Makúk: A New History of Aboriginal-White Relations* (Vancouver: UBC Press, 2008).

11 On discourses of race, see Kay Anderson, *Vancouver's Chinatown: Racial Discourse in Canada, 1875-1980* (Montreal and Kingston: McGill-Queen's University Press, 1991); W. Peter Ward, *White Canada Forever* (Montreal and Kingston: McGill-Queens University Press, 2002); Patricia Roy, *A White Man's Province: British Columbia Politicians and Chinese and Japanese Immigrants, 1858-1914* (Vancouver: UBC Press, 1989); *The Oriental Question: Consolidating a White Man's Province* (Vancouver: UBC Press, 2003); and *The Triumph of Citizenship: The Japanese and Chinese in Canada, 1941-67* (Vancouver: UBC Press, 2007). Representative works on the Chinese community include Edgar Wickberg, ed., *From China to Canada: A History of the Chinese Community in Canada* (Toronto: McClelland and Stewart, 1982). On the Japanese community, see Ken Adachi, *The Enemy That Never Was: A History of the Japanese Canadians* (Toronto: McClelland and Stewart, 1976). On the Sikh community, see Sarjeet Singh Jagpal, *Becoming Canadians: Pioneer Sikhs in Their Own Words* (Madeira Park, BC: Harbour Publishing, 1994).

12 Among notable works see Howard Hiroshi Sugimoto, *Japanese Immigration: The Vancouver Riots and Canadian Diplomacy* (New York: Arno Press, 1978); Timothy J. Stanley, "'Chinamen, Wherever We Go': Chinese Nationalism and Guangdong Merchants in British Columbia, 1871-1911," *Canadian Historical Review* 77 (December 1996): 475-501; Erika Lee, "Hemispheric Orientalism and the 1907

Pacific Coast Race Riots," *Amerasia Journal* 33, 2 (2007): 19-47; Michiko Midge Ayukawa, *Hiroshima Immigrants in Canada, 1891-1941* (Vancouver: UBC Press, 2008); and Lisa Rose Mar, Brokering Belonging: Chinese in Canada's Exclusion Era, 1885-1945 (Toronto: University of Toronto Press, 2010).

13 See Renisa Mawani, *Colonial Proximities: Crossracial Encounters and Juridical Truths in British Columbia, 1871-1921* (Vancouver: UBC Press, 2009).

14 Bernard Cohn, *Colonialism and Its Forms of Knowledge* (Princeton: Princeton University Press, 1996).

15 Mawani, *Colonial Proximities.*

16 As cited in Ward, *White Canada Forever*, 25.

17 Ibid.

18 For details, see Robin W. Winks, *The Blacks in Canada: A History*, 2nd ed. (Montreal and Kingston: McGill-Queen's University Press, 1997), chap. 9.

19 The commission's findings were contained in *Report of the Royal Commission on Chinese Immigration: Report and Evidence* (Ottawa: Royal Commission on Chinese Immigration, 1885).

20 Ibid., 162.

21 See Stanley, "Chinamen."

22 Theodore W. Allen, *The Invention of the White Race*, vol. 1, *Racial Oppression and Social Control* (London: Verso, 1994) documents the transformation of the Irish into part of the white American nation.

23 Alvin Finkel, Margaret Conrad, and Veronica Strong-Boag, *History of the Canadian Peoples*, vol. 2, *1867 to the Present* (Toronto: Copp Clark Pitman, 1993), 116.

24 See D.J. Hall, *Clifford Sifton*, vol. 1, *The Young Napoleon, 1861-1900* (Vancouver: UBC Press, 1981), 263-66.

25 For details on the transnational dimensions of the Natal Act, see Jeremy Martens, "A Transnational History of Immigration Restriction: Natal and New South Wales, 1896-97," *Journal of Imperial and Commonwealth History* 34, 3 (2006): 323-44.

26 Wickberg, *From China to Canada*, 79.

27 Adachi, *Enemy That Never Was*, chap. 1, has one of the best overviews of early migration.

28 See K.T. Homma and C.G. Isaksson, *Homma Tomekichi, The Story of a Canadian* (Surrey, BC: Hancock House, 2008).

29 *Report of the Royal Commission on Chinese and Japanese Immigration* (New York: Arno Press, 1978), 397.

30 Ibid., 397-99.

31 Ibid., 400.

32 On the South Asian communities, see Norman Buchignani, Doreen M. Indra, and Ram Srivastiva, *Continuous Journey: A Social History of South Asians in Canada* (Toronto: McClelland and Stewart, 1985).

33 Jagpal, *Becoming Canadians*, 18.

34 Only nine women immigrated between 1904 and 1920. See Jagpal, *Becoming Canadians*, 23.

35 For a recent English-language study of the unequal treaties with Japan, see Michael R. Auslin, *Negotiating with Imperialism: The Unequal Treaties and the Culture of Japanese Diplomacy* (Cambridge: Harvard University Press, 2004).

36 On this period, see Yuichi Inouye, "From Unequal Treaty to the Anglo-Japanese Alliance, 1867-1902," in *The History of Anglo-Japanese Relations,* vol. 1, *The Political-Diplomatic Dimension, 1600-1930,* ed. Ian Nish and Yoichi Kibata, 131-58 (Basingstoke: Macmillan, 2000).

37 As outlined in Walter LaFeber, *The Clash: US-Japanese Relations throughout History* (New York: W.W. Norton, 1997), 79-81.

38 See Alexander Saxton, *The Indispensable Enemy: Labor and the Anti-Chinese Movement in California* (Berkeley: University of California Press, 1971), 251-52.

39 The protests are contained in Gaimusho henshū, *Nihon gaikō bunsho, taibei imin mondai keika gaiyou fuzokusho* [Documents on Japanese foreign policy: Annexes to summary of the course of negotiations between Japan and the United States concerning the problem of Japanese immigration in the United States] (Tokyo: Gaimusho, 1973).

40 See Erika Lee, "Hemispheric Orientalism and the 1907 Pacific Coast Race Riots," *Amerasia Journal* 33, 2 (2007): 19-47.

41 This section on the race riots and their aftermath is based on John Price, "Orienting the Empire: Mackenzie King and the Aftermath of the 1907 Race Riots," *BC Studies* 156 (2008): 53-81. It was inspired by Sugimoto's *Japanese Immigration,* an edited version of the author's Master's thesis, which was completed in 1966 at the University of Washington.

42 Correspondence from the Seattle branch of the AEL was noted in new business of the 20 June 1907 meeting of the Vancouver Trades and Labour Council (VTLC). See Minute Book of the Vancouver Trades and Labor Council, 20 June 1907, Special Collections, University of British Columbia.

43 The VTLC was in close contact with the Bellingham labour council and anticipated sending a large contingent to participate in Labor Day activities, a move that fell through, however, because of transportation costs. See VTLC Minutes, May-June 1907.

44 Details of the race riot are contained in Gerald N. Hallberg, "Bellingham, Washington's Anti-Hindu Riot," *Journal of the West* 12 (1973): 163-75.

45 For such an account, see "Hindus Beaten by Angry Whites," *The Globe,* 6 September 1907, 1.

46 Basic accounts are contained to various degrees in Sugimoto, *Japanese Immigration;* Ward, *White Canada Forever,* 52-76; Wickberg, *From China to Canada,* 84-87; Roy, *White Man's Province,* 185-226; Adachi, *Enemy That Never Was,* 63-85; Michael Barnholden, *Reading the Riot Act: A Brief History of Riots in Vancouver* (Vancouver: Anvil Press, 2005).

47 For details on international press coverage, see Woan-Jen Wang, "Perspectives on the 1907 Riots in Selected Asian Languages and International Newspapers," *Nikkei Images* 12, 1 (2007): 12-15.

48 Masako Iino, "Japan's Reaction to the Vancouver Riot," *BC Studies* 60 (1983-84): 40.

49 Robert Joseph Gowen, "Canada and the Myth of the Japan Market, 1896-1911," *Pacific Historical Review* 39, 1 (1970): 65.

50 This is hinted at in John Hilliker, *Canada's Department of External Affairs,* vol. 1, *The Early Years, 1909-1946* (Montreal and Kingston: McGill-Queen's University Press, 1990), chap. 1. Racism is not considered in this history.

51 A recent biography of Lemieux includes an account of his voyage to Japan. See René Castonguay, *Rodolphe Lemieux et le Parti liberal 1866-1937: Le chevalier du roi* (Quebec: Les Presses de l'université Laval, 2000), 84-91.

52 Rodolphe Lemieux, "Report: By the Honourable Rodolphe Lemieux, K.C., Minister of Labour, of his Mission to Japan on the subject of the Influx of Oriental Labourers into the Province of British Columbia," 12 January 1908, Sir Wilfrid Laurier Papers, Library and Archives Canada, MG 26, G1, 132060-090, 20-21.

53 Theodore Roosevelt to Henry Cabot Lodge, 11 September 1907, in *The Letters of Theodore Roosevelt,* ed. Elting E. Morrison (Cambridge: Harvard University Press, 1952), 5:790.

54 King wrote three major reports related to the riot: *Report by W.L. Mackenzie King ... Commissioner Appointed to Investigate into the Losses Sustained by the Japanese Population of Vancouver, BC on the Occasion of the Riots in That City in September, 1907* (Ottawa: S.E. Dawson, 1908); *Report of W.L. Mackenzie King, C.M.G., Commissioner Appointed to Enquire into the Methods by which Oriental Labourers Have Been Induced to Come to Canada* (Ottawa: S.E. Dawson, 1908); *Report by W.L. Mackenzie King ... Commissioner Appointed to Investigate into the Losses Sustained by the Chinese Population of Vancouver, BC on the Occasion of the Riots in That City in September, 1907* (Ottawa: S.E. Dawson, 1908).

55 William N. Tilchin, *Theodore Roosevelt and the British Empire: A Study in Presidential Statecraft* (New York: St. Martin's Press, 1997), 174.

56 William Lyon Mackenzie King, *The Diaries of W.L. Mackenzie King* (Toronto: University of Toronto Press, 1983), 25 January 1908.

57 The United States had been developing war plans with Japan since before the turn of the century. See Edward S. Millar, *War Plan Orange: The US Strategy to Defeat Japan, 1897-1945* (Annapolis: Naval Institute Press, 1991).

58 For an assessment of the fleet's popular impact, see Margaret Werry, "'The Greatest Show on Earth': Political Spectacle, Spectacular Politics, and the American Pacific," *Theatre Journal* 57, 3 (2005): 355-82.

59 Theodore Roosevelt to Sir Wilfrid Laurier, 1 February 1908, in *The Letters of Theodore Roosevelt,* ed. Elting E. Morrison, 6:917-18 (Cambridge: Harvard University Press, 1952). Roosevelt's account of the meeting is contained in Theodore Roosevelt to Arthur Hamilton Lee, 3 February 1908, in *The Letters of Theodore Roosevelt*), 5:918-21.

60 Tilchin, *Theodore Roosevelt,* 178.

61 The account of this trip is in the Mackenzie King Papers, *Mission to the Orient,* 3 vols., LAC, MG 26, J13.

62 Ibid., 7-8.

63 The continuous voyage regulation demanded that immigrants travel non-stop from India to Canada. The governments of Britain and India then pressured the steamship companies to not provide direct passage.

64 Mackenzie King, *Report by W.L. Mackenzie King, C.M.G., Deputy Minister of Labour, on Mission to England to confer with the British Authorities on the subject of Immigration to Canada from the Orient and Immigration from India in Particular* (Ottawa, S.E. Dawson, 1908), 10.

65 Winks, *Blacks in Canada*, 300-13.
66 Hugh Johnston, *The Voyage of the* Komagata Maru: *The Sikh Challenge to Canada's Colour Bar* (Delhi: Oxford University Press, 1979).
67 Ibid., 48.
68 Midge Ayukawa, "Good Wives and Wise Mothers: Japanese Picture Brides in Early Twentieth-Century British Columbia," *BC Studies* 105/06 (1995): 103-18.
69 Enakshi Dua, "Exclusion through Inclusion: Female Asian Migration in the Making of Canada as a White Settler Nation," *Gender, Place and Culture: A Journal of Feminist Geography* 14, 4 (2007): 445-66.
70 Paul Yee, *Chinatown: An Illustrated History of the Chinese Communities of Victoria, Vancouver, Calgary, Winnipeg, Toronto, Ottawa, Montreal and Halifax* (Toronto: J. Lorimer, 2005), 112.
71 On the politics, see Roy, *Oriental Question*, chap. 3. On protests from the Chinese community, see Wickberg, *From China to Canada*, chap. 10.
72 Wickberg, *From China to Canada*, 14.
73 Census of Canada, 1901-41, as cited in Ward, *White Canada Forever*, 171.
74 As cited by Lisa Rose Mar, "Beyond Being Others: Chinese Canadians as National History," *BC Studies* 156 (2008): 24. Mar also suggests that the pattern of illegal migration was also adopted by the Japanese and South Asian communities.
75 For the story of the women left behind in China, see Yuen-fong Woon, *The Excluded Wife* (Montreal and Kingston: McGill-Queen's University Press, 1998).
76 Adachi, *Enemy That Never Was*, 137.
77 Ayukawa, "Good Wives and Wise Mothers," 103-18.
78 The major exception is the new work by Australian historians Marilyn Lake and Henry Reynolds, *Drawing the Global Colour Line: White Men's Countries and the Question of Racial Equality* (Carlton: Melbourne University Press, 2008).
79 See Roy, *Oriental Question*, chap. 1.
80 Robert Joseph Gowen, "Great Britain and the Twenty-One Demands of 1915: Cooperation versus Effacement," *Journal of Modern History* 43, 1 (1971): 76-106.
81 For details, see Murashima Shigeru, "The Anglo-Japanese Alliance, 1895-1923," in *The History of Anglo-Japanese Relations*, vol. 1, *The Political-Diplomatic Dimension, 1600-1930*, ed. Ian Nish and Yoichi Kibata (Basingstoke: Macmillan, 2000), 186; and Whitney A. Griswold, *The Far Eastern Policy of the United States* (New York: Harcourt Brace, 1938), 205-6.
82 The classic account of Canada at the conference is G.P. de T. Glazebrook, *Canada at the Paris Peace Conference* (London: Oxford University Press, 1942). A more recent analysis is found in Margaret MacMillan, "Canada and the Peace Settlements," in *Canada and the First World War*, ed. David Mackenzie, 379-408 (Toronto: University of Toronto Press, 2005).
83 Prime Minister of Canada to Prime Minister of United Kingdom, 23 November 1918, in *Documents on Canadian External Relations* (hereafter *DCER*), vol. 2, *The Paris Peace Conference of 1919*, ed. R.A. MacKay (Ottawa: Department of External Affairs, 1967), 3.
84 Margaret MacMillan, *Paris 1919: Six Months That Changed the World* (New York: Random House, 2001).

85 An important study underlining this point is Erez Manela's *The Wilsonian Moment: Self-Determination and the International Origins of Anticolonial Nationalism* (New York: Oxford University Press, 2007).

86 The most important English-language source that focuses on this question is Naoko Shimazu's *Japan, Race and Equality: Racial Equality Proposal of 1919* (London: Routledge, 1998). The primary source for Japanese-language information is Gaimusho, *Nihon gaikō bunsho: Pari kōwa kaigi keika gaiyō* [Documents on Japanese Foreign Policy: Summaries of the proceedings of the Paris Peace Conference] (Tokyo: Gaimusho, 1971). The best concise overview is Paul Gordon Lauren's "Human Rights in History: Diplomacy and Racial Equality at the Paris Peace Conference," *Diplomatic History* 2 (1978): 257-78.

87 Borden discusses this in his memoirs. See Henry Borden, ed., *Robert Laird Borden: His Memoirs* (Toronto: Macmillan, 1938), 2:931.

88 Ibid., 2:955.

89 *DCER*, vol. 2, *Paris Peace Conference*, 92.

90 Borden, *Robert Laird Borden*, 2:944-45.

91 Arthur S. Link, trans. and ed., *The Deliberations of the Council of Four (March 24-June 28, 1919)* (Princeton: Princeton University Press, 1992), 1:336.

92 Ibid., 1:406.

93 John King Fairbank, *Chinabound: A Fifty-Year Memoir* (New York: Harper Colophon, 1983), 162-63.

94 Antony Best, *British Intelligence and the Japanese Challenge in Asia, 1914-1941* (Houndmills: Palgrave Macmillan, 2002), 46.

95 Previous analyses of the Canadian role are: M.G. Fry, "The North Atlantic Triangle and the Abrogation of the Anglo-Japanese Alliance," *Journal of Modern History* 39, 1 (1967): 46-64; Merze Tate and Fidele Roy, "More Light on the Abrogation of the Anglo-Japanese Alliance," *Political Science Quarterly* 74, 4 (1959): 532-54; and J. Bartlet Brebner, "Canada, the Anglo-Japanese Alliance and the Washington Conference," *Political Science Quarterly* 50, 1 (1935): 45-58.

96 Governor General to Colonial Secretary, 15 February 1921, *DCER*, vol. 3, *1919-1925*, ed. L.C. Clark (Ottawa: Department of External Affairs, 1970), 163.

97 Roger Graham, *Arthur Meighen* (Toronto: Clarke, Irwin and Co., 1963), 74.

98 Fry, "North Atlantic Triangle," 48. The English-Speaking Union was founded in 1918 in Britain to promote friendship between the British Empire and the United States.

99 Michael Graham Fry, "The Pacific Dominions and the Washington Conference, 1921-22," in *The Washington Conference, 1921-22: Naval Rivalry, East Asia Stability and the Road to Pearl Harbor*, ed. Goldstein and Maurer (Essex: Frank Cass, 1994), 71. For further details on Loring Christie's role, see Robert Bothwell, *Loring Christie: The Failure of Bureaucratic Imperialism* (New York: Garland, 1988).

100 On immigration and the ending of the alliance, see J.A. Stevenson, "Japanese Problems in Canadian West," *New York Evening Post*, 32 November 1921.

101 Best, *British Intelligence*, 46.

102 Contemporary accounts include Yamato Ichihashi, *The Washington Conference and After: A Historical Survey* (New York: AMS Press, 1969 [reprint original 1928 edi-

tion]); and Raymond Leslie Buell, *The Washington Conference* (New York: Russell and Russell, 1970 [reprint of the 1922 edition]).

103 The most recent study of the conference is Erik Goldstein and John Maurer, eds., *The Washington Conference, 1921-22: Naval Rivalry, East Asian Stability and the Road to Pearl Harbor* (Essex: Frank Cass, 1994). For Canadian reports, see *DCER*, vol. 3, *1919-1925*, 483-518. The official documents are found in *Papers Relating to the Foreign Relations of the United States, 1922*, 2 vols., Department of State Publication 2033 (Washington, DC: Government Printing Office, 1938), vol. 1.

104 As cited in Ian Nish and Yoichi Kibata, eds. *The History of Anglo-Japanese Relations*, vol. 1, *The Political-Diplomatic Dimension, 1600-1930* (Basingstoke: Macmillan, 2000), 8.

105 Ibid.

106 As cited in Sadao Asada, "From Washington to London: The Imperial Japanese Navy and the Politics of Naval Limitation, 1921-1930," in Goldstein and Mauer, *Washington Conference*, 157.

107 William Lyon Mackenzie King, *The Diaries of W.L. Mackenzie King* (Toronto: University of Toronto Press, 1983), 18 October 1927.

108 Wickberg, *From China to Canada*, 160.

109 The shots were probably fired by two Sikh policemen who were used by the British to control the foreign settlement in Shanghai. See Goto-Shibata Harumi, "Anglo-Japanese Co-operation in China in the 1920s," in *The History of Anglo-Japanese Relations*, vol. 1, *The Political-Diplomatic Dimension, 1600-1930*, ed. Ian Nish and Yoichi Kibata (Basingstoke: Macmillan, 2000), 224.

110 Detailed accounts are contained in Pei-kai Cheng and Michael Lestz, with Jonathan D. Spence, eds., *The Search for Modern China: A Documentary Collection* (New York: W.W. Norton, 1999), 257-62.

111 For varied accounts of Manchuria, see previous British sources cited in this chapter as well as Christopher Thorne, *The Limits of Foreign Policy* (London: Macmillan, 1972); and Dorothy Borg, *The United States and the Far Eastern Crisis of 1933-38* (Cambridge: Harvard University Press, 1964). Other sources include Nihon, Chūgoku, Kankoku kyōdō henshū, Nitchūkan 3-goku Kyōtsū Rekishi Kyōzai Iinkai, *Mirai o hiraku rekishi: Higashi Ajia 3-goku no kin-gendaishi* [A History of the Future: A Modern and Contemporary History of Three Countries in East Asia] (Tokyo: Kōbunken, 2005), 104-10; Walter LaFeber, *The Clash: US-Japan Relations throughout History* (New York: W.W. Norton, 1997); Jonathan Spence, *The Gate of Heavenly Peace: The Chinese and Their Revolution, 1895-1980* (New York: Penguin, 1982); Bai Shouyi, *An Outline History of China, 1919-1949* (Beijing: Foreign Languages Press, 1993); John King Fairbank, *The Great Chinese Revolution, 1800-1985* (New York: Perennial Library, 1987).

112 Wickberg, *From China to Canada*, 161.

113 For background on Marler and the establishment of the legation, see Eber H. Rice, "Sir Herbert Marler and the Canadian Legation in Tokyo," in *Canada and Japan in the Twentieth Century*, ed. John Schultz and Kimitada Miwa, 75-84 (Toronto: Oxford University Press, 1991).

114 As cited by Best, *British Intelligence*, 99.

115 See John D. Meehan, *The Dominion and the Rising Sun: Canada Encounters Japan* (Vancouver: UBC Press, 2004), 86-93.

116 For a recent interpretation, see Meehan, *Dominion and the Rising Sun*, 86-92. Earlier accounts include F.H. Soward, "Forty Years On: The Cahan Blunder Re-examined," *BC Studies* 32 (1976-77): 126-38; and Donald Story, "Canada, the League of Nations and the Far East, 1931-1933: The Cahan Incident," *International History Review* 3, 2 (1981): 236-55.

117 Hugh Keenleyside, *Memoirs of Hugh L. Keenleyside*, vol. 1, *Hammer the Golden Day* (Toronto: McClelland and Stewart, 1981), 424-25.

118 On the role of racism and the founding of the IPR, see Lawrence T. Woods, *John Nelson (1873-1936) and the Origins of Canadian Participation in APEC*, Working Paper No. 18, Institute of International Relations, University of British Columbia, October 1997. On the history of the IPR, see Paul F. Hooper, ed., *Remembering the Institute of Pacific Relations: The Memoirs of William L. Holland* (Tokyo: Ryukei Shyosha, 1995).

CHAPTER 2: CHINA AND THE CLASH OF EMPIRES

1 This account of the war is based on: James C. Hsiung and Steven I. Levine, eds., *China's Bitter Victory: The War with Japan, 1937-1945* (Armonk: M.E. Sharpe, 1992); Bai Shouyi, ed., *An Outline History of China, 1919-1949* (Beijing: Foreign Language Press, 1993); John King Fairbank, *The Great Chinese Revolution, 1800-1985* (New York: Harper and Row, 1986); T. Fujitani, Geoffrey M. White, and Lisa Yoneyama, eds., *Perilous Memories: The Asia-Pacific War(s)* (Durham, NC: Duke University Press, 2001); Akira Iriye, *The Origins of the Second World War in Asia and the Pacific* (London: Longman, 1987); Diana Lary and Stephen MacKinnon, eds. *Scars of War: The Impact of Warfare on Modern China* (Vancouver: UBC Press, 2001); Nihon, Chūgoku, Kankoku kyōdō henshū, Nitchūkan 3-goku Kyōtsū Rekishi Kyōzai Iinkai, *Mirai o hiraku rekishi: Higashi Ajia 3-goku no kin-gendaishi* [A History of the Future: A Modern and Contemporary History of Three Countries in East Asia] (Tokyo: Kōbunken, 2005).

2 Honda Katsuichi, *The Nanjing Massacre: A Japanese Journalist Confronts Japan's National Shame*, ed. Frank Gibney, trans. Karen Sandness (Armonk, NY: M.E. Sharpe, 1999), 7-24.

3 Erwin Wickert, ed., *The Good Man of Nanking: The Diaries of John Rabe* (New York: Alfred E. Knopf, 1998), 92.

4 As cited in Iris Chang, *The Rape of Nanking* (New York: Basic Books, 1997), 97.

5 With the assistance of Japanese lawyers, Li filed a defamation suit against a neo-nationalist writer, Matsumura Toshio, who, as part of a campaign to deny the Nanjing massacre, had accused Li of being a false witness. In May 2002, the Supreme Court of Tokyo found in favour of Li and awarded her 1.5 million yen (Cdn$18,000) in compensation.

6 Diana Lary, "A Ravaged Place: The Devastation of the Xuzhou Region, 1938," in Lary and MacKinnon, *Scars of War*, 102.

7 See, for example, Fairbank, *Great Chinese Revolution*, chap. 14.

8 The best known of these is undoubtedly Edgar Snow's *Red Star over China* (New York: Random House, 1938).
9 Iris Chang, *The Rape of Nanking: The Forgotten Massacre* (New York: Basic Books, 1997). See also Timothy Brook, *Collaboration: Japanese Agents and Local Elites in Wartime China* (Cambridge: Harvard University Press, 2005); Takashi Yoshida, *The Making of the "Rape of the Nanking": History and Memory in Japan, China, and the United States* (Oxford: Oxford University Press, 2006).
10 "Quarrelsome," *Vancouver Sun*, 9 July 1937.
11 "The Future of Japan," *Vancouver Sun*, 23 November 1937.
12 "China's Generalissimo," *Toronto Daily Star*, 19 July 1937.
13 "Premature Fireworks in China," *Toronto Daily Star*, 29 July 1937.
14 "Enchainements," *La Presse*, 4 August 1937.
15 "Nanking Strewn with Corpses When It Fell," *Vancouver Sun*, 16 December 1937.
16 "'Wholescale Executions by Japanese Soldiers When Nanking Fell' Eyewitness Report," *Vancouver Sun*, December 1937.
17 "Sack of Nanking," *Vancouver Daily Province*, 20 December 1937.
18 *Vancouver Daily Province*, 4 December 1937.
19 *Calgary Daily Herald*, 18 December 1937.
20 "Fear Felt for Whites in Nanking," *Globe and Mail*, 15 December 1937.
21 "The Tension Growing," *Victoria Daily Times*, 15 December 1937.
22 "Japan Becoming Uneasy," *Victoria Daily Times*, 20 December 1937.
23 "Un empire s'organize," *La Presse*, 15 December 1937.
24 On this tendency in the Chinese community, see Tim Stanley, "'By the Side of Other Canadians': The Locally Born and the Invention of Chinese Canadians," *BC Studies* 156/57 (2007/08): 109-39.
25 Edgar Wickberg, ed., *From China to Canada: A History of the Chinese Community in Canada* (Toronto: McClelland and Stewart, 1982).
26 Ibid., 189.
27 Ibid., 200.
28 Paul Yee, *Chinatown: An Illustrated History of the Chinese Communities of Victoria, Vancouver, Calgary, Winnipeg, Toronto, Ottawa, Montreal and Halifax* (Toronto: J. Lorimer, 2005), 72.
29 See, for example, Brandy Lien Worrall, ed., *Finding Memories, Tracing Routes* (Vancouver: Chinese Canadian Historical Society, 2006); or Mei-fung Lee, *Childhood Lost: Memoir of a Self-Taught Grandma Who Grew Up in a War-Torn Country* (Burnaby, BC: Bauhinea Press, 2006).
30 Kirsten Emiko McAllister, "Narrating Japanese Canadians In and Out of the Canadian Nation: A Critique of Realist Forms of Representation," *Canadian Journal of Communication* 24, 1 (1999), http://www.cjc-online.ca/. However, two decades after redress has been achieved, other, more diverse, representations are being undertaken, such as that by Terry Watada in his novel *Kuroshio*.
31 Based on figures in Tsuneharu Gonnami, *The Perception Gap: A Case Study of Japanese Canadians*, rev. ed. (Vancouver: Institute of Asian Research, 2005), 25-26.
32 "Bankuba no hitori nipponjin, kogun ankan ni issen en" [One Japanese in Vancouver, one thousand yen to the imperial army], 2 August 1937, *Tairiku nippō*.

33 "Iki shitai hachikyūman, horyo susen" [Eighty to ninety thousand abandoned corpses, several thousand prisoners-of-war], 18 December 1937, *Tairiku nippō.*
34 "Shinagun no songai" [Chinese casualties], 27 December 1937, *Tairiku nippō.*
35 For further details on the Japanese community press, see Tamura Norio, *Esunikku jyanarizum: Nikkei kanadajin, sono genron no shori* [Ethnic journalism: Japanese Canadians and their victory for expression] (Tokyo: kashiwa shobō, 2003), 93-94, 103-5.
36 See Ken Adachi, *The Enemy That Never Was: A History of the Japanese Canadians* (Toronto: McClelland and Stewart, 1976), 160-62.
37 "Shinobu Higashi Accepts Post on Dairen Daily," *New Canadian,* 15 April 1939.
38 Pearl S. Buck, "Soul of a Soldier," *New Canadian,* 15 August 1939.
39 "London Paper Asks Nisei View on Tientsin Dispute," *New Canadian,* 1 July 1939.
40 "Japanese MPs Visit City on Way to Confab," *New Canadian,* 15 July 1939.
41 "Col. Drew and Japanese," and "Intolerant Press," *New Canadian,* 15 August 1939.
42 For details, see Patricia Roy, *The Oriental Question: Consolidating a White Man's Province* (Vancouver: UBC Press, 2003), chaps. 6 and 7.
43 Ibid., 197.
44 Ibid., 209.
45 Thomas P. Socknat, *Witness against War: Pacifism in Canada, 1900-1945* (Toronto: University of Toronto Press, 1987), 164.
46 Ibid., 166.
47 "Distinguished Speakers Open Peace Session," *Daily Clarion,* 20 November 1937.
48 "The Chinese Outrage," *Toronto Daily Star,* 7 December 1937.
49 "Condemnation, Big Meeting Unanimously Passes Boycott Resolutions," *Winnipeg Free Press,* 16 December 1937.
50 "Legislators Debate Boycott," *Winnipeg Free Press,* 16 December 1937.
51 Canadian League for Peace and Democracy, *Amplifier* 1, 1 (23 January 1938).
52 Ibid., 20 April 1938.
53 Jean Lumb, *Jin Guo: Voices of Chinese Canadian Women* (Toronto: Women's Press, 1992), 50.
54 "Chinese Boycott Harms Valley Rhubarb Growers," *New Canadian,* 1 February 1939.
55 "The Embargo Council," *New Canadian,* 15 March 1939.
56 Roy, *Oriental Question,* 177-78.
57 For an illuminating view of the situation in the United States, see Margaret Paton-Walsh, "Women's Organizations, US Foreign Policy, and the Far Eastern Crisis, 1937-1941," *Pacific Historical Review* 70, 4 (2001): 601-26.
58 As cited in John D. Meehan, *The Dominion and the Rising Sun: Canada Encounters Japan* (Vancouver: UBC Press, 2004), 152.
59 William Lyon Mackenzie King, *The Diaries of W.L. Mackenzie King* (Toronto: University of Toronto Press, 1983), 30 August 1937.
60 Meehan, *Dominion and the Rising Sun,* 155.
61 Despite the crisis precipitated by the bombing of the *Panay,* "no real change was affected in American policy." See Dorothy Borg, *The United States and the Far Eastern Crisis of 1933-1938* (Cambridge: Harvard University Press, 1964), 543.
62 "Canada-Japan Trade Follows Economic Principles," *New Canadian,* 27 May 1939.

63 See tables 1.1 and 7.1 in Meehan, *Dominion and the Rising Sun*, 11, 147.
64 King, *Diaries*, 8 March 1939.
65 Address to Central Guomindong Headquarters, Chongqing, 26 December 1938, in Pei-Kai Cheng and Michael Lestz, with Jonathon D. Spence, *The Search for Modern China: A Documentary Collection* (New York: W.W. Norton, 1999), 320-21.
66 Fujiwara Akira and Himeta Mitsuyoshi, eds., *Chūgoku ni okeru nihonjin no hansen katsudō* [Japanese anti-war activities in China] (Tokyo: Aoki shoten, 1999).
67 Ibid., 104.
68 For Bethune's biography, see Ted Allan and Sidney Gordon, *The Scalpel and the Sword: The Story of Dr. Norman Bethune* (Toronto: McClelland and Stewart, 1989); Wendell MacLeod, Libbie Park, and Stanley Ryerson, *Bethune: The Montreal Years, an Informal Portrait* (Toronto: James Lorimer, 1978); David Lethbridge, ed., *Bethune: The Secret Police File* (Salmon Arm, BC: Undercurrent, 2003); Larry Hannant, ed., *The Politics of Passion: Norman Bethune's Writing and Art* (Toronto: University of Toronto Press, 1998); and, most recently, Adrienne Clarkson, *Extraordinary Canadians: Norman Bethune* (Toronto: Penguin Canada, 2009).
69 Jean Ewen, *China Nurse, 1932-1939* (Toronto: McClelland and Stewart, 1981), 46.
70 Ibid., 64.
71 Mao Zedong, "In Memory of Norman Bethune" (21 December 1939), in *Selected Works of Mao Tse-tung* (Beijing: Foreign Languages Press, 1967), 2:337-38.
72 See Munro Scott, *McClure: The China Years* (Toronto: Canec, 1977).
73 Rewi Alley, *Rewi Alley: An Autobiography*, 3rd ed. (Beijing: New World Press, 1997).
74 Ibid., 138.
75 Norman Buchignani, Doreen M. Indra, and Ram Srivastiva, *Continuous Journey: A Social History of South Asians in Canada* (Toronto: McClelland and Stewart, 1985), 96.
76 *Special Committee on Orientals in British Columbia, Report and Recommendations*, December 1940 (Ottawa: Edmond Cloutier, 1941).
77 Ibid., 16.
78 Roy, *Oriental Question*, 217.
79 King, *Diaries*, 8 January 1941, 2.
80 This account is from Timothy Brook, *Collaboration: Japanese Agents and Local Elites in Wartime China* (Cambridge: Harvard University Press, 2005), 217-18.
81 Shouyi, *Outline History*, 178.
82 For details, see Meehan, *Dominion and the Rising Sun*, 184-94.
83 For the full text of the charter, see *Foreign Relations of the United States, 1941* (Washington, DC: US Government Printing Office, 1959), 1:367-69.
84 Interestingly, Churchill's personal marked-up draft copy of the Charter has the term "freedom from want" crossed out of the fifth paragraph, which deals with hopes for international collaboration in "the economic field." See http://www.ssa.gov/.
85 As cited in Thomas Borstelmann, *The Cold War and the Color Line* (Cambridge: Harvard University Press, 2001), 29.
86 Christopher Thorne, "Wartime British Planning for the Post-War Far East," in *Anglo-Japanese Alienation, 1919-1952*, ed. Ian Nish (Cambridge: Cambridge University Press, 1982), 208.

87 King, *Diaries,* 26 July 1941, 3.

88 Ibid., 6 November 1941, 3.

89 For example, in what is known as the Southern Anhui Incident, GMD units did cut down a large number of soldiers of the communist-led New Fourth Army as they moved to new positions.

CHAPTER 3: DECEMBER 1941 AND WORLD WAR

1 Don MacPherson, "1939-1945," private memoir, n.d. (mimeographed recollections, personal copy received from Don MacPherson, October 2001, Vancouver).

2 Carl Vincent, "No Reason Why: The Hong Kong Tragedy," in *Canada and Japan in the Twentieth Century,* ed. John Schultz and Kimitada Miwa, 86-101 (Toronto: Oxford University Press, 1991). See also John Ferris, "Worthy of Some Better Enemy? The British Estimate of the Imperial Japanese Army 1919-41, and the Fall of Singapore," *Canadian Journal of History* 28, 2 (1993): 224-56. For a defence of the decision, see Galen Roger Perras, "'Our Position in the Far East Would Be Stronger without This Unsatisfactory Commitment': Britain and the Reinforcement of Hong Kong, 1941," *Canadian Journal of History* 30, 2 (1995): 231-59; and also Kent Fedorowich, "'Cocked Hats and Swords and Small, Little Garrisons': Britain, Canada and the Fall of Hong Kong, 1941," *Modern Asian Studies* 37, 1 (2003): 111-57.

3 See the documentary report submitted to the UN Commission on Human Rights on abuse and veterans' demands for compensation in Brian N. Forbes and H. Cliff Chadderton, *Compensation for Canadian Hong Kong Prisoners of War by Government of Japan* (Ottawa: War Amputations of Canada and Hong Kong Veterans Association of Canada, 1987).

4 On the continuing debate re Pearl Harbor, see Henry C. Clausen and Bruce Lee, *Pearl Harbor: Final Judgement* (New York: DaCapo Press, 1993).

5 The story of collaboration and resistance in south and southeast Asia is beyond the purview of this study. For background, see Li Narangoa and Robert Cribb, *Imperial Japan and National Identities in Asia, 1895-1945* (London: RoutledgeCurzon, 2003); and Joyce C. Lebra, *Japanese-Trained Armies in Southeast Asia* (New York: Columbia University Press, 1977).

6 US Government, *A Decade of American Foreign Policy: Basic Documents, 1941-49* (Washington, DC: Government Printing Office, 1950).

7 As cited in John Dower, *War without Mercy: Race and Power in the Pacific War* (New York: Pantheon, 1986).

8 It needs to be noted that Chiang had only converted to Christianity to please his mother-in-law-to-be when she objected to her daughter's marrying a non-Christian.

9 As cited by Klaus H. Pringsheim, *Neighbours across the Pacific* (Westport, CT: Greenwood Press, 1983), 68.

10 See Ken Adachi, *The Enemy That Never Was: A History of the Japanese Canadians* (Toronto: McClelland and Stewart, 1976), chaps 9-13; Muriel Kitagawa, *This Is My Own: Letters to Wes and Other Writings on Japanese-Canadians, 1941-1948* (Vancouver: Talonbooks, 1985); Keibo Oiwa, *Stone Voices: Wartime Writings of Japanese Canadian Issei* (Montreal: Vehicule Press, 1991); Robert K. Okazaki, *The Nisei Mass Evacuation Group and POW Camp 101, Angler, Ontario,"* trans. Jean M. Okazaki and Curtis T. Okazaki (Scarborough, ON: Markham Litho, 1996); Takeo

Ujo Nakano with Leatrice Nakano, *Within the Barbed-Wire Fence: A Japanese Man's Account of His Internment in Canada* (Toronto: University of Toronto Press, 1980); Ann Gomer Sunahara, *The Politics of Racism* (Toronto: James Lorimer, 1981).

11 Adachi, *Enemy That Never Was*, 199-200.

12 Escott Reid, *Radical Mandarin: The Memoirs of Escott Reid* (Toronto: University of Toronto Press, 1989), 164.

13 As cited by Adachi, *Enemy That Never Was*, 212.

14 Adachi, *Enemy That Never Was*, 234.

15 See Okazaki, *Nisei Mass Evacuation Group*.

16 Dennis McLaughlin and Leslie McLaughlin, *Fighting for Canada: Chinese and Japanese Canadians in Military Service* (Ottawa: Minister of National Defence Canada, 2003), 45.

17 The story of Sam is included in McLaughlin and McLaughlin, *Fighting for Canada*, 49-51; and also in Vivienne Poy, "Calling Canada Home: Canadian Law and Immigrant Chinese Women from South China and Hong Kong, 1860-1990" (PhD diss., University of Toronto, 2003), 118-20.

18 See Roy Ito, *We Went to War* (Stittsville, ON: Canada's Wings, 1984).

19 Hirose's story is told by Ito, *We Went to War*, 182-88, 240-43.

20 See Kim Richard Nossal, "Business as Usual: Relations with China in the 1940s," *Journal of the Canadian Historical Association* 134 (1978): 40.

21 Ronald Takaki, *Double Victory: A Multicultural History of America in World War II* (Boston: Little, Brown and Co., 2000).

22 William Lyon Mackenzie King, *The Diaries of W.L. Mackenzie King* (Toronto: University of Toronto Press, 1983), 25 November 1941, 3.

23 Ibid., 18 February 1942, 2.

24 Ibid., 28 February 1942, 1.

25 Ibid.

26 Ibid., 2.

27 Ibid., 3.

28 Memorandum from Under-Secretary of State to Prime Minister, 28 February 1942, *Documents on Canadian External Relations* (hereafter *DCER*), vol. 9, *1942-43*, ed. J.F. Hilliker (Ottawa: Department of External Affairs, 1980), 1791.

29 Minister of Mines and Resources to Prime Minister, 17 September 1942, *DCER*, vol. 9, *1942-43*, 1793.

30 Ibid., 18 September 1942, *DCER*, vol. 9, *1942-43*, 1794.

31 See related memoranda, *DCER*, vol. 9, *1942-43*, 7.

32 Odlum was a reluctant diplomat who had, in 1941-42, served as Canada's high commissioner to Australia. Although he arrived in Chongqing with the somewhat lesser rank of minister, he was soon elevated to ambassador; the job description was essentially the same. His story has been told by his son, Roger Odlum, in *Victor Odlum: A Memoir* (Vancouver: Petrokle-Tor Publications, 1995).

33 See Chester Ronning, *A Memoir of China in Revolution* (New York: Pantheon Books, 1974).

34 Memorandum from USSEA to Prime Minister, in *DCER*, vol. 9, *1942-43*, 1798.

35 Secret: Memorandum for Canadian Minister to China, 9 January 1943, LAC, RG 25, G2, file 4526-40, box 232, 1.

36 *DCER*, vol. 9, *1942-43*, 1789-820.
37 King, *Diaries*, 15 April 1942, 5.
38 Ibid., 22 April 1943, 2.
39 King, *Diaries*, "Memorandum of Proceedings of Pacific War Council," 20 May 1943, 1.
40 King, *Diaries*, 20 May 1943, 6.
41 Ibid., 1 June 1943, 3.
42 Ibid., 15 June 1943, 2.
43 Canada, *Hansard*, 16 June 1943, 3717.
44 Ibid., 3718.
45 Ibid., 3721.
46 King, *Diaries*, 23 August 1943.
47 Ibid., 24 August 1943, 2.
48 Ibid., 25 August 1943, 4.
49 Ibid., 9 November 1943.
50 Christopher Thorne, *Racial Aspects of the Far Eastern War of 1941-1945* (London: Oxford University Press, 1980), 362.
51 King, *Diaries*, 8 July 1942, 2.
52 Revelations were first made by John Powell, "Japan's Germ Warfare: The US Coverup of a War Crime," *Bulletin of Concerned Asian Scholars* 12, 4 (1980): 2-17, in the United States and in 1982-83 in Japan. See Morimura Seiichi, *Akuma no hōshoku dai, 1-3 bu* [The devil's gluttony, parts 1-3] (Tokyo: Kakkawa bunkō, 2000 and 2001). Other studies in Japanese include a report from the Center for Research and Documentation on Japan's War Responsibility, *Kikan sensō sekinin kenkyū, tokushū: 731 butai no jisso ni semaru* [Report on Japan's war responsibility, special edition: Closing in on the reality of Unit 731] 2 (1993); Tsuneishi Keiichi, *Igakushatachi no soshiki hanzai, kantōgun dai 731 butai* [Doctors organized crime, the Kantō Military Unit 731] (Tokyo: Asahi shimbunsha, 1999); and *731 butai: Seibutsu heiki hanzai no jijitsu* [Unit 731: The truth about crimes related to biological weapons] (Tokyo: Kōdansha gendai shinsho, 1995). The most significant works in English are Peter Williams and David Wallace, *Unit 731: The Japanese Army's Secret of Secrets* (London: Hodder and Stoughton, 1989); and Sheldon H. Harris, *Factories of Death: Japanese Biological Warfare, 1932-45, and the American Cover-Up* (London: Routledge, 1994).
53 Testimony of Xu Jiaxie at the Canadian conference entitled "Preventing Crimes against Humanity: Lessons from the Asia-Pacific War, 1931-1945," First Nations House of Learning, University of British Columbia, Vancouver, 21-22 March 2003.
54 Utsumi Aiko, "Korean 'Imperial Soldiers': Remembering Colonialism and Crimes against Allied POWs," in T. Fujitani, Geoffrey M. White, and Lisa Yoneyama, eds., *Perilous Memories: The Asia-Pacific War(s)* (Durham, NC: Duke University Press, 2001), 202.
55 Ibid., 205.
56 See Leo T.S. Ching, *Becoming Japanese: Colonial Taiwan and the Politics of Identity Formation* (Berkeley: University of California Press, 2001).
57 Among the many works on this topic, see George Hicks, *The Comfort Women: Japan's Brutal Regime of Enforced Prostitution in the Second World War* (New York:

W.W. Norton, 1994); Kang Hyun Yi, "Conjuring 'Comfort Women': Mediated Affiliations and Disciplined Subjects in Korean/American Transnationality," *Journal of Asian American Studies* 6, 1 (2003): 25-55; Yuki Tanaka, *Japan's Comfort Women: Sexual Slavery and Prostitution during World War II and the US Occupation* (London: Routledge, 2002); Yoshimi Yoshiaki, *Comfort Women: Sexual Slavery in the Japanese Military during World War II* (New York: Columbia University Press, 2000); Hayashi Hirofumi, "Japanese Comfort Women in Southeast Asia," *Japan Forum* 10, 2 (1998): 211-19.

58 Testimony of Ahn Jeomsun at the Canadian conference entitled "Preventing Crimes against Humanity."
59 King, *Diaries,* 14 April 1944, 2.
60 Ibid., 3.
61 See Takaki, *Double Victory,* 119-20.
62 Minister in China to SSEA, 3 March 1944, in *DCER,* vol. 11, *1944-1945,* ed. J.F. Hilliker (Ottawa: Department of External Affairs, 1990), pt. 2, 1814.
63 Memorandum from USSEA to Prime Minister, 2 June 1944, *DCER,* vol. 11, pt. 2, 1826.
64 Over 50 million in armaments was sent from Canada, but much of it did not get to China until the end of the war due to logistical impediments and objections from the British and American governments.
65 See compilation of press reports in Foon Sien, ed., *Seventh Anniversary of China's War with Japan* (Vancouver: Chinese National Salvation League of Canada, 1945).
66 As cited in Foon Sien, ed., *Seventh Anniversary,* 7.
67 As cited in Bill Rawling, "Only If Necessary: Canada's War against Japan," in *Contradictory Impulses: Canada and Japan in the Twentieth Century,* ed. Greg Donaghy and Patricia E. Roy (Vancouver: UBC Press, 2008), 113.
68 The 1943 conferences are recorded in the US Department of State, *The Conferences at Cairo and Tehran, 1943* (Washington, DC: GPO, 1961).
69 Department of State, "Agreement Regarding Japan," Yalta Conference, *A Decade of American Foreign Policy: Basic Documents, 1941-49* (Washington, DC: Government Printing Office, 1950).
70 Over 200,000 lives were lost during this battle, the majority civilian casualties. The story is told most eloquently in Okinawaken heiwa kinen shiryokan henshū [Okinawa Peace Memorial Museum, ed.], *Heiwa no kokoro o sekai e* [A Spirit of Peace, for the World] (Itoman: Okinawa, 2001).

CHAPTER 4: HIROSHIMA AND WAR'S END

1 Interview with Kinuko [Doi] Laskey, 21 August 2003, Vancouver, Canada.
2 William Lyon Mackenzie King, *The Diaries of W.L. Mackenzie King* (Toronto: University of Toronto Press, 1983), 736.
3 MacDonald to Howe, 6 August 1945, LAC, MG 27 III, B 20, vol. 13, file S-8-2.
4 Press Release by Honourable C.D. Howe, Minister of Munitions and Supply, n.d., LAC, MG 27 III, B 20, vol. 13, file S-8-2, 1.
5 Ibid., 2
6 Ibid., 3

7 King, *Diaries,* 740-41.
8 Ibid., 741.
9 Their story is told in *Hiroshima wa dō kiroku sareta ka* [Recording Hiroshima] (Tokyo: NHK shuppan, 2003), 205-8. Their ragged and blood-stained clothing hangs on a single rattan mannequin in the "Three in One" exhibit at the Hiroshima Peace Memorial Museum.
10 As cited in Ronald Takaki, *Hiroshima: Why America Dropped the Atomic Bomb* (Boston: Little, Brown and Co., 1995), 46-47.
11 Michael Weiner, "The Representation of Absence, and the Absence of Representation: Korean Victims of the Atomic Bomb," in *Japan's Minorities: The Illusion of Homogeneity,* ed. Michael Weiner (London: Routledge, 1997), 90.
12 "Atomic Kamikaze," *Vancouver Sun,* 7 August 1945.
13 "Atomic Bombing of Japanese Area Said 'Not War at All,'" *Globe and Mail,* 9 August 1945.
14 "Quickest Way Best for Fighting Japs: Use of Atomic Bomb Justified," "What Might Be," "Kills an Evil Power," "First, Nations' Charter: Then the Atomic Bomb," *Globe and Mail,* 11 August 1945.
15 Takaki, *Hiroshima.*
16 "Claims Atomic Bombing Used in Wrong Way," *Globe and Mail,* 18 August 1945.
17 "British Groups Protest Using Atomic Weapon," *Globe and Mail,* 10 August 1945.
18 "Atomic Bomb Saved Million Allied Lives," *Globe and Mail,* 17 August 1945.
19 "Atom Bomb Is Legal," *Vancouver Sun,* 13 August 1945.
20 J. Samuel Walker, "The Decision to Use the Bomb: A Historiographical Update," *Diplomatic History* 14, 1 (1990): 110.
21 Contrary views include works such as Paul Fussell's *Thank God for the Atomic Bomb and Other Essays* (New York: Summit Books, 1988). There are important nuances among scholars who are critical of the decision to use the bomb. Gar Alperovitz, a pathbreaker in critically re-examining the evidence, suggests that Truman and James Byrnes decided to use the bomb to intimidate the Soviet Union. Barton J. Bernstein, on the other hand, rejects Alperovitz's argument, reserving his critique for the way the bombs were used. See also Takaki, *Hiroshima*; and Kyoko Selden and Mark Selden, eds., *The Atomic Bomb: Voices from Hiroshima and Nagasaki* (Armonk, NY/London: M.E. Sharpe, 1989).
22 Tsuyoshi Hasegawa, *Racing the Enemy: Stalin, Truman, and the Surrender of Japan* (Cambridge: Belknap Press, 2005). An earlier study, Marc S. Gallicchio, *The Cold War Begins in Asia: American East Asian Policy and the Fall of the Japanese Empire* (New York: Columbia University Press, 1988), covers similar themes but mainly through the American policy-making process, with little reference to developments in Japan.
23 This was first demonstrated by Alperovitz in his *Atomic Diplomacy: Hiroshima and Potsdam* (New York: Simon and Schuster, 1965), and his subsequent *The Decision to Use the Atomic Bomb* (New York: Vintage, 1996).
24 As cited in Takaki, *Hiroshima,* 29.
25 See Yuki Tanaka, "Indiscriminate Bombing and the Enola Gay Legacy," as posted on Japan Focus, http://www.japanfocus.org/.

26 "Atomic Bombing: The Moral Issue," *Vancouver Sun*, 10 August 1945.
27 Statistics are from Gallup Polls, as cited by Barton J. Bernstein, "Truman and the A-Bomb: Targeting Noncombatants, Using the Bomb, and His Defending the 'Decision,'" *Journal of Military History* 62 (July 1998): 568-69.
28 For accounts of this and other related issues, see Michael J. Hogan, ed., *Hiroshima in History and Memory* (New York: Cambridge University Press, 1996); and Edward T. Linethal and Tom Engelhardt, eds., *History Wars: The Enola Gay and Other Battles for the American Past* (New York: Metropolitan Books, 1996).
29 For the decision in Japanese, see *Hanrei Jihō*, vol. 355, 17; translated into English in *The Japanese Annual of International Law* 8 (1964): 231.
30 The decision and related documents are available online through the International Court of Justice, http://www.icj_cij.org/. For an interesting assessment of the decision and its implications for direct action, see Peter Weiss, "The International Court of Justice and the Scottish High Court: Two Views of the Illegality of Nuclear Weapons," *Waseda Proceedings of Comparative Law* 4 (2001): 149-65.
31 David Bercuson, *Maple Leaf against the Axis: Canada's Second World War* (Toronto: Stoddart, 1995), 270. This brief passage fails to mention that almost all of those killed at Hiroshima and Nagasaki were non-combatants, and it also fails to inform readers that the actual reason for the use of the bomb may rest elsewhere. Bercuson at least mentioned the bomb; Jack Granatstein, for his part, does not even mention Canadian involvement in atomic bomb development in his *Canada's War: The Politics of the Mackenzie King Government, 1939-1945* (Toronto: Oxford University Press, 1975), or in his *Empire to Umpire: Canada and the World to the 1990s* (Toronto: Copp Clark Longman, 1994), co-authored with Norman Hillmer.
32 Robert Bothwell, *Nucleus: The History of Atomic Energy of Canada Limited* (Toronto: University of Toronto Press, 1988), 62.
33 John W. Holmes, *The Shaping of Peace: Canada and the Search for World Order, 1943-1957* (Toronto: University of Toronto Press, 1979), 1:202-3. On the purge, see Adam Chapnick, *Canada's Voice: The Public Life of John Wendell Holmes* (Vancouver: UBC Press, 2009), chap. 6; and Hector Mackenzie, "Purged ... from Memory: The Department of External Affairs and John Holmes," *International Journal* 59, 2 (2004): 375-86.
34 Hugh Keenleyside, *Memoirs of Hugh L. Keenleyside*, vol. 2, *On the Bridge of Time* (Toronto: McClelland and Stewart, 1982), 182.
35 Press Release (n.a.), 31 July 1998, Vancouver.
36 See Leslie Roberts, *C.D.: The Life and Times of Clarence Decatur Howe* (Toronto: Clarke, Irwin, 1957), 135-38; and Richard Rhodes, *The Making of the Atomic Bomb* (New York: Simon and Schuster, 1995), 649.
37 Cindy Kenny-Gilday, "A Village of Widows: The Story of the Dene 'Ore Carriers,'" *Aboriginal Voices* 4, 6 (1999): 44-45.
38 Deborah Simmons, "Sahtú and the Atomic Bomb," available at http://collections.ic.gc.ca/.
39 As cited in Simmons, "Sahtú and the Atomic Bomb." Simmons based her article on the documentary film by Peter Blow, *Village of Widows* (Peterborough, ON: Lindum Films, 1999).

40 Atomic tears continue to be shed as the Sahtu people face government intransigence regarding their claim for redress for their terrible ordeal.
41 Andrew Nikiforuk, "Echoes of the Atomic Age: Uranium Haunts a Northern Aboriginal Village," *Calgary Herald*, 14 March 1998.
42 The story of the Tizard mission is told in David Zimmerman, *Top Secret Exchange: The Tizard Mission and the Scientific War* (Montreal and Kingston: McGill-Queen's University Press, 1996).
43 For details on Maass and his role in the development of weapons of mass destruction, see John Price, "Shroud of Silence: Canada, the United States and the Cover-Up of Japanese Biological Warfare in China," *CAPRN Asia Pacific Working Papers*, ser. 3, Working Paper 1, a joint publication of Canada Asia Pacific Resource Network and the Polaris Institute.
44 Canada, Department of Reconstruction, Canada's Role in Atomic Bomb Drama, Press Release, 13 August 1945, LAC, MG 27, vol. 13, S-8-2, 1.
45 *Documents on Canadian External Relations,* vol. 9, *1942-1943,* ed. J.F. Hilliker (Ottawa: Department of External Affairs, 1980), 470.
46 Ibid., 959.
47 Ibid., 962-63.
48 Ibid., 967.
49 "Minutes of Combined Policy Committee Meeting held at the Pentagon on July 4th, 1945-9:30 a.m.," in ibid., 972-73.
50 See Tanaka, "Indiscriminate Bombing."
51 Hasegawa, *Racing the Enemy*, 298.

CHAPTER 5: SHADES OF LIBERATION

1 Don MacPherson, private memoir, mimeographed recollections, n.d. (personal copy received from Don MacPherson, October 2001, Vancouver).
2 Ibid., 5.
3 Liu's story is based on a presentation by his lawyer, Saikawa Osame, "The Chinese Forced-Labour Lawsuit: The Case of Liu Lianren Lawsuit Team," delivered at the 5th Biennial Conference of the Global Alliance for Preserving the History of World War II in Asia, November 2002, San Diego.
4 Liu's experience is partially paralleled by that of Japanese soldiers who, accidentally or intentionally, became separated from their units in the jungles of Southeast Asia and, fearing punishment, hid themselves away for years. The most recent emergence of such a soldier was in the spring of 2005 in the Philippines. There cannot be many such octogenarians left.
5 Mitsui kōan kabushiki kaisha, *Shiryō: Miike sōgi* [Documents: The miike dispute] (Tokyo: Nihon keieisha dantai renmei, 1963), 16.
6 Central Liaison Office to SCAP, "Chinese Labourers in Japan," 23 October 1945 (personal copy obtained from Neil Burton, October 2005).
7 Ahn Jeomsun, "Wouldn't It Be Okay if I Told This Story? My Heart Aches and I'm Confused ...," paper presented at the "Canadian Conference on Preventing Crimes against Humanity: Lessons from the Asia Pacific War, 1931-1945," 21-22 March 2003, Vancouver, British Columbia.

8 "The Last Surrender," *Vancouver Sun*, 15 August 1945.
9 The Chinese Canadian Association, memorandum and petition, 16 February 1945, British Columbia Archives, P 323.67, C539a, 1.
10 Ibid., 3.
11 Lan Cao and Himilce Novas, *Everything You Need to Know about Asian-American History* (New York: Plume-Penguin, 1996), 126.
12 As cited in Ann Gomer Sunahara, *The Politics of Racism: The Uprooting of the Japanese Canadians during the Second World War* (Toronto: James Lorimer, 1981), 116.
13 Ibid., 116-17.
14 Muriel T. Kitagawa, *New Canadian*, 10 November 1945, as cited in Muriel Kitagawa (ed. Roy Miki), *This Is My Own* (Vancouver: Talonbooks, 1985), 208.
15 State-War-Navy Coordinating Subcommittee for the Far East, "National Composition of Forces to Occupy Japan Proper in the Post-Defeat Period," 24 July 1945, National Diet Library, Tokyo, minutes of the State-War-Navy Coordinating Committee, minutes of the Sub-Committee for the Far East, 1945-1947, SFE-1, Occupation and Aims, 3.
16 State-War-Navy Coordinating Subcommittee for the Far East, "Allied Control Machinery for Japan," 13 September 1945, National Diet Library, Tokyo, minutes of the State-War-Navy Coordinating Committee, minutes of the Sub-Committee for the Far East, 1945-1947, 52.
17 The story of the Occupation has been told by many. In this book I base my account on Japanese sources, particularly the work of Takemae Eiji, including his Japanese works *GHQ* (Tokyo: Iwanami shoten, 1983) and *GHQ no hitobito* [The people of GHQ] (Tokyo: Meiji shoten, 2002), as well as his recent 750-page English tome, *Inside GHQ: Allied Occupation of Japan and Its Legacy* (New York: Continuum, 2002). Other recent notable works include John Dower, *Embracing Defeat: Japan in the Wake of World War II* (New York: W.W. Norton, 1999); Yukiko Koshiro, *Trans-Pacific Racisms and the US Occupation of Japan* (New York: Columbia University Press, 1999); and Herbert P. Bix, *Hirohito and the Making of Modern Japan* (New York: Harper Collins, 2000).
18 Two engaging works on post-surrender Japan are Dower's *Embracing Defeat* and Mark Gayn's *Japan Diary* (New York: William Sloane, 1948).
19 See Koshiro, *Trans-Pacific Racisms*, 70.
20 See Arthur Menzies, "Canadian Views of United States Policy toward Japan, 1945-1952," in *War and Diplomacy Across the Pacific, 1919-1952,* ed. A. Hamish Ion and Barry Hunt, 155-72 (Waterloo, ON: Wilfrid Laurier University Press, 1988); Klaus H. Pringsheim, *Neighbours across the Pacific* (Westport, CT: Greenwood Press, 1983), chap. 3; John W. Holmes, "Canada's Postwar Policies towards Japan," paper presented at the International University Symposium on Japan and Postwar Diplomacy in the Asia-Pacific Region, International House of Japan, 18-19 March 1983, Tokyo; Michael G. Fry, "Canada and the Occupation of Japan: The MacArthur-Norman Years," in *The Occupation of Japan: The International Context*, ed. Thomas Burkman, 130-59 (Norfolk: The MacArthur Foundation, 1984); Roger Bowen, *Innocence Is Not Enough: The Life and Death of Herbert Norman* (Vancouver: Douglas and McIntyre, 1986), chaps. 4 and 5.

21 Accounts of Norman's life in English include Roger Bowen, ed., *E.H. Norman: His Life and Scholarship* (Toronto: University of Toronto Press, 1984); Roger Bowen's dedicated biography, *Innocence Is Not Enough: The Life and Death of Herbert Norman* (Toronto: Douglas and McIntyre, 1986); John Hilliker, "'Sleeping with an Elephant': Canada, the United States and Herbert Norman," paper presented at the Annual Meeting of the American Political Science Association, 1998, Boston; Peyton Lyon, "The Loyalties of E. Herbert Norman," report for Department of External Affairs and International Trade, 18 March 1990; Charles Taylor, *Six Journeys: A Canadian Pattern* (Toronto: Anansi Press, 1977); James Barros, *No Sense of Evil: Espionage, the Case of Herbert Norman* (Toronto: Deneau, 1986); and a short pamphlet, Greg Donaghy, ed., *Herbert Norman: A Documentary Perspective* (Ottawa: Department of Foreign Affairs, 1999). In Japanese, see Nakano Toshiko, *H. nōman: Aru demokuratto no tadotta unmei* [H. Norman: The fate that befell a democrat] (Tokyo: Riburopōto, 1990); Kudō Miyoko, *Higeki no gaikōkan: Hābāto nōman no shogai* [Tragedy's diplomat: The life of Herbert Norman] (Tokyo: Iwanami shoten, 1991).

22 Katō Shūichi and Nakano Toshiko, eds., *E.H. Nōman: Nihon senryō no kiroku* [E.H. Norman: Reports from Occupied Japan] (Tokyo: Jimbun shoin, 1997).

23 John Price, "E.H. Norman, Canada and Japan's Postwar Constitution," *Pacific Affairs* 74, 3 (2001): 383-405.

24 Norman's distinct emphasis on this was pointed out as early as 1974 by John Dower in his edited work, *Origins of the Modern Japanese State: Selected Writings of E.H. Norman* (New York: Pantheon, 1974), 26-27. In Norman's own words, the oligarchy consisted of representatives of the "armed services, business, bureaucracy, and court." See Herbert Norman, "Review of Edwin O. Reischauer, *Japan Past and Present*," *Pacific Affairs* 20, 3 (1947): 359.

25 See Dale Hellegers, "The Konoe Affair," in *The Occupation of Japan: Impact of Legal Reform*, ed. L.H. Redford (Norfolk: MacArthur Memorial, 1975), 173-74; and Kudō, *Higeki no gaikōkan*, 174-76.

26 See Bowen, *Innocence Is Not Enough*, 123; Nakano, *H. nōman*, 116.

27 Ibid., 199.

28 Ibid., 202.

29 See "Telegram from President Harry Truman for Generalissimo Chiang Kai-shek," 1 August 1945, in *Vietnam: A History in Documents*, ed. Gareth Porter (New York: New American Library, 1979), 27.

30 Mark Atwood Lawrence, *Assuming the Burden: Europe and the American Commitment to War in Vietnam* (Berkeley: University of California Press, 2005), 25.

31 Ibid., 68.

32 William J. Duiker, *Ho Chi Minh: A Life* (New York: Hyperion, 2000), 313-16.

33 See also the account by James Eayrs, *In Defence of Canada*, vol. 5, *Indochina: Roots of Complicity* (Toronto: University of Toronto Press, 1983), chap. 1.

34 External Affairs, "Indochina: From the Beginning of the French Occupation until the Appointment of the International Commissions for Supervision and Control" (a background paper), 23 September 1959, LAC, RG 25, vol. 3069, file 5.

35 "Declaration of Independence of the Democratic Republic of Vietnam," 2 September 1945, in Porter, *Vietnam*, 29-30.

36 James S. Olson and Randy Roberts, *Where the Domino Fell: America and Vietnam* (New York: St. Martin's Press, 1991), 21.
37 Mark Philip Bradley, *Imagining Vietnam and America: The Making of Postcolonial Vietnam* (Chapel Hill: University of North Carolina Press, 2000), 134-35.
38 Ibid., 137.
39 Duiker, *Ho Chi Minh*, 361.
40 As cited in Olson and Roberts, *Where the Domino Fell*, 26.
41 Dean Acheson to Walter Robinson in China, 4 October 1948, in Porter, *Vietnam*, 38.
42 This account of developments in South Korea is based on Bruce Cumings, *The Origins of the Korean War: Liberation and the Emergence of Separate Regimes, 1945-1947* (Princeton: Princeton University Press, 1981); and his *Korea's Place in the Sun: A Modern History* (New York: W.W. Norton, 1999). See also George M. McCune, *Korea Today* (Cambridge: Harvard University Press, 1950); Kang Jeong-Koo, "A Critical Evaluation on the US Role in the Division of Korea and the Korean War," unpublished paper (personal copy received from Kang).
43 As cited in Cumings, *Origins of the Korean War*, 145.
44 Ibid., 138; Steven Hugh Lee, *The Korean War* (Harlow, UK: Pearson Education, 2001), 22.
45 Cumings, *Origins of the Korean War*, 145.
46 Sources used to reconstruct developments in the south are also the basis for this discussion, with the addition of Charles K. Armstrong, *The North Korean Revolution, 1945-1950* (Ithaca: Cornell University Press, 2003), which offers a balanced account of political developments in the north.
47 McCune, *Korea Today*, 214.
48 Kim's background is described in Han Hong-koo, "Wounded Nationalism: The *Minsaengdan* Incident and Kim Il Sung in Eastern Manchuria" (PhD diss., University of Washington, 1999).
49 For details, see Hua Qingzhao, *From Yalta to Panmunjon: Truman's Diplomacy and the Four Powers, 1945-1953* (Ithaca: Cornell University Press, 1993). On US troops in northeast China, see Yan Zhiguo, "US Marines in Qingdao: Society, Culture and China's Civil War," in *China and the United States: A New Cold War History*, ed. Xiaobang Li and Hongshan Li, 181-206 (Lanham, MD: University Press of America, 1998).
50 For details on the Soviet role, see Chen Jian, *Mao's China and the Cold War* (Chapel Hill: University of North Carolina Press, 1998), 26-31.
51 As cited in Hua, *From Yalta to Panmunjon*, 119.
52 Odlum to External Affairs, 2 February 1946, LAC, MG 30, E 300, vol. 34, 1.
53 Ibid., 3, emphasis in original.
54 Odlum to MacKenzie King, 27 February 1946, LAC, MG 30, E 300, vol. 34.
55 Odlum to External Affairs, interview with Wang Bingnan, 29 May 1946, LAC, MG 30, E 300, box 37, 2.
56 Robert Rhodes James, ed., *Winston S. Churchill: His Complete Speeches, 1897-1963*, vol. 7, *1943-1949* (New York: Chelsea House Publishers, 1974), 7285.

57 Thomas Borstelmann, *The Cold War and the Color Line: American Race Relations in the Global Arena* (Cambridge: Harvard University Press, 2001), 47.

CHAPTER 6: BOUNDARIES OF RACE AND DEMOCRACY

1 Bowen is the main proponent of this thesis. See his comments on Michael Fry's interpretation of Norman in Michael G. Fry, "Canada and the Occupation of Japan: The MacArthur-Norman Years," in *The Occupation of Japan: The International Context,* ed. Thomas Burkman, 130-59 (Norfolk: The MacArthur Foundation, 1984). See also his chapters in Roger Bowen, *Innocence Is Not Enough: The Life and Death of Herbert Norman* (Vancouver: Douglas and McIntyre, 1986), chaps. 4 and 5. For other views on the Canadian role in the Occupation see Arthur Menzies, "Canadian Views of United States Policy toward Japan, 1945-1952," in *War and Diplomacy across the Pacific, 1919-1952,* ed. A. Hamish Ion and Barry Hunt, 155-72 (Waterloo, ON: Wilfrid Laurier University Press, 1988), 155-72; Klaus H. Pringsheim, *Neighbours across the Pacific* (Westport, CT: Greenwood Press, 1983), chap. 3; and John W. Holmes, "Canada's Postwar Policies towards Japan," paper presented at the International University Symposium on Japan and Postwar Diplomacy in the Asia-Pacific Region, International House of Japan, 18-19 March 1983, Tokyo.

2 For a full account of the machinations regarding the FEAC versus the FEC, see Michael Schaller, *The American Occupation of Japan* (New York: Oxford University Press, 1985), 57-61. On the Canadian role in the FEC, see Keith Stuart Webster, "Canada and the Far Eastern Commission" (MA thesis, University of Victoria, 2008).

3 The Canadian government argued for US military control of Japan but with political control to be invested in a control commission. See Hume Wrong to Canadian Ambassador-Washington, 27 October 1945, LAC, RG 25, vol. 4729, 50061-40, pt. 1.

4 E.H. Norman, "General MacArthur's Remarks to the Far Eastern Advisory Council," 29 January 1946, as cited in Katō Shuichi and Toshiko Nakano, ed. and trans., *E.H. nōman, Nihon senryō no kiroku 1946-48* [E.H. Norman reports from occupied Japan, 1946-48] (Tokyo: Jinbun shoin, 1997), 16. That the staff had stopped work on the Constitution is confirmed by Tanaka Hideo, "The Conflict between Two Legal Traditions in Making the Constitution of Japan," in *Democratizing Japan: The Allied Occupation,* ed. Robert Ward and Sakamoto Yoshikazu (Honolulu: University of Hawaii Press, 1987), 108n3.

5 See John Dower, *Embracing Defeat: Japan in the Wake of World War II* (New York: W.W. Norton, 1999), 362-64. This view had been articulated by the Japan crowd in the State Department, including former ambassador to Japan, Joseph C. Grew. For details, see Robert E. Ward's chapter, "Presurrender Planning," in Ward and Sakamoto, *Democratizing Japan.*

6 MacArthur's full message is contained in "Mr. Max W. Bishop, of the Office of the Political Adviser in Japan, to the Secretary of State," Tokyo, 15 April 1946, *Foreign Relations of the United States* (Washington, DC: US Government Printing Office, 1946), 8:202-5.

7 Canadian Ambassador to US to SSEA, 5 April 1946, LAC, RG 25, vol. 4606-A-40, 2.

8 FEC, Steering Committee-012/4, as contained in Canadian Ambassador to US to SSEA, 8 May 1946, LAC, RG 25, vol. 4606.

9 Canadian Ambassador to US to SSEA, 8 May 1946, LAC, RG 25, vol. 4606-A-40, 2.

10 Positions of individuals are based on John Hilliker and Donald Barry, *Canada's Department of External Affairs*, vol. 2, *Coming of Age, 1946-1968* (Montreal and Kingston: McGill-Queen's University Press, 1995). On Wrong, see ibid., 7.

11 J.R. Maybee to the Canadian Ambassador: Washington, Ex-1790, 18 July 1946, LAC, RG 25, vol. 3649, file 4606-A-40, 1.

12 Irene [Kato] Tsuyuki's story is recounted in Kage Tatsuo, *Nikkei kanadajin no tsuihō* [Exiled Japanese Canadians] (Tokyo: Akashi shoten, 1999), 165-74.

13 Patricia Roy, with J.L. Granatstein, Masako Iino, and Hiroko Takamura, *Mutual Hostages: Canadians and Japanese during the Second World War* (Toronto: University of Toronto Press, 1990), 173.

14 *Canada Is Our Choice*, as reprinted in Muriel Kitagawa, *This Is My Own: Letters to Wes and Other Writings on Japanese Canadians, 1941-1948*, ed. Roy Miki (Vancouver: Talonbooks, 1985), 204.

15 Kitagawa's knowledge of Canadian history is broad; here she refers to Henry Wadsworth Longfellow's epic poem "Evangeline," which derived from the Acadian expulsion in 1755.

16 *New Canadian*, 2 March 1946, 2.

17 Robert K. Okazaki, *The Nisei Mass Evacuation Group and POW Camp 101 Angler, Ontario*, trans. Jean M. Okazaki and Curtis T. Okazaki (Scarborough, ON: Markham Litho., 1996), 119.

18 Kage, *Nikkei kanadajin no tsuihō*, 58.

19 For a different story, see "An Exiled Japanese Canadian: The Experience of Mary Seki," a translation of Kage, *Nikkei kanadajin no tsuiho*, 151-56, in *The Bulletin* (September 1999): 15-17.

20 The directive was adopted on 10 August 1946 while Norman was en route to Japan. See Memorandum from Department of External Affairs to Cabinet Committee on Japanese Problems, 16 April 1947, *Documents on Canadian External Relations* (hereafter *DCER*), vol. 13, *1947*, ed. Norman Hillmer and Donald Page (Ottawa: Canada Communication Group, 1993), 267-68.

21 Ibid., 268.

22 E. Herbert Norman, *Andō Shōeki and the Anatomy of Japanese Feudalism* (Tokyo: Transactions of the Asiatic Society of Japan, 1949), 1.

23 Takemae Eiji, *Inside GHQ: Allied Occupation of Japan and Its Legacy* (New York: Continuum, 2002), 263.

24 For background on Yoshida, see *John Dower, Empire and Aftermath: Yoshida Shigeru and the Japanese Experience, 1878-1954* (Cambridge: Council on East Asian Studies, Harvard, 1979).

25 See Dower, *Embracing Defeat*, chap. 3.

26 Yukiko Koshiro, *Trans-Pacific Racisms and the US Occupation of Japan* (New York, Columbia University Press, 1999), 31.

27 Ibid., 33.

28 Naoko Shibusawa, *America's Geisha Ally: Reimagining the Japanese Enemy* (Cambridge: Harvard University Press, 2006).

29 Koshiro, *Trans-Pacific Racisms*, 110.

30 Ibid., 60.
31 See Michael Schaller, *Douglas MacArthur: The Far Eastern General* (New York: Oxford University Press, 1989), 125.
32 About 60 percent of these babies were abandoned by their fathers according to Shibusawa, *America's Geisha Ally*, 41
33 On Koreans in Japan, see Mark Caprio, *Japanese Assimilation Policies in Colonial Korea, 1910-1945* (Seattle: University of Washington Press, 2009); Sonia Ryang, ed., *Koreans in Japan: Critical Voices from the Margins* (London: RoutledgeCurzon, 2000).
34 Takemae, *Inside GHQ*, 452.
35 Koshiro, *Transnational Racisms*, 115.
36 Ibid., 116.
37 Ibid., 3
38 L.B. Pearson to E.H. Norman, 12 March 1947, LAC, vol. 3342, file 4606-40, pt. 1.
39 Norman to SSEA, 1 February 1947, LAC, vol. 3342, file 4606-40, pt. 1.
40 Details can be found in Takemae Eiji, *Sengo rōdō kaiku: GHQ rōdō seisakushi* [Postwar labour reform: A history of GHQ labour policy] (Tokyo: Tokyo daigaku shuppankai, 1982); and in John Price, *Japan Works: Power and Paradox in Postwar Industrial Relations* (Ithaca: Cornell University Press, 1997).
41 For some of those involved in the United States, see Howard Schonberger, *Aftermath of War* (Kent: Kent State University Press, 1989). For an analysis of the reverse course, see Yamamoto Kiyoshi, *Sengo kiki ni okeru rōdō undō* [The labour movement in the postwar crisis] (Tokyo: Ochanomizu shobo, 1978).
42 Norman to SSEA, No. 14, 1 February 1947, LAC, vol. 3342, file 4606-40, pt. 1.
43 Suzuki penned the work *Jiyū minken* [Freedom and popular rights] (Tokyo: Hakuyōsha, 1948).
44 Norman to SSEAC, no. 313, 19 December 1947, LAC, vol. 3651, file 4606-C-15-40, pt. 1, 2.
45 Canada, *Hansard*, 12 July 1943, 4682-83.
46 The efforts of the Chinese community provincially are recorded in Patricia Roy, *The Triumph of Citizenship: The Japanese and Chinese in Canada, 1941-67* (Vancouver: UBC Press, 2007), 172-75.
47 As cited in Roy, *Triumph of Citizenship*, 168.
48 Edgar Wickberg, ed., *From China to Canada: A History of the Chinese Community in Canada* (Toronto: McClelland and Stewart, 1982), 205.
49 Many of the changes that came about were in tandem with other human rights struggles. For details, see Ross Lambertson, *Repression and Resistance: Canadian Human Rights Activists, 1930-1960* (Toronto: University of Toronto Press, 2005). Unfortunately, Lambertson does not provide a chapter on the struggle for the franchise for Asian Canadians.
50 Roy, *Triumph of Citizenship*, 162.
51 A recent in-depth analysis of the support movement is provided by Stephanie Bangarth, *Voices Raised in Protest: Defending North American Citizens of Japanese Ancestry, 1942-1949* (Vancouver: UBC Press, 2008).

52 As discussed by Greg Robinson, "Two Other Solitudes: Encounters between Japanese Canadians and French Canadians, 1900-50," in *Contradictory Impulses, Canada and Japan in the Twentieth Century,* ed. Donaghy and Roy (Vancouver: UBC Press, 2008), 151.

53 Roy, *Mutual Hostages*, 184.

54 Canada, *Hansard,* 1 May 1947, vol. 3, 2644-46.

55 Escott Reid, "The United States and the Soviet Union: A Study of the Possibility of War and Some of the Implications for Canadian Policy," DCER, vol. 13, *1947,* 372.

56 Memorandum Submitted to the Dominion Government by the Canadian Congress of Labour, 24 April 1945, LAC, CLC series, MG 28, I 103, vol. 314 file 4-28, point 4.

57 David Lewis, *The Good Fight: Political Memoirs, 1909-1958* (Toronto: Macmillan, 1981), 237-41.

CHAPTER 7: ELUSIVE JUSTICE

1 Saikawa Osame, "The Chinese Forced-Labour Lawsuit: The Case of Liu Lianren Lawsuit Team," paper presented at the Fifth Biennial Conference of the Global Alliance for Preserving the History of World War II in Asia, 22 November 2002, San Diego, 3.

2 Kishi's dossier is contained in Awaya Kentarō and Yoshida Yutaka, eds., *Kokusai kensatsukyoku (IPS) Jimmon Chōsho, dai 1 kan-52 kan* [Interrogation record of the International Prosecution Section, vols. 1-52] (Tokyo: Nihon tosho senta, 1993), case no. 77, 14:183-251. A sympathetic account of Kishi's life is found in Dan Kurzman, *Kishi and Japan: The Search for the Sun* (New York: Ivan Obolensky, 1960).

3 Jack Best, "Stag Dinner for Jap Premier," *Ottawa Journal*, 22 January 1960. The article explained that the dinner was "stag" because Kishi was not accompanied by his wife.

4 For reports on this visit, see *Ottawa Journal*, 22 and 23 January 1960; *Montreal Star*, 22 and 23 January 1960; and *Toronto Daily Star*, 18 and 21 January 1960.

5 The former trials took place in Japan and other countries in Asia and mainly dealt with conventional war crimes. For details, see Philip R. Piccigallo, *The Japanese on Trial: Allied War Crimes Operations in the East, 1945-1951* (Houston: University of Texas Press, 1980).

6 A small number of Canadian studies deal with the trial. See Patrick Brode, *Casual Slaughters and Accidental Judgements: Canadian War Crimes Prosecutions, 1944-1948* (Toronto: University of Toronto Press, 1997); John Stanton, "Canada and War Crimes: Judgement at Tokyo," *International Journal*, 55, 3 (2000): 376-400. A retrospective view is found in John S. Brownlee, "The Tokyo Trial Fifty Years Later," in *Japan at Century's End: Changes, Challenges and Choices,* ed. Hugh Millward and James Morrison, 11-20 (Halifax: Fernwood, 1997). Timothy Brook, a China specialist, focuses on the Tokyo Tribunal and the 1937 "Rape of Nanjing" in Timothy Brook, ed., *Documents on the Rape of Nanking* (Ann Arbor: University of Michigan Press, 1999).

7 Kobayashi Yoshinori, "A Word of Recommendation," in *Pāru hanji no nihon muzairon* [Judge Pal's "Japan not guilty" thesis], ed. Masaaki Tanaka, 3-8 (Tokyo: Shogakkan bunko, 2001).

8 Tanaka, *Pāru hanji no nihon muzairon*, 18.

9 In Japanese, see Ajia minshū hōtei junbikai, ed., *Toinaosu Tōkyō saiban* [Reassessing the Tokyo tribunal] (Tokyo: Ryokufu shuppan, 1995); Asahi shimbun Tōkyō saiban kishadan, *Tōkyō saiban, jo-ge* [The Tokyo tribunal, 2 vols.] (Tokyo: Asahi shimbunsha, 1983); or Kojima Noboru, *Tōkyō saiban, jo-ge* [Tokyo tribunal, 2 vols.] (Tokyo: Chuō kōronsha, 1982); Awaya Kentarō, *Tōkyō saiban ron* [Views on the Tokyo tribunal] (Tokyo: Ōtsuki shoten, 1989); and Awaya Kentarō, *Tōkyō saiban e no michi, jo-ge* [The road to the Tokyo tribunal, 2 vols.] (Tokyo: Kodansha, 2006).

10 Utsumi Aiko, "Introduction to *Toinaosu Tōkyō saiban* [Reassessing the Tokyo tribunal]," in Ajia minshū hōtei junbikai, ed., *Toinaosu Tōkyō saiban* [Reassessing the Tokyo tribunal] (Tokyo: Ryokufu shuppan, 1995), 13.

11 See John Dower, *Embracing Defeat: Japan in the Wake of World War II* (New York: W.W. Norton, 1999), chap. 15; or Timothy Brook, "The Tokyo Judgment and the Rape of Nanking," *Journal of Asian Studies* 60, 3 (2001): 673-700.

12 A number of archives, including Library and Archives Canada and the University of British Columbia Archives, hold original copies of the trial transcript. It has since been reproduced in R. John Pritchard, ed., *The Tokyo War Crimes Trial: The Complete Transcripts of the Proceedings of the International Military Tribunal for the Far East in Twenty-two Volumes* (New York/London: Garland, 1981). English-language books on the trial include Chihiro Hosoya, Nisuki Ando, Yasuaki Onuma, and Richard H. Minear, eds., *The Tokyo War Crimes Trial: An International Symposium* (Tokyo: Kodansha, 1986); Richard H. Minear, *Victor's Justice: The Tokyo War Crimes Tribunal* (Princeton: Princeton University Press, 1971); Arnold C. Brackman, *The Other Nuremberg: The Untold Story of the Tokyo War Crimes Trials* (New York: William Morrow, 1987); and, more recently, Tim Maga, *Judgement at Tokyo: The Japanese War Crimes Trials* (Lexington: University Press of Kentucky, 2001).

13 This overview is based on a review of the trial by Herbert Norman as well as other materials as cited. For Norman's view I have relied on an unsigned article by Norman commissioned by the Department of External Affairs and entitled "Observations on the Trial of War Criminals in Japan," *Monthly Bulletin* (February 1949): 12-23; and in Ōkubo Genji, ed. and trans., *Complete Works of Herbert Norman* (Tokyo: Iwanami shoten, 1977), 2:384-402.

14 The latter were tried in other venues, not at the Tokyo Tribunal.

15 Norman/DEA, "Observations," 13.

16 Ibid., 14.

17 Ibid., 21.

18 See Stanton, "Canada and War Crimes," 384.

19 "Dear Mr. Robertson," 23 April 1946, LAC, RG 25, vol. 3641, 4060-C-40 (2), 2.

20 Ibid., 3.

21 E.S. McDougall to Louis St. Laurent, 19 March 1947, LAC, RG 25, vol. 5762, file 104-J (s) pt. 1., 1. (John Stanton first tracked down this document in the archives.)

22 Ibid., 1.

23 Ibid.

24 E.S. McDougall to Louis St. Laurent, 19 March 1947, 2.

25 Ibid.

26 Ibid.
27 Ibid., 3.
28 Handwritten note, signed L.S. StL., 29 March 1947, LAC, RG 25, vol. 5762, file 104-J (s) pt. 1.
29 Norman to Pearson, 5 April 1947, LAC, RG 25, vol. 5762, file 104-J (s) pt. 1, 1.
30 Ibid., 3.
31 Hume Wrong to L.B. Pearson, 21 April 1947, LAC, RG 25, vol. 5762, file 104-J (s) pt. 1.
32 Norman Robertson to SSEA, 8 May 1947, LAC, RG 25, vol. 5762, file 104-J (s) pt. 1.
33 Lord Patrick memorandum, n.d., British National Archive/Public Records Office, Lord Chancellor's Office, LCO 2/2992, 1.
34 Ibid., 2.
35 Ibid., 5.
36 "My Dear Minister," 20 May 1947, LAC, RG 25, vol. 5762, file 104-J (s) pt. 1, 1.
37 On New Zealand, see Ann Trotter, *New Zealand and Japan, 1945-1952: The Occupation and Peace Treaty* (London: Athlone Press, 1990); and Robin Kay, ed., *Documents on New Zealand External Relations,* vol. 2, *The Occupation and Surrender of Japan* (Wellington: Government Printer, 1982), 1499-1748 passim.
38 Ben Bruce Blakeney, "Defense Appeal to General MacArthur, Nov. 21, 1948," as cited in Minear, *Victor's Justice,* 206. That the group of seven authored the final opinion is also suggested by historian Awaya Kentarō in his introduction to Asahi shimbun Tōkyō saiban kishadan, *Tōkyō saiban,* 7.
39 Ienaga Saburō, "The Historical Significance of the Tokyo Trial," in *The Tokyo War Crimes Trial: An International Symposium,* ed. Chihiro Hosoya, Nisuki Ando, Yasuaki Onuma, and Richard H. Minear (Tokyo: Kodansha, 1986), 169.
40 E.H. Norman, no. 526, 2 November 1948, LAC, External Affairs Series, RG 25, vol. 3642, file 4060-C-40, pt. 3.
41 Ibid., 2.
42 Far Eastern Commission, additional information (for use with Press Release No. 53), 1 April 1949, LAC, RG 25, vol. 6196, file 4060-C-40, pt. 4.1.
43 Axel Marschik, "The Politics of Prosecution," in *The Law of War Crimes: National and International Approaches,* ed. T.L.H. McCormack and G.I. Simpson, 65-74 (The Hague/Boston: Kluwer Law International, 1997).
44 See Ian Hancock, "Romani Victims of the Holocaust and Swiss Complicity," in *When Sorry Isn't Enough: The Controversy over Apologies and Reparations for Human Injustice,* ed. Roy L. Brooks, 68-76 (New York: New York University Press, 1999).
45 R. John Pritchard, ed., *The Tokyo War Crimes Trial: The Complete Transcripts of the Proceedings of the International Military Tribunal for the Far East in Twenty-Two Volumes* (New York/London: Garland, 1981), 4546-47.
46 The summary of the trial is from the Chinese Plaintiffs Legal Team Lawsuit against the Japanese Germ Warfare entitled "Anti-Unit 731: Stop the War against Iraq and North Korea," 16 November 2002 (Ichinose Law Office, Tokyo).
47 Revelations were first made by John Powell, "Japan's Germ Warfare: The US Coverup of a War Crime," *Bulletin of Concerned Asian Scholars* 12, 4 (1980): 2-17, in the United States. In Japan they were first made in 1982-83. See Morimura Seiichi, *Akuma no Hōshoku dai 1-3 bu* [The devil gluttony, parts 1-3] (Tokyo: Kakkawa

bunkō, 2000-2001 editions). Other studies in Japanese include a report from the Center for Research and Documentation on Japan's War Responsibility, *Kikan sensō sekinin kenkyū, tokushū: 731 butai no jisso ni semaru* [Report on Japan's war responsibility, special edition: Closing in on the reality of Unit 731] 2 (Winter 1993); Tsuneishi Keiichi, *Igakushatachi no soshiki hanzai, kantōgun dai 731 butai* [Doctors organized crime, the kantoo military unit 731] (Tokyo: Asahi shimbunsha, 1999); and *Unit 731, Seibutsu heiki hanzai no jijitsu* [Unit 731: The truth about crimes related to biological weapons] (Tokyo: Kodansha gendai shinsho, 1995). The most significant works in English are Peter Williams and David Wallace, *Unit 731: The Japanese Army's Secret of Secrets* (London: Hodder and Stoughton, 1989); and Sheldon H. Harris, *Factories of Death: Japanese Biological Warfare, 1932-45, and the American Cover-Up* (London: Routledge, 1994).

48 Joint Publications Research Service (hereafter JPRS), *Moscow Daily Press Summary*, no. 365, 31 December 1949, enclosed with I.B.C. Watkins to Acting SSEA, 6 January 1950, LAC, RG 25, vol. 6196, file 4060-C-40, pt. 4.2, 4-5.

49 As cited in Harris, *Factories of Death*, 218.

50 Bert V.A. Roling, "A Judge's View," *Bulletin of the Atomic Scientists* 37, 8 (1981): 52.

51 Nolan's official three-page report of his activities as associate prosecutor is cursory, and little can be learned other than that he arrived in Tokyo on 8 February 1946 and departed on 7 May 1948 after the trial had ended. See H.G. Nolan to Brooke Claxton, n.d. [June 1948], LAC, RG 25, vol. 3642, file 4060-C-40, pt. 3.

52 Washington (Joint Chiefs of Staff) to CINCAFPAC (for MacArthur), 24 July 1946, RG 153, entry 145, box 73, 000.5, 2.

53 Joseph B. Keenan to Kenneth C. Royall, 20 April 1948, LAC, RG 25, vol. 6196, file 4060-C-40, pt. 4.1, 1.

54 Ibid., 2.

55 The record of the trial is entitled *Materials of the Trial of Former Servicemen of the Japanese Army Charged with Manufacturing and Employing Biological Weapons* (Khabarovsk Trial) (Moscow: Foreign Languages Publishing House, 1950).

56 A. Panyushkin to Hume Wrong, 1 February 1950, LAC, RG 25, vol. 6196, file 4060-C-40, pt. 4.3.

57 David Stansfield to Arthur Menzies, 25 May 1950, LAC, RG 25, vol. 6196, file 4060-C-40, pt. 4.3.

58 JPRS, *Moscow Daily Press Summary*, 20 May 1950, encl. with ibid., 4.

59 This document was an enclosure from Ralph E. Collins to A.R. Menzies, 1 June 1950, LAC, RG 25, vol. 6196, file 4060-C-40, pt. 4.3.

60 Herbert Norman to J.J. McCardle, 13 July 1950, LAC, RG 25, vol. 6196, file 4060-C-40, pt. 4.3, 1.

61 N. Burbridge, memorandum for American and Far Eastern Division, 23 June 1950, LAC, RG 25, vol. 6196, file 4060-C-40, pt. 4.3, 1.

CHAPTER 8: MR. KENNAN COMES TO OTTAWA

1 "Interview with Press Correspondents, Primarily Concerning Plan for United Nations Administration of Japan," 19 March 1947, as reproduced in Supreme Commander for the Allied Powers, *Political Reorientation of Japan, September 1945*

to September 1948 (Washington, DC: US Government Printing Office, 1948), apps. 765-66.

2 See Assistant Secretary of State (Hilldring) to the Political Adviser in Japan (Atcheson), 9 June 1947, *Foreign Relations of the United States* (hereafter *FRUS*), vol. 6, *1947* (Washington, DC: US Government Printing Office, 1972), 461.

3 Secretary of State to General of the Army Douglas MacArthur, 26 June 1947, in *FRUS*, vol. 6, *1947*, 465.

4 Memorandum of conversation, 1 July 1947, *FRUS*, vol. 6, *1947*, 468.

5 The record of these consultations is "British Commonwealth Conference, Canberra: Summary Record of Proceedings, 26 August-1 September 1947," in Robin Kay, ed., *Documents on New Zealand External Relations* (hereafter *DNZER*) (Wellington: Government Printer, 1985) 3:150-64.

6 These papers were found not in the records of the DEA in Canada's national archives but, rather, among Brooke Claxton Papers, LAC, MG 32, B5, vol. 99, Canberra Conference Book 2.

7 Herbert Norman, "Japanese Peace Settlement: Post-War Control Machinery," LAC, MG 32, B5, vol. 99, Canberra Conference Book 2.

8 Herbert Norman, "Japanese Peace Settlement: Territorial Settlement," LAC, MG 32, B5, vol. 99, Canberra Conference Book 2.

9 Herbert Norman, "Japanese Peace Settlement: SCAP Directives and the Peace Treaty," LAC, MG 32, B5, vol. 99, Canberra Conference Book 2, 1.

10 Ibid., 2.

11 Herbert Norman, "Japanese Peace Settlement: Trade Notes," LAC, MG 32, B5, vol. 99, Canberra Conference Book 2, 1.

12 Typescript manuscript from the Australian Archives, CRS A5463, Embassy of Canada in Tokyo, E.H. Norman Library, Ōkubo Genji Collection, box 6-2.

13 Ibid., 4.

14 Ibid., 6.

15 Extract from report by head of delegation to Commonwealth Conference, 2 September 1947, *Documents on Canadian External Relations* (hereafter *DCER*), vol. 13, *1947*, ed. Norman Hillmer and Donald Page (Ottawa: Canada Communication Group, 1993), 229. A full transcript of Norman's presentation to the Canberra Conference is held in the Australian Archives (A5463, Item [2]) and was obtained among the papers of Ōkubo Genji held at the Norman library in the Canadian embassy in Tokyo.

16 Brooke Claxton's report on the conference is contained in Brooke Claxton Papers, LAC, MG 32, B5, vol. 99, Canberra Conference file. Extracts are contained in *DCER*, vol. 13, *1947*, 227-34. Norman's submission, included in the preparatory materials provided Claxton and the delegation, are contained in Canberra Conference Book 2, LAC, MG 32, B5, vol. 99.

17 Extract from report by head of delegation to Commonwealth Conference, 2 September 1947, *DCER*, vol. 13, *1947*, 229-30.

18 Conference communiqué, in "Report on British Commonwealth Conference," Kay, *DNZER*, 3:176.

19 The Canberra Conference envisaged a meeting of the FEC plus Pakistan, and perhaps Burma, to be held in October at the latest; voting would be by a two-thirds majority and the treaty was to be completed by 1948. See extract from report by head of delegation to Commonwealth Conference, 2 September 1947, *DCER,* vol. 13, *1947,* 229-30.

20 Working Group on Japan Treaty, notes on meeting, *FRUS,* vol. 8, *1946,* 349.

21 United States Aide-Memoire to the Soviet Government, 12 August 1947, in Kay, *DNZER,* 3:206.

22 Minutes, meeting of foreign ministers, 18 July 1945, as cited in memorandum from Legal Adviser (Fahy) to the Under-Secretary of State (Lovett), 7 August 1947, *FRUS,* vol. 6, *1947,* 479-80.

23 Chinese Embassy, London, to United Kingdom, Government, contained in Secretary of State for Commonwealth Relations to the Minister of External Affairs, 19 November 1947, Kay, *DNZER,* 3:219.

24 Article 2, Treaty of Friendship and Alliance between the Republic of China and the USSR (Moscow, 14 August 1945).

25 See *FRUS,* vol. 6, *1948,* 663.

26 Memorandum by the director of the Office of Far Eastern Affairs (Vincent) to the Secretary of State, 12 May 1947, *FRUS,* vol. 6, *1947,* 458.

27 For details, see Michael Schaller, *The American Occupation of Japan: The Origins of the Cold War in Asia* (New York: Oxford University Press, 1985), 98-106; and Howard B. Schonberger, *Aftermath of War: Americans and the Remaking of Japan, 1945-1952* (Kent: Kent State University Press, 1989), 178-80.

28 X, "The Sources of Soviet Conduct," *Foreign Affairs* 25 (July 1947): 566-82.

29 For a gender analysis, see Frank Costigliola, "'Unceasing Pressure for Penetration': Gender, Pathology, and Emotion in George Kennan's Formation of the Cold War," *Journal of American History* 83, 4 (1997): 1309-39. On race, see Thomas Borstelmann, *The Cold War and the Color Line: American Race Relations in the Global Arena* (Cambridge: Harvard University Press, 2001), 49-50.

30 The full text is available in *FRUS, 1946,* 6:697-709.

31 X, "The Sources of Soviet Conduct," 568.

32 Memorandum by the Director of the Policy Planning Staff (Kennan) to the Under-Secretary of State (Lovett), 12 August 1947, *FRUS,* vol. 6, *1947,* 487.

33 Ibid., 486.

34 Memorandum by the director of the Policy Planning Staff (Kennan), 14 October 1947, *FRUS, The Far East and Australasia,* vol. 6, *1948,* 536-37; and Annex memorandum by the director of the Policy Planning Staff (Kennan), 14 October 1947, *FRUS,* vol. 6, *1948,* 537-43.

35 Ibid., 537.

36 "Statement to Be Made to Far Eastern Commission by United States Member and Transmitted to SCAP for Information and Released for Publication," *FRUS,* vol. 6, *1948,* 654.

37 "Conversation between General of the Army MacArthur and Mr. George F. Kennan," 5 March 1948, *FRUS,* vol. 6, *1948,* 704.

38 George F. Kennan, *Memoirs, 1925-1950* (Boston: Little, Brown and Co., 1967), 386.

39 Ibid., 387.

40 Kennan letters to Butterworth, 9, 14, and 16 March 1948, NRAW, PPS file, box 19, as cited in Richard B. Finn, *Winners in Peace: MacArthur, Yoshida, and Postwar Japan* (Berkeley: University of California Press, 1992), 204.

41 Non-Western states, Kennan wrote to Dean Acheson in 1949, were "states with coloured populations ... unsteadied by tradition" who were "the neurotic products of exotic backgrounds and tentative western educational experiences, racially and socially embittered against the West." As cited by Mark Bradley in his *Imagining Vietnam and America: The Making of Postcolonial Vietnam* (Chapel Hill: University of North Carolina Press, 2000), x.

42 Report by the director of the Policy Planning Staff (Kennan), 25 March 1948, *FRUS*, vol. 6, *1948*, 691-96.

43 My detailed review of Canadian involvement in Korea at this time was published as "The Cat's Paw: Canada and the United Nations Temporary Commission on Korea," *Canadian Historical Review* 85, 2 (2004): 297-324. For differing perspectives, see Denis Stairs, *The Diplomacy of Constraint* (Toronto: University of Toronto Press, 1974), chap 1; or, more recently, Graeme S. Mount with Andre Laferriere, *The Diplomacy of War: The Case of Korea* (Montreal: Black Rose Books, 2004).

44 Canadian Ambassador to the United States to SSEA, WA 2872, 19 July 1946, LAC, RG 25, vol. 3649, file 6406-A-40, 5.

45 Minutes of meetings of the State-War-Navy Coordinating Committee (hereafter SWNCC), 1944-1947, 29 January 1947, National Archives and Records Administration (NARA), RG 353, 14.

46 Ibid., 15.

47 Minutes of meetings of SWNCC, 1944-1947, 19 March 1947, 6.

48 For a detailed analysis of US policy in Korea, see James I. Matray, *The Reluctant Crusade: American Foreign Policy in Korea, 1941-1950* (Honolulu: University of Hawaii Press, 1985); and also his "Korea: Test Case of Containment in Asia," in *Child of Conflict: The Korean-American Relationship, 1943-1953*, ed. Bruce Cumings, 169-93 (Seattle: University of Washington Press, 1983).

49 Leland M. Goodrich, *Korea: A Study of US Policy in the United Nations* (New York: Council on Foreign Relations, 1956), 29. Other sources used in the reconstruction of events include Leon Gordenker, *The United Nations and the Peaceful Unification of Korea* (The Hague: Martinus Nijhoff, 1959); Shiv Dayal, *India's Role in the Korean Question* (Delhi: S. Chand and Co., 1959); and Evan Luard, *A History of the United Nations*, vol. 1 (London: Macmillan, 1982).

50 *FRUS*, vol. 6, *1947*, 849.

51 The resolution is contained in ibid., 857-59.

52 Department of External Affairs, memorandum for the Canadian delegation to the second session of the General Assembly, 24 October 1947, LAC, RG 25, vol. 5778, file 204-A(S), pt. 1.1.

53 Ibid., 5.

54 Ibid., 12.

55 Canadian Consulate General, New York, to Secretary of State for External Affairs, 6 November 1947, LAC, RG 25, vol. 5778, file 204-A(S), 2.

56 Prime Minister to President of United States, 8 January 1948, in *DCER*, vol. 14, *1948*, 150-51 (emphasis added).

57 John English, for example, in his biography of Lester Pearson, concluded that, because the Soviet Union denied the commission access to the north, UNTCOK "would not act at all, and it did not." See John English, *Shadow of Heaven: The Life of Lester Pearson*, vol. 1, *1897-1948* (London: Vintage UK, 1990), 328. In a biography of Louis St. Laurent, Dale Thomson states that Canada opposed the partition of Korea and withdrew from UNTCOK after it decided to supervise elections in the south alone. See Dale C. Thomson, *Louis St. Laurent: Canadian* (Toronto: Macmillan, 1967), 291.

58 For an account of the rebellion in English, see John Merrill, "The Cheju-do Rebellion," *Journal of Korean Studies* 2 (1980): 139-98. In Korean, see Kim In-duck et al., *Jeju 4.3 Yun-gu* [Research on Cheju 4.3.] (Seoul: Yuk-sa-bi-pyung-sa, 1999); *Reporters of the* Cheju People's Daily Newspaper, 4.3 eun Mal-han-da [4.3 Speaks] (Seoul: Jean-ye-won, 1989); Jeju 4.3 Research Centre, *Yi-je-sa Mal-ham-su-da* [It is only now that we are able to tell] (Seoul: Han-wool, 1994).

59 Norman to Pearson, 22 March 1948, LAC, RG 25, vol. 4729, 50061-40, pt. 1.

60 Kennan and Butterworth to Marshall, *Occupation of Japan,* Part 2, *US and Allied Policy, 1945-1952,* National Archives and Records Administration (NARA), 3-H-21.

61 WA-1527, following for Pearson from Wrong, 20 May 1948, LAC, RG 25, vol. 4730, file 50061-40, pt. 1, 1.

62 Ibid., 3.

63 Arthur Menzies, memorandum on conversations regarding Japan with Mr. M.E. Dening, 27 May 1948, LAC, RG 25, vol. 4730, file 50061-40, pt. 1, 2.

64 Ibid. Dening's racialized views come through strongly in the record of this conversation.

65 Arthur Menzies, memorandum for Mr. Pearson: Kennan's visit, 1 June 1948, LAC, RG 25, vol. 4730, file 50061-40, pt. 1, 2.

66 Arthur Menzies, United States policy for Japan, 3 June 1948, LAC, RG 25, vol. 4730, file 50061-40, pt. 1, 1.

67 Ibid.

68 Ibid., 2.

69 Ibid., 3.

70 Menzies and Collins appear to differ on this question.

71 Menzies, United States policy for Japan, 4.

72 Ibid., 6.

73 Ibid., 6-7.

74 Ibid., 7.

75 Ibid., 8.

76 Ibid., 9.

77 Personal message for Mr. Mackenzie King from Mr. Attlee, 21 July 1948, LAC, RG 25, vol. 4730, file 50061-40, pt. 1, 1.

78 Ibid., 2.

79 Pearson wrote Norman Robertson on 4 August 1948, explaining that Mackenzie King was preoccupied with the Liberal convention but that Robertson might share

with British authorities the content of the draft reply. He also told Robertson that they had shared their views with Kennan and that the matter was basically closed. See Cypher No. 1245, Robertson from Pearson, 4 August 1948, LAC, RG 25, vol. 4730, file 50061-40, pt. 1.

80 Personal message for Mr. Attlee from Mr. Mackenzie King, 23 July 1948, LAC, RG 25, vol. 4730, file 50061-40, pt. 4.

81 As an ultimate objective of the Occupation, the US document stated: "(d) The Japanese people shall be afforded opportunity to develop for themselves an economy which will permit the peacetime requirements of the population to be met." See "United States Initial Post-Surrender Policy for Japan," as reproduced in Supreme Commander for the Allied Powers, *Political Reorientation of Japan, September 1945 to September 1948* (Washington, DC: US Government Printing Office, 1948 [reprint: Westport, CT: Greenwood, 1977]), apps., 423.

82 Potsdam Declaration, as reproduced in ibid., 413.

83 Kennan, *Memoirs*, 376.

84 This draws on my earlier work on the labour movement. See John Price, *Japan Works: Power and Paradox in Postwar Industrial Relations* (Ithaca: Cornell University Press, 1997), chaps. 3 and 4.

85 For details on who was in the lobby, see Schonberger, *Aftermath of War*, chaps. 4-7.

86 Lester B. Pearson, *Mike: The Memoirs of the Right Honourable Lester B. Pearson*, vol. 2, *1948-1957*, ed. John A. Munro and Alex I. Inglis (Toronto: University of Toronto Press, 1973), 188.

CHAPTER 9: CANADA, ASIA, AND "PAX AMERICANA"

1 Memorandum from Under-Secretary of State for External Affairs to Cabinet Committee on Immigration, 26 May 1947, *Documents on Canadian External Relations* (hereafter *DCER*), vol. 13, *1947*, ed. Norman Hillmer and Donald Page (Ottawa: Canada Communication Group, 1993), 293-94.

2 Gurcham S. Basran, B. Sing Bolaria, *The Sikhs in Canada: Migration, Race, Class and Gender* (New Delhi: Oxford University Press, 2003).

3 For details, see *DCER*, vol. 13, *1947*, 298-333.

4 For later developments, see Patricia E. Roy, *The Triumph of Citizenship: The Japanese and Chinese in Canada, 1941-67* (Vancouver: UBC Press, 2007), chap. 7.

5 This paper and extracts of responses to it are reproduced in "Canada and a Bipolar World," in *DCER*, vol. 13, *1947*, 342-461.

6 For an analysis of this debate, see Reg Whitaker and Gary Marcuse, *Cold War Canada* (Toronto: University of Toronto Press, 1994), 120-34.

7 "The United States and the Soviet Union: A Study of the Possibility of War and Some of the Implications for Canadian Policy," in *DCER*, vol. 13, *1947*, 377.

8 Ibid., 381.

9 As cited in Norman Hillmer and Donald Page, "Introduction," in *DCER*, vol. 13, *1947*, xxii.

10 The original proposal for geographic divisions, written by Hugh Keenleyside, suggested four geographic sections (American, Far Eastern, Europe, and Commonwealth), but the four were combined to form only two sections, with American and

Far Eastern together. See John Hilliker, *Canada's Department of External Affairs*, vol. 1, *The Early Years, 1909-1946* (McGill-Queen's University Press, 1990), 242-43.

11 Key primary sources on the topic are the *Foreign Relations of the United States* (hereafter *FRUS*) series for 1945-50, and the so-called "White Paper on China," originally issued by a desperate State Department in 1949 as *United States Relations with China, with Special Reference to the Period 1944-1949* (Washington, DC: Department of State Publication 3573, Far Eastern series 30, 1949). Stanford University Press reissued this in 1967, with the original letter of transmittal to President Truman from Secretary of State Dean Acheson and a new introduction by Lyman P. Van Slyke. Recent works based on Soviet and Chinese materials include Chen Jian, "Re-Reading Chinese Documents: A Post-Cold War Interpretation of the Cold War on the Korean Peninsula," in *Ending the Cold War in Korea: Theoretical and Historical Perspectives*, ed. Moon Chung-in, Odd Arne Westad, and Gyoo-hyoung Kahng, 171-91 (Seoul: Yonsei University Press, 2001); Chen Jian, *Mao's China and the Cold War* (Chapel Hill and London: University of North Carolina Press, 2001); and Xiaobing Li and Hongshan Li, eds., *China and the United States: A New Cold War History* (Lanham/New York/Oxford: University Press of America, 1998).

12 T.C. Davis to External Affairs, 12 May 1947, *DCER*, vol. 13, *1947*, 1621.

13 "General Situation in China," 15 June 1947, LAC, RG 25, vol. 3, 50055-40, 1.

14 Ibid., 5.

15 "General Conditions in China," 7 July 1947, LAC, RG 25, vol. 4, 50055-40, 2.

16 "Official Visit to Shanghai," 23 October 1947, LAC, RG 25, 4558-12-40, 8.

17 "General Conditions in China," 16 January 1948, LAC, RG 25, G 2, 4558-P-40c, box 233, 5.

18 Ronning to External Affairs, 18 November 1946, LAC, RG 25, 50056-40, vol. 2.

19 "Export of Armaments," 2 April 1947, *DCER*, vol. 13, *1947*, 1589.

20 Ibid., 1590.

21 George S. Patterson to External Affairs, 28 January 1947, LAC, RG 25, vol. 2, 50056-40.

22 Minister of Reconstruction to Minister of Finance, *DCER*, vol. 13, *1947*, 1618.

23 External Affairs to High Commissioner in UK, 23 April 1947, *DCER*, vol. 13, *1947*, 1595.

24 C.D. Howe to Secretary of State for External Affairs, 2 June 1947, *DCER*, vol. 13, *1947*, 1624.

25 External Affairs to High Commissioner in UK, 25 September 1947, *DCER*, vol. 13, *1947*, 1626.

26 Escott Reid to Lester Pearson, 16 November 1948, *DCER*, vol. 14, *1948*, 1844-45.

27 Chester Ronning, *A Memoir of China in Revolution* (New York: Pantheon Books, 1974), 136. "Top" is a reference to Ronning's son-in-law Seymour Topping.

28 Enclosure No. 2, memo to the ambassador, April 1949, LAC, RG 25, G 2, 4558-V-40, col. 2.

29 Stephen Beecroft, "Canadian Policy towards China, 1949-1957: The Recognition Problem," in *Reluctant Adversaries: Canada and the People's Republic of China, 1949-1970*, ed. Paul M. Evans and B. Michael Frolic (Toronto: University of Toronto Press, 1991), 48-49.

30 Escott Reid, "Colombo Conference Notes," 9 January 1950, LAC, MG 31, E46, vol. 7, 15, 19.

31 External Affairs, "Commonwealth Meeting on Foreign Affairs," 30 March 1950, LAC, MG 31, E46, vol. 7, 15 (202.2), 2.

32 Notes for Mr. Pearson's broadcast for CBC, 12 January 1950, LAC, MG 31, E46, vol. 7, 15 (202.2), 6.

33 Ibid., 9.

34 External Affairs, "Commonwealth Meeting on Foreign Affairs," 30 March 1950, LAC, MG 31, E46, vol. 7, 15 (202.2), 9.

35 Pearson to Heeney, 17 January 1950, LAC, MG 31, E46, vol. 7, 15 (202.2), 2.

36 Ibid., 3.

37 Ibid., 2.

38 For an interesting retrospective, see Keith Spicer, "Clubmanship Upstaged: Canada's Twenty Years in the Colombo Plan," *International Journal* 25, 1 (1969/1970): 23-33.

39 Nik Cavell, "Technical Assistance and the Colombo Plan," 5 October 1951, Statements and Speeches, Canada, Department of External Affairs, 51/38, 2.

40 "Press Conference," 10 February 1950, Statements and Speeches, Canada, Department of External Affairs; "Commonwealth Meeting on Foreign Affairs," 30 March 1950, LAC, MG 31, E46, vol. 7, 15 (202.2), 3.

41 Beecroft, "Canadian Policy towards China," 50.

42 The main voice for delay in the DEA was that of the Canadian ambassador to the United States, Hume Wrong. See his dispatches from Washington in February and March, *DCER*, vol. 16, *1950*, ed. G. Donaghy, 1775-79.

43 This account of the French colonial war in Vietnam is based on Mark Philip Bradley, *Imagining Vietnam and America: The Making of Postcolonial Vietnam, 1919-1950* (Chapel Hill: University of North Carolina Press, 2000); William J. Duiker, *Ho Chi Minh: A Life* (New York: Hyperion, 2000); George C. Herring, *America's Longest War: The United States and Vietnam, 1950-1975*, 4th ed. (Boston: McGraw-Hill, 2002); Seth Jacobs, *America's Miracle Man in Vietnam: Ngo Dinh Diem, Religion, Race and US Intervention in Southeast Asia* (Durham: Duke University Press, 2004); Mark Atwood Lawrence, *Assuming the Burden: Europe and the American Commitment to War in Vietnam* (Berkeley: University of California Press, 2005); Steven Hugh Lee, *Outposts of Empire: Korea, Vietnam and the Origins of the Cold War in Asia, 1949-1954* (Montreal and Kingston: McGill-Queen's University Press, 1995); Fredrik Logevall, *The Origins of the Vietnam War* (Harlow, UK: Longman/Pearson Education, 2001); James S. Olson and Randy Roberts, *Where the Domino Fell: America and Vietnam* (New York: St. Martin's Press, 1991).

44 This account of the DRV's external efforts is based on Bradley, *Imagining Vietnam and America*, 163-75.

45 As cited in Bradley, *Imagining Vietnam and America*, 167.

46 "Department of State Policy Statement on Indochina," 27 September 1948, *FRUS*, vol. 6, *1948*, 45.

47 Kennan to Acheson, United Nations, 14 November 1949, in *The State Department Policy Planning Staff Papers* (New York: Garland, 1983), 3:189.

48 Mao directly authorized recognition while in Moscow. See Shuguang Zhang and Jian Chen, *Chinese Communist Foreign Policy and the Cold War in Asia: New Documentary Evidence, 1944-1950* (Chicago: Imprint Publications, 1996), 138.
49 William Duiker, *Ho Chi Minh: A Life* (New York: Hyperion, 2000), 421.
50 Chen Jian, *Mao's China and the Cold War* (Chapel Hill: University of North Carolina Press, 2001), chap. 6.
51 Canadian accounts include James Eayrs, *In Defence of Canada, Indochina: Roots of Complicity* (Toronto: University of Toronto Press, 1983); Steven Hugh Lee, *Outposts of Empire: Korea, Vietnam and the Origins of the Cold War in Asia, 1949-1954* (Montreal and Kingston: McGill-Queen's University Press, 1995); Victor Levant, *Quiet Complicity: Canadian Involvement in the Vietnam War* (Toronto: Between the Lines, 1986); Douglas A. Ross, *In the Interests of Peace: Canada and Vietnam, 1954-73* (Toronto: University of Toronto Press, 1984); Charles Taylor, *Snow Job: Canada, the United States and Vietnam, 1954-1973* (Toronto: Anansi, 1978); Ramesh Thakur, *Peacekeeping in Vietnam: Canada, India, Poland, and the International Commission* (Edmonton: University of Alberta Press, 1984). More recent essays include Robert Bothwell, "The Further Shore: Canada and Vietnam," *International Journal* 56, 1 (2000-1), 89-114; Andrew Preston, "Balancing War and Peace: Canadian Foreign Policy and the Vietnam War, 1961-1965," *Diplomatic History* 27, 1 (2003): 73-111.
52 Eayrs, *In Defence of Canada*, 12.
53 Draft memorandum to Cabinet, 21 February 1950, in *DCER*, vol. 16, *1950*, 1838-39.
54 Ibid., 1839.
55 Canada, *Hansard*, 22 February 1950.
56 Cabinet Conclusions, 23 February 1950, http://www.collectionscanada.gc.ca/, page 7.
57 As cited in Duiker, *Ho Chi Minh*, 434.

CHAPTER 10: AMERICA'S PRESTIGE, KOREA'S WAR

1 *Globe and Mail*, 26 June 1950.
2 "US Fighter Plans Downs Yak in Fight over Airfield," *Globe and Mail*, 27 June 1950.
3 The official account of Canada's response to the initial stage of the Korean War is found in Government of Canada, *Canada and the Korean Crisis* (Ottawa: King's Printer, 1950).
4 "War in Korea," *Globe and Mail*, 27 June 1950.
5 D'Arcy Jenish, "Our Forgotten War," *Maclean's*, 26 June 2000, 32.
6 David J. Bercuson, *Blood on the Hills: The Canadian Army in the Korean War* (Toronto: University of Toronto Press, 1999), 229.
7 A dedicated volume on Korea and the Cold War is Moon Chung-in, Odd Arne Westad, and Gyoo-hyoung Kahng, eds., *Ending the Cold War in Korea: Theoretical and Historical Perspectives* (Seoul: Yonsei University Press, 2001). In particular, for a review of the new Chinese sources, see Chen Jian, "Re-Reading Chinese Documents: A Post-Cold War Interpretation of the Cold War on the Korean Peninsula," in Chung-in et al., *Ending the Cold War*, 171-91. For an interpretation of the Soviet documents, see Kathryn Weathersby, "Soviet Documents and Reinterpretation of the Origins of the Korean War," in Chung-in et al., *Ending the Cold War*, 161-69.
8 Blair Fraser, "Win or Lose, the Russians May Get Korea," *Maclean's*, 1 January 1951, 9.

9 The most important works on Kim Il Sung are Korean historian Han Hong-Koo's "Wounded Nationalism: The *Minsaengdan* Incident and Kim Il Sung in Eastern Manchuria" (PhD diss. University of Washington, 1999); and Japanese historian Wada Haruki's *Kin nissei to manshu konichi sensō* [Kim Il Sung and the anti-Japanese war in Manchuria](Tokyo: Heibonsha, 1992). See also Bruce Cumings *North Korea: Another Country* (New York: New Press, 2004), chap. 3; and Charles K. Armstrong, *The North Korean Revolution, 1945-1950* (Ithaca: Cornell University Press, 2003), 26-37.

10 See Chen Jian, *China's Road to the Korean War: The Making of the Sino-American Confrontation* (New York: Columbia University Press, 1994), 109; and Xiaobing Li and Hongshan Li, eds., *China and the United States: A New Cold War History* (Lanham, MD: University Press of America, 1998), 15.

11 See Shen Zhihua, "China Sends Troops to Korea: Beijing's Policy-Making Process," in Li and Li, *China and the United States*, 14-15.

12 The three agreements were outlined in a "Communiqué announcing the Soviet-Chinese Treaty," 14 February 1950. The alliance was formalized in the Treaty of Friendship, Alliance and Mutual Aid between the USSR and the Chinese People's Republic. Both documents are found in Edward H. Judge and John W. Landon, *The Cold War: A History through Documents* (Upper Saddle River, NJ: Prentice Hall, 1999), 58-60.

13 As cited in Shen, "China Sends Troops to Korea," 17.

14 Chen, "Re-Reading Chinese Documents," 181.

15 Kang Jeong-Koo, "A Critical Evaluation on the US Role in the Division of Korea and the Korean War," 7, unpublished paper, given to author.

16 For details, see John Lewis Gaddis and Paul Nitze, "NSC 68 and the Soviet Threat Reconsidered," *International Security* 4, 4 (1980): 164-76; George Kennan, *Memoirs, 1925-1950* (Boston: Little, Brown and Co., 1967); Melvyn P. Leffler, *A Preponderance of Power: National Security, the Truman Administration, and the Cold War* (Stanford: Stanford University Press, 1992). One of the most incisive analyses of this period is offered by David M. Finkelstein, *Washington's Taiwan Dilemma, 1949-1950* (Fairfax, VA: George Mason University Press, 1993). See also Michael Schaller, *The American Occupation of Japan: The Origins of the Cold War in Asia* (New York: Oxford University Press, 1985), 198-200; Department of State, *The China White Paper, August 1949* (Stanford: Stanford University Press, 1967); *NSC 68: A Report to the National Security Council by the Executive Secretary on Unites States Objectives and Programs for National Security*, 14 April 1950. Available online at http://www.coldwarfiles.org/ (George Washington University, National Security Archive). A prime example of the impact of anti-communism is the case of Qian Xuesen, a Chinese scientist living in the United States who was effectively put on ice for five years and then left the country for China, where he became the father of the Chinese rocket program. See Iris Chang, *Thread of the Silkworm* (New York: Basic Books, 1995).

17 Ibid., 270.

18 Department of State, transcript of Secretary of State's press conference, no. 34, 12 January 1950, LAC, RG 25, vol. 6031, 50293-40, part 1-1, 4.

19 Ibid., 12-13.

20 Ibid., 14.
21 Melvyn P. Leffler, a prominent US historian of the Cold War, notes the importance of the exercise but then suggests that Truman wavered, believing that the implementation of NSC-68 and related policies might "lead the United States toward becoming a garrison state." See Melvyn P. Leffler, *The Specter of Communism: The United States and the Origins of the Cold War, 1917-1953* (New York: Hill and Wang, 1994), 94-98.
22 Ellen Schrecker, *Many Are the Crimes: McCarthyism in America* (Princeton: Princeton University Press, 1998), 241, 298.
23 Details of the internal shuffles are contained in Michael Schaller, *The American Occupation of Japan: The Origins of the Cold War in Asia* (New York: Oxford University Press, 1985), 246-72.
24 The most comprehensive account is in Melvyn Leffler, *A Preponderance of Power: National Security, the Truman Administration, and the Cold War* (Stanford: Stanford University Press, 1992), 312-60. For the implications in Asia, see Bruce Cuming's essay, "Introduction: The Course of Korean-American Relations, 1943-1953," in *Child of Conflict: The Korean-American Relationship, 1943-1953*, ed. Bruce Cumings, 3-55 (Seattle: University of Washington Press, 1983).
25 See *NSC-68*, 6-20, passim.
26 *NSC-68*, ibid., 56-57.
27 Steven Casey, "Selling NSC-68: The Truman Administration, Public Opinion, and the Politics of Mobilization, 1950-1951," *Diplomatic History* 29, 4 (2005): 655-90.
28 As cited in Walter LaFeber, *America, Russia and the Cold War, 1945-1984* (New York: Alfred A. Knopf, 1985), 98.
29 Lester Pearson, *Mike: The Memoirs of the Right Honourable Lester B. Pearson*, vol. 2, *1948-1957*, ed. John A. Munro and Alex I. Inglis (Toronto: University of Toronto Press, 1973), 145.
30 Canadian Ambassador to SSEA, 13 January 1950, LAC, RG 25, vol. 6031, 50293-40, pt. 1-1, 1.
31 Ibid., 2.
32 Ibid., 3.
33 See Statement Issued by the President, 27 June 1950, *United States Department of State, Foreign Relations of the United States* (hereafter *FRUS*), vol. 7, 1950, Korea (Washington, DC: US Government Printing Office, 1972), 202-3.
34 Pearson's response is in extract from memorandum from Secretary of State for External Affairs to Prime Minister, 27 June and 4 July 1950, Greg Donaghy, ed., *Documents on Canadian External Relations* (hereafter *DCER*), vol. 16, *1950*, ed. G. Donaghy (Ottawa: Canada Communication Group, 1995), 22.
35 For another view on the issue, see Graeme S. Mount, with Andre Laferriere, *The Diplomacy of War: The Case of Korea* (Montreal: Black Rose Books, 2004).
36 See Greg Donaghy, "Pacific Diplomacy: Canadian Statecraft and the Korean War, 1950-53," in *Canada and Korea: Perspectives 2000*, ed. Rick Guisso and Yong-Sik Yoo (Toronto: University of Toronto Press and the Centre for Korean Studies, 2002), 83. The most comprehensive history of Canada's involvement in Korea remains

Denis Stairs, *The Diplomacy of Constraint* (Toronto: University of Toronto Press, 1974). See, more recently, Steven Hugh Lee's *Outposts of Empire* (Montreal and Kingston: McGill-Queen's University Press, 1995.

37 For details see Korean veterans site, http://www.kvacanada.com/, and the Canadian government synopsis at http://www.canadainternational.gc.ca/.

38 Edgar Wickberg, ed., *From China to Canada: A History of the Chinese Community in Canada* (Toronto: McClelland and Stewart, 1982), 227-28.

39 As reprinted in the *Canadian Unionist,* October 1950, 265.

40 "Minister of Labour's Address," *Trades and Labour Congress Journal* 29, 10 (1950): 35.

41 "65th Convention Liquidates Communism," *Trades and Labour Congress Journal* 29, 10 (1950): 12.

42 ICFTU, "Free Trade Unions Denounce Communist Aggression in Korea," *Information Bulletin,* no. 7, 5 July 1950, 1.

43 ICFTU, as cited in "Free Trade Unions Pledge Continued Support to UN in Korea," *Information Bulletin* 10 (6 September 1950), 2.

44 See Denis Stairs, *The Diplomacy of Constraint* (Toronto: University of Toronto Press, 1974), 110-12.

45 As citied in John English, *Citizen of the World: The Life of Pierre Elliot Trudeau,* vol. 1, *1919-1968* (Toronto: Knopf, 2006), 227.

46 See WILPF, "Brief to the Canadian Government," 28 October 1950, UBC Archives, WILPF Collection, box 5, file 100, 1.

47 The Indian delegation officially abstained in the UN vote, but its opposition was well known, and Lester Pearson was discouraged at his inability to bring India on side (although he blamed the Indian government for the impasse). See Donaghy, "Pacific Diplomacy," 87.

48 Li and Li, *China and the United States,* 27.

49 Canadian Embassy, Nanking to SSEA, 13 September 1950, LAC, RG 25, vol. 6031, 50293-40, pt. 1.2, 1.

50 Extract from Cabinet Conclusions, 9 December 1950, in *DCER,* vol. 16, *1950,* 288.

51 Joint Planning Committee, "War in Korea, Extension of Military Operations to Chinese Territory," LAC, MG 31, ser. E46, vol. 29, pt. 17, 3.

52 Chiefs of Staff Committee, "War in Korea," n.d., LAC, MG 31, ser. E46, vol. 29, pt. 17.

53 For details of Lovestone's activities and collaboration with the CIA, see Ted Morgan, *A Covert Life: Jay Lovestone, Communist, Anti-Communist and Spymaster* (New York: Random House, 1999). On the Chinese operations specifically, see ibid., 202-9.

54 *Montreal Gazette,* 11 November 1950, 1; and "Memorandum from Defence Liaison Division to Under-Secretary of State for External Affairs," 11 November 1950, in *DCER,* vol. 16, *1950,* 1479-80.

55 The truth is recorded in a conversation between Hume Wrong and an official of the US Secretary of State. See "Memorandum of Conversation with Special Assistant to Secretary of State of United States," 2 December 1950, *DCER,* vol. 16, *1950,* 1488-89.

56 Ibid., 1488.

57 Menzies to External Affairs, 21 December 1950, LAC, RG 25, 92-93/002, vol. 7, 7-1-3-1 pt. 1, 1.
58 Ibid., 2.
59 Ibid., 4.
60 Pearson to the Prime Minister, 18 December 1950, LAC, RG 25, vol. 4758, 50069-9-40, 1.
61 Ibid., 2.
62 Memorandum to Cabinet, 28 December 1950, LAC, RG 25, vol. 4758, 50069-9-40, 1.
63 Ibid.
64 External Affairs to Menzies, 29 December 1950, LAC, RG 25, 92-93/002, vol. 7, 7-1-3-1 pt. 1, 1.
65 Ibid., 2.
66 Ibid.
67 See Mark Atwood Lawrence, *Assuming the Burden: Europe and the American Commitment to War in Vietnam* (Berkeley: University of California Press, 2005), 256-57.
68 L.S. St. Laurent, "The Preservation of Civilization," 27 October 1950, no. 50/43, Information Division, Department of External Affairs.
69 Ibid., 4.
70 Ibid., 5.
71 L.B. Pearson, "Canadian Foreign Policy in a Two-Power World," Statements and Speeches, no. 51/14, Information Division, Department of External Affairs.
72 Ibid., 2.
73 L.B. Pearson, "Communism and the Peace Campaign," 20 April 1951, Statements and Speeches, no. 51/17, Information Division, Department of External Affairs, 2.
74 Ibid., 2.
75 Ibid., 4.
76 Ibid., 8.
77 For Endicott's story, see Stephen Endicott, *James G. Endicott: Rebel out of China* (Toronto: University of Toronto Press, 1980); and Reg Whitaker and Gary Marcuse, *Cold War Canada* (Toronto: University of Toronto Press, 1994), 365-83.
78 See Whitaker and Marcuse, *Cold War Canada*, for in-depth treatment of the effects of the Cold War on Canadians.
79 Memorandum for Mr. Reid, 5 March 1951, LAC, RG 25, acc. 92-93/002, vol. 7, file 7-1-3-1, pt. 1.
80 Chen, *China's Road to the Korean War*, 93.
81 Ibid., 93-95.
82 Escott Reid for Pearson, to Hume Wrong, 7 April 1951 (not sent), LAC, RG 25, vol. 4758, 50069-9-40, 3.
83 Laura Belmonte, "Anglo-American Relations and the Dismissal of MacArthur," *Diplomatic History* 19, 4 (1995): 662.
84 Ibid., 665.
85 As cited in Stephen Hugh Lee, *The Korean War* (Harlow, UK: Pearson Education, 2001), 83.
86 "Ridgeway Claims US Doesn't Know What War Is," *Montreal Gazette*, 14 May 1951.

87 Early reports on the bombing suggested that "the Reds staged the bombing themselves for propaganda purposes." See "Air Bombing of Kaesong 'Not by UN,'" *Vancouver Sun*, 1 September 1951. On 12 September, UN High Commander General Ridgeway admitted that a plane from the 3rd Bomber Command had attacked Kaesong "through an error of navigation." See "Allies Admit Plane Strafed 'Truce City,'" *Vancouver Sun*, 11 September 1951.
88 For details on Koje, see Stairs, *Diplomacy of Constraint*, 246-59.
89 Chen, *China's Road to the Korean War*, 111.
90 Accounts of Mackenzie's story may be found in Ted Barris, *Deadlock in Korea: Canadians at War, 1950-1953* (Toronto: Macmillan, 1999), 274-76, 285; and John Melady, *Korea: Canada's Forgotten War* (Toronto: Macmillan, 1983), 119-22, 127-32.
91 Canadian Press report, 10 February 1955, Canadian Press Archives, 155-6-93.
92 Ibid., 155-6-94.
93 General Hong Xuezhi, deputy commander of the CPV forces and head of logistics throughout the Korean War, states that US planes bombed northeast China beginning in late August 1950, targeting Andong, Ji'an, and other regions. See Hong Xuezhi, *Kangmei yuanchao zhanzheng huiyi* [Recollections of the war to resist America and aid Korea] (Beijing: PLA Literature Press, 1992), excerpts of which are translated in Xiaobing Li, Allan R. Millett, and Bin Yu, trans. and eds., *Mao's Generals Remember Korea* (Lawrence: University Press of Kansas, 2001), 114.
94 Pearson to Hume Wrong, 29 May 1952, LAC, RG 25, 92-93/002, vol. 7, 7-1-3-1, pt. 1.
95 Wrong to Pearson, 5 June 1952, LAC, RG 25, 92-93/002, vol. 7, 7-1-3-1, pt. 1, 3.
96 See LAC, RG 25, vol. 5984, file 50267-40, pt. 3-1.
97 For further details, see Roger Bowen, *Innocence Is Not Enough* (Vancouver: Douglas and McIntyre, 1986), chaps 6 and 7.
98 As cited in Escott Reid, *Radical Mandarin: The Memoirs of Escott Reid* (Toronto: University of Toronto Press, 1989), 260.
99 Ibid., 261.
100 "Statement by L.B. Pearson," 26 January 1951, no. 51/2, Statements and Speeches, Department of External Affairs, 8.
101 Ibid., 10.
102 Pearson, *Mike*, 2:170.
103 John Hilliker and Donald Barry, *Canada's Department of External Affairs* (Montreal and Kingston: McGill-Queen's University Press, 1995), 2:47-48; Escott Reid, *Radical Mandarin: The Memoirs of Escott Reid* (Toronto: University of Toronto Press, 1989), 242-43.
104 Hilliker and Barry, *Canada's Department of External Affairs*, 88.
105 L.B. Pearson, "Canadian Foreign Policy in a Two-Power World," Statements and Speeches, no. 51/14, Information Division, Department of External Affairs, 6.
106 Escott Reid, memorandum for Mr. R.M. Macdonnell, 10 September 1952, LAC, MG 31, E46, vol. 7, no. 16, 201.1, 1.
107 As cited in Escott Reid, memorandum for Mr. R.M. Macdonnell: Re-Examination of Canadian Foreign Policy, Policy Papers 1951-1952, LAC, MG 31, E46, no. 16, 201.1, 1.

CHAPTER 11: THE SAN FRANCISCO PEACE TREATY

1 The origins and development of the corporate agenda is meticulously documented in Howard Schonberger, *Aftermath of War* (Kent: Kent State University Press, 1989).

2 Miyazawa Kiichi, *Tokyo-wasinton no mitsudan* [The Tokyo-Washington secret talks] (Tokyo: Chūō Kōronsha, 1999), 40.

3 For details, see Koyama Kōtake and Shimizu Shinzō, *Nihon shakaitō shi* [History of Japanese Socialist Party] (Kyoto: Hōka shoten, 1965); and J.A.A. Stockwin, *The Japanese Socialist Party and Neutralism* (London: Melbourne University Press, 1968).

4 Takemae Eiji, *GHQ* [General Headquarters] (Tokyo: Iwanami shoten, 1985), 203.

5 Hiratsuka Raichō et al., "Hibusōkoku nihon josei no kōwa mondai ni tsuite no yōkō" [An outline of peace issues by women in a demilitarized Japan], in Hiratsuka Raichō chosakushū henshū iinkai, *Hiratsuka raichō chosakushū dai 7 kan* [Collected works of Hiratsuka Raichō, vol. 7] (Tokyo: Ōtsuki shoten, 1984), 101-2.

6 Sebald to Allison, 24 March 1950, *Foreign Relations of the United States* (hereafter *FRUS*), vol. 6, *1950* (Washington, DC: Government Printing Office, 1972), 1154.

7 Pearson's remarks on the peace treaty during the Colombo Conference are contained in Robin Kay, *Documents on New Zealand External Relations,* vol. 3, *The ANZUS Pact and the Treaty of Peace with Japan* (Wellington: Historical Branch, Department of Internal Affairs, 1985), 305-7. Pearson's report about the conference is contained in *Documents on Canadian External Relations* (hereafter *DCER*), vol. 16, *1950,* ed. G. Donaghy (Ottawa: Canada Communication Group, 1996), 1196.

8 SSEA to High Commissioner in United Kingdom, 22 April 1950, in *DCER, 1950,* vol. 16, 1814.

9 Ibid.

10 SSEA Permanent Representative to United Nations, 13 October 1950, in *DCER,* vol. 16, *1950,* 1834-36.

11 Japanese sources on the peace treaty include Nishimura Kumao, *Sanfuransisuko heiwa joyaku, nichibei ampo joyaku* [The San Francisco Peace Treaty and US-Japan Security Treaty] (Tokyo: Chuo koron shinsha, 1999); Murakawa Ichirō, *Daresu to Yoshida Shigeru* [Dulles and Yoshida Shigeru] (Tokyo: Kokusho kankō kai, 1991); Miura Yōichi, *Yoshida Shigeru to san furanshisuko kōwa* [Yoshida Shigeru and the San Francisco Pact], vol. 2. In English, see Michael Schaller, *Altered States: The United States and Japan since the Occupation* (New York and Oxford: Oxford University Press, 1997), and *The American Occupation of Japan* (New York: Oxford University Press, 1985); Seigen Miyasato, "John Foster Dulles and the Peace Settlement with Japan," in *John Foster Dulles and the Diplomacy of the Cold War,* ed. Richard H. Immerman, 189-212 (Princeton: Princeton University Press, 1990); and Walter LaFeber, *The Clash: US-Japanese Relations throughout History* (New York: W.W. Norton, 1997).

12 Memorandum of conversation, 23 April 1951, *FRUS,* vol. 6, *1951,* pt. 1, 985.

13 "Editorial Note," *FRUS,* vol. 6, *1951,* pt. 1, 825.

14 *FRUS,* vol. 6, *1951,* pt. 1, 881-82.

15 Memorandum by Mr. Robert A. Fearey of the Office of Northeast Asian Affairs, 7 February 1951, *FRUS,* vol. 6, *1951,* pt. 1, 865.

16 *FRUS,* vol. 6, *1951,* pt. 1, 901.
17 Provisional United States draft of a Japanese Peace Treaty, *FRUS,* vol. 6, *1951,* pt. 1, 944-50.
18 Memorandum regarding the Japanese Peace Treaty, 10 April 1951, LAC, RG 25, vol. 4615, file 50051-40, pt. 11, 1.
19 Ibid.
20 Ibid., 2.
21 Enclosure to "Note," 18 May 1951, *DCER,* vol. 17, *1951,* ed. G. Donaghy (Ottawa: Canada Communication Group, 1990), 1807-16.
22 Ibid., 1808.
23 Ibid., 1816-22.
24 Memorandum for the Under-Secretary, 23 May 1951, LAC, RG 25, vol. 4615, file 50051-40, pt. 12, 1.
25 High Commissioner for Canada, London to SSEA, 14 June 1951, LAC, RG 25, vol. 4615, file 50051-40, pt. 12, 1-3.
26 C.S. Ronning, memorandum for the minister, 14 June 1951, LAC, RG 25, vol. 4615, file 50051-40, pt. 12, 2.
27 SSEA to Ambassador in United States, 11 July 1951, *DCER,* vol. 17, *1951,* 1823.
28 Ambassador in United States to Secretary of State for External Affairs, 13 July 1951, *DCER,* vol. 17, *1951,* 1825.
29 Memorandum of conversation, 9 July 1951, *FRUS,* vol. 6, *1951,* pt. 1, 1182-83.
30 For details, see Sung-Hwa Cheong, *The Politics of Anti-Japanese Sentiment in Korea: Japanese-South Korean Relations under American Occupation, 1945-1952* (New York: Greenwood Press, 1991), 92-93.
31 France pressed for the inclusion of the Associated States. See memorandum of conversation, 11 June 1951, *FRUS,* vol. 6, *1951,* pt. 1, 1115. The United States and Great Britain agreed to their participation after a formula was found whereby co-signing of the treaty would not infer diplomatic recognition since some states still did not recognize the Associated States. See Secretary, Office of the High Commissioner for the United Kingdom, to the Department of External Affairs, 21 August 1951, *Documents on New Zealand External Relations* (hereafter *DNZER*) (Wellington: Government Printer, 1985), 3:1110.
32 Memorandum of conversation, 19 July 1951, *FRUS,* vol. 6, *1951,* pt. 1, 1204.
33 Ibid.
34 Memorandum from Secretary of State for External Affairs to Cabinet, 27 July 1951, *DCER,* vol. 17, *1951,* 1826.
35 Ibid., 1827. Norman's involvement in the crafting of this memorandum is not clear. On 26 June he had been assigned as acting permanent representative to the United Nations, replacing John Holmes.
36 Memorandum from USSEA (Under-Secretary of State) to SSEA, 8 August 1951, *DCER,* vol. 17, *1951,* 1829.
37 Ibid., 1830.
38 Ibid.
39 Ministry of Foreign Affairs of the Central People's Government of the People's Republic of China to Department of External Affairs, 16 August 1951, *DNZER,* 3:1092.

40 Ibid., 1095.
41 Points 1 to 4 are based on *DNZER*, 3:1095.
42 Memorandum for SSEA to Cabinet, 21 August 1951, *DCER*, vol. 17, *1951*, 1832-33.
43 The Indian Charge (Kirpalani) to the Consultant to the Secretary of State, 23 August 1951, *FRUS*, vol. 6, *1951*, pt. 1, notes 1-14, 1288-91.
44 SSEA to Ambassador in US, September 1951, *DCER*, vol. 17, *1951*, 1497.
45 Dean Rusk made the link explicit in a memorandum to Romulo the day before the treaty signing. See Assistant Secretary of State for Far Eastern Affairs (Rusk) to the Secretary of Foreign Affairs of the Philippines (Romulo), 29 August 1951, *FRUS*, vol. 6, *1951*, pt. 1, 250.
46 See Akira Iriye, *Japan and the Wider World: From the Mid-Nineteenth Century to the Present* (London: Longman, 1997), chap. 9.
47 "Japanese to Korea?" *Vancouver Sun*, 6 September 1951.
48 As cited in Cheong, *Politics of Anti-Japanese Sentiment*, 82.
49 Carlos Romulo in *Conference for the Conclusion and Signature of the Treaty of Peace with Japan, Record of Proceedings* (Washington, DC: Department of State, 1951), 230-31.
50 Memorandum of conversation, 3 September 1951, *FRUS*, vol. 6, *1951*, pt. 1, 1320-23.
51 Ibid., 1337.
52 Ibid., 1324.
53 Ibid., 1333.
54 *Conference for the Conclusion*, 197.
55 Ibid., 231.
56 Pearson's speech is recorded in ibid., 215-19.
57 Ibid., 218.
58 Ibid.
59 "After the Peace Treaty," *Vancouver Sun*, 5 September 1951.
60 This account of the Vancouver meeting is based on the *Vancouver Sun*, 10 September 1951.
61 E.H. Norman, "Notes by Head, American and Far Eastern Division, for Heads of Divisions Meeting," 17 September 1951, *DCER*, vol. 17, *1951*, 1836.
62 E.H. Norman, "Japan since Surrender," n.d., in *Historical and Political Writings [MSS] by Herbert Norman* (compiled by Ōkubo Genji and held as part of the E. Herbert Norman Papers, Special Collections and University Archives, University of British Columbia). This thirteen-page overview of the Occupation was translated into Japanese and included in Ōkubo Genji ed., *Hābāto nōman zenshū, dai 2 kan* [Complete works of Herbert Norman, vol. 2] (Tokyo: Iwanami shoten, 1977), 419-32. According to Okubo, Norman's wife Irene gave him this article, which he dates as having been written in February 1953, probably for use as an official background paper for the government or possibly as a presentation.
63 For the draft letter, see *FRUS*, vol. 6, *1951*, pt. 2, 1445. For the letter signed by Yoshida, see ibid., 1466-67.
64 See memorandum by the Consultant to the Secretary (Dulles) to the Secretary of State, 26 December 1951, *FRUS*, vol. 6, *1951*, pt. 2, 1467-70. Dulles would become the next US secretary of state.

65 Memorandum for the minister, 23 January 1952, LAC, RG 25, vol. 3651, file 4606-C-14, pt. 1)
66 Ibid. Pearson's comments are handwritten on Norman's memo but were later transcribed for inclusion in a memo to Hume Wrong.
67 Canadian Ambassador to United States to SSEA, 26 January 1952, LAC, RG 25, vol. 3651, file 4606-C-14, pt. 1, 1.
68 SSEA to Canadian Ambassador, 6 February 1952, LAC, RG 25, vol. 3651, file 4606-C-14, pt. 1, 2.
69 Canadian Ambassador to the United States to SSEA, 14 February 1952, LAC, RG 25, vol. 3651, file 4606-C-14, pt. 1, 1.
70 Lester Pearson, memorandum of a conversation with Mr. John Foster Dulles, March 14, 15 March 1952, LAC, RG 25, vol. 6031, file 50293-40, pt. 2.2.
71 On regional impacts and territorial issues, see Kimie Hara, *Japanese-Soviet/Russian Relations since 1945: A Difficult Peace* (London: Routledge, 1998); Hara, *Sanfuranshisuko heiwajoyaku no moten: Ajia taiheiyo chiiki no reisen to "sengo mikaiketsu no shomondai"* [Blind spots of the San Francisco Peace Treaty: Re-thinking the cold war in the Asia-Pacific region and the "unresolved problems" since the Second World War] (Hiroshima: Keisui-sha, 2005); and Hara, *Cold War Frontiers in the Asia-Pacific: Divided Territories in the San Francisco System* (London: Routledge, 2007).
72 Yoshida Shigeru, *Japan's Decisive Century, 1867-1967* (New York: Praeger, 1967), 81.

CHAPTER 12: RACISM, WAR CRIMES, AND THE KOREAN WAR

1 Interview with Shin Hyun-can and Park Chong-Soon, Hwang Bang-li village, Yangjun County, Kyongi Province, Korea, 6 April 2004. My deepest appreciation to Kim Gwi-Ok and Chong Ae-Yu for their assistance in locating Shin's family, in travelling to the village, and in interpreting during the interview.
2 Interview with Kim Dong-choon, Seoul, Korea, October 2003
3 Sang-Hun Choe, Martha Mendoza, and Charles J. Hanley, *The Bridge at No Gun Ri: A Hidden Nightmare from the Korean War* (New York: Henry Holt, 2001).
4 As cited in ibid., 122-23.
5 Department of the Army, Inspector General, *No Gun Ri Review* (January 2001) available at http://www.army.mil/nogunri/.
6 Ibid., xiv.
7 Muccio to Rusk, 26 July 1950, as cited in Sahr Conway-Lanz, "Beyond No Gun Ri: Refugees and the United States Military in the Korean War," *Diplomatic History* 29, 1 (2005): 59.
8 Bill Boss, wire copy, Canadian Press Archives (hereafter CPA), Korea War File 155 [3]-85.
9 Bill Boss, "Local Soldier on Trial for Murder of Korean Civilian," *Moncton Transcript*, 15 December 1951 (CPA, Korea War File, 155 [3]-84).
10 Bill Boss, *Saint John Telegraph Journal*, 18 December 1951 (CPA, Korean War File, 155 [3]-85).
11 Bill Boss, "Contradictory Evidence Heard at Court Martial," *St. John Telegraph*, 17 December 1951 (CPA, Korea War File 155 [3]-84).
12 "Convicted Soldier Freed by Ottawa," Canadian Press, 14 June 1952.

13 Canadian Press Files, 155 (3)-17, "Court Martials Planned under Canadian Board."
14 "The Censorship That Helps the Enemy," *Maclean's*, 15 October 1951.
15 See Chris Madsen, *Another Kind of Justice: Canadian Military Law from Confederation to Somalia* (Vancouver: UBC Press, 1999), 109-10.
16 Brent Watson, *Far Eastern Tour: The Canadian Infantry in Korea, 1950-1953* (Montreal and Kingston: McGill-Queen's University Press, 2002), 171-74.
17 Canadian Press files, 155 (4)-84.
18 Watson, *Far Eastern Tour*, 172.
19 The veterans organized to construct a wall of remembrance in 1997. See Ted Barris, *Deadlock in Korea: Canadians at War, 1950-1953* (Toronto: Macmillan, 1999), 290-97.
20 Based on a Bill Boss report, Canadian Press files, 135 (3)-36.
21 See George Barrett, *Globe and Mail*, 21 August 1951, Canadian Press files, 155 (3)-18.
22 Pierre Berton, "The Real War in Korea," *Maclean's*, 1 August 1951, 2. Berton recounts his experiences in more detail in his autobiography *My Times: Living with History, 1947-1995* (Toronto: Seal Edition, 1996), 78-103.
23 Ibid., 96.
24 Ibid., 100.
25 "Correspondent Raps Integration of Army," *Vancouver Sun*, 7 September 1951.
26 Elmore Philpott, "Bill Boss Warns West," *Vancouver Sun*, 6 September 1951.
27 For individual reports on the trip, see LAC, MG 32, B5, vol. 97, 25CDN Infantry Brigade.
28 Frank Lowe, "Reports Koreans Mistreated by Canadians Declared False," *Montreal Daily Star*, 22 November 1951.
29 As cited by Watson, *Far Eastern Tour*, 50.
30 Retired parliamentarian Margaret Mitchell, who worked in Korea in 1953-54, provides further evidence of the systemic nature of the problem in her observation: "[Many of the soldiers] hated the country and the people, and counted the days and hours until they could either go home or go on leave to Japan. I hated their racist attitudes, and cringed when they called the Koreans 'gooks.'" See Margaret Mitchell, *No Laughing Matter: Adventure, Activism and Politics* (Vancouver: Granville Island Publishing, 2008), 22.
31 Lt.-Col. Herbert Fairlie Wood, *Strange Battleground: Official History of the Canadian Army in Korea* (Ottawa: Queen's Printer, 1966), 101.
32 *8th Cavalry Regiment Journal*, as reproduced in Choe et al., *Bridge at No Gun Ri*, 6 (photographic plates).
33 Ibid., 75.
34 Ibid.
35 As cited in Choe et al., *Bridge at No Gun Ri*, 208.
36 "Kill Any Man in Red Areas, Airmen Told," Canadian Press file, 155 (2)-4.
37 Ted Barris, *Deadlock in Korea: Canadians at War, 1950-53* (Toronto: Macmillan, 1999), 84.
38 As cited in Conrad C. Crane, *American Airpower Strategy in Korea, 1950-1953* (Lawrence: University of Kansas Press, 2000), 32.

39 Ibid., 44.
40 Ibid., 46.
41 The first thorough analysis of the bombing campaign is found in Callum A. MacDonald, *Korea: The War before Vietnam* (New York: The Free Press, 1986). Much of Crane's later study confirms the MacDonald research.
42 As cited in Michael Schaller, *Douglas MacArthur: The Far Eastern General* (New York: Oxford University Press, 1989), 209.
43 George Barrett, "US Hell Buggies Shell Seoul from Seven Miles," *Globe and Mail*, 12 February 1951.
44 Lester Pearson to Hume Wrong, 2 March 1951, LAC, MG 26 N1, vol. 17, Wrong, H.H., 1948-1953, 1.
45 Hume Wrong to Lester Pearson, 7 March 1951, LAC, MG 26 N1, vol. 17, Wrong, H.H., 1948-1953, 1.
46 As cited in David Jay Bercuson, *True Patriot: The Life of Brooke Claxton, 1898-1960* (Toronto: University of Toronto Press, 1993), 224.
47 As cited in MacDonald, *Korea*, 235.
48 This campaign is described in James I. Matray, *Historical Dictionary of the Korean War* (New York: Greenwood Press, 1991), 12-13, but his description leaves the impression that indiscriminate bombing only began in July 1952 and that, prior to this, the air force had been restricted to providing tactical support for ground troops.
49 As cited in MacDonald, *Korea*, 241.
50 Stephen Endicott, *Rebel out of China* (Toronto: University of Toronto Press, 1980), 291.
51 For analysis of the Soviet documents, see Milton Leitenberg, "New Russian Evidence on the Korean War Biological Warfare Allegations: Background and Analysis," and Kathryn Weathersby, "Deceiving the Deceivers: Moscow, Beijing, Pyongyang, and the Allegations of Bacteriological Weapons Use in Korea," both in *Cold War International History Project*, Bulletin 11 (winter 1998), available at http://www.wilsoncenter.org/.
52 See Stephen Endicott and Edward Hagerman, *The United States and Biological Warfare: Secrets of the Early Cold War and Korea* (Bloomington: Indiana University Press, 1998); and Endicott and Hagerman, "Twelve Newly Released Soviet-Era 'Documents' and Allegations of US Germ Warfare during the Korean War," *Asian Perspective* 25, 1 (2001): 249-57 (also on internet H-Diplo, 5 July 1999).
53 For information on the British response, see Tom Buchanan, "The Courage of Galileo: Joseph Needham and the 'Germ Warfare' Allegations in the Korean War," *History* 86, 284 (2001): 507-22.
54 As cited in Department of External Affairs, minutes, 19 May 1952, LAC, RG 25, vol. 2137, ser. B-3, 1951-China, pt. 2-April.
55 Reg Whittaker and Gary Marcuse, *Cold War Canada: The Making of a National Insecurity State, 1945-1957* (Toronto: University of Toronto Press, 1994), 376.
56 E.S. McDougall to L.B. Pearson, 15 June 1952, LAC, RG 25, vol. 5920, file 50208-40, pt. 2-2.
57 Escott Reid, memorandum for the minister, 15 May 1952, LAC, RG 25, vol. 5919, file 50208-40, pt. 1.2.

58 Escott Reid, memorandum for Mr. Freifeld, 6 May 1952, LAC, RG 25, vol. 5919, file 50208-40, pt. 1.2.

59 The abridged version is entitled *Report of the International Scientific Commission for the Investigation of the Facts Concerning Bacterial Warfare in Korea and China* (Prague: Hsinhua News Agency, n.d.).

60 John Bryden, *Deadly Allies: Canada's Secret War, 1937-1947* (Toronto: McClelland and Stewart, 1989); Donald H. Avery, *The Science of War: Canadian Scientists and Allied Military Technology during the Second World War* (Toronto: University of Toronto Press, 1998).

61 Chiefs of Staff Committee, minutes of 298th meeting, 25 August 1944, LAC, RG 24, vol. 8082, file 11272-2, 7, 3.

62 George W. Merck to Harvey H. Bundy, 14 December 1944, LAC, RG 25, vol. 5919, file 50208-40, pt. 1-1.

63 C.J. Mackenzie to R.M. Macdonnell, 28 December 1944, LAC, RG 25, vol. 5919, file 50208-40, pt. 1-1.

64 R.M. Macdonnell to General G.V. Henry, 2 January 1946, LAC, RG 25, vol. 5919, file 50208-40, pt. 1-1.

65 O. Maass to Mjr. J.C. Bond, 24 January 1949 and enclosure, McGill University Archives, MG 1050, Otto Maass C.2, box 2104c.

66 Telephone conversation between Dr. O. Maass and Gen. A. Waitt, 22 January 1949, McGill University Archives, MG 1050, Otto Maass C.2, box 2104c.

67 Joint Publications Research Service, *Moscow Daily Press Summary*, 20 May 1950, 4.

68 David Stansfield to Arthur Menzies, 25 May 1950, LAC, RG 25, vol. 6196, file 4060-C-40, pt. 4.3.

69 Other studies include Robert Harris and Jeremy Paxman, *A Higher Form of Killing: The Secret History of Chemical and Biological Warfare* (New York: Random House, 2002); and Brian Balmer, *Britain and Biological Warfare: Expert Advice and Science Policy, 1930-65* (Basingstoke: Palgrave, 2001).

70 Chiefs of Staff Committee, minutes of a special meeting, 3 July 1950, LAC, RG 25, vol. 5919, file 50208-40, pt. 1.1, 1.

71 G.B. Reed, Canadian views on BW, 27 June 1950, LAC, RG 25, vol. 5919, file 50208-40, pt. 1.1, 1.

72 Ibid., 2.

73 H.G. Richards to Chief of the Air Staff, 25 October 1951, LAC, RG 24F, vol. 4220, file 700-900-267-1, 1.

74 A.L. Wright to Chairman, Defence Research Board, 7 December 1951, LAC, RG 24F, vol. 4220, file 700-900-267-1, 1.

CHAPTER 13: VIETNAM

1 Memorandum from Acting Secretary of State for External Affairs to Cabinet, 1 November 1952, *Documents on Canadian External Relations* (hereafter *DCER*), vol. 18, *1952*, ed. D. Barry (Ottawa: Canada Communication Group, 1990), 1552-55.

2 Ibid., 1552.

3 Ibid., 1553.

4 Ibid., 1554.

5 Memorandum from Under-Secretary of State for External Affairs to Secretary of State for External Affairs, 24 December 1952, *DCER*, vol. 18, *1952*, 1556-57.
6 The best source on Chinese influence in Vietnam in this period is Quiang Zhai, *China and the Vietnam Wars, 1950-1975* (Chapel Hill: University of North Carolina Press, 2000).
7 On the Bao Dai solution, see Steven Hugh Lee, *Outposts of Empire: Korea, Vietnam and the Origins of the Cold War in Asia, 1949-1954* (Montreal and Kingston: McGill-Queen's University Press, 1995), 43-54.
8 See Frederick Logevall, *The Origins of the Vietnam War* (Essex: Pearson Education, 2001), 16-22; and James S. Olson and Randy Roberts, *Where the Domino Fell: America and Vietnam* (New York: St. Martin's Press, 1991), chap. 2.
9 See George C. Herring, *America's Longest War: The United States and Vietnam, 1950-1975,* 4th ed. (Boston: McGraw-Hill, 2002), 38-39.
10 As cited in ibid., 40.
11 The official account of conference proceedings is *The 1954 Geneva Conference: Indo-China and Korea* (New York: Greenwood Press, 1968), combining "Documents relating to the Discussion of Korea and Indo-China at the Geneva Conference, April 27-June 15, 1954" and "Further Documents relating to the discussion of Indo-China at the Geneva Conference, June 16-July 21, 1954," originally issued in June and August 1954, respectively (London: Her Majesty's Stationery Office, n.d.).
12 According to Ilya V. Gaiduk, *Confronting Vietnam: Soviet Policy toward the Indochina Conflict, 1954-1963* (Stanford: Stanford University Press, 2003), this was Molotov's swan song as a Soviet diplomat.
13 Transcript, "Press Conference, New Delhi," 24 February 1954, LAC, MG 31, E46, vol. 29, 29-12, 8.
14 CANDEL, Paris to SSEA, 22 April 1954, LAC, MG 26, Indochina, 1954-57, 3.
15 See Ramesh Thakur, *Peacekeeping in Vietnam: Canada, India, Poland, and the International Commission* (Edmonton: University of Alberta Press, 1984), chap. 2.
16 Holmes recounts his Geneva experience in John Holmes, "Geneva: 1954," *International Journal* 22, 3 (1967): 457-83; and also in Holmes, *The Shaping of Peace*, vol. 1, *Canada and the Search for World Order, 1943-1957* (Toronto: University of Toronto Press, 1979). Pearson's autobiography does not include anything on Geneva.
17 Pearson to St. Laurent, 6 May 1954, LAC, MG 26, Indochina, 1954-57, 1.
18 Liu Guangtai, *Langning Zhuan* [Biography of Chester Ronning] (Shijiazhuang: Hebei Education Publishing House, 1999), 313.
19 This account is disputed by Wang Bingnan, who said it "couldn't have happened," and that, "in the memoirs of several Americans, including Nixon and Kissinger, it [wasn't] mentioned." See Wang Bingnan, *Zhong-Mei Huitan Jiunian Huigu* [Reminiscences of nine years of China-US talks] (Beijing: World Knowledge Publishing House, 1985),
20 Pearson to St. Laurent, 6 May 1954, LAC, MG 26, Indochina, 1954-57, 3.
21 Ibid., 4.
22 Ibid., 2.
23 Dominion London to DomCan, The Hague, 17 May 1954, LAC, MG 26, Indochina, 1954-57, 1.
24 Ibid., 2.

25 Interview with General Bedell Smith, 20 May 1954, LAC, MG 26, Indochina, 1954-57, 5.
26 Ibid., 4.
27 For Pearson's 4 May speech and Ronning's 11 June presentation, see *1954 Geneva Conference*, 31-34, and 79-84, respectively.
28 There were separate agreements for each of the three countries: Cambodia, Laos, and Vietnam.
29 One perspective is reflected in Chen Jian, *Mao's China and the Cold War* (Chapel Hill and London: University of North Carolina Press, 2001), 141-44, while another is reflected in William J. Duiker, *Ho Chi Minh: A Life* (New York: Hyperion, 2000), 458-61.
30 "Indochina: Krishna Menon's Views," 30 June 1954, LAC, MG 26, N-1, vol. 34.
31 Liu Guangtai, *Langning Zhuan*, 314.
32 Memorandum, 30 June 1954, LAC, MG 26, Indochina, 1954-57, 1.
33 Ibid., 3.
34 Memorandum, 20 July 1954, LAC, MG 26, Indochina, 1954-57, 3.
35 This interpretation challenges Douglas Ross's thesis that Canadian policy was a floating mean between alliance with the US anti-communist containment program and sympathy towards new, left-wing, nationalist, anti-colonialist governments such as India. See Douglas A. Ross, *In the Interests of Peace: Canada and Vietnam, 1954-73* (Toronto: University of Toronto Press, 1984), 42.
36 "Establishment of the International Commissions for the Supervision and Control," 28 July 1954, *DCER,* vol. 20, *1954*, ed. G. Donaghy and P. Kelly (Ottawa: Canada Communication Group, 1997). See Foreign Affairs and International Trade Canada, http://www.dfait-maeci.gc.ca/.
37 As cited in James Eayrs, *In Defence of Canada,* vol. 5, *Indochina: Roots of Complicity* (Toronto: University of Toronto Press, 1983), 53.
38 According to Holmes, *Shaping of Peace*, 414.
39 Chargé d'affaires, Washington to External Affairs, 19 August 1954, LAC, RG 25, vol. 4625, 50052-A-40, pt. 2.
40 Tran Thi Lien, "The Catholic Question in North Vietnam: From Polish Sources, 1954-56," *Cold War History* 5, 4 (2005): 427-49.
41 See Thakur, *Peacekeeping in Vietnam*, 135.
42 Delegatio Apostolica to Honourable Lester Pearson, 1 September 1954, LAC, RG 25, vol. 4625, 50052-A-40, pt. 2.
43 Lester Pearson to Giovanni Panico, 7 September 1954, LAC, RG 25, vol. 4625, 50052-A-40, pt. 2.
44 Lansdale's autobiography sheds some light on these events. See Edward Lansdale, *In the Midst of Wars: An American's Mission to Southeast Asia* (New York: Harper and Row, 1972).
45 NSC 5429/2 was adopted on 12 August 1954 and approved by Eisenhower on 20 August.
46 As cited in Seth Jacobs, *America's Miracle Man in Vietnam: Ngo Dinh Diem, Religion, Race and US Intervention in Southeast Asia* (Durham: Duke University Press, 2004), 135.

47 Jacobs, *America's Miracle Man*, 132.
48 Thomas A. Dooley, *Deliver Us from Evil: The Story of Vietnam's Flight to Freedom* (New York: Farrar, Straus, and Cudahy, 1956).
49 Christina Klein, in her *Cold War Orientalism: Asia in the Middlebrow Imagination, 1945-1961* (Berkeley: University of California Press, 2003), analyzes the changes in postwar Orientalism, suggesting that changes in American attitudes towards race mitigated the extent of Orientalism in the 1950s. I argue in my conclusion that this misconstrues the nature of the changes that took place.
50 *Third Interim Report of the International Commission for Supervision and Control in Vietnam, February 11, 1955 to April 10, 1955*, 25 April 1955 (Hanoi), LAC, MG 26, N-1, vol. 34.
51 Thakur, *Peacekeeping in Vietnam*, 135.
52 Escott Reid, *Radical Mandarin: The Memoirs of Escott Reid* (Toronto: University of Toronto Press, 1989), 277.
53 Jacobs, *America's Miracle Man*, 27-29.
54 Truong Nhu Tang, with David Chanoff and Doan Van Toai, *A Viet Cong Memoir* (New York: Vintage, 1985), 34.
55 See Jacobs, *America's Miracle Man*, chap. 5.
56 Ibid., 209.
57 Olson and Roberts, *Where the Domino Fell*, 60-61.
58 Jacobs, *America's Miracle Man*, 215.
59 For a recent reassessment, see Jessica M. Chapman, "Staging Democracy: South Vietnam's 1955 Referendum to Depose Bao Dai," *Diplomatic History* 30, 4 (2006): 671-703.
60 Jacobs, *America's Miracle Man*, 189.
61 See Thakur, *Peacekeeping in Vietnam*, 141-73.
62 Lett went on to become chief justice in British Columbia. See Reginald H. Roy, *Sherwood Lett: His Life and Times* (Vancouver: UBC Press, 1991).
63 Pearson to Lett, 24 August 1954, Vancouver City Archives, MSS 361, 550-E-1, file 1), 2.
64 Ibid., 4.
65 Canadian Commissioner, Hanoi, to External Affairs, 9 September 1954, LAC, RG 25, vol. 4625, 50052-A-40, pt. 2, 1.
66 Ramesh Thakur provides detailed voting breakdowns in *Peacekeeping in Vietnam*, 178-79.
67 Lett spent Christmas dinner in 1954 with Ho Chi Minh and the leadership of the Viet Minh. "Uncle Ho was at his genial best and saw to it the party was lively," stated Lett in a letter home to his wife. See "O.M." to Missus, 25 December 1954, Vancouver City Archives, MSS 361, 550-E-2, file 1, 4.
68 Hanoi Commissioner to External Affairs, 4 July 1955, LAC, RG 25, vol. 4632, 50052-A-40, pt. B, 2.
69 Ibid., 2.
70 Teletype, Saigon to External, 20 July 1955, LAC, RG 25, vol. 4632, 50052-A-40, pt. 14.
71 Canadian Delegation to External, 22 July 1955, LAC, RG 25, vol. 4632, 50052-A-40, pt. 14.

72 Memorandum summarizing telegram from US ambassador in Saigon, 20 July 1955, LAC, RG 25, vol. 4632, 50052-A-40, pt. 14.
73 "Indochina," 18 February 1954, LAC, MG 26, N1, vol. 34.
74 External Affairs to Heads of Posts Abroad, 8 March 1955, *DCER,* vol. 18, *1955,* 535-36.
75 Diary of Secretary of State for External Affairs, January-February 1955, *DCER,* vol. 18, *1955,* 514.
76 Andrew Preston, "Balancing War and Peace: Canadian Foreign Policy and the Vietnam War, 1961-1965," *Diplomatic History* 27, 1 (2003): 73-111.
77 The key academic works in this regard are Eayrs, *In Defence of Canada*; Victor Levant, *Quiet Complicity: Canadian Involvement in the Vietnam War* (Toronto: Between the Lines, 1986).
78 Douglas A. Ross, *In the Interests of Peace: Canada and Vietnam, 1954-73* (Toronto: University of Toronto Press, 1984), 64.
79 Robert Bothwell, "The Further Shore: Canada and Vietnam," *International Journal* 56, 1 (2000-1): 89.

CONCLUSION

1 Robert Bothwell, *Alliance and Illusion: Canada and the World, 1945-1984* (Vancouver: UBC Press, 2007), 132.
2 Paula S. Rothenberg, *White Privilege: Essential Readings on the Other Side of Racism* (New York: Worth, 2008), 2.
3 For in-depth treatment of this topic, see Andrew F. Cooper, *Canadian Foreign Policy: Old Habits and New Directions* (Scarborough, ON: Prentice Hall, 1997). For Cooper's more recent views, see his "Canadian Foreign Policy after September 11: Patterns of Change and Continuity," in *Canadian Politics,* ed. James Bickerton and Alain Gagnon, 447-66 (Toronto: Broadview Press, 2004).
4 As cited in Emily S. Rosenberg, *A Date Which Will Live: Pearl Harbor in American Memory* (Durham, NC: Duke University Press, 2003), 182.
5 Sophie Bessis, *Western Supremacy: Triumph of an Idea?* (London: Zed Books, 2003), 54-55.
6 It is beyond the scope of this study to satisfactorily describe the substantial decline of white supremacy because it occurs only after the 1950s and is related to the rise of Quebec nationalism, among other factors. For the US transition see Thomas Borstelmann, *The Cold War and the Color Line: American Race Relations in the Global Arena* (Cambridge: Harvard University Press, 2001), final chapter and epilogue.
7 On this question, see Greg Robinson's *A Tragedy of Democracy: Japanese Confinement in North America* (New York: Columbia University Press, 2009).
8 For details on the process, see Tetsuden Kashima, *Judgement without Trial: Japanese American Imprisonment during World War II* (Seattle: University of Washington Press, 2004), 174-75.
9 The historical significance of this process is outlined by Roy Miki in *Redress: Inside the Japanese Canadian Call for Justice* (Vancouver: Raincoast Books, 2005), esp. chap. 12.

10 For details see Patricia Roy, *The Triumph of Citizenship: The Japanese and Chinese in Canada, 1941-67* (Vancouver: UBC Press, 2007), chaps. 7 and 8.
11 The government abstained in the first vote on the draft declaration and then voted for it in the plenary sessions. For details, see *Documents on Canadian External Relations*, vol. 14, *1948*, ed. H. Mackenzie (Ottawa: Canada Communication Group, 1994), 350-68. Another new volume that treats some of the same issue is Robert Teigrob, *Warming Up to the Cold War: Canada and the United State's Coalition of the Willing, from Hiroshima to Korea* (Toronto: University of Toronto Press, 2009).
12 Reid to J.W. Holmes, 13 March 1959, LAC, MG 31, E46, vol. 13, 1.
13 Reg Whitaker and Gary Marcuse, *Cold War Canada: The Making of a National Insecurity State, 1945-1957* (Toronto: University of Toronto Press, 1994), 12-13.
14 For details, see Carolyn Eisenberg, *Drawing the Line: The American Decision to Divide Germany, 1944-1949* (Cambridge: Cambridge University Press, 1996).
15 Memorandum Submitted to the Dominion Government by the Canadian Congress of Labour, 24 April 1945, LAC, Canadian Congress of Labour Series, MG 28 I103, col. 314, file 4-28, point 4.
16 John Brebner, *North Atlantic Triangle: The Interplay of Canada, the United States and Great Britain* (New York: Columbia University Press, 1945), xi.
17 Ibid., xi.
18 Ibid., 305.
19 Ibid., vii.
20 Michael G. Fry, *Illusions of Security: North Atlantic Diplomacy, 1918-22* (Toronto: University of Toronto Press, 1972).
21 Michael G. Fry, John J. Kirton, and Mitsuru Kurosawa, eds., *North Pacific Triangle: The United States, Canada, and Japan at Century's End* (Toronto: University of Toronto Press, 1998).
22 See B.J.C. McKercher and L. Aronsen, eds., *The North Atlantic Triangle in a Changing World: Anglo-American-Canadian Relations, 1903-1956* (Toronto: University of Toronto Press, 1996); and Phillip Buckner and R. Douglas Francis, eds., *Canada and the British World: Culture, Migration, and Identity* (Vancouver: UBC Press, 2006).
23 Erika Lee, "The 'Yellow Peril' and Asian Exclusion in the Americas," *Pacific Historical Review* 76, 4 (2007): 538.
24 Marilyn Lake and Henry Reynolds, *Drawing the Global Colour Line: White Men's Countries and the Question of Racial Equality* (Carlton, Victoria: Melbourne University Press, 2008).
25 Edward P. Kohn, *This Kindred People: Canadian-American Relations and the Anglo-Saxon Idea, 1895-1903* (Montreal and Kingston: McGill-Queen's University Press, 2004), 197, 205.
26 Statistics Canada, Table A125-163, *Origins of the Population, Census Dates, 1871 to 1971*, available at http://www.statcan.ca/.
27 Michael H. Hunt, *Ideology and US Foreign Policy* (New Haven: Yale University Press, 1987), 162.
28 On the alliance, see Tony Smith, "New Bottles for New Wine: A Pericentric Framework for the Study of the Cold War," *Diplomatic History* 24, 4 (2000): 567-91.

29 Gyan Prakash, "Subaltern Studies as Postcolonial Criticism," *American Historical Review* 99, 5 (1994): 1475.
30 For example, see Ueno Chizuko, *Nationalism and Gender* (Melbourne: Trans Pacific Press, 2004); Elaine H. Kim and Chungmoo Choi, *Dangerous Women: Gender and Korean Nationalism* (New York: Routledge, 1998); Mariko Asano Tamanoi, *Under the Shadow of Nationalism: Politics and Poetics of Rural Japanese Women* (Honolulu: University of Hawaii Press, 1998); Stefan Tanaka, *Japan's Orient: Rendering Pasts into History* (Berkeley: University of California Press, 1993).
31 Alexis Dudden, "Japanese Colonial Control in International Terms," *Japanese Studies* 25, 1 (2005): 1-20.
32 Rumi Sakamoto, "Race-ing Japan," in *Japanese Cultural Nationalism at Home and in the Asia Pacific*, ed. Roy Starrs, 179-92 (Folkestone, UK: Global Oriental, 2004).
33 For insights into postwar struggles, see Jo-Anne Lee, "Gender, Ethnicity, and Hybrid Forms of Community-Based Urban Activism in Vancouver, 1957-1978: The Strathcona Story Revisited," *Gender, Place and Culture: A Journal of Feminist Geography* 14, 4 (2007): 381-407; and Ross Lambertson, *Repression and Resistance: Canadian Human Rights Activists, 1930-1960* (Toronto: University of Toronto Press, 2005).
34 Bob Wing, "Crossing Race and Nationality: The Racial Formation of Asian Americans, 1852-1965," *Monthly Review* 57, 7 (December 2005), 2.
35 See Robin W. Winks, *The Blacks in Canada: A History*, 2nd ed. (Montreal and Kingston: McGill-Queen's University Press, 1997), chap. 10; and R. Bruce Shepherd, *Deemed Unsuitable* (Toronto: Umbrella Press, 1997).
36 Renisa Mawani, "Cross-Racial Encounters and Juridical Truths: (Dis)Aggregating Race in British Columbia's Contact Zone," *BC Studies* 156/57 (2007/08): 141-71.
37 Sherene Razack's suggestion of three stages in the evolution of Canada's national mythologies (represented metaphorically by the legal concept of terra nullius – empty or uninhabited lands; the "true north, strong and free" – hardy European settlement; and a current stage that involves a stable Canada threatened by the chaos accompanying developing world immigration) is a useful starting point. See Sherene E. Razack, ed., *Race, Space and the Law: Unmapping a White Settler Society* (Toronto: Between the Lines, 2002), 3-4. Jan Noel, ed., *Race and Gender in the Northern Colonies* (Toronto: Canadian Scholars' Press, 2000) is an excellent compendium on the black experience in the border colonies.
38 Enakshi Dua, "Exclusion through Inclusion: Female Asian Migration in the Making of Canada as a White Settler Nation," *Gender, Place and Culture: A Journal of Feminist Geography* 14, 4 (2007): 445-66.
39 Borstlemann, *Cold War and the Color Line*, 46.
40 The process of articulating and demanding redress for internment in the 1980s also had its own dynamics, including the necessity to create a narrative that not only refuted previous racialized notions of the community but that also created new portraits (i.e., of Japanese Canadians as loyal Canadians). See Kirsten Emiko McAllister, "Narrating Japanese Canadians In and Out of the Canadian Nation: A Critique of Realist Forms of Representation," *Canadian Journal of Communication* 24, 1 (1999), available at http://www.cjc-online.ca/.

41 Statistics Canada, Table A125-163, *Origins of the Population, Census Dates, 1871 to 1971*, available at http://www.statcan.ca/.

42 See John Gabriel, *Whitewash: Racialized Politics and the Media* (London: Routledge, 1998), as cited in Yasmin Jiwani, *Discourses of Denial: Mediations of Race, Gender, and Violence* (Vancouver: UBC Press, 2006), 17.

Select Bibliography

PRIMARY SOURCES

Archives

British National Archive/Public Records Office, London

Lord Chancellor's Office (LCO)

Canadian Press Archives, Toronto

E.H. Norman Library Archives, Embassy of Canada in Tokyo

Ōkubo Genji Collection

Library and Archives Canada (LAC)

Brooke Claxton Papers, MG 32

C.D. Howe Papers, MG 27 III

Department of Defence, RG 24

Department of Reconstruction, MG 27

Defence Research Board, RG 24F

Escott Reid Papers, MG 31

External Affairs, RG 25

Hugh Keenleyside Papers, MG 31 E102

Louis St. Laurent Papers, MG 26 L

Lester Pearson Papers, MG 26 N1

Mackenzie King Papers, MG 26, J 1-5

Mary Kitagawa papers, MG 31E 26

Sir Wilfrid Laurier Papers, MG 26 G

McGill University Archives

Otto Maass Papers, MG 1050

National Archives and Records Administration (NARA), Washington, DC

National Diet Library, Tokyo, Japan
Minutes of State-War-Navy Coordinating Committee
Awaya Kentarō and Yoshida Yutaka, eds. *Kokusai kensatsukyoku (IPS) Jimmon Chōsho, dai 1 kan-52 kan* [Interrogation record of the International Prosecution Section, vols. 1-52]. Tokyo: Nihon tosho senta, 1993.
University of British Columbia, Special Collections and University Archives
Gwen and Howard Norman Collection
Ōkubo Genji Collection
Roger Bowen Collection
Women's International League for Peace and Freedom Collection
Vancouver City Archives
Sherwood Lett Collection, MSS 361

Serials

Bulletin (Vancouver)
Chinese Times
Documents on Canadian External Relations (DCER). Ottawa: Canada Communication Group, various editors and years
Documents on New Zealand External Relations (DNZER). Wellington: Government Printer, various years
Foreign Relations of the United States (FRUS). Washington, DC: US Government Printing Office, various years
Globe and Mail
House of Commons Debates (*Hansard*)
Maclean's
New Canadian
The *Province* (Vancouver)
Statements and Speeches, Department of External Affairs, Canada
Tairiku nippō
Trades and Labour Congress Journal
Vancouver Sun

Unpublished Materials and Interviews

Ahn Jeomsun. Testimony at conference entitled "Preventing Crimes against Humanity: Lessons from the Asia-Pacific War, 1931-45," First Nations House of Learning, University of British Columbia, Vancouver, 21-22 March 2003.
Kang Jeong-Koo. "A Critical Evaluation on the US Role in the Division of Korea and the Korean War." Unpublished paper given to the author in Yeosu, Korea.
MacPherson, Don. "1939-1945." Private memoire. N.d.
Rape of Nanking Redress Coalition. "50 Years of Denial: Japan and Its Wartime Responsibilities." A paper presented to A Symposium Marking 50th Anniversary of San Francisco Peace Treaty, 6-9 September 2001, San Francisco.
Stainton, Michael. "George Leslie Mackay and the Poll Tax." Unpublished paper presented at Canadian Asian Studies Association-East Asia Council, Quebec City, November 2007.

Xu Jiaxie. Testimony at Conference entitled "Preventing Crimes against Humanity: Lessons from the Asia-Pacific War, 1931-45," First Nations House of Learning, University of British Columbia, Vancouver, 21-22 March 2003.

Interviews

Dean, Elsie, 8 April 2002, Vancouver

Endicott, Stephen, 13 December 2003, Toronto

Fraser, George, 14 November 2003, Vancouver

Kim Dong-choon, October 2003, Yeosu, South Korea

Laskey, Kinuko and David, 21 August 2003, Vancouver

Menzies, Arthur, 12 December 2002, Ottawa

Powells, Cyril and Marjorie, April 2002, Vancouver

Shin Hyun-chan, 6 April 2004, Hwang Bang-li, Yangjun County, South Korea

SECONDARY SOURCES

Adachi, Ken. *The Enemy That Never Was: A History of Japanese Canadians.* Toronto: McClelland and Stewart, 1976.

Ajia minshū hōtei junbikai, ed. *Toinaosu Tōkyō saiban* [Reassessing the Tokyo tribunal]. Tokyo: Ryokufu shuppan, 1995.

Allan, Ted, and Sidney Gordon. *The Scalpel and the Sword: The Story of Dr. Norman Bethune.* Toronto: McClelland and Stewart, 1989.

Allen, Theodore W. *The Invention of the White Race.* Vol. 1: *Racial Oppression and Social Control.* London: Verso, 1994.

Alley, Rewi. *Rewi Alley: An Autobiography.* 3rd ed. Beijing: New World Press, 1997.

Alperovitz, Gar. *Atomic Diplomacy: Hiroshima and Potsdam.* New York: Simon and Schuster, 1965.

–. *The Decision to Use the Atomic Bomb.* New York: Vintage, 1996.

Anderson, Benedict. *Imagined Communities: Reflections on the Origin and Spread of Nationalism.* London: Verso, 1983.

Anderssen, Erin. "Hong Kong Veterans to Get $18-Million." *Globe and Mail,* 12 December 1998.

Armstrong, Charles K. *The North Korean Revolution, 1945-1950.* Ithaca: Cornell University Press, 2003.

Asada, Sadao. "From Washington to London: The Imperial Japanese Navy and the Politics of Naval Limitation, 1921-1930." In *The Washington Conference, 1921-22: Naval Rivalry, East Asia Stability and the Road to Pearl Harbor,* ed. Erik Goldstein and John Maurer, 147-90. Essex: Frank Cass, 1994.

Asahi Shimbun Tōkyō saiban kishadan. *Tōkyō saiban jo, ge* [The Tokyo tribunal, 2 vols.]. Tokyo: Asahi shimbunsha, 1983.

Auslin, Michael R. *Negotiating Imperialism: The Unequal Treaties and the Culture of Japanese Diplomacy.* Cambridge: Harvard University Press, 2004.

Avery, Donald H. *The Science of War: Canadian Scientists and Allied Military Technology during the Second World War.* Toronto: University of Toronto Press, 1998.

Awaya Kentarō. "Introduction." In Asahi Shimbun Tōkyō saiban kishadan, *Tōkyō saiban jo, ge* [The Tokyo tribunal, 20 vols.]. Tokyo: Asahi Shimbunsha, 1983.

–. *Tōkyō saiban ron* [Views on the Tokyo tribunal]. Tokyo: Ōtsuki shoten, 1989.

Awaya Kentarō, and Yoshida Yutaka, eds. *Kokusai kensatsukyoku (IPS) Jimmon Chōsho, dai 1 kan-52 kan* [Interrogation record of the International Prosecution Section, vols. 1-52]. Tokyo: Nihon tosho senta, 1993.

Ayukawa, Midge Michiko. *Hiroshima Immigrants in Canada, 1891-1941*. Vancouver: UBC Press, 2008.

Bacchi, Carol Lee. *Liberation Deferred? The Ideas of the English-Canadian Suffragists, 1877-1918*. Toronto: University of Toronto Press, 1983.

Backhouse, Constance. *Colour-Coded: A Legal History of Racism in Canada, 1900-1950*. Toronto: Osgoode Society for Canadian Legal History/University of Toronto Press, 2001.

–. "The White Women's Labor Laws: Anti-Chinese Racism in Early Twentieth Century Canada." *Law and History Review* 14, 2 (1996): 315-68.

Bai Shouyi. *An Outline History of China, 1919-1949*. Beijing: Foreign Languages Press, 1993.

Balmer, Brian. *Britain and Biological Warfare: Expert Advice and Science Policy, 1930-65*. Basingstoke: Palgrave, 2001.

Bannerji, Himani, ed. *The Dark Side of Nation: Essays on Multiculturalism, Nationalism and Gender*. Toronto: Canadian Scholars' Press, 2000.

–. *Returning the Gaze: Essays on Racism, Feminism, and Politics*. Toronto: Sister Vision Press, 1993.

Barnholden, Michael. *Reading the Riot Act: A Brief History of Riots in Vancouver*. Vancouver: Anvil Press, 2005.

Barrett, George. "US Hell Buggies Shell Seoul from Seven Miles." *Globe and Mail*, 12 February 1951.

Barris, Ted. *Deadlock in Korea: Canadians at War, 1950-53*. Toronto: Macmillan, 1999.

Barros, James. *No Sense of Evil: Espionage, the Case of Herbert Norman*. Toronto: Deneau, 1986.

Bates, M. Searle, and Kenneth Scott Latourette. "The Future of Japan: An American View." *Pacific Affairs* 17, 2 (1944): 190-203.

Bellow, Walden, ed. *Ho Chi Min, Down with Colonialism!* London: Verso, 2007.

Belmonte, Laura. "Anglo-American Relations and the Dismissal of MacArthur." *Diplomatic History* 19, 4 (1995): 641-67.

Bennett, Neville. "White Discrimination against Japan: Britain, the Dominion and the United States, 1908-1928." *New Zealand Journal of Asian Studies* 3, 2 (2001): 91-105.

Bercuson, David J. *Blood on the Hills: The Canadian Army in the Korean War*. Toronto: University of Toronto Press, 1999.

–. *Maple Leaf against the Axis: Canada's Second World War*. Toronto: Stoddart, 1995.

–. *True Patriot: The Life of Brooke Claxton, 1898-1960*. Toronto: University of Toronto Press, 1993.

Berton, Pierre. *My Times: Living with History, 1947-1995*. Toronto: Seal Edition, 1996.

Bessis, Sophie. *Western Supremacy: Triumph of an Idea?* London: Zed Books, 2003.

Best, Antony. *British Intelligence and the Japanese Challenge in Asia, 1914-1941*. Hampshire: Palgrave, 2002.

Bhabha, H.K. *Nation and Narration*. London: Routledge, 1990.

Bickerton, James, and Alain Gagnon, eds. *Canadian Politics*. Toronto: Broadview Press, 2004.

Bix, Herbert P. *Hirohito and the Making of Modern Japan*. New York: HarperCollins, 2000.

Blow, Peter, dir. *Village of Widows*. Documentary film. Lindum Films, Peterborough, ON, 1999. Available at http://www.mercurycenter.com/.

Borden, Henry, ed. *Robert Laird Borden: His Memoirs*. Vol. 2. Toronto: Macmillan, 1938.

Borg, Dorothy. *The United States and the Far Eastern Crisis of 1933-38*. Cambridge: Harvard University Press, 1964.

Borstelmann, Thomas. *The Cold War and the Color Line: American Race Relations in the Global Arena*. Cambridge: Harvard University Press, 2001.

Bothwell, Robert. *Alliance and Illusion: Canada and the World, 1945-1984*. Vancouver: UBC Press, 2007.

–. "Eyes West: Canada and the Cold War in Asia." In *Canada and the Early Cold War 1943-1957*, ed. Greg Donaghy, 59-70. Ottawa: Department of Foreign Affairs and International Trade, 1998.

–. "The Further Shore: Canada and Vietnam." *International Journal* 56, 1 (2000-1): 89-114.

–. *Loring Christie: The Failure of Bureaucratic Imperialism*. New York: Garland, 1988.

–. *Nucleus: The History of Atomic Energy of Canada Limited*. Toronto: University of Toronto Press, 1988.

Bothwell, Robert, Ian Drummond, and John English. *Canada, 1900-1945*. Toronto: University of Toronto Press, 1987.

Bowen, Roger, ed. *E.H. Norman: His Life and Scholarship*. Toronto: University of Toronto Press, 1984.

–. *Innocence Is Not Enough: The Life and Death of Herbert Norman*. Vancouver: Douglas and McIntyre, 1986.

Brackman, Arnold C. *The Other Nuremberg: The Untold Story of the Tokyo War Crimes Trials*. New York: William Morrow, 1987.

Bradley, Mark Philip. *Imagining Vietnam and America: The Making of Postcolonial Vietnam, 1919-1950*. Chapel Hill: University of North Carolina Press, 2000.

Brebner, John. *North Atlantic Triangle: The Interplay of Canada, the United States and Great Britain*. New York: Columbia University Press, 1945.

British Columbia, Ministry of Education. *Canada and the Holocaust: Social Responsibility and Global Citizenship*. Victoria: Ministry of Education, 2000.

British Columbia and Vancouver Island: A Complete Handbook. London: W. Penny, 1858.

Brode, Patrick. *Casual Slaughters and Accidental Judgements: Canadian War Crimes Prosecutions, 1944-1948*. Toronto: University of Toronto Press, 1997.

Brook, Timothy. *Collaboration: Japanese Agents and Local Elites in Wartime China*. Cambridge: Harvard University Press, 2005.

Brook, Timothy, ed. *Documents on the Rape of Nanking*. Ann Arbor: University of Michigan Press, 1999.

Brooks, Roy L., ed. *When Sorry Isn't Enough: The Controversy over Apologies and Reparations for Human Injustice*. New York: New York University Press, 1999.

Bryden, John. *Deadly Allies: Canada's Secret War, 1937-1947*. Toronto: McClelland and Stewart, 1989.

Buchanan, Tom. "The Courage of Galileo: Joseph Needham and the 'Germ Warfare' Allegations in the Korean War." *History* 86, 284 (2001): 507-22.

Buchignani, Norman, Doreen M. Indra, and Ram Srivastiva. *Continuous Journey: A Social History of South Asians in Canada*. Toronto: McClelland and Stewart, 1985.

Buckely, Roger. *Occupation Diplomacy: Britain, the United States and Japan, 1945-1952*. Cambridge: Cambridge University Press, 1982.

Buckner, Phillip, and R. Douglas Francis, eds. *Canada and the British World: Culture, Migration, and Identity*. Vancouver: UBC Press, 2006.

Buell, Raymond Leslie. *The Washington Conference*. New York: Russell and Russell, 1970. (Reprint of the 1922 edition.)

Byrnes, James F. *Speaking Frankly*. New York: Harper and Bros., 1947.

Canada. *Canada and the Korean Crisis*. Ottawa: King's Printer, 1950.

Canadian League for Peace and Democracy. *Amplifier* 1, 1 (23 January 1938).

Castonguay, René. *Rodolphe Lemieux et le Parti liberal, 1866-1937: Le chevalier du roi*. Quebec: Les Presses de l'Université Laval, 2000.

Center for Research and Documentation on Japan's War Responsibility. *Kikan sensō sekinin kenkyū, tokushū: 731 butai no jisso ni semaru* [Report on Japan's war responsibility, special edition: Closing in on the reality of Unit 731] 2 (Winter 1993).

Chamberlain, Muriel E. *European Decolonisation in the 20th Century*. London: Longman, 1998.

Chang, Iris. *The Rape of Nanking: The Forgotten Massacre*. New York: Basic Books, 1997.

Cheju 4.3 Research Institute. *Records of the US Department of State Relating to the Internal Affairs of Cheju-do, 1945-1950*. Cheju 4.3 Research Institute, reprint.

Cheju sasam sageon jinsang kyumeong mit heesaengja myongyeh hyebok wiwanhye. *Cheju sasam sageon jinsang chosa bogoseo* [Report on the investigation into the truth regarding the Cheju April 3rd incident]. Seoul: Danmul inshwe jeonbo, 2003.

Chen Jian. *China's Road to the Korean War: The Making of the Sino-American Confrontation*. New York: Columbia University Press, 1994.

–. *Mao's China and the Cold War*. Chapel Hill and London: University of North Carolina Press, 2001.

–. "Re-Reading Chinese Documents: A Post-Cold War Interpretation of the Cold War on the Korean Peninsula." In *Ending the Cold War in Korea: Theoretical and Historical Perspectives*, ed. Moon Chung-in, Odd Arne Westad, and Gyoo-hyoung Kahng, 171-91. Seoul: Yonsei University Press, 2001.

Chen, Zhongping. "Chinese Minority and Everyday Racism in Canadian Towns and Small Cities: An Ethnic Study Case of Peterborough, Ontario, 1892-1951." *Canadian Ethnic Studies* 34, 1 (2004): 71-91.

Cheng, Pei-kai, and Michael Lestz, with Jonathan D. Spence, eds. *The Search for Modern China: A Documentary Collection*. New York: W.W. Norton, 1999.

Cheong, Sung-Hwa. *The Politics of Anti-Japanese Sentiment in Korea: Japanese-South Korean Relations under American Occupation, 1945-1952*. New York: Greenwood Press, 1991.

Ching, Leo T.S. *Becoming Japanese: Colonial Taiwan and the Politics of Identity Formation*. Berkeley: University of California Press, 2001.

Chizuko, Ueno. *Nationalism and Gender*. Melbourne: Trans Pacific Press, 2004.

Choe, Sang-Hun, Martha Mendoza, and Charles J. Hanley. *The Bridge at No Gun Ri: A Hidden Nightmare from the Korean War*. New York: Henry Holt, 2001.

Clausen, Henry C., and Bruce Lee. *Pearl Harbor: Final Judgement*. New York: DaCapo Press, 1993.

Cooper, Andrew F. *Canadian Foreign Policy: Old Habits and New Directions*. Scarborough, ON: Prentice Hall, 1997.

Craft, Stephen G. *V.K. Wellington Koo and the Emergence of Modern China*. Lexington: University of Kentucky Press, 2004.

Crane, Conrad C. *American Airpower Strategy in Korea, 1950-1953*. Lawrence: University of Kansas Press, 2000.

Cribb, Narangoa, and Robert Cribb, eds. *Imperial Japan and National Identities in Asia, 1895-1945*. London: RoutledgeCurzon, 2003.

Cuff, R.D., and J.L. Granatstein. *Ties That Bind: Canadian American Relations in Wartime, from the Great War to the Cold War*. Toronto: Samuel Stevens Hakkert, 1977.

Cumings, Bruce, ed. *Child of Conflict: The Korean-American Relationship, 1943-1953*. Seattle: University of Washington Press, 1983.

–. *Korea's Place in the Sun: A Modern History*. New York: W.W. Norton, 1997.

–. *North Korea: Another Country*. New York: New Press, 2004.

–. *The Origins of the Korean War: Liberation and the Emergence of Separate Regimes, 1945-1947*. Princeton: Princeton University Press, 1981.

Dayal, Shiv. *India's Role in the Korean Question*. Delhi: S. Chand and Co., 1959.

Denoon, Donald, Gavan McCormack, Mark Hudson, and Tessa Morris-Suzuki, eds. *Multicultural Japan: Paleolithic to Postmodern*. Cambridge: Cambridge University Press, 2001.

Dirlik, Arif. *The Postcolonial Aura: Third World Criticism in the Age of Global Capitalism*. Boulder: Westview Press, 1997.

Donaghy, Greg, ed. *Canada and the Early Cold War, 1943-1957*. Ottawa: Department of Foreign Affairs and International Trade, 1998.

–. *Herbert Norman: A Documentary Perspective*. Ottawa: Department of Foreign Affairs, 1999.

Donaghy, Greg, and Patricia E. Roy, eds. *Contradictory Impulses: Canada and Japan in the Twentieth Century*. Vancouver: UBC Press, 2008.

Dooley, Thomas A. *Deliver Us from Evil: The Story of Vietnam's Flight to Freedom.* New York: Farrar, Straus, and Cudahy, 1956.

Dower, John. *Embracing Defeat: Japan in the Wake of World War II.* New York: W.W. Norton/New Press, 1999.

–. *Empire and Aftermath: Yoshida Shigeru and the Japanese Experience, 1878-1954.* Cambridge: Council on East Asian Studies, Harvard University, 1979.

–. *War without Mercy: Race and Power in the Pacific War.* New York: Pantheon, 1986.

Dua, Enakshi, and Angela Robertson, eds. *Scratching the Surface: Canadian Anti-Racist Feminist Thought.* Toronto: Women's Press, 2006.

Dudden, Alexis. *Japan's Colonization of Korea: Discourse and Power.* Honolulu: University of Hawaii Press, 2005.

Duiker, William J. *Ho Chi Minh: A Life.* New York: Hyperion, 2000.

Eayrs, James. *In Defence of Canada, Indochina: Roots of Complicity.* Toronto: University of Toronto Press, 1983.

Eisenberg, Carolyn. *Drawing the Line: The American Decision to Divide Germany, 1944-1949.* Cambridge: Cambridge University Press, 1996.

Elizalde, Dolores, ed. *Las Relaciones Internacionales en el Pacifico (Siglos XVIII-XX): Colonizacion, Decolonizacion y Encuertro Cultural.* Madrid: Consejo Superior de Investigaciones Cientificas, 1997.

Endicott, Stephen. *James G. Endicott: Rebel Out of China.* Toronto: University of Toronto Press, 1980.

Endicott, Stephen, and Earl Willmott. "Canadian Missionaries and the Chinese Revolution of 1949: The Sympathetic Observers." Paper presented at the International Symposium on the Dissemination of Protestant Christianity in Modern China and East Asia and on "Missionary Cases," Chongqing-Nanjing, November 1994.

Endicott, Stephen, and Edward Hagerman. *The United States and Biological Warfare: Secrets of the Early Cold War and Korea.* Bloomington: Indiana University Press, 1998.

English, John. *Shadow of Heaven: The Life of Lester Pearson.* Vol. 1: *1897-1948.* London: Vintage, 1990.

Evans, Paul M., and B. Michael Frolic. *Reluctant Adversaries: Canada and the People's Republic of China, 1949-1970.* Toronto: University of Toronto Press, 1991.

Ewen, Jean. *China Nurse, 1932-1939.* Toronto: McClelland and Stewart, 1981.

Fairbank, John King. *Chinabound: A Fifty-Year Memoir.* New York: Harper Colophon, 1983.

–. *The Great Chinese Revolution, 1800-1985.* New York: Perennial Library, 1987.

Ferguson, Niall. *Colossus: The Rise and Fall of the American Empire.* New York: Penguin Books, 2004.

Finkel, Alvin, Margaret Conrad, and Veronica Strong-Boag. *History of the Canadian Peoples.* Vol. 2: *1867 to the Present.* Toronto: Copp Clark Pitman, 1993.

Finkelstein, David M. *Washington's Taiwan Dilemma, 1949-1950.* Fairfax, VA: George Mason University Press, 1993.

Finn, Richard B. *Winners in Peace: MacArthur, Yoshida, and Postwar Japan*. Berkeley: University of California Press, 1992.

Fiset, Louis, and Gail M. Nomura, eds. *Nikkei in the Pacific Northwest: Japanese Americans and Japanese Canadians in the Twentieth Century*. Seattle: University of Washington Press, 2005.

Flaras, Augie, and Jean Leonard Elliot. *Unequal Relations: An Introduction to Race and Ethnic Dynamics in Canada*. 4th ed. Toronto: Prentice Hall, 2003.

Fry, Michael G. "Canada and the Occupation of Japan: The MacArthur-Norman Years." In *The Occupation of Japan: The International Context*, ed. Thomas Burkman, 130-59. Norfolk: The MacArthur Foundation, 1984.

–. *Illusions of Security: North Atlantic Diplomacy, 1918-22*. Toronto: University of Toronto Press, 1972.

Fry, Michael G., John Kirton, and Kurosawa Mitsuru, eds. *The North Pacific Triangle: The United States, Japan, and Canada at Century's End*. Toronto: University of Toronto Press, 1998.

Fujitani, T., Geoffrey M. White, and Lisa Yoneyama, eds. *Perilous Memories: The Asia-Pacific War(s)*. Durham, NC: Duke University Press, 2001.

Fujiwara Akira, and Himeta Mitsuyoshi, eds. *Chugoku ni okeru nihonjin no hansen katsudo* [Japanese anti-war activities in China]. Tokyo: Aoki shoten, 1999.

Fukunaga Fumio. *Senryōka chūdō seiken no keisei to hōkai* [The rise and fall of moderate government under the occupation]. Tokyo: Iwanami shoten, 1997.

Fussell, Paul. *Thank God for the Atomic Bomb and Other Essays*. New York: Summit Books, 1988.

Gabriel, John. *Whitewash: Racialized Politics and the Media*. London: Routledge, 1998.

Gaiduk, Ilya V. *Confronting Vietnam: Soviet Policy toward the Indochina Conflict, 1954-1963*. Stanford: Stanford University Press, 2003.

Gallicchio, Marc S. *The Cold War Begins in Asia: American East Asian Policy and the Fall of the Japanese Empire*. New York: Columbia University Press, 1988.

Goldberg, David Theo. *The Racial State*. Oxford: Blackwell, 2002.

Goldstein, Erik, and John Maurer, eds. *The Washington Conference, 1921-22: Naval Rivalry, East Asia Stability and the Road to Pearl Harbor*. Essex: Frank Cass, 1994.

Goodrich, Leland M. (Council on Foreign Relations). *Korea: A Study of US Policy in the United Nations*. New York: Greenwood, 1956.

Gordenker, Leon. *The United Nations and the Peaceful Unification of Korea*. The Hague: Martinus Nijhoff, 1959.

Graham, Roger. *Arthur Meighen*. Toronto: Clarke, Irwin and Co., 1963.

Granatstein, Jack. *Canada's War: The Politics of the Mackenzie King Government, 1939-1945*. Toronto: Oxford University Press, 1975.

–. *Who Killed Canadian History?* Toronto: HarperCollins, 1998.

Granatstein, Jack, and Norman Hillmer. *Empire to Umpire: Canada and the World to the 1990s*. Toronto: Copp Clark Longman, 1994.

Granger, Serge. *Le lys et le lotus: Les relations du Québec avec la Chine de 1650 à 1950*. Montreal: VLB Éditeur, 2005.

Griswold, Whitney A. *The Far Eastern Policy of the United States.* New York: Harcourt Brace, 1938.

Hall, D.J. *Clifford Sifton.* Vol. 1: *The New Napoleon, 1861-1900.* Vancouver: UBC Press, 1981.

Han Hong-Koo. "Wounded Nationalism: The Minsaengdan Incident and Kim Il Sung in Eastern Manchuria." PhD diss., University of Washington, 1999.

Hardt, Michael, and Antonio Negri. *Empire.* Cambridge: Harvard University Press, 2000.

Harries, Meiron and Susie. *Sheathing the Sword: The Demilitarization of Japan.* London: Hamish Hamilton, 1987.

Harris, Robert, and Jeremy Paxman. *A Higher Form of Killing: The Secret History of Chemical and Biological Warfare.* New York: Random House, 2002.

Harris, Sheldon H. *Factories of Death: Japanese Biological Warfare, 1932-45, and the American Cover-Up.* London: Routledge, 1994.

Hasegawa, Tsuyoshi. *Racing the Enemy: Stalin, Truman, and the Surrender of Japan.* Cambridge: Belknap Press of Harvard University Press, 2005.

Hellwig, Tineke, and Sunera Thobani, eds. *Asian Women: Interconnections.* Toronto: Women's Press, 2006.

Herring, George C. *America's Longest War: The United States and Vietnam, 1950-1975.* 4th ed. Boston: McGraw-Hill, 2002.

Hier, Sean P., and B. Singh Bolaria, eds. *Race and Racism in 21st-Century Canada.* Peterborough, ON: Broadview Press, 2007.

Hilliker, John. *Canada's Department of External Affairs.* Vol. 1: *The Early Years, 1909-1946.* Montreal and Kingston: McGill-Queen's University Press, 1990.

Hilliker, John, and Donald Barry. *Canada's Department of External Affairs.* Vol. 2: *Coming of Age, 1946-1968.* Montreal and Kingston: McGill-Queen's University Press, 1995.

Hiratsuka Raichō chosakushū henshū iinkai. *Hiratsuka Raichō chosakushū dai 7 kan* [Collected works of Hiratsuka Raichō] Tokyo: Ōtsuki shoten, 1984.

Hobson, John. *The Eastern Origins of Western Civilization.* Cambridge: Cambridge University Press, 2004.

Hogan, Michael J., ed. *Hiroshima in History and Memory.* New York: Cambridge University Press, 1996.

Holmes, John W. "Canada's Postwar Policies towards Japan." Paper presented at the International University Symposium on Japan and Postwar Diplomacy in the Asia-Pacific Region, International House of Japan, Tokyo, 18-19 March 1983.

–. *The Shaping of Peace.* Vol. 1: *Canada and the Search for World Order, 1943-1957.* Toronto: University of Toronto Press, 1979.

Homma, K.T., and C.G. Isaksson. *Homma Tomekichi: The Story of a Canadian.* Surrey, BC: Hancock House, 2008.

Honda Katsuichi. *The Nanjing Massacre: A Japanese Journalist Confronts Japan's National Shame.* Ed. Frank Gibney, trans. Karen Sandness. Armonk, NY: M.E. Sharpe, 1999.

Hong Xuezhi. *Kangmei yuanchao zhanzheng huiyi* [Recollections of the war to resist American aggression and aid Korea]. Beijing: PLA Literature Press, 1992.

Hopper, Helen M. *A New Woman of Japan: A Political Biography of Kato Shidzue.* Boulder: Westview Press, 1996.

Hopper, Paul F, ed. *Remembering the Institute of Pacific Relations: The Memoirs of William L. Holland.* Tokyo: Ryukei shyosha, 1995.

Horne, Gerald. *Race War: White Supremacy and the Japanese Attack on the British Empire.* New York: New York University Press, 2004.

Hosoya, C., ed. *The Tokyo War Crimes Trial: An International Symposium.* Tokyo: Kodansha, 1986.

Hsu Shuhsi. *The War Conduct of the Japanese.* Hankou, China: Kelly and Walsh, 1938.

Hunt, Michael H. *Ideology and US Foreign Policy.* New Haven: Yale University Press, 1987.

Huttenback, Robert A. *Racism and Empire: White Settlers and Colored Immigrants in the British Self-Governing Colonies, 1830-1910.* Ithaca: Cornell University Press, 1976.

Iacovetta, Franca. *Gatekeepers: Reshaping Immigrant Lives in Cold War Canada.* Toronto: Between the Lines, 2006.

Ichihashi, Yamato. *The Washington Conference and After: A Historical Survey.* New York: AMS Press, 1969 [1928].

Ienaga Saburō. *Taiheiyo sensō dainihan* [The Pacific war, 2nd ed.]. Tokyo: Iwanami shoten, 1997.

–. *The Pacific War, 1931-1945.* New York: Pantheon Books, 1978.

Ignatieff, Michael. *Empire Lite: Nation-Building in Bosnia, Kosovo and Afghanistan.* London: Penguin, 2003.

Innis, Harold A. *A History of the Canadian Pacific Railway.* Toronto: University of Toronto, 1971 [1923].

Inoue, Kyoko. *MacArthur's Japanese Constitution.* Chicago: University of Chicago Press, 1991.

International Organizing Committee for the Women's International War Crimes Tribunal. *Women's International War Crimes Tribunal: Judgement.* Tokyo: Violence against Women in War Network Japan, 2002.

Ion, A. Hamish. *The Cross and the Rising Sun.* Waterloo: Wilfrid Laurier University Press, 1990.

Ion, A. Hamish, and Barry Hunt, eds. *War and Diplomacy across the Pacific, 1919-1952.* Waterloo: Wilfrid Laurier University Press, 1988.

Iriye, Akira. *The Origins of the Second World War in Asia and the Pacific.* London: Longman, 1987.

Ito, Roy. *We Went to War.* Stittsville, ON: Canada's Wings, 1984.

Jacobs, Seth. *America's Miracle Man in Vietnam: Ngo Dinh Diem, Religion, Race and US Intervention in Southeast Asia.* Durham, NC: Duke University Press, 2004.

Jagpal, Sarjeet Singh. *Becoming Canadians: Pioneer Sikhs in Their Own Words.* Madeira Park, BC: Harbour Publishing, 1994.

Jiwani, Yasmin. *Discourses of Denial: Mediations of Race, Gender, and Violence.* Vancouver: UBC Press, 2006.

Johnson, Chalmers. *Blowback: The Costs and Consequences of American Empire.* New York: Henry Holt, 2000.

Johnson, U. Alexis. *The Right Hand of Power.* Englewood, NJ: Prentice-Hall, 1984).

Johnston, Hugh. *The Voyage of the* Komagata Maru: *The Sikh Challenge to Canada's Colour Bar.* Delhi: Oxford University Press, 1979.

Joint Publications Research Service. *Moscow Daily Press Summary* Washington, DC: Government Printing Office, 1951.

Judge, Edward H., and John W. Langdon. *The Cold War: A History through Documents.* Upper Saddle River, NJ: Prentice Hall, 1999.

–. *A Hard and Bitter Peace: A Global History of the Cold War.* Upper Saddle River, NJ: Prentice Hall, 1996.

Kage Tatsuo. *Nikkei Kanadajin no tsuiho* [Exiled Japanese Canadians]. Tokyo: Akashi shoten, 1999.

Kang, Hildi. *Under the Black Umbrella: Voices from Colonial Korea, 1910-1945.* Ithaca: Cornell University Press, 2001.

Kashima, Tetsuden. *Judgement without Trial: Japanese American Imprisonment during World War II.* Seattle: University of Washington Press, 2004.

Katō Suichi, and Toshiko Nakano, ed. and trans. *E.H. nōman, Nihon senryō no kiroku 1946-48* [E.H. Norman reports from occupied Japan, 1946-48]. Tokyo: Jinbun shoin, 1997.

Kay, Robin, ed. *Documents on New Zealand External Relations.* Vol. 2: *The Occupation and Surrender of Japan.* Wellington: Government Printer, 1982.

–. *Documents on New Zealand External Relations.* Vol. 3: *The ANZUS Pact and the Treaty of Peace with Japan.* Wellington: Government Printer, 1985.

Keenleyside, Hugh. *Memoirs of Hugh L. Keenleyside.* Vol. 1: *Hammer the Golden Day.* Toronto: McClelland and Stewart, 1981.

–. *Memoirs of Hugh L. Keenleyside.* Vol. 2. *On the Bridge of Time.* Toronto: McClelland and Stewart, 1982.

Keibo, Oiwa. *Stone Voices: Wartime Writings of Japanese Canadian Issei.* Montreal: Vehicule Press, 1991.

Kennan, George F. *Memoirs, 1925-1950.* Boston: Little, Brown and Co., 1967.

Khong, Yuen Foong. *Analogies of War: Korea, Munich, Dien Bien Phu and the Vietnam Decisions of 1965.* Princeton: Princeton University Press, 1992.

Kim, Elanine H., and Chungmoo Choi. *Dangerous Women: Gender and Korean Nationalism.* New York: Routledge, 1998.

Kim Ik Ruhl. "The Truth about Cheju 4.3." In *Cheju 4.3 Uprisings,* ed. Cheju 4.3 Research Institute. Papers presented at the 50th Anniversary Conference of the 3 April 1948 Chejudo Rebellion, Tokyo, 1998.

Kim In-duck et al. *Jeju 4.3 Yun-gu* [Research on Cheju 4.3]. Seoul: Yuk-sa-bi-pyung-sa, 1999.

King, William Lyon Mackenzie. *The Diaries of W.L. Mackenzie King.* Toronto: University of Toronto Press, 1983.

Kitagawa, Muriel. *This Is My Own: Letters to Wes and Other Writings on Japanese Canadians, 1941-1948.* Ed. Roy Miki. Vancouver: Talonbooks, 1985.

Klein, Christina. *Cold War Orientalism: Asia in the Middlebrow Imagination, 1945-1961.* Berkeley: University of California Press, 2003.

Kohn, Edward P. *This Kindred People: Canadian-American Relations and the Anglo-Saxon Idea, 1895-1903.* Montreal and Kingston: McGill-Queen's University Press, 2004.

Kojima Noboru. *Tōkyō saiban jo, ge* [Tokyo tribunal, 2 vols.]. Tokyo: Chuō kōronsha, 1982.

Korean Overseas Culture and Information Service. *A Handbook of Korea,* 10th ed. Seoul: Korean Overseas Culture and Information Service, 1990.

Koshiro, Yukiko. *Trans-Pacific Racisms and the US Occupation of Japan.* New York: Columbia University Press, 1999.

Kovel, Joel. *Red Hunting in the Promised Land: Anti-Communism and the Making of America.* New York: Basic Books, 1994.

Koyama Kōtake and Shimizu Shinzō. *Nihon shakaitō shi* [History of the Japan Socialist Party]. Kyoto: Hōka shoten, 1965.

Kudō Miyoko. *Higeki no gaikōkan: Hābāto nōman no shōgai* [Tragic diplomat: The life of Herbert Norman]. Tokyo: Iwanami shoten, 1991.

Kudō Yoroshi. *Ruporutājyu nihonkoku kempō* [Reporting on the Japanese constitution]. Tokyo: Asahi shimbunsha, 1997.

Kurzman, Dan. *Kishi and Japan: The Search for The Sun.* New York: Ivan Obolensky, 1960.

LaFeber, Walter. *America, Russia and the Cold War, 1945-1984.* New York: Alfred A. Knopf, 1985.

–. *The Clash: U.S.-Japan Relations throughout History.* New York: W.W. Norton, 1997.

Lake, Marilyn, and Henry Reynolds. *Drawing the Global Colour Line: White Men's Countries and the Question of Racial Equality.* Carlton, Victoria: Melbourne University Press, 2008.

Lam, Truong Bun. *Colonialism Experienced: Vietnamese Writings on Colonialism, 1900-1931.* Ann Arbor: University of Michigan Press, 2000.

Lambertson, Ross. *Repression and Resistance: Canadian Human Rights Activists, 1930-1960.* Toronto: University of Toronto Press, 2005.

Langdon, Frank. *The Politics of Canadian-Japanese Economic Relations, 1952-1983.* Vancouver: UBC Press, 1983.

Lansdale, Edward. *In the Midst of Wars: An American's Mission to Southeast Asia.* New York: Harper and Row, 1972.

Lary, Diana, and Stephen MacKinnon, eds. *Scars of War: The Impact of Warfare on Modern China.* Vancouver: UBC Press, 2001.

Lawrence, Mark Atwood. *Assuming the Burden: Europe and the American Commitment to War in Vietnam.* Berkeley: University of California Press, 2005.

Lee, Erika. "Hemispheric Orientalism and the 1907 Pacific Coast Race Riots." *Amerasia Journal: A Journal of Feminist Geography* 33, 2 (2007): 19-47

–. "The 'Yellow Peril' and Asian Exclusion in the Americas." *Pacific Historical Review* 76, 4 (2007): 537-62.

Lee, Jo-Anne. "Gender, Ethnicity, and Hybrid Forms of Community-Based Urban Activism in Vancouver, 1957-1978: The Strathcona Story Revisited." *Gender, Place and Culture* 14. 4 (2007): 381-407.

Lee, Steven Hugh. *The Korean War*. Harlow, UK: Pearson Education, 2001.

–. *Outposts of Empire: Korea, Vietnam and the Origins of the Cold War in Asia, 1949-1954.* Montreal and Kingston: McGill-Queen's University Press, 1995.

Leffler, Melvyn P. *A Preponderance of Power: National Security, the Truman Administration, and the Cold War.* Stanford: Stanford University Press, 1992.

–. *The Specter of Communism: The United States and the Origins of the Cold War, 1917-1953.* New York: Hill and Wang, 1994.

Leitenberg, Milton. *The Korean War: Biological Warfare Allegations Resolved.* Stockholm: Centre for Pacific Asia Studies, 1998. Reprinted as "Resolution of the Korean War Biological Warfare Allegations," in *Critical Reviews in Microbiology* 24, 3 (1998): 169-94; revised version published as "New Russian Evidence on the Korean War Biological Warfare Allegations: Background and Analysis." In *Cold War International History Project Bulletin* 11 (Winter 1998).

Lethbridge, David, ed. *Bethune: The Secret Police File.* Salmon Arm, BC: Undercurrent, 2003.

Levant, Victor. *Quiet Complicity: Canadian Involvement in the Vietnam War.* Toronto: Between the Lines, 1986.

Lew, Ki-baik, and Carter J. Eckert et al. *Korea Old and New: A History.* Seoul: Ilchokak Publishers for the Korea Institute, Harvard University Press, 1990.

Li, Xiaobing, and Hongshan Li, eds. *China and the United States: A New Cold War History.* Lanham/New York/Oxford: University Press of America, 1998.

Li, Xiaobing, Allan R. Millett, and Bin Yu, trans. and ed. *Mao's Generals Remember Korea.* Lawrence: University Press of Kansas, 2001.

Linethal, Edward T., and Tom Engelhardt, eds. *History Wars: The* Enola Gay *and Other Battles for the American Past.* New York: Metropolitan Books, 1996.

Link, Arthur S., trans and ed. *The Deliberations of the Council of Four.* Vol. 1: *March 24-June 28, 1919.* Princeton: Princeton University Press, 1992.

Liu Guangtai. *Langning Zhuan* [Biography of Chester Ronning]. Shijiazhuang: Hebei Education Publishing House, 1999.

Logevall, Fredrik. *The Origins of the Vietnam War.* Essex, UK: Pearson Education, 2001.

Loomba, Ania. *Colonialism/Postcolonialism.* London: Routledge, 1998.

Lu, David John, ed. *Japan: A Documentary History – The Late Tokugawa Period to the Present.* Armonk, NY: M.E. Sharpe, 1996.

Luard, Evan. *A History of the United Nations,* Vol. 1. London: Macmillan, 1982.

Lundestad, Geir. "Empire by Invitation? The United States and Western Europe, 1945-1952." In *The Cold War in Europe,* ed. Charles S. Maier, 143-68. New York: Markus Weiner Publishers, 1991.

Lyon, Peyton. *The Loyalties of E. Herbert Norman.* Report for External Affairs and International Trade, 18 March 1990. In *Labour/Le Travail* 28 (Fall 1991): 219-59.

MacDonald, Callum A. *Korea: The War before Vietnam.* New York: The Free Press, 1986.

Mackenzie, David, ed. *Canada and the First World War.* Toronto: University of Toronto Press, 2005.

MacLeod, Wendell, Libbie Park, and Stanley Ryerson. *Bethune: The Montreal Years, an Informal Portrait.* Toronto: James Lorimer, 1978.

MacMillan, Margaret. *Paris 1919: Six Months That Changed the World.* New York: Random House, 2001.

Madsen, Chris. *Another Kind of Justice: Canadian Military Law from Confederation to Somalia.* Vancouver: UBC Press, 1999.

Maga, Tim. *Judgement at Tokyo: The Japanese War Crimes Trials.* Lexington: University Press of Kentucky, 2001.

Maier, Charles S. *The Cold War in Europe.* New York: Markus Weiner Publishers, 1991.

Manela, Ezra. *The Wilsonian Moment: Self-Determination and the International Origins of Anti-Colonial Nationalism.* New York: Oxford University Press, 2007.

Mao Zedong, "In Memory of Norman Bethune" (21 December 1939). In *Selected Works of Mao Tse-tung.* Vol. 2. Beijing: Foreign Languages Press, 1967.

Mar, Lisa Rose. *Brokering Belonging: Chinese in Canada's Exclusion Era, 1885-1945.* Toronto: University of Toronto Press, 2010.

Materials of the Trial of Former Servicemen of the Japanese Army Charged with Manufacturing and Employing Biological Weapons [Khabarovsk Trial]. Moscow: Foreign Languages Publishing House, 1950.

Matray, James I. *Historical Dictionary of the Korean War.* New York: Greenwood Press, 1991.

–. *The Reluctant Crusade: American Foreign Policy in Korea, 1941-1950.* Honolulu: University of Hawaii Press, 1985.

Mawani, Renisa. *Colonial Proximities: Cross-Racial Encounters and Juridical Truths in British Columbia, 1871-1921.* Vancouver: UBC Press, 2009.

McClintock, Anne. *Imperial Leather: Race, Gender and Sexuality in the Colonial Contest.* New York: Routledge, 1995.

McCormack, Gavan. *Cold War Hot War: An Australian Perspective on the Korean War.* Sydney: Hale and Iremonger, 1983.

McCune, George M. *Korea Today.* Cambridge: Harvard University Press, 1950.

McKenzie, Fredrick Arthur. *The Tragedy of Korea.* London: Hodder and Stoughton, 1908.

McKercher, B.J.C., and L. Aronsen, eds. *The North Atlantic Triangle in a Changing World: Anglo-American-Canadian Relations, 1903-1956.* Toronto: University of Toronto Press, 1996.

Meehan, John D. *The Dominion and the Rising Sun: Canada Encounters Japan.* Vancouver: UBC Press, 2004.

Melady, John. *Korea: Canada's Forgotten War.* Toronto: Macmillan, 1983.

Miki, Roy. *Redress: Inside the Japanese Canadian Call for Justice.* Vancouver: Raincoast Books, 2005.

Millar, Edward S. *War Plan Orange: The US Strategy to Defeat Japan, 1897-1945.* Annapolis: Naval Institute Press, 1991.

Minear, Richard H. *Victor's Justice: The Tokyo War Crimes Tribunal.* Princeton: Princeton University Press, 1991.

Mitsui kōan kabushiki kaisha. *Shiryō: Miike sōgi* [Documents: The miike dispute]. Tokyo: Nihon keieisha dantai renmei, 1963.

Miyazawa Kiichi. *Tokyo-Wasinton no mitsudan* [The Tokyo-Washington secret talks]. Tokyo: Chūō kōronsha, 1999.

Mommsen, Wolfgang J. *Theories of Imperialism.* Chicago: University of Chicago Press, 1980.

Moon Chung-in, Odd Arne Westad, and Gyoo-hyoung Kahng, eds. *Ending the Cold War in Korea: Theoretical and Historical Perspectives.* Seoul: Yonsei University Press, 2001.

Moore, Joe. *Japanese Workers and the Struggle for Power, 1945-1947.* Madison: University of Wisconsin Press, 1983.

Morgan, Ted. *A Covert Life: Jay Lovestone, Communist, Anti-Communist and Spymaster.* New York: Random House, 1999.

Morimura Seiichi. *Akuma no hōshoku, dai 1-3 bu* [Devil's gluttony, parts 1-3]. Tokyo: Kakkawa bunkō, 2000-01.

Morrison, Elting E., ed. *The Letters of Theodore Roosevelt.* Vols. 4 and 5. Cambridge: Harvard University Press, 1952.

Morton, Desmond. *A Short History of Canada,* 5th ed. Toronto: McClelland and Stewart, 2001.

Murphey, Rhoads. *East Asia: A New History.* New York: Pearson, 2004.

Nakano, Takeo Ujo, with Leatrice Nakano. *Within the Barbed Wired Fence.* Toronto: University of Toronto, 1980.

Nakano, Toshiko. *H. nōman: Aru demokuratto no tadotta unmei* [H. Norman: The fate that befell a democrat]. Tokyo: Riburopōto, 1990.

NHK. *Hiroshima wa dōkiroku sareta ka* [Recording Hiroshima]. Tokyo: NHK shuppan, 2003.

Nish, Ian, ed. *Anglo-Japanese Alienation, 1919-1952.* Cambridge: Cambridge University Press, 1982.

Nish, Ian, and Yoichi Kibata, eds. *The History of Anglo-Japanese Relations, 1600-2000.* Vol. 1: *The Political-Diplomatic Dimension, 1600-1930.* Basingstoke: Macmillan, 2000.

–. *The History of Anglo-Japanese Relations, 1600-2000.* Vol. 2: *The Political-Diplomatic Dimension, 1931-2000.* Basingstoke: Macmillan, 2000.

Nitobe Inazo. *Japan: Some Phases of Her Problems and Development.* New York: Charles Scribner's Sons, 1931.

–. *Lectures on Japan.* Tokyo: Kenkyusha, 1936.

–. *Thoughts and Essays.* Tokyo: Teibi Publishing Company, 1909.

Noel, Jan, ed. *Race and Gender in the Northern Colonies.* Toronto: Canadian Scholars' Press, 2000.

Norman, E. Herbert. *Andō Shōeki and the Anatomy of Japanese Feudalism.* Tokyo: Transactions of the Asiatic Society of Japan, 1949.

–. "Japan since Surrender," n.d. In *Historical and Political Writings [MSS] by Herbert Norman,* comp. Ōkubo Genji, E. Herbert Norman Papers, Special Collections and University Archives, University of British Columbia.

–. *Origins of the Modern Japanese State: Selected Writings of E.H. Norman.* Ed. John Dower. New York: Pantheon, 1974.

Nossal, Kim Richard. *The Politics of Canadian Foreign Policy.* Scarborough, ON: Prentice-Hall, 1997.

Odlum, Roger. *Victor Odlum: A Memoir.* West Vancouver, BC: Petrokle-Tor Publications, 1995.

Okazaki, Robert K. *The Nisei Mass Evacuation Group and POW Camp 101, Angler, Ontario.* Trans. Jean M. Okazaki and Curtis T. Okazaki. Scarborough, ON: Markham Litho, 1996.

Ōkubo Genji, ed. and trans. *Hābāto nōman zenshū* [Complete works of Herbert Norman]. Tokyo: Iwanami shoten, 1977.

Olson, James S., and Randy Roberts. *Where the Domino Fell: America and Vietnam.* New York: St. Martin's Press, 1991.

Oshiro, George. "Nitobe Inazō and Japanese Nationalism." In *Japanese Cultural Nationalism: At Home and in the Asia Pacific,* ed. Roy Starrs, 61-77. Folkestone, UK: Global Oriental, 2004.

–. *Nitobe Inazō: Kokusai shugi no kaitakusha* [Nitobe Inazo: Interpreter of internationalism]. Tokyo: Chūō daigaku shuppanbu, 1992.

Panikkar, K.M. *Asia and Western Dominance.* London: George Allen and Unwin, 1953.

Pauwels, Jacques. *The Myth of the Good War: America in the Second World War.* Toronto: James Lorimer, 2002.

Pearson, Lester B. ("T"). "Canada and the Far East." *Foreign Affairs* 13, 3 (1935): 388-97.

–. *Diplomacy in a Nuclear Age.* Oxford: Oxford University Press, 1959.

–. *Mike: The Memoirs of the Right Honourable Lester B. Pearson.* Vol. 2: *1948-1957.* Ed. John A. Munro and Alex I. Inglis. Toronto: University of Toronto Press, 1973.

Pickersgill, J.W., and D.F. Forster. *The MacKenzie King Record.* Vol. 4: *1947-1948.* Toronto: University of Toronto Press, 1970.

Porter, Gareth, ed. *Vietnam: A History in Documents.* New York: New American Library, 1979.

Prakash, Gyan. "Subaltern Studies as Postcolonial Criticism." *American Historical Review* 99, 5 (1994): 1475-90.

Pratt, Mary Louise. *Imperial Eyes: Travel Writing and Transculturation.* London: Routledge, 1992.

Price, John. "The Cat's Paw: Canada and the United Nations Temporary Commission on Korea." *Canadian Historical Review* 85, 2 (2004): 297-324.

–. *Japan Works: Power and Paradox in Postwar Industrial Relations.* Ithaca: Cornell University Press, 1997.

Pringsheim, Klaus H. *Neighbours across the Pacific.* Westport, CT: Greenwood Press, 1983.

Pritchard, R. John, ed., *The Tokyo War Crimes Trial: The Complete Transcripts of the Proceedings of the International Military Tribunal for the Far East in Twenty-Two Volumes.* New York/London: Garland, 1981.

Razack, Sherene E., ed. *Race, Space and the Law: Unmapping a White Settler Society.* Toronto: Between the Lines, 2002.

Reid, Escott. *Radical Mandarin: The Memoirs of Escott Reid.* Toronto: University of Toronto Press, 1989.

Rhodes, Richard. *The Making of the Atomic Bomb.* New York: Simon and Schuster, 1995.

Roberts, Leslie. *C.D.: The Life and Times of Clarence Decatur Howe.* Toronto: Clarke, Irwin, 1957.

Robinson, Greg. A *Tragedy of Democracy: Japanese Confinement in North America.* New York: Columbia University Press, 2009.

Ronning, Chester. *A Memoir of China in Revolution.* New York: Pantheon, 1974.

Rosenberg, Emily S. *A Date Which Will Live: Pearl Harbor in American Memory.* Durham, NC: Duke University Press, 2003.

Ross, Douglas A. *In the Interests of Peace: Canada and Vietnam, 1954-73.* Toronto: University of Toronto Press, 1984.

Rothenberg, Paula S. *White Privilege: Essential Readings on the Other Side of Racism.* New York: Worth, 2008.

Roy, Patricia E. *The Oriental Question: Consolidating a White Man's Province.* Vancouver: UBC Press, 2003.

–. *The Triumph of Citizenship: The Japanese and Chinese in Canada, 1941-67.* Vancouver: UBC Press, 2008.

–. *A White Man's Province: British Columbia Politicians and Chinese and Japanese Immigrants, 1858-1914.* Vancouver: UBC Press, 1989.

Roy, Patricia, with J.L. Granatstein, Masako Iino, and Hiroko Takamura. *Mutual Hostages: Canadians and Japanese during the Second World War.* Toronto: University of Toronto Press, 1990.

Saccone, Richard. *Koreans to Remember.* Seoul: Hollym, 1993.

Said, Edward. *Culture and Imperialism.* New York: Vintage, 1994.

–. *Orientalism.* London: Routledge, 1978.

Samson, Jane. *Race and Empire.* Harlow, UK: Pearson Longman, 2005.

Satō Tatsuo. *Nihonkoku kempō seiritsu-shi* [History of the establishment of Japan's constitution]. 2 vols. Tokyo: Yūhikaku, 1962, 1964.

Saxton, Alexander. *The Indispensable Enemy: Labor and the Anti-Chinese Movement in California.* Berkley: University of California Press, 1971.

Schaller, Michael. *The American Occupation of Japan: The Origins of the Cold War in Asia.* New York: Oxford University Press, 1985.

Schonberger, Howard B. *Aftermath of War: Americans and the Remaking of Japan, 1945-1952.* Kent: Kent State University Press, 1989.

Schrecker, Ellen. *Many Are the Crimes: McCarthyism in America.* Princeton: Princeton University Press, 1998.

Schultz, John, and Kimitada Miwa, eds. *Canada and Japan in the Twentieth Century.* Toronto: Oxford University Press, 1991.

Selden, Kyoko, and Mark Selden, eds. *The Atomic Bomb: Voices from Hiroshima and Nagasaki.* Armonk, NY/London: M.E. Sharpe, 1989.

Shen I-yao. Trans. Shi Yi. *A Century of Chinese Exclusion Abroad.* Beijing: Foreign Language Press, 2006.

Shepherd, R. Bruce. *Deemed Unsuitable.* Toronto: Umbrella Press, 1997.

Shimazu, Naoko. *Japan, Race and Equality: Racial Equality Proposal of 1919.* London: Routledge, 1998.

Skelton, O.D. *The Life and Letters of Sir Wilfrid Laurier.* Vol. 2. Toronto: Oxford University Press, 1921.

Smythe, Lewis Strong Casey. *War Damage in the Nanking Area, December 1937 to March 1938.* Shanghai: Mercury Press, 1938. (Urban and Rural Surveys, by Dr. Lewis Strong Casey Smythe and assistants, on behalf of the Nanjing International Relief Committee, compiled June 1938.)

Snow, Edgar. *Red Star over China.* New York: Random House, 1938.

Spence, Jonathan. *The Gate of Heavenly Peace: The Chinese and Their Revolution, 1895-1980.* New York: Penguin, 1982.

Spivak, G.C. *A Critique of Postcolonial Reason: Toward a History of the Vanishing Present.* Cambridge, MA.: Harvard University Press, 1999.

Stairs, Denis. *The Diplomacy of Constraint.* Toronto: University of Toronto Press, 1974.

Stockwin, J.A.A. *The Japanese Socialist Party and Neutralism.* Carlton, Victoria: Melbourne University Press; London, New York: Cambridge University Press, 1968.

Stoler, Ann Laura. *Carnal Knowledge and Imperial Power: Race and the Intimate in Colonial Rule.* Berkeley: University of California Press, 2002.

Sugimoto, Howard Hiroshi. *Japanese Immigration: The Vancouver Riots and Canadian Diplomacy.* New York: Arno Press, 1978.

Sunahara, Ann Gomer. *The Politics of Racism: The Uprooting of the Japanese Canadians during the Second World War.* Toronto: James Lorimer, 1981.

Supreme Commander for the Allied Powers. *Political Reorientation of Japan, September 1945 to September 1948.* Washington, DC: US Government Printer, 1948.

Suzuki Yasuzō. *Jiyū minken* [Freedom and popular rights]. Tokyo: Hakuyōsha, 1948.

Takaki, Ronald. *Double Victory: A Multicultural History of America in World War II.* Boston: Little, Brown and Co., 2000.

–. *Hiroshima: Why America Dropped the Atomic Bomb.* Boston: Little, Brown and Co., 1995.

Takemae Eiji. *GHQ* [General headquarters]. Tokyo: Iwanami shoten, 1985.

–. *GHQ no hitobito* [The people of GHQ]. Tokyo: Meiji shoten, 2002.

–. *Inside GHQ: Allied Occupation of Japan and Its Legacy.* New York: Continuum, 2002.

–. *Sengo rōdō kaiku: GHQ rōdō seisakushi* [Postwar labour reform: A history of GHQ labour policy]. Tokyo: Tokyo daigaku shuppankai, 1982.

Tamanoi, Mariko Asano. *Under the Shadow of Nationalism: Politics and Poetics of Rural Japanese Women.* Honolulu: University of Hawaii Press, 1998.

Tanaka Masaaki. *Pāru hanji no nihon muzairon* [Justice Pal verdict: Japan not guilty]. Tokyo: Shogakkan, 2001.

Tanaka, Stefan. *Japan's Orient: Rendering Pasts into History.* Berkeley: University of California Press, 1993.

Tanaka, Yuki. "Indiscriminate Bombing and the Enola Gay Legacy." As posted on *Japan Focus*, http://www.japanfocus.org/.

Taylor, Charles. *Six Journeys: A Canadian Pattern.* Toronto: Anansi, 1977.

–. *Snow Job: Canada, the United States and Vietnam, 1954-1973.* Toronto: Anansi, 1978.

Teigrob, Robert. *Warming Up to the Cold War: Canada and the United States' Coalition of the Willing from Hiroshima to Korea.* Toronto: University of Toronto Press, 2009.

Thakur, Ramesh. *Peacekeeping in Vietnam: Canada, India, Poland, and the International Commission.* Edmonton: University of Alberta Press, 1984.

Thomson, Dale C. *Louis St. Laurent: Canadian.* Toronto: Macmillan, 1967.

Thorne, Christopher. *The Limits of Foreign Policy.* London: Macmillian, 1972.

–. *Racial Aspects of the Far Eastern War of 1941-1945.* London: Oxford University Press, 1982.

Tilchin, William N. *Theodore Roosevelt and the British Empire: A Study in Presidential Statecraft.* New York: St. Martin's Press, 1997.

Timperley, Harold John. *Japanese Terror in China.* New York: Modern Age Books, 1938.

–. *What War Means: The Japanese Terror in China – A Documentary Record.* London: Victor Gollancz, 1938.

Tran, Nhung Tuyet, and Anthony Reid, eds. *Viet Nam: Borderless Histories.* Madison: University of Wisconsin Press, 2006.

Trotter, Ann. *New Zealand and Japan, 1945-1952: The Occupation and Peace Treaty.* London: Athlone Press, 1990.

Truong, Nhu Tang, with David Chanoff and Doan Van Toai. *A Viet Cong Memoir.* New York: Vintage, 1985.

Tsuneishi Keiichi. *Igakushatachi no soshiki hanzai: Kantōgun dai 731 butai* [Doctors organized crime: The Kanto military unit 731]. Tokyo: Asahi shimbunsha, 1999.

–. *Unit 731, Seibutsu heiki hanzai no jijitsu* [Unit 731: The truth about crimes related to biological weapons]. Tokyo: Kōdansha gendai shinsho, 1995.

Ueno, Chizuko. *Nationalism and Gender.* Melbourne: Trans Pacific Press, 2004.

United States, Department of State. *The Conferences at Cairo and Tehran, 1943.* Washington, DC: US Government Printing Office, 1961.

Van Slyke, Lyman P., ed. and intro. *The China White Paper.* Stanford: Stanford University Press, 1967. Originally issued as *United States Relations with China, with special Reference to the Period 1944-1949* (Department of State publication 3573, Far Eastern Series 30).

Vetter, Hal. *Mutiny on Koje Island.* Rutland, VT: Charles E. Tuttle, 1964.

Wada Haruki. *Chosen sensō zenshi* [The history of the Korean war]. Tokyo: Iwanami shoten, 2002.

–. *Kin nissei to manshū kōnichi sensō* [Kim Il Sung and the anti-Japanese war in Manchuria]. Tokyo: Heibonsha, 1992.

Wala, Michael. *The Council on Foreign Relations and the American Foreign Policy in the Early Cold War.* Oxford: Berghahn Books, 1994.

Wang Bingnan. *Zhong-Mei huitan Jiunian Huigu* [Reminiscences of nine years of China-US talks]. Beijing: World Knowledge Publishing House, 1985.

Ward, Peter W. *White Canada Forever.* Montreal and Kingston: McGill-Queen's University Press, 2002.

Ward, Robert, and Sakamoto Yoshikazu eds. *Democratizing Japan: The Allied Occupation.* Honolulu: University of Hawaii Press, 1987.

Watson, Brent. *Far Eastern Tour: The Canadian Infantry in Korea, 1950-1953.* Montreal and Kingston: McGill-Queen's University Press, 2002.

Weathersby, Kathryn. "Deceiving the Deceivers: Moscow, Beijing, Pyongyang, and the Allegations of Bacteriological Weapons Use in Korea." *Cold War International History Project Bulletin* 11 (1998).

Weiner, Michael, ed. *Japan's Minorities: The Illusion of Homogeneity.* London: Routledge, 1997.

Whittaker, Reg, and Gary Marcuse. *Cold War Canada: The Making of a National Insecurity State, 1945-1957.* Toronto: University of Toronto Press, 1994.

Wickberg, Edgar, ed. *From China to Canada: A History of the Chinese Community in Canada.* Toronto: McClelland and Stewart, 1982.

Wickert, Erwin, ed. *The Good Man of Nanking: The Diaries of John Rabe.* New York: Alfred E. Knopf, 1998.

Wiener, Michael, ed. *Japan's Minorities.* London: Routledge, 1997.

Williams, Peter, and David Wallace. *Unit 731: The Japanese Army's Secret of Secrets.* London: Hodder and Stoughton, 1989.

Winks, Robin W. *The Blacks in Canada: A History*, 2nd ed. Montreal and Kingston: McGill-Queen's University Press, 1997.

Woods, Lawrence T. "John Nelson (1873-1936) and the Origins of Canadian Participation in APEC," Working Paper No. 18, Institute of International Relations, University of British Columbia, October 1997.

Woodsworth, Charles J. *Canada and the Orient: A Study in International Relations.* Toronto: Macmillan, 1941.

Woon, Yeun-fong. *The Excluded Wife.* Montreal and Kingston: McGill-Queen's University Press, 1998.

Yahuda, Michael. *The International Politics of the Asia-Pacific, 1945-1995.* London: Routledge, 1996.

Yamamoto Kiyoshi. *Sengo kiki ni okeru rōdō undō* [The labour movement in the postwar crisis]. Tokyo: Ochanomizu shobo, 1978.

Yoshida, Takashi. *The Making of the "Rape of the Nanking": History and Memory in Japan, China, and the United States.* Oxford: Oxford University Press, 2006.

Young, Robert J.C. *Postcolonialism: An Historical Introduction.* Oxford: Blackwell, 2001.

Yu, Henry, ed. *Pacific Canada: Beyond the 49th Parallel,* special issue of *Amerasia Journal* 33, 2 (2007).

–. "Refracting Pacific Canada." *BC Studies* (double issue) 156/57 (2007/08).

Zhang, Shu Guang, and Jian Chen. *Chinese Communist Foreign Policy and the Cold War in Asia: New Documentary Evidence, 1944-1950*. Chicago: Imprint Publications, 1996.

Zimmerman, David. *Top Secret Exchange: The Tizard Mission and the Scientific War*. Montreal and Kingston: McGill-Queen's University Press, 1996.

Index

Page numbers in *italics* refer to photographs.

Printed and bound in Canada by Friesens

Set in Futura Condensed and Warnock by Artegraphica Design Co. Ltd.

Copy editor: Joanne Richardson

Proofreader: Dianne Tiefensee

Indexer: Annette Lorek

Cartographer: Eric Leinberger